Applying Psychology

THIRD EDITION

Virginia Nichols Quinn
Northern Virginia Community College

McGraw-Hill, Inc.

New York St. Louis San Francisco Auckland Bogotá Caracas Lisbon
London Madrid Mexico City Milan Montreal New Delhi
San Juan Singapore Sydney Tokyo Toronto

APPLYING PSYCHOLOGY

This book is printed on acid-free paper.

7 8 9 0 DOC DOC 9 0 9

P/N 051339-2

This book was set in Palatino by Ruttle, Shaw & Wetherill, Inc.
The editors were Brian L. McKean, Laura Lynch, and Fred H. Burns;
the production supervisor was Kathryn Porzio.
The cover was designed by Rafael Hernandez.
The photo editor was Debra P. Hershkowitz.
New drawings were done by TecDocPubInc.
R. R. Donnelley & Sons Company was printer and binder.

Cover illustration: John Graham Diary, 1937, 3 × 5 in., May 7th–May 10th 1937, *ink, pencil, and colored pencil on paper. John Graham Papers, Archives of American Art, Smithsonian Institution, Washington, D.C.*
John Graham (1881–1961) was a central figure among American avant-garde artist from the late 1920s through the 1940s. He helped such renowned artists as Stuart Davis, Arshile Gorky, and Jackson Pollack gain their recognition and fame. His intense interest in psychology, particularly Jungian approaches, is evident from the notes on the calendar pages. The author of numerous books on art, his approach demonstrated his keen love for diversity. Although an expert on the cubism and surrealism of the European art scene, he became a collector of African art and through his writings stimulated American artists' interest in the primitive art of Mexico.
His diary pages reflect the nature of this text; while appearing simple at first glance, closer inspection reveals complexities. John Graham personalized his calendar with many comments. Hopefully each copy of this text also will acquire a unique flavor after each student individualizes it with his or her own responses, comments, and notes.

Library of Congress Cataloging-in-Publication Data

Quinn, Virginia Nichols.
    Applying psychology / Virginia Nichols Quinn.—3rd ed.
      p.   cm.
    Includes bibliographical references and index.
    1. Psychology.   2. Psychology, Applied.   I. Title.
  BF121.Q56   1995
  158—dc20
                                       94-33045

About the Author

VIRGINIA NICHOLS QUINN has been a professor of psychology at Northern Virginia Community College for more than twenty years. She received her bachelor's degree from Hunter College, where she majored in psychology and minored in mathematics and education. She completed her master's degree and course work for her doctorate in psychometrics at Harvard University. Her professional experiences in applying psychology include teaching children who have behavioral problems, working as a consultant in decision making and problem solving for the United States Department of Defense, and serving as the director of psychology at a children's rehabilitation hospital. In addition, she has applied psychological principles to politics in her successful campaign for mayor of Round Hill, Virginia, and in her role as a member of school boards and planning commissions. Her strongest concern is to make psychology understandable, practical, and useful to students. She is the author of numerous study guides and test banks to accompany psychology texts.

Contents

Preface

In preparing the preface for the first and second editions of this text, I recalled my father's annoyance when I decided to continue studying for a doctorate at Harvard. He pounded his fist on the kitchen table and warned, "Virginia, you're going to educate yourself right out of humanity; no one will be able to talk to you!" He feared that I would bury myself in textbooks and lose my sense of reality. I hope the first two editions proved that even after a lengthy education, I can still talk with most people and remain an active member of humanity.

I also hope that this text demonstrates that books (or at least this textbook) can be closely connected to reality, even useful. A good text should not be only for those who already know something about the subject. This text is designed for beginning students who have little or no knowledge of psychology. The tone of the text is conversational and should read as easily as a newspaper or magazine article. Students should be able to enjoy the content and concentrate on the topics without struggling to understand what they are reading.

The content includes basic topics in psychology and describes their application across a broad range of everyday experiences, including—but not limited to—work, education, consumer concerns, community and civic programs, social and environmental interests, sports, mental health, human relations, forensics, and a variety of vocational interests. Cartoons, illustrations, photos, and clippings from newspapers and magazines are used to spark interest and show the relevance and importance of psychology. The intent of this text is not only to maintain the integrity of traditional psychology by acknowledging the basic research required but also to make psychology useful, so students will be enticed into continuing their study either formally or informally.

For many decades psychologists have known that students learn more when they read actively rather than passively. Psychologists have also confirmed that practice and feedback are critical to learning. *Applying Psychology* does just this by putting these basic principles in psychology to use. As a result, this is not an ordinary text that can be read passively. This book has been designed for students to use, write in, and personalize with their own notes. Each chapter has several unique features including:

Chapter Outline   At the beginning of each chapter an outline previews the major topics to be included.

Features   A variety of newspaper and magazine articles and other information are highlighted to show the relevance and application of psychological principles.

Exercises   After each new concept is discussed, the student has the opportunity to interact with the material and demonstrate an ability to apply the newly acquired knowledge.

Feedback   This section of the chapter either provides reinforcement for material that was learned correctly or alerts the student to the need for further review of the text.

Checkpoints   Each chapter is broken into readable units based on the length of the average attention span. After reading about one-third of a chapter and completing the required exercises, the student reaches a checkpoint with review questions. Answers can be checked at the end of the chapter.

Running Glossary   All key terms are defined in the margin where they first appear.

Chapter Inventory   This list of specific learning objectives appears at the conclusion of each chapter. Students can use these objectives as a checklist for review and exam preparation.

Among the important new features in this edition are the emphasis on cultural diversity and the inclusion of more information on the brain and physiological processes.

TACT (*Team Assisted Computerized Testing*) is a special new option that accompanies this text. I developed *TACT* to help students prepare for their exams. A Harvard study found that students who review for tests with study groups achieved higher grades than students who studied alone. However, students who commute to college usually have great difficulty setting study places and schedules with others. Jobs, lengthy drives, family responsibilities, and a multitude of other factors often prohibit group work. The *TACT* program (available in IBM format) allows students to work with two other (simulated) students. The program contains 240 questions; 15 questions for each chapter.

It would be impossible to list the names of the thousands of students who studied the manuscript and the first and second editions of this text and offered comments for making this edition more useful and explicit. But to each and every student, I am most grateful. Many ideas in the text came from reviewers for the first and second editions: Alice Brown, Southwest Virginia Community College; James D'Amato, Rockland Community College; Jim Eison, Roane Community College; Eugene Fichter, Northern Virginia Community College; Normal Halls, Westfield State College; Donald Murdock, Suffolk County Community College; Marlene Polkovich, Special Intermediate Vocational School, Wisconsin District No. 916; Robert Rea, Charles County Community College; Robert Sands, State University of New York, Agricultural and Technical College at Alfred; Thomas Bond, Thomas Nelson Community College; Ronald Caldwell, Blue Mountain Community College; James Dailey, Vincennes University; Nancy Dash, C. S. Mott Community College; Pauline Gillette, Northern Virginia Community College; Harriette B. Ritchie, American River College; Mary A. Rogers, Inver Hills Community College; Caroline Roth, Northern Virginia Community College; Linda Truesdale, Midlands Technical College; Everette K. Wagner, San Antonio College.

I am grateful for the comments, suggestions, and intelligent criticisms offered by the reviewers for the third edition: James M. Dailey, Vincennes University; Alma Hollinsead, Solano Community College; Ogretta MacNeill, College of the Holy Cross; Laura Thompson, Midlands Technical College; and J. Oscar Williams, Jr., Diablo Valley College.

A special tribute must be paid to my husband, Paul, who was supportive and encouraging in spite of my grumpy moods as deadlines approached. Finally, thanks must go to my father who, by pounding his fist, left me with something to prove persistently!

Virginia Nichols Quinn

Examining the Methods of Psychology

The proper study of mankind is man.
—ALEXANDER POPE

How can you properly study mankind? It sounds like a tall order! Suppose you are wandering college halls in search of ways to learn about yourself as well as other people. You could probably get help from professors of history, anthropology, sociology, literature, art, political science, and many other disciplines. Many subjects focus on people's behavior. History records behavior; sociology observes behavior; and literature, art, and political science inform you about behavior. But only one discipline attempts to use scientific methods to explain why people behave the way they do—psychology. The viewpoints of psychologists and the methods they use to learn about human behavior are the subjects of this chapter.

The chapter begins by examining the five main views of psychology. Each view has a slightly different emphasis on what the focus of psychology should be. The possible specializations in psychology are listed and discussed briefly. The next section emphasizes the importance of proper methodology and interpretation. After the description of each method, a caution note is added for emphasis on possible pitfalls and misuses of each method. Finally, the diverse population that psychology must study is discussed, and the ethical requirements of psychologists are considered.

psychology Scientific study of human behavior and thought processes

applied psychology approach involving practical uses of the study of behavior and thoughts

Psychology is the scientific study of human behavior and thought processes. *Applied psychology,* as the name suggests, emphasizes the practical uses of psychology rather than its history and theories. Applied psychology gained importance in the late 1960s.

In an often-quoted speech before the American Psychological Association, Miller (1969) recommended:

> The secrets of our trade need not be reserved for highly trained specialists. Psychological facts should be passed out freely to all who need and can use them. . . . There are simply not enough psychologists, including non-professionals, to meet every need for psychological services. The people at large will have to be their own psychologists, and make their own applications of established principles.

Unfortunately, applying psychology is not as simple as many people believe. Some people have a mistaken notion that with minimal effort psychologists can analyze and understand the causes and nature of behavior. Indeed, in several popular paperbacks, authors promise to resolve your every problem and bring instant happiness after an hour of reading. Book advertisements promise their products will help you to control pain, relieve grief, and remove stress. They also pledge increased sexual desire and performance and improved popularity to readers. However, such promises are not likely to be fulfilled. Learning to apply psychology is complex. First, you must recognize the basic principles of psychology. You also need to understand the methods of psychology and their limitations. Finally, you need to know when to apply the principles and methods.

Even skilled psychologists have been sharply criticized for not taking the required time in applying psychology. Several radio and television stations around the United States offer call-in therapy. A listener calls the station and reports a problem on the air to a psychologist. The psychologist usually probes the listener and offers advice within two to five minutes. Since the conversation between the psychologist and the caller is broadcast, listeners can apply the advice to themselves or be informed or entertained by the predicaments of other people. Several of the problems that radio and television psychologists face are described in Feature 1-1.

Some psychologists maintain that the radio method is effective in educating masses of people about the applications of psychology. Other psychologists feel that call-in psychology is harmful because the advice is hasty and can be misinterpreted and misapplied.

Exercise 1-1

Check five items on the following list that are important to the study of applied psychology.

_____ Reading history

_____ Learning practical uses

_____ Observing everyday behavior

_____ Analyzing theory

_____ Using principles of psychology

_____ Finding quick, simple solutions

_____ Reading how-to pop psychology books

_____ Using the methods of psychology

_____ Learning when to use the methods and principles of psychology

_____ Entertaining an audience

You may compare your answers to those in the Feedback section at the end of the chapter.

Views of Psychology

Although most psychologists agree that all aspects of human behavior must be studied, they disagree on which aspects are of greatest importance. The disagreement is friendly. There are five major views of behavior: behaviorist, gestalt, psychoanalytic, humanist, and cognitive. Many psychologists do not adhere to a single view but are eclectic in their approach, choosing a view to fit a particular situation.

FEATURE 1-1 PSYCHOLOGY IN THE NEWS

Would-Be Stars, Beware: Cameras Never Blink

"Media psychology has come a long way since Joyce Brothers first scandalized many of her colleagues by going public," says Sonya Friedman, "but there are still plenty of personal and professional pitfalls for those who enter the glare of the spotlight. . . ."

Friedman, author of *Men Are Just Desserts, Smart Cookies Don't Crumble,* and *A Hero Is More Than Just a Sandwich;* columnist for *The Ladies Home Journal* and *The Detroit Free Press,* and host of a daily television show and weekly radio program, said her 15 years working in the media have given her the chance "to make every single mistake" there is.

"Walking the tightrope between the caring profession of psychology and a commercial endeavor like hosting a radio program or offering advice in a newspaper column is far from easy," Friedman said.

"What is easy," she laments, "is to fail to maintain professionalism when people dangle money and fame in front of you." Her watchword is "credibility," she said, and her credo is "Do no harm."

A basic rule in the electronic media is that the time constraints of on-air advice shows must be followed, she said. "You are not practicing therapy on the air."

Nevertheless, she believes that even within five minutes of air time, a psychologist can do a lot of good: to offer a glimmer of hope to someone with a problem, and point out a direction for a resolution. "You have a chance to open a window." After such shows, Friedman said she returns calls to those who seem seriously troubled.

Far from endeavoring to dispel apprehension about entering the mine-strewn field of television, Friedman warned: "When you screw up on air, 20,000 people just heard you. . . ."

Source: Landers, S. (1987, November). Would-be stars, beware: Cameras never blink. *APA Monitor.*

Behaviorism.

behaviorism Belief that psychology should be scientific and based on observable events

Behaviorism began in the United States about eighty years ago with John Watson. Watson felt that psychology should be scientific and based on observable events that two or more people agree upon. According to the behaviorist view, only behaviors that can be observed and agreed upon are worthy of interest in psychology. People's inner thoughts and feelings are only of importance if they are expressed in overt actions or affect their behavior in some way. Behaviorists hold that, except for a few reflexes, all behavior is learned. People learn to respond to certain stimuli. Skinner (1938), a leader in the behaviorist perspective, maintained that behavior is shaped by consequences. Behaviors that are rewarded increase in frequency, and those that are punished decrease. For example, if you received $100 every time you said "psychology," you might find yourself repeating the word constantly. On the other hand, if you were whipped for using the word, you would probably cease to use it. Applications of the behaviorist perspective are discussed in detail in Chapter 3.

Gestalt Psychology.

gestalt School of psychology that emphasizes patterns of organization in behavior

Around the same time that the behaviorist movement began in the United States, the *gestalt* perspective emerged in Germany. The German word "gestalt" does not have an exact English equivalent. It is translated as a form, shape, pattern, or organized whole. The basic belief of the gestaltists is that the whole is greater than the sum of its parts. Clearly, this is the opposite of everything you learned in geometry!

But the gestaltists compare behavior to music rather than mathematics. Think of your favorite tune. If you looked at each note individually, you could never create the melody. However, you could change every note and still play the melody in a different key. The pattern, or organization, of the notes is of prime importance. According to the gestalt view, human behavior loses its meaning if it is broken into components. They argue with behaviorists that the organization of behavior is more important than are outward actions. Psychology, in the gestalt view, should focus on sensory, perceptual, and insight processes. Chapter 2 considers sensory and perceptual gestalt applications. Insight and problem solving are discussed in Chapter 5.

Psychoanalysis.

psychoanalysis View that psychology should focus on unconscious feelings

Psychoanalysis is the oldest of the five perspectives, tracing its beginnings to the writings of Sigmund Freud more than 100 years ago. According to the psychoanalytic view, people are controlled by impulses buried in their unconscious. We are unaware of most of our motives and feelings. Our outward behavior is like the tip of an iceberg; beneath our conscious outward behavior is a vast unconscious.

The psychoanalytic view has been called the third great blow for humans. First, Galileo stated that the earth is not the center of the universe. Next, Darwin announced that humans and apes had a common ancestor. And Freud delivered the final blow by stating that humans are controlled by unconscious impulses. Since we are unaware of our unconscious, we must be psychoanalyzed to learn of these inner unknown feelings. Many of our unknown feelings are sexual and aggressive urges. Methods used in psychoanalysis are covered in Chapter 11.

Humanistic Psychology.

humanistic psychology View that emphasizes the importance of self-direction and personal growth

Humanistic psychology began in the 1950s with the works of Carl Rogers and Abraham Maslow. Humanists believe that people

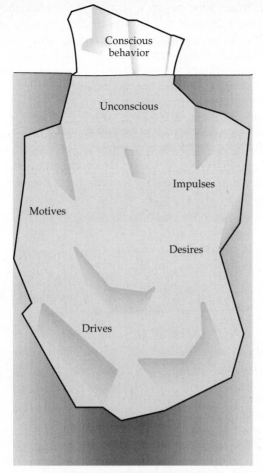

FIGURE 1-1. Psychoanalytic iceberg.

are constantly growing, changing, and struggling to reach their full potential. They maintain that psychologists should focus on the importance of self-
direction. Free will and the ability to make choices independently are critical to humanists. The real world is what you believe it to be. You are unique.
Since no one else fully comprehends your world, you must make your own
choices. Chapter 11 discusses the methods used by humanists in counseling
sessions.

Cognitive Psychology. The *cognitive* view is the most recent development
and emphasizes the processes that our minds use. Cognitive psychologists are
interested in how we think, remember, solve problems, create mental images,
and form our beliefs. The development of computers promoted a greater interest in cognitive psychology. As scientists became more interested in programming computers to solve simple and complex problems, psychologists began
to use more scientific approaches to study how people solve problems. Currently, cognitive psychology has expanded to include dreaming, hypnosis,
meditation, and the effects of drugs on thinking.

**cognitive psychol-
ogy** View that fo-
cuses on how the
mind processes in-
formation

The Eclectic View. *Eclectic* psychologists choose among behaviorist, gestalt, psychoanalytic, humanist, and cognitive methods, according to the problem they are facing. Most psychologists are eclectic, accepting and respecting the work of all five views.

Exercise 1-2

Read the following play and decide which viewpoint each character is demonstrating: *behaviorist, gestalt, psychoanalytic, humanist, cognitive,* or *eclectic.* State the reason for your choice.

SCENE: It is 8 P.M. in the bedroom of a two-year-old boy. The boy is standing by his bed surrounded by his mother, father, grandfather, Uncle Gustavo, and Aunt Rhea, all psychologists.

BOY (*crying*): I won't go to bed by myself. I want to sleep in someone else's bed. I'm scared of the dark.

MOTHER: Poor child, he doesn't even know why he's afraid. Probably something horrible happened to him in the dark when he was a newborn in the hospital. Now he will never stay alone in a dark room. Someday I'll have to work with him to get this problem out of his unconscious.

UNCLE GUSTAVO: Don't waste your time! Just put some cookies by his bed. If he eats his favorite oatmeal cookies in the dark, he won't mind staying here.

AUNT RHEA: Oh, Gustavo, you're always trying to look at the petty aspect of behavior. This poor child may have trouble understanding what darkness is. Maybe his eyes don't adapt easily.

GRANDFATHER: Let me have a chat with the boy and find out how he is thinking.

FATHER: I agree that cookies aren't the answer. But let me ask you, son, what happens when the room is dark?

BOY: Terrible dreams come out of the closet.

FATHER: Do you want me to close the door so the dreams can't come out?

BOY: Sure, but ask Uncle Gustavo to bring me the cookies and Aunt Rhea to check my eyes, and I'd like to talk to Mom about when I was a baby and have a chat with Grandpa about how I think.

a. Mother: _____

   Reason: _____

b. Father: _____

   Reason: _____

c. Uncle Gustavo: _____

   Reason: _____

d. Aunt Rhea: _____

   Reason: _____

e. Grandfather: _____

   Reason: _____

f. Boy: _____

   Reason: _____

   You may check your answers in the Feedback section.

Subspecialties of Psychology

If you browse through a typical college catalog, you will notice many offerings in the psychology department (see Feature 1-2). Undergraduate students study in a number of different fields of psychology. However, if training in psychology continues in graduate school, students must usually choose an area of specialization. Feature 1-3 lists brief descriptions of common subspecialties. Psychologists who specialize while in graduate school are not necessarily locked into a subfield. As their interests change, they sometimes take up new specializations.

Psychotherapists

Psychotherapists are sometimes confused with other professionals who work closely with people who have emotional problems. A psychotherapist is a

---

FEATURE 1-2

Undergraduate Courses Offered at Eastern Washington University, Cheney, Washington

General Psychology	Intelligence and Experience
Psychology Applied to Human Problems	Madness in Literature
Environmental Psychology	Human Sexuality
Career Development	Psychology in the Secondary Schools
Seminar/Special (Individual Studies)	Co-op Field Work
Theories of Personality	Advanced Conditioning and Learning
Abnormal Psychology	Sensation and Perception
Foundations of Psychotherapy	Biological Basis of Behavior
Scientific Principles of Psychology	Human Psychophysiology
Psychological Statistics I	Stress and Coping
Psychological Statistics II	Clinical Psychology of Adult Life and Aging
Research Methods in Psychology	Animal Behavior
Principles of Clinical Assessment	Social Psychology
Conditioning and Learning	Social Psychology of Interpersonal Behavior
Human Memory and Cognition	Group Dynamics
Behavioral Health Therapy	Industrial and Organizational Psychology
Drugs and Behavior	Managerial Psychology
Psychology of Women	Workshops, Short Courses, Conferences
Discovering Women in Science	Directed Study

professional with special training in managing or treating emotional problems and mental illness. Psychotherapists include psychologists, psychiatrists, and psychiatric social workers. Perhaps you have wondered about the differences in training among these three types of professionals. Although their functions sometimes overlap, there are some clear contrasts in both the education and roles of each of the three general types of psychotherapists.

Psychiatrists. Psychiatrists are medical doctors who have several years of special training in psychological disorders. They are the only type of therapist who can prescribe medications. Since most forms of psychosis and psychosomatic illness require medication along with psychological treatment, psychiatrists usually supervise the management of these disorders. Severe forms of anxiety and any emotional problem that has a medical element usually require the assistance of a psychiatrist.

Psychologists. Not all psychologists are psychotherapists; some specialize in research or in other areas and applications. The most advanced degree in psychology is a Ph.D. or Psy.D. Many psychologists have medical training but few have a medical degree. Specific course requirements vary in each state. There are two specialties in psychology that focus on therapy: clinical psy-

---

FEATURE 1-3

Subspecialties in Psychology

Clinical psychologist Performs therapy and handles emotional problems

Comparative psychologist Works with lower animals such as rats, mice, pigeons, or monkeys; uses experimental procedures in a laboratory setting

Consumer psychologist Studies and evaluates emotional appeals, marketing, packaging, and advertising methods

Counselor Tests, advises, and suggests resources for additional assistance

Cross-cultural psychologist Studies how human behavior is the same or varies in diverse cultures

Developmental psychologist Studies changes that occur with each age, from prenatal stages through old age

Educational psychologist Improves methods of teaching, studying, learning, and testing

Engineering psychologist Develops improvements in equipment design

Environmental psychologist Assists in planning communities and buildings, emphasizing human needs

Experimental psychologist Develops scientific methods to find causes of behavior

Forensic psychologist Studies crime prevention and motivation and causes of crime

Health psychologist Helps people develop healthier lifestyles and avoid illness

Industrial and organizational psychologist Organizes job allocation and working conditions for optimal production

Personality psychologist Assesses individual differences and tests patterns of behavior

Physiological psychologist Studies the biological causes of behavior

Psychometrician Constructs tests to measure intelligence, achievement, aptitude, and personality; designs experiments and applies statistics

School psychologist Evaluates students to diagnose learning or emotional problems that may interfere with success in school.

Social psychologist Studies attitudes, prejudices, group interactions, and leadership

Engineering psychologists are involved in the design of complex control panels on aircraft.

chology and counseling psychology. Most states require licenses to practice in either of these two areas. Clinical psychologists specialize in psychological testing and in methods for performing therapy. Counseling psychologists focus more on educational and vocational aspects of adjustment. However, often they are also concerned with personal, social, and emotional problems. Counseling psychologists may have either an Ed.D. or a Ph.D.; some have only an M.A. or Ed.M. in counseling.

Psychiatric Social Worker. Psychiatric social workers may have either a master's degree or a doctorate in social services or social work and must be licensed for private practice as therapists. Most often they deal with people who need social services. They refer people to appropriate agencies and help.

The terms psychiatrist, psychologist, and psychiatric social worker are regulated by state laws. Only persons with appropriate education and experience are licensed to use the titles. What about a woman who calls herself a "mental health counselor" or a man who lists his titles as "mind therapist" and "psychohealer"? Chances are they are both quacks, persons who are neither trained nor qualified in psychology or psychiatry. Lists of members of the American Psychiatric Association and the American Psychological Association are available at most public libraries. Qualifications can be checked by looking up a therapist's name in one of the indexes.

Exercise 1-3

Briefly describe the type of training you would expect each of the following therapists to have had.

a. Clinical psychologist:

_____

b. Psychiatrist:

_____

c. Psychiatric social worker:

_____

d. Mind therapist:

_____

e. Counseling psychologist:

_____

Please check your descriptions against those found in the Feedback section.

Checkpoint

Use the following questions to check your understanding of this portion of the chapter. Choose and mark the one correct response to each question.

1. What is the purpose of applied psychology?
   a. To expose the history of psychology
   b. To study the theories of psychology
   c. To use the discoveries of psychology
   d. To use the findings of history, sociology, and other disciplines
2. What does psychology study?
   a. Human behavior
   b. Animal thinking
   c. Unconscious thoughts
   d. Human perception
3. Who is most likely to state, "The whole is more than the sum of its parts"?
   a. A behavioral psychologist
   b. A psychoanalyst
   c. A gestalt psychologist
   d. A humanist
4. Suppose you wanted a young woman to wear her red sweater. If you held a behavioral view, what might you do?
   a. Discuss her perception of the color red.
   b. Give her a reward for wearing the sweater.
   c. Point out her unconscious need to wear red.
   d. Let her discuss her attitudes and associations with red.

5. Which view of psychology is primarily concerned with behavior that can be observed and agreed upon?
   a. The behaviorist view
   b. The gestalt view
   c. The psychoanalytic view
   d. The humanist view

6. Bing's psychologist told him that he should not blame himself for being aggressive. He is controlled by unconscious impulses. What view does his psychologist probably hold?
   a. A behavioral view
   b. A gestalt view
   c. A psychoanalytic view
   d. A humanist view

7. What would a humanist psychologist emphasize?
   a. Organization
   b. Impulses
   c. Rewards
   d. Choices

8. Which type of psychologist is most interested in how your mind processes information?
   a. Behavioral
   b. Cognitive
   c. Psychoanalytic
   d. Humanistic

9. Which of the following professionals is likely to accept and practice more than one view of psychology?
   a. A psychoanalyst
   b. A behaviorist
   c. A gestalt psychologist
   d. An eclectic psychologist

10. At what stage do most psychologists specialize?
    a. In high school
    b. As undergraduate students in college
    c. As graduate students and thereafter
    d. Never

11. Which of the following therapists is a physician?
    a. Psychiatric social worker
    b. Clinical psychologist
    c. Psychiatrist
    d. Mind therapist

12. What is a psychotherapist?
    a. A therapist who focuses on the unconscious
    b. A person who specializes in vocational interests
    c. A professional who treats emotional problems or disorders
    d. A physician who works with children

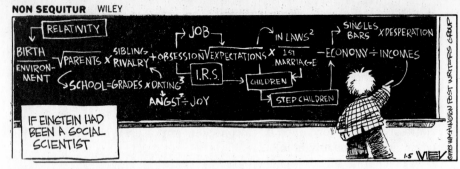

FIGURE 1-2. Measurements in the social sciences are more complex than in the natural sciences.

13. Which types of psychologists are psychotherapists?
    a. Clinical and counseling
    b. Environmental and forensic
    c. School and social
    d. Educational and developmental
14. Which of the following professions is not governed by state licensing?
    a. Psychologists
    b. Psychiatrists
    c. Psychiatric social workers
    d. Mind therapists

Check your responses against the Checkpoint Answer Key at the end of the chapter. If you had difficulty with any question, reread the text. If you had little or no difficulty answering the questions or have resolved problems that you might have had, you are ready to continue with the next portion of the chapter.

METHODS OF PSYCHOLOGY

You may have heard that psychology is just "common sense." Sometimes the findings do make sense; however, they must be based on evidence. Psychologists of all types use a variety of different techniques to gather their evidence. Psychology is a social science and is considered a borderline science. Every attempt is made to use scientific methods, but, as you can imagine, it is difficult to measure human behavior accurately. Natural sciences measure weights of materials and components of chemicals, while psychologists are faced with the difficult task of measuring humor, motivation, adjustments, and changes in people. Methods used in psychology have limitations, so read the cautions carefully.

Observation

observation Research method that requires watching and recording behavior without interference or interpretation

Observation requires watching people and recording what happens. The psychologist does not meddle or interfere with what people are doing. Sometimes a one-way mirror is used because people often change their behavior when they believe they are being watched.

FIGURE 1-3. Sometimes it's difficult to avoid making insinuations from observations.

Recording of observations must be factual. Psychologists note what happens without making any interpretations or inferences. For example, if someone laughs, the psychologist records the laughter. No inference is made about the cause of the laughter. Whether the laughter was caused by something funny, a joyous feeling, nervousness, or an attempt to cover up fears cannot be determined through observation alone.

Caution! Beware of insinuations based on observation. Since inferences should not be made from observations, behavior cannot be explained. For example, suppose you observed that there were a large number of bearded men in a particular town. All you can conclude is that the town has a large number of bearded men. There are innumerable reasons for their beards. Perhaps beards are in vogue, or women prefer men with beards, or razor blades are expensive. Maybe the men are trying out for Santa Claus roles. The list of possible causes could be as long as this book. Suppose you saw a woman lift up papers and stare around the desk surface beneath them. Next she rubbed the desk with the palm of her hand. What can you conclude? Is she looking for a small object, brushing dust, or wiping a spot? If you are a cautious observer, you will not conclude anything. You will simply record her behavior.

Exercise 1-4

Have you heard the joke about the psychologist and the frog? It seems the psychologist was observing a frog's response to a bell. The psychologist rang a bell. The frog jumped. The psychologist immediately wrote down that the frog jumped. The psychologist cut off one of the frog's legs and again rang the bell. The frog jumped. The psychologist noted that the frog jumped. A second leg was cut from the frog and the bell was rung. The psychologist again recorded her observation of the frog jumping. She then cut off the frog's third leg. The frog once again jumped in response to the ringing bell. The psychologist noted the behavior. Finally, the psychologist cut off the frog's fourth leg and rang the bell. The frog did not move. The psychologist wrote in her notes, "When frog's fourth leg is cut, frog becomes hard of hearing."

From what you know about the technique of observation, criticize the psychologist's conclusion.

_____

_____

_____

Please turn to the Feedback section to check your criticism.

Case Study

case study In-depth study of one individual, usually including tests, biographical and family histories, and interviews

The *case-study* method is used primarily by clinical psychologists working with troubled persons. A case study is an in-depth examination of one individual. The purpose is to learn as much as possible about the person's problems. The technique is expensive and takes several sessions for completion.

Psychologists usually begin by acquiring biographical information that relates to the problem. In the case of a child, psychologists usually interview parents and request reports from teachers and other significant people who know the youngster. They then interview the troubled person and begin extensive testing. Depending on the type of problem, intelligence, aptitude, achievement, perception, and personality tests may be administered. Based on the evaluation of the test results, biographical information, and interviews, recommendations are made to alleviate the problems. Such recommendations may include therapy, a change in classes or jobs, a new direction in leisure activities, or improved communication with authorities and family members.

Caution! A case study is a valuable source of information on the one person being studied. However, since each individual is unique, you cannot apply the results of one case study to any other individual. For example, if Bilbo attends weekly concerts as a child and develops an intense interest in composing music, you cannot generalize that other children who attend concerts will develop similar interests. Likewise, people react differently to alcoholic parents, family fighting and abuse, and cultural pressures.

"Now think carefully. The answer
you give will represent the opinion of
millions of Americans."

FIGURE 1-4. One would hope that this woman is
part of a carefully selected sample.

Survey

Have you ever received a call asking you which television program you were
watching? Or perhaps you have received a questionnaire enclosed with an
appliance or some equipment that you purchased. The questionnaire might
have asked unusual questions, from the number of bathrooms in your house
to how much time you spend vacationing. In both instances, someone was
conducting a survey. Think back on how you responded—or if you responded.

The purpose of a psychological *survey* is to determine the attitudes and
behaviors of a large group of people. Usually everyone in the group cannot be
questioned; thus, psychologists choose only a sample of the group. The sample
might include half the group or as little as 5 or 10 percent of the group.

If only a small percentage of people are chosen for the sample, they must
be selected carefully. Caution must be taken to be sure that the sample has the
same important attributes as the population they represent. For example, suppose the officials of a college wanted to determine whether students felt that
instructors were giving them higher grades than they deserved. They only
want to survey 10 percent of the students. If the college is half male and half
female, their sample should reflect that. Similarly, the sample should include
the same distribution of subject majors and age groups as the total college
population. Even more important, the sample's grades should reflect the distribution of the total college population.

Suppose grades were distributed on a *normal curve*, as shown in Figure 1-5.
Indeed it would be unusual to have such a perfect assortment of grades, but

survey Poll to de-
termine attitudes
and behaviors of a
group of people

normal curve Bell-
shaped frequency
distribution

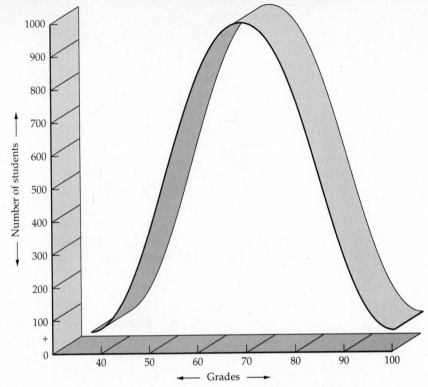

FIGURE 1-5. Grade distribution, total college population.

assume for convenience that most students in the college have grades between 60 and 80. An equal number have grades between 80 and 90 and 50 and 60. Very few have grades above 90 or below 50. The sample must show the same distribution of grades if it is to represent everyone in the college (see Figure 1-6).

After carefully selecting the sample, the college administrators would need to be accurate in wording their questions. Students may honestly feel that they are graded too leniently. However, they may fear their grades will drop if they admit their true feelings to college officials. Researchers have found that people do not always respond honestly to surveys. When drivers were surveyed, 62 percent claimed they always wore seat belts. But when the researchers looked in cars at random intersections, only 30 percent were buckled up (Associated Press, 1987). The article in Feature 1-4 offers another example of a difference between survey responses and actual behavior.

Often questions are worded in a general way to draw out one response. For example, most people are in favor of such general concepts as peace and education and are opposed to violence and pollution. If asked, "Are you in favor of world peace?" most would reply, "Yes." However, responses might vary considerably if people were asked how world peace could be achieved. Good questions should bring out a variety of responses.

Once the questions are written and a list of names has been carefully

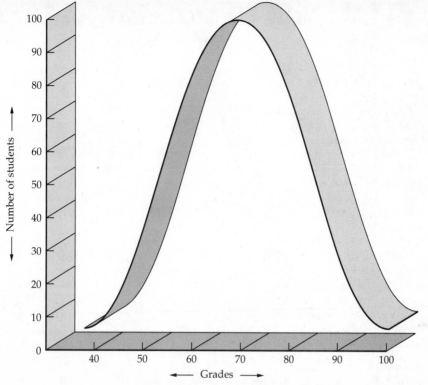

FIGURE 1-6. Grade distribution, sample.

selected for a sample, how can you get the questions to the people in the sample? The cheapest method is by telephone, but you will be limited to people who have telephones and listed numbers. People without phones or with un-listed numbers will be left out. To be sure, they may have different attitudes from the rest of your sample. You cannot assume that their thinking would be the same as the rest of the group.

Another alternative is to mail the questionnaires. Think about question-naires you have received in the mail. If you are like most people, you neither completed them nor returned them. Usually, less than 10 percent of the people return questionnaires received by mail. A 15 percent return is considered high by psychologists. Unfortunately, evidence from such a small percentage of a sample cannot be of much use. Those who took the time to answer questions are not necessarily typical of the people who chose not to respond.

The most accurate method for conducting surveys is through personal interviews. However, it is also the most time-consuming and costly method. As a result, surveys using the interview method are usually either overwhelm-ingly expensive or derived from samples that are too small to permit drawing any conclusions.

Caution! When reading the results of a survey, first note when the survey was taken. World events change! People do modify their thinking and change

VCRs: No Family Affair

Ask your average owner of a videocassette recorder what's so wonderful about having a VCR and he or she may well say that it's a great way for the family to spend time together. But watch that same family in action and you're likely to find quite a different story: VCR use is, by and large, a solitary sport.

In Great Britain, where VCR ownership resembles that in the United States, more than 40 percent of all houses have VCRs. In those with children, that figure rises to more than 50 percent. Psychologist Barrie Gunter of England's Independent Broadcasting Authority and sociologist Mark R. Levy of the University of Maryland surveyed more than 400 households in four regions of England to find out who watches what with whom.

Almost three-quarters of the respondents agreed with the statement, "Watching video is often an enjoyable way for my family to spend some time together." But video-use diaries painted a different picture. Almost 60 percent of the videotapes played during a two-week period were watched alone. Only 22 percent were viewed with adults from the same household and a mere 6 percent were viewed with children from that household.

By comparison, broadcast-television viewing was far more sociable: Only 24 percent of TV programs viewed directly off the air were viewed alone; 42 percent were watched in the company of other adults and another 17 percent with both adults and children from the same household.

Source: Grant, E. (1988, January). VCRs: No family affair. *Psychology Today.*

their minds. American attitudes toward Iraq were relatively neutral until Kuwait was invaded. Similarly, attitudes toward fashions, education, activities, and relationships constantly sway.

Judge the wording of the questions used. Were the questions worded to bring out only one response? The choice of words in the question should be neutral and not show any bias.

Read the results of surveys conscientiously. Check the size and representatives of the sample. If they are not stated, chances are good that the poll is hiding something. The conclusion that "three out of four homemakers surveyed recommended Slowpoke baking powder" could mean that only four homemakers were surveyed. All four may be major stockholders in the Slowpoke Company. Conclusions should be based on a large representative sample.

Survey conclusions can be worded to convey totally different impressions (see Feature 1-5). It is usually best to read survey results directly rather than accept another person's interpretation. As in observation, facts are important and inferences should be avoided.

Exercise 1-5

State the main difference between the case-study method and the survey method.

_____

_____

_____

"Excuse me, sir. Are you interested in going to Heaven?"

FIGURE 1-7. An example of a general question designed to bring forth an obvious response.

Exercise 1-6

A librarian has been campaigning to have more city funds allocated to buying books. He decided to prove that most of the people in the city felt there were not enough books in the library. He conducted a survey by asking people who checked out books, "Would you like more books in the library?" Ten people were asked and nine responded "yes." The tenth person was uncertain. The librarian concluded: "Ninety percent of the people in our city want more funds allocated for library books. No one opposes additional funding for the library." Criticize the librarian's survey method in each of the following areas:

a. Selection of the sample: _____

_____

_____

b. Size of sample: _____

_____

_____

c. Wording of the question: _____

_____

_____

d. Conclusion: _____

Please turn to the Feedback section to check your answers.

Correlation Method

Suppose you want to find out whether high school students who travel tend to get higher grades. Look at the roster in Feature 1-6 and imagine these were

---

FEATURE 1-5 PSYCHOLOGY IN THE NEWS

Religion in America: A Rashomon Result

One more set of statistics that can be read several ways comes from a new survey of American attitudes and values. The official version is below at left; at right, an alternate—equally accurate—reading, based on the same data, by Carin Rubenstein, a social psychologist and associate editor of *Psychology Today*.

- "Forty-nine percent of Americans say they have made a personal commitment to Christ which they feel has changed their lives."
- "Twenty-six percent of the American public over the age of 14, representing more than 45 million people, are highly religious."
- "Blacks are far more likely to be highly religious than whites. . . . Women are more inclined than men to be highly religious. . . . Those with lower, rather than higher, incomes [and] . . . levels of education are more likely to be highly religious. There is a steady increase in religious involvement of Americans as they grow older."

- More than half of Americans (51 percent) say they have not made an important commitment to Christ.
- Fifty percent of the American public over the age of 14, representing more than 87 million people, have low religious commitment.
- In general, underprivileged groups and minorities—Blacks, women, the poor, the uneducated, and the elderly—are the most religious.

- According to a press release, "The . . . report detects a religious current sweeping the United States today, finding America is a nation of people committed to religious beliefs."

- An alternate release might read: "The report detects strong religious faith only among underprivileged Americans, finding privileged America a nation of people largely indifferent to religion."

Source: Rubenstein, C. (1981, July). Religion in America: A Rashomon result. *Psychology Today.*

your results. There appears to be a clear relationship, or *correlation*, between the number of miles traveled during the past year and the grade-point average of students. What can you conclude? Does travel improve ability or knowledge? Do good students yearn to travel? Or do students from enriched homes travel and do well in school? All could be true. There is simply not enough information to prove a cause.

correlation Relationship between scores on two variables

Suppose a psychologist found a correlation between the number of churches in a community and the amount of alcohol consumed. Is is not likely that the people are drinking in church. Nor is it probable that after drinking, people build churches. One factor does not necessarily cause the other, although it might. In this case, there is most likely an underlying factor related to both the amount of alcohol consumed and the number of churches—namely, the population of the community.

Read the article in Feature 1-7. While the researchers found a positive correlation between the amount of television viewing and young people's cholesterol level, they avoided concluding that watching television causes a rise in cholesterol or that high cholesterol causes young people to crave television. The possibility that those who watch more television also exercise less or have more time to eat fatty foods are more plausible explanations to be explored.

Rather than simply inspecting a roster of numbers, psychologists use statistical formulas to compute correlations. Correlations can be positive or negative. A *positive correlation* means that as one variable increases, so does the other. Likewise, as one variable decreases, so does the other. The example of grade-point average and distance traveled was a positive correlation. *Negative correlations* are equally important. In a negative correlation, as one factor increases, the other decreases. For example, there is a negative correlation between the amount of alcohol consumed and the ability to drive a car. As the amount of alcohol people drink increases, their scores on driving tests will decrease. While correlation is a useful method for studying many relationships, it does have limitations.

positive correlation When one variable increases, the other also increases

negative correlation When one variable increases, the other decreases

---

FEATURE 1-6

Travel in Past Year

Name		Grade-Point Average	Name		Grade-Point Average
Jim B.	850 miles	4.0	Harry T.	200 miles	2.2
Karen J.	740 miles	3.9	Irene Y.	160 miles	2.0
Saki L.	720 miles	3.8	Bill B.	140 miles	1.6
Lorenzo A.	550 miles	3.5	Lin C.	110 miles	1.4
Clyde B.	400 miles	3.2	Cork C.	60 miles	1.0
Juan C.	360 miles	3.0	Justine G.	50 miles	0.8
Nora H.	300 miles	2.7	Ed C.	30 miles	0.6
Miguel B.	220 miles	2.4			

Caution! Correlation is *not* causation. Too often when a strong relationship is found between two variables, readers or listeners conclude that one factor causes the other. There can be many other possible explanations for the relationship. For example, suppose there is a positive relationship between the number of peaches eaten and the number of cases of poison ivy. There is no evidence that peaches cause poison ivy. Nor can you conclude that poison ivy causes a craving for peaches. In all probability, peaches and poison ivy grow during the same season.

The Experiment

The *experiment* is the only method that can determine whether one factor causes another. Although other methods can reveal relationships, they cannot provide any information on the cause of the relationship. In a psychological experiment conditions are "controlled" so that causes can be discovered. The psychologist begins with a *hypothesis,* or educated guess about a relationship. The hypothesis may be formed after checking the results of case studies, a survey, or a correlation study.

Suppose a survey checked children's school grades and vitamin-pill consumption. If a strong positive correlation was found, a psychologist might wish to determine whether vitamin pills cause improved achievement. The hypothesis would be, "Children who take vitamin pills are more successful in school than children who do not." Success in school will be measured by achievement tests.

The psychologist needs two groups: an *experimental group* and a *control group.* Both groups are equal in school achievement at the beginning of the experiment and are alike in every way. Students are *randomly assigned* to either

experiment Research technique using controls to find causes of specific behaviors

hypothesis Educated guess that gives a tentative explanation and a basis for research

experimental group Group that receives treatment being investigated in an experiment

control group Group of research participants that are the same as the experimental group, with the exception of the variable being studied

random assignment Assignment based on chance alone

FEATURE 1-7 PSYCHOLOGY IN THE NEWS

Television's Cholesterol Connection

New research suggests a link between television viewing and high blood cholesterol levels among children and young adults.

Kurt V. Gold and Thomas K. Hei of the University of California, Irvine, studied 1,066 males and females aged 2 to 20 and discovered that more than half of those who had cholesterol readings of at least 200 milligrams per deciliter of blood—a level considered high by the American Academy of Pediatrics—said they watched more than two hours of television daily. Previous studies have shown that elevated cholesterol during youth may lead to clogged arteries and heart disease later in life.

Hei stresses that watching television doesn't cause high cholesterol, but it may indicate a sedentary lifestyle. Kids who habitually watch television, he says, tend to eat more food, especially the fatty "junk" foods that elevate blood cholesterol.

He advises pediatricians to ask about children's viewing habits during routine checkups and to consider ordering cholesterol tests for those with additional cardiac risk factors.

Source: (1990, November 24). Television's cholesterol connection. *Science News.*

NATIONAL RESEARCH FOUNDATION

WE'D LIKE A FEDERAL GRANT TO TEST THE HYPOTHESIS THAT MONEY CAN'T BUY EVERYTHING!

THAVES 9-1
© 1992 by NEA, Inc.

FIGURE 1-8. Do you think their hypothesis was based on a case study, survey, or correlation study?

the experimental group or the control group. Random assignment requires that the students be chosen for each group purely by chance. The experimenter may put the names of all students in a hat and draw names to be assigned to the experimental group and control group. The students are not told which group they are in.

The psychologist then gives the experimental group a vitamin pill every morning. The control group receives a pill that looks and tastes like a vitamin pill but is only a *placebo,* an inert substance. If the control group did not receive anything, the psychologist could not be certain that vitamins alone were causing success. It is possible that simply receiving a free pill every morning could make students work better. All conditions must be exactly the same for both groups, except for the content of the pills.

placebo Inert substance or fake treatment often used on a control group in an experiment

Just believing they received vitamins could affect students' work. Beecher (1959) reported experiments that found a placebo injection (saline solution) was 70 percent as effective as morphine for reducing pain. People who believe they took something often feel better and work harder. Thus, it is important that people in the control group believe they are taking something too.

At the end of the experiment both groups would again be administered achievement tests. Their scores on the tests would be compared. A mathematical formula can be used to decide whether the differences between the two groups' scores are large enough to be statistically significant, that is, not just the result of chance. If all other conditions were carefully controlled and the differences are statistically significant, the psychologist can conclude that the differences are probably caused by the vitamins.

Caution! Control is a key factor in experiments. All factors other than the condition being tested must be controlled. It is critical that subjects not know whether they are in an experimental or control group. Often the novelty of participating in an experiment can produce exceptional results!

When reading experiments, check to be sure a control group was used. Without a control group, you cannot be certain of a cause-and-effect relationship. For example, consider the experiment described. An improvement in achievement scores among students who took vitamin pills for a month would not prove that vitamin pills caused the achievement. Possibly all children improve their achievement scores within a month! Their success on the test could be attributed to variables other than vitamins.

Exercise 1-7

State the key difference between the conclusions that can be reached after a correlation study and after a controlled experiment.

_____

_____

Exercise 1-8

List five steps needed in a controlled experiment.

a. _____

b. _____

c. _____

d. _____

e. _____

You may check your answers in the Feedback section.

Checkpoint

Use the following questions to check your understanding of this portion of the chapter. Choose and mark the one correct response to each question.

15. What does a cautious observer do?
    a. Interfere with behavior
    b. Infer causes
    c. Record behavior
    d. Draw cause-and-effect conclusions
16. Which type of psychologist is most likely to use a case-study method?
    a. A clinical psychologist
    b. An experimental psychologist
    c. A comparative psychologist
    d. A consumer psychologist
17. What is included in a case study?
    a. An experiment, a survey, and tests
    b. A case history, interviews, and tests
    c. A survey, observation, and an experiment
    d. A correlation, tests, and a survey
18. A company decides to take a telephone poll of how people will vote in a coming election. What is wrong with this survey technique?
    a. The sample is not representative.
    b. The sample will be too large.

c. The technique is too costly.

d. The technique is too time-consuming.

19. Assume you want to survey a small representative sample from a tiny town of 100 people. One-quarter of the town residents are over 65. What percentage of your sample should be over 65?

a. 5 percent

b. 10 percent

c. 12$\frac{1}{2}$ percent

d. 25 percent

20. What is the main disadvantage of mailing questionnaires?

a. People are more dishonest on questionnaires received in the mail.

b. Only a small percentage of people return the questionnaires.

c. It is a time-consuming and costly method.

d. Many people do not receive their mail.

21. The results of a study reported that 80 percent of the doctors surveyed recommend soaking your feet in Relaxy Solutions. What can you conclude?

a. A large number of doctors were surveyed.

b. A small number of doctors were surveyed.

c. The pollster is not revealing the number of doctors surveyed.

d. No doctors were surveyed.

22. A study reported that the number of windows in men's houses correlates with the number of neckties they own. What conclusions can be reached?

a. Owning neckties causes men to buy houses with many windows.

b. Living in a house with many windows causes men to purchase neckties.

c. People give neckties to men who live in houses with many windows.

d. No cause-and-effect conclusion can be reached.

23. Which of the following methods can determine causes?

a. The survey

b. Observation

c. Correlation

d. The experiment

24. A psychologist gave children an arithmetic test. She gave them lollipops for a month and then retested them. Their scores on the test improved. What does her experiment lack?

a. Observation

b. Adequate testing

c. A survey

d. A control group

Check your responses against the Checkpoint Answer Key at the end of the chapter. If you had difficulty with any question, reread the text. If you had little or no difficulty answering the questions or have resolved problems that you might have had, you are ready to continue with the final portion of this chapter.

culture Norms, beliefs, values, and ways of life that are shared by a group of people

Suppose a psychologist wanted to predict how a child somewhere in the world would turn out. The psychologist had to forecast the future behavior of the child based on only one fact. What would be the most useful fact to have?

If you answered "culture," you know the most important factor in predicting human behavior. Although culture has been recognized as a key to human behavior since the days of Hippocrates and the early Greeks, only recently have psychologists accepted that cultural diversity should be recognized in *all* mainstream research (Betancourt & Lopez, 1993). In the past, only cross-cultural psychologists compared the behavior of people in different cultures. They attempted to find out which behaviors were the same in all cultures and which behaviors differed across cultures. Only rarely did their studies examine the underlying causes of the differences of behavior in each culture.

What is *culture*? Psychologists have not agreed on a set definition, but most agree that culture includes the norms, beliefs, values, and ways of life that are shared by a group of people. Each culture defines the roles and responsibilities of family members, how people communicate and express their emotions, and whether the individual or the group is more important. Cultures often have spiritual beliefs and religious rituals.

Aspects of Diversity

Diversity includes more than differences in general culture. It also involves differences in race, ethnic group, socioeconomic class, gender, and special conditions such as physically or emotionally handicapped and mentally gifted or retarded. Many people confuse the terms *race* and *ethnic group*.

race Genetic background of Caucasoid, Negroid, or Mongoloid

ethnic group Group that shares common nationality, culture, or language

You probably have seen questionnaires that asked you to indicate your race by checking whether you are Asian, American Indian, Black, Latino, or White. Yet, Latinos can be White, Black, Asian, American Indian, or any combination of these. The term *race* is often misused to include ethnic groups. Many anthropologists argue that, technically, there are only three races, Caucasoid, Negroid, and Mongoloid. People in the three different racial groups are more alike than they are different, even in physical and genetic characteristics. Many differences that researchers have attributed to race were really based on ethnic differences (Zuckerman, 1990). *Ethnic groups* usually have a common nationality, culture, or language. Your ethnic group probably taught you some specific customs that have been used for generations. Whether your ethnic group is Irish, Italian, Russian, Lebanese, Nigerian, Bolivian, Korean, Japanese, or Icelandic, it is an important part of your culture but it does not indicate your race.

socioeconomic class Level of financial and social power

Another important aspect of diversity is *socioeconomic class*, your level of financial and social power. Even within the same culture, race, and ethnic groups, people who are wealthy and powerful usually have different attitudes, concerns, and behaviors than do people who are poor and oppressed. Sometimes research that suggests ethnic differences is really revealing differences in socioeconomic class. For example, Frerichs et al. (1981) reported that more Latinos suffered from depression than did Anglos or African Americans. How-

..... AND THEN THEY PUT ON THEIR UGLIEST CLOTHING AND LAY THEIR EGGS IN THESE LITTLE HOLES.

FIGURE 1-9. Might these be cross-cultural psychologists from another planet?

ever, when differences in socioeconomic class were considered, the ethnic differences disappeared. Depression is really related to being poor and oppressed rather than to any ethnic group. The same issue may apply to the relationship between *gender* and depression. If a culture gives less power and financial resources to women, can you be certain that the reason more women than men suffer from depression is biological?

The factors involved in diversity are closely intertwined. It is not easy to clearly distinguish whether behaviors are caused by race, ethnic background, socioeconomic class, gender, or special conditions, such as physical or emotional impairments. Research is suggesting that race and gender are probably less significant than culture and socioeconomic class.

Exercise 1-9

Read the following description and indicate the aspects of diversity of the person described.

Arax was born in the South Bronx area of New York City. Both of her parents had immigrated from Armenia. Arax looked just like her beautiful Armenian mother with clear white skin and rich black hair. Her parents struggled to provide for her. Her father worked as a janitor in an apartment building where his uncle lived and her mother worked long hours in a neighborhood grocery store that was owned by an Armenian friend. Since most of her family's friends spoke Armenian, Arax had a difficult time adjusting to English in school, had a stuttering problem, and at first was a poor student. Students made fun of her and she hated going to school. Her parents valued education and arranged for an older Armenian girl to tutor Arax in English. Her parents could not afford speech therapy so Arax's stuttering still persists. As her ability to speak English improved, Arax became more comfortable in school but had less contact with her Armenian relatives.

Arax is now a successful high school student at the Bronx High School of Science. Although she has many American friends, she still treasures her Armenian background.

a. Cultural values _____

b. Race _____

c. Ethnic group _____

d. Socioeconomic class _____

e. Gender _____

f. Unusual conditions _____

Please check the Feedback section.

Cultural Bias in Psychology

culture-bound
Limited to one culture

Most research in psychology is conducted in the United States and, as Betancourt and Lopez (1993) noted, is based primarily on the findings of Anglo-Americans studying Anglo-Americans. As a result psychology is considered *culture-bound*; the findings can apply to only one culture. To be certain that a theory applies to everyone, it would have to be tested rigorously in various parts of the world (Lonner, 1988). Clearly, one culture is overrepresented in the study of psychology—middle class Euro-Americans. Even more limiting is the fact that male college students are the most likely subjects in psychological experiments. Women, African Americans, Asians, Hispanics, and people of lower socioeconomic status are underrepresented.

Culture affects researchers as well as subjects. Much of what psychologists emphasize in their research is based on such Euro-American values as individual achievement, self-understanding, motivation, and career interests. The norms that are established in these areas are for Euro-Americans and cannot be applied to cultures that do not share the same values. Indeed some psychologists have described people of other cultures who do not score well on these dimensions as "culturally deprived." While these individuals may be "deprived" of a Euro-American culture, most likely they are enriched in their own culture.

Cultural Awareness

The United States has long been known as a "melting pot." People from diverse cultures were expected to blend and adjust to the American way of life. Currently there is a new trend in psychology toward accepting and even cherishing and nurturing diversity (Szapocznik and Kurtines, 1993). Many American college students have had little or no personal contact with other cultures or ethnic groups. Since no culture can exist in isolation, psychologists have recognized the importance of studying cultural diversity. Cross-cultural psychology and ethnic studies are essential parts of the curriculum (see Feature 1-8).

As psychologists are becoming more sensitive to the diversity of people, many new multinational networks and organizations for cross-cultural psychology are beginning. The American Psychological Association publishes guidelines for clinical psychologists who treat ethnically and culturally diverse clients (APA, Office of Minority Affairs, 1990). The excerpt in Feature 1-9 demonstrates how behaviors that are normal in one culture may be problematic in another.

In Defense of Ethnic Studies

A college friend advised me during my junior year to limit the number of ethnic-studies courses I was taking. Why? His reasoning was that top-flight professional schools and employers don't take kindly to too many courses in Black and Chicano studies on a student's academic transcript. . . .

Are ethnic-studies programs as intellectually and academically bankrupt as their detractors claim? No. In fact, my positive ethnic-studies experiences at Pomona College in California both reinforced the exact opposite and confirmed my suspicion that ethnic-studies programs are merely the scapegoats of unfair political battles currently being waged in American higher education and in the larger society. . . .

So, contrary to allegations that ethnic-study courses lack intellectual and academic rigor, I found that they demanded tough assignments, critical analysis and extensive classroom discourse. . . .

Ethnic-studies programs complement the otherwise narrow focus of traditional liberal arts curricula with different viewpoints and perspectives that can sensitize students' thinking. They also promote a sometimes utopian but necessary appreciation of cultural pluralism. . . .

But if educators sacrifice this important component of the liberal-arts curricula for egotistical or ideological reasons alone, American education at large will only stand to suffer, because de-emphasizing ethnic studies makes liberal education illiberal.

Source: Sarpong-Kumankumah, J. (1992, August). In defense of ethnic studies. *Essence.* p. 134.

While there is evidence that all humans share the same biological processes and basic feelings, we have little to go on in determining how cultures create differences in attitudes and expressions. Psychologists are faced with the task of providing some universal principles, theories that apply to everyone regardless of culture, race, ethnic group, gender, or special conditions. Finding objective scientific evidence on cultural similarities and differences is an important step in short-circuiting the stereotypes and prejudices to be discussed in Chapter 14.

The Psychiatry of Culture and the Culture of Psychiatry: Cultural Bias and Mental Health

Since illness categories reflect cultural principles, we must be careful not to let our own cultural bias exert a hidden damaging effect on our scientific research and therapies. For example, many Plains Indians hear the voice of a recently deceased relative calling them from the afterworld. The experience is culturally typical for members of these communities, and therefore by definition cannot be abnormal. On the other hand, for an adult White North American it might well be a hallucination with serious implications for mental health. . . .

Source: Kleinman, A. *The Harvard Mental Health Letter.* (1991, July). The psychiatry of culture and the culture of psychiatry: Cultural bias and mental health. p. 5

The hope is that an increased understanding among cultures will improve communication and provide alternatives to violence and war.

Exercise 1-10

For each of the following categories indicate how psychologists can reduce bias and broaden their perspective.

a. Topics being researched _____

_____

_____

b. People selected for experiments _____

_____

_____

c. Clinical treatment of people from diverse backgrounds _____

_____

_____

Please check your responses in the Feedback section.

ETHICS

Although there are federal regulations for scientific research, the American Psychological Association (APA) established an additional broad set of ethical guidelines to protect the records and welfare of persons who are being studied or are participating in research (American Psychological Association, 1992). According to the APA guidelines, research psychologists are expected to:

- Respect the dignity and welfare of participants and protect them from both physical and mental harm.
- Use language that is reasonably understandable and inform participants of the nature of the research.
- After the nature of the research has been described, have the people willing to participate in experiments sign *informed consent* documents.
- Allow participants to withdraw from an experiment at any time.
- Avoid deception and inform participants of the purpose and procedures immediately following their involvement.
- Keep records confidential and guarantee the participants' right to privacy.

informed consent
Document signed by subjects in an experiment after the nature of the research and any risks have been explained

The APA ethical code also sets standards of conduct for psychologists involved in clinical or counseling practice, teaching, advertising, and forensics, along with strict guidelines for the use of animals in research.

Checkpoint

Use the following questions to check your understanding of this final portion of the chapter. Choose and mark the one correct response to each question.

25. Which aspect of your life is most likely to affect your future?
    a. Your race
    b. Your genetic makeup
    c. Your size
    d. Your culture

26. Which of the following is an example of a race?
    a. Mongoloid
    b. Asian
    c. Latino
    d. American Indian

27. Maria is a Catholic domestic worker from Guatemala. She has just arrived in the United States. What is her ethnic group?
    a. Catholic
    b. Domestic workers
    c. Guatemalan
    d. American

28. Which of the following aspects of diversity is related to depression?
    a. Gender
    b. Race
    c. Socioeconomic class
    d. Ethnic group

29. Why is psychology considered culturally biased?
    a. Most psychologists are prejudiced.
    b. Most research has focused on White American males.
    c. Most researchers distort the results of their experiments.
    d. Minority subjects are often mistreated.

30. How is the focus of psychology changing?
    a. Diversity is being studied.
    b. Ethical standards are being reduced.
    c. Fewer experiments are needed.
    d. Less training is required.

31. According to the ethical regulations of the American Psychological Association, what must psychologists tell subjects in their experiments?
    a. Whether they are in the experimental group or control group
    b. The theories behind the experimental hypothesis
    c. The purpose and methods of the experiment
    d. The names of other subjects in the experiment

CHAPTER INVENTORY

Use this list of objectives as a review checklist. You should be able to do each task outlined in the objectives. If you can, you may feel confident that you have mastered the material in this chapter.

1. Describe the nature of applied psychology.
2. Distinguish among the views of psychology: the behaviorist, the gestalt, the psychoanalytic, the humanist, and the cognitive.

3. Recognize that most psychologists are eclectic and define the term.
4. Distinguish among psychologists, psychiatrists, and psychiatric social workers.
5. Briefly describe the subspecialties of psychology.
6. Identify psychology as a borderline science, and recognize the need for scientific methods.
7. Describe the procedure used in observation, and specify the cautions and limitations.
8. Identify the purpose of case studies, and describe the procedures used.
9. Explain the procedure required in a survey, and recognize the importance of sample selection and sample size.
10. State the limitations and cautions associated with the survey method.
11. Distinguish between correlation and causation.
12. Recognize the experiment as the only method that determines causes.
13. List the steps required in an experiment, and explain the need for control groups.
14. Describe the importance of culture in predicting behavior.
15. Identify and define six aspects of diversity.
16. Recognize that psychology has been culturally bound.
17. Explain why psychology needs to address issues of diversity.
18. List six ethical guidelines established by the American Psychological Association.

Feedback

The correct answers to the exercises follow. If you did not answer an exercise correctly, review the preceding pages and return to the exercise to correctly complete it.

1-1. You should have checked the following:
Learning practical uses
Observing everyday behavior
Using principles of psychology
Using the methods of psychology
Learning when to use the methods and principles of psychology

1-2. a. Psychoanalytic: concerned with past events buried in his unconscious
b. Humanist: accepts the view that dreams are in the closet
c. Behavioral: wants to reward desired behavior
d. Gestalt: concerned with perception and understanding
e. Cognitive: concerned with the process of the mind
f. Eclectic: accepted all the views

1-3. a. A Ph.D., specializing in testing and therapy
b. An M.D., with additional training and an internship in psychological disorders
c. A master's or doctorate, specializing in family and marital problems and community social services
d. Probably a quack!
e. An M.A., an Ed.M., an Ed.D, or a Ph.D. in counseling, specializing in educational and vocational adjustment

1-4. The psychologist was recording observations correctly until the end of the experiment. The correct observation should have been "When frog's fourth leg is cut, frog does not jump." (Admittedly, the psychologist's conclusion was funnier!)

1-5. The case-study method examines one person in depth, while the survey method samples the attitudes of many people.

1-6. a. The sample was not carefully selected to represent everyone in the city. People who do not use the library were excluded.
  b. Only ten people were questioned. Although the population of the city was not stated, chances are the sample was only a fraction of the percentage of the entire population—too small to be accurate.
  c. The question did not include anything about allocating money in the city budget.
  d. The conclusion did not state the size of the sample or the selection method used. The librarian inferred that people wanted more city money, although the question made no reference to funding. The conclusion should be factual rather than inferential.

1-7. After a correlation study, one can only conclude that a relationship does or does not exist. After an experiment, one can conclude whether or not one factor is causing another.

1-8. a. Formulate an hypothesis.
  b. Assign subjects to experimental and control groups.
  c. Check to be sure the two groups are similar.
  d. Control all conditions except the factor being tested.
  e. Test both groups to see if there are significant differences.

1-9. a. Value hard work and education
  b. Caucasoid
  c. Armenian
  d. Working class/lower middle class
  e. Female
  f. Language problems and a speech defect (stuttering)

1-10. a. Include values from other cultures.
  b. Select more women, African Americans, Asians, Hispanics, and people of lower socioeconomic status.
  c. Learn about typical behaviors in other cultures; use scientific evidence on cultural similarities and differences.

Checkpoint Answer Key

1. c; 2. a; 3. c; 4. b; 5. a; 6. c; 7. d; 8. b; 9. d; 10. c; 11. c; 12. c; 13. a; 14. d; 15. c; 16. a; 17. b; 18. a; 19. d; 20. b; 21. c; 22. d; 23. d; 24. d; 25. d; 26. a; 27. c; 28. c; 29. b; 30. a; 31. c.

Perceiving

Genius, in truth, means little more than the faculty of
perceiving in an unhabitual way.
—WILLIAM JAMES

Imagine you are watching a group of Hawaiian women dancing to soft and lilting ukelele music. Your Hawaiian friend, watching with you, exclaims, "What a beautiful story!" You keep staring but neither see nor hear any story. You merely hear a pleasant melody and see some women waving their arms and wiggling. As your friend explains the meaning of each dance movement, you begin to recognize a charming story about the wind.

Or suppose you are starving and you start eating a juicy steak, only to have someone complain that the cook used a heavy hand on the salt. The steak tasted delicious at first. But as you continue eating, you begin to detect a terribly salty flavor.

Obviously no ingredients were added to your steak, nor did the dancers' movements change. Why did your perception of the steak and the Hawaiian dancers change? In this chapter you will learn about conditions that affect your perception and methods you can use to improve your perception.

Senses are the only source of information from the outside world. In the first portion of this chapter, the differences between internal and external sensation are examined. The relationship between attention and perception is considered, and some common attention-getting techniques are described. The next portion of the chapter investigates some of the conditions that influence the interpretive aspect of perception and also looks at some common illusions.

Finally, methods for improving perception and evidence on extrasensory perception are reviewed.

35

PERCEIVING

WHAT IS PERCEPTION?

Perception is a process that combines both sensing and interpreting. Information from the outside world comes through our senses. The information is then interpreted, and this interpretation gives meaning to what is sensed. For example, when you hear your alarm clock ring, the actual sound you hear is the *sensation*. How you construe the meaning of the alarm is your *interpretation*. If it is 7 A.M. on a weekday, you would probably interpret the alarm as a signal to get moving and begin the day. However, the same alarm may have a different meaning on a holiday. You might perceive yourself as absurd for setting the alarm, or you might snicker at the alarm and roll over. In both instances, the sensation (the ring) was the same, but your interpretation changed because of other factors.

perception Process that combines both sensing and interpreting

sensation Bringing stimuli from the outside world into the nervous system

interpretation Inferring meaning from what is sensed by comparing it with previously stored information.

Exercise 2-1

a. Imagine you are driving along a road and notice a red hexagonal sign. You read the word "Stop." You immediately take your foot off the gas pedal and begin to apply the brakes. Which part of your experience involved sensation, and which involved interpretation?

Sensation:

_____

_____

Interpretation:

_____

_____

b. How might your interpretation have changed if you were walking along the same road and saw the same sign?

_____

_____

Check your responses in the Feedback section at the end of the chapter.

External Senses

Usually the sources of information from the outside world are thought of as the senses of seeing, hearing, smelling, tasting, and touching. Improving each of these senses—perhaps with contact lenses, hearing aids, or sinus surgery—could involve physiological changes. But even after all these corrections and improvements, our senses would still be limited. For example, look at the frame in Figure 2-1. You can probably see three or, possibly, four dots.

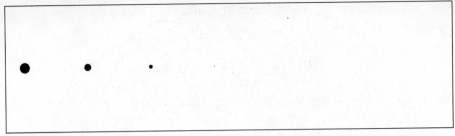

FIGURE 2-1. How many dots do you see?

Actually there are eight dots in the frame. Several dots are so small that you are not consciously aware of them. Similarly, you probably have neither heard nor smelled a flea. Their sounds and odors are beneath our sensory *thresholds,* and we cannot perceive them consciously. A threshold is the smallest amount of a stimulus that we are aware of sensing: the tiniest image, the softest sound, the faintest scent, or the blandest taste and texture. To find your hearing threshold, turn down your radio or stereo to the point where you can just barely detect the sound. If you lower the volume any further, the sound will seem to disappear. The level of sound you can just barely hear is your threshold.

threshold Smallest amount of stimuli that a person is aware of; stimulus a person can barely sense

Role of the Brain in Perception

Your brain is amazing! It picks up messages from each of your external senses and allows you to see, hear, smell, taste, and feel. It then collects and stores this information so you can use it to interpret future sensations. Scientists believe the human brain is the most complex structure in the universe. In addition to ruling perception, your brain controls your moods, memory, movements, body functions, and imagination.

The outer surface of the brain is called the *cortex* (from the Latin word for bark). The cortex consists of deep folds of nerve tissue. If unfolded, the entire surface of the cortex would be about the size of an office desk. Most of your thinking and perception results from nerve impulses moving across your cortex.

cortex Outer surface of the brain that processes all perception and complex thoughts

At first, nerve impulses travel from your sensory organ to a specialized receiving area in your cortex (see Figure 2-2). For example when you hear notes of a song on the radio, the signal is sent from your ears to the auditory (hearing) cortex of your brain. The nerve impulse is then passed on to other regions of the brain, where the sounds can be interpreted and compared with other notes you have heard. If you have heard the song before, you will recognize it.

Subliminal Stimuli

What about the radio sounds beneath your threshold? Some believe that you sense these sounds and the nerve impulses travel to the specialized area of your brain, even though the sounds seem inaudible to you. The sounds, sights, and other stimuli beneath your threshold are considered *subliminal.* Research on hypnosis has confirmed that unconscious influences are possible.

subliminal Stimulus beneath a person's sensory threshold

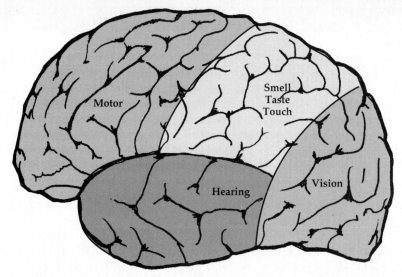

FIGURE 2-2. Specialized areas of the brain's cortex receive sensory messages.

Even patients under anesthesia may have some awareness. As reported in Feature 2-1, people under anesthesia may be influenced by what they hear. Might we also be unconsciously influenced by subliminal information? Wolfe (1983) found that we can see things without conscious awareness. But it is not clear whether subliminal messages can definitely change our behavior.

A few studies during the 1950s implied that people could easily be influenced by subliminal suggestions and be totally unaware of them. Movie houses experimented with subliminal flashes of "Buy popcorn" in their films; some claimed major increases in popcorn sales. The implications were alarming. However, these experiments were not carefully controlled. The increased sales could have been attributed to weather conditions, the type of audience attracted to particular films, changes in refreshment displays, or many other possible factors. As you read about the results of subliminal experiments, check to be sure that the experimenters used proper controls. Controlled laboratory studies have not shown evidence that subliminal advertising is effective.

The study of the use of subliminal stimuli to change behavior continues. During the 1980s there was a suspicion that devil messages were recorded backward on music albums. Many were frightened that these subliminal messages could change people. However, Vokey and Reed (1985) found no evidence that these messages could affect attitudes or behavior. More recently a group of psychologists had college students listen to subliminal tapes that were designed to increase either their memory or their self-esteem (Greenwald et al., 1991). However, after five weeks of listening to the subliminal tapes, students did not improve their scores on either memory or self-esteem tests. But there was an interesting result. The researchers intentionally mislabeled half the tapes. Students who listened to self-esteem tapes thought they were listening to subliminal messages to improve their memory. Conversely, students

Hear No Evil

For years doctors have suspected that when patients are under anesthesia, they can hear what's being said around them. Now studies in the United States and Britain suggest that anesthetized patients not only hear but also unconsciously "absorb" what is being said in the surgical area.

M. Ghoneim, an anesthesiologist at the University of Iowa, conducted a study in which a group of anesthetized patients were read a list of words. The day after surgery they were shown a list of word fragments. More than half of the patients filled out the fragments to complete the words they heard under anesthesia, but they had no conscious recall of hearing them. The same groups of patients had been told to touch their ears or noses. After the anesthesia they were still touching the body parts dictated by the surgeon but had no recollection of being told to do so. As far as Ghonheim is concerned, this confirms that "some information processing functions in the brain continue to work during general anesthesia."

In Great Britain, anesthesiologists Carlton Evans and P. H. Richardson at St. Thomas's Hospital in London have shown that suggestions made during anesthesia can help speed recovery from surgery. Patients who were given positive suggestions, such as "You will not feel sick," recovered sooner and had fewer complications than patients who had received no encouragement.

How do these messages influence recovery or lodge suggestions in the minds of anesthetized patients? No one is sure, but, writes Evans in the British medical journal *Lancet*, "It is clear from our finding that these suggestions did get through in some way and improved their recovery from surgery."

Source: Gurney, O. (1990, March). Hear no evil. *Omni*.

---

listening to subliminal memory tapes thought they were hearing about self-esteem. Even though the tapes had actually improved neither memory nor self-esteem, students "thought" they had improved in the area on the label of the tape. Students who had listened to memory tapes perceived their self-esteem as improving and students who had listened to self-esteem tapes perceived their memory as improving. People believed in subliminal influences that never happened. To date there simply is not enough evidence to decide whether or not subliminal cues affect people.

Exercise 2-2

A rather dull-witted psychology instructor wants to find out whether students respond to subliminal suggestion. After a long, monotonous lecture, he writes on the blackboard in $\frac{1}{4}$-inch letters "What time is it?" He observes several students checking their watches and proclaims, "Aha! You reacted to the subliminal message!"

a. From what you know about the meaning of the word "subliminal," what is wrong with this experiment?

_____

_____

_____

b. What other factors might make you question the instructor's conclusion?

_____

_____

_____

Check your answers in the Feedback section.

Internal Senses

The senses of hearing, seeing, smelling, touching, and tasting give information about the external world. There are also senses that provide internal information. Do you want to get in touch with some of your internal senses? Turn off a few of your external senses. Close your eyes and cover your ears. Saunter around the room for a few minutes. (If you are on a busy street, on a cliff, or in a crowded area, wait until later.) Without visual or sound cues, you will have to rely on internal senses. Take time out. Do your strolling now, and come back to complete the next two exercises.

Exercise 2-3

Record your experiences from your perceptual stroll by answering the following questions about your internal senses.

a. Were you more aware of your steps and movements? _____

b. Did you go astray or veer to the left or right when you were trying to walk a straight path? _____

c. What problems did you have in maintaining your balance, or equilibrium?

_____

d. Could you tell if there was an obstacle near you or if you were going through a doorway or narrow space? _____

e. How much time did you spend strolling? Did the time pass slowly or quickly? _____

Exercise 2-4

Each of the questions in Exercise 2-3 related to one internal sense. Based on your experiences and responses to these questions, list five internal senses.

a. _____

b. _____

c. _____

d. _____

e. _____

You may check your answers in the Feedback section.

Perception and Attention

Perception is strongly influenced by attention. Unfortunately, if you daydream during a lecture, little or nothing will reach your brain. Attending is not always easy, so so you take notes and make conscious efforts to remain alert. Did you notice an error in the last sentence? You probably were concentrating on the content and although your eyes saw the word "so" repeated, you ignored it. Likewise you were probably not focusing any attention on your thumb until you read this sentence. You simply cannot attend to every stimulus around you, so only certain things are selected. Have you ever driven down a highway with your gas needle nearing "empty"? Chances are you became preoccupied with the location of gas stations. Another day when your tank was full but your stomach was empty, the gas stations might have been overlooked, but every diner and restaurant would have caught your eye. Attention is usually focused on needed things. If you are hungry or thirsty right now, you might have a problem keeping your attention focused on the reading rather than on the refrigerator.

Advertisers often appeal to needs and interests as a sure way to attract attention. They insinuate that popularity will increase because houses are cleaner or teeth are brighter. But since advertisers are not always certain of the needs of their audience, they have to draw on other principles to gain attention. Their most common techniques will be considered.

Contrasts. Perhaps the most basic way to invite interest is to create some sort of change. Contrasts in color, shape, size, movement, and mood are usually effective attention-getters. A small red barn in the midst of white limestone skyscrapers would be apt to catch your eye. Attention-getting fluorescent colors may soon be used on highway signs (see Feature 2-2). A lecturer is more likely to hold your attention when she frantically waves her arms and hops around than when she stands motionless behind a lectern. Creating contrasts is as old as vaudeville. A good program would never feature a number of slapstick comedians followed immediately by several comic monologues. We need a

---

FEATURE 2-2 PSYCHOLOGY IN THE NEWS

Highway Hues: Forget the Blues

Fluorescent yellow and orange should be the highway designer's colors of choice for catching a driver's eye, according to two engineers from Ohio University in Athens.

Helmut T. Zwahlen and Uma D. Vel tested detection and color recognition of four fluorescent and six nonfluorescent, 12-by-6-inch targets, which they placed in full sunlight against backgrounds representing fall colors, spring foliage, or a typical city. They flashed the targets 20, 30, and 40 degrees to the right of the line of sight of a dozen volunteer "drivers," who noted the colors they saw.

The volunteers detected fluorescent yellow best and recognized fluorescent orange more readily than other colors. The results indicated that drivers glancing to the side see the fluorescent colors much better than they see the nonfluorescent counterparts.

Source: Pennisi, E. (1992, July). Highway hues: Forget the blues. *Science News.*

FIGURE 2-3. The man with the novel label will surely attract more attention than Ed, Nancy, Bill, John, or Ted.

variety of moods to hold our attention. You may want to check how often television commercials use the principle of change and variation to hold your attention. Look for color contrasts and changes in settings, moods, and movements.

Changes in Intensity. Another way to win attention is through changes in intensity. Ever notice that radio and television commercials tend to be louder than the rest of the program? Flashing lights on movie marquees and neon signs also exploit our interest in contrasting intensities.

Repetition. Repetition is another key to attention. A friend who accepts your invitation with a "yes, yes, yes," will attract more notice than someone who merely responds, "yes." Candidates for political office pass out bumper stickers and buttons in hopes that the repetition of their names will hold your attention. Likewise, advertising slogans and product names are frequently repeated many times in magazine ads and commercials. But if repetition is overdone, it can become monotonous and boring, and attention will be lost to a more interesting stimulus.

Novelty. One sure way to divert your interest is through novelty. If, as you continue your reading, a large purple blob crossed the room ringing a fire siren, your interest would undoubtedly stray from this book. Commercials frequently appeal to an attraction to novelty. Rabbits that beat drums, cats that eat from elegant crystal glasses, and elves with baking abilities are only a few.

Social Insinuations. Social insinuations can also attract our interest. If everyone else appears interested in something, we assume it worthy of our attention. Perhaps as children you and your friends were involved in a prank of putting your ears to the sidewalk as if there were some unusual sounds emerging. Soon others would join you in response to the insinuation that there was something worth hearing under the sidewalk. Similarly, ads frequently suggest that products are popular or praised and approved by famous people.

Exercise 2-5

Assume you have been selected as campaign manager for a woman who is running for mayor. The woman is not well known in the community, and your immediate goal is to have her gain the attention of voters. Based on your knowledge of techniques for attracting attention, indicate which of the following alternatives would be preferable and why.

a. Have her appear at social occasions wearing (1) neutral colors and conservative dress or (2) bright colors and striking clothes.

Alternative: _____

Reason: _____

b. Hang (1) conventional rectangular posters on walls or (2) hexagonal posters from wires.

Alternative: _____

Reason: _____

c. In the local paper, place (1) half-page ads in three locations or (2) a single full-page ad.

Alternative: _____

Reason: _____

d. Have her make a short promotional speech (1) on a local music program or (2) on a local talk show.

Alternative: _____

Reason: _____

e. Either (1) surround her with people who appear intrigued and ask her questions, or (2) have her travel alone.

Alternative: _____

Reason: _____

Compare your choices and reasons with those given in the Feedback section.

Distraction and Pain Control

Sometimes it is desirable to be distracted from stimuli. Pain is one example. Although it is important to feel pain so that you know if you have a sore throat or an infected toe or tooth, there are times when you want to turn off some of the pain experience. In experiments psychologists have shown that people can experience relief from pain when distracted. Some considerate and imaginative dentists have used this advice and supply stereophonic headphones or small television sets. Others are more conventional and hand out magazines. Distraction is an important factor in natural childbirth. Attention is diverted to concerns with breathing and monitoring the progress of the labor. The mother is so concerned with her role in delivery that she is less aware of the pain she is experiencing. Indeed in some cultures women seem to experience no pain at childbirth but the man "goes to bed and groans" (Rumpel, 1988).

Both Olshan (1980) and Beers and Karoly (1979) found that pain can be relieved through mental exercises. If you are suffering from severe stomach discomfort, you might pretend your pain is caused by running furiously up Mount Everest. Imagine the fame, the crowds, and the awards awaiting you, the fastest person to climb Mount Everest! Perhaps a little farfetched, but it may help. Next time you have a nagging headache or sore muscles, try to focus your attention on something fascinating and see if you perceive less pain.

Checkpoint

Use the following questions to check your understanding of this portion of the chapter. Choose and mark the one correct response to each question.

1. Which two processes are always involved in perception?
   a. Attention and subliminal stimuli
   b. Subliminal stimuli and sensation
   c. Sensation and interpretation
   d. Internal sensation and distraction

2. Which of the following stimuli would be beneath your sensory threshold?
   a. A bright light bulb that almost blinds you
   b. The odor of a grain of salt
   c. The low-pitched tones of a bass
   d. A lecture that you are ignoring

3. Where does perception occur?
   a. In each sensory organ
   b. In the lower part of the brain
   c. In the cortex of the brain
   d. External to the body

4. What does current research on subliminal stimuli suggest?
   a. Almost everyone is constantly influenced by subliminals.
   b. Only visual subliminal stimuli affect behavior.
   c. There is not enough evidence to determine the influence of subliminal stimuli.
   d. People cannot be affected by subliminal stimuli.

5. Which of the following contain three internal senses?
   a. Senses of balance, nearness, and time
   b. Senses of balance, touch, and smell
   c. Senses of vision, hearing, and touch
   d. Senses of hearing, time, and taste

6. A woman is engrossed in her work. She suddenly looks at the clock and realizes she has worked through her lunch hour. Which of the following reasons best explains why she had not noticed the time?
   a. Her attention was focused on her work rather than on the clock.
   b. The clock's ticking was only a subliminal cue.
   c. There are social insinuations about clock-watching.
   d. Her work may have been painful.

Listed on the left are techniques for winning attention. Match the statement on the right that provides the best example of each technique.

7. _____ Repetition

8. _____ Novelty

9. _____ Changes in intensity

10. _____ Social insinuations

11. _____ Contrasts in color, shape, or size

a. A woman paints a white stripe on her black car.
b. A teacher raises his voice and screams, "Quiet!"
c. The crowd around a store bargain table grows constantly.
d. A mother nags constantly, "Don't forget to clean your room."
e. A man squirts everyone he sees with a water pistol.

Use the Checkpoint Answer Key at the end of the chapter to verify your responses. If you had any difficulty with a question, carefully reread the text. If you had little or no difficulty answering the questions or have resolved any problems that you might have had, you are ready to continue with the next portion of this chapter.

FACTORS AFFECTING INTERPRETATION

Having discussed sensation and attention, we can move on to the interpretation of perception. Interpretation implies that meaning is inferred from what is sensed. Because each person has had different experiences, needs, and emotions, no two people interpret reality in quite the same way. Have you ever looked at a priceless modern painting and found it absurd and senseless? Apparently it had meaning for at least one other person and probably for many others. Individual differences in perception are important. It would be a boring world if everyone viewed reality in exactly the same way. But sometimes these differences can present problems. Ask any police officer who has tried to determine what occurred at a traffic accident! Sometimes there will be as many perceptions as there are observers. This section of the chapter will investigate some of the main factors that cause varying interpretations in perception: expectation, cultural factors, and needs, motivations, and emotions. It will also examine some common illusions.

Expectation

F. Scott Fitzgerald stated, "We do not first see and then define; we first define and then see." Past experience and learning often point out what should be

FIGURE 2-4. The debate participants have strong differences in their perception of global warming.

expected. For example, if you were in a card game with some people who had cheated you before, you would be on guard for deceptive actions. Simple coughs or foot tapping might be interpreted as trickery. Previous experience has a strong influence on perception. The article in Feature 2-3 reminds us that even professional judges can be biased by their expectations.

People have some idea of what exists out there, and to some extent this determines what is perceived. Ask one of your professors to check your grade on a "jest." Based on past experience the teacher will probably assume you said "test." It is doubtful that anyone had ever before expressed concern over a score on a "jest."

Past knowledge also provides a frame of reference. If a boss is accustomed to a secretary who makes at least five errors on every page typed, a replacement who makes only two errors on each page would be perceived as a good typist. However, the replacement secretary would be rated far lower when compared with more efficient coworkers in the organization. The appraisal of the secretary's competency changes when the frame of reference shifts. Likewise, how you judge a film will depend on whether you compare it with one that won an Oscar or an old rerun of a B movie. The frame of reference will make an impressive difference.

Exercise 2-6

A woman accustomed to her Irish family's simple cooking decides to try eating at a Mexican restaurant. As she is seated the waiter presents her with a

Memories Trip Up Gymnastics Scores

Two Canadian psychologists offer advice to ambitious gymnasts: In athletic meets perform your warm-ups as flawlessly as possible to avoid taking a scoring tumble in actual competition. The reason: Gymnastics judges display unconscious scoring biases in favor of gymnasts who perform warm-ups with no slip-ups, report Diane M. Ste.-Marie and Timothy D. Lee of McMaster University in Hamilton, Ontario.

. . . Judges' unintentional memories for warm-up moves cut two ways. If a warm-up proceeds perfectly, a duplicated performance in competition gets an optimal score and a flawed performance gets a better score than it deserves, the psychologists assert. However, if the warm-up contains a flub, a flawed competitive performance receives a minimal score and an error-free routine scores undeservedly low.

While the 8 percent contrast in accuracy between judges' ratings . . . appears relatively small, it could easily affect competition standings, the researchers add. For instance in the 1988 Olympics, the women's gold medalist scored 79.675 out of 80 and the 10th-place finisher scored 78.550, a difference of less than 2 percent.

Source: (1991, March 9). Memories trip up gymnastics scores. Science News.

platter of tortilla chips and salsa. She asks if the salsa is "hot," and the Mexican waiter assures her that the sauce is very mild. As she swallows a chip dipped in the salsa, her mouth feels afire and she quickly begins gulping her water. Using the concept of *frame of reference,* describe the possible causes of the differences in the perception of the salsa.

You may check your description of the causes with those in the Feedback section.

Sometimes you are told what to expect. Your own past experiences and frame of reference will then have less importance. Look at the professor in

FIGURE 2-5. Professor Ahman Oramouz.

FIGURE 2-6a. Stimulus figure.

"Seven"   "Four"

FIGURE 2-6b. Reproduced figure.

Figure 2-5. You expect to see a man, and you probably do. Take another look. Could it be a mouse? The figure will switch from man to mouse depending on what you expect to see.

In one experiment two groups of subjects were shown the same stimulus figure shown in Figure 2-6a. One group was told it was the number "7" and the other group was told it was the number "4." When the two groups were asked to reproduce the figures, their drawings resembled those in Figure 2-6b. Being told what to expect had a clear impact on what was perceived.

Many initiation rituals are based on telling people what to perceive. One gimmick involves passing around a pair of peeled grapes to blindfolded initiates. The initiates are told they are feeling the eyes of a dead person. Even if you have never experienced this type of ritual, you can probably imagine the horror that accompanies the resulting perception. Although the participants are touching ordinary grapes, the expectation of something horrible changes their perception.

Uniforms have been used to influence our expectations and perceptions. As the excerpt in Feature 2-4 reports, we have specific expectations from people in uniforms. If you met a woman dressed as a nun, you probably would expect her to be holy and somewhat reserved. As a result, you would most likely see her as religious and self-controlled, rather than as a rowdy materialist.

Exercise 2-7

A psychologist named Sirpola (1935) told one group of subjects that he would present words related to boats. He then presented the stimulus words: "sael," "dack," and "wharl." The group interpreted the words as "sail," "deck," and "wharf."

He presented the same stimulus words to a second group of subjects. This time he said the words would be related to animals.

a. Give an educated guess on how the words were interpreted.

"sael": _____

"dack": _____

"wharl": _____

b. Why did the two groups give such different responses?

_____

_____

_____

Check your answers in the Feedback section.

In another investigation, a psychology professor introduced the same male guest lecturer to two different classes. The first class was told to expect a rather cold, dull, uninteresting person. The second class was told to expect a warm, intelligent, friendly lecturer. The lecturer presented identical information in the same manner to both groups. The groups perceived him differently and ac-

FEATURE 2-4 PSYCHOLOGY IN THE NEWS

Standard Issue

. . . One function of service apparel is to communicate a company's selling points, whether it be cleanliness, professionalism, safety or just good taste. Thus, like a chameleon, service apparel assumes the properties of the group it represents. It embodies the group's ideals and attributes, allowing its wearer to transmit the dominant values of the company or organization. Effective uniforms can go a long way toward establishing a desirable impression: the hygienic nurse, the brave soldier, the law-and-order police officer.

Uniforms help to boost customers' confidence in an organization or business. Since many services (such as an airplane flight) cannot be inspected before they are bought, consumers are reluctant to take a chance on an unknown provider. By contributing to a recognizable and familiar image, uniforms enhance company credibility and lessen consumer hesitancy.

Lynn Shostack, a services-marketing consultant based in New York, has proposed that the more abstract the service, the greater the consumer's need for tangible evidence of its quality. As Harvard marketing professor Theodore Leavitt has

observed, in the extreme case the marketer must essentially create a physical surrogate for the product. For example, while airplane customers are actually buying a ride from point A to point B, their choice of a carrier is often based on such things as food quality, the attentiveness of flight attendants and perhaps even the feeling evoked by the airline's color scheme.

As people deal with a service business over time, they are likely to be served by several individuals in the same roles. For example, a hotel guest may encounter different employees on different shifts during the course of a stay. The continuity of uniform can smooth over fluctuations in service quality and personnel by providing a consistent picture of the provider, regardless of who happens to represent the organization at a given time. The very presence of a uniform implies coherent group structure—someone who wears the uniform and a superior who authorizes that person to wear it. . . .

Source: Solomon, M. (1987, December). Standard issue. *Psychology Today.*

FIGURE 2-7. How do you suppose poor Bernie will be affected by the suggestion of itching?

cording to their expectations: The first group found his lecture boring and did not ask questions; the second group found him warm and stimulating and asked many questions. This experiment has been replicated successfully many times. The results suggest that telling someone what to perceive in another person will influence what is experienced.

Exercise 2-8

A party is moving rather slowly, and there are many awkward silences and pauses. The host corners you in the kitchen and pleads for help. You agree to assist with the introductions. From what you know about expectations and perceptions, suggest the type of introductions that might help get the party going.

_____

_____

_____

_____

Compare your suggestion with the one in the Feedback section.

You probably have less difficulty detecting subtle differences in features among persons who are similar to you.

Cultural Factors

Do you recall the problem of interpreting the movements of the Hawaiian dancers described in the beginning of the chapter? Clearly a cultural factor was responsible. As discussed in later parts of this chapter, psychologists also know that culture can affect how people experience pain and are influenced by illusions.

Perhaps the most interesting effect of culture is how you perceive people with backgrounds similar to yours versus your perception of people from different cultures. If you are like most people, you can easily identify subtle differences in individuals within your own group but tend to view people of other races, ethnic groups, and ages as very much alike. Caucasians think that all Afro-Americans are similar, old people see young people as alike, and young people think all old people are the same (Brewer & Lui, 1984; Linville & Jones, 1980). People in your "in-group" (your college friends) are seen as more diverse than people in "out-groups" (people of other ethnic or racial groups). People in "out-groups" tend to be stereotyped (Judd and Park, 1988).

Since you know more about your own group, you will be critical of biased stereotypes presented by the media. As suggested in Feature 2-5, you probably will not be as critical when the media gives biased treatment of "out-groups."

Six students of different cultural backgrounds are meeting for the first time at a college student council meeting. Harry is English, Dominic is Italian, Eric is Swedish, Ho is Chinese, Sadaka is Japanese, and Kim is Korean. Harry, Dominic, and Eric recognized each other by name immediately but have difficulty distinguishing between Ho, Sadaka, and Kim. Likewise, Ho, Sadaka, and Kim quickly identified each other but are still confusing Harry, Dominic, and Eric. What is the probable cause of their perceptual problems?

_____

_____

_____

You may compare your response with the one given in the Feedback section at the end of this chapter.

Needs, Motivations, and Emotions

Earlier in this chapter, needs and motivations were mentioned as factors affecting attention. Needs and motivations constantly interact and create emotions. It is difficult to separate the roles of these three factors, but there has been considerable research on how they work together to affect perception.

One group of psychologists studied how financial needs affect the perception of coin size. Middle-class college students were asked to adjust the size of a light to approximate the sizes of a penny, a nickel, a dime, and a quarter. The students were then hypnotized and told they had a history of poverty. The hypnotist suggested they lacked even the basic necessities. While still under hypnosis the students were again asked to adjust the size of the light to the

---

FEATURE 2-5 PSYCHOLOGY IN THE NEWS

Psychology: Group Involvement and Media Bias

When the news media cover issues that matter to specific groups of people, they are fair and accurate—except when it comes to your own group. Then bias really shows and it's clearly unfavorable to your side.

That, a news story shows, is what most people think, no matter what group they belong to or what issue they hold dear.

"Involvement in a group means you're almost certain to consider the media's treatment of your group as biased against you," said Al Gunther, who studies mass media and public opinion at the University of Wisconsin at Madison.

Gunther's study . . . looked at nationwide sam-
ples of people belonging to seven groups whose interests are frequently in the news: Republicans, Democrats, Roman Catholics, born-again-Christians, African-Americans, Hispanics, and labor unionists. The survey asked respondents to give their opinions of how fairly the news media covered each of the groups.

In every group the preponderant opinion was the coverage of issues affecting other groups was "quite likely fair," whereas coverage pertaining to the subject's group was usually biased.

Source: Resberger, B. (1992, November 30). Psychology: Group involvement and media bias. *The Washington Post.*

size of the same four coins. They adjusted the light to sizes significantly larger than each coin. During a second hypnosis session, the same students were told they had wealthy backgrounds and enjoyed many sumptuous luxuries. This time they adjusted the light to a smaller size than they had in their normal condition. Figure 2-8 shows the results of the experiment. Although it is impossible to separate the roles of needs, motivations, and emotions in the perception of the subjects, it is clear that all three factors interacted to change the perception of coin size.

The old adage "love is blind" illustrates how emotions affect perception. Even unattractive people seem incredibly beautiful when you feel deep emotions for them. And when you feel this sense of love, warmth, and well-being, you usually have a more favorable perception of the whole world. Each type of emotion influences perception differently. If you are fearfully walking through a dark alley, you are apt to perceive every sound and shadow as looming danger. Because of your fearful state, you interpret even ordinary stimuli as potential threats to your safety.

Psychologists use perceptions to learn more about underlying emotional states and to analyze personalities. They use ambiguous pictures or inkblots and ask for a description of what is seen. Each person's perception is considered an expression of personal emotions, motivations, and needs. Chapter 9 discusses this method of personality assessment in more detail.

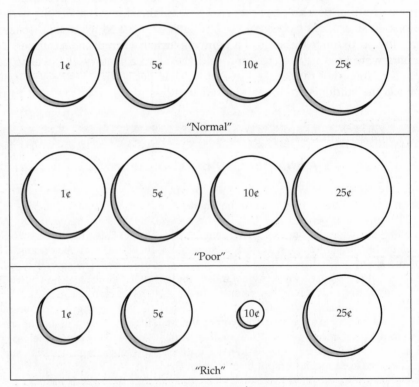

FIGURE 2-8. Average size of light spots judged equal to coin size.

Two women, Mrs. S. and Ms. T., belong to the same recreation club. They were given an outline of the club and were asked to draw a plan of how the facilities were arranged. Examine the correct plan of the club and the sketches made by Mrs. S. and Ms. T. (see Figures 2-9, 2-10, and 2-11 on pages 53 to 55). Based on their perceptions of the club, see what you can learn about the needs and motivations of each woman.

a. Which areas of the club were emphasized by both women?

_____

b. Which areas of the club were emphasized only by Mrs. S.?

_____

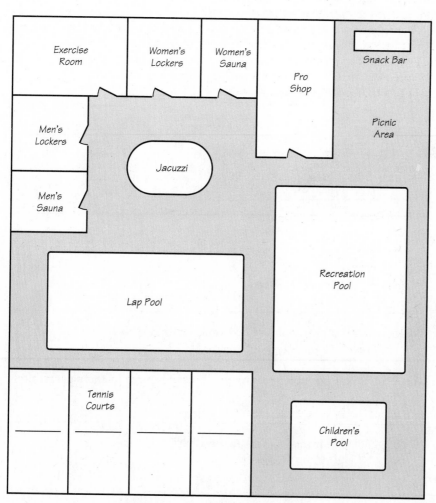

FIGURE 2-9. Correct club plan.

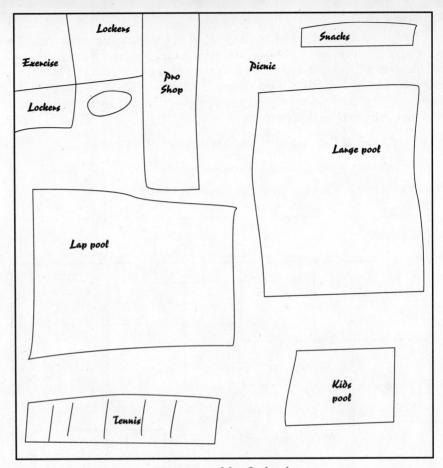

FIGURE 2-10. Mrs. S. sketch.

c. Which areas of the club were emphasized only by Ms. T.?

_____

d. Which areas did both women minimize or forget?

_____

e. What are some possible reasons for the differences in their perceptions of the club?

_____

Please check your answers in the Feedback section.

Illusions

illusion Misinterpretation or error in perception

Illusions are misinterpretations or errors in perception. Look at two common visual, or optical, illusions in Figure 2-12. In both the Muller-Lyer and Ponzo

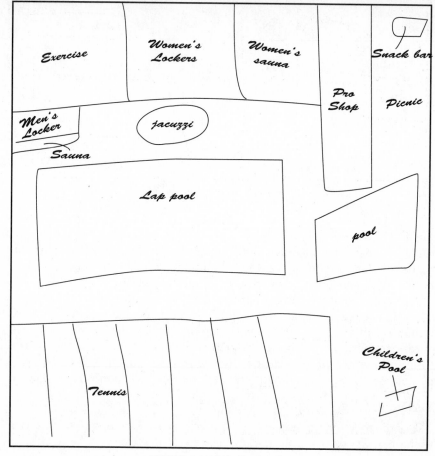

FIGURE 2-11. Ms. T. sketch.

illusions the horizontal lines are the same length. In the Muller-Lyer illusion the bottom line appears longer, and in the Ponzo illusion the upper line looks longer. If all but the horizontal lines were removed from the drawings, it would be obvious that the two lines are equal. The other lines in the drawing cause you to misinterpret their size.

If you were raised in a culture where most buildings are rectangular in shape, you are more susceptible to the Muller-Lyer illusion. Segall and others (1990) found that rural Africans who did not live among rectangular buildings did not misinterpret the size of the lines, while Africans living in cities were caught by the illusion. So your culture can be blamed for some perceptual errors.

But, your brain must accept the blame for some perceptual errors, too. Look at Figure 2-13, an illusion known as the KANIZA triangle. Do you see a triangle? The lines of the triangle are incomplete and the visual cortex of your brain creates lines where none exist.

Illusions can be bothersome and problematic. Pilots who rely solely on

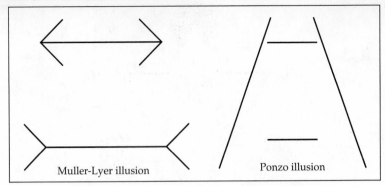

FIGURE 2-12. Muller-Lyer illusion and Ponzo illusion.

their own senses can misinterpret their altitudes or flight attitude. This would be a dangerous situation were it not for aircraft instruments. Pilots are taught to use instruments in situations where visual illusions are likely.

Beauty experts, clothing designers, and interior decorators all use their knowledge of illusion to improve appearances. Eye shadow is used to create the illusion of deep-set eyes; obese men wear suits with vertical stripes to appear slimmer; and rooms are painted white and equipped with small-scale furniture to appear more spacious. Examine your friends and your environment more closely, and you will probably find many examples of illusions.

Checkpoint

Use the following questions to check your understanding of this portion of the chapter. Choose the one best response to each question.

12. Perception includes sensation and interpretation. What does interpretation involve?
    a. Giving meaning to what is sensed
    b. Finding the cause of sensation
    c. Knowing what to expect
    d. Correcting illusions

13. After hearing a local choral group sing, a woman exclaims, "They are the best singing group in the world!" What is her probable frame of reference?
    a. All the singing groups in the world
    b. Singing groups she has heard before
    c. The orchestra that accompanied the group
    d. Her mood on the day she heard the group

14. Which of the following explanations would best account for a man hearing ghost footsteps in his attic?
    a. He has heard ghost footsteps in other attics.
    b. He believes in ghosts and expects to hear footsteps.
    c. The Muller-Lyer illusion has distorted his perception.
    d. His financial needs have distorted his perception.

FIGURE 2-13. KANIZA triangle.

15. If you were told that a certain new job was fun, how would your perception of the job most likely be affected?
    a. You would find the job more difficult.
    b. You would view the job as disappointing.
    c. You would find the job boring.
    d. You would find the job enjoyable.

16. Which of the following persons is most likely to detect a slight sunburn on an Irish-American teenager?
    a. An elderly African-American man
    b. An elderly Native-American woman
    c. A young Asian man
    d. An Irish-American teenage girl

17. In a study of middle-class college students, a group of psychologists had the students adjust the size of a light to approximate the sizes of coins. What did the results of this study suggest?
    a. Expectation affects perception.
    b. Expectation does not affect perception.
    c. Needs and emotions affect perception.
    d. Needs and emotions do not affect perception.

18. What is an illusion?
    a. An error in sensation
    b. An error in interpretation
    c. An incorrect frame of reference
    d. An error caused by needs

19. Which of the following is the best example of an illusion?
    a. A student is tense about an exam and views everything negatively.
    b. A poor girl sees money as more important than grades.
    c. A fat man appears thinner when he wears oversized clothes.
    d. A man who is late for work tries to sneak by his employer's desk.

Check your responses against the Checkpoint Answer Key at the end of the chapter. If you had difficulty with any question, reread the text. If you had little or no difficulty answering the questions or have resolved problems that you might have had, you are ready to continue with the final portion of this chapter.

PERCEPTION IN ACTION

Having looked at the basic principles of sensation, attention, and perception, you will now have an opportunity to actively apply some of these ideas to improve your own perception. In this portion of the chapter you will be considering steps you can take to improve your own sensitivity, awareness, and perception. You will also examine some common and not-so-common perceptual impairments. The chapter concludes by defining types of extrasensory perception (ESP) and checking the evidence from studies of ESP.

Improving Perception

Perhaps you have been wondering what steps you could take to improve your own perception and interpretation of things around you. As mentioned earlier in the chapter, no one can perceive everything. There is always selection in choosing which part of the environment deserves your attention. Factors like past experiences, emotions, motivations, and what other people infer have a strong influence on the interpretation of surroundings. In many ways these factors can also limit and restrict interpretations and resulting perceptions. By using your awareness of these restricting factors, you can enhance and increase your perceptual abilities. Here are a few hints that may be useful in improving your perception:

1. Identify your own needs and emotions. If you are having a "down" day, admit it to yourself and realize that your resulting perceptions may be distorted.
2. Acknowledge your own frame of reference, and concede that others may be using different frames of reference.
3. Try to broaden your view by taking a different perspective. Exchanging positions with another person can create a totally new perception.
4. Differentiate between what you are sensing and what you are interpreting or inferring. There is often a great difference between what is observed and what is inferred.
5. Be suspicious when you are told what to perceive. Search for other possibilities.
6. Recognize techniques that are used to attract your attention, and try to maintain control over undesirable distractions.
7. Remember that you can be fooled by illusions.

Exercise 2-11

Now check your ability to use these hints. In each of the following examples a person is demonstrating a problem in perceiving accurately. Using the hints just listed, explain what each person should do to improve perception.

a. Jim told Juan that their new office building had a faulty heating system. Bob felt chilly as soon as he entered the building, even though the temperature was 72 degrees.

_____

_____

b. Claire woke up with a hangover and a severe backache. She looked in the mirror and saw a face full of wrinkles. Actually Claire was an extremely attractive and youthful-looking person.

_____

_____

c. Marsha drove through a red light. She said she had trouble concentrating on her driving because of all the blinking lights from nightclubs and casinos.

_____

_____

d. Sidney, a chain smoker, cannot understand why nonsmokers are so finicky about sitting near smoke.

_____

_____

e. When Bill saw Meg in a slinky black dress, he was sure she had lost 10 pounds. Actually Meg's weight was the same.

_____

_____

f. Jerome's boss gave him a poor evaluation because she noticed that Jerome spent time staring out the window or off into space. She felt Jerome was a daydreamer. Jerome had been having difficulty with eyestrain, and his doctor had told him to look into the distance periodically to relax his eyes.

_____

_____

You may check your responses in the Feedback section.

Sensory and Perceptual Impairments

Thus far, the discussion of perception has focused on the problems and limitations of people with normal sensory and perceptual abilities. As you know, there are many individuals who have perceptual impairments. Three of the more common types of impairments are blindness, deafness, and dyslexia. People who suffer from these conditions have specific limitations and must learn ways to compensate for their problems.

Blindness and Low Vision. Perhaps you have thought of blind individuals as being able to read braille or walk around with the aid of a cane or seeing-eye dog. Surprisingly, less than 20 percent of the 600,000 blind Americans can read braille, and only about 10 percent can make their way around with canes and seeing-eye dogs. Low vision and blindness are sensory impairments. Many people with visual impairments can make use of contrasts in lights and shadows. However, blind people must rely heavily on their other external senses and on their internal senses. Remember the blindfolded stroll you took while reading the first part of this chapter? Just as you were more aware of your other senses when you were blindfolded, blind persons constantly depend on these other senses. Many blind people show an unusual ability to picture their surroundings through the use of other senses.

There is some hope that total blindness may be eliminated in the near future. Efforts are being made to develop a system that will allow a blind person to see through a glass eye. The glass eye will contain a tiny camera. Wires from the camera will go to a miniature computer placed in an eyeglass frame. The picture messages from the computer will be sent to electrodes that are permanently placed in the visual cortex of the brain. Presently, scientists have enabled blind persons to see individual letters. For example when the camera is focused on the letter "B," a dot-matrix–printed image of the letter appears on the visual cortex of the blind person. The image is similar to the letter images displayed on stadium scoreboard screens. Although this present system probably will not provide normal vision, it may help to give some visual information to the blind.

Deafness and Hearing Impairments. Deafness is another sensory impairment and can become a severe problem in babies and young children because it is difficult to detect. Many parents are not aware that their child has hearing limitations until it is time for the child to speak. Since hearing-impaired persons make use of touching objects, vibrations, and lip-reading, often deafness is not discovered until the child is almost two years old. By then the child is already handicapped in the development of language abilities. If found early enough, many types of hearing loss are correctable with either medication, hearing aids, or surgery. But not all deafness is congenital. Hearing losses can result from exposure to a noisy environment. Although after the age of thirty everyone becomes progressively deaf to the higher frequencies, people who work or live in noisy settings will show a more rapid rate of hearing loss (see Feature 2-6). Intense sounds such as a firecracker explosion or a gunshot may cause permanent damage with only one brief exposure. If you have ringing in your ears or sounds seem muffled, you may have experienced hazardous noise exposure. Noise damage can occur at any age, even infancy.

Just as modern technology is giving hope to the blind, there is also hope for the deaf. Scientists are currently working on microphones that can send electrical signals to electrodes implanted in the brain. With the aid of these electronic systems, it may be possible to bring hearing to the deaf.

dyslexia Perceptual impairment that results in reading, writing, and/or listening problems; reversed, scrambled, or confused message is sent to the brain

Dyslexia. *Dyslexia* is a type of perceptual impairment that affects the ability to read, write, and/or listen. Dyslexia has many different forms. Some dyslexic

Risk of Hearing Loss Is Growing, Panel Says

Millions of Americans are unwittingly suffering a hearing loss because of exposure to loud noises at home, on the job, and during recreational activity, a Federal advisory panel said today.

Experts convened by the National Institute of Health said millions are being exposed to irreversible and untreatable hearing damage because of an increasingly noisy environment.

While some efforts have been made to reduce occupational noise exposure, the experts said too little attention has been paid to potential hearing damage caused by devices like stereo music players and snowmobiles. The panel estimated that more than 10 million Americans have suffered some hearing loss because of exposure to excess noise.

The conference chairman, Dr. Patrick E. Brookhouser, director of Boys Town National Research Hospital in Omaha, said . . . "Everybody who has two ears has an interest in preserving their hearing, . . . Our increasingly noisy environment places more and more people at risk. Many of the individuals who are losing their hearing don't know it."

The panel said sounds with an intensity of less than 75 decibels are unlikely to cause hearing loss even over a long duration of exposure. The sound of ordinary speech is about 65 decibels, and 75 decibels is equivalent to the noise from a dishwasher or vacuum cleaner.

But exposure to sound levels above 85 decibels are potentially dangerous if endured for 8 hours a day for prolonged periods, the report said. And higher levels could cause permanent damage from shorter durations. The panel noted that 85 decibels is roughly equivalent to the sound of a power lawn mower or a food blender.

Source: Leary, W. E. (1990, January 25). Risk of hearing loss is growing, panel says. *The New York Times.*

---

persons read a scrambled or reversed message. For example, "was" might be read as "saw," "517" could be interpreted as "751," or the concepts of "hot" and "cold" might be confused. The errors in perception may involve reversals, mirror images, or some other type of confusion. Although there continues to be much research, the exact cause of dyslexia is uncertain. Studies have shown that people with dyslexia are usually average or above in intelligence and have no clear evidence of brain damage. Nelson Rockefeller, Woodrow Wilson, and Albert Einstein were among the famous dyslexics. Although the cause of dyslexia has not been determined, effective programs have been developed to help individuals adjust to their perceptual distortions. Research on the nature of dyslexia continues (see Feature 2-7).

Exercise 2-12

Consider three of the more common forms of perceptual impairment: blindness, deafness, and dyslexia. In your own words, describe the steps that a person with each of these impairments can now take to adapt.

a. Blindness: _____

b. Deafness: _____

c. Dyslexia: _____   61

Exercise 2-13

Now take a look into the future. What steps might be taken to alleviate each of the disorders discussed in Exercise 2-12?

a. Blindness: _____

b. Deafness: _____

c. Dyslexia: _____

You may compare your responses with those in the Feedback section.

extrasensory perception (ESP) Ability to perceive and/or influence objects without using external senses

parapsychology Field of psychology that focuses on extrasensory perception

telepathy Ability to understand what another person is thinking, without the use of the senses; mind reading

Extrasensory Perception

Many psychologists believe that people have the ability to perceive or influence objects and events without the normal use of the senses. This ability is called *extrasensory perception*. The study of ESP is relatively new to the field of psychology and is included in the field of parapsychology. *Parapsychology* studies behavior that cannot be explained by either physics or physiology. These behaviors are labeled "psi events." The main psi events of interest in parapsychology are:

Telepathy. *Telepathy* is another word for mind reading and has been a central theme in many fantasies and science-fiction stories. People communicate without speaking or seeing each other. Each knows what the other person is

FEATURE 2-7 PSYCHOLOGY IN THE NEWS

Dyslexia: Reading Words, Missing Letters

"Although dyslexics take longer to read and understand words, they can still improve their reading skills and accomplish much," asserts psychologist Maggie Bruck of McGill University in Montreal. "The bad news is that a core problem in dealing with letters and their corresponding sounds doesn't go away."

No good evidence exists as to whether instruction that emphasizes the ways in which sounds "hang on letters" substantially improves the reading skills of adult dyslexics, Bruck notes.

The causes and exact nature of dyslexia remain uncertain. Bruck and many other researchers define it as a disorder in which a healthy person with a normal IQ exhibits word recognition and other reading skills far below standard levels for his or her age. Some educators view dyslexia as a condition that affects all facets of language, including reading, writing, and listening.

Comparisons of dyslexics with good readers of the same age or the same reading level indicated that dyslexics always lag far behind in the ability to match letters to individual sounds that make up words. However as dyslexics get better at recognizing words, they compare favorably with good readers on tests of knowledge about larger segments within words, such as syllables.

"Dyslexics can learn to compensate for this difficulty," Bruck maintains. "We see remarkable progress in many adults who have been dyslexic since childhood and who are willing to work hard at becoming better readers."

Source: Bower, B. (1992, October 3). Dyslexia: Reading words, missing letters. *Science News.*

thinking. In some cases, identical twins have claimed telepathic ability between themselves.

Clairvoyance. *Clairvoyance* is an ability to perceive objects or events that are beyond the reach of the normal senses. A clairvoyant person might be able to describe a traffic jam more than 100 miles away.

Precognition. *Precognition* is the ability to foresee the future and know what is going to happen. Jeanne Dixon became famous for this ability when she predicted the assassination of President Kennedy. You may have experienced a weak version of precognition in the form of a premonition—possibly a vague feeling that something was going to happen to a close friend or relative. Perhaps it was nothing definite, but if the person did get sick you may have taken this as proof of your precognitive ability.

Psychokinesis. *Psychokinesis* (PK) is the ability of a mind to manipulate physical objects. In a PK demonstration a person may bend forks and spoons or make clocks and watches begin to tick.

Do these abilities really exist? Although remarkable phenomena have been demonstrated in nightclubs and on television, the evidence from laboratory experiments is less convincing. Individuals who seem to have outstanding ESP one day will have no such ability the next day. People who claim ESP abilities state they cannot function normally in a sterile laboratory environment. Many supposed "extrasensory" powers can be explained by trickery and the use of illusions.

Most psychologists doubt the existence of psi events, but evidence is still being collected. Watch for their findings, and check your own ESP! As suggested in Feature 2-8, belief in psi phenomena is widespread.

clairvoyance Ability to perceive objects or events that are not within the reach of the senses

precognition Ability to foresee future events

psychokinesis (PK) Ability of the mind to manipulate physical objects without the use of any physical contact

Checkpoint

Use the following questions to check your understanding of the final portion of this chapter. Choose the one best response to each question.

FEATURE 2-8 PSYCHOLOGY IN THE NEWS

Believe It or Not

People express a "surprising degree" of credence in psychic and supernatural phenomena, according to a random, nationwide telephone poll of 1,236 U.S. adults conducted last June. Although these beliefs often conflict with traditional religious views, they emerge among deeply religious folk almost as often as among the nonreligious, report George H. Gallop, Jr., and Frank Newport of the Gallop Organization in Princeton, N.J.

The poll results include the following: One in four people believe in ghosts, one in six cite communications with someone deceased, one in four say they have communicated "telepathically" with another person, one in ten claim to have seen or been in the presence of a ghost, one in seven say they have seen a UFO, one in four believe in astrology and about half believe in extrasensory perception.

Source: (1991, March 9). Believe it or not. Science News.

20. You see a man shuffling through papers on his desk. You do not want to confuse observation and inference. What would be your observation?
    a. A man has misplaced a paper.
    b. A man is shuffling through papers.
    c. A man is looking for a missing paper.
    d. A man is annoyed with his carelessness.

21. What are three of the more common perceptual impairments?
    a. Blindness, deafness, and dyslexia
    b. Deafness, dyslexia, and illusion
    c. Blindness, telepathy, and psychokinesis
    d. Dyslexia, clairvoyance, and precognition

22. How do blind people know that they are going through doorways?
    a. They rely on their internal and other external senses.
    b. They use extrasensory perception.
    c. They use computer-brain implants.
    d. They have psychedelic experiences.

Match the term on the left with one phrase from the list on the right. Only one phrase can be correctly related to each term.

23. _____ Dyslexia

24. _____ Psychokinesis

25. _____ Parapsychology

26. _____ Clairvoyance

27. _____ Precognition

28. _____ Telepathy

29. _____ Illusion

a. Ability to foresee the future
b. Reading the thoughts of another person
c. Receiving scrambled or reversed messages
d. A field of psychology that includes ESP
e. Ability to manipulate objects through the use of the mind
f. An error in interpretation
g. Ability to see something beyond the range of normal vision

Check your responses against the Checkpoint Answer Key at the end of the chapter. If you had difficulty with any question, reread the text. If you had little or no difficulty answering the questions or have resolved problems that you might have had, you are ready to check yourself against the chapter inventory that follows.

CHAPTER INVENTORY

Use this list of objectives as a review checklist. You should be able to do the tasks outlined in the objectives and apply them to everyday examples. If you can, you may feel confident that you have mastered the material in this chapter.

1. Define perception.
2. Distinguish between sensation and interpretation.

3. Identify the limitations of the senses.
4. Provide examples of thresholds and subliminal stimuli.
5. Describe the role of the brain in perception.
6. Summarize the problems encountered in the study of subliminal stimuli.
7. Distinguish between internal and external senses and identify five internal senses.
8. Explain five ways to gain attention.
9. Describe the role of distraction in pain control.
10. Explain how expectation influences interpretation.
11. Describe how cultural factors affect perception.
12. Describe how needs, motivations, and emotions influence interpretation.
13. Define illusions and give three examples.
14. Identify seven ways to check and improve perception.
15. Consider three types of perceptual impairment, and recognize possible ways to improve these conditions.
16. Categorize the study of ESP as a field in parapsychology.
17. Identify and explain four areas of study in parapsychology.
18. Recognize problems encountered in the study of extrasensory perception.

Feedback

The correct answers to the exercises follow. If you did not answer an exercise correctly, review the preceding pages and return to the exercise to complete it correctly.

2-1. a. The color, shape, and letters on the sign that you saw would be your sensation. The meaning that you gave the sign, "Stop your car," involved interpretation.

  b. If you were walking you probably would not stop, since your interpretation would be different. You would not interpret the sign as applying to you.

2-2. a. Subliminal stimuli are beneath the threshold. Letters of 1/4-inch would probably be above the visual threshold for students in front seats. Likewise, students may have been able to guess the letters being written if they saw his hand movements.

  b. The instructor did not control a number of factors. Check to see how many you identified:

    1. His lecture was long and monotonous; perhaps this caused the students to check their watches.
    2. It is also possible that students normally check their watches toward the end of a lecture.
    3. The instructor's behavior is not reported; perhaps he checked his watch.
    4. Likewise, if one or more students who were able to read the message began checking the time, this may have influenced other students.
    5. The term "several students" is vague; this may have been a small percentage of the class.

2-3. Some typical responses to a blindfolded stroll follow:

   a. "I noticed every step I took." "I put my foot down carefully each time to be sure there wasn't a step or something in front of me." "I was really conscious of every move I made."

   b. "I thought I was walking straight, but I found myself in the middle of the room." "I kept moving toward the left; once I was almost against the wall." "I had trouble figuring out which way was straight ahead; I was veering to the right."

   c. "I was afraid I'd lose my balance, so I kept my arms outstretched." "I started to get dizzy." "I didn't have any trouble with balance."

   d. "Even though I couldn't see anything, I could tell when I was going through a doorway." "I could tell when I moved from a big room into a narrow hall." "I didn't know what it was, but I knew there was something big in front of me."

   e. "I was sure I had been walking for at least ten minutes, but it was less than four minutes." "Time sure passed slowly; I was aware of every second."

2-4. Each experience related to one of the following internal senses:

   a. Sense of movement
   b. Sense of direction
   c. Sense of balance
   d. Sense of nearness
   e. Sense of time

2-5. a. Alternative 2: Bright colors and striking clothes will make her stand out in the group and draw attention to her, giving her more visibility and future recognition.

   b. Alternative 2: Hexagonal posters suspended from wires might attract more attention because of their novelty.

   c. Alternative 1: Repetition is a useful technique in gaining attention.

   d. Alternative 1: The contrast from music to speaking would attract more attention.

   e. Alternative 1: An atmosphere of intrigued and interested people would create a social insinuation that she was an interesting and popular candidate.

2-6. The Mexican waiter and the Irish woman are using different frames of reference. The Mexican waiter is comparing the salsa with highly spiced hot food, and the woman is comparing the salsa with mild, relatively bland food.

2-7. a. Seal, duck, and whale.

   b. The subjects were told what to expect, and this influenced their perception.

2-8. Introductions suggesting that each guest is an exciting person would probably help get the party moving. For example: "Sam, meet Bob Taylor. Bob had me in hysterics the last time we met. He's a super story teller. Some of the pranks his kids have pulled are really incredible. Tell Sam about the time your daughter ended up on top of a flagpole." Or "Jane, don't tell me you haven't met Angela. Angela has just returned from a fascinating vacation. She went to a resort that gave instructions on ski-boarding, and now she's an expert!"

2-9. Harry, Dominic, and Eric are all of European cultures and would recognize even subtle differences among each other. Likewise, Ho, Sadaka, and Kim are all of Asian backgrounds and would be more aware of subtle differences in their facial features. Both the European students and the Asian students would have a tendency to stereotype people from "out-groups" and miss perceiving differences.

2-10. a. Both women emphasized the pro shop and the lap pool.
b. Mrs. S. emphasized the snack bar, picnic area, large pool, and children's pool.
c. Ms. T. emphasized the exercise room, women's sauna and locker area, and tennis courts.
d. The men's lockers and sauna were minimized or forgotten.
e. Personal emotions, needs, and motivations probably are the key reasons for the inaccuracies in the perception of the club. It is likely that Mrs. S. has children and uses the pools, snack area, and shop. Ms. T. probably plays tennis, swims laps, and uses the exercise and locker facilities.

2-11. a. Juan needs to be suspicious of what he has been told to perceive.
b. Claire should identify her own needs and emotions. She should admit that she is having a bad day and that her perceptions may be distorted.
c. Marsha needs to recognize the techniques that are used to attract attention and try to maintain control over undesirable distractions.
d. Sidney might try to broaden his perspective by sitting in a smoking area without lighting a cigarette.
e. Bill should remember that illusions can be deceiving.
f. Jerome's boss must learn to differentiate between observation and inference.

2-12. a. A blind person can adapt to the impairment by using other external and internal senses more fully. Learning braille and using a cane or seeing-eye dog are other possibilities.
b. A deaf person must also rely on other senses. Medication, hearing aids, and surgery might be helpful.
c. A dyslexic person would benefit from a special program designed to help with adjustment to distorted perception and peripheral vision.

2-13. a. In the future, blind people will be aided by the use of an electronic camera that is wired to the brain and electronic microchips.
b. Deaf individuals will be aided by an electronic microphone wired to the brain and electronic microchips.
c. The exact cause of dyslexia may be determined in the future, and possibly there will be a cure.

Checkpoint Answer Key

1. c; 2. b; 3. c; 4. c; 5. a; 6. a; 7. d; 8. e; 9. b; 10. c; 11. a; 12. b; 13. b; 14. d; 15. c; 16. d; 17. c; 18. b; 19. c; 20. b; 21. a; 22. a; 23. c; 24. e; 25. d; 26. g; 27. a; 28. b; 29. f.

Learning and Changing Behavior

Give me a dozen healthy infants, well-formed, and
my own specified world to bring them up in and I'll
guarantee to take any one at random and train him
to become any type of specialist I might select—
doctor, lawyer, artist, merchant chief, and yes, even
beggarman and thief, regardless of his talents,
penchants, tendencies, abilities, vocations, and the
race of his ancestors.

—JOHN WATSON

Have you ever wondered why your behavior changes when you are with
different individuals or groups? Perhaps you have been in some situations
where you tended to joke and see humor in everything. Yet in other situations,
people might have only seen your serious side. Sometimes you may act shy
and uncertain, and at other times you are outspoken and friendly. Why do you
keep changing? Psychologists would say that it has something to do with your
learning.

If you are at a party and everyone is laughing merrily at your stories and jokes, you are apt to tell a few more. Your history teacher, however, might scowl when you try to introduce some humor into the class discussion. Only your sober and serious comments will be encouraged. Or perhaps you have been around people you thought to be much smarter than you. You probably felt a bit uneasy and were afraid to say something that might make you sound stupid or foolish. You appeared shy and hesitant. But, since you are accepted pretty well among your close friends, you have no such fears and concerns. You are more likely to say what you think.

Learning is constantly influencing your behavior. Somehow learning is usually associated with classroom instruction. In reality, most learning occurs elsewhere. Almost everything you do involves some learning. Whether you are eating ice cream with a spoon, choosing a fishing rod, knitting an afghan, playing poker, or cheering at a rock concert, your behavior involves learning. In this chapter you will take a closer look at learning and consider its relationship with performance. You will examine more closely the reasons that behavior changes and how you can influence the behavior of other people, as well as change your own. Two major forms of learning, classical conditioning and instrumental, or operant, conditioning, will be described and applied to many different kinds of situations. You will also weigh the ethical problems in using conditioning.

WHAT IS LEARNING?

If almost everything you do involves *learning*, you may wonder how to differentiate between learned and unlearned behavior. Other than a few basic reflexes and some haphazard actions, almost everything you do has been learned in some way. Learning happens internally. It cannot be seen or touched. In fact, it cannot even be measured accurately. Psychologists usually measure learning by looking for a change in performance. If performance shows a relatively lasting change, then they infer that learning occurred.

learning Relatively lasting changes in behavior that are caused by experience or practice

Suppose that last year a boy was introduced to the water for the first time. The child showed some random movements of his arms and legs and then nearly sank. This year you see the child at the beach swimming a strong crawl for about 20 feet. You could rightly assume that the boy had learned to swim. Even though you did not see the learning, you assume it occurred, because the child's performance has changed. It is likely that the child has had some experiences in the water since you saw him a year ago. It was during these experiences and practice that learning happened. Now, every time the boy jumps in the water, he is able to swim. His new ability is lasting, or relatively permanent.

Now imagine that you go to a bowling alley with a woman who has never bowled before and who admits to be lacking in athletic talent. You manage to push her fingers into the holes in the bowling ball. Suddenly she drops the ball on the floor. The ball rolls down the alley, and she has a strike. Was her strike the result of learning? Clearly it does not sound as if she has learned much about the sport, other than how to get her fingers out of the ball. Psychologists look for more permanent changes in performance before assuming that learning has occurred. If she could bowl a strike with some consistency, it could be concluded that she had learned. Such chance behaviors as her first strike do not provide enough evidence to pass judgment on learning.

In judging whether a situation involves learning, look for two important conditions: (1) a relatively permanent change in behavior and (2) some experience or practice that caused the change. Experiences could include observing other people and reading, as well as practicing. The woman in the bowling-alley example had an experience, but it is doubtful that it caused a lasting change in behavior.

Learning is not necessarily positive. People learn to steal, cheat, lie, and swindle. In each of these cases, both requirements for learning are present. Similarly, people can learn to litter, pollute, waste natural resources, and spoil the environment.

Performance as a Measure of Learning

When there is a lasting change in performance, you can infer that learning has occurred. But learning is only one factor; in reality many other factors may also influence performance. Even if you studied endlessly for a midterm exam and felt that you had thoroughly mastered the subject matter, a sleepless night or fever and nausea could affect your performance on the test. Or suppose during the test you had an attack of hiccups or the person next to you had a sneezing fit. A low grade would not necessarily mean you had not learned much. Performance is used as a measure of learning, because learning itself is not observable or measurable. It is important to remember that such factors as motivation, distraction, and health can also affect performance.

Exercise 3-1

A middle-aged automobile mechanic has been taking accounting courses in the evenings. He is now considering changing his career. Although he has always been respected as a mechanic, he has recently been distracted from his work (see Figure 3-1). He spends time planning and thinking about his new career. In breaking in a new employee, he was unable to think of the names of even simple parts of the engine. In your own words describe why this man's present performance may not be a good measure of what he has learned about automobile repair.

_____

_____

_____

_____

You may check your answer in the Feedback section at the end of this chapter.

FIGURE 3-1.

CLASSICAL CONDITIONING

Since performance is observable and can be measured, behavioral psychologists limit their measurement of learning to measurement of changes in performance. They have identified two techniques that cause changes in performance. Behavioral psychologists believe that classical conditioning and instrumental, or operant, conditioning are responsible for almost all learning. *Classical conditioning*, an approach that uses associations and relationships, will be considered first. Reflexes and emotional respondents play the key roles in classical conditioning.

classical conditioning Form of learning based on pairing a stimulus that elicits a reflex or emotional response with a neutral stimulus, so that the neutral stimulus will eventually elicit the reflexive or emotional response

"Reflexes. . .amazing!"

FIGURE 3-2. Perhaps an exaggerated example of the common knee-jerk reflex.

Reflexes

There are many behaviors that occur in all people whenever special stimuli are presented. For example, if someone were to slip a pickle in your mouth, you would begin to salivate. Likewise, if this book caught fire and suddenly burned your fingers, you would pull your hands away from it. Because these behaviors always occur in all people and do not require any learning, they are called *reflexes.*

reflex Response that is always elicited after a given stimulus and does not require learning

You are probably familiar with several common reflexes. If you hit someone in the center of the knee, you are likely to be kicked with a knee-jerk reflex. Or if you are walking along the beach and a gust of wind blows some sand in your eyes, you will experience an eye-blink reflex. A whiff of pepper will make you sneeze. If someone tickles the sole of your foot, you will scrunch your toes. Medical books have recorded many such reflexes in humans.

Emotional Respondents

emotional respondent Emotion that is always elicited by a given stimulus and does not require learning; an emotional reflex

An *emotional respondent* is an emotional reflex, or a feeling that always results from a certain stimulus. Fear is a common emotional respondent. Normal people find pain unpleasant and become fearful. Fear is the normal response to pain, and no learning is required. Anger is another common emotional respondent. Love and joy, more positive feelings, are also considered emotional respondents. If you have ever been infatuated with someone, you probably have experienced some positive emotional respondents. Joy and bliss are possibilities. Each emotional reaction is felt internally in response to some specific type of stimulus. The outward expression of the emotion may vary according to your learning and past experience. But whether you ran up and hugged the

"Harriet's diet? . . . coming along just fine . . .
easy as pie . . . piece of cake . . . bowl o' cherries . . . ."

FIGURE 3-3. Harriet seems to be having an emotional response to the stimulus of his words.

person or simply stood and giggled, you experienced the same internal feeling. Similarly, if someone held a knife against your back, you would undoubtedly experience fear as an emotional respondent. How you expressed the fear would vary according to your cultural background and previous learning experience.

Both reflexes and emotional respondents happen automatically in response to specific stimuli. Whenever something is thrown in your eye, you blink. If an electric shock is sent through the seat of your chair, you rise. A painful experience causes fear and anxiety, and a pleasurable encounter causes joy and happiness.

Exercise 3-2

The following scenario includes three reflexes and five emotional respondents. Draw one line under each reflex and two lines under each emotional respondent.

Clyde, whose union is on strike, has become addicted to watching an afternoon soap opera. This afternoon he notices that it is time for his series to begin and gets himself a cold beer. As he opens the bottle, it fizzes and squirts in his eye. He blinks and becomes annoyed. He then carries his beer over to his favorite chair and settles down to a half-hour of feeling comfortable. The program begins. The charming, innocent heroine is being threatened by a surly, vicious woman. Clyde grows tense. He nervously picks up a cigarette and burns his finger. He pulls his hand away and wraps it around the cold beer. He turns his attention back to the television screen. The evil woman is choking the lovely heroine and kills her. Clyde watches the heroine fall and feels overwhelmed with sadness. He attempts to turn off the television set. But there is a short in the switch, and Clyde gets a sharp electric shock. He pulls his hand away and feels afraid to touch the set again.

You may compare your answers to those in the Feedback section.

The Process of Classical Conditioning

Through classical conditioning you can learn to blink your eye, even when something is not thrown into it. You can automatically rise from your chair without the use of an electric shock. Similarly, people can have fears and anxieties without undergoing a painful experience. The reflex responses and emotional respondents will occur with associations.

Suppose a woman is sitting in a chair wired so that electric shocks can be passed into the seat. A psychologist is trying to use classical conditioning to make her rise from the chair every time he scratches his head. (Psychologists sometimes perform strange experiments!) He has observed that she reflexively rises from the chair whenever an electric shock is sent to her seat.

FIGURE 3-4.

Now when he administers the electric shock, he simultaneously scratches his head.

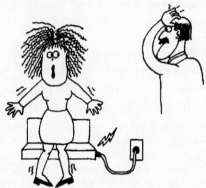

FIGURE 3-5.

Soon she will associate the head scratching with the electric shock. When she sees him scratch, she will anticipate the shock and rise from her chair. Eventually she will rise from the chair whenever he scratches his head, even if the shock has not been administered.

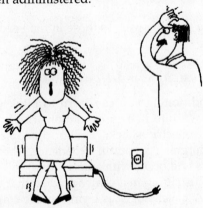

FIGURE 3-6.

Imagine how ridiculous she might feel rising from a chair just because a man scratched his head!

The classical-conditioning process has three stages:

1. A reflex is observed, and the stimulus that causes the reflex is identified. In the example the reflex was withdrawal, or rising from the chair. The stimulus that caused the reflex was the electric shock.
2. Another stimulus is paired with the stimulus that causes the reflex. The psychologist scratched his head at the same time he administered the electric shock. This pairing is repeated many times.
3. The new stimulus causes a reflexive response, even when the original stimulus is removed. The woman rose when the psychologist scratched his head, even when the electric shock was not put through her chair.

Exercise 3-3

A psychologist wishes to use the knee-jerk reflex to make a man kick his leg in response to a whistle. In your own words, specify what should occur in each stage of classical conditioning.

a. Stage 1: _____

b. Stage 2: _____

c. Stage 3: _____

You may check your description in the Feedback section.

The process of classical conditioning follows the same pattern when emotional respondents are used in place of reflex reactions. In the first step, a stimulus that elicits an emotional response is identified. For example, most people would respond with fear and fright to the stimulus of having a gun pointed at them. In the second stage, this stimulus (the pointed gun) is paired with another stimulus that does not usually cause a fearful reaction—perhaps an old sneaker. This pairing is repeated many times. Each time you are handed an old sneaker, a gun is pointed at your head. Eventually you will become frightened when handed the sneaker, even if the gun does not appear. Although this is hardly a common example, there are many instances where such classically conditioned fears occur. Someone who, on four different occasions, had been fired from a job on Tuesday may develop a fear of going to work on Tuesdays. Or a person who has had a number of different painful experiences in a dentist's office may have an unpleasant sensation when detecting the smell of the dentist's cologne. Think of your own fears. Can you trace the causes?

Checkpoint

Use the following questions to check your understanding of this portion of the chapter. Choose and mark the one correct response to each question.

1. How do psychologists measure learning?
   a. By reaction time of basic reflexes
   b. By relatively permanent changes in performance
   c. By quantity and quality of practice
   d. By motivation and interest

2. Which of the following is an example of learning?
   a. A boy falls down when he is pushed.
   b. A woman feels pain when she smashes her finger in the car door.
   c. A girl throws a candy wrapper in a trash basket.
   d. A man sneezes whenever he inhales snuff.
3. How is learning related to performance?
   a. Learning and performance are always the same.
   b. Learning is the opposite of performance.
   c. Learning is one of many factors that affect performance.
   d. Learning is measurable, and performance is inferred.
4. Some behaviors happen automatically and without learning. What are these behaviors called?
   a. Reflexes
   b. Associations
   c. Experiences
   d. Reactions
5. Which of the following is the best example of an emotional respondent?
   a. You blink whenever your grapefruit squirts in your eye.
   b. You always ask for advice when you are lost.
   c. You do your homework at the same time every night.
   d. You become frightened whenever you feel pain.
6. How are reflexes and emotional respondents alike?
   a. They occur automatically and can be used in classical conditioning.
   b. They require learning and practice and are influenced by motivation.
   c. They involve fears and can be removed through classical conditioning.
   d. They involve pleasurable experiences and should be increased by using classical conditioning.
7. A doctor who gives painful shots to children always wears a white coat. Through classical conditioning the children learn to associate the white coat with the painful needle. How will these children probably react when they see a barber who wears a white coat?
   a. They will be frightened.
   b. They will be relieved.
   c. They will feel confused.
   d. They will suffer from bed-wetting.
8. What is the first step in classical conditioning?
   a. Removing a stimulus
   b. Identifying a reflex or emotional respondent
   c. Pairing a stimulus with a reflex or emotional respondent
   d. Pairing a reflex with an emotional respondent

Use the Checkpoint Answer Key to verify your responses. If you had any difficulty with a question, carefully reread the text. If you had little or no difficulty answering the questions or have resolved any problems that you might have had, you are ready to continue with the next portion of this chapter.

You are probably now aware of the importance of classical conditioning in forming some of your fears, attitudes, and superstitions. Next you will look at how you can use classical conditioning to help yourself, whether you are acting, pretending, or trying to overcome some fear or anxiety. The uses of classical conditioning in controlling undesirable behavior will also be examined.

Acting and Pretending

Actors frequently use classical conditioning to make themselves feel emotions so they can portray them in a more convincing way. One technique taught in many acting schools requires potential actors and actresses to think of experiences in their lives that caused strong emotions. An unhappy love affair or the loss of a close relative might be used to bring on feelings of sadness and some honest tears. If a play involved a crying scene, dwelling on these past experiences and associating them with the scene could help an actor again be moved to tears. Likewise, a scene requiring a frightened reaction might require the actor to envision the approach of a poisonous snake. Actors and actresses who use this technique feels that it helps them to appear less phony in portraying feelings, since they are actually experiencing the emotions.

You have probably been in situations where you wanted to hide your true feelings. Watching a clumsy man spill his soup on his lap might strike you as amusing, but undoubtedly you would not want to embarrass the man further. Taking a hint from acting schools, you might find it profitable to dwell on a serious experience, like a final exam. Your sincere, serious expression would certainly cover your amusement.

Exercise 3-4

A close friend has invited you and his boss to a Sunday brunch. Your friend is anxious to make a good impression and wants the boss to enjoy herself. You are finding the boss to be a complete bore, telling old "moron" jokes. When she asks, "Why did the moron throw his clock out the window?" you pretend not to know, since you want to be polite to your friend. When she finishes with "He wanted to see time fly," you manage a courteous laugh. The dull boss then continues her monologue of moron jokes. How might you use the principles of classical conditioning to make yourself appear honestly amused by her supposed wit?

_____

_____

_____

_____

Compare your response with the answer given in the Feedback section.

Most fears are acquired through classical conditioning. A boy is bitten by a nasty little dog and develops a fear of all dogs. Even though the dogs do not bite him and may even appear friendly, the boy fears the sight of them. The appearance of any dog is associated with the pain a dog once caused. As the boy grows older, the fear may become bothersome and embarrassing.

Classical conditioning techniques could help him control his fear. A psychologist would want to remove the emotional respondent of fear and replace it with a more pleasant emotional respondent. Sitting on his mother's lap and being hugged would probably bring the boy a feeling of relaxation and joy. At first he could be shown a picture of a dog while being hugged. Perhaps he could then progress to a toy dog and finally to a real one, using the same pleasant association. If the psychologist achieves the desired goal, eventually the appearance of the dog will be a pleasant emotional experience rather than a painful one.

This gradual method for removing fearful associations is sometimes referred to as *desensitization*. As Feature 3-1 reports, psychologists began using desensitization to reduce fear of flying many years ago. The same technique has been successful in removing fear of heights and of crowds.

desensitization
Therapeutic approach that uses a gradual method of classical conditioning to remove fears

Exercise 3-5

A thirty-five-year-old woman dropped out of high school twenty years ago because of failing grades. She felt humiliated every time a test was returned to her because she usually had the lowest grade in the class. She is now taking a psychology class at her local community college and has an intense fear of taking exams. Her instructor announced that the first test will be next week. She has begun to panic!

Her psychology instructor, Professor Allheart, knows she has become an expert on baseball trivia during the past twenty years. First the good professor asks her several true-false questions about baseball facts. Her responses are

---

FEATURE 3-1 PSYCHOLOGY IN THE NEWS

Grounding the Fear of Flying

The behavior modification technique of desensitization has been reported successfully with at least part of the sweaty-palm, white-knuckle group of airplane travelers. Desensitization involves a step-by-step exposure of the person to progressively fearful situations connected with the phobia. In successful cases, the phobic situation gradually becomes associated with positive, relaxed feelings rather than with anxious or hysterical ones.

Researchers at the New Jersey Medical School in Newark have developed an audio-visual therapy program—using film clips and tapes—to help persons with a fear of flying. In their initial study, the investigators reported that 78 percent of fifty-one people who had previously refused to fly were able to fly after treatment. In addition, the subjects underwent significant attitude changes about flying and, in some cases, about other fears and phobias, as well.

Source: (1978, December 9). Grounding the fear of flying. *Science News.*

perfect, and she feels pleased and proud. Next she is given a short written test on baseball, and again she feels successful. As a final step the woman is given an exam of baseball questions interspersed with psychology questions.

a. What method is the professor using? _____

b. Why might this method help remove the woman's anxieties and fear of

exams? _____

Check your responses with those in the Feedback section.

Unwanted Behavior

The principles of classical conditioning have been used by psychologists to help people rid themselves of such undesirable behavior as bed-wetting (enuresis) and drug and alcohol addiction. Recent studies have shown that bed-wetting can usually be cured through classical conditioning, except in rare cases where the lack of control is complicated by emotional and physiological problems. Bed-wetting occurs when a child does not awaken when the bladder is full. As a result, the child wets the bed. A psychologist invented a device that consists of a wired sheet that detects urine. As soon as it begins to flow, an alarm rings to awaken the child. The training routine follows the standard procedures of classical conditioning. The sound of an alarm causes a reflex response of waking up. The alarm is paired with the initial flow of urine, a sign that the bladder is full. At first the child will awaken when the alarm rings and will begin to associate the ringing of the alarm with a full bladder. After several nights the child will awaken to a full bladder, whether or not the alarm rings. A similar device for snoring is described in Feature 3-2.

FEATURE 3-2 PSYCHOLOGY IN THE NEWS

Antisnore Device

Man's eternal quest for a truly effective way to prevent snoring has led him over the centuries to any number of ingenious, if often impractical, devices, some merely useless, some ridiculous, others downright painful.

One of the earliest was a chin strap that held the snorer's jaw shut. Another triggered a piercing wail whenever the hapless sleeper lost control of his mandible. Next was a device that violently shook his pillow at the faintest sound, followed by a web of wires that broadcast antisnoring propaganda via an earplug.

None of these Rube Goldberg cures proved popular, either with the snorer or with his or her bedmate. Too often the devices woke up the wrong person or incorrectly activated themselves because they couldn't tell the difference, say, between a snore and the sound of passing traffic.

So it remained for one Anthony R. Dowling, an Australian inventor from the Sydney suburb of Vaucluse, to develop a compact, self-contained electronic mechanism worn in the outer ear. It will detect snoring via the vibrations it causes in the head and auditory canal, then emit a buzzing sound that is inaudible to a sleeping partner. Gradually this behavior modifier—complete with a combination microphone/speaker—will break a snorer's habit, according to patent documents Dowling has filed.

Source: Nobbe, G. (1987, November). Antisnore device. *Omni.*

emetic Substance that causes vomiting

Controlling alcohol and drug addiction involves a slightly different procedure. One technique that has been used with some success involves lacing drinks with a substance that causes vomiting. If a person drinks such a substance, called an *emetic*, the normal reflex response is to throw up. If the substance is mixed and paired with alcoholic beverages, the association can become so strong that the alcoholic will feel nausea at the sight of a drink. There is one serious limitation in this technique: It is extremely difficult to have an alcoholic agree to take the treatment.

Medical Uses

People who are suffering and want to change their condition are more likely than alcoholics to be aided by classical conditioning. Patients receiving chemotherapy for cancer often feel nauseated as a side effect. Most associate food (rather than their medication) with the nausea and refuse to eat full nutritious meals. Broberg and Bernstein (1987) fed children coconut and root-beer–flavored lifesavers after chemotherapy and before their next meal. The children associated the candy rather than the meal with their nausea. When compared with children who were not fed lifesavers, the children who ate the flavored lifesavers were twice as likely to eat a test meal.

Many medications have severe side effects. Allergy victims often suffer from sleepiness as a side effect of their medicine. Sampson and Jolie (1984) combined allergy medicine with a strong odor. Children associated the odor with the medication and eventually their allergic reactions were relieved by the odor alone.

Exercise 3-6

Briefly describe how each of the following individuals could use classical conditioning.

a. An actress who must pretend she is nauseated:

_____

_____

b. A girl who is afraid of the sight of blood and wants to become a physician:

_____

_____

c. A boy with enuresis:

_____

_____

d. A physician who wants his cancer patients to eat nutritious food:

_____

_____

You may compare your descriptions with those given in the Feedback section.

81

LEARNING AND CHANGING BEHAVIOR

OPERANT CONDITIONING

Although classical conditioning accounts for many of your fears and attitudes, most behavioral psychologists believe your actions are influenced by the feedback you receive. Suppose you are blindfolded and told to throw a ball at a target. You keep throwing the ball but no one tells you when or if you are close to the target. Without feedback, or knowledge of your degree of success, you cannot improve your skill. You need to hear such comments as "Good throw" or "Really close," or even some negative information such as "Way off," in order to improve. You will try to win favorable comments and avoid the derogatory remarks. You learn to do things that may result in rewards and avoid behavior that may result in punishment. For example, handing in work assignments on time might result in a few words of praise from your boss. You might even eventually earn a bonus, raise, or promotion. In contrast, sleeping at your desk could bring complaints and cost you your job. If you want to have an income, you behave in ways that will allow it to continue. Having an income might be considered a reward; losing your job, a punishment.

The type of learning that occurs because of rewards and punishments is labeled either *operant conditioning* or *instrumental conditioning*. Both terms refer to the same technique, a method of conditioning based on rewards, or positive reinforcers, and punishments, or other negative reinforcers. In classical conditioning, association is the significant feature. In operant conditioning, reinforcers and punishments are the key. Reinforcers and punishments provide feedback.

operant (instrumental) conditioning Type of learning that occurs because of positive or negative reinforcements

Positive Reinforcement

Suppose someone asked you to sit on top of a flagpole for twelve hours and promised you a reward. The reward was a stick of gum. Would you be likely to repeat the flagpole-sitting behavior? Chances are you would not unless there was a severe gum shortage and you craved gum. Although the gum was a reward, it would not serve as a *positive reinforcement*. The result of a positive reinforcement is an increase in the same behavior. What would it take to make you climb up and sit on top of the flagpole again? Perhaps a good positive reinforcer for you would be a new car or a headline in the newspaper or a screen test from a movie studio. If these did not serve as reinforcers, maybe you would sit there for an invitation to the White House or a tour of the Greek islands. Perhaps just smiles of approval from your friends would work. For a positive reinforcement to be effective and increase behavior, it must be appropriate. Finding the right reinforcer can be difficult. Some can be rewarded with money; others seek only attention and approval.

positive reinforcement Rewards that increase the likelihood of a behavior

Behavioral psychologists believe your entire personality is shaped by reinforcers. If you are talkative, your parents and friends have probably found appropriate ways to reinforce your conversation. Simply paying attention and listening is a way of showing approval and is a positive reinforcement. You may have learned some successful flirting techniques or ways of hedging an answer when you are uncertain. Again, approval was the likely reinforcer.

For a reinforcement to be effective, it should occur immediately or as soon as possible following the desired behavior. If a man is training his dog to beg and delays the dog-biscuit reward for an hour after the begging behavior, the pet will not recognize the biscuit as a reward for begging. Instead, the dog may connect the biscuit with more recent behaviors that may have included barking, chewing the furniture, or chasing a cat.

Exercise 3-7

A man serves his wife breakfast in bed, complete with a good French champagne and fresh strawberries. His wife consumes her breakfast with little conversation or comment. Two weeks later when she reads about positive reinforcements in her psychology class, she decides that she would like her husband to serve breakfast in bed more frequently. When she goes home she gives him a penny.

List two things wrong with her positive reinforcement.

a. _____

b. _____

Compare your answers with those in the Feedback section.

Negative Reinforcement

negative reinforcement Removal of an unpleasant stimulus to increase the likelihood of a behavior

Like positive reinforcements, *negative reinforcements* are also used to increase behavior. However, while positive reinforcements are pleasant stimuli presented after you behave as desired, negative reinforcements are the removal of unpleasant stimuli when you behave as desired. For example, suppose your roommate constantly nags you to pick up your messy clothes and clean the room. If you keep your area tidy, the nagging stops. Nagging, the negative reinforcer, is increasing the likelihood of your cleanup behavior. You want to escape from the nagging, so you pick up your clothes and maintain a neat

FIGURE 3-7. The positive reinforcement certainly is effective in increasing asking behavior.

*"Daddy will stop singin' if you pretend you're
asleep."*

FIGURE 3-8. In this cartoon, it appears that "Daddy's
singing" is a negative reinforcement to increase sleeping behavior.

room. In many instances, the desire to escape negative reinforcement is indeed
effective in increasing specific behaviors.

Punishment

The result of *punishment* is a weakened behavior or a decrease in its likelihood.
Punishment can be effective. A study by Sherman and Berk (1984) found that
men who were arrested for wife beating were less likely to beat their wives
during the next six months than were men who were not arrested. The experiment was carefully controlled, and the men were only arrested for twenty-
four hours.

In other cases, however, punishment seems to be ineffective. Thieves who
are sent to jail steal again as soon as they are released. A dog that has been hit
for eating food off the table will often continue to gobble what it can find when
the owner is not around. A teenage girl who is "grounded" because she
sneaked out of the house will try to come up with a more creative plan to get
out without being caught.

Furthermore, many studies have found disadvantages and problems with

punishment An
unpleasant stimulus
that decreases the
likelihood of a be-
havior.

punishment. Generally punishment will suppress a response only for a short time. In most cases the undesired response will reappear later. If your kid brother annoys you by tapping his foot all through dinner, you might decide that an appropriate reaction would be a swift kick under the table. Your "punishment" might eliminate the behavior for the present, but chances are his undesired foot-tapping behavior will reappear. Similarly, a mother who washes her daughter's mouth with soap to clean up her language may find that the cleaning will not last very long, particularly if the mother is not around. Unfortunately, people often punish others when they are angry and upset. As a result, the punishment seems unreasonable and little is learned.

Guidelines for Punishment

Effective punishment can help eliminate an undesirable behavior. However, if the punishment is not chosen carefully, there can be unexpected side effects.

Sometimes what we thought was a punishment can have elements of positive reinforcement. A teacher may believe she is punishing a six-year-old boy when she shouts, "Mike, don't tell me you are out of your seat again. You never sit still!" In reality, Mike is gaining the attention he is seeking. Classmates turn and notice him, and the teacher becomes totally preoccupied with his problem. What she thought was a punishment turns out to be positive reinforcement. The next time Mike feels a need for attention, he will know that getting out of his seat and walking around the classroom will win the notice he wants. Similarly, a hockey player put in the penalty box for a clash and fight often gets cheers from the crowd. His rowdy behavior may well increase because of the attention of the crowd. The article in Feature 3-3 presents some creative punishment strategies.

Psychologists have developed several guidelines for punishment. Four important rules are:

- Avoid combining rewards with punishments.
- Punish immediately, or reinstate the situation that caused the need for punishment.
- Avoid inadequate punishment.
- Make the punishment suit the crime.

Exercise 3-8

Imagine that the town council of your community has been considering ways of dealing with the litter problem in the parks and streets. After several public hearings on the matter, four ordinances are proposed. Based on the recommended guidelines for punishment, which ordinance would you recommend and why?

a. Any individual who litters or in any way disturbs the beauty of the town's parks and streets will be fined the sum of $1. The fine must be paid within two years of the offense.

b. Any individual who litters or in any way disturbs the beauty of the town's parks and streets will be fined a sum of no less than $2000. The fine must be paid within one hour of the offense.

c. Any individual who litters or in any way disturbs the beauty of the town's parks and streets will be fined a sum of $20 and given a work assignment of two hours with the town's sanitation crew, to be completed within seven days of the offense.

d. Any individual who litters or in any way disturbs the beauty of the town's parks and streets will be given a work assignment of one hour with the town's sanitation crew. Those attending the town's schools will be excused from class in order to complete the work assignment.

_____

_____

_____

_____

_____

_____

Check your choice and reason with those in the Feedback section.

FEATURE 3-3 PSYCHOLOGY IN THE NEWS

Instead of a Hit, Sinatra: Teachers Try "Creative Detention" as Discipline

High school history teacher Bruce Janu knows how to hurt a kid. Sure it's brutal, but after Janu makes his smart alecks and troublemakers listen to Frank Sinatra once, they usually don't mess with him again.

"Some of the kids sit there and grimace when I'm playing Frank," said Janu, of Riverside High near Chicago. Janu said that his misbehaving students, weaned on the wailing guitars of Megadeth and Pearl Jam, sometimes beg for leniency when they hear Old Blue Eyes crooning "My Way" or "New York, New York."

In the old days, Joseph Cifelli, the principal of Cedarbrook Middle School in Cheltenham Township, Pa., said students caught fistfighting would automatically get a three-day suspension. But in this new era, where teachers see no point to sending students home to watch MTV, offenders have to report to the "Nature Center."

There, they are charged with caring for a greenhouse of plants and animals ranging from an alligator to a finch.

"The kids who are fighting have to talk it out there," said Cifelli, "and the plants and animals have a calming effect on them." . . .

In Alexandria, Va., when eight students were caught spray painting a black-tar parking lot in a rainbow of colors, they were sentenced to redo it in basic black.

The penalty could have been stiffer "but they didn't write anything obscene," said John Porter, principal of T. C. Williams High School. He also made them cough up the $200 cost for the repair. . . .

Constantly, the teachers said, they have to be on the lookout for new techniques. Janu, the musically minded disciplinarian, said that when Frank Sinatra wears off, he has another idea: Tony Bennett.

Source: Jordan, M. (1993, February 7). Instead of a Hit, Sinatra: Teachers Try "Creative Detention" as Discipline. *The Washington Post.*

Types of Punishment

Several categories or types of punishment have been identified. Coopersmith (1967) described three types.

corporal punishment Inflicting bodily harm to decrease undesirable behavior

Corporal Punishment. *Corporal* refers to the body, and corporal punishment involves inflicting bodily harm when a person behaves in an undesirable way. A spanking, a whipping with a switch, a slap across the face, and a punch in the nose would all qualify as corporal punishments. Parents who use corporal punishment teach their children that physical force leads to control. As a result their children are likely to become hostile and aggressive and use violence to gain control.

Withdrawal of Love and Approval. Parents sometimes reprimand their children for misbehavior by threatening to remove their love from the children. Statements like "If you go outside the yard again, I won't love you anymore" or "I hate you because you just spilled your juice" are examples. If this technique is used persistently, the child will feel that the parents' love is weak and undependable. The child is given the impression that love and affection have to be earned. As a result the child may become anxious and show such symptoms as nail biting, bed-wetting, or thumb-sucking.

management Conditioning method that allows a person to choose alternatives of reward or punishment

Management. *Management* permits the person to escape the punishment and gain a reward. A parent who states "If you don't eat your spinach, you may not have dessert" is permitting the reward of dessert for a desired behavior (eating spinach) and a punishment of no dessert for the undesired behavior (not eating spinach). Of the three techniques Coopersmith found this to be the most effective.

Checkpoint

Use the following questions to check your understanding of this portion of the chapter. Choose and mark the one correct response to each question.

9. A psychologist is using the technique of desensitization to help a person overcome a fear of thunder. What will the psychologist do?
   a. Be sure that the person never hears thunder.
   b. Have the person associate the thunder with an eye-blink reflex.
   c. Gradually increase the loudness of thunder while associating it with a pleasant stimulus.
   d. Give the person drugs that will cause emotional confusion whenever exposed to thunder.

10. How is classical conditioning used in controlling bed-wetting?
   a. An electric shock is given as punishment for bed-wetting.
   b. A special antidepressant drug is associated with an alarm.
   c. An emetic is given whenever the child wets the bed.
   d. An alarm is rung whenever the bed is wet, so that the child learns to awaken to a full bladder.

11. Which of the following is a key element in operant conditioning?
    a. Reflexes
    b. Emotional respondents
    c. Reinforcements
    d. Fears

12. A young boy polished his father's shoes. The father gave his son a book in the hope that the boy would repeat the shoe-shining behavior. The boy has not shined a shoe since. Which of the following best describes the role of the book?
    a. A reward and a positive reinforcement
    b. A reward but not a positive reinforcement
    c. A positive reinforcement but not a reward
    d. A punishment and a positive reinforcement

13. What are the two most important characteristics of a good positive reinforcer?
    a. Appropriate and immediate
    b. Emotional and immediate
    c. Appropriate and emotional
    d. Sensitive and emotional

14. What is the relationship between punishment and negative reinforcement?
    a. Negative reinforcement decreases behavior and punishment increases behavior.
    b. Punishment decreases behavior and negative reinforcement increases behavior.
    c. Negative reinforcement requires corporal punishment.
    d. Punishment and negative reinforcement are the same.

15. Which of the following is considered the most effective method of punishment?
    a. Corporal punishment
    b. Withdrawal of love
    c. Withdrawal of approval
    d. Management

16. Kathy is tired of having her young sister, Jane, monopolize the telephone for hours. What should Kathy do to help cut down on Jane's telephone talking?
    a. Kick Jane whenever she talks on the phone.
    b. Refuse to talk to Jane if she spends more than ten minutes on the phone.
    c. Promise Jane unlimited use of the phone if she can limit her calls to five minutes—otherwise, no phone use for a week.
    d. Tell Jane that if she spends more than five minutes on each phone call she will be despised by the rest of the family.

Check your responses against the Checkpoint Answer Key at the end of the chapter. If you had little or no difficulty answering the questions or have resolved problems that you might have had, you are ready to continue with the final portion of this chapter.

You are probably familiar with the conflicting adages, "Spare the rod and spoil the child" and "You can catch more flies with honey than with vinegar." Which should you believe? Will you spoil a child by not using punishments, or is it better to stick with rewards? Most psychological research concludes that a child disciplined with rewards will show better emotional adjustment than one disciplined with punishments. If a child is punished harshly by parents and teachers, he or she is likely to develop an aversion, or dislike, for them. In addition the child will tend to avoid activities associated with the parents and teachers. Family activities and school studies could become unpopular.

Further, since punishment is generally either painful or frustrating, it can lead to aggression. A study by Bandura and Walters (1959) found that boys who were severely punished for aggression at home tended to be overly aggressive in school. Punishment is most effective and least damaging when a rewarding alternative is offered. If a father scolds his daughter for not completing her homework, he should also praise her when she does complete her assignments. Unfortunately, repeated corporal punishments can result in child abuse. Parents who use punishments rather than rewards may cause serious problems for preschool children, as described in Feature 3-4.

As mentioned in the previous section, a punishment that draws attention to a person can serve more as a positive reinforcement than as a punisher. One way the teacher could avoid this dilemma is to put more emphasis on Mike's positive behavior. Remarks such as "Look at how nicely Mike is sitting in his seat. I wish everyone would sit and work like that" would give Mike a re-

---

FEATURE 3-4 PSYCHOLOGY IN THE NEWS

Chronic Pain Traced to Abuse

When preschoolers complain of abdominal, head, or chest pain that seems to have no physical cause, it may mean that they are depressed as the result of abuse, say Javad Kashani, professor of psychiatry at the University of Missouri at Columbia, and Gabrielle Carison, a professor of psychiatry at the University of New York at Stony Brook.

With a team of mental health and education professionals, they studied 1000 preschoolers referred to a child-development unit over a five-year period beginning in 1981.

Nine children, six boys and three girls ages 3–6, were diagnosed as having a major depressive disorder. All nine expressed somatic complaints while none of the control group, chosen from the original pool of 1000, complained of physical pain. The depressed preschoolers also were much more likely to report feelings of sadness, suffer sleep changes and fatigue and loss of appetite. All of the depressed children had been abused or severely neglected, versus 22 percent of the control subjects.

Complaints of bodily pain decreased as the children got older, according to the researchers.

In describing their study in the March issue of *The American Journal of Psychiatry*, they comment, "We hypothesize that the helplessness, fear, and frustration experienced by abused preschoolers by virtue of their small size, limited abilities, and immature defenses may increase their vulnerability to depression."

Source: Landers, S. (1987, June). Chronic pain traced to abuse. *APA Monitor.*

warding alternative. Punishment would be still more effective if she offered an alternative directly: "If you stay in your seat, you can play a special game. If you walk around, you will not play the game."

Punishment situations arise far beyond the classroom and home. Prisons are a prime example of attempts at punishments that sometimes work and sometimes do not. Statistics on repeat offenders are alarming. Again it seems that punishment is more effective when it is combined with a positive experience or alternative.

Exercise 3-9

A father is shopping at a supermarket with his two-year-old son. His son persistently tries to gain attention with chatter, but the father is preoccupied with his shopping list. The boy then looks at his surroundings and begins pointing to items on the shelves. He screams that he wants cookies, candies, strange cereals, and other impractical items. His father becomes embarrassed by the sudden outburst and begins scolding him. His child continues to scream, now even louder. To keep peace the father reaches for the nearest bag of lollipops and stuffs one in the boy's mouth. Even this does not satisfy the boy, and his loud crying continues.

From what you have read about rewards and punishments, suggest how this father might avoid a similar episode the next time he takes his son to the supermarket.

_____

_____

_____

_____

Compare your suggestion with the ones given in the Feedback section.

Shaping

A mother might complain that she would indeed love to reward her teenage son for keeping his room clean, but she never has the opportunity. It would be a long wait for a neat room. Consequently, she may resort to punishment for his untidiness. What sort of alternatives does this mother have? One possibility is *shaping*, sometimes referred to as a "method of approximations." Shaping requires a series of steps. The first thing to do is to define the objective, or the target behavior. In this case the target behavior would be having her son completely clean his room. However, any small step that her son takes in the direction of the target behavior is rewarded. When her son picks up his sneakers to wear them, the mother notices how much better the floor looks without his tennis shoes. She rewards her son with an extra half hour before curfew. The next step might require her son to pick up his wet towels, as well, before he is permitted the added time at night. After he has mastered picking up his sneakers and wet towels, he will also need to pick up his dirty socks and underwear for the reward. Finally, her son will be rewarded with added curfew time only if his room is totally tidy and spotless.

shaping Rewarding each behavior in a sequence that will eventually lead to a target behavior

Shaping is based on the principles of operant conditioning and is widely used by psychologists. There are two basic methods of shaping. The first type was descibed in the example of the teenager learning to keep his room orderly. The mother rewarded a sequence of behaviors, beginning with very simple steps, and finally arrived at the target behavior. Schools use this type of shaping. In first grade you were promoted if you could recognize the letters of the alphabet and sound them out in simple words. In second grade your reward of promotion would only be given if you could read simple sentences and perform some basic addition and subtraction. Each reward was a reinforcement that would help lead to your target behavior of being an informed, literate person, skilled in language, mathematics, science, and the humanities. You certainly could not expect your twelfth-grade teacher to reward you for achievements on the first-grade level. Likewise your first-grade teacher would not be giving many rewards if she were waiting for twelfth-grade abilities. This shaping method has also been used by clinical psychologists working with withdrawn children. Many of these children will not even approach another person. Initial rewards are given when the child sits in a chair near the psychologist. Next the child is rewarded only if eye contact with the psychologist is achieved. Eventually these children are expected to converse with the psychologist before receiving their rewards.

The second type of shaping is the reverse of the first type; it permits a person to perform the final step of behavior and be rewarded. This approach is frequently used in teaching an infant self-feeding. The mother or father puts food on a spoon, then places the spoon in the baby's hand and helps the baby aim the spoon toward the mouth. The final step of putting the food in the mouth is done by the baby, usually accompanied by cheers of enthusiasm from the proud parents. On subsequent trials the baby will do its own aiming for the mouth. Eventually, filling the spoon, aiming, and inserting in the mouth will be required before the parents cheer and the baby receives the reward of food. Most ski instructors now use a technique called "graduated length method," or GLM. This is really a shaping technique that permits a beginner to accomplish the target behavior of skiing down a slope, even though the person is on very short skis. Gradually the task is made more difficult by increasing the length of the skis. The more traditional methods for teaching skiing used the first type of shaping. The beginner was kept on a relatively flat surface until some basic skills could be demonstrated. Then the person could be taken to a slight incline until snowplow turns and stops were accomplished. Only after the necessary components were mastered could a person be taken up a lift to complete the target behavior of skiing down the slope.

Exercise 3-10

Two methods of shaping have been described. One breaks the target behavior into component steps. The other allows the person to perform the target behavior with some help, gradually removing the help. Assume you have been assigned as a swimming instructor at a summer camp. You want to find out which method of shaping is more effective in teaching swimming to ten-year-old children. You are assigned two groups of children. Each group is to be instructed with only one shaping technique. Describe how you would instruct each group.

Group a:

_____

_____

_____

Group b:

_____

_____

_____

You may check your instructional techniques in the Feedback section.

Behavior Modification

Behavior modification techniques are an application of shaping. Again, the first step is to identify a target behavior. Then each progressive step toward the target behavior is rewarded. Careful records are kept to show progress toward the target behavior. Behavior may be used either to help others or for self-help.

behavior modification Technique that uses principles of conditioning to reach a desirable goal

Nord (1970) reported an interesting use of behavior modification by a hardware company. The business was having problems with employees being late and absent from work. To reward the employees who came to work on time every day, they had a monthly drawing for home appliances. Employees who had been late or absent during the month were not eligible. At the end of six months, the company held a special drawing for a color television set. Only those employees who had been to work on time every day for six months could participate. They found that employees with colds or mild problems were coming to work rather than staying at home as they had done in the past. After the program was in effect for one year, absenteeism and lateness were reduced by 75 percent.

Businesses are eager to use behavior modification to cure absenteeism. One manufacturing company had each present worker pick a playing card each day. In each department, the employee with the best poker hand at the end of the week won $20 (Pedalino and Gamboa, 1974). Attendance improved by 18 percent and remained high as long as poker hands were dealt. Another manufacturing plant distributed daily bingo numbers. When their bingo cards were filled, workers could spin a wheel and win from $5 to $25. Once again behavior modification was effective in reducing absenteeism and tardiness.

Recently behavior modification has been used in pain-control clinics. Here the concern has been with patients who become so totally preoccupied with their pain that they cannot take an interest in anything else. In most cases these patients have not been able to receive help in any other way. They are usually the worst cases. The staff members of pain clinics are instructed to walk away from any patient who begins to talk or complain about pain. The only time a patient is permitted to discuss pain is during an appointment with a physician who asks about the location and extent of the pain. Only "well" behaviors are rewarded. Staff members give special attention to patients who talk about subjects other than pain or who become involved in other activities. Patients are encouraged to keep busy and show an interest in a variety of subjects. The success of this type of behavior-modification program has varied. But usually more than half of the patients have been helped.

In a sense absenteeism, tardiness, and complaining could be considered bad habits. These bad habits have been controlled through behavior modification. Would you care to use the same method to control your own bad habits? Perhaps you bite your nails, overeat, or lose your temper too easily. Or perhaps you want to improve yourself in some way. You might want to study more, get more exercise, or be more sociable. You can use the same behavioral approaches to control your bad habits and improve yourself by using the five steps of behavior modification.

1. Identify a target behavior, such as losing 25 pounds, jogging 2 miles, or controlling your temper. This is your ultimate goal.
2. Establish a baseline. Record your present status. This means you must write down your present weight, the distance you now jog, or the number of times you lose your temper each day.
3. Identify a suitable reinforcer. Find a reward that will motivate you. It can be something simple, such as a bubble bath, a cold beverage, or a half hour of listening to favorite records. Or it can be a night on the town, a new outfit, or a canoe trip. Make a list of your favorite things, and then find the ones that will be most appropriate for you.
4. Set subgoals, or steps, toward the target. Your subgoals might be losing 2 pounds each week or jogging a 1/4 mile, then a 1/2 mile, then 1 mile, and finally 2 miles.
5. Write down your weight loss, your jogging distance, or the number of temper outbursts.

Exercise 3-11

Ken is a compulsive overspender. If he has a plastic credit card in his pocket, he feels he can buy anything, whether or not he can afford it. He has been lured into buying such frivolous items as a monogrammed leather case for his tennis racket and a sterling-silver toothpick. His bills are mounting. Last month he charged more than $880. He could pay his present bills within six months if he could prevent himself from continuing his useless spending.

Sailing is Ken's favorite sport, but he never seems to have enough money to sail with his friends. One group is planning some inexpensive weekend sailing trips at a local lake. They are also arranging a magnificent voyage up the inland waterway of the Atlantic coast next year.

Ken wants to change his spendthrift behavior. List what he might do to help himself by using the five steps of behavior modification.

a. _____

b. _____

c. _____

d. _____

e. _____

Compare your list with the one found in the Feedback section.

Imitation and Modeling

Many of your present skills and attitudes were acquired by imitating other people. This type of learning is labeled *modeling*, or observational learning. If you see other people rewarded for a behavior, you tend to imitate it. If they are punished, you probably avoid similar behaviors, at least for the present. Many childhood behaviors are based on modeling. Children learn to walk, talk, and use facial expressions similar to the ways of their parents. They use imitation also to learn the skills required in their cultures. Whether performing a tea ceremony in Japan or hunting animals in Africa, children learn by imitating their parents.

modeling Learning that occurs by observing and imitating others

Unfortunately children even imitate some negative behaviors. A mother who fakes a headache whenever she is criticized is likely to find that her daughter will claim a similar malady whenever she is scolded. Several studies have shown that children can even learn aggression from their parents. Parents who show hostile actions and use physical punishments tend to have more aggressive children than do parents who use verbal punishments and control. In one experiment (Bandura, Ross, & Ross, 1963) children watched a film of adult actors hitting a clown doll with a hammer. After the film the children were given a similar doll. Interestingly, they also struck it and behaved aggressively. Children who had not seen the film played peacefully with the clown doll.

"Maybe giving your daddy his shot first wasn't such a good idea, after all!"

FIGURE 3-9. Parents do not always model ideal behavior.

Some children do not have appropriate models to imitate. Asch (1988) noted that disabled youngsters rarely have opportunities to see disabled adults, either in person or in the media. As a result they lack positive models to imitate.

Modeling techniques have also been used to help people overcome phobias. In Bandura's (1969) study, adults who had a strong fear of snakes viewed a film showing people playing with snakes. At the beginning of the film, a plastic snake was used. As the film progressed, a real snake was introduced, and contact became closer and more daring. The phobic viewers could stop the film whenever it became too upsetting and restart with a less frightening scene. People with snake phobias have also been helped by watching live models handling snakes. In fact, the live models have been even more successful than films have in helping individuals conquer their phobias.

Exercise 3-12

A five-year-old girl hits her three-year-old sister. Her mother scolds "Don't ever hit your little sister!" and spanks the five-year-old. Why might this spanking increase hitting behavior in her children?

_____

_____

Check your response in the Feedback section.

Extinction

Since some learning results in undesirable behavior, sometimes a behavior needs to be unlearned or extinguished. For example, suppose a baby girl finds her tongue and sticks it out. Her parents laugh and applaud. She enjoys their attention and amusement. However, when the girl is three or four years old, this behavior will no longer be amusing. It is more likely to be deemed rude and annoying. How can the behavior be extinguished? If parents and friends discontinue their laughter and applause whenever the tongue appears, *extinction* will probably occur.

extinction Weakening or diminishing of a response; removal of the positive reinforcer to decrease the likelihood of a behavior

The first step in extinction is determining what is reinforcing the behavior. If the reinforcer is repeatedly and consistently withheld, the undesirable act will probably not continue. Assume you were kind enough to bring a woman at work a cup of coffee every morning for a week. If she neither drank it nor thanked you, you probably would not continue to bring coffee. Without any reinforcement your coffee-serving behavior would cease.

Perhaps you are wondering about using punishment to extinguish behavior. Punishment is usually not an effective method in extinction if the original positive reinforcer is not removed. A girl who is punished for fighting, but always gets what she wants when she fights for it, is likely to continue to show fighting behavior. The general rule for extinction is to remove the positive reinforcer.

Exercise 3-13

Juan brings his girlfriend, Dora, a bouquet of dandelions and hollyhocks every Saturday night. To be polite she always thanks him and puts them in a vase. Dora hates both dandelions and hollyhocks and dislikes most flowers. What could she do to extinguish Juan's flower-bearing behavior?

_____

_____

_____

_____

_____

_____

Check your suggestion in the Feedback section.

ETHICAL CONCERNS

As psychologists come closer to learning how to control their fellow human beings through conditioning techniques, there has been an increasing debate about the ethics of controlling another person's behavior. Many psychologists feel that such control could restrain personal freedom. Others claim conditioning could create a better world by eliminating undesirable and selfish behavior. They see behavior modification as an important advance in the treatment of psychological problems (Hill, 1985). Think about the many uses and possible abuses of conditioning. Is society moving closer to a better world or merely restricting freedom?

Checkpoint

Use the following questions to check your understanding of the final portion of this chapter. Choose the one best response to each question.

17. Which of the following methods of discipline leads to better emotional adjustment in children?
    a. Positive reinforcement of appropriate behavior
    b. Negative reinforcement of inappropriate behavior
    c. Corporal punishment for inappropriate behavior
    d. Extinction of appropriate behavior

18. Why is scolding not always an effective form of negative reinforcement?
    a. There is no corporal punishment.
    b. It creates attention—a powerful positive reinforcement.
    c. It tends to extinguish behavior.
    d. It is not easily imitated and modeled.

19. Initially a father rewards his son for pulling on his socks. Next the son is rewarded only if he puts on both his shoes and socks. Eventually the son is rewarded only when he fully dresses himself. What technique is the father using?
    a. Negative reinforcement
    b. Modeling
    c. Extinction
    d. Shaping

20. What is the first step in behavior modification?
   a. Identify the goal.
   b. Extinguish old behaviors.
   c. Record progress.
   d. Imitate a model.

21. What is the purpose of behavior modification?
   a. To increase motivation
   b. To change behavior
   c. To model desirable behavior
   d. To model undesirable behavior

22. Which of the following is the best example of modeling?
   a. You read about a man who won $1000 for holding his breath for three minutes. You practice holding your breath.
   b. You kick your friend whenever he lights an unpleasant-smelling cigar.
   c. You ignore a woman whenever she uses foul language.
   d. You are pleasant only to people who punish you.

23. What is the best method for extinguishing behavior?
   a. Present a negative reinforcer.
   b. Present a positive reinforcer.
   c. Remove the negative reinforcer.
   d. Remove the positive reinforcer.

24. What are the concerns of psychologists regarding the use of conditioning methods?
   a. That use of the methods is often ineffective
   b. That use of the methods could restrict freedom
   c. That the methods do not use sufficient negative reinforcement
   d. That there is no difference in the methods between positive and negative reinforcement

Check your responses against the Checkpoint Answer Key at the end of the chapter. If you had difficulty with any question, reread the text. If you had little or no difficulty answering the questions or have resolved problems that you might have had, you are ready to check yourself against the chapter inventory that follows.

CHAPTER INVENTORY

Use this list of objectives as a review checklist. You should be able to do the tasks outlined in the objectives and apply them to everyday examples. If you can, you may feel confident that you have mastered the material in this chapter.

1. Define learning.
2. Distinguish between learning and performance.
3. Describe the roles of reflexes and emotional respondents in classical conditioning.
4. List three stages in the process of classical conditioning.
5. Explain how classical conditioning can be used in acting, controlling fears, eliminating unwanted behavior, and helping medical patients.

6. Describe operant conditioning.
7. Define positive reinforcement and specify two important conditions.
8. Distinguish between negative reinforcement and punishment.
9. Identify four guidelines for punishment and describe three categories of punishment.
10. Identify the strengths and weaknesses of positive and negative reinforcements.
11. Recognize attention as a positive reinforcer.
12. Explain and give examples of two types of shaping.
13. Describe the uses of behavior modification.
14. Outline five steps in the behavior-modification process.
15. Describe how learning occurs through modeling.
16. State the necessary conditions for extinction.
17. Discuss the controversy of the ethics of conditioning.

Feedback

The correct answers to the exercises follow. If you did not answer an exercise correctly, review the preceding pages and return to the exercise to correctly complete it.

3-1. The automobile mechanic is no longer motivated to work on engines. His interest in accounting is undoubtedly distracting him from his work.

3-2. The three reflexes were: "He blinks," "He pulls his hand away," and "He pulls his hand away." The five emotional respondents were: "becomes annoyed," "feeling comfortable," "Clyde grows tense," "feels overwhelmed," and "feels afraid."

3-3. a. Stage 1: Striking a man on the center of his knee will cause him to kick.
   b. Stage 2: Each time you strike the man in the center of his knee, blow a whistle. Repeat this many times.
   c. Stage 3: Blow the whistle but do not strike the man's knee. Watch him kick.

3-4. You might try thinking about some hysterically funny situation or joke. Perhaps a favorite cartoon or old comedy film would get you through the situation.

3-5. a. Desensitization
   b. Through the gradual approach, the woman will begin to feel successful when she takes exams. It should help to remove some of her anxiety.

3-6. a. She could think about how she felt the last time she had the flu or a virus. Associating someone or an object from the set with a disgusting or distasteful food would also help.
   b. She could listen to her favorite relaxing music while looking at pictures of blood cells. She might then progress toward seeing a finger with a tiny drop of blood. Again she would need a pleasant association. Gradually she might progress until her fear is removed.
   c. He would profit from an alarm device based on classical conditioning. Whenever urine flows, an alarm would awaken him. He would asso-

ciate the alarm with his full bladder and eventually awaken even without the alarm.

d. The physician could give chemotherapy patients a strongly flavored candy that they would associate with their nausea.

3-7. a. The reinforcement was not immediate. It came far too late.

b. The reinforcement was not appropriate. One penny hardly seems an adequate reward for such service!

3-8. Ordinance *c* should have been the one you favored. It provides for adequate punishment, appropriate for the offense. Although the punishment is not immediate, it occurs within a reasonably short time of the offense. It also provides a reinstatement of the circumstances by forcing the person to return to the scene. Each of the other ordinances violates at least one guideline.

3-9. It would help if the father would pay some attention to his son when the son is behaving appropriately. When they are about to go on a shopping expedition, he could offer the boy a choice: If the boy behaves nicely, they will spend time together on a favorite activity; if he misbehaves, he will be by himself.

3-10. Group *a*: This group could be taught the components of swimming. They might begin by learning to put their heads in the water. Next they would be expected to take arm strokes with their heads in the water before they were praised. Kicking techniques might come next. Finally they would only be praised if they could coordinate arm strokes, kicks, and breathing. Group *b*: This group would start out swimming with assistance. Gradually the assistance would be removed. They might begin by learning to swim on a paddleboard or with water wings. Next they would swim while you held one hand beneath their stomachs. You would gradually use less strength holding them until they were swimming on their own.

3-11. a. The target behavior is not to put any charges on his accounts.

b. He presently spends $880 in one month.

c. Sailing seems a suitable reinforcer.

d. If Ken can go for a full week without charging any items, he should reward himself with a weekend sailing trip. If he can keep it up for a year, he should allow himself to go on the island-waterway voyage.

e. He should note what he charges each week.

3-12. The mother is showing her daughter that authority is established by spanking or hitting. The next time the little girl wants to show her authority, she may imitate her mother's behavior.

3-13. If Dora removes her positive reinforcement of thanking Juan and putting the flowers in a vase, she could extinguish his behavior. She might say nothing and simply let the flowers wither on a table or on the floor.

Checkpoint Answer Key

1. b; 2. c; 3. c; 4. a; 5. d; 6. a; 7. a; 8. b; 9. c; 10. d; 11. c; 12. b; 13. a; 14. b; 15. d; 16. c; 17. a; 18. b; 19. d; 20. a; 21. b; 22. a; 23. d; 24. b.

Improving Memory

"The horror of the moment" the King said, "I shall
never, never forget."
"You will though," said the Queen "if you don't
make a memorandum of it."
—Lewis Carroll, *Through the Looking Glass*

MEMORY
    The Stages of Memory
    Improving Long-Term Memory
    Improving Depositing
    Improving Retrieval
FORGETTING
    Repression
    Suppression
    Amnesia

    Fading and Distortion
    Interference
    Positions
    Drugs
IMPROVING STUDY METHODS
    Improving Time Schedules
    Improving Concentration
    Preparing for Tests
    Taking Tests

Where were you on the evening of last October 25th? Unless that date was
your birthday, anniversary, or other significant occasion, it is doubtful that you
can recall your whereabouts. Yet if you were given a few clues, or even a choice
of two or three possibilities, you might have less difficulty remembering.

How can you improve abilities like memory? Without memory, learning
would be impossible. In this chapter you will look at three stages of memory
and consider why memory sometimes succeeds and sometimes fails. With a
better understanding of the memory process, you should be able to improve
your study skills, your ability to score well on tests, your performance at work,
and your ability to recall people and events. This chapter will help you learn
ways to sharpen your memory and minimize forgetting.

MEMORY

Take a moment and imagine what it would be like not to have a memory. You
would not know who you are, where you are, or what day it is. You would be
incapable of speaking, reading, writing, eating with a fork, or taking a shower.
Even if someone told you your name you could not remember it. But you

99

would not realize that you were lacking a memory, since you would be unaware that you ever possessed the capacity to retain anything.

Now that the importance of memory has been established, take another moment and consider the many things you do remember. In addition to factual information, such as dates in history and mathematical truths learned in school, you are capable of remembering an enormous assortment of trivial information. Right this minute, you can probably state which drawer is used to store your socks, the number of windows in your bedroom, and whether you have milk in the refrigerator and gas in your car.

Many psychologists have compared the human memory to a filing cabinet. The analogy suggests that you pick out special information from the environment and store it in your brain. If you file it correctly, you will be able to retrieve it easily from your brain file. But if you misfile it or forget where it is filed, you will have trouble retrieving or remembering the information.

Exactly where is this file? It is difficult to envision a huge file cabinet in every human brain. Certainly memories are not stored in file folders. But the analogy is not totally ridiculous. There has been some evidence that memories may leave a *trace*, or impression in the brain. Just which portion of the brain stores the memory traces has been a subject of some controversy.

trace Memory impression stored in the brain

Although there is uncertainty about the location of memory, there is agreement about the human brain's capacity. People use only a tiny portion of their memory potential. Are you wondering how you can make more efficient use of your memory capacity? Certainly, increasing memory is an extremely noble goal. The first step is to examine the process, or stages involved, and check where improvement can be made.

The Stages of Memory

Most views of memory describe three stages: sensory register, short-term memory, and long-term memory. Each stage is part of the memory process. The main difference between each stage is the length of time involved. The sensory register is the first step in the memory process and lasts only a few milliseconds. It is difficult to imagine such a fleeting time span. The next phase is short-term retention, lasting only a few seconds. Long-term retention, the final stage in memory, can last a lifetime. Figure 4-1 shows the relationship between the three stages of memory. Read on to find out why there is such a difference in capacity at each stage.

Sensory Register. As you see, hear, feel, or experience anything from the external world, it first enters the senses and the *sensory register* of your brain. The sensory register records everything that you sense. Information in the sensory register decays rapidly. The record lasts less than a second and is usually lost. Only a fractional percentage of sensations are passed along into short-term memory. As you are sitting and reading this chapter, a sizable amount of information is entering your sensory register. Hopefully the words you are reading and the concepts they present will be passed along to short-term and long-term retention. Among the stimuli that will probably be lost are such things as a horn honking or a bird chirping outside your window. Your

sensory register First stage of memory when information that is sensed is briefly recorded and rapidly decays if not passed along to short-term memory

sensory register takes in far more information than can be processed, so most inputs will be lost.

Short-Term Memory. *Short-term memory* is similar to attention span. If you looked up the telephone number of a local restaurant, you could probably retain it just long enough to dial the number. If a friend asked you to repeat the number an hour later, you would have to return to the phone directory. Short-term memory has both a limited duration and a limited capacity. Although there are individual differences, for most people only about seven items can be manipulated at a time. Your short-term memory can probably handle a telephone number within your dialing area, but if the area code is added, you may have a problem.

Since items can be stored either individually or in chunks, many people find it profitable to group information or items. For example, if you wish to remember the phone number "627-4357," it will consume the seven spaces in the average short-term retention. However, if you convert the numbers to letters and meaningful words, you could translate the number to "NAP-HELP." Now you need to retain only two words and would have room for five additional items. Grouping individual items together to allow for additional short-term retention is called *chunking*. According to Chase and Simon (1973), chess masters use chunking. When they glance at a board, they see patterns rather than individual chess pieces. After a quick peek at a board, lasting only two or three seconds, a chess master can reproduce the entire arrangement on the board perfectly. It would clearly be beyond the capacity of the average short-term memory to handle the location of thirty-two chess pieces.

short-term memory Second stage of memory when information is stored for less than thirty seconds

chunking Grouping individual items together into units, to increase short-term retention

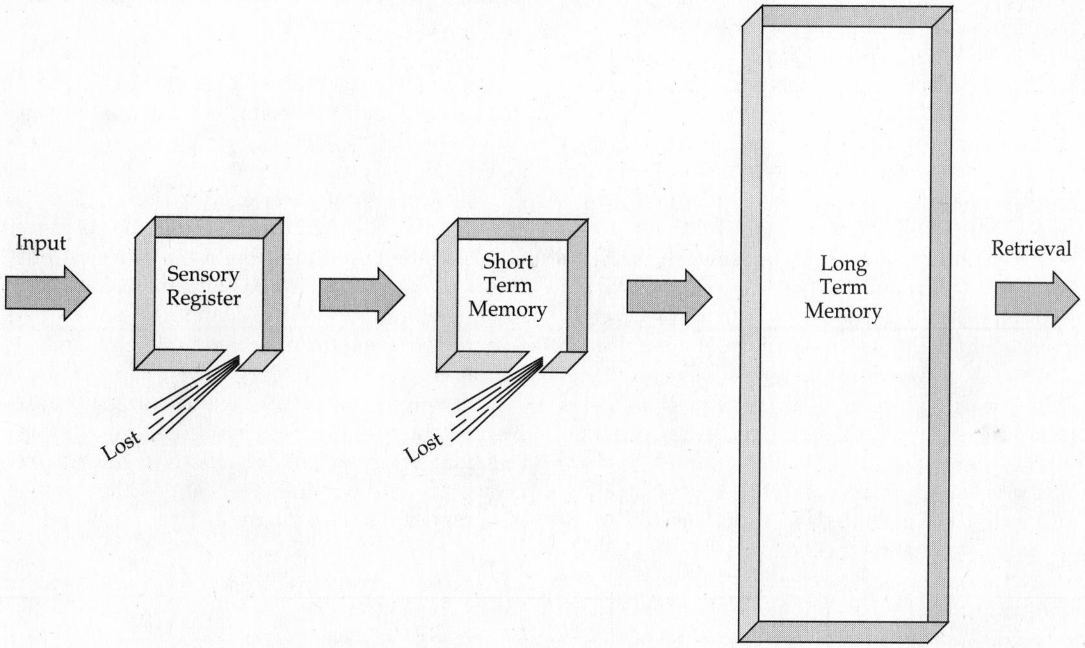

FIGURE 4-1. Stages of memory.

The study of verbal memory reported in Feature 4-1 found that memory experts use smaller chunks than other people do. Experts are also aware of the importance of intonation and rhythm as they memorize. Have you ever noticed how easily you remember musical lyrics?

Short-term retention is usually most efficient during the first few seconds. Efficiency begins to diminish in about twelve seconds, and after twenty seconds, items will fade away unless they are passed along to long-term memory. Practice and rehearsal help to maintain items in short-term memory. If you repeat a phone number over and over again to yourself, you are more likely to remember it if you hear a busy signal the first time you dial. On the other hand, if you are distracted or need to retain some new information in your short-term memory, chances are you will find yourself with your finger poised to dial and no idea which numbers should be struck. Rote rehearsal has been found to be an effective method in increasing retention.

Klatzky (1975) reports that by repeating information to yourself either

---

FEATURE 4-1 PSYCHOLOGY IN THE NEWS

Memory, Chunk-Style

Can you recite the second sentence of the Pledge of Allegiance? Most people say, "Of course," and then think through the entire pledge before realizing it consists of a single sentence.

People often memorize the pledge, as well as passages such as the Gettysburg Address, as a chunk, verbatim. Although most prose does not lend itself to this kind of memorization, some people, such as actors, can easily learn and recall substantial, albeit unremarkable, tracts. Among their tricks: Experts break passages into smaller chunks than novices do and use specific words from the text as cues to help them remember the rest.

Researchers selected eight expert memorizers from the Indiana University drama department and compared their abilities with those of eight novices. Initially, people had twenty minutes to learn each of two three-paragraph passages. Later in the week their recall of the passages was tested at least six times. The researchers, Indiana University psychologist Margaret Jean Intons-Peterson and psychologist Mary M. Smyth of the University of Lancaster, England, used word-for-word transcriptions to analyze their rehearsal strategies.

Even the novices were able to remember substantial tracts of prose, Intons-Peterson and Smith

report (*Journal of Experimental Psychology: "Learning, Memory, and Cognition,"* Vol. 13, pp. 490-500). Verbatim recall was high, approaching 85 percent even after four days. The researchers found, however, that experts learned and recalled the material more quickly.

Why? Experts included fewer words per chunk as they memorized than the novices did. They also focused more on specific words—for example, initial words of sentences and paragraphs—to help jog their memories.

The experts also consciously searched for a certain intonation while memorizing the passages, experimenting until they found the "correct" one. When trying to recall the passage, they often made brief, preliminary efforts, continuing only when they remembered the preferred intonation and cadence.

Nonprofessionals can copy some of the experts' techniques, says Intons-Peterson: "Alter intonation, use numbers and bits of humor as retrieval cues and pay special attention to beginnings of paragraphs and sentences."

Source: Simon, C. (1988, March). Memory, chunk-style. *Psychology Today.*

silently or aloud, you create a memory that can endure almost indefinitely. There has also been some evidence that what you hear can be retained longer than what you see. If you want to remember the name of someone you just met, use the name as you are talking with the person. The repetition of the name will act as a rehearsal, and you will be hearing your own voice. Next time you look up a phone number or fill your tank with gas, try saying the number out loud or calling out the cost of the gasoline. Then, if there is a delay in reaching the number or in paying your gas bill, you will impress everyone with your outstanding short-term memory.

Long-Term Memory. *Long-term memory*, as the term implies, lasts much longer than does short-term memory. Most studies have suggested that anything that is remembered more than five minutes is considered to be in long-term memory. Memories can last hours, days, months, years, or a lifetime. With so many memories lasting for such long durations, long-term memory must have a vast capacity. The exact capacity has never been determined, but even after 100 years of memories, new material can still be stored. You need to sort through an immense supply of information to find a correct response in long-term memory. As a result, retrieval, or recall, from long-term memory is generally slower and more difficult than is recall from short-term memory.

> **long-term memory**
> Third stage of memory; items remembered more than five minutes are likely to be stored there indefinitely

Exercise 4-1

Indicate whether each description is an example of sensory register, short-term memory, or long-term memory.

a. A woman recognizes a man she met at a party the previous night.

_____

b. A baby feels a breeze come across his face.

_____

c. An old man reminisces about his childhood.

_____

d. A waitress at a fast-food chain takes an order for three hamburgers, two

french fries, and five milkshakes. _____

Check your answers in the Feedback section.

Improving Long-Term Memory

You probably have seen advertisements for books and lectures that promised to improve your memory. There are a number of tricks and gimmicks that have been successful in increasing the efficiency of long-term retention. Most techniques focus on one of two aspects of memory: depositing or retrieving information.

articulate = 9.

Improving Depositing

mnemonics
Method that gives meaning and organization to help memory

Most of the systems for improving the deposit of memories in the brain use *mnemonics*. Mnemonics or mnemonic devices give meaning and organization to help memory. "Thirty days hath September. . . ." is without doubt the best-known mnemonic in the English language. If you have ever studied music, you are familiar with the mnemonic for remembering the notes associated with the five lines of the treble clef, "Every Good Boy Does Fine."

Mnemonics are not limited to use by children. Mathematics students who want to memorize the first fifteen digits in the decimal expansion of π use the expression "How I want a drink, alcoholic of course, after the heavy lectures involving quantum mechanics." By counting the number of letters in each word, they can recite the extended value of π as 3.14159265358979. Astronomy students could use the mnemonic "*M*ercury's *v*ery *e*ager *m*other *j*ust *s*erved *us* *n*ine *p*otatoes" to recall the names of the planets in the order of their distances from the sun, *M*ercury, *V*enus, *E*arth, *M*ars, *J*upiter, *S*aturn, *U*ranus, *N*eptune, and *P*luto.

Psychologists have identified several formal mnemonic systems for remembering lists. The pegword system and the method of loci have been used with success in a variety of situations. If you have a list of things to remember, try these procedures to see which works most successfully for you.

pegword Method for improving memory, using a poem to attach mental image associations with items on a list that is to be retained.

Pegword. First memorize and practice reciting the following poem. Keep repeating it even after you think you have memorized it perfectly. Extensive studying enhances long-term retention.

1 is a bun	6 is sticks
2 is a shoe	7 is heaven
3 is a tree	8 is a gate
4 is a door	9 is a lion
5 is a hive	10 is a hen

Next create as vivid an image as possible for each item—bun, shoe, tree, and so on. The poem can help you learn ten unrelated items by using association of mental images. For example, if you want to remember to purchase ten or fewer items on your way home one evening, you could associate each item with a number line from the poem and conjure some sort of image in your mind. Figure 4-2 shows a possible set of images that could help a person remember to bring home a number of unrelated items. Any item can be hooked onto each "peg," and ridiculous images will be remembered even more easily than sensible ones. One advantage to the system is that you can usually recall items backwards as well as forward. The main disadvantage is that you are limited to ten items. Some systems extend the pegs up to twenty and thirty, but these systems have been less successful than has the ten-pegword method.

loci Mnemonic device that associates locations along a familiar path with items to be remembered

Loci. This method is sometimes referred to as the "house method." The first step is to walk through your house, apartment, or other familiar location and assign a number to each piece of furniture or fixture that you pass. Most individuals can be successful with about twenty items. After mastering twenty locations, you can gradually increase the number. Once the list of locations is

poem	list	image

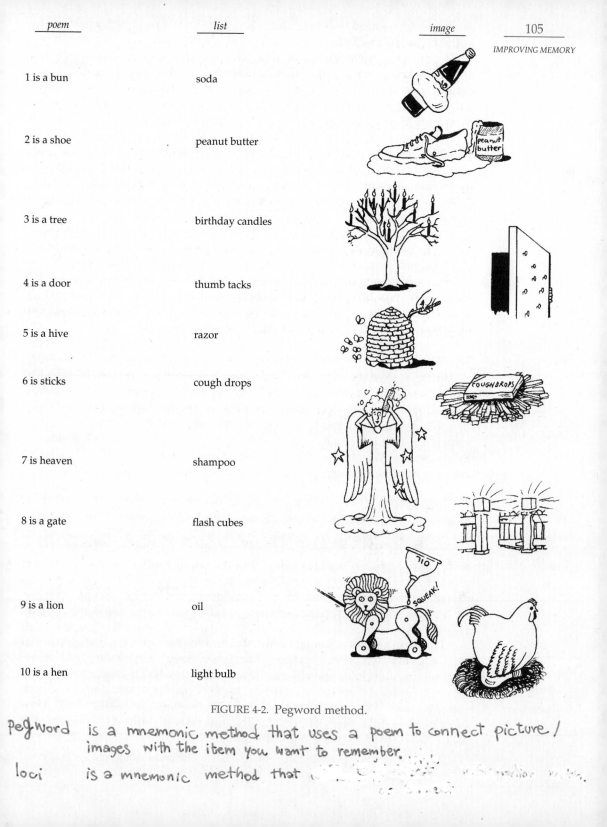

1 is a bun   soda

2 is a shoe   peanut butter

3 is a tree   birthday candles

4 is a door   thumb tacks

5 is a hive   razor

6 is sticks   cough drops

7 is heaven   shampoo

8 is a gate   flash cubes

9 is a lion   oil

10 is a hen   light bulb

FIGURE 4-2. Pegword method.

Pegword is a mnemonic method that uses a poem to connect picture / images with the item you want to remember.

loci is a mnemonic method that ...

established, you need to overlearn the locations just as you overlearned the list in the pegword method.

Again, as in the pegword method, the next step is to associate each item on the list to be memorized with a location. Assume that as you enter the front door of your home the first thing you see is an umbrella stand. This would be number 1 on your loci list. You would then continue with each item as you come to it. Perhaps an easy chair, an ottoman, a coffee table, a planter, a sofa, a CD player, a rocker, an end table, a bar stool, a wood stove, and a log bin could be items 2 through 12. Using the previous list, your associations could be an umbrella stand filled with soda, your easy chair smeared with peanut butter, the ottoman set with birthday candles, and thumb tacks nailed into your coffee table. Your list could continue throughout your house, using as many locations as you wished.

The method is surprisingly effective. Bower (1973) found that students using the method of loci could recall two or three times more than could students using traditional rote-memory methods. The method of loci also helped the students keep the list in correct order. Students were given five lists with twenty words on each. Subjects using the loci method recalled an average of 72 percent of the items, while the control group, using traditional memory methods, recalled an average of only 28 percent.

Exercise 4-2

In the early days of Rome, orators never read their speeches; they had to recite them from memory. History books state that the great Roman orator Cicero memorized his speeches by using a mnemonic technique. Supposedly he walked through his garden and numbered each part that he passed. He then associated each topic that he wished to address in his speech with a location in his garden. When it was time to deliver his oration, he simply thought of the images of his garden and was able to recite his speech perfectly.

a. What mnemonic device was Cicero using? _____

b. What other method might have been useful to Cicero?

He can use poem and image to connect what subject he will speeches

c. Why was Cicero's method better than the alternative?

because the pegword allow he remember only 10 items.

Compare your responses with the answers given in the Feedback section.

There are a variety of other techniques for improving the deposit of material into long-term retention. Psychologists have advised that organizing information into meaningful units will assist memory. If you had a long grocery list, it would be helpful if you divided the list into vegetables, meats, dairy products, canned goods, paper products, and cleaning materials. Thorndike (1977) demonstrated the importance of organization and meaningfulness by showing the following passage to two groups of subjects.

A farmer wanted his mule to go into the barn. The mule would not go in, so he asked his dog to bark and scare it in. The dog refused to bark, so the farmer asked his cat to scratch the dog to make it bark. The cat would not scratch the dog unless it got some milk, so the farmer asked the cow to provide some milk. The cow gave the farmer the milk, the farmer gave the milk to the cat, the cat scratched the dog, whereupon the dog barked and scared the mule into the barn.

One group of subjects was shown the passage as it appears above. A second group was shown the passage with the first two sentences at the end. Recall was much better when the first two sentences were at the beginning so that subjects were aware of the purpose of the animal activity. When the sentences were at the end, the passage was less meaningful and recall was not as good.

It is easier to remember meaningful information. Undoubtedly you would have less trouble memorizing a speech written in English than one written in Russian or an unfamiliar language. The purpose of mnemonics is to give meaning through associations. These strategies, coupled with concentration and overlearning, can usually improve the depositing of memories.

Several studies have shown that women tend to remember stories better when the main character is referred to as "she" or "her" rather than "he" or "him" (Hamilton and Henley, 1982; Crawford and English, 1984). In earlier decades most textbooks contained only masculine forms of pronouns and rarely used female examples. The use of unbiased pronouns is likely to increase memory in women since they are better able to relate to what they read.

Exercise 4-3

A spelling teacher has given the following list of words to his students: psychiatry, neighbor, seize, lieutenant, psalm, retrieve, psychology, reign, brief, psychotherapy.

a. Show how the students can organize the words into three groups so they will be better able to remember the correct spelling.

Group 1   Group 2   Group 3

_____   _____   _____

_____   _____   _____

_____   _____   _____

_____   _____   _____

b. Why will this grouping help students remember the correct spelling?

_____

_____

You may compare your responses to those in the Feedback section.

Improving Retrieval

Have you ever had an answer or a name "on the tip of your tongue"? This expression is often used to describe a failure to retrieve information that you

FIGURE 4-3. Wouldn't you love to know which technique Mr. Total Recall uses?

once deposited. Although the deposit was successful, you are experiencing a problem in locating and picking up the memory. You have all had the experience of seeing an actor or famous person whose name you were unable to recall, although you were certain you knew it. Frequently, after some sorting and associating, the correct name emerged.

free association
Following a sequence of associated, spontaneous personal thoughts

Free association is considered an effective method for improving retrieval. Klatzky (1980) reports that it helps to tap into areas that are associated. For example, if you misplace an assignment, it will probably help to retrace your steps. Go back to your desk and walk through the rooms and places you have been. The reenactment will jar your memory. The more similarity between the present cues and those that existed when the information was deposited in your memory, the better your chance of accurate retrieval. Looking at an old photo will often elicit old memories that would not ordinarily be retrieved.

On the other hand, slight changes in appearance can make retrieval difficult. If you meet a coworker at the beach or on a hike, she will most likely be dressed differently. The change in appearance will make it more difficult to recognize her. One system that usually helps with the recall of names is the alphabetic system. There is some evidence that words beginning with the same letter are associated in memory. A quick run through each letter of the alphabet will sometimes help you recall the first letter of her name. Once you have the first initial, the name is considerably easier to recall.

to retrace your step

Use the following questions to check your understanding of this portion of the chapter. Choose and mark the one correct response to each question.

1. It is believed that memories leave impressions on the brain. What are these impressions called?
   a. Memory images
   b. Memory traces
   c. Files
   d. Memory potentials

2. Which stage of memory has the shortest duration?
   a. Sensory register
   b. Short-term memory
   c. Long-term memory
   d. Retrieval

3. Imagine your boss has called you and asked you to come into her office immediately with three pencils, a ballpoint pen, two paper clips, an eraser, and six rubber bands. Which of the following methods would be most effective for assuring that you remember all the items?
   a. Change your setting so that you will not be bored.
   b. Cover your eyes so that you will not be distracted.
   c. Repeat the list to yourself over and over again.
   d. Go through the alphabet until you come to the letter of each item.

4. How many items or "chunks" can your short-term memory handle?
   a. About three
   b. Exactly five
   c. About seven
   d. Exactly ten

5. Which of the following techniques are favored by memory experts?
   a. Using large chunks and distraction
   b. Using large chunks and rhythm
   c. Using small chunks and distraction
   d. Using small chunks and rhythm

6. Which of the following is the best example of long-term memory?
   a. Looking at the page numbers as you turn the pages
   b. Feeling an itch at the end of your nose
   c. Blinking your eyes when dust blows
   d. Giving the answers to Checkpoint questions

7. A man uses the name "Roy G. Biv" to help him recall the colors of the spectrum as red, orange, yellow, green, blue, indigo, and violet. Which technique is he using?
   a. A mnemonic device
   b. The method of loci
   c. The pegword method
   d. Overlearning

use first letter of colors and creat the name.

8. In which situation would the pegword method be most effective?
   a. You want to remember people's faces.
   b. You want to remember people's names.
   c. You want to remember a list of ten items.
   d. You want to remember a list of fifty items.

9. If you wanted to use the method of loci to help you remember a list, what would be your first step?
   a. Memorize the poem "1 is a bun. . . ."
   b. Walk through your home and identify each location you pass.
   c. Divide the list into meaningful groups of items.
   d. Repeat aloud the list of items over and over again.

10. Assume that you need to memorize fifty words. Which type of words would be easiest to remember?
    a. Words in a foreign, unfamiliar language
    b. Words that are part of a meaningless passage
    c. Words that are part of a meaningless passage written in a foreign language
    d. Words that are part of a meaningful passage

11. A woman has forgotten where she put her keys. She last remembers seeing them in the ignition of her car as she drove home from work. Which of the following suggestions would probably be the most useful in helping her locate the keys?
    a. Use the method of loci.
    b. Use the pegword method.
    c. Go through the alphabet.
    d. Retrace her steps from the car.

Check your responses against the Checkpoint Answer Key at the end of the chapter. If you had difficulty with any question, reread the text. If you had little or no difficulty answering the questions or have resolved problems that you might have had, you are ready to continue with the next portion of this chapter.

FORGETTING

Forgetting can be embarrassing, inconvenient, and unpleasant. Why do you forget? There are several possibilities. First, it is possible that you are not aware that the event occurred. Your sensory register may not have received the input. This type of problem is not usually referred to as forgetting, since you never really experienced or learned the information. Second, although you experienced something, you never processed it into short-term and long-term memory. As you saw in Figure 4-1, many memories of events are transitory and fleeting and are not stored in either short-term or long-term memory. The third possibility has been of greatest concern to psychologists. Items or events have been stored in long-term memory but are now difficult to retrieve. Several explanations have been given to describe why this type of retrieval problem occurs. Among the reasons offered are repression, amnesia, fading from disuse, distortion, interference, and drugs.

Exercise 4-4

There are three possible reasons for forgetting something: (1) You never sensed it, (2) you sensed it and processed it for a fleeting moment but did not store it in your long-term memory, (3) you stored it in long-term memory but are unable to retrieve it. For each of the following examples of forgetting, indicate whether the cause is (1), (2), or (3).

a. Guido memorized a poem last night and now cannot remember the third line.

_____ (3) _____

b. Gladys watched the weather forecast on the news last night but was daydreaming about her summer vacation. She cannot remember whether showers were forecast for today.

_____ (2) _____

c. Mabel was so excited when she heard she had won the Irish Sweepstakes that she forgot she was brewing coffee. She burned the bottom of the pot.

_____ (1) ✗ 3 _____

d. Everyone laughed when Bill forgot to wear a tie to the party. No one had told him it was a formal occasion.

_____ (1) _____

Compare your answers to those in the Feedback section.

Repression = 9

One possible explanation for being unable to retrieve memories is *repression*. Repression is unconsciously motivated forgetting. It is an unconscious blocking of things that are frightening or threatening. Traumatic events and anxiety-provoking people and situations can be painful if they are retrieved from long-term memory. Everyone has encountered some form of repression. Having difficulty recalling an unpleasant happening is a type of represssion. According to Freud, it is a way of protecting yourself from remembering things that are distressing. These unbearable thoughts remain buried in the unconscious and can be revealed only through hypnosis or dreams.

Children who suffer from sexual abuse often are afraid to report the incident. The memory is so painful that it is repressed but usually it resurfaces at some time in adulthood. Viewing a movie on incest, being sexually victimized again, or seeing the family member may bring the memory out of repression.

Although repression can account for some forgetting, it is a limited explanation. Repression only applies to highly unpleasant emotional experiences. People often forget pleasant or neutral experiences as well. Further, most examples of repression are based on observations of patients in clinical settings. There has been little experimental evidence.

repression Forgetting that is caused by unconscious blocking of thoughts or events that are threatening or frightening

suppression Consciously and intentionally avoiding unpleasant thoughts and memories

Suppression

Have you ever wanted to forget something? Perhaps you did something embarrassing or foolish and wanted to suppress the memory. *Suppression* is a conscious effort to avoid thinking about an event. Since you are aware of the event, suppression is different from repression. As a result of your awareness, as pointed out in Feature 4-2, forgetting is more difficult.

Women who have been raped try desperately to avoid memories of the assault. Many are unwilling to acknowledge that they were victims and suppress thoughts for months or years after the attack. Unfortunately, suppressing the painful thoughts does not remove the emotional side effects which may include excessive fears, phobias, and depression.

Amnesia

amnesia Loss of memory or a memory gap that includes forgetting personal information that would normally be recalled

Amnesia is a disorder that displays the most extreme form of repression. Because of its dramatic effect, amnesia has been used as the subject of novels, films, and soap operas. The symptoms include a loss of personal information. Amnesia victims forget who they are, where they are from, and almost all other personal information. Interestingly, they retain basic memories. They remember how to add, subtract, read, write, dress, and cook.

FEATURE 4-2 PSYCHOLOGY IN THE NEWS

Suppress Now, Obsess Later

How to get rid of an unwanted thought? Psychologist Daniel M. Wegner has found that the usual strategy—trying hard not to think about it—can backfire: The more we try to suppress unwanted thoughts, the more likely we are to become preoccupied with them.

Wegner and his colleagues told a group of college students not to think about white bears and then asked them to dictate their ongoing thoughts into a tape recorder and ring a bell each time a white bear came to mind.

Not thinking about white bears proved difficult for the students: They rang the bell or mentioned the bear more than once a minute during a five-minute session. In other words, actively trying to suppress an idea paradoxically makes us think about it.

Why is it so difficult to get rid of unwanted thoughts? In trying not to think about a white bear, the researchers explain, we must first think about it.

What's a worrier to do? The researchers repeated the experiment but this time told another group of students to think about a red Volkswagen if they happened to think of a white bear. Using a single distracting thought did the trick; it helped the students to avoid thinking of the dreaded white bear.

This strategy, the researchers suggest, may prove useful in the treatment of obsessive thinking, as well as in the treatment of addictions such as smoking. But they admit that more work needs to be done before we fully understand thought suppression. "In the meantime," they say, "it seems clear that there is little to be gained in trying not to think about it."

Source: Neath, J. (1987, December). Suppress now, obsess later. *Psychology Today.*

There are several forms of amnesia. The best-known and most often popularized form is *hysterical amnesia*. In this type of amnesia, there is no organic or physical reason for the problem. Hysterical amnesia usually occurs after a traumatic event and is generally temporary.

Amnesia can have physiological causes. Alcoholism, drug abuse, disease, injuries, nutritional deficiencies, and brain damage are possible contributors. Amnesia from physiological causes can be either temporary or permanent and is labeled *organic amnesia*.

A third type of amnesia, called *global demential amnesia*, is characterized by an absentmindedness about the present. This form is common in older, senile patients who have excellent recall about their earlier lives but have difficulty keeping apprised of the present. Most often this form of amnesia is permanent.

Like repression, amnesia is a limited explanation of why forgetting occurs. It is not nearly as common as the media suggest and can only account for a tiny percentage of forgetting.

hysterical amnesia Amnesia that has no organic or physical cause; usually occurs after a trauma and is temporary

organic amnesia Amnesia that has physiological causes

global demential amnesia Type of amnesia characterized by an absentmindedness about present events

Exercise 4-5

A Princeton student reported that he met Albert Einstein while strolling across campus one day. They stopped and chatted for a few minutes, and the student invited Einstein to join him for lunch. Albert Einstein asked in which direction he had been walking when he came upon the student. When the student indicated the direction, Einstein stated that he had already eaten and politely thanked the student for the invitation.

Which type of amnesia was Einstein experiencing? ___global___

You may check your answer in the Feedback section.

Fading and Distortion

There has been some evidence that memories will fade with time if they are not used. This is possibly an accurate explanation of forgetting in short-term retention. However, fading does not provide a complete explanation for long-term forgetting. Strangely, people often forget valuable information and remember things that are totally useless.

However, several experiments (Loftus, 1975; Loftus et al., 1978) have shown that memories can become distorted with time. New memory material changes to conform with information that was previously learned. As additional material is learned, old information becomes incorporated. Experimental subjects have watched slides and films of accidents involving cars striking either a pedestrian or another vehicle. In one situation slides showed a green car passing. The experimenter asked the subjects if the blue car passing had a ski rack. When asked the color of the passing vehicle, most of the subjects recalled it as blue rather than green. Control subjects were not given the color blue when asked about the passing vehicle. They remembered the car as green.

In another situation subjects were asked to estimate the speed of the car when it "smashed" into another vehicle. These subjects overestimated the speed considerably. Control subjects who were asked to estimate the speed when the car "hit" the other vehicle gave fairly accurate estimates.

113

When you observe a crime scene, your memory of exactly what happened is likely to become distorted.

Exercise 4-6

From what you know about distortion of memories, why might the warning "Beware eyewitness testimony!" be accurate?

_____

_____

You may compare your answer with the one given in the Feedback section.

Interference ⇐ n. แทรกแซง, n. รบกวน, อีรุงตุงนัง

Interference is the most popular explanation for why forgetting occurs. It is similar to the distortion explanation but gives clearer details. You forget because other information interferes with your remembering. According to the interference description of forgetting, there are two types of obstructions to remembering: proactive interference and retroactive interference.

Proactive Interference. Proactive means "acting forward." *Proactive interference* refers to instances when previous memories block the recall of more recent learnings. If you have trouble learning the French phrase for "goodbye" because you keep thinking of the German phrase that you previously learned, you are experiencing a proactive interference: You have difficulty remembering "au revoir" because you keep remembering the old "auf wiedersehn." Or suppose you meet a new psychology instructor named Professor

---

proactive interference Forgetting that occurs because of confusion with previously learned material

Kassel, who reminds you of your old girlfriend Flora Belle. You may have difficulty remembering the professor's correct name and want to call her Flora Belle. In proactive interference, earlier learning interferes with new learning.

Retroactive Interference. Retroactive means "acting backward." *Retroactive interference* refers to instances where recent learning blocks the recall of previous memories. If, after finally learning the French phrase "au revoir," you have trouble remembering the German phrase "auf wiedersehn," you are experiencing retroactive interference. New learning interferes with your ability to recall something from the past. If the next time you meet your old girlfriend Flora Belle, you have difficulty remembering her name and have an urge to call her "Professor," retroactive interference will be contributing to your forgetting. Figure 4-4 shows how proactive and retroactive interference can cause forgetting.

retroactive interference Forgetting that occurs because of confusion with newly learned material

Exercise 4-7

Indicate whether each of the following is an example of proactive or retroactive interference.

a. You have difficulty learning the metric system because you keep thinking of inches, feet, and yards.

_____ Proactive.

b. You have trouble learning the scissor kick with your sidestroke swimming and keep going back to your old flutter kick.

_____ Proactive.

c. After reading the book *Gone with the Wind*, you went to see the movie. Now you have trouble remembering what was in the book and keep thinking of the film.

_____ Retroactive.

d. When you first learned to drive, you used a car with a standard shift. For the past five years you have been driving a car with an automatic transmission. You are asked to drive a car with a standard transmission and find yourself forgetting to use the clutch and treating the car as if it were automatic.

_____ Retroactive.

Check your responses against those given in the Feedback section.

Positions → What is positions? How difference.

Are you familiar with a poem that begins "Twas the night before Christmas"? Chances are you can recall the first few lines. But if you are asked to continue, you may have difficulty. It is also likely that you can recall the closing lines "Merry Christmas to all and to all a good night!" Similarly, young children usually have no difficulty singing the first line of the alphabet song "A, B, C, D," and enjoy ending with a robust "X, Y, Z." It is the middle part of the song that creates confusion.

FIGURE 4-4. Proactive and retroactive interference.

primacy effect Explanation of why the first things learned are easier to remember

recency effect Explanation of why the last things learned are easier to remember

Psychologists have reasoned that you have little difficulty remembering the first part because of a *primacy effect.* For the first thing you learn, you will not be bothered by any proactive interference. Most people can remember the first few bars of any tune they hear, the picture on the cover of a magazine, and their first date. The last items learned are also easier to remember. They are fresh in your mind and not bothered by retroactive interference. This is called a *recency effect.*

Think about the last party you attended. If you remember the first people you met when you entered and the last few people you spoke with before leaving, you experienced primacy and recency effects. Most students find that they have little difficulty remembering the first part of their assigned reading. The end of the chapter is also easier to recall. The middle section is most difficult; it has no primacy and recency advantages. Unfortunately, the middle portion is affected by both proactive and retroactive interference. Students usually need to apportion more time to the middle section since it will be more difficult to remember.

Exercise 4-8

Assume you have been asked to give an address to a local civic group. Several friends have come to your aid and have helped write an outstanding five-page speech. Now you need to memorize the talk so that it will sound as if it were your own. Based on what you have learned about interference and positions, describe a strategy for remembering the speech. Keep in mind the sections that are likely to be easy or difficult to learn.

_____

_____

_____

_____

You may compare your strategy with the ones described in the Feedback section.

Drugs = What is problem of drugs?

Recent studies have shown that certain drugs given in carefully controlled doses can help people remember. McGaugh (1983) reported that the hormones epinephrine and norepinephrine enhance memory. There has also been evidence (McGaugh, 1970) that some more common drugs, such as nicotine and caffeine, will speed up the incorporation of information in long-term memory. However, if the dosage of even these ordinary drugs is not carefully controlled, memory can be disrupted and poisoning is possible.

Most drugs impede memory. For example, tranquilizers have a strong negative impact on memory. A recent study found that the tranquilizer diazepam (commercially known as Valium) actually blocks memory for up to six hours.

Many studies (Birnbaum et al., 1978; Darley et al., 1973; Miller et al., 1978; Nahas, 1979; Peterson, 1984; Relman, 1982; Wetzel et al., 1982) have concluded that both marijuana and alcohol have a detrimental effect on memory. The greatest impairment is the ability to transfer information from short-term to long-term memory. People who have had several drinks or have been smoking marijuana can usually carry on a conversation, recalling and retrieving information from the past. They can also remember new things for a few seconds. The usual problem is in forming lasting memories. After an evening of being high at a party, many individuals will have difficulty the next morning recalling their own behavior at the celebration.

If you have been drinking or smoking marijuana, intake of information will be more difficult than will retrieval. Experiments have shown that sober subjects can recall information from the past both when intoxicated or sober. But if a subject is intoxicated when learning information, recall will diminish when the subject is sober (Parker, Birnbaum, and Noble, 1976). The subject will actually recall better if intoxicated. This situation is sometimes referred to as "state dependence." Recall is best if you are in the same state that you were in when you learned the information. A student who likes to have a few beers while studying will probably perform better on an exam if he is sipping some brew. But, keep in mind that memory is best when you have not been drinking or smoking marijuana at all. About 10 percent of people who seek help for alcohol problems have serious brain damage and memory problems (NIAAA, 1982).

Checkpoint

Use the following questions to check your understanding of this portion of the chapter. Choose and mark the one correct response to each question.

12. Which of the following reasons for forgetting has been of greatest concern to psychologists?
    a. Failure to sense information
    b. Failure to process material in short-term memory
    c. Inability to retrieve material from long-term memory
    d. Inability to retrieve material from short-term memory

13. What is repression?
    a. An unconscious blocking of painful memories
    b. A conscious retrieval of pleasant memories
    c. A hypnotic method for recalling dreams
    d. A clinical technique for observing amnesia patients

14. How are suppression and repression related?
    a. Both are unconscious.
    b. Both are conscious.
    c. Suppression is conscious and repression is unconscious.
    d. Repression is conscious and suppression is unconscious.

15. When is hysterical amnesia most likely to occur?
    a. After brain damage
    b. After excessive alcoholic consumption
    c. After a traumatic experience
    d. With senility

16. Which of the following provides the most popular explanation of forgetting?
    a. Repression
    b. Amnesia
    c. Fading
    d. Interference

17. A student just read her assignment in sociology. Now she is studying psychology. She is having difficulty reading her psychology assignment because she keeps thinking of her sociology. What is she experiencing?
    a. Proactive interference
    b. Retroactive interference
    c. A primary effect
    d. A recency effect

18. A tap dancer claims he finds it easy to remember the first few steps of any dance routine but becomes confused as he gets further along. Why does he have less difficulty with the first part?
    a. There is a recency effect.
    b. There is a primacy effect.
    c. There is less repression.
    d. There is a state dependence.

19. Shelley took a Valium to help her relax during her history exam. What is likely to happen?
    a. She will be relaxed and remember the material she learned.
    b. She will be relaxed, but her memory will be blocked.
    c. She will not be relaxed, but her memory will be enhanced.
    d. She will not be relaxed and will feel a need for alcohol.

20. Wally had seven martinis and met an attractive girl, Eleni. The next day he could recall neither her name nor her address. In which of the following situations would Wally be most likely to remember Eleni?
    a. After sleeping
    b. After drinking seven martinis
    c. After drinking several cups of coffee
    d. After smoking marijuana

   Check your responses against the Checkpoint Answer Key at the end of the chapter. If you had difficulty with any question, reread the text. If you had little or no difficulty answering the questions or have resolved problems that you might have had, you are ready to continue with the next portion of this chapter.

IMPROVING STUDY METHODS

In all probability you are wondering how to use your knowledge of memory and forgetting to improve your own study skills. There is no uniform set of study habits that works for everyone. Diverse study systems seem to benefit different individuals. However, there are a few general suggestions that psychologists have found profitable for most people. Several methods have been discovered that can improve concentration, apportionment of time, and test preparation.

Improving Time Schedules

One of the most important skills that you can learn in college is how to plan your time to study successfully. The best students are not necessarily the most intelligent. Often they are students who have learned how to organize their time and use self-discipline. Most of us have experienced the stress of feeling that there is too much to do and too little time. In truth, there rarely is enough time to do everything. But if you set your priorities and plan your time carefully, you will experience less stress and your grades will probably improve.

   One system for planning your time for a semester suggests three types of calendars (Quinn and Daughtry, 1988). The first calendar is used for long-range plans, for an entire term. The second calendar sets your short-term plans, on a weekly basis. The final calendar sets your immediate plans, or daily list of activities.

Long-Range Plans. Buy or make a calendar that has a large space for each day of the entire term. This calendar will be used to plot the entire semester. First mark vacations and holidays so blocks of free time will be obvious. Next, fill in days with work, family, or other responsibilities. As soon as you receive course outlines from your instructors, fill in key dates for tests, midterms, deadlines for assignments or papers, and final examinations. Next add major social events, perhaps concerts, dances, or sports events.

Then add deadlines that you set for yourself. Remember the importance of breaking long assignments into sections. When setting deadlines for yourself, give yourself some space before the official deadline. This will help you avoid the stress of time pressures. Use some method for distinguishing fixed dates from deadlines that you have assigned yourself; perhaps different colored inks or print for fixed deadlines and script for personal deadlines. A typical term calendar is shown in Figure 4-5.

By actually writing a schedule for yourself, you can avoid procrastination. If a term paper is due in ten weeks, you can break the assignment into weekly tasks. You might use the first week to research several possible topics. The following week you could select the topic. Then give yourself two weeks to read and take notes. By week five you could begin your outline. This would give you four weeks for writing and a week to edit and revise the paper.

A completed term calendar shows a clear picture of the entire semester. Hang this calendar in a conspicuous place, such as over your desk or on your closet door.

Short-Range Plans. Once your term calendar is completed, you are in a good position to plan each week. For most people, Sunday is a good day to develop a weekly plan. Again, it is best to begin by filling in fixed obligations: work hours, class times, and commuting time. It's a good idea to enter these in the manner you have chosen to indicate fixed deadlines in the long-range plans.

As you begin to fill in study times, consider the time of day when you are most efficient. Many people find that they work best at a particular time of day. Some feel more efficient in the morning, while others reach a peak during the afternoon or evening hours. Still others perform evenly throughout the day. It is always helpful to study during your peak time.

There are several important general principles to remember in planning a study schedule. To avoid interference, it is best to study just before and just after class. In most cases distributed practice is more efficient than massed practice, so it is better to study for thirty minutes a day over a ten-day period than to study for five hours on one day (see Feature 4-3). This is particularly true if you find the subject dull and boring. If the material is stimulating and exciting, spacing is less important.

Schedule times for your most difficult subjects first. Be sure to include some fun and leave some free time. Figure 4-6 shows the schedule of a student taking

FIGURE 4-5. A term calendar.

sixteen credit hours, commuting fifteen minutes each way, and working six hours each week.

Immediate Plans. If you function well at night, you may want to take ten or fifteen minutes to plan the next day; otherwise save the planning until morning. Make a daily list of accomplishments or a simple checklist of what you want to do. Again you may separate necessary from unnecessary (but desirable) items by using print and cursive script or different colored inks. Figure 4-7 shows a typical daily list.

Exercise 4-9

Ms. L. is a working parent who is also taking two courses at a community college. Lately she has been feeling stressful because two term papers and two final exams are scheduled for completion within three days. Although it may be too late to correct her current problems, describe three types of calendars that Ms. L. could use to help her use her time more efficiently.

a. _____

_____

b. _____

_____

c. _____

_____

Please compare your descriptions with the list in the Feedback section.

FEATURE 4-3 PSYCHOLOGY IN THE NEWS

Spaced-Out Memory

Remember the old grade-school maxim: "Say a new word ten times quickly and it's yours"? Now the results of a long-term study by a pair of psychologists may turn that bromide into an old wives' tale. In fact, say Harry Bahrick of Ohio Wesleyan University in Delaware, Ohio, and Elizabeth Phelps of Princeton University in New Jersey, if you want a new word to stick in your brain for the long haul, it's best to space out the initial repetitions over a much longer period of time.

Beginning in 1979, Bahrick and Phelps had a group of students learn the Spanish equivalents of fifty English words. Some of the students learned the Spanish words in "forced feedings," with many repetitions of the word in a single day. Others learned them at a much slower rate, in some cases receiving repetitions only after intervals of thirty days. Eight years later, the students were tested for long-term recall. Those who had learned the words in one-day "cram sessions" recalled only 6 percent, while those who learned them over thirty-day intervals remembered as many as 25 percent.

Would the "spaced-out" method work for learning more complex knowledge systems like music or math? Although its effectiveness is difficult to determine scientifically without special teaching methods and specific long-term tests, Bahrick's hunch is that "the principles will apply to almost any subject you'd learn in school—music, mathematics, even what you know about baseball."

Source: Lawren, B. (1988, February). Spaced-out memory. *Omni.*

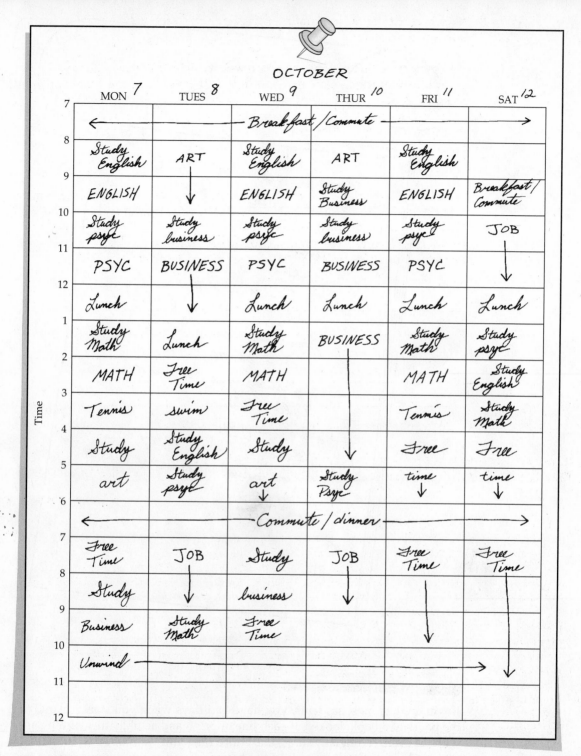

FIGURE 4-6. A weekly calendar.

123

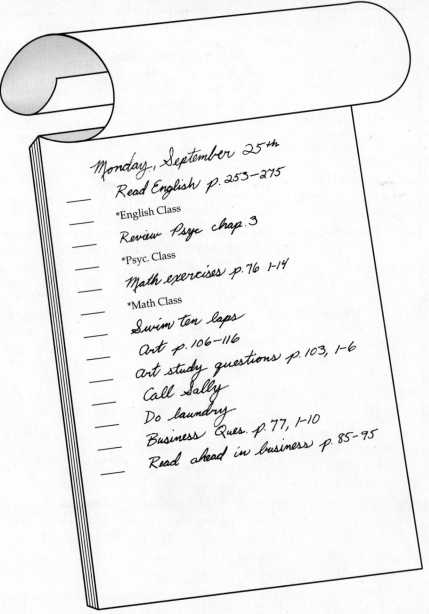

FIGURE 4-7. A daily list of activities.

Improving Concentration

If you are like most students, you have had days when you stared blankly at the pages of a book, looked at each line of print, and actually turned the pages without ever reading anything. The entire time you were daydreaming about something else. This is more likely to happen if you are studying a subject that does not interest you. You might even look for distractions, stare out the window, or listen for unusual sounds. How can you avoid this type of preoccupation? Most techniques for improving concentration try to minimize distractions and keep you active with the material you need to learn.

One important factor in minimizing distractions is the location of the study area. There is evidence that study sessions are more productive when a special area is set aside for work. When distracting thoughts occur, it is best to leave the work area. Return again only when studying will continue. It is also important to keep your study area free of photographs or other items that may cause your mind to wander. Sitting in an upright position is preferable to relaxing on a sofa or easy chair. Although there are individual differences, many students find that soft music will block out intermittent sounds and noises that would be more distracting (Lapp, 1987).

Keeping your mind focused on your studies is usually easier if you are actively involved with the material to be learned. Students find it useful to underline important points using highlighters or ink pens to brighten words. Others prefer to outline or write notes in the margin. These techniques, along with making flash cards of important terms and concepts and making up exams, all seem to work equally well. Recent research at Harvard University suggests that students who keep active by working in groups with other students are more successful (see Feature 4-4). The important factor is to keep alert and involved with the subject. Studies have shown that active study results in more learning than does passive study.

One procedure for keeping study active that has had exceptional success is labeled the SQ3R method, a mnemonic for "Survey, question, read, recite, and review." The first step is to survey the assignment by checking the major headings and gaining a general impression about the subject you will be studying. After checking the headings, make up a general question for each topic. Next begin reading, but as you read search for the answers to your questions. Then recite the answers to your questions. It is preferable to recite aloud so

SQ3R Mnemonic for survey, question, read, recite, and review; a successful approach to studying

---

FEATURE 4-4 PSYCHOLOGY IN THE NEWS

How Undergraduates Can Succeed: Study Together, and in Small Classes

College students who study together, meet frequently with advisors, and enroll in at least one small class every semester are most likely to excel, according to a report by Harvard University.

After five years of study the Harvard researchers concluded that the most effective strategy for an undergraduate to pursue is to make alliances with fellow students, faculty members, and advisors and not try to brave college alone.

"The thing for a student to avoid," said Richard J. Light, a professor of education at Harvard who was director of the assessment project, "is signing up for large classes, drifting in and out anonymously, sitting in the eighth row working quietly and then going back to the library or a dorm room and applying the seat of the pants to the seat of the chair."

Source: De Palma, A. (1991, November 6). How undergraduates can succeed: Study together and in small classes. *The New York Times.*

By studying together, these students are more likely to excel.

that you get additional sensory input. The final step is to review, emphasizing the areas where you had difficulty answering your own questions. An important asset of this method is that you receive feedback and find out whether you have mastered the subject or need to spend more time studying.

Exercise 4-10

Read the following scenario and list five ways that Arsenio could improve his study habits.

Arsenio curled up on the sofa to begin reading his economics assignments. The midterm was the next morning, and he had postponed the reading until the night before so that the material would be fresh in his mind. He hated economics and decided to turn on the television to keep himself awake. As he began the reading, his mind drifted toward the program he was half watching. He closed his eyes and began daydreaming. He began to realize how tired he was and soon dozed off into a sound sleep.

a. _____Survey_____

b. _____Question._____

126

c. _Read_

d. _recite_

e. _review_

Compare your list with the one given in the Feedback section.

Preparing for Tests

Memory is usually measured through one of three methods: recall, recognition, or relearning. Most instructors use either the recall method (essay questions), or the recognition method (multiple-choice tests). Only rarely will relearning be used as a measure.

Essay tests measure memory through ability to recall information and are graded subjectively. Although teachers usually expect specific answers, they are often influenced by the appearance and organization of a response. If two tests are submitted having the same content, the test written neatly with pen rather than pencil and put in correct grammatical form tends to receive a higher grade. Although this tip will not improve your ability, it could improve your test score.

On multiple-choice tests, you must recognize a correct answer imbedded among several wrong alternatives. Recognition is a more sensitive measure than is recall. Multiple-choice tests can detect learning that might not be picked up on a recall test. For example, although you may not be able to name every country in Europe, you probably could select the European nations from a list of countries thoughout the world. A common problem with multiple-choice questions is guessing. Many instructors penalize wrong responses. It is usually wise to determine whether points will be deducted for guessing.

While cramming for tests is never recommended, it is extremely popular. Everyone is occasionally caught in a situation where cramming is necessary. If you must cram, you might find these suggestions useful:

- Use cues in your study setting that you can recreate during the test. If possible study at your desk in the room where you will take the test. Or chew a strongly flavored gum (perhaps grape or strawberry) while cramming and again while taking the test. The strong flavor will act as a cue for your memory. The article in Feature 4-5 reports that even aromas can act as a cue for memory. You could use a different aroma for each course—but you may want to check with your instructor before bringing chocolate bars or mothballs into the testing room.

- Eat lightly and avoid alcohol and too much caffeine. Heavy meals will make you drowsy, and alcohol will dull your memory. While one or two cups of coffee may help keep you awake, too much caffeine will make you jittery.

- Keep active with your reading material. Use the strategies discussed earlier in the chapter: Mark your book with highlighters, take notes, recite the material aloud, use the SQ3R method, and call or meet with classmates for discussion.

Memory: It Seems a Whiff of Chocolate Helps

The power of an odor to stimulate memory, familiar to anybody in whom a whiff of perfume or cologne has stirred thoughts of a long-lost lover, has proved itself in a research laboratory.

College students who smelled chocolate during a word exercise and again the next day did better at remembering the answers than others denied the memory-evoking aroma.

The researcher, Frank Schab, said a memory strategy based on odor could help students studying for multiple exams or airline pilots training for emergencies.

"His work provides the first firm scientific evidence that odors can help bring back memories," said Brian Lyman of the Monell Chemical Senses Center in Philadelphia.

Mr. Lyman said odors, unlike sights and sounds, are processed through the brain's limbic system, which is involved in emotions. This might help odors bring back memories with emotional overtones, he said.

In one study 72 Yale undergraduates were presented with a list of 40 common adjectives and told to write down the opposite of each word. They were not told that the next day they would be asked to recall the words they had written.

Each student was exposed to a chocolate smell during the word exercise only, during the later recall test only, on both occasions, or on neither.

All students were told to imagine the smell of chocolate on both occasions.

Those who were exposed to the smell of chocolate during the word exercise and again in the recall test recalled an average of 21 percent of the words they had written. That was significantly better than the best average from the other groups, 17 percent.

A follow-up experiment showed that the same odor must be present upon both learning and testing to get a memory benefit. There were no differences in the effect between men and women.

Schab also found that chocolate and mothball odors worked equally well, suggesting that a smell's pleasantness does not affect its power to stimulate memory.

Such research has many potential applications, Mr. Schab said. For example students studying for exams in several subjects at a time might benefit from using a different odor for each topic. And using a particular odor when training pilots to handle an emergency, and again when that emergency occurs, might "bring back a lot of information about how to do things, what to do next, what to look for," he said.

Source: Associated Press. (1990, July 10). Memory: It seems a whiff of chocolate helps. The New York Times.

- Take a short break about every hour. Walk around, stretch, have a light snack, or drink water, but be prepared to concentrate when you return to studying.
- Use a variety of mnemonic techniques for improving depositing, including pegword, the method of loci, and meaningful associations.
- Sleep if you become too groggy to concentrate. If you continue to study when you are overtired, you will lose your concentration. It is better to sleep for a few hours and then return to studying.

Taking Tests

In taking any test, the best approach is to answer the easy questions first. This will leave additional time for the more difficult items. When you come to troublesome questions, you can sometimes jog your memory by using free association. Jot down anything that comes into your mind. Free association can help in retrieval. But never waste too much time on one question. By budgeting your time, you can have a few minutes at the end to reread the test.

Many people suffer from test anxiety. Perhaps you have walked into exam rooms with sweaty palms, butterflies in your stomach, and a dry mouth. These are only some of the symptoms. Unfortunately, another symptom is difficulty in retrieving memories. Your mind goes blank, and you cannot think of any answers while you are completing the test. As soon as the exam is handed in and you leave the room, your anxiety ends. The correct responses become apparent to you—but it is too late.

A moderate amount of anxiety seems to help test performance. You are alert and eager to do well. But a high level of anxiety is detrimental. Psychologists have suggested three techniques for helping individuals overcome test anxiety. The first is to use desensitization. By writing out answers and imagining a test situation where you are completely relaxed, you can help to make yourself less sensitive to becoming anxious. This desensitization technique for removing anxieties and fears was discussed in Chapter 3.

The second suggestion is to overlearn. Even when you think you understand and know the information completely, keep studying. This will increase your confidence and keep the answers more available when anxiety strikes. This strategy is used by actors in plays; they learn their parts so well that regardless of how much stage fright they experience, the words of their role just flow from them.

The third technique is to put yourself into a relaxed state before entering the examination room. Panic exchanges with classmates can intensify test anxiety. Think of something soothing, perhaps the sound of waves splashing on the shore as you sit on the sand soaking up sunshine, or maybe a quiet snowfall while you nap by a fire. This method is only useful if you tend toward high anxiety. Seek the help of a professionally trained psychologist or counselor if the problem is sufficiently distressful and self-help measures have failed. Remember, moderate anxiety is helpful. You do not want to doze off during the test.

Checkpoint

Use the following questions to check your understanding of this portion of the chapter. Choose and mark the one correct response to each question.

21. Which type of time-planning calendar should you develop first?
    a. Long-range
    b. Weekly
    c. Daily
    d. Hourly

22. Dwanda has a term paper due next month. What advice would you give her?
    a. Be sure to be free the night before the paper is due.
    b. Procrastinate; most teachers accept late papers.
    c. Try to pace yourself so that the paper will be ready early.
    d. Relax and enjoy yourself now, so you will be rested when you have to work.

23. Abe finds history boring. How should he plan to study?
   a. Cram before the final.
   b. Study in short blocks of time.
   c. Study in long blocks of time.
   d. Avoid studying and wait until an interest develops.

24. What is the first step in the SQ3R method?
   a. Study
   b. Select
   c. Speculate
   d. Survey

25. What do techniques for improving concentration stress?
   a. Keeping actively involved with the material to be learned
   b. Keeping yourself comfortable while you are studying
   c. Surrounding yourself with items of interest
   d. Cramming and massed practice

26. Bertha walked into her final exam in math and felt jittery. Her mouth was dry, her palms were sweaty, and her stomach felt nervous. Suddenly she could not remember a single formula. What was Bertha experiencing?
   a. Global demential amnesia
   b. Organic amnesia
   c. Test anxiety
   d. Fading

27. Which of the following would be most useful in increasing the confidence of a person who usually experiences test anxiety?
   a. Taking new responsibilities
   b. Avoiding active study
   c. Underlearning
   d. Overlearning

Check your responses against the Checkpoint Answer Key at the end of the chapter. If you had difficulty with any question, reread the text. If you had little or no difficulty answering the questions or have resolved problems that you might have had, you are ready to check yourself against the chapter inventory that follows.

CHAPTER INVENTORY

Use the list of objectives as a review checklist. You should be able to do the tasks outlined in the objectives and apply them to everyday examples. If you can, you may feel confident that you have mastered the material in this chapter.

1. Name the three stages of memory, and describe what occurs during each.
2. Outline one way to improve short-term memory.
3. Distinguish between the two aspects of long-term memory: depositing and retrieving.
4. Describe how mnemonics, the pegword system, the method of loci, meaningfulness, and organization can improve depositing.

5. Explain the importance of association and alphabetics in retrieval.
6. List three possible reasons for forgetting, and identify the possibility of greatest interest to psychologists.
7. Describe repression, suppression, fading, and distortion, and recognize their limitations as explanations of forgetting.
8. Specify three types of amnesia.
9. Define and give examples of proactive and retroactive interference and primacy and recency effects.
10. Explain how drugs can affect memory.
11. Identify ways to improve time schedules using long-range, short-range, and immediate plans.
12. Explain how active studying can improve concentration.
13. Specify three methods used to measure memory.
14. Describe how to prepare for tests and avoid test anxiety.

Feedback

The correct answers to the exercises follow. If you did not answer an exercise correctly, review the preceding pages and return to the exercise to correctly complete it.

4-1. a. Long-term memory
b. Sensory register
c. Long-term memory
d. Short-term memory

4-2. a. The method of loci
b. The pegword method
c. By using the method of loci, Cicero could make his speech as long as he wished; his use of the pegword method would have limited the length.

4-3. a.

Group 1	Group 2	Group 3
psychiatry	neighbor	lieutenant
psalm	seize	retrieve
psychology	reign	brief
psychotherapy		

b. This grouping will help students learn the correct spelling because the lists are organized according to similar spellings. This will improve the depositing of the spelling of each word in long-term memory.

4-4. a. 3
b. 2
c. 3
d. 1

4-5. Global demential amnesia

4-6. Psychological experiments have shown that eyewitness testimony can be distorted. The type of question asked from the witness could distort a memory and change a response.

4-7. a. Proactive interference
b. Proactive interference
c. Retroactive interference
d. Retroactive interference

4-8. Since the middle portion will be more difficult to learn than the first portion and the end, it will take more time to learn it. You could simply apportion more time to the center section. Or you might break the speech into smaller units and begin with a different unit each time you work on memorizing the speech. In this way different sections would be benefiting from primacy and recency effects.

4-9. a. Term calendar with key dates for assignments, major work projects, and family responsibilities
b. Weekly calendar with class times, work hours, and parenting responsibilities.
c. Daily checklist of activities to be completed

4-10. a. Arsenio should sit in a straight-backed chair rather than on a sofa.
b. He should space his studying rather than cramming the night before an exam, particularly when he dislikes a subject.
c. He should not allow distractions to creep in when he is studying. The television program is apt to take his mind off his work.
d. When he begins to notice that he is not attending to his studies, Arsenio should leave the area and return only when he is ready to resume his work.
e. He could call classmates and discuss the subject.

Checkpoint Answer Key

1. b; 2. a; 3. c; 4. c; 5. d; 6. d; 7. a; 8. c; 9. b; 10. d; 11. d; 12. c; 13. a; 14. c; 15. c; 16. d; 17. a; 18. b; 19. b; 20. b; 21. a; 22. c; 23. b; 24. d; 25. a; 26. c; 27. d.

Thinking and Problem Solving

There is no more miserable human being than one in
whom nothing is habitual but indecision. —W. JAMES

THINKING	CREATIVE THINKING
Scripts	Characteristics of Creative
Logical Thinking	Thinkers
Predicate Thinking	Improving Creativity
Magical Thinking	Teaching Creativity
Critical Thinking	MEASURING THINKING
Problem Solving	ABILITIES
Artificial Intelligence	Intelligence Tests
	Other Standardized Tests

Have you ever considered how many problems you solve during the course of a day? No doubt some problems are simple, such as choosing what to wear or what to eat for breakfast. Others, however, may be more complicated. Perhaps you must find a way to make a deposit in your overdrawn checking account, or find a way to study when you have out-of-town guests. The solutions you choose for some problems can have an important impact on your life. Your choice of a major in college or a first job will most likely influence your entire career in some way.

This chapter will consider ways to improve your problem-solving abilities. Thinking, the basis of problem solving, will be considered first. Next, the focus will be on the steps involved in problem solving and how to use creative approaches. Finally, you will learn how psychologists measure thinking and problem-solving abilities.

THINKING

Whether you are remembering your childhood, daydreaming about television stardom, trying to fix a leaky faucet, or painting a mural, you are thinking. The term "thinking" is very broad and complex. It includes processes from preoc-

133

cupation and daydreaming to complex problem solving and creating new ideas. Psychologists often refer to the thinking process as "cognition." *Cognition* refers to any mental activity, whether conscious or unconscious.

cognition Mental or thought process

Thoughts come in various forms. Sometimes you think in images. For example, if asked to come up with a scheme for rearranging your living room furniture to make room for a new piano, you would undoubtedy think in images. On the other hand, if asked to explain your position on a new increase in electric rates, you may rely more on words. Some thoughts are in the form of neither words nor images. Ideas such as peace, kindness, and coldness are concepts. Concepts are formed from experiences. Most thoughts involve a combination of images, words, and concepts. It is not always easy to distinguish among them. Think about your last vacation. Can you separate the images, words, and concepts in your thoughts? Thinking seems so natural that most of us are unaware of the complexity of our thought processes.

cerebrum [seh-REE-bruhm] Upper part of the brain that is the center of thinking

cerebellum [sehr-uh-BELL-um] Small section attached to the brain stem that controls balance

brain stem Lower part of the brain that controls heartbeat and breathing

The part of the brain that you exercise when you think is called the *cerebrum*. The cerebrum is located at the top of your brain (see Figure 5-1) and allows you to understand numbers, interpret language, use logic, make decisions, appreciate music, and create imaginary ideas. The cerebrum covers about 85 percent of your brain. Two other parts, the *cerebellum* and the *brain stem* comprise the other 15 percent. Your cerebellum controls your body balance and your brain stem is responsible for maintaining your heartbeat and breathing.

The cerebrum, sometimes referred to as "a thinking cap," is divided into two parts, a right hemisphere and a left hemisphere. The two hemispheres are

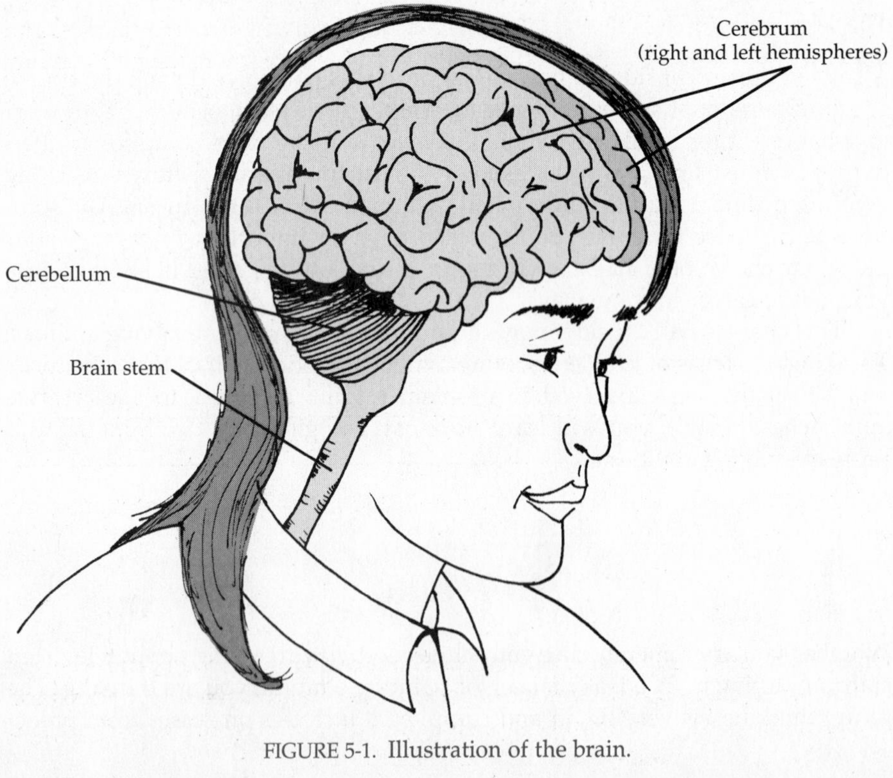

FIGURE 5-1. Illustration of the brain.

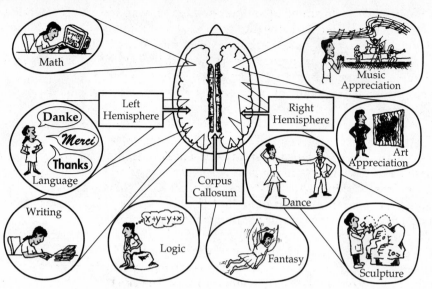

FIGURE 5-2. Left and right hemispheres of the brain.

connected by a bundle of nerves called the *corpus callosum.* Researchers have studied the special jobs performed in each hemisphere and, although their findings are a bit sketchy, generally have determined that the left side of the brain deals with language, mathematics, logical thinking, and problem solving. The right hemisphere takes care of sensing rhythm and color, imagination and fantasy, music and art, and spatial relationships. Researchers have found that the two hemispheres do not operate independently and sometimes assume each other's functions. The hemispheres work together to process information, with messages crossing the corpus callosum.

corpus callosum [KOR-pus kah-LOW-sum] Bundle of nerves that connects the right and left hemispheres of the brain

Exercise 5-1

Assume you are writing a song about your best friend. Describe the roles of your right and left hemispheres. Explain how the two hemispheres would communicate.

_____

_____

_____

Compare your response with the one listed in the Feedback section at the end of this chapter.

Scripts

Often we do some impressive thinking without realizing it. Schank and Abelson (1983) noted that a great amount of thought is often required to understand even the simplest, very boring little story or *script*. A script is very short and we automatically fill in details. Consider the script:

script Brief story that requires you to fill in information

FIGURE 5-3. Could this be the way your right brain sees the field?

> Jane threw a bridal shower for Cathy. Cathy received fifteen irons and fifteen mixers. She went to the returns department the next day.

This script is indeed a very boring little story. However, think of all the blanks you need to fill in to understand even this simple story. If you were an immigrant from another culture, the script would be very difficult to understand. First, you need to know both what it means to "throw a bridal shower" and the purpose of a bridal shower. You also need to know what irons and mixers are and that most people only need one of each. You also have to fill in the fact that these items were gifts that were purchased at a store and could be returned. Fortunately, if you are familiar with this cultural ritual, most of this thinking happens automatically!

Exercise 5-2

Read the following script from Minsky (1983), and indicate three things you had to fill in to understand the story.

> Jane was invited to Jack's birthday party. She wondered if he would like a kite. She went to her room and shook her piggy bank. It made no sound.

a. _____

b. _____

c. _____

Please check your list in the Feedback section at the end of the chapter.

Logical Thinking

Whether or not you have ever taken a formal course in logic, chances are you use logical thought many times every day. However, you may not be aware of the sequence of steps in your logical-thought process. Logical thought consists of two beliefs and a conclusion based on the beliefs, or *premises*. The first belief is called the "major premise" and the second belief is labeled the "minor premise." Logically enough, the conclusion is called the "conclusion."

premise Belief

Consider the sequence of logical thought:

Major premise	If the traffic light is red, I must stop my car.
Minor premise	The traffic light is red.
Conclusion	Therefore, I must stop my car.

This logical sequence is reasoned by millions of individuals many times each day. In most cases the thought process is unconscious, and people are not even aware that they have thought logically. Most decisions require logical thought. When judging whether you are sick enough to stay home from work, you might reason:

Major premise	If I have a fever, I should not go to work.
Minor premise	I have a fever.
Conclusion	Therefore, I should not go to work.

Conversely,

Major premise	If I do not have a fever, I should go to work.
Minor premise	I do not have a fever.
Conclusion	Therefore, I should go to work.

Assuming that your premises are true, if you follow a logical thought sequence, you will reach a valid conclusion. Unfortunately, sometimes people base their thinking on false premises. For example, the major premise: "If I do not have a fever, I should go to work" would not be true if it is Sunday and you only work on weekdays. Even though your logic is correct, your conclusion would be false.

Predicate Thinking

The thought process is not always logical. Freud identified a type of nonlogical thought process that he labeled *predicate thinking*. Predicate thinking is based on sentence structures. When two sentences have the same predicates, or endings, people unconsciously associate the subjects, or beginnings. Advertisements often appeal to predicate thinking. Advertisers might make statements like "Distinguished men drink Boozy brand liquor" or "Good mothers buy Sticky brand cake mix." They hope you will use nonlogical thought and reason that:

predicate thinking Nonlogical thought that unconsciously associates subjects of sentences that have the same predicates or endings

- Distinguished men drink Boozy brand liquor.
- I drink Boozy brand liquor.
- Therefore, I am a distinguished man.

or

- Good mothers buy Sticky brand cake mix.
- I buy Sticky brand cake mix.
- Therefore, I am a good mother.

Exercise 5-3

Read each of the following thought sequences. If it is possible to reach a logical conclusion, write the correct conclusion. If the sequence is an example of predicate thinking and is not logical, simply put an "X" on the final line.

a. If there is a blizzard, the college will be closed.
   There is a blizzard.

_____

b. Young women wear modern hairstyles.
   Matilda wears modern hairstyles.

_____

c. A smart person reads Genius magazine.
   Han reads Genius magazine.

_____

d. Whenever I am in the bathtub, the telephone will ring.
   I am in the bathtub.

_____

Compare your conclusions with the ones in the Feedback section.

Magical Thinking

Did you ever shake hands with a famous person and swear you would never wash your hand? Or perhaps you collected an autograph or possession from a celebrity. If you thought that something would "rub off" from the well-known person, you indulged in *magical thinking*. While you may not believe in magic, your emotions caused your thinking to become irrational. The article in Feature 5-1 describes some examples of magical thinking.

magical thinking
Irrational thought processes

Public attitudes about AIDS provide a common example of magical thinking. Many people who know that the disease cannot be transmitted with casual contact still avoid coming close to AIDS victims. Magical thinking requires scrapping your logical thought and focusing on your gut-level reactions. The result is irrational behavior.

Critical Thinking

Distinguishing among logical thinking, predicate thinking, and magical thinking requires critical thinking. You must evaluate the statements and make judgments based on reason. Recently, educators have expressed concern about developing critical thinking skills in children. In the past, children who argued were often considered rebellious. Mexican and Mexican-American children, as

Contagious Thoughts: Under a "Magical Law," Good and Evil Prove as Infectious as Germs

A young woman contemplates slipping into a sweater previously worn by her ex-boyfriend, but she finds the garment repulsive. "It's the fact that he could somehow transmit—uh, somehow the object would pick up some negativeness," she explains to a research psychologist. "I'm not saying it would smell or have dandruff on it, but it would be creepy because he's a creepy person."

A man in the same study rejects a thoroughly laundered sweater once worn by a hepatitis victim. "I'd feel it was contaminated in some way, not only that I could get hepatitis from it, but that it was somehow contaminated, it's just not clean," he tells an experimenter. "I don't really think you could get (hepatitis) that way."

Do these cases represent rare lapses into superstition or "magical thinking" on the part of otherwise rational folks? Just the opposite, asserts psychologist Carol Nemeroff of Arizona State University in Tempe. Her research indicates that many adults routinely subscribe to what Nemeroff calls "the magical law of contagion," a traditional belief noted in many non-Western cultures by anthropologists. From isolated New Guinea tribes to crowded New York streets, contagion beliefs hinge on the conviction that all sorts of sources—including friends, enemies, food, blood and hair—contain some sort of contagious entity or "essence" that transfers physical, psychological or moral qualities to others through direct or indirect contact.

Source: Bower, B. (1991, August 31). Contagious thoughts: Under a "magical law," good and evil prove as infectious as germs. *Science News.*

well as children from many other cultures, are supposed to respect their elders and learn not to argue or question them (Greenfield, 1992). Often these children have difficulty adjusting as critical thinking becomes a stronger part of the American education curriculum.

Without critical thinking skills, we can easily be misled by propaganda and deceptive advertising. Ennis (1985) and Paul (1984) identified several guidelines for critical thinking:

- Separate logical ideas from emotional arguments.
- Try to see both sides, for and against, the issue being proposed.
- Don't be afraid to question a weak-sounding argument.
- Look for inconsistencies in statements.
- Wait for enough evidence and don't rush to conclusions.

If we use these guidelines, we will be less susceptible to hoaxes.

Exercise 5-4

For each the following claims, indicate which of the above guidelines for critical thinking would help you make a proper evaluation.

a. There are eight good reasons why you should chew Gummy gum.

_____

b. I'm in favor of increasing spending on government services and salaries and reducing taxes.

_____

FIGURE 5-4. Educators are eager to develop critical thinking skills.

c. I can't stand small children, so there's no way I'd vote for a new school in this community.

_____

d. We need to expand the highway for more bicycle space, and anyone who questions it must be pretty stupid.

_____

You may check your responses in the Feedback section at the end of the chapter.

Problem Solving

Although logical thinking can be an important aspect of problem solving, there are also other factors involved. Many problems are solved by trial and error, where there is no system; you just take chance guesses. This process drags on and is not efficient. Psychologists have suggested a more practical series of steps for solving problems.

Define the Problem. In order to solve a problem, someone needs to admit that a problem exists. Short people are familiar with the problem shown in Figure 5-5. Unfortunately few store managers have recognized and defined the problem, so tall customers and salespeople continue to reach for items or allow short persons to leave without purchases.

Find the Facts. Often the facts will make the solution obvious. The comedian Norm Crosby gave a humorous example of ignoring some facts.

FIGURE 5-5. A tall person may not recognize this problem.

I have a friend who went through a harrowing experience recently. He locked his car with the keys in the ignition. He stood there for two hours with a wire coat hanger trying unsuccessfully to fish out the keys through a narrow opening in the window. It was awful. His wife sat inside the car crying her heart out.

Look for Possible Solutions. Once you understand the problem and have gathered all the facts, you will then search for possible solutions. Most people will base their selection of possible solutions on past experiences. If a solution once worked on a similar problem, chances are it will be successful once again. The difficulty with such an approach is that it tends to limit your thinking and view. This difficulty is referred to as a *mental set,* or an inability to get out of a rut. For example, check yourself by reading the following:

mental set Limited view of possible solutions and a tendency to rspond in the same way regardless of the problem

There are a number of words in the English language where the letters "*olk*" are pronounced "*oke*." Remember President *Polk*? Of course there is the word *folk*. And what do you call the white part of an egg?

If you responded yolk, you were in a mental set. (The yellow part of an egg is the yolk; the white part is called the albumin.)

functional fixedness Using objects only for their known purposes and being unable to think of other possible uses to solve problems

One variation of mental set that can restrain thinking is called *functional fixedness*. Functional fixedness involves the use of objects. The more you use an object for one purpose, the less likely you are to think of other possible uses. For example, suppose ice has formed on your car windshield and you are without a scraper. What else could you use to scrape the ice? Credit cards in your wallet or a spatula from your kitchen might do the job. Of course the usual function of a credit card or spatula is not for ice scraping. If you can think beyond the usual purposes of objects, you can often come up with alternative solutions to your problems. Anyone who has used a coin to tighten a screw or a newspaper as a shield from the rain has, in a sense, overcome functional fixedness.

Choose a Solution and Evaluate the Effectiveness. After reviewing possible solutions, select what appears to be the best alternative. Then test this solution to be sure it works. If the solution is useful, your problem is solved. If the solution does not work, you must again study the alternative answers and make a selection. The process will continue until an effective solution emerges.

Exercise 5-5

Martin has a problem. Within the next three weeks, he needs $200 for books. He has decided to use a systematic approach to find a solution to his problem:

a. Define the problem.
b. Find the facts.
c. Consider possible solutions.
d. Choose a solution and evaluate its effectiveness.

The flow diagram in Figure 5-6 shows the actual steps he took. Divide the diagram into four sections. Label each section to show which step in his systematic approach is being used. The first section has been done for you.

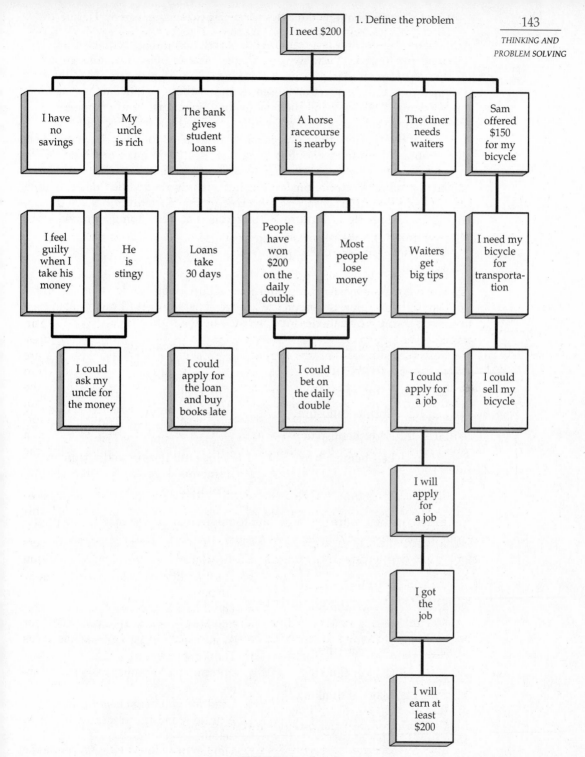

FIGURE 5-6.

Artificial Intelligence

Artificial intelligence (AI) is a term that describes computer programs that solve problems by "thinking" the way people do. Most of these programs are based on sets of rules similar to logical thinking. One AI program, MYCIN, was designed to diagnose infectious diseases and is about as efficient as most doctors (Mason, 1985). In fields such as geology, insurance, and engineering, AI programs have solved problems far more quickly than people could.

One of the most exciting aspects of AI research is the knowledge we have gained about the human thought process. Researchers must break down the thought process into steps in order to write programs. As a result we have gained far more appreciation for the human mind's abilities in evaluating scripts, using common sense, and even recognizing a friend (Schank and Hunter, 1985). The article in Feature 5-2 suggests that developing common sense for a computer is a difficult task.

Checkpoint

Use the following matching questions to check your understanding of this portion of the chapter. Listed on the left are six areas of the brain. Match each area with the appropriate description listed on the right.

1. _____ Cerebrum		a. Helps you maintain your balance
2. _____ Cerebellum		b. Provides a bridge between the two sides of the brain
3. _____ Brain stem		c. Represents the upper-85-percent portion of the brain, involved in thinking
4. _____ Corpus callosum		d. Helps with logical thinking and language
5. _____ Right hemisphere		e. Helps with images and imagination
6. _____ Left hemisphere		f. Maintains your heartbeat and breathing

Listed on the left are ten important terms. Match each term with one phrase from the list on the right.

7. _____ Cognition	a. A belief
8. _____ Script	b. The inability to use an object for a new purpose
9. _____ Logical thinking	c. The thinking process
10. _____ Premise	d. Random guessing at answers
11. _____ Predicate thinking	e. Associating subjects of sentences
12. _____ Critical thinking	f. Thinking in a rut
13. _____ Magical thinking	g. Computer programs that solve problems
14. _____ Trial and error	h. Used for valid conclusions
15. _____ Mental set	i. A little story that requires filling in details
16. _____ Functional fixedness	j. Making judgments based on reason
17. _____ Artificial intelligence	k. Irrational notions usually based on emotions

So Who's That Talking: Human or Machine?

It has been 41 years since Alan M. Turing, the British mathematician, formulated a simple test to answer the question, "Can machines think?" In the intervening years scientists and philosophers have engaged in a sometimes bitter debate over Mr. Turing's puzzle.

In one camp are those who believe the brain is simply a biological machine, and despite its immense complexity there is no reason in principle why a suitably programmed computer should not be able to mimic it. Their opponents respond that the human mind is inherently different from a machine and can never be reduced to a set of computations.

Computer scientists have recently made significant progress in what is referred to as "natural language." Programs that understand simple English phrases have been available on personal computers for a number of years. But these programs also stumble easily, failing to comprehend many statements that even children construe correctly. A computer program might be easily confused by information that humans take for granted: for example, that a child is always younger than its parent.

Researchers ... have been trying to build a program with a common-sense knowledge base equivalent to that of a young child. The project, which is expected to be completed in 1994, will eventually include as much as a billion bytes of information and about 100 million statements. A byte is a string of ones and zeros that contains the basic information processed by digital computers ...

Source: Markoff, J. (1991, November 5). So who's talking: Human or machine? *The New York Times*.

CREATIVE THINKING

One area of thinking that computers have not invaded is creative thinking. Psychologists have difficulty agreeing on the exact definition of *creativity*. However, most psychologists view creativity as an ability to see things in a new and unusual way and to come up with unique solutions to problems. Creativity is the opposite of mental set. It provides an original path from humdrum ideas and dull, routine views. Creative thinking lends excitement and helps find new solutions to old problems. The article in Feature 5-3 describes a creative and

creativity Ability to see things in a new way and come up with unusual solutions

Simple Plot

During World War I when Harrigan was in France, his wife wrote to him. "There isn't an able-bodied man left in Ireland," she said, "and I'm gonna have to dig up the garden myself."

Harrigan wrote back, "Don't dig up the garden. That's where the guns are." The letter was censored and soldiers came to the house and dug up every square foot of the garden. "I don't know what to do," wrote Mrs. Harrigan to her husband. "Soldiers came and dug up the whole garden."

Harrigan wrote back, "Now plant the potatoes."

Source: Baker, L. (1992, September). Simple plot. *The Saturday Evening Post*.

humorous solution to a problem. Psychologists agree that creativity is not the same as intelligence measured by standard intelligence tests. Often people with high IQs are not at all creative.

Some researchers base their evaluations of creativity on the production of a result or an accomplishment. They look for such socially valued products as inventions, art, or musical works as signs of creativity. Although there is some relationship between creative ability and accomplishments, according to Barron and Harrington (1981), this relationship is very low.

Exercise 5-6

The man in Figure 5-7 seems pleased with his invention. Would most psychologists consider his invention creative? Why or why not?

_____

_____

_____

You may check your answer in the Feedback section.

Characteristics of Creative Thinkers

Do you view creative people as wild, imaginative, and different? Andreason (1987) found that creative writers may have more emotional mood swings than other people do. Most people who have made creative contributions are considered nonconforming, independent, confident, and moody.

*"I've done it. . .I've invented the world's first
solar-powered lighting device."*

FIGURE 5-7.

But apparently creativity also requires hard work. Madigan and Elwood (1984) stressed the importance of curiosity and persistence. They described the story of the invention of Velcro by the creative Swiss inventor George de Mestral. While hunting, de Mestral and his dog became covered with burrs. As he struggled to remove the burrs, de Mistral became curious about why the burrs stuck so well to his clothes. He studied the burrs under his microscope and discovered hundreds of tiny hooks on each burr. He spent years of persistence trying to find a way to attach these types of hooks to tape. The final result was Velcro.

Other creative persons report similar experiences. Beethoven labored long hours writing, tearing up, and rewriting his works. The Nobel prize winner Thomas Mann claimed he struggled to make himself write three pages each day.

Exercise 5-7

Read the following list of adjectives, and check those which describe common characteristics of creative thinkers.

_____ Conforming

_____ Confident

_____ Independent

_____ Boring

_____ Moody

_____ Intelligent

_____ Curious

_____ Persistent

Compare your checks with answers in the Feedback section at the end of the chapter.

Improving Creativity

How can you become more creative? A variety of suggestions have evolved. Many psychologists suggest jotting down every idea that occurs to you, whether good or bad. Trying to think of only good ideas can be both stifling and frustrating. The time for being creative is not the time to exercise your critical thinking. Give yourself plenty of time. Some psychologists suggest acting out and drawing diagrams to help you visualize problems. They recommend talking to yourself out loud and walking through the problem as you act it out. It is always useful to follow in the steps of well-known creative thinkers and be persistent. Papalia and Olds (1988) have identified several steps to becoming more creative:

- Make a conscious effort to be original and develop new ideas.
- Don't worry about what other people may think.

- Try to think with a broad perspective and avoid cultural taboos in your thinking (such as racial or gender stereotyping).
- If you are not right at first, explore other alternatives and try new routes.
- Keep an open mind and question your assumptions.
- Look for explanations for odd and puzzling facts.
- Overcome functional fixedness and look for unconventional ways to use objects.
- Change your habitual ways of doing things and force yourself to try new approaches.
- Have brainstorming sessions with other people: Generate as many new ideas as possible without evaluating them until the end of the session.
- Be objective and imagine your ideas were produced by a stranger when you evaluate them.

Exercise 5-8

Mr. C wants to increase creativity in his toy-manufacturing company. He has developed a list of ideas. Place a + sign beside each idea that is likely to improve creativity and a − sign beside each idea that might hamper creativity.

_____ Avoid ideas that our computer can't handle.

_____ Take your time and come up with plenty of ideas.

_____ Feel free to be unconventional.

_____ Talk out your ideas.

_____ Eliminate ideas that might be expensive.

_____ Stick with the toy company's image.

_____ Think of unconventional ways to use our equipment.

Compare your responses to those in the Feedback section.

Teaching Creativity

Many courses have been developed to teach creative thinking. However, according to Mayer (1983), creativity improves only on the specific tasks being taught. The creative skills learned do not seem to work in other situations. Perhaps we need more creative approaches to teaching creativity!

Checkpoint

Use the following questions to check your understanding of this portion of the chapter. Choose and mark the one correct response to each question.

18. Which of the following types of thinking is found in humans but not in computers?
    a. Logical
    b. Mathematical
    c. Creative
    d. All of the above

FIGURE 5-8. How would you encourage Calvin's creativity?

19. Which of the following is the opposite of creativity?
    a. Intelligence
    b. Mental set
    c. Persistence
    d. Scripts

20. Bill invented an exercise machine. What characteristics must it have to be considered creative?
    a. New and original
    b. Conforming and acceptable
    c. Working and inexpensive
    d. Humdrum and expensive

21. What is the relationship between creative ability and creative achievement?
    a. There is a high relationship.
    b. There is a high negative relationship.
    c. There is a slight relationship.
    d. There is no relationship.

22. Which of the following conditions has been linked to creativity?
    a. Schizophrenia
    b. Paranoia
    c. Cocaine addiction
    d. Mood swings

23. What are two common characteristics of creative persons?
    a. Humor and conformity
    b. Curiosity and persistence
    c. Impulsiveness and dependence
    d. Acceptance and timidity

24. Which of the following statements is likely to kill creative ideas?
    a. Take your time.
    b. Talk to yourself.
    c. Come up with lots of different ideas.
    d. That's not the way the boss usually does it.

25. Peter just completed a course in creative poetry writing. What is likely to happen?

a. His poetry writing will become more creative.
b. His poetry writing will become less creative.
c. His poetry writing will not change.
d. All of his creative skills will improve.

Check your responses against the Checkpoint Answer Key at the end of the chapter. If you had difficulty with any question, reread the text. If you had little or no difficulty answering the questions or have resolved problems that you might have had, you are ready to continue with the next portion of the chapter.

MEASURING THINKING ABILITIES

Along with a set of physical characteristics, each person has a unique pattern of abilities and talents. In discussing thinking abilities, the emphasis thus far has been on general characteristics that can be applied to most people. At this point you may be wondering how you compare with other people. Psychologists have a number of testing instruments that can be used to measure and compare talents and abilities. You are probably most familiar with intelligence and achievement tests, since they are used more often than other instruments are. It is difficult to attend school without taking a number of standardized intelligence and achievement tests. *Standardized* means that the test has been tried on a large population and one score may be compared with the scores of other individuals and groups. But other types of standardized tests are also available—from tests of neurological and motor abilities to tests of creative, artistic, and musical talent.

standardized test Test that has a uniform set of instructions for administration and scoring; the results can be compared with the scores of a larger population.

Intelligence Tests

intelligence Ability to learn or adapt

Psychologists do not completely agree on the definition of the concept of *intelligence*. However, most of their explanations infer an ability to learn and adapt in a very broad sense. Many psychologists have jokingly defined intelligence as "what intelligence tests measure." While intelligence is a concept, intelligence tests use concrete criteria that is believed to be related to the concept of intelligence. Your score on an intelligence test is used to compute your *intelligence quotient (IQ)*. Attempts to measure intelligence have been far from perfect, and, clearly, many intelligence tests available measure something far removed from an ability to learn.

intelligence quotient (IQ) Score on an intelligence test that is used to classify individuals.

One major problem in measuring intelligence is the number of elements that can contribute to the ability to learn. Some have argued that intelligence is innate: You are born with certain abilities and capacities. But factors like cultural exposure, health, and nutrition have been found to influence intelligence. Intelligence tests have not been successful in measuring innate abilities. However, results of individual intelligence tests are helpful in planning educational programs.

There are two common types of intelligence tests: individual tests and group tests.

Individual Tests of Intelligence. For the most part, psychologists prefer individual tests. This means that the individual works alone with the psychologist in answering questions and performing tasks. During the testing session the psychologist can observe the person's behavior and deal with any specific difficulties that are encountered. Many psychologists prefer the Wechsler scales because they reveal patterns of abilities. The strengths and weaknesses of each person are made clear. The results of Wechsler tests can be used to prescribe special methods of instruction based on the person's pattern of abilities.

Group Tests of Intelligence. In a group test there is more opportunity for error. Group tests are often administered by classroom teachers, clerks, secretaries, and other individuals who may not have been trained in testing. Behavior is not noted, and there is more room for misjudgment. An individual who misunderstands the directions could lose credit for an entire section of the test. Likewise a good guesser or cheater could achieve a high score. People who do not read well generally score poorly on group tests. Group tests are less expensive, but they are also less accurate.

Exercise 5-9

When Ted was in grade two, he took a group intelligence test with his class. He remembers the day because he had a heavy cold and neither a tissue nor a handkerchief. He kept sniffing and looking around to borrow a tissue. The teacher who was administering the test thought he was cheating and made him start over. He was too upset to explain. He had to complete the test in the remaining ten minutes and never even saw the last page.

a. List five reasons why Ted's resulting IQ score of 82 may not be accurate.

1. _____

3. _____

4. _____

5. _____

b. Suggest a way for Ted to find more accurate information about his ability to learn.

_____

_____

Please check your responses with those in the Feedback section.

Classification. As stated before, intelligence tests result in a score that is your intelligence quotient, or IQ. The IQ classification system is based on the scores obtained on individual tests, but most group tests have adopted the same labels.

Score	Classification
0–24	Profound mental retardation
25–39	Severe mental retardation
40–54	Moderate mental retardation
55–65	Mild mental retardation
66–89	Below average
90–109	Average
110–119	Bright normal
120–129	Superior
130 and above	Very superior

The use of classification and labeling based on IQ scores has been sharply criticized. Even the best test of intelligence can result in errors of five to ten IQ points. As reported in Feature 5-4, children who have been absent from school show significant drops in their IQ scores and may be mislabeled. A teacher who identifies a child as mildly retarded or below average in intelligence is not likely to seek challenging tasks to stimulate the child. Many schools use track systems that separate children into educational channels according to their scores on group tests. Children in the lower tracks usually are given fewer opportunities. These children often are from families or school systems that have less stimulating activities.

Cultural Factors. Since absence from school can cause a drop in IQ scores, it is clear that the environment has a definite influence on IQ scores. There is also evidence that children from differing cultures score poorly on IQ tests developed using White American criteria. Several early studies found that

FEATURE 5-4 PSYCHOLOGY IN THE NEWS

The Educated IQ

In the contentious field of intelligence testing, some researchers argue that IQ scores represent a measure of stable general intelligence that underlies achievement at school and work. But a review of nearly 200 studies charting IQ development indicates that IQ rises as people spend more time in school, regardless of the schooling . . .

Even the most basic schooling fosters thinking and problem-solving skills tapped by most IQ tests, asserts psychologist Stephen J. Ceci of Cornell University in Ithaca, N.Y.

Ceci notes several trends in the data: Small but significant IQ drops occur during summer vacation, especially among youngsters living in poor areas; children who attend school intermittently experience steadily declining IQs; children who be-

gin school late or who drop out have lower IQs than their peers; fluctuations in IQ scores closely parallel peaks and valleys in academic achievement scores, suggesting that both measures respond to similar school influences; and average IQs rose dramatically from 1952 to 1982 in 14 industrial nations as the average level of education for citizens in those countries increased.

Other factors, including genetics, affect individual IQs, Ceci acknowledges, but the studies suggest that the magnitude of the educational effect ranges from losing one-quarter of an IQ point to six IQ points per year of missed school.

Source: (1991, September 21). The educated IQ. *Science News.*

Blacks in the United States score about 15 points lower than Whites on IQ tests (Mackenzie, 1984). However, as educational opportunities for Blacks are improving, so are their IQ test scores. Unfortunately about half of Black children still live below the poverty level. What happens when Black children are raised in White upper-middle-class homes? Scarr and Weinberg (1976) studied Black children who had been adopted into affluent White homes in Minnesota and found that their IQ scores were comparable to White children adopted into similar homes.

Some argue that racial differences in IQ scores may also have a hereditary, or genetic, cause. But there is no apparent support for this argument. When Scarr and her colleagues (1977) investigated Black children of varying amounts of African heritage, they found that racial heritage did not influence IQ scores. The Mackenzie study (1984) compared the IQ scores of German children whose mothers were German but whose fathers were American military serving in World War II. Regardless of the color of the father's skin, the children had almost identical IQ scores.

While cultural factors cause clear differences in IQ scores between White children and Black children, as you can imagine, the differences become even stronger when White American children are compared with children from totally different cultural environments. Our intelligence tests are based on White American and Western European values which place importance on speed and analysis skills. Some cultures, like the Cree Indians in northern Canada, favor working slowly, patiently, and carefully and being self-sufficient and good (Berry and Bennett, 1992), values that are totally apart from the criteria on IQ tests.

Different cultures attach different values to certain skills. In parts of Africa, hunting skills are critical, and in China, mastering a written word is of prime importance (Rumpel, 1988). Black Americans are encouraged by their communities to develop spontaneous, creative, interactive, and broad thinking skills (Heath, 1989). But most educators in the United States value language ability and mathematical and spatial skills, and that is what most IQ tests measure.

IQ tests have a cultural bias, and language presents an additional problem. People who are unfamiliar or uncomfortable with the English language are at a clear disadvantage. Psychologists have attempted to devise tests that do not require language, in an attempt to make *culture-free tests*. But even the simplest nonverbal tasks seem to be influenced by cultural values and understandings. Accepting that it may be impossible to develop a culture-free test, psychologists have also attempted to produce a *culture-fair test*, a test that deals with experiences common to many cultures. Once again, these attempts have not been successful, since the required tasks are more familiar to some cultural groups than to others (Anastasi, 1988).

culture-free test
Test with no culture-linked content

culture-fair test
Test that uses experiences common to many cultures

At this point you may be wondering why psychologists continue to use IQ tests when the tests discriminate against so many people. IQ tests are usually good predictors of school success. Since schools in the United States stress the values of our culture, students who share these values and skills tend to do well both on IQ test and in school performance. IQ tests are culturally biased but so are our schools. Psychologists are now attempting to devise appropriate ways to test people from other cultures. Geisenger (1992) has proposed some solutions to the testing of Hispanics and has outlined areas for further research. Helms (1992) favors measuring such additional factors as cultural dependence and alternative thinking, and adding more items that reflect diversity. In the meantime separate norms for different cultures are recommended. Currently, IQ scores are only one estimate of innate intelligence, and a biased estimate at that.

Exercise 5-10

Twara is an eight-year-old Cree girl who recently came to the United States from northern Canada. She had never attended school and when tested for placement in an American school was found to have an IQ of 65. The school recommended placing her in a special class for mildly mentally retarded students.

a. List two reasons why Twara's IQ score may not reflect her true intelligence.

1. _____

_____

2. _____

_____

b. Explain why this placement could have a negative effect on Twara.

_____

_____

Please compare your responses with those listed in the Feedback section at the end of the chapter.

Scope of Intelligence Tests. Several psychologists have argued that current intelligence testing has an extremely narrow focus. Gardner (1983) pointed out that traditional IQ tests really only measure three things: language ability, mathematical/logical reasoning, and spatial/perceptual skills. Gardner believes there are other aspects of intelligence. He includes musical ability, bodily ability, intrapersonal ability (self-understanding), and interpersonal ability (understanding of others). Gardner (1985) found that intelligence tests correlate well only with schoolwork. They do not correlate well with later growth and accomplishments.

Wagner and Sternberg (1985) argued that intelligence tests do not measure practical skills. They contend that there are nonacademic skills that are not taught but are closely related to business success. Such skills include:

- The ability to adapt to new or unexpected situations
- The ability to have sudden insights when solving problems
- The ability to size things up and learn from examples rather than instruction

The article in Feature 5-5 shows the difference between standard IQ test questions and the types of questions suggested by Sternberg.

A Different Sort of I.Q. Test

Standard I.Q. tests measure, in the main, two varieties of intelligence—verbal and logical-mathematical. But according to critics like Robert Sternberg, a Yale psychologist, tests should measure other key elements of intelligence, such as insight. The first two questions on this quiz, which is taken from Dr. Sternberg's book *Intelligence Applied*, are standard I.Q. questions that he says rely for their answers on specific skills a child learns in school. But the other questions, he says, measure the sort of intelligence not found on standard I.Q. tests and depend for answers on such mental skills as insight, thinking in novel ways and detecting fallacies. The answers appear below.

STANDARD I.Q. QUESTIONS:

1. TENNIS is to RACQUET as BASEBALL is to:
   a. Club
   b. Strike
   c. Bat
   d. Home run
2. In the following series what number comes next? 3, 7, 12, 18
   a. 24
   b. 25
   c. 26
   d. 27

INSIGHT QUESTIONS

3. Aeronautical engineers have made it possible for a supersonic jet fighter to catch up with the bullets fired from its own guns, with sufficient speed to shoot itself down. If a plane, flying at 1000 miles an hour, fires a burst, the rounds leave the plane with an initial velocity of about 3000 miles an hour. Why won't a plane that continues to fly straight ahead overtake and fly into its own bullets?
4. If you have black socks and brown socks in your drawer, mixed in a ratio of 4 to 5, how many socks will you have to take out to make sure of having a pair of the same color?
5. In the Thompson family, there are five brothers, and each brother has one sister. If you count Mrs. Thompson, how many females are there in the Thompson family?

NOVEL-THINKING QUESTIONS

In solving the following analogies, assume that the statement given before the analogy is true, whether it actually is true or not, and use that assumption to solve the analogy.

6. LAKES are dry.
   TRAIL is to HIKE as LAKE is to:
   a. Swim
   b. Dust
   c. Water
   d. Walk
7. DEER attack tigers.
   LION is to COURAGEOUS as DEER is to:
   a. Timid
   b. Aggressive
   c. Cougar
   d. Elk
8. DIAMONDS are fruits.
   PEARL is to OYSTER as DIAMOND is to:
   a. Mine
   b. Tree
   c. Ring
   d. Pie

INFERENCE QUESTIONS

The following problems require detecting the relationship between the first two items and finding a parallel relationship between the second two. In answering, explain what those relationships are.

9. VANILLA is to BEAN as TEA is to LEAF.
10. ATOM is to MOLECULE as CELL is to ORGANISM.
11. UNICORN is to SINGLE as DUET is to BICYCLE.
12. NOON is to EVE as 12:21 is to 10:01.

ANSWERS

1. c
2. b
3. Gravity pulls the bullets down; thus unless a pilot consciously dives to run into the bullets, they will not hit the plane.
4. Three.

(continued)

5. Two. The only females in the family are the mother and her daughter, who is the sister to each of her brothers.
6. d
7. b
8. b
9. Vanilla comes from a bean, and tea, from a leaf.
10. Atoms combine to form a molecule; cells combine to form an organism.
11. A unicorn and a single both refer to one of something; a duet and a bicycle both refer to two of something.
12. Each of the terms of the analogy reads the same, both forward and backward.

Source: Goleman, D. (1986, November 9). A different sort of IQ test. *The New York Times*.

Exercise 5-11

Imagine that Gardner and Sternberg decided to write a new IQ test together. They both agree that they want to expand the scope of questions beyond the usual questions on language ability, logical reasoning, and perceptual skills. List seven additional areas that they would test.

a. _____

b. _____

c. _____

d. _____

e. _____

f. _____

g. _____

Check your list in the Feedback section.

Other Standardized Tests

achievement test Test designed to measure past accomplishments, usually in academic subjects

Most standardized tests other than IQ tests measure either achievement or specific aptitudes. *Achievement tests* are designed to measure academic success. Your score on a standardized achievement test may be compared with the average scores of other students. Most achievement tests give a *grade-level score*. This means that your score was roughly the same as the average student with a certain number of years of schooling. A girl with a reading grade level of 10.0 reads at about the same level as most tenth-grade students who took the test.

aptitude test test of potential used to predict future achievements in a given area.

Aptitude tests are supposed to differ from achievement tests. Aptitude indicates potential, while achievement suggests specific accomplishments. However, in truth, most aptitude tests measure accomplishments. One of the best predictors of future performance is your present achievement. Have you ever taken the Scholastic Aptitude Test (SAT) or American College Testing (ACT) program? Both are aptitude tests used to predict academic success in higher education. However, both include tests of reading comprehension, general knowledge, and other skills associated with academic accomplishments.

FIGURE 5-9. Traditional IQ tests do not measure
practical skills.

Like intelligence tests, college aptitude tests are culturally biased. They also underpredict women's performances (Rosser, 1987). Women tend to have lower SAT scores but have higher college grades than men do. Since SAT scores are often used for scholarships and placement in honors programs, women lose out on many opportunities (Unger and Crawford, 1992). Yet, among the Asian-American population there are much smaller differences between men and women (Bronstein and Quina, 1991). Standardized aptitude tests do not predict college success well for Hispanics. Duran (1983) found better predictors in such factors as motivation level, social commitment, language proficiency, and parental interest in educational achievement.

Aptitude tests have a broader latitude than does measurement of academic potential. Psychologists have developed tests of psychomotor abilities, athletic potential, mechanical ability, musical and artistic talent, and creativity. In most cases these aptitude tests are based on skills and attributes possessed by accomplished people in the specific fields.

The development of the computer has clearly increased interest in problem solving and the process of thinking. Further, the computer has eased the development and scoring of tests, making evaluations less expensive and more available. Perhaps future abilities testing will be done by electronic devices!

"You're kidding! You count S.A.T.s?"

FIGURE 5-10. If so, heaven will have fewer women and minorities . . .

Checkpoint

Use the following questions to check your understanding of this final portion of the chapter. Choose and mark the one correct response to each question.

26. Mrs. T claims the test she is using is standardized. What can you assume?
    a. It is an achievement test.
    b. It is an intelligence test.
    c. It has never been used before.
    d. It was tried on a large population.

27. Which of the following factors is a problem in measuring intelligence?
    a. People will not take intelligence tests.
    b. Many factors influence intelligence.
    c. There is no classification system for intelligence.
    d. There are no tests that show strengths and weaknesses.

28. What is the advantage of individual intelligence tests over group tests?
    a. Psychologists can observe behavior.
    b. Individual tests are shorter.
    c. Individual tests are cheaper.
    d. All of the above.

29. Why are the Wechsler scales considered the most useful individual tests?
    a. They measure creative and artistic abilities.
    b. They show patterns of strengths and weaknesses.

    c. They do not require the presence of a psychologist.

    d. They can be connected to electronic devices.

30. What is one disadvantage of group tests?

    a. They are more expensive.

    b. They require many psychologists.

    c. They are difficult to score.

    d. They are less accurate.

31. What is one problem that often arises from the current classification system for IQ scores?

    a. Standardization

    b. Functional fixedness

    c. Mislabeling

    d. Predicate thinking

32. Why are current IQ tests being criticized?

    a. They are too narrow in focus.

    b. They are too broad in focus.

    c. They are used too often.

    d. They are not used enough.

33. Which of the following areas is not measured on traditional IQ tests?

    a. Verbal ability

    b. Insight

    c. Reasoning

    d. Perceptual skills

34. Millie, a first grader, has a reading grade-level score of 3.0. What does this mean?

    a. Millie has the reading ability of a 3-year-old.

    b. Millie is in the bottom 3 percent of her class.

    c. Millie reads at the level of most third graders.

    d. Millie is in the top 3 percent of her class.

35. Which area is supposed to be measured by SAT and ACT?

    a. Intelligence

    b. Achievement

    c. Insight

    d. Aptitude

Check your responses against the Checkpoint Answer Key at the end of the chapter. If you had difficulty with any question, reread the text. If you had little or no difficulty answering the questions or have resolved problems that you might have had, you are ready to check yourself against the chapter inventory that follows.

CHAPTER INVENTORY

Use this list of objectives as a review checklist. You should be able to do each of the tasks outlined in the objectives and apply them to everyday examples. If you can, you may feel confident that you have mastered the material in this chapter.

1. Define cognition and differentiate among three forms of thought.
2. Identify the areas of the brain involved in thinking.
3. Explain how scripts are used.
4. State the sequence of logical thought, and distinguish among logical, predicate, and magical thinking.
5. Describe critical thinking.
6. Isolate four steps involved in problem solving.
7. Explain how mental set and functional fixedness can impair problem solving.
8. Define artificial intelligence.
9. Describe creativity, and identify the characteristics of creative thinkers.
10. Identify ways to improve creativity.
11. Specify the limitations of teaching creativity.
12. Describe the purpose of intelligence tests.
13. Explain the limitations of group intelligence tests.
14. Discuss the problem of cultural bias in IQ tests.
15. Identify the narrow focus of traditional intelligence tests.
16. Explain the difference between aptitude and achievement.

Feedback

The correct answers to the exercises follow. If you did not answer an exercise correctly, review the preceding pages and return to the exercise to correctly complete it.

5-1. Your right hemisphere would contribute the musical tune, the rhythm, and any imagination or fantasy. Your left brain would provide the words. Communication between the two halves would cross through the corpus callosum.

5-2. You might have listed any three of the following:
   a. People bring gifts to birthday parties.
   b. A kite is a possible gift.
   c. Kites cost money.
   d. Money is kept in piggy banks.
   e. Money in piggy banks makes a sound.
   f. Piggy banks with no money make no sound.

5-3. a. Therefore, the college will be closed.
   b. X
   c. X
   d. Therefore, the telephone will ring (assuming that the premises are really true).

5-4. a. Try to see both sides. (Are there reasons why you should not chew it?)
   b. Look for inconsistencies in statements.
   c. Separate logical ideas from emotional arguments.
   d. Don't be afraid to question a weak-sounding argument.

5-5. See Figure 5-11.

5-6. Most psychologists would not consider his invention creative. Windows are not unusual, and he has not developed a new solution.

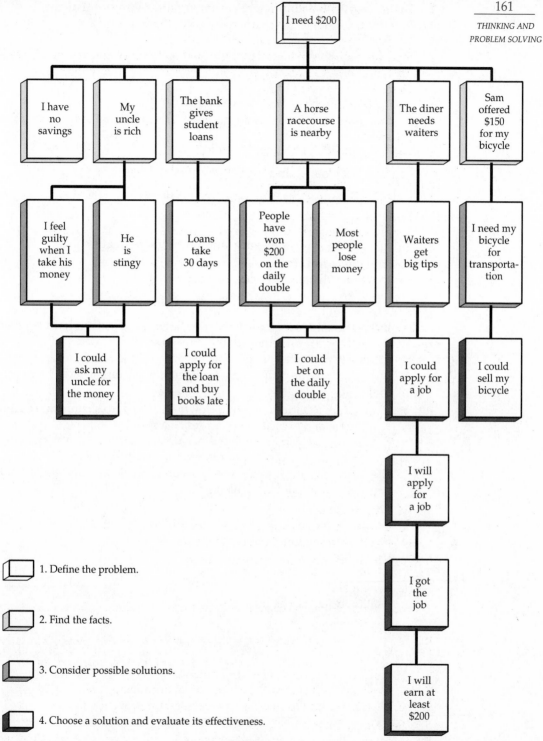

FIGURE 5-11.

5-7. _____√_____ Confident

_____√_____ Independent

_____√_____ Moody

_____√_____ Persistent

5-8. _____−_____ Avoid ideas that our computer can't handle.

_____+_____ Take your time and come up with plenty of ideas.

_____+_____ Feel free to be unconventional.

_____+_____ Talk out your ideas.

_____−_____ Eliminate ideas that might be expensive.

_____−_____ Stick with the toy company's image.

_____+_____ Think of unconventional ways to use our equipment.

5-9. a. 1. Ted was sick.
  2. He was distracted by his need for a tissue.
  3. The teacher who was administering the test was not aware of the problem.
  4. Ted became upset when he was accused of cheating. This compounded his difficulties.
  5. He did not have enough time to complete the test.
 b. Ted could take an individual intelligence test, administered by a psychologist.

5-10. a. 1. In Twara's culture, working slowly is valued, so she probably took her time and earned lower scores as a result.
  2. Her absence from school and her unfamiliarity with American requirements could cause her to score lower than her true ability.
 b. She would receive less stimulation than normal students would, and her mind would not be challenged.

5-11. a. Musical ability
 b. Bodily ability
 c. Self-understanding
 d. Understanding of others
 e. Ability to adapt to new situations
 f. Insight ability
 g. Ability to size things up

Checkpoint Answer Key

1. c; 2. a; 3. f; 4. b; 5. e; 6. d; 7. c; 8. c; 9. i; 10. a; 11. h; 12. e; 13. k; 14. d; 15. f; 16. b; 17. g; 18. c; 19. b; 20. a; 21. c; 22. d; 23. b; 24. d; 25. a; 26. d; 27. b; 28. a; 29. b; 30. d; 31. c; 32. a; 33. b; 34. c; 35. d.

Developing

Age only matters when one is aging. Now that I have
arrived at a great age, I might as well be 20.
—Pablo Picasso (at 80)

How far back can you remember? Can you recall events from the first year of your life? The second or third years? Chances are you have a few blurry memories of your early childhood. Yet, undoubtedly, many incidents from that period affected the type of person you are today. Such factors as far back as your mother's health during her pregnancy, the absence or presence of your father, and the type of discipline that your parents used had strong impacts on your development.

Your recall of school-age events is probably a bit sharper. Here, teachers and peers became major influences. Peers became even more significant during your adolescence. In this chapter you will not only consider these earlier stages of development, but you will also focus on the responsibilities of adult life and the changes and adjustments required in your continued development through middle and old age.

The process of development begins with conception. As incredible as it may seem, every human began with the uniting of two cells. How people grow, change, and face adjustments is the focus of developmental psychology. In this chapter you will begin by looking into the importance of a decision to become a parent and the responsibilities and knowledge required. Next you will look at each stage of development, from conception through old age, and consider the characteristics and problems encountered.

PARENTHOOD

Although it is best if parenthood is the result of a carefully considered decision, many individuals became parents accidentally. Numerous unwanted babies are born. A steadily increasing number of babies are born out of wedlock to teenage mothers. Although some are welcomed, most are not. Current estimates suggest that there are more than 1 million abortions in the United States each year. These abortions are the result of unwanted and unplanned pregnancies.

Since parenting requires considerable responsibility and commitment, psychologists feel that it is best to learn about child rearing prior to pregnancy. As the child develops, parents tend to become involved in current problems and adjustments, and they have less time to learn. Although there have been rumors claiming the existence of a maternal instinct that permits any woman to rear children perfectly, there has been no support for this claim. Women are no more talented than men are in rearing children. There is neither a maternal nor a paternal instinct. Both mothers and fathers need to learn about child development to be effective parents.

In addition to their having an understanding of the nature of human development, it is also useful for both parents to understand how children are likely to affect their marriage. It is important for parents to consider and agree upon a desirable family size, their roles as parents, and the type of discipline preferred. By sharing ideas and reaching agreement about child-rearing methods, parents are more likely to be consistent and relaxed in caring for children.

Effects of Children on a Marriage

Occasionally couples who are having difficulties with their marriage will decide to have a child, believing the baby will bring them closer together. This decision usually results in a broken marriage. It is indeed rare for a child to save a marriage that is floundering. The presence of a new baby usually has a strong emotional impact on both mother and father. There is very little time for transition in adjusting to a new baby. The infant is suddenly there, so husband and wife must abruptly shift to roles of father and mother. Both the transition and commitment are more immediate than in marriage.

There is an additional responsibility, since parents realize that they cannot divorce their children. Spitz (1965) noted that the presence of a child often exposes problems and jealousies that were previously unnoticed. A husband who was insecure about his relationship with his wife will often be jealous of the attention that she focuses on their offspring. Husbands and wives who are immature may find the responsibility of caring for a child burdensome. The child will then become the subject of arguments over duties and obligations.

Even in mature relationships, the presence of an infant may be expected to

"There—isn't this better than having a real baby?"

FIGURE 6-1. Adjusting to a real baby requires far more than manipulating the switches on a TV set.

cause some disruptions. But parents who are happy with each other and with the newborn infant are willing to make the required adjustments.

Family Size and Planning

Quite often family size does not result from choice. In the past decade there has been an apparent increase in infertility among married couples in the United States. If you were given a choice, would you prefer to be an only child, a member of a large family, or one of two siblings? Each of these family sizes has advantages and disadvantages. Although only children generally gain more materially and have more adult attention, many complain of loneliness and more pressure from their parents. Members of larger families are rarely lonely. Some complain of a lack of privacy, where others grumble about not having enough attention from their parents. There is often competition among brothers and sisters. This competition within the family has been labeled *sibling rivalry* by psychologists. Sibling rivalry is common even in families where there are only two or three children. Although lack of sibling rivalry may be considered an advantage of being an only child, the only child may feel competitive and have difficulty sharing when interacting with other children.

sibling rivalry Competition between brothers and sisters in a family

Exercise 6-1

Each of the following statements was made by a misinformed individual. Help set the person straight by supplying correct information.

a. "Why bother with child psychology? All women have a maternal instinct and know exactly how to raise children."

b. "My wife and I are not getting along. We argue constantly. We have decided to start a family so we can have a common interest."

---

c. "When and if I ever meet someone I want to marry, I plan to have at least ten children. Children in large families are always happier."

---

d. "I would never have more than one child. Only children have every advantage and no disadvantages."

You may compare your responses with the ones given in the Feedback section.

Parental Roles

Traditionally in the American family, child care, emotional support, and housework were part of the roles of mothers and wives. Fathers set rules and provided authority in the family. They were also the source of financial support and contact with the community. Although the traditional roles may still be encountered in some homes, more often the mother works outside the home and the father exhibits less authority and participates more in household duties and child care.

Many fathers-to-be begin adjusting to their new roles during their wife's pregnancy. Although the woman plays the primary role in carrying the child, the expectant father plays a significant role in providing emotional support. Women who share their feelings and concerns with their husbands during pregnancy can usually deepen their relationships. Women who turn their feelings inward and do not communicate their feelings often find that their husbands feel neglected. Usually men are just as eager as women are to become parents. Interestingly, several studies have reported that expectant fathers have even more anxiety than their wives do about the well-being of the baby (Lamb, 1979; Greenberg and Morris, 1974; Lynn, 1974). In studies of single parents, fathers demonstrate equal competence with mothers in child care (Lamb, 1987).

With the increasing number of divorces and remarriages, stepparenting is becoming more common. Even when a couple has an outstanding relationship, raising stepchildren will present problems. Usually the child has lived with a single (biological) parent, and adjustment to changes in the roles of the familiar parent creates tension. The article excerpt in Feature 6-1 suggests some positive steps that stepparents can take. (Chapter 12 covers male and female roles in marriages in greater detail.)

Child-Rearing Styles

Psychologist Diana Baumrind (1967, 1970) differentiates among three styles of child rearing. Think about your own childhood. How did your parents discipline you? Discipline is a way of regulating behavior. Did they use a set of rigid rules? If you were told what to do without any reasons or explanations,

Parenting in Stepfamilies

Discipline may be a problem because the biological parent and the stepparent have different feelings about the children and unequal authority in the household. Single parents have often disliked handling discipline and feel relieved that a stepparent will take that role. But at the beginning children have little concern about the approval of stepparents and are therefore unwilling to obey them. The biological parent, the only one with the authority to enforce rules, needs to take an active role at first; the stepparent is a "parent helper" as one stepmother decribed herself. . . .

But eventually a stepparent must earn the right to discipline the children by developing a satisfying relationship with them. All the best research suggests that stepparents repeat the pattern of first-marriage families—nurturance before discipline. The cooperation of the remarried parent is essential. An adult emerging from an emotionally close single-parent household may find it difficult to make room for the stepparent in the child's life. Sharing the child may seem like a loss. But in fact, a warm relationship between stepparent and stepchild moves the family toward satisfactory integration by shifting the balance of power toward more equality between the adults.

Children need time alone with each adult so that they can feel less cut off from the biological parent and get to know the stepparent. It is also important to establish enjoyable family rituals to provide shared memories.

Stepparents can often adopt a parental role quickly with very young children, who have relatively few loyalty conflicts unless the biological parents are angry at each other or there is hostility between the stepparent and the biological parent of the same sex. But it usually takes a number of years for older children to form an attachment to a stepparent. . . .

Remarried couples may have to devote special effort to changing their relations with the children, using outside assistance if necessary, as the following example indicates:

When Marcia and Tom remarried, Marcia had two children with whom she had lived for three years—9-year-old Ben and 7-year-old Dora. Marcia and Tom's father's and Marcia's first husband had all been the family disciplinarians, so Marcia asked Tom to discipline the children. He was glad to comply because he thought Marcia had been too lenient. But whenever he corrected the children, they ran to their mother and told her how mean he was. Then Marcia and Tom argued; Marcia defended her children and accused Tom of not loving them; Tom felt betrayed and alienated.

After one especially bad argument, Marcia arranged for the couple to see a family therapist. The therapist pointed out that Tom was trying to discipline Dora and Ben although he had not worked out a relationship with them and had little idea what to expect from children of their ages. The therapist pointed out that the pattern of the male disciplinarian could not be simply duplicated in a remarriage. He suggested that Marcia discipline the children with support from Tom, and that Tom develop his relationship with them by accompanying them in activities they enjoyed. The therapist also recommended that they take a parenting course together, and he advised them to find books on stepfamily life both for themselves and for the children.* As Marcia and Tom met the therapist several times in the next few months, their handling of the children slowly changed and the family atmosphere improved greatly.

*Such books are often difficult to obtain; many are available through Stepfamily Association of America, 215 Centennial Mall South, No. 212, Lincoln, NE 68508, 402/477-STEP.
Source: Visher, J. H., & Visher, E. B. (1992, January). Parenting in stepfamilies. *Harvard Mental Health Letter.*

your parents were using an *authoritarian* approach. In an authoritarian environment, a parent might tell a child to wear mittens. If the child asks "Why?" the parent would reply "Because I said so!" If the child does not comply, the mittens are forced on and the child is spanked for not adhering to the rule. The parents would use the same method to be certain the child ate balanced meals, went to bed on time, shared toys, and completed chores. The child would not

authoritarian discipline Regulating the behavior of others by rigid rules

permissive approach Method using little or no discipline

democratic approach Method using explanations and reasoning for rules

be given choices. In an authoritarian home, parents make the decisions and use external force and punishment to be sure that rules are kept.

Perhaps your home atmosphere was far looser and less structured. In a *permissive approach*, little or no discipline is used. If your parents chose this rearing style, you had few rules, limits, or boundaries. A child raised by permissive parents would be asked, "Would you like to wear mittens today?" and would be allowed to wear them or not wear them regardless of the weather. Similarly, the child would choose meals and bedtime and participate with other children and family activities as he or she desired. This style of child rearing is sometimes chosen by parents who were raised in an authoritarian atmosphere. They resent the approach used on them and select a permissive style in protest against their own parents' methods. Some parents are afraid to confront their children. Others believe that children must learn by their own mistakes. Such parents, as well as those who are too busy or are disinterested, will often choose a permissive approach.

Both the authoritarian and permissive styles of child rearing are extremes. Most American parents choose a middle ground. If you were raised in the United States, chances are you were reared in a more *democratic* environment. In a democratic home, children are given rules and restrictions, but the rules are usually accompanied by an explanation. A child might be cautioned to wear mittens because the weather is cold or to go to bed because everyone feels better after a good rest. If the child can give a good reason for not keeping a rule, parents will listen and perhaps grant an exception. The aim in a democratic approach to discipline is to have children learn to control their own behavior.

But not all cultures share this value of independent control in children. The Zinacantecos, a Mayan group in southern Mexico, value total obedience in children. American students who must learn from authoritarian teachers in Zinacantan have difficulty adjusting. One college student described her problems in learning to weave from a Zinacanteco teacher:

> "When I began taking back-strap loom weaving from Tonik, an older Zinacanteco woman, I became increasingly restless, when after two months of what I called observation and what she called learning, I had not touched the loom. Many times she would call my attention to an obscure technical point, or when she would finish a certain step she would say, "You have seen me do it. Now you have learned." I wanted to shout back, "No, I haven't! Because I have not tried it myself." However, it was she who decided when I was ready to touch the loom, and my initial clumsiness brought such comments as, "Cabeza de pollo!" (chicken head) "You have not watched me! You have not learned!" (Turok, 1972, pp. 1–2).

Authoritarian parenting is common in Asian-American and Hispanic homes. Since most American schools are based on democratic methods, students from these authoritarian settings have the same difficulties adjusting to a democratic environment that the American student (described above) faced adjusting to an authoritarian environment. The emphasis on independence and self-direction in American schools is the opposite of the family emphasis on obedience and conformity and may put these youngsters at a disadvantage (Steinberg et al., 1992). Changing cultural surroundings can change attitudes about methods of discipline. Greenfield (1992) noted that while parental strictness (authoritarian discipline) is seen as a sign of love within Korea, the same level of strictness is resented by Korean American and Korean Canadian teenagers.

Exercise 6-2

Indicate what type of discipline each of the following examples illustrates: authoritarian, permissive, or democratic.

a. Kim's usual bedtime is 8 P.M. She told her mother that she wanted to stay up later tonight to watch a special Halloween program on television. Her mother agreed to let her stay up a half-hour later, since Kim could sleep later the next morning.

---

b. Carlos is expected to study every evening from 7 P.M. until 9 P.M. He is not permitted to make or receive phone calls during study time. Last night he called a friend during study time to check on the pages required in his social studies assignment. His father prohibited Carlos' phone use for the remainder of the month and told him he would not listen to excuses.

---

c. Nelson wants to have a friend over for dinner tonight. His mother explains that she only has enough pork chops for members of the family. She suggests that Nelson invite his friend the next night when his father will be preparing a large batch of spaghetti.

---

d. Julie throws toys all around her house. Her parents often trip and have difficulty walking from room to room. They believe that Julie will decide if the toys need to be picked up.

You may check your responses with those in the Feedback section.

PRENATAL CONCERNS

The first stage of development begins with conception. The greatest percentage of a person's growth occurs between conception and birth. The importance of prenatal care cannot be overemphasized. The health of the mother during pregnancy will have a marked influence on the life of the child she is carrying. Since illnesses such as rubella (German measles), syphilis, tuberculosis, and certain types of influenza can adversely affect the fetus, prompt medical treatment is important. A mother who has the virus for acquired immune deficiency syndrome (AIDS) can infect her fetus. Infants infected with AIDS have had head and facial abnormalities at birth (Marion, Wiznia, Hutcheon, and Rubinstein, 1986).

Drillien and Ellis (1964) pointed to evidence that women with adequate diets were more likely to have healthy babies and uncomplicated births than were malnourished women. The National Center for Health Statistics (1986) recommends a weight gain of about 26 to 35 pounds during pregnancy. Women who gain less weight are more likely to miscarry, have a stillborn baby, or have a baby weighing under 5 pounds. Women who gain more than 35 pounds put their fetus at risk.

A pregnant woman's use of drugs, alcohol, tobacco, and caffeine can have noticeable effects on her unborn child. Perhaps the most severe problems occur from addictive drugs. Each year more than 40,000 children are born with brain damage related to their mothers' alcohol use. The most common problem is known as *fetal alcohol syndrome (FAS)*, a disorder characterized by physical, mental, and behavioral abnormalities in babies whose mothers consumed large amounts of alcohol during their pregnancies. The article in Feature 6-2 describes the lifetime problems faced by victims of FAS.

fetal alcohol syndrome (FAS) Disorder characterized by physical, mental, and behavioral abnormalities in babies whose mothers drank large amounts of alcohol during pregnancy.

Although we know that FAS is the leading cause of mental retardation in the United States, pregnant women continue to drink and use other drugs. Almost 300,000 babies are born at below normal weights, usually because they were prenatally exposed to alcohol, nicotine, or illegal drugs (Newman and Buka, 1991). The article in Feature 6-3 points out that the United States does not have adequate treatment programs for addicted women.

Engstrom et al. (1964) confirmed that women who are tense and unhappy

---

FEATURE 6-2 PSYCHOLOGY IN THE NEWS

Alcohol's Fetal Harm Lasts a Lifetime

Pregnant women who abuse alcohol may hand down a lifetime legacy of disabling mental and behavioral problems to their offspring, according to the first systematic study of the long-term consequences of fetal alcohol syndrome (FAS).

Adolescents and adults assigned a diagnosis of FAS during childhood often appear alert and verbal, but they cannot live independently, hold down jobs, or succeed in school because of poor concentration, social withdrawal, impulsiveness, failure to consider the consequences of their actions, and related problems, report psychologist Ann P. Streissguth of the University of Washington in Seattle and her colleagues. Mental retardation also persists among a majority of those with FAS, they point out. However, the debilitating behavioral problems plague those with normal and low IQs alike.

FAS, a mix of physical, mental, and behavioral abnormalities afflicting many babies born to mothers who drink heavily during pregnancy, represents the leading cause of mental retardation in the United States.

"[FAS] is not just a childhood disorder," Streissguth's team writes . . . "There is a predictable long term progression of the disorder into adulthood." . . .

The long-term problems associated with FAS make these individuals unsuitable for current job-training programs, the researchers argue. Prenatal brain damage may permanently disrupt the ability to concentrate, think abstractly, and function independently, even among those with normal intelligence, the scientists add. Nevertheless, they call for the development of remedial programs for adult FAS victims.

Source: Bower, B. (1991, April 20). Alcohol's fetal harm lasts a lifetime. *Science News.*

about their pregnancies have more problems in the prenatal stages and more difficult deliveries at birth. The investigators also found that children of anxious pregnant women are generally less well adjusted throughout their development. Pregnant women who are experiencing stress should seek help and support.

Sometimes expectant parents are concerned about the possibility of their child inheriting an illness present in either or both of their families. Genetic counselors can usually provide mathematical odds but cannot be certain. A technique called *amniocentesis* is generally a better predictor. A physician takes a sample of the fluid the fetus is floating in. There is a very slight risk of hurting the fetus, but the procedure permits the detection of Down syndrome, Turner syndrome, sickle-cell anemia, Rh disease, and other possible birth defects.

amniocentesis Procedure involving the removal of fluid samples from the uterus of an expectant mother to detect possible disease or genetic defects

THE BIRTH PROCESS: APPROACHES AND ORIENTATIONS

In recent years there has been an increasing concern about the conditions that surround the birth of an infant. Many American mothers receive an anesthetic

---

FEATURE 6-3 PSYCHOLOGY IN THE NEWS

Better Research, More Help Needed for Pregnant Addicts

Thanks to a recent public education effort, policy-makers and the public are increasingly aware of how a pregnant woman's substance abuse can harm her fetus and cause problems throughout childhood. But they're less attuned to the pain the woman herself experiences as a result of her addiction.

Norma Finklestein, Ph.D., and Hortensio Amaro, Ph.D., spoke on the need for more services and more unbiased research on these women respectively . . .

At present, treatment programs are primarily designed for and made available to men, according to the psychologists. In addition, pregnant addicts face social and psychological barriers to using the limited resources. And more data are needed to design gender-sensitive treatment plans for addicted women—now, addicted men capture most of the research attention, the psychologists noted . . .

Despite the large number of pregnant women and mothers addicted to drugs and alcohol—a 1991 NIDA survey reported that 7.7 percent of all

American women used an illicit drug in the past month of the survey—policymakers, treatment providers, and the public have traditionally downplayed the needs of women addicted to drugs and alcohol, Dr. Finklestein said in her presentation . . .

As in the past, people today view women addicts "as 'fallen' women, as sexually promiscuous, weak-willed and negligent of their children," she said. And if a woman is pregnant, "there is even greater contempt for her, since she is blamed for harming her fetus." . . .

Pregnant addicted women and mothers also face psychological barriers to treatment, Dr. Finklestein added. These include not wanting to put their children in foster care while they're in treatment, fear of losing custody of their children; and their societally induced belief "that they are terrible people and 'bad mothers,' " she said . . .

Source: De Angelis, T. (1992, November). Better research, more help needed for pregnant addicts. *APA Monitor.*

just prior to the birth of the baby. Some receive a general anesthetic, so they are completely unconscious at the time of birth. Others receive regional anesthetics, so they are awake but are not aware of pain. In both situations the drugs they receive are passed into the infant's bloodstream. Haire (1972) found that babies of mothers who had received anesthetics had a greater chance of birth injury and respiratory problems. Brazelton (1970) noted that the drugs affected the motor activities and muscular responses of the baby during its first week of life. Their findings have been substantiated by many other studies during the past decade. As a result, there has been a recent increase in the number of drugless childbirths.

Lamaze method
Preparation for active and conscious participation in the birth process

The most popular form of drugless childbirth is the *Lamaze method*. This method is often referred to as "prepared childbirth," since the expectant mother must begin preparing for the birth several months before the baby is due. She learns to use breathing and muscular reactions in response to uterine contractions. She feels less pain because she is distracted by her need to control her breathing and muscles. (Chapter 2 described the relationship between distraction and pain.) The baby benefits, since the mother does not usually need drugs. As an added benefit, the mother is awake and alert and can enjoy the birth experience. Often, the father assists and plays a supporting role.

Leboyer method
Childbirth method that attempts to minimize shock to the newborn infant

A more controversial approach to childbirth has been suggested by Leboyer (1975). Leboyer advised that delivery rooms should be dimly lit and the baby handled gently, in an attempt to minimize the shock of birth. In the *Leboyer method*, the baby is not slapped. Rather the infant is placed in a warm bath and then laid on the mother's belly. Among the criticisms hurled against this technique are concerns about exposing the baby to germs from the water and the mother's body, and worries that the physician may not see problems because of the poor lighting.

A recent study suggests that women in labor benefit greatly from one-to-one personal support by a woman who has experienced a normal labor. The women who provided the support were called "doulas" (a Greek word for an experienced mother who helps new mothers). The researchers trained the doulas in hospital procedures for three weeks. Each woman in labor was assigned a doula who stayed by her side, encouraged her, explained the process of labor, and soothed her as necessary. Women who were assisted by doulas had shorter labors, required less anesthetics and labor-inducing drugs, and had fewer Cesarean and forceps deliveries (Bower, 1991).

Exercise 6-3

Anita, who is one month pregnant, has several bad habits. She has three cups of coffee with breakfast and is a constant gum chewer. She swears, smokes at least twenty cigarettes each day, and sips cola beverages all afternoon. At about 5 P.M. Anita switches to wine. She usually has two or three drinks and then eats an enormous dinner. She is excited about becoming a mother and wants to do the right things for her baby. Her friends have told her that it is best to have a general anesthetic at delivery. She believes that she will be more relaxed if she does not feel the pain.

Anita is now asking for your advice. Which of her bad habits should be eliminated? Do you agree with her friends about the use of a general anesthetic?

You may compare your advice with that given in the Feedback section.

PATTERNS OF DEVELOPMENT

Development is a continuous process that begins at conception. Once infants are born, they begin to experience complex changes physically, intellectually, and emotionally. The changes are gradual and occur throughout the lifespan. As a convenience, psychologists have separated the lifespan into stages and identified specific changes that may be expected during each period. When you are considering changes and adjustments at each stage, remember that the transition from each stage to the next is gradual rather than sudden. A child does not awaken on a third birthday with an abrupt change from babyhood to early childhood. Similarly the age groups assigned to each are general. There are vast individual differences. One person may progress to young adulthood at sixteen, while another will still be battling adolescent problems at twenty-four.

Age	Stage
Birth–3 years	Babyhood
3–6 years	Early childhood
6–12	Later childhood
12–18	Adolescence
18–40	Young adulthood
40–65	Mature adulthood
Over 65	Aging adult

Checkpoint

Use the following questions to check your understanding of this portion of the chapter. Indicate whether each statement is true or false.

1. _____ Women have a natural ability to rear children because of their maternal instinct.

2. _____ The birth of a child will usually strengthen a weak marriage.

3. _____ Only children often feel lonely.

4. _____ Competition among brothers and sisters is called "sibling rivalry."

5. _____ Childbearing is a woman's task; the expectant father has no role.

6. _____ Authoritarian parents do not give their children choices.

7. _____ In a permissive home, children are restricted but are given explanations.

8. _____ All cultures use democratic methods of discipline.

9. _____ The greatest percentage of growth occurs during the prenatal period.

10. _____ The alcoholic drinking of a pregnant woman rarely affects her unborn child.

11. _____ Anxious women tend to have problems delivering their babies.

12. _____ Amniocentesis is a technique for detecting some genetic abnormalities in an unborn infant.

13. _____ Mothers who receive anesthetics during childbirth tend to have healthier babies.

14. _____ The Lamaze method of childbirth is natural and does not require any preparation.

15. _____ Each stage of development is distinct, with sudden changes occurring between stages.

Use the Checkpoint Answer Key to verify your responses. If you had any difficulty with a question, carefully reread the text. If you had little or no difficulty answering the questions or have resolved any problems that you might have had, you are ready to continue with the next portion of this chapter.

BABYHOOD

The firstborn baby is often a shock to new parents. The newborn rarely resembles babies seen in advertisements. Since advertisements are aware of the shortcomings of a newborn's appearance, they use babies between six and twelve months old. Infants are called *neonates* during their first two weeks of life. They usually have wrinkled, blotchy red skin and large heads that may be misshapen. Their necks are impossible to find beneath folds of skin. Nonetheless parents are usually so overjoyed with their offspring that they see beauty in the appearance.

neonate Newborn infant, usually less than two weeks old

Most neonates sleep two-thirds of the time, about sixteen hours each day. They follow a pattern of awakening when hungry and crying until fed. After feedings they remain alert and active a few minutes, then sleep for two or three hours until hunger strikes again. Some neonates experience difficulty sleeping and spend more time crying. Birns et al. (1966) found crying neonates can be soothed by rocking them gently, humming in low tones, or speaking in a soothing manner. Some neonates are easier to comfort than others are. There is also considerable variation in which method is most effective. There are vast individual differences in neonate irritability. Unfortunately many parents fear they might spoil their new baby if they show it attention. In reality, it is impossible to spoil neonates. They are totally reliant on others for survival. Affection and handling comfort them and help to relieve irritability. Unhappy neonates who are not shown attention tend to become more agitated and restless. Fathers can play an important role in relieving their infant's discomforts, since neonates usually respond to the lower frequencies of male voices.

What can neonates do? There is evidence that neonates can recognize the voices of their mothers and that they start learning at or before birth. The average neonate can see best at distances of about 8 inches, although others see best at spans from 7 to 15 inches. According to Pick and Pick (1970), other distances appear blurred.

Exercise 6-4

Assume you are baby-sitting for a ten-day-old baby girl. The mother fed her and has left. The baby was awake and moving her hands and feet for five minutes. She then began crying. Her crying is growing louder. List three things you could do to soothe the baby.

a. _____

b. _____

c. _____

Turn to the Feedback section to check your list.

As the infant progresses from the neonate period through the babyhood stage, its need for affection remains powerful. A baby who feels accepted and loved by parents will feel worthy and lovable and will develop a positive self-concept. By consistently satisfying their baby's needs, parents can help their infant develop a sense of trust. By the end of their first year, most babies can differentiate between strangers and familiar persons. Babies who have developed a sense of trust will feel secure with people they know, but they may be skeptical of strangers.

One area of concern for many parents is how and when to feed the baby. Common questions are, "Is it better to bottle-feed or breast-feed our baby?" and "Should we use a feeding schedule or feed the baby on demand?" In response to the first question, there are some advantages to breast-feeding infants. The infant is provided with natural immunities passed through the mother's milk. The mother is not burdened with expense and the task of keeping formula available. However, the mother's freedom is somewhat restricted, and if she is feeling depressed, burdened, or tied down by the baby, breast-feeding may tire her and increase her despondency. According to Mussen et al. (1978) the attitude and affection of the parent at feeding time are more important than whether the bottle or breast is used. If the parent is affectionate, talking to and touching the baby, the style of feeding will not matter.

The answer to the second question, whether to adhere to a feeding schedule, will depend on the lifestyle of the parents. Studies have shown that babies who are fed on demand are at least as healthy as those fed on strict schedules. Though feedings should be relaxed and happy times for the infant, the parents' comfort and the convenience of the schedule are also a prime concern. Parents who awaken at precisely 7 A.M., have breakfast at 7:30 A.M., lunch at noon, and dinner at exactly 7 P.M. will probably be more at ease if their baby is on a schedule. In contrast, parents who awaken sometime between 6 and 10 A.M., sometimes skip breakfast and opt for a late brunch, nibble during the afternoon, and have dinner when they feel hungry will probably be more comfortable with a demand schedule. If the feedings are accompanied by warmth and affection, the baby will eventually adjust to either method.

"Sorry, Mrs. Martin . . . we let you, then everybody
would want to do it."

FIGURE 6-2. Thanks to the store manager, the children will
be able to explore their environment!

In addition to affection, the baby also needs stimulation. Even during the first months of life, babies prefer new and novel things (Fantz, 1958). Infants enjoy mobiles and having their cribs moved to vary their view. Babies are usually fascinated when they enter a new room and surroundings. They need to explore and manipulate objects. Touching, smelling, and listening are important. Once babies begin to crawl, their curiosity becomes heightened. Although playpens are safe places, babies also need to be able to investigate their environment. Children need to see new areas. Walks through the neighborhood and visits to stores and other people's homes will keep them stimulated.

During their first two years, babies play alone. They explore their surroundings, hande toys, and engage in make-believe. They often talk to themselves while playing. Language begins with babbling and cooing. Although most one-year-olds can understand simple conversation, they usually can only speak a few words. Between one and two years, most babies learn to utter some word combinations. Words are usually mispronounced; for example, a blanket might be called a "blah-blah." You are probably familiar with this type of baby talk. Should baby talk be corrected? Most psychologists would suggest that it not be corrected, since it might frustrate the child. However, parents should not repeat the baby-talk mispronunciation. Rather, they should enunciate the word correctly. Otherwise the child could be subject to future ridicule by other children.

Two-year-olds usually have some problems communicating. Because they lack vocabulary, they will try to make themselves understood by repeating their statements in louder voices. A child may ask, "Cookie?" If the father answers "No," the child will say in a louder voice "Cookie!" as if the father did not hear or understand the first request. It usually helps if the parent informs the child that the request or message has been understood. If the father responds "I know you want a cookie right now, but I would rather you ate your lunch first. Finish your lunch and then have a cookie. If you want your cookie, eat some lunch." Two-year-olds need to be addressed in explicit terms. Often they are confused and frightened by idioms and expressions that they interpret literally. Figure 6-3 illustrates some common misunderstandings.

Dreams create another area of confusion. Many two-year-olds believe that dreams come in through the window or the closet. Young children often fear

Tommy grew up overnight.

He plays the piano by ear.

It's raining cats and dogs.

He's the spitting image of his father.

I'm all thumbs.

I was tied up at work.

CANEVARI

FIGURE 6-3. Interpretations.

the darkness of their rooms and have difficulty verbalizing and talking about these worries. Simple rituals such as pulling shades, closing closet doors, and using a night light can help allay these fears.

In the American culture, the most important accomplishment of babyhood is the development of independence. Progressing from newborns who are totally dependent on parents, babies gradually learn to understand, speak, walk, feed themselves, become toilet-trained, and partially dress themselves by the time they are three. They should be encouraged to try things on their own. As babies become more accomplished, they also try to assert their independence. You have probably heard the expression, "the terrible two's." Two-year-olds are pleased with their skills and want to be recognized as individuals. "No" becomes a popular word in these youngsters' vocabularies. They have their own ideas and are unwilling to accept adult rules as readily as they did the previous year.

Exercise 6-5

In each of the following instances, a couple is expressing disagreement about their baby. Assume you have been asked to help them resolve their differences. For each of the following conflicts, indicate the person with whom you agree.

a. GEORGE: There is something wrong with Chester; he doesn't like strangers. Whenever a strange person picks him up, he cries.

   HELEN: Chester is normal. Now that he is almost one year old, he knows the difference between friends and strangers. He trusts people he knows, so he is perfectly normal.

   George _____ or Helen _____

b. MARSHA: We shouldn't put Lalla in a crib by herself to drink her bottle. We should talk to her and let her know we care while she is being fed.

   OTTO: Nonsense! We shouldn't distract her while she is drinking. She needs to be more independent now that she is six months old.

   Marsha _____ or Otto _____

c. JUANITA: Now that we have a baby, we'll have to be far more organized. Babies have to eat every four hours. I'm going to be a nervous wreck trying to stick to a schedule, but I guess it's best for little Elliot.

   HENRI: I think little Elliot will get along just fine without a set schedule. Why don't we just feed him when he acts hungry? We always eat when we're hungry.

   Juanita _____ or Henri _____

d. PATRICK: Let's keep our little baby Bridget in her crib most of the time. If she stays in the same spot, she'll be more secure. If we move her around, she will become confused.

   KATHLEEN: I think we should let Bridget see different things. She needs more stimulation than just the view from her crib.

   Patrick _____ or Kathleen _____

e. SIDNEY: Little Alicia always calls cookies "kakaks." I think we should call a cookie "cookie" so she learns the right word.
   DIANE: Oh, Alicia is so cute with her baby talk. Let's not spoil it by letting her hear the right word.

   Sidney _____ or Diane _____

f. NELLIE: I think that something is wrong with Larry. All of a sudden he is afraid to go to bed at night. He cries and claims he is scared. I'll bet it's just a big act to get attention. We probably should punish him for crying.
   BOB: Larry is only two and maybe is afraid at night. Lots of two-year-olds have fears. Don't punish him. Maybe we can figure out what's bothering him.

   Nellie _____ or Bob _____

Turn to the Feedback section to check your choices.

EARLY CHILDHOOD

Early childhood has traditionally been referred to as the "preschool" period. However, today an increasing number of children between the ages of three and six are attending some sort of nursery school or day-care program. Most programs at these schools and facilities focus more on structured playing than on academic learning. Whether day care helps or hinders development in early childhood is not clear. While day-care children show some initial gains in intellectual development, home-care children catch up quickly when they enter preschool or a kindergarten (Clarke-Stewart, 1989). Studies of social development of day-care children have shown mixed results (Haskins, 1985; Phillips et al., 1987). Day-care facilities and preschool programs vary widely in quality. Some offer stimulating activities with warm and enthusiastic caregivers, while others are overcrowded and boring, with an inadequate supply of caregivers. It is difficult to reach any conclusion about whether children should or should not attend day-care or preschool programs. While the American culture stresses the importance of a strong mother-child relationship, Polynesian families do not see this relationship as essential. According to Lonner (1988), as many as one-half of Samoan children are passed to several different foster families during their childhood and show no adverse effects. The quality of care is probably the most important factor.

Playing is an important occupation in early childhood. Through play activities the young child can often let out aggressive feelings and other emotions. A child who is frustrated by the demands of older brothers and sisters or playmates can release feelings by throwing a doll or stuffed animal against the wall or punishing it in some way. Positive emotions can also be expressed. Hugging and showing affection to dolls and stuffed animals are common in young children.

But play provides far more than emotional expression. The preschool child learns primarily through play activities (Piaget, 1952). Until age two or three most children play alone or parallel to other children. Even if several two-year-olds are sitting on the floor together, each is usually playing independently. Each watches and copies the other children. By the time a child is three, social play usually begins. Children play socially with each other and must learn to understand and talk to each other. In the process of learning to share and take turns, they may quarrel, which should be expected. Social play is considered the most important activity of preschool children. If other children are not available for interaction, the preschool child's development will suffer. Children who live in isolated areas or do not have playmates should be taken to places where they can meet other children and learn to play happily and successfully.

Play activities also help young children develop motor coordination. Running and skipping games, block building, and seesaw and slide activities all help to develop gross motor coordination. Coloring, cutting, pasting, and doing simple jigsaw puzzles aid in the development of fine motor skills. These activities are generally included in nursery-school programs. If a child is not exposed to an organized preschool program, he or she should be given opportunities to learn and benefit from such play activities.

Many children who do not have playmates spend considerable time watching television. Unfortunately these children are not learning important social skills and developing crucial motor skills. If children learn about people from watching television, they are likely to develop inaccurate and unfavorable views of people from minority groups. Although television has supported more roles for African Americans, they are still underrepresented and the percentage of roles for other minorities has not improved. Unfortunately most non-Black minorities are portrayed as either victims of violence or criminals (Liebert and Sprafkin, 1988). Most television programs stereotype people with disabilities as either suffering martyrs or superheroes who have overcome handicaps. Realistic portrayals are rare.

Not only should parents monitor the types of programs being watched, but they should also take heed of the advertisements. The advertisements that seem to influence children most recommend low-nutrition foods. Young children's eating habits are a source of frustration for most parents. Because the growth rate slows down during early childhood, there is less interest in food. As a result, early childhood is a period of picky eating. As suggested in the humorous clipping in Feature 6-4, mealtime is often a continuation of play activities. Since children's appetites are diminished, parents have the difficult task of being certain that nutritious foods are eaten.

How can parents enforce rules about eating? Further, what is the best way to discipline a preschool child? According to Kohlberg (1969, 1976), most young children base their morality and sense of right and wrong on rewards and punishments. Actions that are punished are presumed to be bad. Rewarded actions are considered good. Young children base their values on the attitudes of their parents and other people they care for. Ginott (1969) warned parents to criticize and scold children's actions rather than personalities. For example, a young boy who clutters his toys on the kitchen floor should not be personally accused of being "sloppy" or "stupid." Instead, the punishment should be focused on the disarray of the toys. An appropriate scolding might be, "When you throw your toys all over the kitchen floor, I get annoyed. The room looks sloppy and someone could get hurt." Ginott feels strongly that positive alternatives should be offered. A parent might add, "The room will look tidy if you put your toys in the bin. Then it will be safe for us." By following Ginott's advice, parents can help their children develop a better understanding of values, as well as a positive self-image.

Exercise 6-6

Assume that you must develop a set of guidelines for a new day-care center for children ages three to six. For each heading make some suggestions for the program. The first has been done for you.

a. Social play: Allow time for the children to interact with each other. Play group games and have activities that require sharing and taking turns.

b. Gross motor activities: _____

_____

_____

c. Fine motor skills: _____

_____

_____

d. Television: _____

_____

_____

FEATURE 6-4 PSYCHOLOGY IN THE NEWS

How to Eat Like a Child—and Other Lessons in Not Being a Grown-Up

Peas: Mash and flatten into thin sheet on plate. Press the back of the fork into the peas. Hold fork vertically, prongs up, and lick off peas.

Mashed potatoes: Pat mashed potatoes flat on top. Dig several little depressions. Think of them as ponds or pools. Fill the pools with gravy. With your fork, sculpt rivers between pools and watch the gravy flow between them. Decorate with peas. Do not eat.

Alternative method: Make a large hole in center of mashed potatoes. Pour in ketchup. Stir until potatoes turn pink. Eat as you would peas.

Spinach: Divide into little piles. Rearrange into new piles. After five or six maneuvers, sit back and say you are full.

French fries: Wave one french fry in air for emphasis while you talk. Pretend to conduct orchestra. Then place four fries in your mouth at once and chew. Turn to your sister, open your mouth, and stick out your tongue coated with potatoes. Close mouth and swallow. Smile.

Source: Ephron, D. (1979, June). How to eat like a child. *Saturday Evening Post.*

e. Meals: _____

_____

_____

f. Discipline: _____

_____

_____

You may check your answers in the Feedback section.

LATER CHILDHOOD

Later childhood, the period from age six to the onset of puberty, brings many changes. Although physical growth is initially slow, there is vast intellectual, moral, and social expansion. But school-age children still need time to play to improve their health and motor coordination. The absence of exercise can make children more prone to heart disease in later years. Ismail and Gruber (1967) found that physical exercise in school-age children also improves academic achievement.

According to Piaget (1952), around age seven most children make several major advances in intellectual development. Memory improves and becomes more organized. Children are suddenly capable of solving more difficult problems and become more aware of their achievement. They distinguish between make-believe and reality and lose their belief in Santa Claus. They compare themselves with their friends and make judgments about school performance, as well as athletic and social skills.

During the elementary school years, children become more aware of their own sex. They tend to select playmates of the same sex and the same racial and ethnic backgrounds and play together in groups. This is often referred to as the "gang age." By puberty, most narrow their friendships to one or two close companions.

Moral development proceeds as the children accept the standards and rules of their friends and teachers. Many of the popular elementary-school games involve rules. At this stage children have a better understanding of the meanings of rules and ideas of morality are based on whether accepted rules are kept or broken (Kohlberg, 1976). This is indeed an improvement over early childhood when morality was strictly based on rewards and punishments.

Checkpoint

Use the following questions to check your understanding of this portion of the chapter. Choose and mark the one correct response to each question.

16. What is a neonate?
    a. A premature baby
    b. A newborn baby
    c. An irritable baby
    d. An unloved baby

FIGURE 6-4. Remember the "Simon Says" rules?

17. What have psychologists found to be the best technique for feeding babies?
    a. Breast feeding
    b. Bottle feeding
    c. Some breast feeding and some bottle feeding
    d. Either breast or bottle feeding, accompanied by affection

18. According to psychologists what type of feeding schedule should parents follow for their babies?
    a. A fixed four-hour schedule
    b. A fixed three-hour schedule
    c. A demand schedule
    d. A schedule they feel comfortable with

19. In addition to affection, what else do babies need?
    a. Rules
    b. Standards
    c. Stimulation
    d. Interaction with other babies

20. How should parents handle a little girl who uses baby talk?
    a. Permit her to use baby talk and use the same pronunciation so she will feel she is correct.
    b. Permit her to use baby talk but use the correct pronunciation so she can hear the right sounds.
    c. Criticize her and make her say the word correctly.
    d. Punish her for baby talk and listen only when she speaks correctly.

21. What is the most important activity of a preschool child?
    a. Social play
    b. Reading
    c. Watching television
    d. Keeping rules

22. Don is an eight-year-old boy. What types of friends would you expect him to associate with?
    a. A group of eight-year-old boys
    b. A group of eight-year-old girls
    c. One or two eight-year-old boys
    d. One or two eight-year-old boys and one or two eight-year-old girls

23. During which stage do most children learn to accept rules and standards of morality?
    a. The neonate stage
    b. Babyhood
    c. Early childhood
    d. Later childhood

Use the Checkpoint Answer Key to verify your responses. If you had any difficulty with a question, carefully reread the text. If you had little or no difficulty answering the questions or have resolved any problems that you might have had, you are ready to continue with the final portion of this chapter.

ADOLESCENCE

Clearly, massive changes occur between conception and age twelve. From a microscopic organism, a grown child finally emerges. Then, through physical, social, and mental changes, the child must develop into an adult. The period of shifting from a child to an adult is termed *adolescence.*

Levinson (1986) views the onset of adolescence as the continuation of the preadulthood stage (stage 0). It is a time when young people gain independence as they separate from their parents, both physically and emotionally. By the end of adolescence, there is a sense of independence and an urge to get away from the family (Levinson's stage 1).

Physical Changes

Toward the end of later childhood, sexual change, or puberty, begins. Secondary sexual characteristics develop: enlarged hips and breast development in girls, and muscular development and voice changes in boys. Both sexes begin to grow pubic hair. Puberty is completed when primary sexual functioning occurs. Girls menstruate and boys develop a larger penis with potential for ejaculation. The ages for pubertal changes vary widely. Generally girls undergo puberty about two years before boys.

Social Changes

Adolescence is often viewed as a stormy period, a time of critical changes that have lasting effects. Recently psychologists have advised that adolescence may not be as turbulent as had been forecast in the past. When you recall your own teenage years, you probably remember some of your worries and fears. If you were like most adolescents, you had a clique, or a group of friends that you preferred. The clique might have been a formal group such as a club, sorority, or fraternity. But more likely, it was an informal group. Within the clique you probably had one or two best friends. Undoubtedly you worried about what your friends thought of you.

Most adolescents have deep concerns about what their peers think. They are conformists within their cliques. They dress alike and use the same language expressions. Adolescents of the 1950s used terms like "neat" and "spiffy"; the 1960s brought "cool" and "groovy"; while the 1970s introduced "funky" and "funkadelic"; and youths in the 1980s, "bad." Most adolescents prefer peers who are similar to themselves. The majority choose friends of the same race, economic group, and opinions. They constantly pressure each other to conform to the standards of the clique. There is a great deal of ethnic segregation among adolescents. Steinberg et al. (1992) reported that students from one ethnic group rarely know students from other ethnic groups. Often teenagers develop social fears. Shyness is common, and such tasks as speaking before a class are often dreaded.

Although most adolescents prefer to be with their friends, they also need time for themselves. Adolescence is sometimes referred to as a time of identity crises, or a period when each individual must assert independence. Most fluctuate between dependence on parents and attempts to assert independence. Rebellion against parents is common in adolescence. It usually takes the form of questioning, arguments, and unwillingness to adhere to family rules. Although teenagers want to assert their freedom, they still depend upon the natural affection of their parents. Parent abuse can result from adolescent rebellion that is not handled properly.

Adolescent suicides have created a growing concern. The national suicide rate for adolescents has increased by 200 percent since 1950. Wealthy areas have experienced an even greater increase in adolescent suicides.

Drugs are another problem. If their parents use alcohol or other drugs, adolescents are more likely to follow. But generally peers are even more influ-

"We're just pleased he can still get into the Christmas spirit."
FIGURE 6-5. One adolescent's independent approach to the holiday spirit . . .

ential than parents. Although there is evidence of a general slowdown in illegal drug use nationwide, urban and affluent areas are still battling the problem.

Intellectual Development

The conversion from childhood to adulthood during the adolescent period requires expansion of mental activity as well. Fortunately, comprehension of abstract concepts increases, as does the ability to handle them. The adolescent begins to understand individual human rights and dignity. With this understanding, a sense of justice and conscience develops. According to Rogers (1972), the adolescent also has a better ability to plan for the future. The average 15- or 16-year-old can think about what is likely to occur in ten or twenty years and plan for the changes.

Exercise 6-7

Listed below are examples of changes that occur during adolescence. Indicate whether each change is physical, social, or mental.

a. _____ Fourteen-year-old Tony is an excellent pianist. He used to love to show off before groups. Lately he cringes and blushes when his parents ask him to play a tune for their friends.

b. _____ Fifteen-year-old Shakti stormed out of the house when her parents asked her to remove the dishes from the dishwasher. She shouted, "Everyone tells me what to do. I never have time to myself."

c. _____ Peter seems more understanding now that he is sixteen. He had been annoyed that his father never attended religious services with the family. Yesterday he told his father that people must act according to their own conscience.

d. _____ Poor thirteen-year-old Ned! The instructor asked him to withdraw from choir. He had been a boy soprano, but now he can never be certain of the note he will sing.

e. _____ Now that Gaya is thirteen, she refuses to wear many of her clothes. She will only wear jeans with a certain label and shirts with an insignia. She claims, "That's what all my friends wear, and I don't want to look strange!"

You may check your answers in the Feedback section.

STAGES IN ADULT DEVELOPMENT

The study of adult development is recent. Levinson (1986) maintains that all adults go through the same basic sequence of stages. After interviewing adults in a research project, he concluded that throughout our adult lives, we are creating a *life structure,* or pattern. Sometimes we build on the structure and sometimes we change the structure, but we generally go through the same developmental periods:

life structure Basic pattern of a person's life

Stage	Description	Ages
0	Preadulthood	Conception to age 22
1	Early adult transition	17–22
2	Entry life structure for early adulthood	22–28
3	Age 30 transition	28–33
4	Culminating life structure for early adulthood	33–40
5	Midlife transition	40–45
6	Age 50 transition	50–55
7	Culminating life structure for middle adulthood	55–60
8	Late adult transition	60–65

YOUNG ADULTHOOD

There is no set age when adolescence is completed. Many people in their thirties still show some adolescent problems. But usually some adult responsibilities are accepted during the late teens. Individuals who remain in school for an extended time or remain at home with parents mature more slowly. A young man who completes a bachelor's degree, continues for a master's, then a doctorate is apt to be associating with younger people. If he writes home for checks and avoids work and social responsibility, he is likely to prolong his adolescence. Acceptance of adult responsibility requires important decisions. Among the most crucial are choosing a marriage partner and a career (see Chapters 12 and 16). The young adult years usually begin with goals and hopes. Both Sheehy (1976) and Gould (1975) sampled individuals in their twenties and described them as ambitious and striving. Sheehy labeled the stage "the trying twenties." Levinson (1986) viewed the twenties as the "entry life structure for early adulthood." It is a time when we have chosen a lifestyle and are totally independent.

Sheehy (1976), Gould (1975), and Levinson (1986) also studied young adults in their thirties, and described the early thirties as a time of reassessing (Levinson, stage 3). There was a yearning to fill in missing features. Childless couples began to think of raising children. Women who had been at home began to explore possible careers. Couples married for seven or more years were becoming discontent with marriage and were "looking around." By the late thirties adults settle down and become more satisfied (Levinson, stage 4). Sheehy labeled this contentment as "rooting."

The twenties and thirties are a period of many changes. Although immaturities are common in the early twenties, by the completion of the young-adult stage, a mature person is expected to have emerged. How can you tell if you are a mature person?

Most psychologists believe that a mature person accepts responsibility and some specific personal characteristics. Take inventory and see how you rate on this list of attributes of maturity.

- Ability to think for yourself. If you are mature, you can make up your own mind based on your own values. You may seek other opinions, but the final decision will be your own.
- Willingness to accept responsibility for decisions. If you make a mistake, you can recognize your weakness and accept the blame.
- Control of fear and anger. Although you still have worries and irritations, you have better control. You no longer panic and fly into a rage or burst into tears.
- Willingness to work. Rather than shirk responsibility you want to contribute to society and become financially independent. You prefer not to rely on parents and relatives for money.
- Capacity for sexual love and lasting relationships. You are able to show your inner feelings and accept the feelings of another person in a deep and intimate relationship.

Exercise 6-8

In the following scenario, draw one line under each sign of immaturity and two lines under each indication of maturity.

Natalie is 28 and works as a hairstylist at a local shop. She enjoys her work, but her employer is considering firing her. She tends to lose her temper and become abusive when customers do not care for the way she styles their hair. Yesterday she told a man that no one could ever style his horrible hair well—his hair was just too thin and wispy. Her boss told her she could continue only if she could learn to control her temper.

Natalie has a very close boyfriend, and she discussed her problem with him. He listened and was sensitive to her concerns. But Natalie is having trouble deciding whether to change careers. She plans to call her mother tonight and find out what she should do.

Check your responses in the Feedback section.

After settling down in the late thirties and enjoying what Sheehy labeled "rooting," most people experience an "uprooting," or sense of dissatisfaction, sometime during their forties. Physical deterioration becomes obvious. The forties usually bring face wrinkles, thickening waistlines, and gray or thinning hair. However, men and women who have been pleased with their lifestyle and accomplishments tend to experience fewer problems in coping with the changes of middle age.

The changes that occur during mature adulthood have inspired a variety of expressions such as "middle-age revolt," "midcareer crisis," and "middle-age slump." All refer to the recognition of losing youth and accepting the coming of old age. Levinson (1986) labeled this period, stage 5, the "midlife transition." It is a time when we question our values and assess our accomplishments, realizing that time is limited. The first part of life is over. The excerpt in Feature 6-5 provides some current insights into middle age.

In addition to facing their own problems, most mature adults must also care for aging parents, and, in some cases, face the death of one or both parents. There is often a sense of loneliness during the middle age period. Children are growing up and leaving or planning to leave the home. Husbands and wives now must relate to each other as spouses rather than as parents.

In the past, considerable emphasis was directed at women's adjustments to menopause during middle age. Recently psychologists have found that many beliefs about menopause cannot be proved. For example, depression is not necessarily associated with the hormonal changes of menopause. The symptoms of depression are brought on by psychological reasons. Also, interest and enjoyment of sex do not diminish with menopause. More often, sex life improves because there is less anxiety about pregnancy. Yet surveys have shown that negative beliefs about menopause still prevail and the beliefs cause more problems than does the menopause itself (Adler, 1991). Women who work generally adjust better to middle age than do women who have remained at home. This suggests that social and psychological factors tend to be at least as important as the physical changes in women during mature adulthood.

Depression during middle ages is equally common among both men and women. Men who have been doing heavy physical work are often upset by their diminishing strength. Although there is no decline in the efficiency of men who work in offices or in production these men begin to realize that their fruitful working years may be ending.

Mature adulthood is not necessarily a depressing period. Men and women who have been pleased with their relationships and accomplishments usually enjoy these years and make excellent adjustments. According to Levinson, during this time we go through stages 6, 7, and 8. We have a stronger sense of ourselves and our lifestyles. Ideally, this stage brings a stronger acceptance of oneself and one's lifestyle.

Exercise 6-9

Lewis and Stella are both forty. They have been married twenty years and have an eighteen-year-old daughter. Lewis works on the docks as a longshore-

The New Middle Age

When the American Board of Family Practice asked a random sample of 1,200 Americans when middle age begins, 41 percent said it was when you worry about having enough money for health care concerns, 42 percent said it was when your last child moves out and 46 percent said it was when you don't recognize the names of music groups on the radio anymore.

However it is defined, middle age remains one of the least studied phases in life. "It's the last uncharted territory in human development," said MacArthur Foundation president Adele Simmons in 1989, announcing a $10 million grant to fund the largest scholarly look ever at this period. Team leader Gilbert Brim and his colleagues . . . are now partway through their eight-year effort, trying to answer, among other things, why some people hit their strides at midlife and others hit the wall. . . . "Midlife is full of changes, of twists and turns; the path is not fixed," says Brim. "People move in and out of states of success."

In particular, Brim's group debunks the notion of a "midlife crisis." "It's such a mushy concept—not like a clinical diagnosis in the medical field," he says. But Brim adds, "what a wonderful idea! You could load everything on that—letting people blame something external for what they are feeling." Other scholars agree that very few people suffer full-blown crackups—and that dumping the spouse for a bimbo is more the stuff of fiction—or fantasy—than reality. So is the Gauguin syndrome:

running off to Tahiti at 43. People do have affairs and end up with different mates—but that is often after marriages have failed for reasons other than midlife malaise.

Still, the mythology persists. . . .

What does commonly happen, experts say, is a more subtle acceptance of life's limitations. One key task may be to change your self-image. "A lot of the more tangible rewards come in the first half of life, such as good grades, first jobs, early promotions, marriage, first children," says psychologist Robert E. Simmons. . . . After that "it's harder and harder to rely on external gratifications because there aren't as many. So one is thrown back more on one's internal self-esteem system." That can mean finding new forms of satisfaction—from coaching Little League to taking up the saxophone to tutoring kids in school. . . .

Contrary to conventional wisdom, many people find that the 50's is actually a period of reduced stress and anxiety. "In terms of mental health, midlife is the best time," says Ronald Kessler. One tantalizing bit of biomedical research has found that between 40 and 60, people actually lose cells in their coeruleus, the part of the brain that registers anxiety, which may explain the "mellowing" many people feel in middle age. . . .

Source: Beck, M. (1992, December). The new middle age. *Newsweek.*

man loading and unloading ships. Stella has never worked and is wondering whether to look for a job. Assume they have asked for your help in planning for mature adulthood. Tell them what to expect and how to make a better adjustment.

a. Lewis: _____

_____

_____

_____

_____

b. Stella: _____

Turn to the Feedback section to compare your advice.

OLDER ADULTHOOD

In past years, developmental psychologists focused only on the early stages of development. Few ventured beyond the adolescent years. Recently there has been an increasing interest in gerontology, the study of old age. The population of the United States is growing older. The 1985 census found that 13 percent of the population is over age sixty-five.

Aging causes some loss of vitality. As a result, the aging adult usually spends more time visiting doctors and thinking about death (Kalish and Reynolds, 1976). Taking precautions about physical health, diet, and exercise can create a healthier old age. Eubie Blake, the famous jazz piano player and

Physical exercise is important for maintaining vitality in old age.

composer, joked at age 96, "If I had known I was going to last this long, I would have taken better care of myself."

Unfortunately, much of the general public, including high school and college students, views old people negatively and develops an attitude of *ageism*. Among White Americans, older adults are often stereotyped as rigid, unwilling to change, and senile. Loss of memory in old age is the result of disease and is not an inevitable part of the aging process. Only about 6 percent of older adults suffer from mental impairment, with Alzheimer's disease the leading cause. Younger people who have negative stereotypes of older people often talk down, speaking slowly and using an exaggerated tone called "elderspeak" (Wingfield et al., 1989). In Hispanic and African-American families, older people are more likely to receive respect. Grandparents help with child rearing and contribute to family decisions (Markides and Kraus, 1986).

ageism Negative stereotyping of older adults.

Retirement probably has the most severe impact on aging adults, particularly if they have not planned for it. In addition to planning finances, aging adults should plan to develop their interests. Travel, reading, hobbies, school, volunteer work, or even beginning a new career are all possibilities. Unfortunately, retirement is sometimes very sudden. The U.S. Bureau of Labor reported that the suicide rate after forced retirement is twelve times more than normal. Often suicide results because people feel unnecessary and have lost their sense of meaningfulness in life.

In the past, families included aging parents and grandparents in their homes. Currently, there has been an increase in the number of aging adults in retirement communities, nursing homes, and residences for the aged. Efforts are made to help improve their attitudes about the enjoyment and importance of life. The article in Feature 6-6 suggests that there are some good times in nursing homes! The poet Kenneth Koch (1977) visited nursing homes and taught elderly people to write poems. One woman expressed the meaningfulness she found in the experience:

> Motherless, fatherless, sisterless
> All gone and no more
> I felt so lonely
> Yet within me I felt a joy of joyfulness
> When I read poems relating to things around me
> Like the sun in the skies
> It gives me hope for the future
> —MARY ZAHORJKO (age 94)

Neugarten (1980) has raised hopes that people may be changing their attitudes about aging. She feels that age is becoming more irrelevant. There are many "young-old" persons who are vigorous and healthy. Age itself is a poor predictor of lifestyle. Fewer young-old people are willing to adhere to the traditional and formal elderly role. An increasing number of aging adults are working, involved in community affairs, and generally enjoying their lives. As Neugarten jokes, "Aging is 'in.'"

Exercise 6-10

By planning ahead you can make better adjustments when you are an aging adult. For each area listed, mention one way planning could improve your adjustment.

a. Physical: _____

b. Financial: _____

c. Interests: _____

d. Attitudes: _____

You may check your answers in the Feedback section.

DEATH AND DYING

Have you ever noticed that people avoid using the word "death"? Rather than saying a woman died, friends and relatives will say, "She passed away" or "She is no longer with us." Even doctors and nurses will say, "The patient expired." Perhaps you have even wondered why death insurance is called "life insurance."

Older people are likely to experience the death of spouses, friends, brothers, and sisters, and sometimes even their own children. Frequently, older adults need to express their grief, but the need is ignored.

Until recently death had been a taboo subject, a topic to be avoided. Even when people were dying of a fatal disease, friends and relatives would reassure them and hint that they could live. Weisman (1972) called it a conspiracy of silence. The dying person never heard honest reactions and responses. Kübler-Ross (1969) helped to make death a more comfortable subject. After spending time with patients who were dying, she identified five stages in their reactions.

Denial. At first patients insist that it is a mistake. They are certain the diagnosis is wrong or something has been overlooked.

Anger. Patients then ask, "Why me?" and become annoyed with God or fate or whoever is responsible. It is not unusual for patients to blame their doctors.

Depression. There is a loss of interest and a sense of hopelessness and despair.

FEATURE 6-6 PSYCHOLOGY IN THE NEWS

Visit with a Fortune Teller

The new patient in the nursing home was tall and healthy looking. He was not in a wheelchair, used no apron walker or crutches, not even a cane. As he made his way to the dining room or elsewhere, he noticed an old lady in a wheelchair in the hall who seemed to observe him with unconcealed curiosity. It became bothersome, so one day he stopped at her chair and spoke to her.

After introducing himself, he said: "I notice when I pass your chair, you seem to watch me with more than usual interest. Is there something wrong?"

"No, it's just that you look so much like my fourth husband," she answered.

"That's interesting," he said, "How many times have you been married?"

"Three times," she replied.

Source: Townsend, I.M. (1992, July/August). Visit with a fortune teller. *Saturday Evening Post.*

Bargaining. Patients make promises in exchange for a longer life. Some promise their doctors to give up smoking, alcohol, or sugar, if the doctor can help them survive. Others promise God they will lead a better life.

Acceptance. During the last stage, patients become void of feelings. Although not joyful, they develop an inner peace and finally accept death.

Kübler-Ross's stages were criticized by Kastenbaum and Costa (1977). They argued that not all dying patients experience every stage. Further, the stages do not always occur in the same order. They were also concerned that friends and relatives who are familiar with the five stages would be less understanding and empathetic toward the dying. They could assume an attitude that "It's just a stage."

The recent interest and concern about death and dying has encouraged the hospice movement in the United States. A *hospice* is a comfortable place for dying patients. Hospice care may be provided in the dying person's home or in a special facility. Understanding and the dignity of death are of prime importance. Patients and their families are encouraged to share their feelings, talk about death, and even plan their funerals. As a result, dying patients develop a healthier attitude toward death, and emotional, moral, and practical issues are resolved.

hospice Place for terminally ill patients where understanding, feelings, and dignity are primary concerns, along with health care.

Checkpoint

Use the following questions to check your understanding of the final portion of this chapter. Match each term on the left with the expression on the right that provides the best example.

24. _____ Adolescence

25. _____ Secondary sexual characteristics

26. _____ Primary sexual functioning

27. _____ Clique

28. _____ Peers

29. _____ Identity crisis

30. _____ Trying twenties

31. _____ Rooting

32. _____ Midlife transition

33. _____ Gerontology

34. _____ Hospice

a. A group of friends, "the crowd"
b. Rebelling against parents and finding yourself
c. Period of change from a child to an adult
d. Friends in the same age group
e. Enlarged hips, breast development, voice change
f. A comfortable place for the dying
g. Contentment that occurs in the late thirties
h. Onset of menstruation
i. A period of ambition and striving
j. The study of aging
k. Changes that occur in the forties and fifties

Check your responses against the Checkpoint Answer Key at the end of the chapter. If you had difficulty with any question, reread the text. If you had little or no difficulty answering the questions or have resolved problems that you might have had, you are ready to check yourself against the chapter inventory that follows.

Use this list of objectives as a review checklist. You should be able to do each of the tasks outlined in the objectives and apply them to everyday examples. If you can, you may feel confident that you have mastered the material in this chapter.

1. Outline the focus of developmental psychology.
2. Explain the importance of parenting decisions.
3. Describe how children affect marriages.
4. Describe the factors involved in parental decisions on family size, parental roles, and type of discipline.
5. Identify concerns during the prenatal stage.
6. Describe three approaches to childbirth.
7. List seven stages of development.
8. Describe the lifestyle of a neonate.
9. Identify three needs during babyhood.
10. Identify the needs and problems of early and later childhood.
11. List and describe Levinson's developmental periods.
12. Distinguish among the physical, social, and mental changes in adolescence.
13. Outline common problems encountered during young adulthood.
14. Define maturity and list five attributes of it.
15. Recognize the changes and characteristics of mature adulthood.
16. Describe recent changes in the study of problems of the aged.
17. Specify the five stages of death identified by Kübler-Ross, and give three areas of criticism.

Feedback

The correct answers to the exercise follow. If you did not answer an exercise correctly, review the preceding pages and return to the exercise to correctly complete it.

6-1. a. Women do not have a maternal instinct. Everyone must learn about development and child rearing.

   b. Children rarely, if ever, help a shaky marriage. If anything the pressures of raising children will worsen the problems that presently exist.

   c. It is best if both partners agree on family size. Children in large families are not necessarily happier. Many feel they lack parental attention and must compete with many brothers and sisters.

   d. Although only children do have advantages, they often suffer from loneliness and can have problems adjusting to other children.

6-2. a. Democratic
   b. Authoritarian
   c. Democratic
   d. Permissive

6-3. Anita should not drink coffee, cola beverages, or alcohol. She should give up smoking and ignore the advice of her friends. The anesthetic could have a harmful effect on her baby.

6-4. a. Rock the baby.
    b. Speak in soft, soothing tones.
    c. Hum in a low voice.

6-5. a. Helen
    b. Marsha
    c. Henri
    d. Kathleen
    e. Sidney
    f. Bob

6-6. b. Organize some running and jumping games. Allow the children to make buildings with wooden or Styrofoam blocks. If possible, visit a park with swings, slides, and seesaws.
    c. Arrange cutting and pasting activities, along with coloring and painting. Have simple jigsaw puzzles available.
    d. Although there may be a few educational television programs that would be beneficial, television time should be limited. Programs with biases against minorities should be avoided. The children should spend most of their time in active play.
    e. Meals should be as nutritious as possible, but you should realize that children in this age group often have limited appetites.
    f. Children should be rewarded for desirable behavior. When children misbehave they should understand that they are being punished for their actions. They should be helped to understand the proper way to act.

6-7. a. Social
    b. Social
    c. Mental
    d. Physical
    e. Social

6-8. Signs of immaturity include: "She tends to lose her temper," "She told a man that no one could ever style his horrible hair well," and "She plans to call her mother tonight and find out what she should do." Signs of maturity include: "works as a hairstylist," "enjoys her work," and "has a very close boyfriend."

6-9. a. Lewis should realize that his physical strength may be diminishing. He might want to investigate activities that do not require the strength of his present job. He should also realize that his relationship with his wife may change when his daughter leaves the home.
    b. Stella will probably have a sense of loneliness when her daughter leaves. She will probably make a better adjustment if she has a job or an outside interest. She should prepare herself for a closer relationship with her husband.

6-10. a. Through proper diet, exercise, and health care, you can enter the aging years as a healthier person.
     b. If you face the reality of retirement, you can make plans for a retirement fund or income.

c. Since you will have more leisure time, you can plan areas of interest to pursue.

d. If you keep active and alive with interests and ideas, you will find more enjoyment.

Checkpoint Answer Key

1. F; 2. F; 3. T; 4. T; 5. F; 6. T; 7. F; 8. T; 9. T; 10. F; 11. T; 12. T; 13. F; 14. F; 15. F; 16. b; 17. d; 18, d; 19. c; 20. b; 21. a; 22. a; 23. d; 24. c; 25. e; 26. h; 27. a; 28. d; 29. b; 30. i; 31. g; 32. k; 33. j; 34. f.

Motivation

The last temptation is the greatest treason:
To do the right thing but for the wrong reason.
—T. S. ELIOT

Twenty-seven passengers step off a bus at a terminal in Chicago. Eight rush for restrooms. Four run with outstretched arms to people who have been waiting for them. Another four stroll into a snack bar. One young woman carefully checks to be sure the locks on her luggage are secure. She slowly inspects each surface for scratches. Two men, who apparently met on the bus, ask for directions to the nearest bar. A teenage girl looks around nervously and appears confused. Three elderly women head for the terminal exit door and gaze skyward at the tall buildings. Two middle-aged men seat themselves in the lobby. One reads a newspaper, while the other stares into space. A woman with a crying two-year-old boy angrily warns him to be quiet.

What causes such different behaviors? Perhaps you have wondered why people in similar settings behave so differently from one another. Unfortunately, you can never be certain that you are guessing the correct causes of behavior. The reasons for behavior are studied by psychologists interested in motivation. In this chapter, you will learn more about *motivation*—why people behave the way they do.

Psychologists interested in motivation examine factors that cause behavior. These may include thinking, feeling, acting, or any possible combination of the three. Motivation for behavior is an immensely complex subject. Sometimes you can identify your motivation, but often you cannot. Whether you are aware

motivation Needs and incentives that cause people to behave as they do

198

of it or not, sometimes your motivation is based on physiological needs such as hunger, thirst, and a need for rest. At other times your motivation will reflect such psychological needs as desire for approval or a craving for love. Or your motivation may be influenced by the attitudes of your parents and friends. In this chapter you will examine human basic needs and higher goals. You will also consider how incentives and outside influences can increase motivation.

WHAT IS MOTIVATION? ⇒ What =?

Perhaps, as you turned to this chapter, you had an inkling that motivation is closely related to achievement and success. Indeed, there is a sharp relationship between motivation and success. However, motivation can also cause many behaviors besides achievement and success. It can cause eating, drinking, sleeping, driving a car, and even cutting a college class. A person who is not motivated is either dead or in an intensely deep coma. Motivation is based on internal needs that push and drive you. If you can determine your needs, you can explain why you behave the way you do. You can identify your motivation.

Conscious and Unconscious Motivation ⇒ What =?, How different?

Uncovering needs and identifying motivation are not always easy. People often become puzzled when asked to explain their behavior. Finding excuses for displeasing behaviors can be particularly thorny. The comedian Flip Wilson has managed to keep his motivation cloaked with his joke, "The devil made me do it." Supposedly, Flip is totally unaware of how he could possibly intentionally do anything evil. Many psychologists would agree with him and assume that he was unconsciously motivated.

Have you ever found it difficult to explain your own behavior? It is usually relatively simple to reason that you ate a big dinner because you were hungry. Or you might be able to explain that you are working hard so that you can get a raise or a good grade. These are examples of conscious motivation. But people also do things they cannot explain. Maybe you have occasionally found yourself walking around aimlessly. Or possibly you have sat in the driver's seat of your car without your car keys. Freudian psychologists believe that much human behavior is caused by *unconscious motivation*. As a result most people are often not conscious, or aware, of what causes their behavior. For example, some people are constantly late for appointments and meetings. Even though they make a conscious effort to get an early start, nonetheless they end up being late. Freudian psychologists would blame their tardiness on unconscious motivation, maybe an unconscious desire to make an entrance and be noticed.

Another type of unconscious motivation is *repression,* described in detail in Chapter 4. Repression is motivated forgetting. A student who failed a midterm and must appear for a conference with the instructor might forget to keep the appointment. The student is being truthful and honestly forgets! The thought of being shamed by a teacher is too distressing to think about consciously. As a result, the student is unconsciously motivated to get rid of any thoughts of

---

incentive (n.) Something that encourages you to work harder, start new activities.

intense (adj) Serious and making you feel strong emotions or opinions.

thorny (adj) a question, problem, etc. that is complicated and difficult.

Cloak (v) to deliberately hide facts, feelings etc. So that people do not see or understand them. (adj) be cloaked in s Covered in S.T.

unconscious motivation Motives, feelings, and impulses that are not in a person's awareness but nonetheless may influence the individual's behavior

repression Forgetting that is caused by unconscious blocking of thoughts or events that are threatening or frightening

---

Conscious motivation is behavior that people intend to do

Unconscious motivation is behavior that people aren't aware of

the embarrassing meeting. Unconscious motivation helps remove personal guilt for behavior, since your actions or lack of actions are labeled unintentional.

Exercise 7-1

For each of the following examples, indicate whether the motivation appears to be *conscious* or *unconscious*.

a. Meg has a boring economics professor who drones on during class in a dull monotone. Meg makes a special effort to take notes so she will keep herself alert during his lectures.

b. George notices that a ladder is extended across the sidewalk where he is walking. George scoffs at superstitions and ridiculous people who think walking under ladders will bring bad luck. Yet he walks out into the street to avoid stepping under the ladder.

c. Saundra keeps a special "birthday book" and prides herself in remembering to send cards and notes to friends and relatives on their special days. Although her younger sister's birthday is recorded in the book, Saundra has forgotten to send her a birthday card for the past four years.

d. The last few times Tri wore his wild red-striped ski hat on the slopes, several attractive girls seemed to notice him. Tri plans to wear his wild ski hat on his next trip to Aspen.

Turn to the Feedback section to check your answers.

Needs and Incentives

incentive Reward that motivates behavior

Needs and *incentives* are the pushes and pulls of motivation. Some of our motivations are biologically or emotionally based, and they push us. These pushing forces such as hunger, thirst, and curiosity are considered needs. Other motivations result when we are pulled by an incentive, perhaps a slice of cheesecake, a frosty lemonade, or a sensuous member of the opposite sex. Consider someone at a pie-eating contest, gulping his tenth pie. It is unlikely that a hunger need has anything to do with his continued eating. It is far more likely that he is being pulled by an incentive, perhaps a cash prize, a ribbon, or the attention given a winner.

As you probably suspected, most of our motivations result from a combination of pushes and pulls. We lack something such as food, sleep, approval, or respect, and we are driven to satisfy these needs. We push ourselves. In addition to this pushing, we sometimes experience some pulling. Even if our need is only slight, we often can be pulled by an enticing incentive.

Whether their motivation is conscious or unconscious, people have a broad range of needs. Some needs are shared by everyone. For example, everyone is motivated to stay alive and survive. Food, rest, oxygen, and other necessities for life are common to all people. Other needs vary from one person to the next. For example, some people need to drive a fancy sports car and wear designer clothes. Others may need to travel to far-off lands and live among different cultures. Undoubtedly, you have heard of individuals who had a need to climb high mountains or do missionary work in underdeveloped countries. Strangely, some people even feel a need to write psychology books!

Exercise 7-2

Suppose some neighborhood children set up a lemonade stand on a hot summer day. You are out cutting grass and doing yard work. After an hour you need to quench your thirst and you buy a large glass of lemonade. The children are thrilled when you buy a second glass, and they explain that you are their first customer. Although you are no longer thirsty, you buy a third glass because you know this will please them.

How were the first two glasses motivated by a need and the third, motivated by an incentive? How were you "pushed"? How were you "pulled"?

I was motivated to buy 2 glasses of lemonade to   _my thirst._

Please compare your response with the one in the Feedback section at the end of the chapter.

Survival Needs = what=?

Most Americans experience only a mild form of survival need. Survival needs are biological necessities required to continue living. You may have believed yourself starving or dying of thirst. But chances are your needs were minimal when compared with people who had beyond doubt been without water or food for days.

Keys et al. (1950) studied men who had been fed just enough to stay alive

FIGURE 7-1. It appears a dental plan would be an enticing incentive that would take care of his needs.

during World War II. They found that the men became preoccupied with food thoughts and fantasies. The men delighted in reading cookbooks and exchanging favorite recipes. They forgot about wives, girlfriends, and sex. They became apathetic, dispirited, and irritable.

There has been considerable evidence that thirst needs are even stronger than hunger needs are. When any physiological needs are not satisfied, personality changes generally result. Persons who have been without sleep for extended periods have been known to become anxious and hallucinate. Have you ever been in steady, persistent pain for a prolonged time? You probably noticed your own personality change. In all likelihood, you were easily irked and had difficulty concentrating. Your interest and motivation were concentrated on how to relieve yourself of some pain and become more comfortable.

The human body constantly tries to keep a balanced, stable condition. The maintaining of this balanced condition is called *homeostasis*. Homeostasis acts like a thermostat in regulating your body temperature. You sweat when your body is too hot and shiver (produce heat) when you are too cold. Or you might remove or put on a sweater. Similarly, you feel hungry and eat and stop eating when you feel satisfied or full.

Why do some people eat more than others do? Some researchers believe that the thermostat for weight, or "fatostat," varies in different people. Each person has a different *set point* for weight. Your set point is your usual weight. Have you ever lost several pounds and regained the weight very quickly? Bennet and Gurin (1982) reported that people who diet fall below their set points. Their bodies then feel deprived and they eat more. This explains why people often gain weight after dieting.

Exercise 7-3

Several studies have suggested that children who eat a good nutritious breakfast tend to perform better in school. From what you have learned about problems encountered by men who had hunger needs in Keys's study, explain why a school breakfast program could help undernourished children.

_____

_____

Compare your response with the one given in the Feedback section.

Curiosity and Arousal

Most people seek a moderate amount of stimulation or arousal. They avoid boredom but also avoid too much stimulation. If you are alone with nothing to do, you may turn on your stereo or television, or pick up a magazine. Likewise, if you are at a crowded party with blaring music and loud chatter, you might seek some fresh air and quiet.

There are, however, large individual differences in the amount of stimulation that people need. Farley (1986) described two extremes of arousal needs, *type T* (capital T) and *type t* (lower case t). Type T individuals are thrill seekers. They need more risks and adventures than other people do, to get revved up. As a result they like to experiment, prefer novelty, and enjoy conflicts and

homeostasis Ability of vital functions to maintain a stable condition

set point Mechanism that maintains a person's usual weight

type T personality High-thrill-seeking personality

type t personality Low-thrill-seeking personality

[Handwritten marginal and interlinear notes:]

thetic (adj) not excited not caring about S.T., not interested in thing and unwilling make an effort to nge and improve things.

(adj) thinking or worrying about S.T.

(adj) getting annoyed quickly or easily.

a lot wit the re that yo do no pay a to the othe thin

emonourished (adj) healthy and weak cause you have... t had enough d

et point refers to ur usually weight.

meostasis refers to e actions that gulated your dy temperature tably

If [undernourished children] had a school breakfast program they would not be preoccupied with food. If clause

(รูปภาพไม่ชัด) under fat.

น. การฝึก, การปฏิบัติ. What 9 & How different 9.

arousal (n.) excitement .especially sexual excitement.

People with type T personalities enjoy risky sports such as bungee jumping.

the
on

[A school breakfast program could help undernourished children] to learn because they would not be preoccupied with food.

excitement. At the opposite end of the spectrum are the type t's (little t's). These people like certainty, stability, and a sense of peace. Most people fall in the middle of the type T ←——————→ type t spectrum and seek a moderate amount of stimulation.

Connect with "becauses"
S + V + O
[insert the answer in a gramatical wa

Farley (1992) stressed that under ideal circumstances, type T children can be highly creative. However if these high-sensation–seeking youngsters are not properly stimulated, they may seek their own excitement through delinquency, drugs, or other dangerous and illegal actions. The article in Feature 7-1 points out that type T college students were more likely to drive recklessly if they thought they had drunk alcohol, even if they had only had a placebo. They used the notion that they had been drinking as an excuse to indulge in risky driving. Farley recommends that parents of type T children identify the trait early and try to channel their children's energies into creative activities, adventure weekends, sports, and stimulating discussions and activities.

Exercise 7-4

How would Farley describe Edgar (Figure 7-2)? Why?

_____

_____

Check your response in the Feedback section.

Safety and Security Needs → what=?
'How different?

Chances are you take many precautions to be certain you are safe and secure. You live in some type of shelter, whether it be an apartment, a house, a teepee, or a barn. This shelter protects you from rain, snow, and other unfavorable elements. But undoubtedly your motivations and concerns for safety and security extend well beyond your need for shelter. Do you have locks on your doors and windows? How about flashlights and hurricane lanterns? If you keep a spare tire in your car and maintain health and auto insurance, you are responding to your motivation to satisfy safety and security needs. Our country supports a national military force; towns and cities have police and fire departments. These groups all attest to our needs for safety and security.

Checkpoint

Use the following questions to check your understanding of this portion of the chapter. Choose and mark the one correct response to each question.

1. What do psychologists interested in motivation study?
   a. Actions and overt behavior
   b. Factors that cause behavior
   c. Achievement and success
   d. Repression

(handwritten margin notes:) fety and security ds refer to why e causes why ople need S.T. protect themselves to be alive.

FEATURE 7-1 PSYCHOLOGY IN THE NEWS

Some "Drive" Recklessly after Drinking Placebos

In the past several years, research has shown that a certain kind of person—high in risk-taking behavior, hostility, and related measures—is more likely than others to get involved in traffic accidents after having a few stiff drinks.

Recently, psychologist David McMillen of Mississippi State University has added a twist to that finding: These "sensation seekers" are prone to reckless driving when they only *think* they've consumed alcohol.

"Most of us think, 'I've had something to drink; I'd better be careful,'" said McMillen. "Here's a group that doesn't do that. If you're a high-sensation seeker, and you merely think you've had alcohol, it apparently releases you" to engage in potentially destructive behavior, he said.

The study . . . included 96 college students shown to be either high- or low-sensation seekers based on their completion of the Sensation Seeking Scale (SSS).

Before receiving any drinks, the subjects each played a video driving game in which players

"drive" along a roadway and can pass cars and accelerate using a pedal. They were told to drive the video car as they would their own . . .

The team found that those with high SSS scores who thought they had consumed alcohol—whether or not they actually had—changed lanes and passed cars significantly more than high-sensation seekers who didn't think they had had any alcohol, whether or not they had.

Conversely, low-sensation seekers who thought they had consumed alcohol changed lanes and passed cars less often than average—and less often than low-sensation–seeking subjects who didn't think they'd received alcohol.

The findings are in keeping with other researchers' findings about higher accident rates among those higher in sensation and hostility scores . . .

Source: DeAngelis, T. (1991, May). Some "drive" recklessly after drinking placebos. *APA Monitor.*

(handwritten at bottom:) 1 b d d b c 6

*"Edgar's need for entertainment
is at a bare minimum."*
FIGURE 7-2.

2. What is the difference between conscious motivation and unconscious motivation?
   a. Unconscious motivation causes guilt and conscious motivation does not.
   b. Conscious motivation is repressed and unconscious motivation is not.
   c. People are aware of unconscious motivation but are unaware of conscious motivation.
   d. People are aware of conscious motivation but are unaware of unconscious motivation.

3. Which of the following is an example of an incentive?
   a. Food
   b. Hunger
   c. Thirst
   d. Curiosity

4. Which of the following is the strongest need?
   a. Hunger
   b. Thirst
   c. Safety
   d. Stimulation

5. What is the purpose of homeostasis?
   a. To increase your arousal
   b. To keep your body in stable condition
   c. To meet safety and security needs
   d. To identify unconscious motivation

6. Ted is described as a type T. Which activity would he probably prefer?
   a. Sitting by a plant
   b. Reading a book
   c. Riding a roller coaster
   d. Sleeping

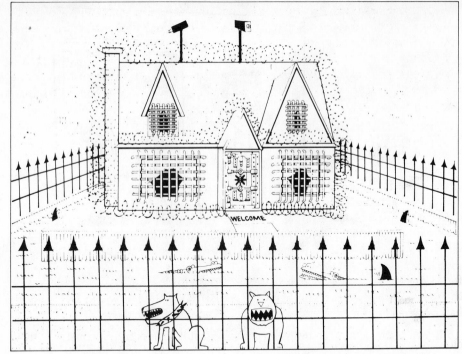

FIGURE 7-3. Some safety and security needs can be intense!

Use the Checkpoint Answer Key to verify your response. If you had any difficulty with a question, carefully reread the text. If you had little or no difficulty answering the questions or have resolved any difficulty you might have had, you are ready to continue with the next portion of this chapter.

THE NEED TO AFFILIATE = what 9

The needs for love and belongingness are sometimes called *affiliation needs*. If you have ever felt lonely or isolated, you have experienced a need to affiliate. Affiliation is not limited to romantic or parental love. You also need friends who accept you. There are immense differences in affiliation needs. Some people are satisfied with one or two close, deep friendships. Others crave superficial relationships with large groups. Some fluctuate between group and individual friendships. Selection of friends usually changes with development. People look for ways to please others and win their approval. Most are selective, seeking acceptance from only certain friends and associates. It would clearly be impossible to win everyone's approval!

Groups such as Alcoholics Anonymous and Weight Watchers are designed to motivate people through their need for affiliation and social approval. Many individuals drink or eat because they feel unwanted or lonely. Although eating

[handwritten margin notes:]
iliate (n.) = a small company, organization etc.
-v.) ① be affiliated with/to sth if a group or organization is affiliated to a larger one, is related to it or controlled by it
② affiliate yourself to sth to join or become related to a larger group or organization

affiliation need
Motivation to associate with other people and feel loved

and drinking are physiological needs, they are often also associated with affiliation. Whether you are enjoying a formal dinner party or a few beers with some friends, your purpose is not solely to satisfy hunger and thirst needs. Alcoholics Anonymous and Weight Watchers recognize the social implications of eating and drinking. The groups were formed to approve refraining from alcohol and excessive food. To win acceptance from the groups, you must keep sober and thin.

Just as there are differences in the types and number of friends needed, there are also wide variations in the intensity and strength of the need to belong and be accepted by others. Crowne and Marlowe (1964) developed a test to measure the need for social approval. They then used subjects who had either extremely high or extremely low scores on their tests. Next, the high and low scorers were asked to do a chore. They were told to put twelve spools in a box, lifting only one at a time. When the box was full, they had to empty it and repeat placing each spool back in the box. Sound like fun? Interestingly, the subjects who had high scores on the need-for-approval test claimed they enjoyed the task. They were also far more enthusiastic about the scientific usefulness of the experiment than were the low scorers. High scorers even stated they had learned something from the experiment. Evidently the low scorers had less need to be approved and could recognize a dull chore!

High needs for approval and affiliation can also be identified through clothes. Wearing sorority and fraternity pins and team or club windbreakers and dressing alike are ways of demonstrating a need to belong. Adolescents often show remarkable conformity in their dress. Men and women who frequent singles bars or attend every mixer and dance usually have strong affiliation needs.

Advertisers capitalize on the need for love and belongingness. Many ads begin with a negative appeal. Jim is lonely and disapproved of by everyone. He has either dandruff, messy hair, bald spots, bad breath, a bad odor, or ill-fitting underwear. However, after using the advertised product, his problem is solved and he gains popularity. The advertisers are appealing to your need for approval. They hope you will believe their product will gain you the same popularity Jim had. Check magazines, newspapers, and your television for this type of ad.

Exercise 7-5

Read the following scenario and check each sentence that demonstrates a need for affiliation and approval.

Helen, a twenty-year-old college junior, is tired of living alone. Next Tuesday she will move into an apartment with three other girls. Right now she is planning a "moving-out" party. She plans to invite everyone she knows. Helen had never had a party in her apartment before because she was afraid it might annoy her landlord.

Tonight she is going to a friend's party and intends to invite every new person she meets. She wants everyone to think she has many friends. A big moving-out party will prove she is popular!

You may check your checks in the Feedback section.

achievement need
Motivation to ac-
complish tasks and
be a success

Our American culture emphasizes the importance of individual achievements. As a result most of us have developed *achievement needs.* Achievements can be any accomplishment, from getting an office with a view or getting a personal secretary to maintaining the clearest complexion on campus. An achievement is a demonstration of success. Think of some achievements that you felt gave you status among others. Did you ever receive the highest grade on an exam or earn enough money for a car or an unusual vacation? Perhaps you have won a contest!

Some contests require an accomplishment, while others are based strictly on luck. Often people feel a sense of achievement in winning contests based more on chance than on actual accomplishments. Bingo and sweepstake addicts delight in the possibility of winning huge sums of money easily. Studies have shown that only rarely are these individuals strong achievers at work. Strong achievers usually want to feel personally responsible for their own success.

Games of chance do not require individual efforts. According to McClelland (1961), people with strong needs for achievement like to use their own skills and want to improve themselves. They prefer tasks that require some effort but are not impossible. If they have control of their jobs and can set their own goals, they feel more satisfied with themelves. A high achiever would prefer a game of chess to a game of poker.

The goals achievers usually set for themselves are those that everyone else will believe are symbols or signs of success. They want to do well and enjoy getting positive feedback from others. Men and women with strong needs for achievement like to get pats on the back. Feedback from others is more important than money is. Adams and Stone (1977) reported that high achievers will even spend their leisure time in activities that will reflect achievement.

Why do some people have strong needs for achievement? McClelland found that the need for achievement is related to parent attitudes. Parents who are high achievers themselves usually demand independence from their children. The children must become self-reliant at a relatively early age. As a result, the children develop a sense of confidence and find enjoyment in their own achievements.

On the other hand, parents who have low needs for achievement are more protective of their children. They help their children perform everyday tasks such as dressing and feeding far more than is necessary. Their children have less freedom and usually have low achievement needs.

Achievement motivation is strongest in cultures that stress individual accomplishments. Although achievement motivation has been studied across cultures, very little research has concentrated on American minorities. Adelson (1980) argued that if socioeconomic status is included in studies of achievement motivation, social class is a better predictor of motivation than is race. A recent study (Steinberg et al., 1992) found that all adolescent American minorities agreed that school success would help them find a good job. But the researchers found significant differences in ethnic views of how a *poor* education would affect their chances for employment. Asian-American students, who tend to

— look for Verbs

— look for subj - obj

have the highest school grades among minorities, had the strongest fears about their job opportunities if they did poorly in school and claimed that their parents would be upset by poor grades. As a result, they spent twice as much time on their homework as did other students. African-American and Hispanic students, who score lower grades in school, were more optimistic about their chances of finding a job without a good education. They spent less time on their studies, were less likely to believe that school success results from hard work, and saw their parents as having lower standards for achievement.

But as the excerpt in Feature 7-2 suggests, we are seeing some changes. While African-American adolescents may believe that job success is possible without a good education, their parents are seeing things differently and are

FEATURE 7-2 PSYCHOLOGY IN THE NEWS

Students Forty and Over

African-Americans 40 and older know that a thirst for knowledge springs from more than just the fountain of youth, as evidenced by the increased numbers of older students making their presence felt at colleges nationwide. Statistics tracking the trend are hard to come by, but educators say over the last five years, and most notably recently, older students are becoming more common on campus.

Roger Richardson, director of African-American student services at New York University, says this year he has seen more older students seeking information about returning to school than in the last four years. "This year there has been a significant number of returning students 40 and over," he says. . . .

At a time when overall black enrollment is lagging behind that of the early 80s, why are older students donning backpacks and burning the midnight oil? One 47-year-old student at California State University, Los Angeles, says two things made him go to college for the first time so late in life. "I had gone through a divorce. My wife had a master's degree, and I thought it was time for me to get a degree. I also wanted to be a role model for young black men."

. . . Another who succeeded at U.C. Berkeley is Eric Morton, 58, who walked away with bachelor's degrees in English and African-American studies, an A average, top honors and three awards this year. A former journalism student during the late 50s, he says he wasn't a serious student back

then and got sidetracked with his involvement in the Civil Rights Movement and politics that included working on campaigns for such heavyweights as Julian Bond, Coleman Young and Ronald Dellums. But as the political activism of the 60s and 70s slowed, he says, "I felt like a mercenary with no job." He returned to the corporate world only to find it high-tech. "It seemed like I had been passed by. I was floundering, but I kept working to take care of the kids," says the single parent of three grown children. He took courses at junior colleges, and in 1989 he entered U.C. Berkeley after hearing about its Re-entry program. . . .

Not only did he benefit from his determination, but he has inspired his children, too. "What I thought would put a strain on us didn't. Everybody kicked it up a notch. One daughter who had just graduated from high school and wasn't doing so well in college suddenly became serious. She said she had to do better than me," he chuckles. His son, who was already at Berkeley and had not been fulfilling his potential, got motivated and was soon tutoring dad. He graduated a year before Eric.

As for Eric, he says the lack of black professors who are motivators is tremendous, and he plans to be one. He's not stopping until he gets his doctorate degree in African-American studies. . . .

Source: Nance-Nash, S. (1992, October/November). Students 40 and over. *Upscale.*

returning to school in increasing numbers. Changes in parental attitudes are likely to affect future generations.

Exercise 7-6

From what you have learned about people's needs for achievement, indicate whether each of the following is apt to be a high achiever or a low achiever. State the characteristic of a high or low achiever that the person is demonstrating.

[handwritten: Chandra is high achiever, because she want to show her achievement to other people.]

a. Chandra was furious when she learned that her new office would not have a carpet. *[handwritten: too high, because she wan't their new office have a carpet. That can]*

b. Reverend Williams always studies the faces of her congregation when she gives a sermon. She wants to be sure she is inspiring her audience. *[handwritten: high. She wan't to get feedback that she feel success. check or so express her acheivement. possitive]*

[left margin handwritten: because he]

c. Claude can only work if he has a midmorning break. He needs some relaxation to concentrate for a full morning. *[handwritten: (reason) high a low. The people who has a high acheivement needs should work or can]*

[left margin handwritten: ecause]

d. When Mark learned he would not be paid for his overtime, he said, "Forget it. I won't work for free!" *[handwritten: low a. He The high achiever usually want to get feed back when Concentrate positive they did it Money isn't big factor to work but accomplisht is in]*

e. Julian has been practicing basketball skills at every opportunity. He wants to be able to score a basket from every possible angle. *[handwritten: High]*

[left margin handwritten: She doesn't want to, initiative (in-ish ativ) take or She doesn't want to take a proactive role.]

f. Laura's boss asked her to develop a project that she would enjoy performing. Laura became upset and announced that she hated to define her own work. She would rather just follow orders. *[handwritten: High a low.]*

g. Joshua never walks to his junior high school alone. His mother accompanies him to be sure he will not be harmed by other children or traffic. *[handwritten: low]*

h. Wanda spends half her salary on sweepstakes and raffle tickets. *[handwritten: low a]*

i. Naomi is afraid that she will not be able to support herself if she does not do well in high school. _____ ~~#~~

You may check your answers in the Feedback section.

Workaholics = What
What is characteristic

Workaholism results when the need to achieve runs wild. *Workaholics* develop a passion for their work. Some are driven to work as much as twelve or fifteen hours every day, including weekends. The term "workaholic," generally used by lay people rather than psychologists, is based on "alcoholic," a word that implies a negative excess. However, unlike alcoholics, workaholics are usually respected. They love their jobs and are having fun. They are successful and enjoy themselves.

workaholic Person who prefers work to socializing and relaxing

Although workaholics are usually respected by coworkers and friends, their families tend to be less enthusiastic. It is not uncommon for workaholics to skip meals, limit their social conversation, and even work their way through holidays.

Perhaps you are wondering about yourself. Undoubtedly, you have worked during a lunch hour. Possibly, you have stayed up all night completing a term paper or project. But for workaholics, these are routine events. Almost every night there is some project or task that requires their concentration. Whether the job be fine-tuning the engine of a car, writing an article for the newspaper, or keeping a spotless kitchen, workaholics cannot pull themselves away. No job is too menial or unimportant. Are you generally inclined to shout "Thank God it's Monday" rather than join the usual chorus of "T.G.I.F."? If so, you might want to check yourself on the quiz in Feature 7-3. Although this quiz is not a scientific analysis, it does allow you to compare yourself with people who have been termed workaholics.

Exercise 7-7

In your own words, describe one positive and one negative aspect of work-aholism.

a. Positive: _____

b. Negative: _____

Check your descriptions in the Feedback section.

> *Why people fear of Competition.*

Fear of Competition = What.

What about people who are afraid to achieve? Psychologists believe the fear of competition is usually related to a different need, the need for love and be-longingness. They are afraid they will lose valued friendships and affection if they compete and become successful. Fear of competition and fear of success are closely related.

Quiz: Are You a Workaholic?

Who are work addicts and what makes them tick? What's wrong with being a workaholic, and more importantly, what's right about it? Despite disparate circumstances, most workaholics share common characteristics. In order to identify workaholics, I've developed a quiz based on these characteristics. If you wonder whether you're a workaholic—or if you think you might be working or living with one—take this test and see.

yes   no

_____

1. *Do you get up early, no matter how late you go to bed?*
As one management consultant confessed, "I'd get home and work until [about] 2 a.m. and then get up at 5 a.m. and think, 'Gee, aren't I terrific!'"

_____

2. *If you are eating lunch alone, do you read or work while you eat?*
Robert Moses, New York's long-time Parks Commissioner, reportedly considered lunches a bore and a bother because he couldn't bear to interrupt work. He used a large table as a desk so lunch could be served right there.

_____

3. *Do you make daily lists of things to do?*
Ever-present appointment books and cluttered calendars are a hallmark of workaholics. Indeed, their main way of wasting time, admits Dr. Elizabeth Whelan, a Harvard University epidemiologist, may be looking for lost lists!

_____

4. *Do you find it difficult to "do nothing?"*
It was claimed that David Mahoney, the handsome, hard-working chairman of Norton Simon, Inc., abandoned transcendental meditation because he found it impossible to sit still for 20 minutes.

_____

5. *Are you energetic and competitive?*
President Johnson once asked Doris Kearns, then a White House Fellow, if she were energetic. Kearns replied, "I hear you need only five hours of sleep, but I need only four so it stands to reason that I've got even more energy than you."

_____

6. *Do you work on weekends and holidays?*
In *Working,* author Studs Terkel related that the president of a Chicago radio station confessed that he regularly works in his home on weekends. But, he added, "when I do this on holidays, like Christmas, New Year's, and Thanksgiving, I have to sneak a bit so the family doesn't know what I'm doing."

_____

7. *Can you work anytime and anywhere?*
Two associates at Cravath, Swaine and Moore, one of Manhattan's most prestigious law firms, were said to have bet about who could bill the most hours in a day. One worked around the clock, billed 24 hours and felt assured of victory. His competitor, however, having flown to California in the course of the day, worked on the plane and billed 27.

(continued)

Horner (1969) was a pioneer in the study of fear and success in women. She gave college students one sentence and asked them to complete an essay. Male students were given the sentence: "After first-term finals, John finds himself at the top of his medical school class." Female students were given the same sentence, with the name "Ann" substituted for "John." The men had a positive attitude toward "John." Only about 10 percent of the male students had any negative comments. Interestingly, almost two-thirds of the women had negative attitudes toward "Ann." They described her as either unpopular and rejected or a guilty cheat or a hoax. Studies by Maccoby and Jacklin (1974) and Monahan and Shaver (1974) have supported Horner's findings.

Although fear of competition had been more common among women, more recent studies have found that men are also becoming susceptible. Pike and Kahill (1983) used Horner's descriptions of John and Ann and found that male physicians showed a higher fear of competition than did female physicians. Many men feel insecure about achieving at the expense of personal friendships and health. As our culture permits more diverse roles for males and females, their motivations are becoming more similar. The changing roles of men and women are discussed in more detail in Chapter 12.

Need for Power

Some people constantly try to dominate and control others. They are motivated by a *need for power*. People with a strong need for power tend to argue and dominate conversations. Competitive sports like tennis are popular with them.

power need Motivation to dominate and rule others

They also <u>accumulate</u> such <u>prestige</u> symbols as gold and platinum credit cards and expensive cars. If they cannot demonstrate their power, they often suffer from chronic high blood pressure and illness (McClelland, 1985).

Checkpoint

Use the following questions to check your understanding of this portion of the chapter. Choose and mark the one correct response to each question.

7. Which of the following describes an individual trying to fulfill a need for love and belongingness?
   a. Joshua always tries to locate a policeman when he walks through a lonely park in the dark.
   b. Jill spends all her spare time reading about people from other cultures.
   c. Nigel is new in town and just joined the local teen club.
   d. Nancy is working nights and weekends to be sure she gets a promotion.

8. What is an affiliation need?
   a. A need to belong
   b. A need to achieve
   c. A physiological need
   d. A curiosity need

9. Assume that you asked two groups of individuals to scrub a floor with a toothbrush. Group A had a high need for social approval and group B had a low need for social approval. Based on the results of the study by Crowne and Marlowe, how would you expect the groups to react?
   a. Both groups would enjoy the task.
   b. Group A would enjoy the task more than group B would.
   c. Group A would enjoy the task less than group B would.
   d. Both groups would refuse to do the task.

10. An advertisement shows a couple in an empty room. No one has showed up at their party because they serve the wrong brand of pretzels. In the next scene they announce that they are switching to a superior brand. Suddenly crowds of people come swarming to their party! To which need is the advertiser appealing?
    a. Physiological
    b. Curiosity
    c. Love and belongingness
    d. Achievement

11. How can esteem and self-esteem needs best be met?
    a. Through achievements
    b. Through affiliation
    c. Through curiosity
    d. Through failures

12. Which of the following families are most likely to have children with a high need for achievement?
    a. The Marsallas, who are extremely protective of their children
    b. The Potters, who encourage their children to be independent
    c. The Bernsteins, who keep their children surrounded by friends
    d. The Murphys, who limit their children's friendships

c   ə.

13. Which of the following factors has the greatest influence in motivating students to achieve in high school?
    a. Fear of not getting a good job
    b. Optimism about getting a good job
    c. Concern about the attitudes of friends
    d. Lack of concern about friends

14. Which of the following individuals could be described as a workaholic?
    a. Bill likes to drink beer when he works.
    b. Todd waits until the night before exams and then crams.
    c. Karen rarely has a meal without studying or making a list at the same time.
    d. Linda prefers to work when there are other people around.

15. Which need is most closely related to the fear of success?
    a. Curiosity
    b. Achievement
    c. Esteem
    d. Love and belonging

Use the Checkpoint Answer Key to verify your responses. If you had any difficulty with a question, carefully reread the text. If you had little or no difficulty answering the questions or have resolved any problems that you might have had, you are ready to continue with the final portion of this chapter.

MASLOW'S HIERARCHY OF NEEDS

Trying to sort and organize every possible need seems like a monstrous task. Yet Abraham Maslow (1970), one of the most important contributors to the field of motivation, managed to classify human needs or motivations into a pyramidlike hierarchy. People progress upward to the top of the pyramid, when they have satisfied each need along the way.

At the base of his pyramid, Maslow placed everyday *physiological needs* required for survival—needs for food, drink, rest, elimination, and so on. On the next level, Maslow put *need for stimulation* and escape from boredom. The need to explore and satisfy curiosity would be included on this second level. *Safety and security needs* follow. The next step up his pyramid is a *need for love and a sense of belonging.* At this fourth level, friendships become important. A move to the upper levels of the hierarchy involves the *need to feel respected by others.* The final level is reached by very few people. It involves carrying out one's total potential. Maslow labeled the top step of his hierarchy *self-actualization.*

self-actualization Highest need on Maslow's hierarchy; need to grow and fulfill potential

Maslow felt that people move up and down this pyramid throughout their lives. Indeed, people can move to different steps or needs on the pyramid within a single day. His pyramid is like a ladder people climb throughout their lives: stepping on each rung to reach the next. Suppose a person is on a high rung. For example, a woman may have progressed to the point where she is looking for approval and self-esteem. Suddenly, a man points a gun in her back. She will abruptly descend the hierarchy to satisfy her need for safety and

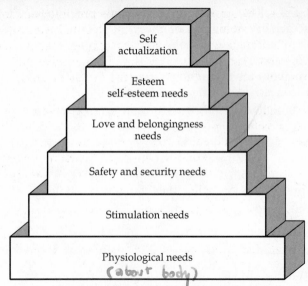

FIGURE 7-4. Maslow's hierarchy of needs.

security. Whenever a rung in the hierarchy "breaks," the person must return down to that level to satisfy the need. However, usually that person's progress back up to the higher level will occur rapidly.

Maslow's hierarchy has met criticism. Some argue that people often experience several needs at the same time. Further, there are wide individual differences. Maslow's hierarchy cannot explain why people will starve or be tortured rather than give up their personal beliefs.

Exercise 7-8

Max has stayed awake for two days and two nights preparing a design project for his drafting class. He wanted to impress his instructor and classmates with his planning ability. Suddenly he no longer cares about his project. He just wants to go to bed. Explain what has happened to Max's motivation, according to Maslow's hierarchy of needs.

_____

_____

_____

You may check your response in the Feedback section.

SELF-ACTUALIZATION

Maslow himself had difficulty finding a precise definition for self-actualization. He felt that all people have some inner talents or abilities that they want to use, or actualize. If all lower needs are met, people can grow and develop by using these abilities. This growth is a continuous process that allows individuals to find self-fulfillment and realize their full potential. Maslow emphasized the importance of individual growth, a goal that is often used in therapy. While individualism is stressed in our culture, this goal is not universal in all cultures. Many societies favor values that emphasize the family or groups (Greenfield, 1992).

In his attempt to identify some characteristics of people who have reached the level of self-actualization, Maslow studied the lives of forty-nine people whom he believed to be self-actualizers. Among those studied were Albert Einstein, Eleanor Roosevelt, Abraham Lincoln, Thomas Jefferson, William James, and Jane Addams. Among the common characteristics of self-actualizers were:

Honesty. They have an ability to be objective and do not show selfish interest.

Creativity. They are spontaneous and natural and enjoy trying new approaches.

Acceptance. They have total acceptance of themselves and are willing to accept others for what they are.

Appreciation. They possess an ability to become fully absorbed, enjoying even simple and basic experiences.

Sense of Humor. They can recognize cleverness and whimsy and will laugh easily.

Sensitivity. They experience a deep feeling of sympathy for other people.

According to Maslow, self-actualization is extremely rare. He screened about 3000 students and found only one self-actualized person. Although self-actualization is slightly more likely among older individuals, it is far from common. Most people never move above the level of esteem. They never reach self-actualization and fully develop their potential.

Slightly more common than self-actualization are what Maslow called *peak experiences.* A peak experience is an extremely brief, momentary sense of total happiness or fulfillment. For a few seconds, or perhaps a minute, there is a sense of self-actualization. This feeling could come from such experiences as watching a spectacular sunset, holding a baby, running a marathon, creating a sculpture, or greeting a returned love. Peak experiences give the same feeling of aliveness and wholeness that self-actualizers encounter. However, the feeling ends abruptly.

peak experience Brief sense of overwhelming total fulfillment, approximating self-actualization

Exercise 7-9

Beth works at a hospital emergency room in an inner city and often encounters patients and families that are frightened and untrusting. She takes time to talk with people even when they are rude. Her supervisor has criticized her for wasting time, but Beth has strong feelings about the physical and emotional pain that patients and their loved ones are feeling. She shows sympathy in the emergency room but also tries to be lighthearted and actually cheers herself along with those she is helping. While she does not overlook rudeness, she tries to focus on positive qualities in people and looks for whimsy. Which qualities of self-actualization is Beth demonstrating?

_____

_____

_____

Please check your answers in the Feedback section.

INTRINSIC AND EXTRINSIC MOTIVATION

intrinsic motivation Performing activities because they are, in themselves, rewarding and enjoyable

Absolutely everything you do is caused by either intrinsic or extrinsic motivation. If you are *intrinsically* motivated, you are performing the activity because you enjoy it. The activity is rewarding in itself. For example, assume you like to watch football games on Sunday afternoons. Just watching the game brings good feelings. A friend who finds football games uninteresting would would not have this intrinsic motivation.

extrinsic motivation Performing activities only for an outside, or external, reward

Now, assume you want this friend to join you. You might have to provide an *extrinsic* motivator. An extrinsic motivator supplies an outside reward. Perhaps you could offer your friend some tasty snacks or concert tickets or cash for watching the game with you. These external rewards would provide extrinsic motivation for sitting through a boring experience.

Although you and your friend would be doing the same thing, namely, watching the football game, your motivations would be different. As a result, you would be likely to watch a football game the following Sunday. However, if there are neither snacks nor concert tickets nor cash, your friend is not likely to be by your side.

Think of some things that motivate you intrinsically. You probably need no external rewards for eating a tasty meal or sleeping in a cozy bed. But what about studying? If you enjoy learning in itself, you are intrinsically motivated. Perhaps there is some subject or activity that holds so much interest for you that you quickly become totally absorbed. Painters and writers often become so engrossed in their work that they lose all sense of time and outside distractions. This total concentration on an activity, psychologists call *flow*. People

flow State of concentration that permits complete absorption in an activity

who achieve a state of flow enjoy their work thoroughly and their performance usually improves. (See Feature 7-4 for more information on flow.)

If you have no intrinsic interest in a course and you are studying strictly to earn credits and an eventual degree or certificate, you are extrinsically motivated. Perhaps you have both types of motivation in studying. If you enjoy learning but also look forward to a good grade, a degree, and maybe a well-paid job, you qualify for both intrinsic and extrinsic motivation.

Psychologists have been interested in the effects of extrinsic motivation on intrinsic motivation. They found that when extrinsic motivation is introduced, intrinsic motivation tends to decrease. Among the evidence are experiments by Deci (1972, 1975). For one experiment, Deci found subjects who enjoyed doing puzzles and were intrinsically motivated. He divided the subjects into two groups. One group was told they would receive $1 for each correct puzzle solution. The second group would receive no external reward. After this experience, he allowed each subject to be alone and choose an activity. The subjects who were to be paid spent far less time on puzzles than did those who were not to be paid. Deci concluded that the money had shifted their interest to external benefits, and as a result, intrinsic motivation was reduced.

Deci (1971) found only one type of external reward that could increase intrinsic motivation. Verbal praise was effective in enhancing intrinsic interest. Although material rewards caused subjects to lose intrinsic motivation, praise and social approval intensified intrinsic attraction.

FEATURE 7-4 PSYCHOLOGY IN THE NEWS

The Power of Concentration

... Milaly Csikszentmihalyi is a man obsessed with happiness. For more than two decades, most recently as a professor of psychology and education at the University of Chicago, he has been trying to identify with some exactness what people mean when they say they are enjoying themselves, how they achieve that enjoyment and how the successful ones manage to keep themselves from falling out of it. More precisely Csikszentmihalyi (pronounced Chick-SENT-me-hi) finds himself focusing on one aspect of human experience that he calls flow.

Flow is a state of concentration that amounts to absolute absorption in an activity. In this state, action flows effortlessly from thought and you feel strong, alert and unself-conscious. Flow is that marvelous feeling that you are in command of the present and performing at the peak of your ability. Time stands still. A split second takes forever. You're a batter, say, and the baseball is coming toward you and it's suspended there, growing larger and larger; your body is in harmony with the moment and you swing, and connect! Dancers know they are in the flow when they seem to transcend themselves and experience a heightened awareness of their bodies. Painters know it when they enter a private dialogue with the canvas. Some surgeons know it; some athletes and writers, too. In fact, research suggests that flow may be a common aspect of human existence. ...

Csikszentmihalyi and his colleagues have found that there is a formula for achieving flow. You must be faced by a challenge—almost any challenge will do—that is not too great for the skills you have to meet it. If the challenge is too great you will be anxious, and anxiety kills flow. If your skills are too great you will be bored, and that is just as bad. The task must also represent an advance, a new complexity. Other activities, such as eating so as not to be hungry, may be satisfying, but they do not produce flow. They do not involve challenge or growth. ...

Societal attitudes may also obstruct flow. Dr. Jean A. Hamilton, a research psychiatrist in Washington, says that our society values extrinsic motivation—the desire for external rewards, such as money or fame—over intrinsic motivation, from which flow arises. ... In Dr. Hamilton's view, because of the emphasis on extrinsic motivation, some people rarely experience pure enjoyment and feel deeply unsatisfied with the lives they have chosen. ...

One approach Dr. Hamilton uses to help patients get in the flow is to find out when they last experienced something resembling total absorption. Was it as a child reading comics, or playing ball? She then tries to encourage whatever ember of flow she finds. ...

Source: Flaste, R. (1989, Oct. 8). The power of concentration. *The New York Times Magazine.*

Exercise 7-10

Ted, a fourteen-year-old boy, always loved to chop and split wood. It gave him a sense of power and strength to see the wood break into segments. Several neighbors noticed how well he performed this task and offered to pay him $5 an hour to prepare wood for their fireplaces. Ted's parents are concerned. He no longer has any interest in cutting wood for them. He will only do it for a fee.

a. From what you have learned about intrinsic and extrinsic motivation, explain why Ted lost much of his interest in chopping and splitting wood.

_____

_____

b. How might Ted's intrinsic interest be restored?

_____

_____

You may compare your answers with those in the Feedback section.

Job Satisfaction

Both intrinsic and extrinsic factors affect job satisfaction. Herzberg (1968) referred to intrinsic motivation as a *growth factor* and extrinics motivation as a *hygiene factor*. According to Herzberg, people can be satisfied in one of these areas and dissatisfied in the other.

The growth aspect of a job provides a person with a sense of achievement and recognition. If the work itself is enjoyable and gratifying, a person will be happy and satisfied. Performing tasks will allow personal growth and a feeling of accomplishment. The person will be intrinsically motivated to work.

The hygiene area involves extrinsic motivators, namely working conditions and benefits. Administration, salary, fringe benefits, and job security are a part of the hygiene factor.

But even if the salary and working conditions are terrific, you can still dislike your job. People who take jobs solely for money or other external rewards can become extremely unhappy. Hygiene factors can keep you from being dissatisfied, but they can never make you like your job. Clearly, money can increase productivity. However, neither money nor any other external factor can make you enjoy your work and feel satisfied. Any happiness attained from hygiene factors is at best temporary. If you were given a substantial raise, you would undoubtedly be thrilled. However, your joy about the raise would only be short-lived. Soon you would be looking for another raise.

Since hygiene and other external factors can bring only brief and fleeting satisfaction, psychologists have focused most of their attention on growth and other intrinsic motivation. They have investigated ways to improve morale and job satisfaction through job enrichment. Job enrichment implies increasing responsibility and freedom and allowing more variety.

One type of enrichment that is gaining popularity is *flex-time*. Each em-

flex-time Program that permits employees to schedule their own hours of work

ployee is permitted to work hours that fit in with their tasks and projects, as well as with other needs. Employees are responsible for writing their own schedules. For example, if a particular job requires working late on Monday night, a person could choose to sleep late one morning or leave early on Friday. Four-day work weeks are as feasible as six-day work weeks. Workers may decide when they prefer to do their jobs and work at a time when they are most motivated.

Another form of enrichment was tried at a Volvo automobile plant some years ago. Each person at the plant was given added responsibilities. Their jobs were made more diverse, and they were permitted to make more decisions. Gyllenhammer (1977) found that this approach not only improved morale but also increased productivity. Currently, five Volvo plants have adopted this type of job enrichment.

Management by objectives (MBO) is undoubtedly the most famous of the many attempts at job enrichment. MBO is a system that requires the employer to set goals. Each employee then decides on personal strategies or objectives to help reach the goals. In a sense, employees design their own jobs. They are then held individually responsible for accomplishing their own goals.

management by objectives (MBO) System that requires managers to set goals and employees to develop their own strategies to accomplish the goals

For example, assume that a woman works for a community recreation center. Her employer sets a goal of attracting more teenagers to the center. The woman may set any objectives she wishes to help reach her employer's goal. Her list of objectives could include booking a rock concert, scheduling teen dances and hayrides, or creating a competitive sports program. Since she is selecting her own strategies, presumably her intrinsic motivation for their ac-

"Hopefully maintenance will take the hint and turn the heat up a notch."

FIGURE 7-5. Although these workers will be pleased when the office is heated, a comfortable temperature alone will not make them like their work.

complishment will be increased. She has a greater sense of responsibility for achieving her own objectives.

Although MBO makes sense as a theory, it is not always an effective way to increase motivation and growth. First, not all jobs are conducive to this approach. How can tollbooth workers or short-order cooks possibly set their own objectives? In addition, MBO has sometimes created problems. Both the employer and the employee must fully understand each other. This often requires exceptional communication skills. If there is any misunderstanding, pressures and tension will usually result.

A recent investigation of work motivation (Katzell and Thompson, 1990) uncovered a need for employers to pay more attention to individual differences. Employers need to develop motivational practices that are suited to workers who are diverse in terms of ethnic background, culture, age, and gender. As workers place more emphasis on their own self-actualization and flow, employers will face new challenges.

Exercise 7-11

Imagine you are job hunting. You want to be certain you will be satisfied with both the hygiene and growth aspects of your new job. List three hygiene and three growth conditions that would help you feel satisfied with the job.

Hygiene   **Growth**

_____   _____

_____   _____

_____   _____

You may check your lists in the Feedback section.

Opposing Incentives

Sometimes incentives can pull you in opposite directions. You like the hours and location of one job but prefer the salary of another. The stronger incentive will usually pull you.

Dieting is an example of opposing incentives. On the one hand you are pulled by the appeal of food, and on the other hand you are drawn toward a slimmer appearance. Usually the food is a stronger incentive and the diet fails. Some recent research has shown that spouses can help strengthen incentives toward a slimmer appearance by lending their encouragement and support.

But according to Stuart and Davis (1972) some husbands have difficulty helping their wives lose weight. Stuart studied a group of women who had difficulty losing weight. He found their husbands were strengthening the food incentive. Although they knew their wives were trying to diet, they constantly tempted them with appealing refreshments. The men had a variety of reasons for wanting to keep their wives obese. Some liked to use their wives' weight as a tactic in arguments, calling their wives "fat slobs." Others used their wives' fatness as an excuse for extramarital affairs. Still others preferred to keep their wives unattractive, fearing that slimmer wives might become unfaithful. Clearly, none of these men could encourage their wives' dieting and provide the required incentives.

Next time you diet, plan to keep your kitchen free of food incentives. If you can find a mate who will encourage slimness, you will be more likely to lose weight!

Checkpoint

Use the folowing questions to check your understanding of this final portion of the chapter. Indicate whether each statement is true or false.

16. _____ According to Maslow, higher needs must be met before lower needs are.

17. _____ Maslow's hierarchy cannot explain some human behaviors.

18. _____ Most people self-actualize by the time they reach college.

19. _____ People who reach the level of self-actualization can enjoy very simple experiences.

20. _____ Peak experiences are usually brief.

21. _____ An artist who is paid for his paintings is likely to have increased intrinsic motivation.

22. _____ Social approval tends to diminish intrinsic motivation.

23. _____ An improvement in health benefits will make the hygiene aspect of a job more satisfying.

24. _____ If the hygiene aspect of a job is satisfying, you will have increased intrinsic motivation at work.

25. _____ Job enrichment helps to improve intrinsic motivation and growth.

26. _____ Management by objectives is a form of job enrichment.

27. _____ Employee morale will improve if the employer makes more decisions.

Check your responses against the Checkpoint Answer Key at the end of the chapter. If you had difficulty with any question, reread the text. If you had little or no difficulty answering questions or have resolved problems that you might have had, you are ready to check yourself against the chapter inventory that follows.

CHAPTER INVENTORY

Use this list of objectives as a review checklist. You should be able to do each of the tasks outlined in the objectives and apply them to everyday examples. If you can, you may feel confident that you have mastered the material in this chapter.

1. Define motivation.
2. Distinguish between conscious and unconscious motivation.
3. Describe the roles of needs and incentives in motivation.
4. Explain why physiological needs must be met.
5. Identify and describe stimulation and safety and security needs.
6. Recognize love and belongingness as affiliation needs and provide examples.
7. Specify how advertisers exploit the need for love and belongingness.
8. Distinguish between the characteristics of individuals with high and low needs to achieve.
9. Describe the characteristics of workaholism.
10. Describe the need for power.
11. Explain how fear of success can interfere with achievement.
12. Identify the order of the steps on Maslow's hierarchy of needs.
13. Explain the relationship between Maslow's hierarchy of needs and individual motivation.
14. List and explain the characteristics of individuals who have reached self-actualization.
15. Distinguish between intrinsic and extrinsic motivation, and describe their relationship.
16. Describe how growth and hygiene factors affect job satisfaction.
17. Identify three types of job enrichment.
18. Define incentive and provide one example of how incentives affect motivation in dieting.

Feedback

The correct answers to the exercises follow. If you did not answer an exercise correctly, review the preceding pages and return to the exercise to correctly complete it.

7-1. a. Conscious
   b. Unconscious
   c. Unconscious
   d. Conscious

7-2. You were "pushed" to buy the first two glasses because you had been deprived of fluid and were motivated by your thirst need. You were "pulled" to ask for the third glass of lemonade by the incentive of pleasing the children.

7-3. A child who is undernourished will be preoccupied with a need for food.

7-4. Edgar is a type t. There is little or no risk or excitement in watching a plant. Edgar seems to enjoy certainty and stability.

7-5. Every sentence described affiliation and approval needs and should have been checked.

7-6. a. High achiever: The carpet would give her a higher status. High achievers are conscious of status.
   b. High achiever: High achievers enjoy getting positive feedback from others.

   c. Low achiever: A high achiever would prefer an activity that reflected achievement.

   d. Low achiever: High achievers are motivated more by a sense of accomplishment than they are by money.

   e. High achiever: High achievers like to improve their personal skills.

   f. Low achiever: High achievers prefer to be independent and set their own goals.

   g. Low achiever: Low achievers usually have overprotective parents.

   h. Low achiever: Low achievers prefer games of chance to games of skill.

   i. High achiever: Higher achievers worry that not doing well in school will affect their employment chances.

7-7. a. Workaholics are successful, enjoy themselves, and are respected.

   b. It is difficult to socialize with workaholics.

7-8. Max had been working at the esteem, self-esteem level. A lower need arose. Max fell back to his physiological need for sleep.

7-9. Honesty (unselfish interest), acceptance (of others in spite of their rudeness), appreciation (enjoys simple experiences), sense of humor, sensitivity.

7-10. a. Ted had an intrinsic motivation to chop wood. When external rewards (extrinsic motivation) in the form of money were introduced, Ted's intrinsic motivation diminished. Extrinsic motivation tends to diminish intrinsic motivation.

   b. If Ted is not paid for chopping and splitting wood but is praised for his fine work, his intrinsic motivation might be restored.

7-11.

Hygiene	Growth
Good administration	Flex-time
Good salary and fringe benefits	A job with responsibility
Good job security	Management by objectives

Checkpoint Answer Key

   1. b; 2. d; 3. a; 4. b; 5. b; 6. c; 7. c; 8. a; 9. b; 10. c; 11. a; 12. b; 13. a; 14. c; 15. d; 16. false; 17. true; 18. false; 19. true; 20. true; 21. false; 22. false; 23. true; 24. false; 25. true; 26. true; 27. false.

Understanding Emotions

The main thing in life is not to be afraid to be
human.
—PABLO CASALS

Have you ever played a game with a computer and felt like a complete loser? Whether you were losing a game of soccer, football, or chess—or were simply not able to follow computer-generated notes—you might have found yourself becoming angry and frustrated. Undoubtedly you have also experienced a few wins over a computer. Recall the sense of satisfaction and glee you felt. Your opponent, the computer, can never sense or feel these emotions.

Emotions are one area where humans are clearly superior to machines. But, unfortunately, emotions are not always helpful; sometimes they can interfere with intellectual abilities. When you felt upset about losing to a computer, you might have been dwelling on your feelings rather than on better strategies for winning. Similarly, you might have felt so proud of your victories that your concentration was broken. In this chapter you will learn ways to improve your understanding, expression, and handling of emotions.

Emotions separate humans from machines. However, it is extremely difficult to define and measure specific human emotions. Most psychologists rely on self-reports and bodily, facial, and physiological changes to estimate likely emotions. In this chapter you will learn how each of these measures is used. You will also become acquainted with some basic human emotions: anger, fear, and joy. Attention will be focused on conflicts that lead to frustration and on the stress that emotions can cause.

WHAT ARE EMOTIONS?

Emotions are internal feelings that arouse people to act or to change within themselves. These feelings can be pleasant, unpleasant, or mixed. Emotions are rarely pure. Consider the case of a father waiting for his fifteen-year-old daughter to come home from a Saturday-night party. The clock strikes 1 A.M. The father paces the floor. The phone rings. It is his daughter. She announces she is about to leave the party and will be home in twenty minutes. This poor father is feeling a variety of emotions. He is pleased that his daughter was considerate and called him. He is relieved that she is safe. But he is also angry that he is being deprived of his sleep because of her late hours. It is likely he also has some concerns and fears about her trip home. Is the driver of her car sober? Are the other drivers on the road lucid enough to be cautious? Perhaps he becomes angry with himself for worrying about her. It would be difficult to describe the many emotions he is experiencing. Most psychologists would say he is feeling a form of all three of the basic emotions: joy, anger, and fear.

emotion Feeling that arouses an individual to act or change

Identifying this man's emotions was simplified because his situation was described. But suppose you stopped in to visit him without knowing his daughter was out. (Admittedly, 1 A.M. would be a strange hour for a casual visit!) How could you assess his emotions? You might ask him to describe how he felt. But his feelings were so mixed, he might have trouble sorting and recognizing each of them. And even if he were able to separate his different emotions, he might prefer not to disclose one or more of them to you.

As an alternative you could choose to observe him. Perhaps you could detect a worried expression or a face flushed with anger. But could you be certain that anger was causing the flushing? Maybe his flushing results from embarrassment. It is 1 A.M. and he may feel awkward if you learn that his daughter is still out. You watch him pace the floor. But again you cannot be certain whether he is angry, fearful, or joyfully exercising. Observation provides awareness that emotions are being experienced, but we need additional information before we can determine precisely which emotions.

So you open a bag filled with stethoscopes, blood-pressure gauges, and an assortment of other devices that measure physiological changes. But all you learn is that indeed he is experiencing physiological changes. You conclude that he is feeling some intense emotions. But which emotions and how intense?

Clearly the techniques currently available for measuring and determining emotions are less than adequate. However, each can in some way help give a better understanding of the emotional changes humans experience.

Exercise 8-1

Based on the example of the father awaiting his daughter, identify three methods used to infer types of emotions being experienced. Explain one shortcoming of each method.

a. _____

_____

b. _____

_____

c. _____

_____

Check your answers in the Feedback section.

Subjective Reports of Emotions

Suppose a psychologist approached you and asked you to describe your present emotions. Do you feel happy? Fearful? Guilty? Embarrassed? Annoyed? None of these terms describing emotions has a clear or precise definition. All require subjective opinions. Your ideas of happiness may differ widely from the ideas of the person next to you. There are significant individual differences in the interpretation of personal emotions.

If you are like most people, you feel inhibited about discussing emotions openly with a stranger. You could probably best assist the psychologist by describing some recent events in your life and your feelings about them. You may have been experiencing some subtle emotions that are difficult to recognize. Knowledge of a situation often aids in surmising emotions. It is easy to imagine the emotions of a person walking into a surprise party or of someone being handed back a paper graded A. Similarly, psychologists can infer emotions when events are described.

sensitivity training
Form of group therapy that requires total honesty and trust among members

One technique that has been used to help people recognize and express their emotions is *sensitivity training,* which is usually done in groups of ten to twenty people. A psychologist or trainer is with the group but does not lead them.

According to Carl Rogers (1970), the group goes through several stages. Initially the group expects the trainer to lead them. When they realize the trainer is not directing their session, there is a general sense of confusion. Group members feel frustrated and annoyed. They resist exposing their own feelings. Soon one or two individuals begin to express past feelings, perhaps old arguments with close friends or their problems in choosing a college. Next members begin to express their unhappiness with the lack of structure and direction within the group. They begin to attack each other and make negative remarks. Rogers believes these negative comments are a way of testing the reactions of other members of the group. Once it is established that the group can accept true feelings, the members develop a trusting attitude. Finally, deeper emotions are described. The atmosphere becomes open, and personal defenses are broken down. Members are expected to express their feelings honestly. They confront anyone who is dishonest or hides behind a mask.

Clearly, these groups provide an intense emotional exchange. Those who have benefited from the sessions claim a greater awareness of their own emotions, as well as an increased sensitivity to the feelings of other people. But although some persons profit from the experience, others remain unaffected. Unfortunately, still others may be harmed. Total openness can be painful, particularly when group members are severely critical. Hartley et al. (1976) studied the effects of participating in sensitivity training sessions. The emotional damage rate ranged from less than 1 percent to almost half the group!

Exercise 8-2

Recently, Lucy was dismissed from college for poor grades. Yesterday she lost her job as a salesclerk because a customer complained about her attitude. Lucy is upset and confused about her emotions. She is considering signing up for a sensitivity training session with a local psychologist.

a. How might Lucy benefit from the session? _____

_____

_____

b. Why might Lucy become further upset by the session? _____

_____

_____

You may compare your responses with those in the Feedback section.

Observing Facial Expressions and Body Language

Studies of facial expressions date back over 100 years. Early studies focused on muscle changes and were performed by anatomists rather than psychologists. Anatomists focus on structural and physical changes rather than emotions. Because of the extensive research of Paul Ekman and his colleagues (Ekman, 1980, 1982, 1992, 1993; Ekman and Friesen, 1978; Ekman et al., 1980), psychologists have been directing more attention to facial expressions as a measure of emotion.

Ekman developed a system for mapping facial muscle changes, called *Facial Action Coding System*, or FACS. He then used this system to identify facial changes that people can use to express emotions. He found more than 7000 possible combinations of muscle changes. But most of these changes were not associated with any specific emotion. Ekman and his colleague, Friesen, practiced in front of mirrors and learned to control their own facial muscles. This gave them an awareness of precise muscle changes that accompany different emotions. They then developed a guide for using their FACS system to identify each emotion.

Ekman points out the difference between *spontaneous* and *deliberate* changes in facial expressions. Spontaneous changes occur immediately and are not planned. You hear a hysterically funny joke and break into a wide grin. On the other hand, actors and actresses must learn to use facial changes and gestures to express emotions. Their actions are deliberate. Have you ever pretended to be surprised at a gift you really expected? To show surprise, you raised your eyebrows, wrinkled your forehead, and opened your eyes and mouth widely.

You may have observed in the past others who expressed surprise spontaneously, or you may have recalled your facial changes from a previous experience. You deliberately imitated a facial expression. Paul Ekman and his colleagues (1988) found some subtle differences between spontaneous and deliberate facial expressions. Smiles that result from actual joy (see Figure 8-1, left) include the outer muscles that surround the eyes. Smiles used to hide negative emotions tend to involve muscles around the lips and eyes that are usually linked to disgust (see Figure 8-1, right). Trying to camouflage true feelings results in a different use of facial muscles.

But can we use facial expressions to determine whether people are lying? One psychologist has proposed that those who can catch liars are probably checking facial expressions even though they are totally unaware of their strategy (See Feature 8-1). Undoubtedly future research will investigate this possibility.

Psychologists are also interested in distinguishing between expressions of emotion common to all people and those that vary from culture to culture. Most of the evidence suggests that facial expressions are universal. Smiles, tightened lips, and frowns express the same emotions in New York, Hong Kong, and Santiago. However, the frequency and intensity of use of these expressions vary according to culture. According to Morris et al. (1979), culture has a stronger influence on body language than it does on facial expressions. Body language is a way of showing feelings without using words. Waving a fist, applauding, kissing, and embracing are examples of body language. Most body language is cultural and varies from one society to the next. For example, clapping hands means appreciation and applause in one culture and worry and anxiety in another.

Some societies discourage open displays of emotions, particularly unpleasant ones. A person who shows sadness or anger is not respected. The stories and novels in these cultures usually relate tales of heroes and heroines who can hold in emotions with exceptional control. Other groups expect emotions to be expressed openly. They use more gestures, movements, and voice changes. Psychologists have found that body language as a method of expressing emotions is usually similar within families. Some families tend to show emotional outbursts. They jump up and down, cheer loudly at games, and wave their arms frantically when angry. Others are more stoic: They applaud politely and hold in their anger. One study found that married couples grow to look alike as a result of using similar facial expressions (Hall, 1987).

Think about the methods members of your family use to express emotions. Do you use some of the same body language?

FIGURE 8-1. (Picture credit: Paul Ekman)

Mr. Clarke, a senior personnel manager, is interested in hiring someone for a dangerous international job. He is interviewing people from several different countries. As he describes the frightening aspects of the assignment, he watches their facial expressions. (He is an expert at FACS.) Only those applicants who show no signs of fear in the use of their facial muscles are considered for the job.

His assistant, Mr. Lewis, prefers to focus on body language. He notices whether the candidates pace the floor, shift their weight from foot to foot, or twiddle their thumbs as the dangerous job is described.

a. Whose method do you prefer, Mr. Clarke's or Mr. Lewis's? _____

   Why? _____

   _____

b. What is the weakness of both techniques? _____

   _____

   _____

Compare your responses to those in the Feedback section.

FEATURE 8-1 PSYCHOLOGY IN THE NEWS

To Catch a Liar . . .

Numerous laboratory studies have found that people often cannot see through the lies of others. And don't expect a "how-to" manual for aspiring deception detectives any time soon. A new study indicates that the best lie catchers display no awareness of their rare ability or the strategies they use to ferret out fabricators.

"We don't know what makes a person a good lie catcher," says Mark G. Frank of the University of California, San Francisco, who directed the study. "No personality study has yet been linked to this ability."

Frank's team videotaped 20 male college students telling lies to an experimenter described to them as an expert in lie detection. Volunteers first devised an alibi for a mock theft of $50 left in the laboratory and then offered an opinion about a controversial social issue, such as capital punishment, either consistent or contrary to their actual sentiments.

A total of 79 male and female college students carefully perused the videos, and most of them correctly identified liars about half the time, a rate that can be achieved by guessing, Frank asserts. But a few participants nearly always separated liars from truth tellers. Those who excelled at detecting lies about the mock theft proved equally adept at separating true from false opinions. However, they reported no awareness of their skill and could think of no specific reasons for their success at sniffing out liars.

Good lie catchers may track facial expressions and other nonverbal signals with particular ease, Frank proposes. Studies are now underway to investigate this possibility. . . .

Source: Bower, B. (1992, August 29). To catch a liar . . . *Science News.*

Culture has a strong influence on how people express their emotions.

Physiological Changes with Emotion

None other than Hippocrates, the father of modern medicine, once wrote, "It is more important to know what kind of person has a disease, than to know what kind of a disease a person has." Hippocrates recognized that emotional factors are crucial to the understanding of internal bodily changes. For many years, as modern medicine progressed, Hippocrates' ideas were lost. There was a stricter emphasis on medical, surgical, and technological methods. However, current estimates suggest that approximately 80 percent of all physiological and medical problems have emotional components. Hippocrates had a valid point!

Undoubtedly, you are aware of some physiological changes that accompany your own emotions. Think of how your body reacts when you experience stress. Stress can be caused by an overabundance of any emotion. Although fear and anger are most commonly associated with stress, excessive joy can likewise be a cause.

Perhaps you have had butterflies in your stomach, a dryness in your mouth, or a pounding heart. All three are common reactions to stress. Other body reactions that you may have noticed in intense emotion include faster breathing, sweating, facial flushing, dilation of eye pupils, and a tightening of muscles. There are also other changes that can only be measured by technical instruments. In times of stress there are many increases in bodily functions. Blood pressure, heart rate, the amount of blood discharged to muscles, the rate and depth of breathing, the flow of adrenalin, and the electric resistance of the skin all increase.

Recent research has attempted to determine whether each different emotion can produce a specific or unique change. Levinson (1992) found that negative emotions such as anger, fear, and sadness produced more intense physical changes than did positive emotions. Levinson noted this same pattern among males and females, young and old subjects, and people of western and non-western cultures. Scientists are curious about which areas of the brain are involved in specific emotions. Studies of brain-damaged individuals suggest that the left side of the brain is involved in positive emotions, like joy, and the right side handles the negative emotions of fear and anger (Davidson, 1992). The article excerpt in Feature 8-2 reports that the right frontal lobes have more electrical activity in times of sadness and the left frontal lobes have increased electrical activity when happiness is experienced. Figure 8-2 illustrates the location of these areas of the brain.

Although the results of current studies indicate that separate hemispheres of the brain are activated for positive and negative emotions, we still cannot determine which specific emotion is being experienced. With constant technical advances scientists are now able to focus on distinguishing the brain activity for each emotion and examining the accompanying biochemical changes (Baum et al., 1992).

Exercise 8-4

Respond to the questions below regarding the person in Figure 8-3.

a. Assuming Mr. Herkimer is experiencing some intense emotions, list three reactions his body may be encountering.

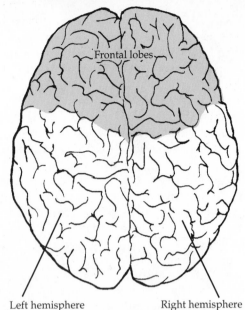

Left hemisphere   Right hemisphere

FIGURE 8-2. Frontal lobes of the right and left hemispheres of the brain.

FEATURE 8-2 PSYCHOLOGY IN THE NEWS

Where Emotions Come From

Twenty years ago, much was made of reports that the brain's left and right hemispheres seemed to "specialize" in different types of thinking, though media accounts of the "right brain/left brain" division were greatly oversimplified. Now a growing body of work suggests that the two sides of the brain may play distinct emotional roles, perhaps because such a division of labor is more efficient. Neurologists have known for many years that stroke patients whose right hemispheres have been damaged have trouble both expressing emotions and perceiving the emotional signals of others. They will understand the statement, "I am angry," for example, but fail to detect the speaker's injured tone or the angry expression on his face. . . .

The brain's right and left hemispheres may divide negative and positive emotions as well. When subjects report feeling emotions such as fear and disgust, their right frontal lobes show increased electrical activity, according to studies by Richard Davidson at the University of Wisconsin

and Donald Tucker at the University of Oregon. Sadness seems to diminish activity in the left frontal lobe as measured by an electroencephalogram (EEG), while certain positive emotions like happiness and amusement increase it.

Right and left asymmetries may even prove to be a marker of differences in overall temperament. In a series of studies Davidson and his colleagues have found that infants more prone to distress when separated from their mothers showed increased activity in the right frontal lobe, as do people with a more pessimistic outlook. People who at some point in their lives have been clinically depressed show increased left frontal lobe activity compared with subjects who have never been depressed. . . .

Source: Goode, E. E., with Schrof, J. M. & Burke, S. (1991, June 24). Where emotions come from. *U.S. News & World Report,* 54-60, 62.

"Have a seat, Mr. Herkimer, and I'll get your file."

FIGURE 8-3.

b. Which portion of his brain is probably showing increased electrical activity?

Please check your responses in the Feedback section.

The Pros and Cons of Physical Responses to Emotions

Generally your body's response to stress helps you. With the many increases in functioning, you are better prepared for emergencies. Because of increases in blood flow and adrenalin, you have additional strength. You can run faster and have more energy. You have probably heard tales of little old ladies who were able to lift cars in order to save loved ones. Perhaps you have even had a burst of strength yourself when you felt emotional stress. A drowning person often finds additional stamina and manages to swim. Similarly, athletes often surpass all of their previous achievements in an important contest. They feel intense emotion when the big event occurs. Remember the Olympic hockey game in 1980? No one imagined the American team had a chance of winning!

Unfortunately, physiological reactions that accompany emotions do not always cause pleasant results. Continuous stress can make physical problems more likely. Dry coughs, ulcers, headaches, high blood pressure, strokes, and heart attacks can result from prolonged physiological changes. In studying voodoo deaths, Seligman (1974) reported that people can die from fear. A person who believes a voodoo threat will undoubtedly experience intense fear. At times of intense fear, heart rate increases rapidly. After a prolonged increase in rate, the heart begins to compensate by slowing down. Occasionally the heart overcompensates, slowing down to a halt, causing death.

Exercise 8-5

In your own words, describe one example of how emotions can cause physical changes that are helpful and two examples of changes that are harmful.

a. Helpful: _____

_____

b. Harmful: _____

_____

You may compare your examples to those in the Feedback section.

Measuring Physical Changes in Emotion

polygraph Instrument commonly known as a lie detector that measures changes in heart beat, blood pressure, breathing, digestive activity, and electric resistance on the skin surface

The best-known device for measuring physical changes resulting from emotions is the *polygraph,* more commonly known as a lie detector because it is frequently used to check truthfulness. The polygraph is a machine that measures heartbeat, blood pressure, breathing, digestive activities, and electric resistance on the surface of the skin. A number of electrode plates are attached to the body of the person being checked. The plates are then connected to a machine that will record physical changes on a printout sheet. The assumption is that lying causes intense emotion. Since intense emotion results in physiological changes, the machine should record a noticeable variation whenever a person lies. Conversely, there should be little or no physiological change when a person is truthful.

Imagine you are hooked up to a polygraph machine. In the usual procedure, you would be asked a number of neutral questions that would not arouse any emotion. Neutral questions might include "What is your name?" or "What did you have for breakfast this morning?" Since these questions do not usually arouse emotions, it would be assumed that your heart rate, blood pressure, and other physiological functions were at their normal levels. These levels would be recorded as your baseline. Next you would be asked critical questions such as, "Were you with Louis the night he was murdered?" or "Where did you hide the stolen car?" Any printout variation from your baseline printout would make the examiner suspicious that you were emotionally aroused.

But does this emotional arousal mean that you are lying? The accuracy of polygraphs as lie detectors has been disputed. Just being strapped to a machine and being questioned can arouse emotions. Also there are immense individual differences in emotional arousal when lying takes place. Some people can lie easily, while others feel intense emotion with even a mild uncertainty. Cheating on polygraphs is not uncommon. Subjects can tense their muscles and dwell on upsetting thoughts when the examiner is asking neutral questions. Since physical stress can provide the same changes as emotional stress, lie detector cheaters can bite the corner of their tongues or press their foot against a nail in their shoe on neutral questions. This will produce a high baseline. When critical questions are asked, little change will be detected. Unfortunately, polygraphs have been wrong and innocent people have been jailed!

Psychologists agree that no single method is effective for measuring emotions. Even the combinations of verbal reports, facial expression, body language, and polygraphs do not always give accurate results. Newer strategies for examining electrical and chemical changes are costly and do not provide clear-cut results. However, if a variety of measures are used, mistakes are less likely.

Checkpoint

Use the following questions to check your understanding of this portion of the chapter. Choose and mark the one correct response to each question.

1. Emotions are feelings that arouse a person. What type of feelings are they?
   a. Internal feelings
   b. Pleasant feelings
   c. Unpleasant feelings
   d. Pure feelings

2. Assume you want to assess the current emotions of another person. The person is giving you a verbal description of present feelings. Which of the following would be most useful in your assessment of the person's emotions?
   a. An understanding of the person's inhibitions
   b. An understanding of the person's frustrations
   c. An understanding of the situation that aroused the emotions
   d. An understanding of the people who were present when the emotion was aroused

3. What is the purpose of sensitivity training?
   a. To permit people to understand the physiological changes that accompany emotions
   b. To help people interpret the facial expressions and body language of others
   c. To allow people to change their own facial expressions by practicing in front of mirrors
   d. To help people understand and express their emotions openly

4. Which of the following is most likely to be affected by a person's cultural experiences?
   a. Facial expression
   b. Body language
   c. Physiological changes
   d. Inner feelings

5. Which of the following gives the best description of the cause of stress?
   a. Fear and anger
   b. Mild feelings of emotion
   c. Intense emotion
   d. Unpleasant experiences

6. Many studies have attempted to associate each emotion with specific physiological changes. What can we conclude from these studies?
   a. Emotions do not produce physiological changes.
   b. All emotions produce identical physiological changes.
   c. Fear is the only emotion that produces physiological changes.
   d. There is some evidence that each emotion may cause specific changes but further study is needed.

7. What happens to your energy level at times of stress?
   a. It remains constant.
   b. It increases.
   c. It decreases.
   d. It decreases then increases.

8. According to Seligman, what is the cause of voodoo deaths?
   a. Inhibitions about expressing emotions
   b. Lack of understanding of facial expression
   c. Inappropriate body language
   d. Bodily reactions to fear

9. What is the purpose of a polygraph machine?
   a. To determine which emotion a person is experiencing
   b. To determine why a person is lying
   c. To measure physiological changes
   d. To determine whether a person has criminal tendencies

10. Why is the polygraph not always an effective lie detector?
    a. It is difficult to measure heart rate and blood pressure.
    b. Many intense emotions are not accompanied by physiological changes.
    c. Emotions can be aroused for reasons other than lying.
    d. The machine cannot measure physiological changes.

11. What is the best method for measuring emotions?
    a. Verbal reports
    b. Facial expression and body language
    c. Polygraphs
    d. A combination of the above

Use the Checkpoint Answer Key to verify your responses. If you had any difficulty with a question, carefully reread the text. If you had little or no difficulty answering the questions or have resolved any difficulty you might have had, you are ready to continue with the next portion of this chapter.

TYPES OF EMOTIONS

Many psychologists believe there are only three basic emotions: anger, fear, and joy. All other emotions are considered variations on one or more of these three emotions. For example, hatred, rage, and hostility are forms of anger. Jealousy and guilt are based on fear. Love and happiness are fundamentally feelings of joy. Sadness is likely to be a combination of fear and anger.

Have you ever wondered why you become angry or fearful or joyful?

Anger, joy, and fear have separate and distinct causes. After studying the causes of each of these three basic emotions, you will look at possible ways to handle and control them.

Anger

Anger is indeed an unpleasant emotion. Think of the last time you felt angry with yourself or with someone else. Anger usually is aroused by *frustration* associated with a situation that is beyond your control. For example, assume you had a long, hard day at work and are anxious to get home at a reasonable hour. Your car engine will not turn over. You have no idea what is wrong, and there is nothing you can do about it. You feel frustrated and your frustration leads to anger. Frustration occurs whenever you cannot reach a desired goal. Psychologists have found that frustration often results in some form of anger or resentment. If you become irritated and kick the car, your behavior is fairly normal.

frustration Feeling that results whenever you cannot reach a desired goal

There are many possible reasons why you cannot reach a desired goal. Sometimes you simply lack the ability. For example, in the case of your car failing to start, you were unable to diagnose the problem and correct it. In addition to feeling irritation toward the car, you may have been annoyed with yourself for not learning ways to troubleshoot engine problems. Often people aspire to goals far beyond their abilities. A shy man may wish to be a super-salesman or a woman with limited finances and intelligence may wish to become a nuclear physicist.

Frustration can also result from confusion about goals. Sometimes people feel pulls in more than one direction. Kurt Lewin (1935) specified three types of goal confusion or conflict that people experience. Each of these three types of conflicts leads to a feeling of frustration.

Approach-Approach Conflicts. Of the three types of conflicts, these are the least frustrating. In an *approach-approach conflict* there are two desirable

approach-approach conflict Conflict that results from choosing between two desirable goals

FIGURE 8-4. Approach-approach conflict.

goals. But you cannot possibly reach both of them at the same time. Maybe there are two good parties in different parts of town at the exact same time on the same night. You must miss one, but which one? Or assume a rich aunt hands you $70,000 to buy yourself a new car. Both a Mercedes and a Porsche look appealing. You must make a choice, but indeed it is a pleasant dilemma. In an approach-approach conflict, you always win, even if you must lose another appealing alternative. As a result, approach-approach conflicts are only mildly frustrating.

Avoidance-Avoidance Conflicts. These are the most frustrating of the three types of conflicts. You must choose between two undesirable goals. Did your mother ever tell you to clean your messy closet or go to bed? Assuming you disliked cleaning closets and were not tired, you experienced an *avoidance-avoidance conflict*. The thought of wasting hours cleaning a cluttered closet was dreadful, but the notion of suffering hours of boredom was also unappealing. The usual reaction to an avoidance-avoidance conflict is to attempt to escape. Perhaps you threatened to run away from home. When no escape is possible, facing the conflict is inevitable. The result is being forced to make an unpleasant choice. The choice is accompanied by intense frustration and anger.

Approach-Avoidance Conflicts. These are the most common of the three types of conflicts. Usually a goal has both positive and negative aspects. Eating a piece of chocolate fudge will provide a delicious taste. But it will also cause tooth decay and, perhaps, unwanted pounds. Studying for an exam will result in a better grade, but it will require an evening away from friends.

A student choosing a college is often involved in a complicated *approach-avoidance conflict*. Perhaps the college with the best program is expensive or a long way from home. A nearby college is good but only has a few specialized

avoidance-avoidance conflict Conflict that results from being forced to choose between two undesirable goals

approach-avoidance conflict Conflict that results from weighing the positive and negative aspects of a single goal

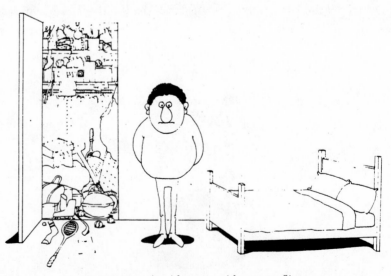

FIGURE 8-5. Avoidance-avoidance conflict.

courses. On the other hand, the student could skip college and take a full-time job. The job will provide more money now, but future income will be limited. When the positive and negative aspects of more than one goal are judged, a multiple approach-avoidance is faced. Most people constantly face multiple approach-avoidance conflicts. Beginning with deciding what to wear and choosing a breakfast, you are repeatedly weighing the pros and cons of your alternatives. However, clothing and breakfast choices rarely cause severe frustration. Major decisions on colleges, jobs, marriages, and divorces create far more anxiety.

In approach-avoidance conflicts, the approach tendency is usually stronger at first. Consider a woman who accepts a leading role in a play. She looks forward to the applause on opening night and has an approach tendency. But she knows she feels nervous when performing before groups and has a slight feeling of avoidance. As the goal comes closer, the avoidance tendency increases. By opening night she has butterflies in her stomach and intense stage fright. Think about some of your own approach-avoidance conflicts. Have you ever backed out of an event at the last minute because of an increasing avoidance tendency?

FIGURE 8-6. Approach-avoidance conflict.

Exercise 8-6

Indicate whether each of the following persons is experiencing an approach-approach conflict, an avoidance-avoidance conflict, or an approach-avoidance conflict.

a. Kim wants to take roller-blading lessons but is afraid she will fall and make a fool of herself. _____

b. Mike cannot decide whether to order a delicious, juicy steak or luscious lobster Newburg. _____

c. Josh hates going to Spanish class but will fail the course if he cuts another class. _____

d. Juan is having trouble deciding whether to vacation at a mountain resort or at the ocean. _____

e. Esther is having fun at the beach but is afraid she will suffer a severe sunburn if she remains much longer. _____

f. Inez is looking forward to entertaining her friends at a dinner party but dreads having to cook for an entire day. _____

Exercise 8-7

Using the information from Exercise 8-6, indicate:

a. Which individual will probably experience the most frustration and anger?

_____

b. Which persons will probably feel the least frustration and anger? _____

_____

Turn to the Feedback section to check your answers.

Anger and Aggression

Regardless of the type of conflict, the outcome is frustration. Reactions to frustration differ, and some people can tolerate more frustration than others can. Sometimes escape is attempted, but often anger results. People use a variety of methods to express their anger, with *aggression* being one of the most common means. Aggression includes a wide range of behaviors, from petty quarreling to extreme physical violence. The goal in aggression is to either verbally or physically hurt or destroy another person or object.

There are immense differences in aggressive tendencies among people. Speilberger (1992) pointed out that some people express their anger immediately by arguing and slamming doors. Others just boil inside themselves but do not show their feelings. Some people just withdraw from situations when they sense frustration and anger. Psychologists differ in their explanations of

aggression Behavior that hurts or destroys another person, either verbally or physically, or both

why such variations occur. Whether aggressive tendencies are inherited or learned remains a controversial issue. However, psychologists are examining both physiological and learning explanations.

Recent research has found that people who have neurological or brain impairments show more frequent aggression. Causes of this impairment could be genetics, brain damage from accidents or fights, or alcohol or drug abuse (Foster et al., 1992). As we gain more information about the areas of the brain involved in emotions, we will know more about the physical origins of aggression.

Psychologists have also found that people learn to be aggressive by relying on past experiences. If in the past aggressive behavior gave a successful outlet for frustration and anger, aggression will be tried again. Research by Bandura and Walters (1963) concluded that aggressive behavior can also be learned from others. They found that children raised by aggressive adults tended to be more aggressive than were children reared by adults who emphasized cooperation and peaceful behavior. Berkowitz (1968) noted that normally only certain stimuli or cues will lead to aggression.

Cultural factors play a role in aggression. Nisbett (1993) found that the people of the U.S. South and West are more likely to have violent responses to anger than are people in other parts of the country. Regardless of social class, economic level, or race, people living in southern regions were more likely to use violence in response to insults.

Since aggressive behavior can be learned, psychologists have questioned whether films and television programs featuring aggression influence the behavior of viewers. Experiments with children have had mixed results. Although some studies found that children who watched violent television programs behaved more aggressively, others found the young viewers to behave less aggressively. Apparently individual childen react differently to seeing violence on a screen. Several correlation studies found that children who watch more violence on television tend to be less empathetic toward victims. But, some psychologists argue that violent programs can provide a healthy outlet for aggressive feelings. Watching a hero whack a villain may help a viewer release personal anger that has been pent up. Research in American prisons found that aggressive films do not appear to cause an increase in prison violence. Whether violence can actually be controlled through films is the subject of present research.

Exercise 8-8

Little Victor's parents often have violent fights. His mother throws pots and pans, and his father has broken vases and windows. Victor is frequently spanked and beaten for misbehaving. In an attempt to control Victor's aggression, his parents do not permit him to watch television programs or movies that show violence.

Little David's parents quarrel occasionally but generally are calm and cooperative. Although they limit the amount of time David may watch television, they allow him to view whatever programs he wishes. David often chooses aggressive shows and films.

Which child is more likely to show aggressive and violent behavior? Why?

_____

_____

_____

Turn to the Feedback section to check your choice and reason.

Handling Anger

There are several options in handling anger. First, you can express your feelings *directly*. If a woman annoys you, you can tell her so in an angry voice or shake your fist at her. If your car will not start, you can kick it. If your boss chastises you, you could empty your wastebasket on his head. Direct anger allows you to vent your feelings. It also helps others to know and understand your feelings. However, there are times when it is, obviously, not the best option.

A second alternative is to express anger *indirectly*. Sometimes you cannot or should not show anger toward the person or object responsible for your frustration. Instead you place your anger or aggression on a person or object that is less threatening to you. Since your anger changes places from one object to another, indirect anger is often labeled *displacement*. Have you ever had a teacher who seemed to pick on you? You probably were wise if you avoided a direct expression of your anger. Direct anger may have increased the friction. If you acted in a friendly manner toward the teacher but slammed down your books or became irritable with a loyal friend, you were displacing your anger. Although this alternative allows you to release your anger, it is definitely unfair to whoever receives the brunt of your emotions. Figure 8-7 shows the classic example. A man is harassed by his boss. The man takes his anger out on his wife who, in turn, scolds her child. The child vents anger on the family pet.

A third option is to hold in, or *internalize*, anger. Rather than express anger openly, you hold it inside yourself. Averill (1976) found that anger is often considered a negative, or "bad," emotion. As a result people try to hide their anger and bottle it within themselves. This attitude toward anger can be unhealthy. As anger builds up and becomes more intense, stress results. As mentioned earlier in the chapter, stress causes physiological changes that can be unpleasant and harmful to general health. People who internalize their feelings of anger are more likely to suffer a number of possible physical disorders.

A final alternative is to *control* the onset of the feeling of anger. The first step in controlling anger is to find the cause. Sometimes the cause of anger can be avoided. If a coworker's lunchtime bragging irritates you, your answer may be a different table in the lunchroom. Unfortunately the solution is rarely that simple. More often people find themselves in situations that are unavoidable. But preparation and planning can help.

Psychologists have developed a number of suggestions for controlling anger. Usually the first step is to determine how hostile you are. Feature 8-3 contains some questions from a hostility-level test. Take a moment to give yourself the test.

How can you take control of your hostility and anger? Talking to yourself in a positive way can be beneficial. Likewise, showing a sense of humor can often break intense anger. By finding something amusing in the situation, you can make tension crumble. One strategy for managing anger uses the acronym RETHINK (Rovner, 1991):

R—Recognize whether you are really angry or just experiencing fear, stress, shame, or fatigue.

E—Empathize with the person who is the target of your anger.

T—Think about the situation. Is there some humor or a solution?

H—Hear what the other person is saying.

I—Integrate love and respect when you speak.

N—Notice changes in your body when you are angry. Gain control by counting to ten.

K—Keep your attention on the present subject. Avoid dredging up old grudges and wounds.

For 25 years a professor of psychiatry has used this painting to teach students about frustration and projected hostility.

FIGURE 8-7. A classic example of indirect anger or displacement.

How Hostile Are You?

Find out how hostile you are on the road, in a supermarket line, and at the office by answering these questions devised by Dr. Redford Williams of Duke University.

1. I am in the express checkout line at the super-market, where a sign reads: "No more than 10 items, please!"
   A. I pick up a magazine to pass the time.
   B. I glance ahead to see if anyone has more than 10 items.

2. My spouse, boyfriend or girlfriend is going to get me a birthday present.
   A. I prefer to pick it out myself.
   B. I prefer to be surprised.

3. Someone is speaking very slowly during a conversation.
   A. I am apt to finish his or her sentences.
   B. I am apt to wait until he or she finishes.

4. Someone treats me unfairly.
   A. I usually forget it rather quickly.
   B. I am apt to keep thinking about it for hours.

5. The person who cuts my hair trims off more than I wanted.
   A. I tell him or her what a lousy job he or she did.
   B. I figure it'll grow back, and I resolve to give my instructions more forcefully next time.

6. I am riding as a passenger in the front seat of a car.
   A. I take the opportunity to enjoy the scenery.
   B. I try to stay alert for obstacles ahead.

7. At times I have to work with incompetent people.
   A. I concentrate on my part of the job.
   B. Having to put up with them ticks me off.

8. Someone bumps into me in a store.
   A. I pass it off as an accident.
   B. I feel irritated at the person's clumsiness.

9. Someone is hogging the conversation at a party.
   A. I look for an opportunity to put him or her down.
   B. I soon move to another group.

10. There is a really important job to be done.
    A. I prefer to do it myself.
    B. I am apt to call on my friends or co-workers for help.

11. Someone criticizes something I have done.
    A. I feel annoyed.
    B. I try to decide whether the criticism is justified.

12. Another driver butts ahead of me in traffic.
    A. I usually flash my lights or honk my horn.
    B. I stay farther behind such a driver.

13. I see an overweight person walking down the street.
    A. I wonder why these people have such little self-control.
    B. I think that he or she may have a metabolic defect or a psychological problem.

14. There have been times when I was very angry with someone.
    A. I have always been able to stop short of hitting them.
    B. I have, on occasion, hit or shoved them.

15. I recall something that angered me previously.
    A. I feel angry all over again.
    B. The memory doesn't bother me as much as the actual event did.

RATING YOUR HOSTILITY

The questions . . . are excerpted from the much longer test Dr. Redford Williams administers to patients. Responses to 15 questions won't determine whether your hostility level is a health risk, but they can suggest whether you would benefit from defusing hostile thoughts.

Questions 1, 2, 6, 10, and 13 are designed to measure cynicism, which Dr. Williams describes as a "mistrusting attitude" toward people's motives and a tendency to be "constantly on guard" against others' misbehavior. If you answered two or more with the responses in parentheses—1(B), 2(A), 6(B), 10(A), 13(A)—your cynicism level is high.

(continued)

Physical exercises have also been effective in controlling anger. Using the added physical strength that intense emotions produce can help to release some pressure. Jogging, racquetball, hitting punching bags, and lifting weights are effective ways to use up physical energy.

Relaxation exercises have also been beneficial in controlling anger. One type of relaxation exercise stresses tensing and relaxing muscles in various parts of your body: your arms, your legs, your feet, and even your nose and tongue. Another relaxation exercise emphasizes deep breathing.

Exercise 8-9

Judy has spent the past two months working diligently on her psychology term paper. Her professor refuses to grade it because it was submitted one hour late. Judy feels her face flush with anger and her heart pound.

Indicate how Judy might behave if she handles her anger directly, indirectly, and internally.

a. Direct anger: _____

_____

b. Indirect anger: _____

_____

c. Internalized anger: _____

_____

Exercise 8-10

Describe three possible methods Judy could use to control her anger.

a. _____

b. _____

c. _____

You may check your responses in the Feedback section.

Joy

Joy, clearly the most pleasant of the three basic emotions, is the most difficult to define. Joy has been vaguely described as an active positive feeling of exhilaration and pleasure. Joy is a transient emotion and can last a few seconds, minutes, or hours. Joy that lasts and endures longer has been labeled happiness. Happiness, however, requires more than the active pleasure of joy. In his research on happiness, Freedman (1978) found that joy can only last when a person also has a sense of contentment and inner peace. A lottery winner will experience an immediate emotion of joy when the winning number is called and again when the money is awarded. However, whether this joy will endure and lead to happiness is another question. Psychological research has found that lottery winners rarely experience lasting joy or happiness from their winnings.

Freedman surveyed 100,000 people to find out the relationship between lifestyles and happiness. He found that married couples tend to be happier than both couples who are living together and single individuals. Money did not help procure happiness. Once a basic standard of living was met, increases in income did not cause increases in happiness. Age and specific religions did not influence happiness either. However, Myers (1992) did find that people who are religiously active are more satisfied with their lives. Nonetheless, social relationships seem to have the strongest bearing on joy and happiness.

Happiness is indeed a desirable state. Not only does it provide positive personal feelings, but it can also have other beneficial outcomes. Happiness is good for your health, and can even enhance learning.

Exercise 8-11

Professor Bliss is working on a formula for happiness. Student assistants have made five suggestions for components of happiness: joy, social relationships, money, age, and inner peace. According to Freedman's research, which of the suggested five components should be included in his formula?

You may check your response in the Feedback section.

Fear

Fear involves a sense of danger. The most common reaction is to attempt to escape from the fearful situation. Fears may be either realistic or unrealistic. Some realistic fears are essential and are necessary for survival. Vicious dogs, moving cars, poisonous snakes, burning buildings, contagious diseases, and toxic foods should be feared and avoided. Realistic fears are specific. Not all dogs are feared, only those that are threatening. If you have realistic fears, an affectionate puppy that jumps on your lap will not precipitate a fear reaction. Normally parked cars, garter snakes, campfires, common head colds, or healthy breakfasts would not arouse realistic fears.

Have you ever feared failing an exam? Your grade probably reflected whether your fear was realistic or unrealistic. If you scored a D or an F, you undoubtedly had a realistic fear.

Advertisers capitalize on realistic fears. They feature such scenes as a lone woman stranded out in a frigid snowstorm by a car that will not start. If you have ever feared this type of situation, you are a perfect target for their new battery. You are probably also familiar with ads that show a family being forced to move from their attractive home and begin an impoverished lifestyle. Someone lacked an appropriate life insurance policy. Scare tactics are common in commercials and letters advertising smoke detectors, burglar alarms, and automobile and theft insurance. The ads threaten an unpleasant, fearful outcome if their product is not purchased.

Checkpoint

Use the following questions to check your understanding of this portion of the chapter. Match the term on the left with the correct phrase from the list on the right.

12. _____ Anger	a.	Hurting another person or object
13. _____ Frustration	b.	An unhealthy approach
14. _____ Approach-approach conflict	c.	An unpleasant basic emotion
	d.	Caused by a blocking or confusion of goals
15. _____ Avoidance-avoidance conflict	e.	Least frustrating conflict
16. _____ Approach-avoidance conflict	f.	Indirect anger
	g.	Method for controlling anger
17. _____ Aggression	h.	Most frustrating conflict
18. _____ Displacement	i.	Most common conflict
19. _____ Internalized anger	j.	Basis for scare tactics used in ads
20. _____ Relaxation exercises	k.	Most pleasant emotion
21. _____ Social relationships	l.	Most common reaction to fear
22. _____ Joy	m.	Important for happiness
23. _____ Escape		
24. _____ Realistic fears		

Check your responses against the Checkpoint Answer Key at the end of the chapter. If you had difficulty with any question, reread the text. If you had little or no difficulty answering the questions or have resolved problems that you might have had, you are ready to continue with the next portion of this chapter.

EMOTIONAL STRESS

As mentioned earlier in the chapter, *stress* is caused by intense emotion. Whether the intense emotion is anger, fear, joy, or a combination of all three, the result will be stress. Stress creates physiological changes that can be dangerous. If you are feeling emotional stress, you are more likely to drive your car carelessly. You also might either go on an eating binge or have difficulty eating. Stressful people often drink or smoke more than usual.

stress Tension caused by intense emotion

Sources of Stress

Holmes and Rahe (1967) suggested that major events are the prime cause of stress. They published a list that identifies a number of important experiences that produce intense emotion. Items are ranked from the most stressful to the least stressful. A quick glance at Feature 8-4 will reveal that both happy and

SOCIAL READJUSTMENT RATING SCALE

Life Event	Answer	Point Value
Death of spouse	yes	100
Divorce	yes	73
Marital separation	yes	65
Jail term	yes	63
Death of close family member	yes	63
Personal injury or illness	yes	53
Marriage	yes	50
Fired from work	yes	47
Marital reconciliation	yes	45
Retirement	yes	45
Change in family member's health	yes	44
Pregnancy	yes	40
Sex difficulties	yes	39
Addition to family	yes	39
Business readjustment	yes	39
Change in financial status	yes	38
Death of close friend	yes	37
Change to different line of work	yes	36
Change in number of marital arguments	yes	33
Mortgage or loan over $10,000	yes	31
Foreclosure of mortgage or loan	yes	30
Change in work responsibilities	yes	29
Son or daughter leaving home	yes	29
Trouble with in-laws	yes	29
Outstanding personal achievement	yes	28
Spouse begins or stops work	yes	26
Starting or finishing school	yes	26
Change in living conditions	yes	25
Revision of personal habits	yes	24
Trouble with boss	yes	23
Change in work hours, conditions	yes	20
Change in residence	yes	20
Change in schools	yes	20
Change in recreational habits	yes	19
Change in church activities	yes	19
Change in social activities	yes	18
Mortgage or loan under $10,000	yes	17
Change in sleeping habits	yes	16
Change in number of family gatherings	yes	15
Change in eating habits	yes	15
Vacation	yes	13
Christmas	yes	12
Minor violation of the law	yes	11

Chance of illness within two years depends on score: 150 or less, 30% chance; 151 to 299, 50% chance; 300 or above, 80% chance.

Source: Holmes, T. H., & Rahe, R. H. (1967). The social readjustment rating scale. *Journal of Psychosomatic Research, 2,* 213–218.

unhappy experiences can produce stress. Research has found that people who experience stress are more susceptible to a number of diseases and physical problems.

Most people face an assortment of daily stresses that do not appear on the list. Whether you are late for class or lose your wallet or receive a huge bill in the mail, you are likely to experience intense emotion. Some psychologists argue that these daily hassles are more stressful than major events are (De-Longis et al., 1982; Kanner et al., 1981). They claim that we are prepared for major problems and usually handle them well. However, everyday irritations can bog us down and make us more susceptible to physical problems. Some researchers have identified uplifts or positive events that can increase our resistance to physical problems (Cohen and Hoberman, 1983). A list of typical hassles and typical uplifts is shown in Feature 8-5.

Exercise 8-12

Read the following list of events that happened to a college student one day. Identify each event as a major event, a hassle, or an uplift.

a. Favorite song is played on the radio _____

b. Can't find the car keys _____

c. Stuck in heavy traffic on the way to class _____

d. Closest friend attempted suicide _____

e. Receives notice of election to Phi Beta Kappa honor society _____

f. Uncle sends check for $100 _____

FEATURE 8-5

"Hassles" and "Uplifts"

TYPICAL HASSLES	TYPICAL UPLIFTS
1. Too many responsibilities	1. Relating well with your spouse or lover
2. Concerns about physical appearance	2. Having enough time to do what you want
3. Being lonely	3. Being visited, phoned, or sent a letter
4. Not enough personal energy	4. Having enough money for entertainment and recreation
5. Concerns about getting ahead	5. Being with children
6. Not enough time for entertainment and recreation	6. Free time
7. Job dissatisfactions	7. Music
8. Concerns about the meaning of life	8. Getting unexpected money
9. Fear of rejection	9. Spending time with family
10. Too many things to do	10. Sex

Source: Adapted from Kanner, Coyne, Schaefer, & Lazarus (1981).

Handling Stress

Whether our problems are major events or minor hassles, we must find a way to handle the stress, or cope. Coping requires a constant effort to manage the demands that make us feel stressful. Shaver and O'Connor (1986) identified three categories of successful coping:

1. Attacking your problem
2. Rethinking your problem
3. Accepting your problem but lessening the physical effects of the stress it causes

When you *attack* a problem, you confront it directly. You define your problem, consider your options, and choose one or more options as your solution. Imagine you receive the stressful news that your grade-point average is too low to permit you to continue in college. First, you would define your problem as being dismissed from college. Next, you would consider your options. You could consider other colleges, perhaps institutions that are less difficult and competitive. You might also consider working or trying a different career. Another option might be to appeal your case to an academic dean. Your final step would be to choose your best option. According to Pearlin and Schooler (1978), people who attack problems have an increased feeling of control and effectiveness.

Rethinking a problem involves changing your initial judgment. You decide that the situation is not a problem after all. You might see a negative situation as character-building. After being dropped by a college, a student might be grateful to be free of academic and money pressures. Often people can see humor in stressful situations. The man in Figure 8-8 is clearly rethinking the traffic problem!

The final approach to coping involves *accepting* a problem and taking steps to avoid any physical effects. If you feel stressed and upset, you might take time out to enjoy some recreation. This approach is useful when problems can be neither avoided nor solved. A mother of several active preschool children will clearly need to arrange for some personal time for fun and rest.

Exercise 8-13

Each of the following persons is coping with stress. Indicate whether the coping strategy involves attacking the problem, rethinking the problem, or accepting the problem (but lessening the physical effects).

a. Ms. A. suffered a neck injury in a car accident. She claims the incident has helped her to better understand people who have constant pain.

_____

b. Mr. N is with a new date and has been waiting more than thirty minutes for service in a restaurant. He begins to crack jokes about the slow service and decides the delay is permitting extra conversation time.

_____

"Hey, is this great traffic, or what?"

FIGURE 8-8. An example of rethinking a problem.

c. Mr. W. was given a poor evaluation by his boss. He considered quitting, transferring to another department, and appealing his evaluation. He decided to file an appeal.

_____

d. Mrs. H. works in an office next to a woman with a loud, high-pitched voice. Mrs. H. plans a quiet jog through the park every lunch hour to relieve her tension.

_____

Please check your answers in the Feedback section.

Stress and the Immune System

Research has provided strong evidence that stressful experiences can weaken our immune systems. Maier and Laudenslager (1985) reported that past stressful experiences weaken our present immune systems. When you are stressed, your body produces a hormone called *cortisol*. Cortisol gives you added energy and maintains your blood pressure but unfortunately also weakens your immune system. Perhaps you have found that after a period of being under pressure, you become ill. After long hours of stressful studying for finals, students often suffer from colds and viruses during exam week. The article excerpt in Feature 8-6 and Figure 8-9 confirm the link between stress and the common cold.

cortisol Hormone released in times of stress that converts protein to energy, maintains blood pressure, and weakens the immune system

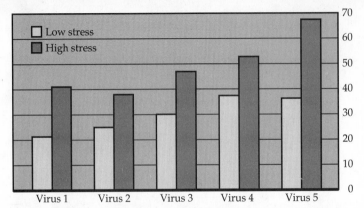

FIGURE 8-9. Stress and cold viruses. The number of study subjects with low psychological stress and high stress who got colds after deliberate exposure to five viruses.
(*Source: New England Journal of Medicine.*)

Stress and Illness

While stress can make you more prone to illness, being ill often introduces new stressors. You fall behind in your work. You must consume unappetizing medicines. You worry about whether the medicine will succeed. You might wonder if you should call your doctor or get another opinion. Indeed, illness presents much additional stress.

How you cope with the stress of an illness can affect your recovery. Although most research has focused on heart disease (see Chapter 9), there has been some recent research on emotional control of cancer. David Spiegel and his colleagues (1989) reported that female cancer patients who participated in

---

FEATURE 8-6 PSYCHOLOGY IN THE NEWS

To Avoid Catching a Cold, Don't Worry About It

Medical researchers have confirmed what many people instinctively believe: you are more likely to catch a cold when you feel "stressed out."

In the clearest demonstration yet of the relationship between emotions and infections, researchers in Pittsburgh and Britain found that high levels of psychological stress could nearly double a person's chances of catching a cold by lowering resistance to viral infection. . . .

Although few health professionals doubt that emotional distress plays a role in many ailments, from heart attacks and cancer to allergies and ulcers, precise studies of the relationship and a full understanding of the mechanisms involved are wanting. During the last decade, numerous studies have demonstrated an effect of undue stress on the immune system, one line of defense against disease. . . .

Source: Brody, J. (1991, August 29). To avoid catching a cold, don't worry about it. *The New York Times*, A-24.

*"Nurse, please show Mr. Fillmond to a larger
room so we can use the big needle."*

FIGURE 8-10. Another stress of being ill . . .

support groups lived an average of two years longer than did their counterparts
who did not receive emotional support. Similar findings are reported in the
news clip in Feature 8-7. Although presently there are insufficient data to prove
that cancer and other illnesses can be controlled through emotions, research
and experimentation are continuing.

Checkpoint

Use the following questions to check your understanding of the final portion of the chapter. Choose and mark the one correct response to each question.

25. Which type(s) of intense emotion can cause stress?
  a. Only anger
  b. Both anger and fear
  c. Both fear and joy
  d. Anger, fear, or joy
26. According to Holmes and Rahe, which events are stressful?
  a. Happy experiences
  b. Unhappy experiences
  c. Both happy and unhappy experiences
  d. Minor problems

27. Some psychologists argue that daily hassles are more stressful than major events are. According to research, what can increase our resistance to the stress of these hassles?
   a. Uplifts
   b. Major problems
   c. Illness
   d. Other hassles

28. Raoul is making a constant effort to manage the demands that make him feel stressful. What is he doing?
   a. Relaxing
   b. Coping
   c. Lowering his immunity
   d. Resisting

29. Ms. P. has defined a problem, considered her options, and chosen a solution. Which method of coping did she use?
   a. Attacking the problem
   b. Rethinking the problem
   c. Accepting the problem
   d. All of the above

30. What conclusion can presently be reached concerning the relationship between emotions and cancer?
   a. Emotional problems are the cause of cancer.
   b. Cancer cannot be controlled by emotions.

FEATURE 8-7 PSYCHOLOGY IN THE NEWS

Doctors Find Comfort Is a Potent Medicine

"Comfort always, cure rarely," was a motto of medicine in times long gone, when bedside manner was more potent than any medicines.

Now, in a movement that counters the rush to high-technology, high-turnover medicine, some physicians are urging that the lost art of comforting be revived. They are spurred by a steady march of scientific findings demonstrating how heavily patients' emotional states can affect the course of their diseases.

For example, among 100 patients preparing to go through bone marrow transplants for leukemia, 13 were found to be highly depressed and 12 of them died within a year of the transplant. But 34 out of the 87 who were not depressed were still alive after two years, a recent study at the University of Minnesota showed.

Of the patients who felt they had strong emotional support from their spouses, family or friends, 54 percent survived the transplants after two years. But the two-year survival rate of those who said they had little social support was only 20 percent. . . .

And in a study done at Mount Sinai Hospital in New York City and Northwestern University Medical School in Chicago, elderly patients admitted for a fractured hip were also checked for and given mental health care if they needed it. They left the hospital two days sooner, on average, than patients who, as is standard in most orthopedic units, received only care for their fractures. . . .

Source: Goleman D. (1991, November 26). Doctors find comfort is a potent medicine: Support can be more effective than chemotherapy. The New York Times, C-1.

c. Emotional care makes medical treatment unnecessary for cancer.
d. Emotional factors play a role in the treatment of cancer.

Check your responses against the Checkpoint Answer Key at the end of the chapter. If you had difficulty with any question, reread the text. If you had little or no difficulty or have resolved problems that you might have had, you are ready to check yourself against the chapter inventory that follows.

CHAPTER INVENTORY

Use this list of objectives as a review checklist. You should be able to do all of the tasks outlined in the objectives and apply them to everyday examples. If you can, you may feel confident that you have mastered the material in this chapter.

1. Define emotions.
2. Identify three methods for measuring emotions, and describe the limitations of each.
3. Explain the nature and purpose of sensitivity training.
4. Summarize the role of facial expression and body language in the expression of emotions.
5. Describe the role of culture in the expression of emotions.
6. Identify physiological changes that accompany emotions.
7. Criticize the use of the polygraph as a lie detector.
8. Identify three basic emotions.
9. Recognize frustration as a cause of anger.
10. Provide examples of three types of conflict that can cause frustration.
11. Describe the roles of the brain and of learning in the development of aggression.
12. Specify four options in handling anger, and describe a technique for controlling hostility and anger.
13. Explain the relationship between joy and happiness.
14. Distinguish between realistic and unrealistic fears.
15. State the causes of stress and recognize examples of stressful events.
16. Identify three methods of handling stress.
17. Discuss the relationships among stress, illness, and the immune system.

Feedback

The correct answers to the exercises follow. If you did not answer an exercise correctly, review the preceding pages and return to the exercise to complete it correctly.

8-1. a. Verbal descriptions: People are not always aware of their own emotions. Even if they are aware, they are not always willing to share their feelings with others.
      b. Observation: Observation does not allow you to distinguish between emotions. The same behavior can represent several different emotions.

c. Measuring physical change: Physical changes do not allow you to distinguish between emotions. Several different emotions can cause the same physical changes.

8-2. a. Lucy may gain a better understanding of her feelings. She may also profit from an honest exchange and acceptance from the group.

b. Lucy may have difficulty accepting sharp criticism from the group. It could be painful for her.

8-3. a. Mr. Clarke's observation of facial expression is probably more reliable. Facial expression is less influenced by past environment and is likely to be more consistent in people from different cultures.

b. Neither method distinguishes between spontaneous and deliberate behavior. A candidate could be acting just to get the job.

8-4. a. Mr. Herkimer may be having stomach butterflies, a dry mouth, a pounding heart, an increase in blood pressure, a change in the amount of blood sent to muscles, breathing changes, a flow of adrenalin, and an increase in skin resistance.

b. The right hemisphere (temporal lobe).

8-5. a. Emotions can provide a sudden burst of energy that can be helpful.

b. Continuous high levels of emotions can increase the likelihood of physical problems. Intense emotions can cause extreme changes in heart rate, and even death.

8-6. a. Approach-avoidance

b. Approach-approach

c. Avoidance-avoidance

d. Approach-approach

e. Approach-avoidance

f. Approach-avoidance

8-7. a. Josh

b. Mike and Juan

8-8. Victor is more likely to show aggressive and violent behavior. A child's behavior is more likely to be influenced by the behavior of parents than by television.

8-9. a. Judy would confront the professor directly. She might express the unreasonableness of not accepting the paper or ask if the professor always submitted work on time.

b. Judy would displace her anger onto someone or something else. She might throw a book against the wall or start an argument with an unsuspecting friend.

c. Judy would not express her anger but would keep it inside. She might begin to feel nauseated, her throat might become dry, or she might otherwise feel physically uncomfortable.

8-10. a. She could RETHINK the problem, convincing herself that the paper was not that important. She might even try to say something amusing to break the tension.

b. She could try to get some physical exercise. Jogging or a fast-paced game of tennis might help her consume some of her emotional energy.

c. She could try to relax either by taking deep breaths or by alternately tensing and relaxing muscles in her body.

8-11. Joy, social relationships, and inner peace
8-12. a. Uplift
b. Hassle
c. Hassle
d. Major event
e. Major event
f. Uplift
8-13. a. Rethinking the problem
b. Rethinking the problem
c. Attacking the problem
d. Accepting the problem

Checkpoint Answer Key

1. a; 2. c; 3. d; 4. b; 5. c; 6. d; 7. b; 8. d; 9. c; 10. c; 11. d; 12. c; 13. d; 14. e;
15. h; 16. i; 17. a; 18. f; 19. b; 20. g; 21. m; 22. k; 23. l; 24. j; 25. d; 26. c; 27. a;
28. b; 29. a; 30. d.

Adjusting

You cannot care for others unless you care for
yourself first.
—LILLADEE BALLENGER

Imagine you are at a carnival. There are exciting sideshows and booths with games all around you. Your attention is suddenly drawn to a sign reading, "Gelda the Great, Fortune Teller—Learn your future for only $10." You walk over to Gelda's tent and see another poster: "Gelda knows your past and everything about you." Intrigued and curious you pay the $10 and enter Gelda's mysterious, dark tent.

Gelda is sitting at a round table in the midst of candles, a crystal ball, and zodiac posters. As you seat yourself across from her, Gelda begins to prove she knows you well. "Gelda knows all. You are a sensitive person, but other people do not fully understand you. You care for others and worry about what they think of you. You have a good sense of humor and enjoy laughing and being amused. You have a tendency to put off things that you do not like to do. Then you feel guilty."

Amazing! Gelda quickly described your personality and some of your adjustment problems rather well. But she also summarized a few characteristics that are common to almost all humans. Fortune tellers often use similar generalizations. These general attributes are found in most people. Psychologists have devised some more efficient ways to evaluate individual personalities and adjustments. In this chapter you will study common adjustment problems, as well as some better methods than Gelda's for assessing adjustment and personality.

In our culture, your adjustments are based on your self-concept or how you view yourself. Methods that you use to protect your self-concept will be explored. You will review several methods psychologists use to measure personality and consider the shortcomings of each technique. A variety of adjustment problems will be described. Finally, you will learn a few ways to maintain a healthy personality

WHAT IS ADJUSTMENT?

You are probably not aware of the many simple adjustments you make routinely. Have you ever told a joke and no one laughed? You immediately adapted to the silence either by repeating the punch line, explaining the joke, or excusing the silence with a statement like, "I guess you had to be there!" Or perhaps you have gone to a party in casual clothes only to find everyone in their fanciest attire. Here, you might have excused your appearance with continued explanations that you had not realized the party was semiformal, or with jokes about going fishing after the festivities. In each of these situations, you had to make adjustments in your thinking and behavior.

Not all adjustments are simple. Marriages, deaths, new jobs, and new friends require some major changes in thinking and behaving. Adjustment is the continuing process of adapting and fitting yourself to your surroundings and meeting the needs of the moment. You must adapt to constant demands and stresses.

Adjustments require both *internal* and *external* changes. Changes in the individual's attitudes, feelings, emotions, and motivation are internal adjustments. External changes are observable behaviors that are based on internal adjustments. Because of new attitudes and feelings, adjustments in outward behavior are made. External changes include such social changes as new roles and relationships.

Suppose a woman tries on last year's summer clothes and notices they are a bit snug. She wants to look better and become more physically fit. She decides to sign up for an exercise class. Her internal attitude about her weight and shape required an adjustment when she noticed the change in her appearance since last summer. This internal adjustment provoked another internal change: a motivation to change her appearance. As a result of her internal adjustments, the woman made an external adjustment, namely, taking on a new role as a participant in an exercise class. External adjustments are caused by internal changes. Internal changes result from changes in self-concept or attitudes about yourself.

Exercise 9-1

Assuming that the gentleman in Figure 9-1 is prepared to make some adjustments, describe one internal adjustment and one external adjustment that would be appropriate.

FIGURE 9-1.

a. Internal: _____

_____

b. External: _____

_____

Please compare your answers with those in the Feedback section.

Self-Concept

self-concept Collection of beliefs that a person has about his or her own self-image

self-esteem Personal regard that people have for their own worth

Your *self-concept* is your own image or picture of yourself. Your opinions of your health, appearance, disposition, influence on others, abilities, and weaknesses are part of your self-concept. A self-concept is a collection of beliefs based on your judgment of yourself; it is not necessarily accurate. *Self-esteem* is another way of viewing self-concept: A person with high self-esteem has a positive self-concept, while a person with low self-esteem has a negative self-concept.

This strong emphasis on *self* is unique to North American and western European cultures. Most cultures (including Asian, African, Latin-American and many southern European) stress the importance of groups and communities. They rely on extended families and clans to provide care (Lonner, 1988; Kitayama and Markus, 1992). Often people from these cultures see the American view as selfish. However, since most adjustment studies have come from western cultures, the emphasis has been with a strong bias toward "self."

In our American culture, most people have a strong need to check themselves and their appearances. Even homes without radios, televisions, dishes, sofas, or tables have at least one and probably several mirrors. Few people can pass a mirror without at least a brief glance at themselves. The appearance aspect of a self-concept is easy to check. However, attitudes toward appearance can vary. One man may believe that the hair stubble on his chin looks distinguished, while another man may think that it appears unkempt.

Your opinions about yourself are usually based on the attitudes of other people toward you. The process of developing a self-concept begins with parents. The name that is chosen for a child often reflects the parents' attitude. For example, Reginald Randolph Wallingford III may be expected to become sophisticated. In a study of attitudes toward names, Marcus (1976) found that John was expected to be kind and trustworthy; Ann would not be aggressive; Agnes would be old, while Robin would be young and bright; and Tony would be sociable.

Often parents select names that reflect their hopes and expectations for their child's adjustment and personality. However, regardless of the name parents choose, encouragement, love, praise, and interest from parents have been found to aid the development of positive self-concepts or high self-esteem in babies and children. Children who are constantly scolded and rarely shown affection are likely to develop poor self-concepts or low self-esteem. Children with low self-esteem have less self-confidence and develop feelings of inferiority. They are likely to have difficulty interacting with other children and becoming accepted by them. As a result children with poor self-concepts often develop behavior problems that elicit negative attitudes from peers, teachers, team coaches, and other group leaders. This further corrodes self-esteem. Problems in self-concept that occur as early as first grade have been found to affect a child's entire future.

As children develop, they begin to compare themselves with others, silently asking such questions as "Am I as nice as Sol is?" "Am I as good-looking as Dana is?" or "Can I work as hard as Leslie does?" The opinions of friends become critical and far more important than the views of parents as adolescence approaches. Apparently teenagers think highly of each other. A study by David Myers (1980) found that most high school seniors have high self-esteem. However, a more recent study reported in Feature 9-1 found clear gender differences in self-satisfaction.

Each person has an *ideal self*, a glamorous or dream self. The ideal self is a goal, the way a person would like to be. Usually an ideal self is based on attributes that are likely to be respected by parents, peers, teachers, and significant people. Your ideal self may change in different social situations. At a party you may want to appear as an attractive flirt, but at a town meeting you might hope to have people view you as a competent leader. In a job interview you may want to impress your potential employer with your efficiency and knowledge, but you probably want your old friends to see you as a warm, relaxed person. Some people are more adept at changing their image than

ideal self Person's goal or dream self

"So the prince and the princess lowered their expectations and lived reasonably contentedly forever after."

FIGURE 9-2. The prince and the princess may have been trying to improve their self-esteem.

others are. If your actual performance meets or comes close to your ideal, you will have high self-esteem.

Studies by Levanway (1955) and Wylie (1957) concluded that people with good self-concepts tend to be more accepting of others. They are also more accepting of their own failures. However, they fail less, since they tend to be better achievers than are people with low self-esteem. High self-esteem is also related to independence and open-mindedness. People with positive self-images will rely on themselves rather than on others and will be more willing to accept criticism and suggestions.

On the other hand, persons with low self-esteem are sensitive to criticism and blame themselves whenever things go wrong. Because they lack confidence, they will succumb to pressure and can usually be manipulated easily. They seek flattery and criticize others to boost their own self-images. Most persons with low self-esteem prefer to work on easy tasks where they can be certain of success. Children with poor self-images are often found playing with friends much younger than themselves. Several studies have shown that low self-esteem is a factor in cheating, drug use, and many forms of delinquency.

Self-esteem does not seem to be related to social class. Lolita Stone (1992) found no significant differences in self-esteem between working-class and middle-class African-American women. However she did find that women with a strong racial identity from both classes tended to have higher self-esteem.

What can be done to boost self-esteem? Accepting your cultural heritage and racial background are important first steps. Reassurance, positive comments, and sincere caring can help you along and play important roles. Rosenbaum (1980) suggested that managers use such techniques as giving special assignments, praising specific jobs, accepting others' opinions and feelings, and

"*Quincy and I love our new house. And you couldn't ask for a better neighbor than Mr. Suggs.*"

FIGURE 9-3. Can you identify two characteristics of low self-esteem that Mr. Suggs appears to have?

FEATURE 9-1 PSYCHOLOGY IN THE NEWS

Girls' Self-Esteem Is Lost on Way to Adolescence, New Study Finds

Girls emerge from adolescence with a poor self-image, relatively low expectations from life and much less confidence in themselves and their abilities than boys. . . .

Confirming earlier studies that were smaller and more anecdotal, this survey of 3,000 children found that at age 9 a majority of girls were confident, assertive and felt positive about themselves. But by the time they reached high school, less than a third felt that way.

The survey, commissioned by the American Association of University Women, found that boys, too, lost some sense of self-worth, but they ended up far ahead of the girls.

For example, when elementary school boys were asked how often they felt "happy the way I am," 67 percent answered "always." By high school, 46 percent still felt that way. But with girls, the figures dropped from 60 percent to 29 percent. . . .

Dr. Carol Gilligan, a professor of education at Harvard and a pioneer in studying the development of girls, said the survey's findings would force a series of more complex questions about what happens to girls' self-esteem during adolescence. . . .

"This work raises all kinds of issues about cultural contributions," she added, "and it raises questions about the role of schools, both in the drop in self-esteem and in the potential for intervention." . . .

Source: Daley, S. (1991, January 9). Girls' self-esteem is lost on way to adolescence, new study finds. *The New York Times,* B-1, B-6.

asking for opinions on how to solve problems in order to bolster the self-esteem of their employees. Since persons with high self-esteem tend to achieve and accomplish more, boosting employees' self-esteem is beneficial to managers and businesses, as well as to each individual's self-image.

Exercise 9-2

Indicate whether each characteristic listed below suggests high self-esteem (a good self-concept) or low self-esteem (a poor self-concept).

a. Is self-confident   _____

b. Communicates and interacts with others   _____

c. Experiences wide differences between ideal
    self and actual behavior   _____

d. Is highly critical of others   _____

e. Is independent   _____

f. Is easily manipulated   _____

g. Is open-minded   _____

h. Is self-reliant   _____

i. Prefers easy tasks   _____

j. Seeks flattery   _____

k. Is willing to accept criticism   _____

You may check your answers in the Feedback section.

Self-Concept and Personality

Even a person who has a good self-concept does not always make proper adjustments. However, a person with a good self-concept is likely to make better adjustments than is someone with a poor self-concept. It is difficult to find criteria that will describe good adjustments and a well-adjusted person. Most often, psychologists look for behaviors that are appropriate for a culture and for the particular situation that a person is confronting.

Methods and styles of adjusting differ according to both cultures and situations. An individual's patterns of adjusting form part of that person's personality. Although there are many definitions of personality, most emphasize adjustment to the environment. Personality is a total picture of patterns of behavior and includes thoughts, feelings, and motives that cannot be observed. Some behaviors and feelings are repeated frequently, while others occur only rarely.

As you face new stresses and demands, you must make adjustments. Your self-concept and personality are constantly changing as you make these adjustments. In the next section of this chapter, you will look at some methods people use to adjust and protect their self-concepts.

Use the following questions to check your understanding of this portion of the chapter. Choose and mark the one correct response to each question.

1. Which of the following individuals is making an external adjustment?
   a. A man who has developed a poor self-concept
   b. A boy who feels unhappy about his appearance
   c. A girl who is satisfied with her grades in school
   d. A woman who applies for a new job

2. How are self-concept and self-esteem related?
   a. A person with a good self-concept has high self-esteem.
   b. A person with a poor self-concept has high self-esteem.
   c. A person with a good self-concept rarely has high self-esteem.
   d. A person with a poor self-concept rarely has low self-esteem.

3. When does development of a self-concept begin?
   a. In babyhood
   b. In first grade
   c. At adolescence
   d. At maturity

4. What is your ideal self?
   a. A high level of self-esteem
   b. A good self-concept
   c. The way you would like to be
   d. Your patterns of adjustment

5. Rucker wants to appear calm and peaceful to his neighbors. However, he finds himself becoming irritated when the people next door burn their smelly garbage. Rucker loses control and pours a bag of trash on his neighbor's front lawn. What did Rucker experience?
   a. A difference in self-esteem and self-concept
   b. A difference in ideal self and self-esteem
   c. A difference in self-esteem and actual performance
   d. A difference in ideal self and actual performance

6. Which of the following persons is likely to have high self-esteem?
   a. Greg, who plays with younger children
   b. Kat, who is independent
   c. Matt, who looks for compliments
   d. Terry, who is easy to push around

7. Which of the following is likely to increase self-esteem?
   a. Criticism
   b. Praise
   c. Pressure
   d. Anger

8. What do most definitions of personality emphasize?
   a. Observable behavior
   b. Thoughts
   c. Adjustments
   d. Independence

Use the Checkpoint Answer Key to verify your responses. If you had any difficulty with a question, carefully reread the text. If you had little or no difficulty answering the questions or have resolved any difficulty you might have had, you are ready to continue with the next portion of this chapter.

DEFENSE MECHANISMS

defense mechanisms Variety of unconscious techniques used to avoid anxiety and protect self-esteem

Maintaining a good self-concept and high self-esteem is not easy. Each day there are many events that could shatter your self-image. If you notice a new blemish or wrinkle on your face, receive a low grade, or are not invited to lunch by the group, you need to take action to protect your self-esteem. The methods you use to protect your self-esteem are called *defense mechanisms*.

Suppression and Repression

suppression Consciously and intentionally avoiding unpleasant thoughts and memories

One way to protect your self-esteem is to avoid thinking about your problem. For example, you might intentionally go to a movie to avoid thinking about an argument. This defense mechanism, a deliberate attempt to avoid stressful thoughts, is labeled *suppression*. Scarlett O'Hara in *Gone with the Wind* is among the more famous practitioners of suppression. Remember her line "I shall think about it tomorrow"? Scarlett was suppressing her unpleasant thoughts. Have you ever felt lonely and intentionally kept yourself busy with chores, sports, or shopping to avoid thinking about your loneliness? If so, you were using suppression.

Suppression is only useful for minor problems. Usually you can only pretend a problem does not exist for a short period. Thoughts and worries tend to come back and may be even more stressful if they have been bottled up. Suppression requires a conscious and voluntary effort and has limited use as a defense mechanism.

repression Unconscious forgetting

Issues that are deeply wounding to self-esteem may be too painful to allow in your consciousness. You unconsciously put them out of your mind with unconsciously motivated forgetting, called *repression*. Repression and suppression were described as reasons for forgetting in Chapter 4. It is common for people to push unpleasant thoughts out of their conscious minds. Since thoughts that are repressed are not conscious, people can only beome aware of them through dreams or hypnosis.

Repression is the most basic defense mechanism. Most other defense mechanisms stem from repression. In its simplest form, repression is unconscious forgetting. Suppose you forget to contribute money to a going-away gift for a close friend. Unconsciously you wish your friend were not leaving. Forgetting appointments, birthdays, weddings, and other important events can be signs of repression. Have you ever met someone who was rejecting and cruel to you? If you have difficulty recalling any of those persons or names, you may be repressing them! Usually thoughts and feelings that are repressed bring on other defense mechanisms.

In your own words describe the key difference between suppression and repression.

_____

_____

_____

You may check your response in the Feedback section.

Other Defense Mechanisms

Assuming that the fellow in Figure 9-4 is deeply worried about being rejected, he may repress the situation. As a result he could forget the name of the woman, their entire conversation, what he was drinking, and where he was that evening. Rather than admit his rejection and suffer, he could also use a number of other unconscious defense mechanisms.

Withdrawal. If the man in Figure 9-4 has trouble talking to women in the future, it could be that he unconsciously fears their rejection. *Withdrawal* usually results when people become intensely frightened or frustrated by a situation. People who fear rejection often avoid or withdraw from social situations. Some-

withdrawal Defense mechanism that involves escaping and removing oneself from unpleasant situations

"Normally I don't let rejection bother me, but . . ."
FIGURE 9-4. The rejection stamped on his forehead may also become buried in his unconscious. Time for some defense mechanisms . . .

times the result is shyness. Often people fear rejection even when it is unlikely. Many famous and likable people have suffered from shyness.

If you have ever tried to escape from an unpleasant situation, you have used a withdrawal defense mechanism. If used cautiously, withdrawal can be a healthy defense mechanism. Often stepping out of a situation can help you gain a better perspective. However, withdrawal can also result in quitting jobs, dropping out of school, separations, and divorces.

fantasy Defense mechanism that involves withdrawing to an imaginary world through daydreams

Fantasy. Sometimes people withdraw into a make-believe, or *fantasy*, world. If the rejected man in Figure 9-4 used a fantasy defense mechanism, he might daydream about his successes with women. He could create his own dream world where he would always be accepted, admired, and loved. Used in moderation, daydreaming and fantasy can be healthy and lead to creative thinking. Everyone daydreams as a method of reducing anxiety. Fantasy can bring a healthy escape from boredom and aid in mental relaxation. Reading a novel or watching a soap opera can provide fantasy escapes. However, if fantasy is used excessively, it can become an unhealthy substitute for activity.

regression Defense mechanism that involves the use of immature and childlike behaviors to cope with problems

Regression. *Regression* is withdrawal into the past. If the rejected fellow regressed in a childlike way, he would behave as a child. He might burst into tears or pout, suck his thumb, throw things, scream, and have a tantrum. Regression requires a return to earlier ways of handling problems. It is generally used when a person is deeply upset and cannot cope in a mature manner. Young children who have been toilet-trained and taught to drink from cups often regress and forget their training when a new baby arrives in their home. The older child does not know how to win parental affection in the new situation. Consequently the child must resort to previous methods for gaining attention and love. The result is regression.

rationalization Defense mechanism that distorts truth to provide excuses for a situation that is unacceptable

Rationalization. *Rationalization* is a distortion of the truth to maintain self-esteem. It provides an excuse or explanation for a situation that is really unacceptable. The man in Figure 9-4 might rationalize that the woman was not really his type and that he was delighted to be rid of her so he could arrive home at a reasonable hour. He might even rationalize that he was just having an unlucky day. Failures are often rationalized as being the result of some external factor, but success is deemed the result of personal abilities.

Most people are unaware of how often they rationalize. Although rationalization is indeed a misuse of logic, it can help to reduce anxiety. Have you ever excused yourself from a poor grade by arguing that the test was unfair or that you were feeling sick when you took the test? Rationalization can also allow you to look at the bright side. If an unpleasant event has already occurred, often little or nothing can be done to change it.

projection Defense mechanism, based on guilt, that involves accusing another of one's own weakness

Projection. *Projection* is based on guilt. Rather than accept his or her own personal weaknesses, a person might project those unacceptable features onto another person. The rejected man could project his rejection onto the lady who stamped him. He would then maintain that it was she who was rejected by everyone. Projection permits you to accuse someone else of your weaknesses.

*"On the other hand, the daily rate is a lot
cheaper than at the ski lodge."*

FIGURE 9-5. The skier's wife is helping him to rationalize his accident.

Perhaps you have heard complaints from one fraternity that members of another fraternity hated them. They could easily be projecting their own feelings
onto the other group. Or maybe you have known a flirt who complained that
every male she met flirted with her. Psychologists often use projective tests to
uncover problems. It is assumed that individuals will project their own feelings
onto the pictures and illustrations in the test material. Projective tests will be
discussed later in the chapter.

Displacement. *Displacement* requires finding a target or victim for pent-up
feelings. The rejected fellow at the bar might ridicule and chastise the bartender
for poor drinks or slow service. Displacement as a form of aggression is discussed in detail in Chapter 8. The chosen victim is usually a safe person,
someone who is not likely to deflate the aggressor's self-esteem. Spouses are

displacement Redi-
rection of feelings
to a substitute per-
son or object when
the true cause of
the feelings is either
an unacceptable or
unavailable target

FIGURE 9-6. The "born loser" is projecting.

often selected. As a result husbands and wives often learn to avoid controversial topics when their mates have had a bad day.

reaction formation
Defense mechanism that causes people to behave in a manner opposite to their unacceptable impulses

Reaction Formation. *Reaction formation* is acting out the exact opposite of unacceptable impulses. People who use reaction formation feel so guilty they bend over backwards to deny their feelings. The result is exaggerated behavior. For example, assume the poor man who was rejected developed a strong hatred for women. He feels guilty about his hatred and unconsciously tries to prove that he really likes women. To prove his acceptance of women, he becomes a leader in the women's rights movement, writing feature articles, soliciting contributions for women's causes, carrying placards, and leading marches for women.

Sometimes parents who really resent their responsibility to rear children will become overprotective. Because a dislike of caring for their own children is considered unacceptable, they try to prove that they really do care. The result is exaggerated behavior and overprotectiveness.

compensation
Healthy defense mechanism that allows persons who are inadequate in one area to turn to areas where they can excel

Compensation. *Compensation* allows a person to make up for inadequacies by doing well in another area. Perhaps the rejected fellow at the bar could go back to work and prove himself an outstanding accountant, attorney, or automobile salesman. Compensation allows someone to de-emphasize weaknesses and play up strengths. A child who is a poor student may try learning clever jokes to become popular. Compensation is a reasonable defense mechanism and usually leads to a healthy adjustment.

sublimation
Healthy defense mechanism that channels unacceptable impulses into positive, constructive areas

Sublimation. *Sublimation* is the most accepted defense mechanism. Unacceptable impulses are channeled into something positive, constructive, or creative. If the man left the bar and wrote a beautiful blues song about rejection and loneliness, he would be sublimating. Some of the finest poetry and folk music have emerged from oppressed groups, examples of their sublimations.

Of the many defense mechanisms, compensation and sublimation are considered the healthiest and most acceptable. Since defense mechanisms are unconscious, usually people are completely unaware of them. Think about some of your own behavior. Can you identify the defense mechanisms you choose most often?

Exercise 9-4

Specify which of the following defense mechanisms is used in each of the following examples:

Repression	Projection
Withdrawal	Displacement
Fantasy	Reaction formation
Regression	Compensation
Rationalization	Sublimation

a. Greg did not complete his biology homework. Rather than be embarrassed in front of the class, he claimed he had a headache and put his head down on his desk. _____

b. Prunella's car broke down. Since she does not have enough money for repairs, she must leave an hour earlier to ride her bicycle or walk to work. Prunella commented that she enjoys the exercise and saving the gas and oil money.

_____

c. Chad had stopped sucking his thumb by the time he was four. At age seven he was told that his parents were divorcing and he would be living with his mother and a "new father." Chad began sucking his thumb again.

_____

d. Julia, a soccer star, tore a tendon in her leg during a game. When her doctor told her she could never play soccer again, Julia worked hard to learn techniques for coaching soccer.

_____

e. Martino was cutting wood and injured his hand with his chain saw. While driving to the emergency room of a local hospital, he recalled the painful shots he received during his last visit there. He missed the turn to the hospital and had to ask for directions to find it.

_____

f. Eric is a big spender. He tips heavily, buys extravagant gifts, and often gambles. When his thrifty wife bought material to make new kitchen curtains, he accused her of squandering money needlessly. He claimed the old, worn curtains were adequate and called her a spendthrift.

_____

g. Little Inez was upset when her mother spanked her. She ran to her toy crib and smacked her doll.

_____

h. Paulette has been trying to support her eight children. They live in an old shack that lacks both heat and plumbing. Paulette likes to daydream about winning a lottery, traveling, and buying fancy clothes.

_____

i. Jeremy has always been a problem to his mother. He never keeps rules and argues with her constantly. In choosing a tattoo, he selected a large heart with "Mom" in the center.

_____

j. Whenever Elizabeth is angry she heads for her piano. She has composed several outstanding jazz tunes.

_____

Turn to the Feedback section to check your responses.

The defense mechanisms you use regularly become part of your style of adjustment and therefore part of your personality. But if most defense mechanisms are unconscious, how can you learn what you are really like? As pointed out in Chapter 1, psychoanalysts would suggest hypnosis and dream analysis to learn about your unconscious. Other psychologists would suggest different techniques.

Measuring personality is a complex task because your personality is constantly changing. You may have developed some characteristics, or traits, that you did not have a few years, or even a few months, ago. Further, there is no single personality test that can ever give a completely accurate picture of what you are presently like. Although no one test or method can give a valid description of your personality, by using a variety of techniques and tests, psychologists can come closer to an accurate assessment.

Techniques for Personality Assessment

projective test Personality test that uses ambiguous stimuli and is designed to measure unconscious feelings

Projective Tests. The purpose of *projective tests* is to uncover unconscious urges and needs. It is assumed that people use projection as a defense mechanism and project their own unconscious feelings onto other persons or objects. One of the oldest projective tests was originated by Rorschach in 1921 (Rorschach, 1942). It consists of a series of ten cards with inkblots on them. The psychologist presents the subject with each of the ten cards. The person is then encouraged to "free-associate," that is, to say whatever comes to mind, about what he or she sees on each card. The psychologist then interprets the subject's responses, according to a standardized scale. The interpretation of Rorschach responses has been refined since the origin of the test. Typical responses of specific disorders, such as depression and simple schizophrenia, have been found. A newer variation on the Rorschach is the Holtzman Inkblot Technique (Holtzman, 1975), involving a set of forty-five cards.

Another type of projective test uses pictures of people in ambiguous real-life situations. The most famous of this type of projective test is the Thematic Apperception Test (TAT). Pictures in the TAT show such scenes as a person lying on a sofa and another figure standing next to the sofa, or a child staring at a violin. The subject taking the test is expected to project unconscious feelings onto the figures in the pictures. For children, there is a special variation of this test, called the Children's Apperception Test (CAT).

Another type of projective test is the widely criticized Draw-A-Person Test (DAP). Here the subject is handed a blank paper and crayon or pencil and simply asked to draw a person. Personality is assessed according to the characteristics and features in the sketch. This test is sometimes expanded to also include separate drawings of a house and a tree. These tests are the least accurate of the projective tests. In his research, Cressen (1978) reported that interpretation of the drawings is strongly influenced by the subject's artistic ability.

There are a number of other types of projective tests that allow open

The Thematic Apperception Test (TAT) uses ambiguous pictures. Persons are asked to describe each picture, projecting their own feelings onto the characters shown. (© 1943 by the President and Fellows of Harvard College; © 1971 by Henry A. Murray)

responses. In word-association tests the psychologist presents a series of words, and the subject is then expected to call out the first word that comes to mind. Another type of projective test requires the subject to complete such sentences as:

- "I always worry a great deal about _____."
- "When I am angry or upset I _____."
- "The happiest time _____."

The major limitation of all projective tests is the subjective nature of their interpretation. Rules for interpretation are clearer on the Rorschach, Holtzman, and TAT than on the other types of projective tests. However, many psychologists find that, in spite of their limitations, projective tests are a good opener in testing sessions. At least they permit individuals to begin talking about their problems.

Self-Report Inventories. Self-report inventories are based on the idea that there are specific personality traits. Each subject is presented with a list of statements about personality characteristics, such as "I feel happiest in a group when I am the person in charge," or "I would rather be alone at home than at a lively party." The person must decide whether, for him or her, each statement is true, false, or somewhere in between. The most popular and most famous personality inventory is the Minnesota Multiphasic Personality Inventory (MMPI), a lengthy and thorough test with 550 items. The primary purpose of the MMPI is to separate normal patterns of responses from patterns associated with mental illness. Another inventory, the California Psychological Inventory (CPI), was designed to identify such normal traits as sociability, self-acceptance, sense of well-being, self-control, tolerance, and responsibility. Although primarily a personality inventory, the CPI also includes assessments of intelligence and achievement. Both the MMPI and the CPI have special scales to detect people who are trying to make good impressions by lying about themselves. However, it is possible to conceal some negative characteristics on these tests. Responses on these inventories depend upon your ability to recall your behavior and attitudes. Often people rationalize and do not fully understand their behavior.

Undoubtedly, you have seen personality inventories in popular magazines and newspapers. Although these quick tests are fun and interesting, they are usually highly inaccurate as measures of personality. It is easy to misinterpret the results of magazine and newspaper inventories since these "tests" are rarely standardized; they are designed strictly for amusement.

Observational and Situational Tests. An interview is probably the most common example of an observational and situational test. The person being interviewed is being carefully observed, with particular attention directed at his or her adjustment to the interview situation. Styles of interviews vary. Sometimes the setting is totally structured and the interviewee must respond to a specific set of questions. At other times the setting is open and the interviewee leads the direction. There are all sorts of variations between these two extremes. (Interviews are discussed in more detail in the final chapter of the text.) Regardless of the style used in the interview, psychologists cannot be certain that the person being interviewed would behave the same way in a natural setting. Some people can put on an act for an interview.

Sometimes psychologists observe individuals in a natural setting and record the types of behavior that occur. For example, a psychologist may observe two five-year-old girls in a playroom. Any aggressive behavior such as hitting, kicking, or pushing is noted. The psychologist may also record crying, teasing, or attempts to embarrass the other girl.

Occasionally psychologists use situational tests; for example, by putting a person in some type of frustrating situation. In one case an individual may be asked to work at length on a boring task, perhaps sorting buttons into boxes. In another case a person may be expected to complete a complex task with time pressures. As the person tries to assemble an elaborate structure, the psychologist keeps reminding the person "You have only two minutes; now, one minute; now, forty-five seconds" and finally, "only eight seconds left." The psychologist then observes and records the person's reactions to frustration.

A common technique for recording observed behavior is a rating scale. Have you ever been asked to complete a questionnaire on another person? On these tests, the items may ask you to indicate on a scale of 1 ("never") to 5 ("always") whether a person is truthful, prompt, friendly, aggressive, responsible, and tidy. Based on your observations, you must rate the person's behaviors. One danger in rating scales is the difficulty in getting truly objective assessments. If the person you are asked to rate is a good friend, you probably would want to be helpful, particularly if your observation might mean a good job or acceptance at a college. Similarly, if you like your friend, you probably have a generally favorable view. As a result you would have a tendency to assess each characteristic in a positive manner. Psychologists call this favorable bias a *halo effect*. Therefore, it is a good practice to use as many judges as possible to assure accuracy on a rating scale.

halo effect Bias that causes a person to overlook another person's specific deficiencies because of one favorable characteristic

Exercise 9-5

List one limitation for each of the following techniques for assessing personality.

a. Projective tests: _____

b. Self-report inventories: _____

c. Interviews: _____

d. Rating scaes: _____

Turn to the Feedback section to check your responses.

Exercise 9-6

What could a psychologist do to overcome these limitations?

_____

_____

Check your answers against those listed in the Feedback section.

Cautions in Personality Assessment

Personality assessment of prospective employees by personnel offices is becoming more common. Often only one test or technique is used. Whether this technique is a rating scale sent to former coworkers and friends, a self-reporting inventory, an interview, or a projective test, the results will have limited validity. A variety of techniques must be used to assure any accuracy. Personality tests are designed for clinical diagnosis and counseling. Any assessment of personality without the consent of the person involved could be considered an invasion of privacy.

Checkpoint

Use the following questions to check your understanding of this portion of the chapter. Match each defense mechanism on the left with the correct definition on the right.

9. _____ Suppression

10. _____ Repression

11. _____ Withdrawal

12. _____ Fantasy

13. _____ Regression

14. _____ Rationalization

15. _____ Projection

16. _____ Displacement

17. _____ Reaction formation

18. _____ Compensation

19. _____ Sublimation

a. Daydreaming and escaping into a make-believe world
b. Distorting the truth to find excuses
c. Using childlike ways to handle upsetting situations
d. Channeling unacceptable urges into constructive and creative areas
e. Making a conscious and deliberate effort to avoid unpleasant thoughts
f. Doing the exact opposite of your unacceptable impulses
g. Forgetting, unconsciously
h. Making up for weaknesses in one area by doing well in another area
i. Escaping unpleasant situations
j. Finding a safe victim for one's aggression
k. Accusing another of one's personal weaknesses

Match each technique on the left with the correct lettered examples listed on the right. There will be more than one example for each technique.

20. _____ Projective tests

21. _____ Self-report inventories

22. _____ Observational and situational tests

a. Minnesota Multiphasic Personality Inventory
b. Rating scales
c. Thematic Apperception Test
d. Rorschach
e. Interviews
f. Draw-a-Person Test
g. CPI

Use the Checkpoint Answer Key to verify your responses. If you had any difficulty with a question, carefully reread the text. If you had little or no difficulty or have resolved any difficulty you might have had, you are ready to continue with the final portion of this chapter.

Personality Types

Although the professional's key purpose in using personality tests is to identify problems in adjustment, some psychologists and physicians have become interested in the use of tests to study the relationship between personality and physical problems. Special tests have been designed to identify personality types that are prone to specific physical disorders. It now appears that personality and adjustment may play a significant role in a leading cause of adult deaths, heart disease.

Two cardiologists, Freedman and Rosenman (1974), found personality type to be a stronger predictor of heart problems than was any other single factor. Among the factors that played lesser roles were smoking, obesity, cholesterol level, and lack of exercise. They labeled the personality type that is prone to heart disease as "type A" and the type that is an unlikely candidate for heart problems, "type B." *Type A* persons are competitive, impatient, organized, and pressured by time. They are easily upset, become obsessed with trivial matters, and lead stressful lives. Recent studies by the American Heart Association (1990) suggest that type A persons experience stronger feelings of hostility and it is their hostility rather than their basic personality that increases their likelihood of developing heart disease. The excerpt in Feature 9-2 explains why stressful people are more likely to have heart attacks.

However, there are benefits to a type A personality. Research by Glass (1977) found that type A people score higher grades and earn more money than do type B people of equal intelligence. His findings are supported by Matthews et al. (1981), who noted that type A psychologists produce the best work. Recent research has found that type A men, although more prone to heart attacks, are more likely to survive than type B men.

Type B persons, on the other hand, are less ambitious, more patient, and can relax more easily. They also smoke less and have lower cholesterol levels. However, even when these two attributes are factored out, they still have fewer heart attacks. Psychologists have used group therapy to help type A persons reduce their feelings of hostility, modify their behavior, and become more like type B persons. But since most psychologists and cardiologists are type A persons themselves, it is often difficult to find relaxed leaders for therapy sessions. However, once a type B is found to lead a group, significant changes do occur among members.

Exercise 9-7

Indicate whether each of the following persons has a type A personality or type B personality.

Side notes:

ADJUSTING
type A personality Behavior characterized by competitiveness and aggression

type B personality Behavior characterized by a relaxed manner

---

FEATURE 9-2 PSYCHOLOGY IN THE NEWS

Stress: The "Type A" Hypothesis

. . . If Type A behavior truly makes one susceptible to coronary artery disease, one reason may be its association with hypertension, smoking and high cholesterol. A recent study noted that 22% of people with newly detected hypertension had Type B personalities; among those with normal blood pressure, about 40% were Type B's. Psychologists who interviewed the hypertensive subjects felt that their potential for hostility was greater. . . .

Brief periods of mental stress also increase "stickiness" of platelets. These small cells gather at the site of an atherosclerotic plaque and further narrow the coronary arteries, raising the question of whether emotional stress contributes to the development of coronary artery disease even in the absence of coronary risk factors. Furthermore, this finding suggests that stress can promote clotting within a coronary artery, thus cutting off blood flow to the heart muscle and causing a heart attack. . . .

Source: (1992, January). Stress: The "type A" hypothesis. *Harvard Heart Letter*, 104.

a. Ulysses is extremely patient. He can work for hours on a tedious, frustrating task. _____

b. Valerie is not interested in a promotion. She prefers her present job where she can take regular lunch hours and relax with her friends. _____

c. Evita is a compulsive student. She studies during every waking moment, since she wants to be certain she graduates with honors. _____

d. Claudio hates to waste time sitting in traffic. He honks his horn and waves his fist at anyone who holds him up. _____

You may check your answers in the Feedback section.

Exercise 9-8

Describe how persons with type A personality can be helped.

_____

_____

_____

Please turn to the Feedback section to check your responses.

ADJUSTMENT PROBLEMS

There are some personality characteristics that do not necessarily lead to physical ailments but nonetheless interfere with daily living and healthy adjustments. If you experience the stress of guilt, insomnia, or culture shock, you face adjustment problems. At best, life will be less than fulfilling and less than perfectly enjoyable. At worst, guilt, insomnia, and culture shock can lead to severe depression.

Guilt

Everyone has felt guilt. Think of some of your own experiences. Perhaps you have called in sick at work on a day when you were perfectly healthy. Or maybe you left a sick friend home alone while you rushed away to have a good time. When was the last time you telephoned or wrote to a lonely grandparent? Guilt arises from moral anxiety. When you violate your own internalized standards or morals, guilt results.

Guilt is natural, normal, and essential for maintaining moral standards and rules within any society. Why do some people experience more guilt than others do? Clearly some people have stronger morals. Rotter (1966) suggested that some people feel more personal responsibility for their actions. He described these people as "internals." Internals believe they control their own fate. Rotter labeled the opposite extreme "externals." Externals believe that they have little or no personal responsibility for what happens to them. They are victims of chance or fate. Phares (1976) found that internals blame themselves for failures and feel more shame and guilt than do externals.

Unfortunately guilt can become excessive, unjustified, and harmful. Needless guilt can lower self-esteem and lead to constant fatigue, sexual frigidity, or even suicide. The causes of painful guilt are often repressed. In such cases, professional help is needed to bring the causes to consciousness. Only then can the appropriateness of the guilt be evaluated. According to Lewis (1992), the simplest method for handling guilt is to own up to your feelings and allow them to dissipate with time. Denying your guilt feelings is dangerous.

Exercise 9-9

Read each of the following statements and indicate whether each remark was likely to be made by an internal or an external person.

a. I'm lucky I got here on time. _____
b. If I'd had a decent teacher, I would have
   passed the course. _____
c. All those years of practice helped me win
   the tennis title. _____
d. It was stupid of me to forget to use sun-
   block; now I have a painful sunburn. _____

Turn to the Feedback section to check your responses.

Insomnia

Insomnia, or inability to sleep, is a common adjustment problem, affecting an estimated 25 million Americans. A person suffering from insomnia may be burdened with worries or guilt at night. While lying awake, the person finds that additional fears are aroused and becomes concerned that sleep may never come. This added worry makes sleep even more difficult and less likely. There is general agreement that sleeping pills cannot cure insomnia (National Institutes of Health, 1984). Although medication may help for a short period, behavior therapy is more effective in the long run (McClusky et al., 1991). The article in Feature 9-3 describes the results of the McClusky study. To avoid problems with insomnia, psychologists recommend a regular schedule that includes daily exercise, a diet free of caffeine (coffee, tea, cola, and chocolate), and a relaxing routine before bed (warm bath, watching television, or listening to music).

insomnia Difficulty getting to sleep, staying asleep, or both

Exercise 9-10

Mr. I suffers from insomnia. Check each suggestion that you would recommend to help cure his problem.

_____ Take sleeping pills.

_____ Eat chocolate.

_____ Avoid coffee.

_____ Exercise every day.

_____ Be active before bedtime.

_____ Take a warm bath before going to bed.

Check your answers against those listed in the Feedback section.

Culture Shock

Have you ever visited a foreign country and had difficulty adjusting to the unusual customs? American women traveling in countries where women are less independent usually experience frustration and stress. Almost everyone has difficulty accepting strange foods, changes in sleeping times, and differences in language and values. All of these problems constitute a disorder that can often be debilitating—culture shock.

If you are not a native of the country you are currently living in, you probably can recall some of your initial problems. Or perhaps some of these problems persist. As mentioned earlier in this chapter, the American culture is in the minority with its focus on "self." Indeed, just reading this chapter would be more difficult for a person from a culture that valued family more than individuals. Greenfield (1992) reported on the difficulties of students from the Philippines, Mexico, and China who are studying in the United States. Their parents expect them to put family needs ahead of their personal school needs. These students are caught in a crisis between their own cultures, which favor

---

FEATURE 9-3 PSYCHOLOGY IN THE NEWS

Two Treatments for Insomnia

Psychologists treating patients who can't get to sleep have found that the commonly prescribed sedative triazalom (Halcion®) is quicker, but behavior therapy is more effective in the long run. The subjects in the experiment were thirty chronic insomniacs who, by their own estimates and the estimates of people who lived with them, needed an average of an hour and 20 minutes to fall asleep.

During the three weeks of treatment, half were given triazolam and half had six sessions of behavior therapy. The procedure consisted of muscle relaxation training and a program known as stimulus control, in which they were given the following advice: go to bed and rise at the same time every day. If you don't fall asleep in a half hour or so, get up and do something else until you become sleepy. Use the bed only for sleep and sex. Do not drink liquids in the evening and do not take naps.

By the second week both groups were falling asleep faster, but patients taking the drug had improved more. By the fourth week patients in behavior therapy had caught up, and they were well ahead at the follow-up five weeks after treatment ended. At that time they were taking an average of 35 minutes to fall asleep, as opposed to an hour or more for the other group, and also felt more rested in the morning. This result may contribute to growing doubt about the value of triazolam, which also has serious side effects—tolerance, rebound insomnia, and occasional memory loss.

Source: (1991, March). Two treatments for insomnia. *Harvard Mental Health Letter,* 6.

family cooperation, and the American culture, which favors individual success. Regardless of the choice made, the result is often stress and guilt.

What can be done to reduce culture shock? Triandis et al. (1988) provided some tips for people with individual values traveling to cooperative cultures and people from cooperative cultures visiting cultures with individual values. For example if you are an American (individual values) visiting China or a Chinese family in your community (cooperative values), to adjust and minimize your culture shock, you should:

- Learn about group memberships and authorities.
- Focus on harmony and cooperation.
- Be patient about developing long-term relationships.
- Be modest and humble in your presentations.
- Explain your social position.

If you are from a culture that emphasizes family cooperation (Mexico) and are visiting a country that stresses individual values (England or the United States), you should:

- Focus on each person's beliefs and attitudes.
- Discuss individual benefits and feel free to be critical.
- Move into business quickly; a few superficial friendly remarks are enough.

A first visit to a foreign country is likely to cause the stressful experience of culture shock.

- Present yourself in a positive light and describe your accomplishments.
- Try to be comfortable when alone, and do not expect to be accompanied by others.

Exercise 9-11

Last summer Betsy traveled from the United States to Scotland and had little or no difficulty adjusting to the new country. This summer Betsy is visiting Thailand and is experiencing culture shock. Give three reasons why her culture shock is stronger in Thailand.

_____

_____

_____

You may check your reasons in the Feedback section.

MAINTAINING A HEALTHY PERSONALITY

The term *mental health* has been used to describe the absence of mental illness or adjustment problems. But just as you may be free of physical illness and still not be healthy, the absence of adjustment problems does not assure a healthy personality. Lack of mental disturbance is merely a minimum condition for a healthy personality. Here is a summary of some suggestions for a mature and healthy personality (Allport, 1961; Johnson, 1971; Mahoney, 1971).

Extend Yourself. If you become genuinely involved in your job, your family, a cause, or anything important to you, you will feel better about yourself.

Reach Out and Show Concern for Others. By showing compassion and warmth, you will develop more tolerance for others, as well as yourself. This will enhance your own security and acceptance of your weaknesses.

Focus on Positive Aspects in Your Life. Often problems cloud thinking. Pogrebin (1980) suggested setting aside one day to indulge in pleasures. Take a day off from work or school and sleep late. Share a relaxed lunch at a restaurant with someone you enjoy. Then go to a movie, play, or athletic event. You might finish the day with your favorite music and a bubble bath. The goal is to enjoy simple pleasures. As an alternative you might force yourself to jot down five things you like about yourself and your life.

Take Responsibility for Yourself. Plan ahead and look to the future. Set objectives for yourself and develop skills that can help you reach your goals. Recognize that you are responsible for your own success.

Relax and Use Your Sense of Humor. Martin and Lefcourt (1983) found that humor improves moods and helps eliminate stress. People who find humorous aspects of bad news are less likely to feel tense and depressed.

And if you should be forced to face adversity, follow the advice in Feature 9-4.

"*Because my genetic programming prevents me from stopping to ask directions—that's why!*"

FIGURE 9-7. Adjustment becomes more difficult when we refuse to ask for help.

FEATURE 9-4 PSYCHOLOGY IN THE NEWS

Coping with Adversity

Dr. Linda James Myers, professor of psychology, psychiatry, and Black studies at Ohio University, tells us how to cope:

Be patient with yourself. If you rush the recovery process and set unrealistic goals, you may not meet your expectation. Recovery won't happen overnight.

Think positively. In very difficult times, one may feel so low that the only way to go is up. But try to identify the good in a situation. Don't view adversity as a limiting experience but rather as an opportunity to enhance your personal growth.

Avoid feeling sorry for yourself. If you choose to wallow in self-pity, you will prolong your suffering and impede the recovery process.

Have a spiritual base. According to Myers, those who are "spiritually grounded" have less difficulty dealing with adversity. Whether it is a strong religious background, a philosophy, or an inner faith, use your spiritual base as a focal point for recovery.

Try to put things in perspective. Adversity can play an important role in our individual growth and development. Negative experiences can be an opportunity for personal growth. It has been said that life is governed by the law of opposites and that to truly know and appreciate good, one must also know bad.

Don't be afraid to ask for help.

Source: Johnson, M. (1993, April). Coping with adversity. *Essence*, 78.

Checkpoint

Use the following questions to check your understanding of the final portion of this chapter. Choose and mark the one correct response to each question.

23. Which of the following quadruplets is in greatest danger of a heart attack?
    a. Fred, who has a hostile personality
    b. Ned, who has a type B personality
    c. Ted, who often feels guilty
    d. Zed, who suffers from insomnia

24. Who is likely to be most ambitious?
    a. A person with insomnia
    b. A person with a type A personality
    c. A person with a type B personality
    d. A person with culture shock

25. What causes guilt?
    a. Depression
    b. Repressed depression
    c. Violation of morals
    d. Atonement for criticism

26. According to Rotter, which of the following persons is likely to believe she is the victim of fate?
    a. Iva, who is an internal person
    b. Edith, who is an external person
    c. Iris, who suffers from insomnia
    d. Gilly, who feels guilty

27. Which of the following behaviors is associated with insomnia?
    a. Type B behavior
    b. External-type behavior
    c. Worry and guilt
    d. Culture shock

28. What should people suffering from insomnia avoid?
    a. Caffeine
    b. Exercise
    c. Regular schedules
    d. Relaxation before bedtime

29. Max, who is from a small town in Nebraska, is visiting the family of his college roommate, Martino, in the Bronx, New York. Martino's family has recently immigrated from El Salvador. Although Max is welcomed warmly, he feels very uncomfortable—the food is different, the apartment is cramped with family, and he has difficulty understanding the language. What is Max experiencing?
    a. Violation of morals
    b. Guilt

c. Hostility
d. Culture shock

Check your responses against the Checkpoint Answer Key at the end of the chapter. If you had difficulty with any question, reread the text. If you had little or no difficulty answering the questions or have resolved problems that you might have had, you are ready to check yourself against the chapter inventory that follows.

CHAPTER INVENTORY

Use this list of objectives as a review checklist. You should be able to do the tasks outlined in the objectives and apply them to everyday examples. If you can, you may feel confident that you have mastered the material in this chapter.

1. Distinghish between internal and external adjustment.
2. Define self-concept, self-esteem, and ideal self.
3. Describe the factors that affect self-esteem, and explain the characteristics of low self-esteem and high self-esteem.
4. Recognize the relationship between adjustment and personality.
5. Define defense mechanisms and explain why they are used.
6. Distinguish between suppression and repression.
7. Define and provide examples of withdrawal, fantasy, repression, rationalization, projection, displacement, reaction formation, compensation, and sublimation.
8. Describe and give examples of projective tests, self-report inventories, and observational and situational tests.
9. Recognize the limitations of each type of personality test, the cautions in personality testing, and the necessity for administering more than one test.
10. Specify two personality types identified by psychologists, and recognize their correlation with heart disease.
11. Name three general adjustment problems.
12. Describe the characteristics and give examples of guilt, insomnia, and culture shock.
13. List five steps toward maintaining a healthy personality and six ways to cope with adversity.

Feedback

The correct answers to the exercises follow. If you did not answer an exercise correctly, review the preceding pages and return to the exercise to correctly complete it.

9-1. a. He will have to adjust his attitude about his importance at work. Apparently he was not missed. He might realize he needs to interact with other people more frequently.
b. He could pick up his telephone and make a few calls. Or he might write a few notes.

9-2. a. High self-esteem
b. High self-esteem
c. Low self-esteem
d. Low self-esteem
e. High self-esteem
f. Low self-esteem
g. High self-esteem
h. High self-esteem
i. Low self-esteem
j. Low self-esteem
k. High self-esteem

9-3. Suppression requires a conscious and deliberate effort to avoid thinking about a problem. Repression is unconscious and cannot be controlled consciously.

9-4. a. Withdrawal
b. Rationalization
c. Regression
d. Compensation
e. Repression
f. Projection
g. Displacement
h. Fantasy
i. Reaction formation
j. Sublimation

9-5. a. In projective tests, interpretation of results is subjective and may differ from one examiner to the next.
b. In self-report inventories, people may try to make a good impression and conceal their faults.
c. In interviews a person could put on an act.
d. In the case of rating scales, many different judges should be used.

9-6. A psychologist should use as many different techniques as possible.

9-7. a. Type B personality
b. Type B personality
c. Type A personality
d. Type A personality

9-8. Type A persons can be helped through group therapy. First they must identify their own type A behavior and situations that are likely to cause stress. Then they can help each other control situations and behavior.

9-9. a. External
b. External
c. Internal
d. Internal

9-10. Avoid coffee.
Exercise every day.
Take a warm bath before going to bed.

9-11. You may have mentioned any of the following: Thailand has group values rather than an individual focus, greater differences in food, a totally different language, and a greater time difference.

Checkpoint Answer Key

1. d; 2. a; 3. a; 4. c; 5. d; 6. b; 7. b; 8. c; 9. e; 10. g; 11. i; 12. a; 13. c; 14. b; 15. k; 16. j; 17. f; 18. h; 19. d; 20. c, d, f; 21. a, g; 22. b, e; 23. a; 24. b; 25. c; 26. b; 27. c; 28. a; 29. d.

Identifying Problem Behavior

Not everything that is faced can be changed; but
nothing can be changed until it is faced.
—James Baldwin

Mindy is a popular college freshman. She is pretty, extremely talkative, and bright. At parties she chats easily about any subject. She seems lighthearted and fun-loving to others. However, Mindy usually feels that her high spirits are not within her control. Her ideas move quickly and she needs to blurt them. She also has a quick temper and will give a strong tongue-lashing to anyone who criticizes her. Her parents feel guilty about her behavior, and her two sisters are embarrassed by her and rarely include her in their plans.

There are times when Mindy becomes quiet. She feels overwhelmingly sad and morose. She avoids other people. Her life seems useless and she fears she is losing control. She has serious thoughts of suicide and considers possible methods she could use. On a few occasions, she has begun to write suicide notes. Is Mindy abnormal? Is her behavior a problem?

Problem behavior is not always easy to define. However, in this chapter you will consider some signs of abnormality, along with problems in diagnosing disorders. You will learn the common symptoms of a variety of anxiety disorders, mood problems, personality confusions, schizophrenias, and organic illnesses. You will also be able to answer the questions about Mindy!

Abnormal means different from normal or average. To be abnormal, behavior must be strangely or markedly different from average or expected behavior. But being unusual is not the only criterion for being considered abnormal by psychologists. Albert Einstein, Hillary Clinton, and Mother Teresa clearly have behaved very differently from the average person. Yet, all have been honored for being different. Their behavior was desirable, if different.

To be considered abnormal, behavior must also be undesirable. Usually people who are workaholics or manage to be active with little or no sleep are considered normal. Only when their behavior upsets or endangers the lives of family and friends or interferes with their own adjustments will they be labeled "abnormal." Usually, abnormal behavior causes emotional distress. Families that are faced with the stress of abnormal behavior of one member often become *dysfunctional* as a reaction. The abnormal behavior upsets the balance of the family, and each member may react differently. Parents, children, and siblings of the abnormal person tend to change their behavior. Some feel anger and resentment or experience shame and try to hide the family problem.

dysfunctional family Family that changes behavior in reaction to the stress of abnormal behavior of one or more members

Now, it is possible to evaluate Mindy: Her uncontrolled talking and morose feelings are not considered average. Further, threats of suicide are undesirable for herself, her family, and her friends. Finally, Mindy seems to be suffering from emotional distress.

Exercise 10-1

List three criteria for abnormal behavior.

a. _____

b. _____

c. _____

Compare your list with the one in the Feedback section.

Problems of Diagnosis

George Albee, a past president of the American Psychological Association, pointed out, "Appendicitis, a brain tumor, and chicken pox are the same everywhere, regardless of culture or class; mental conditions, it seems, are not." It is not easy to diagnose psychological disorders. Psychologists do not always agree on which conditions are really abnormal problems. Further, strange behavior is often only temporary. The extent of a problem may change greatly from time to time. A person may be so mildly depressed that it is difficult to tell whether the behavior is normal or abnormal. At another time the same person may suffer a deep depression that requires intensive treatment.

DSM IV

DSM IV, the fourth edition of the Diagnostic and Statistical Manual of Mental Disorders, published by the American Psychiatric Association, is currently the most widely accepted standard for diagnosing problem behavior. DSM IV describes specific criteria for diagnosing problems. By using DSM IV, clinicians can agree on the diagnoses of the disorders they are treating and understand each other. DSM IV contains descriptions and is not concerned with the causes of disorders. Among the major categories of disorders described in DSM IV are anxiety disorders, abnormal behavior that causes physical problems, changes in identity, mood disorders, substance abuse disorders, personality disorders, schizophrenia, and organic disorders.

Exercise 10-2

Two psychiatrists are discussing a patient's problems. They want to diagnose the patient and find the cause of the disorder. How can DSM IV help them?

_____

_____

_____

_____

Check your response in the Feedback section.

ANXIETY DISORDERS

Anxiety is an uncomfortable feeling. A person has a sense of fearfulness but cannot identify why. The cause of the fear is not immediately present or is vague. Perhaps you have met someone who aroused your anxiety. You felt uncomfortable, fretful, and tense with the person for no apparent reason. Or maybe you have experienced anxiety at the beginning of a new course or job. You have no specific fears but feel some uncomfortable tension. A person who has survived an intensely fearful situation may be left with feelings of anxiety long after the cause of the fear is gone.

anxiety disorder
Continuous state of tension, stress, and fearfulness

Anxiety becomes a major problem, or disorder, when fears are exaggerated or unrealistic. A person suffering from *anxiety disorder* often has such physical symptoms as sweating, shaking, shortness of breath, and a fast heartbeat. Anxiety disorders are somewhat common. Anxiety disorders include phobias, eating disorders, obsessive-compulsive disorders, and post-traumatic stress.

Phobias

phobia Intense, exaggerated, and unrealistic fear

Phobias are the most common forms of anxiety disorders. Phobias are constant, unrealistic fears that interfere with normal living. For instance, if a person fears all animals, even those that are docile and friendly, instead of fearing only threatening animals, such an exaggerated fear is labeled a "phobia." Some phobias are relatively common and do not cause serious negative results. For example, many people feel queasy at the sight of blood or panic at the sight of a harmless snake or mouse. These simple, exaggerated fears rarely interfere with everyday life.

The most severe phobia that clearly interferes with normal living is *agoraphobia*. Agoraphobia is a fear of leaving one's own home. More than half the people who seek treatment for phobias suffer from agoraphobia (Chambless, 1986). These people are unable to go shopping, go to a movie, drive a car, ride a bus, or even walk on a public street.

agoraphobia Most severe phobia, usually accompanied by panic attacks; inability to go out of the house

The list of possible phobias is almost endless. Fifteen of the more common types include:

Acrophobia	Fear of heights
Androphobia	Fear of men
Aquaphobia	Fear of water
Autophobia	Fear of being alone
Cardiophobia	Fear of heart disease
Chrematophobia	Fear of money
Claustrophobia	Fear of closed places
Hemophobia	Fear of blood
Necrophobia	Fear of corpses
Nyctophobia	Fear of the dark
Panophobia	Fear of everything
Phobophobia	Fear of one's own fear
Pyrophobia	Fear of fire
Thanophobia	Fear of death
Toxicophobia	Fear of poison
Triskaidekaphobia	Fear of the number 13
Zoophobia	Fear of animals

A complete list would even mention arachibutyrophobia, fear of peanut butter sticking to the roof of the mouth, and Santa Claustrophobia, a fear of being caught in chimneys! Some phobias can be serious and even life-threatening. Methods for treating phobias are discussed in Chapter 11, Getting Help.

Exercise 10-3

Ms. F. is a nonswimmer. She is concerned about drowning and always wears a life vest when sailing or canoeing. At beaches, she is careful to stay in the water areas that are protected by lifeguards.

Ms. P. is also concerned about drowning. Although she had some swimming lessons as a child, she will no longer go near water. In fact, she refuses to sit in a bathtub, jacuzzi, or water container of any form. She refuses to shower. She even becomes anxious when she is around water fountains.

Explain why Ms. P. is suffering from a phobia and Ms. F. is not.

_____

_____

_____

_____

Please check your explanation against that in the Feedback section.

Eating Disorders

anorexia nervosa
Prolonged refusal to eat, resulting in a severe weight loss

Anxiety is believed to cause eating disorders. One eating disorder, *anorexia nervosa*, generally begins when young girls grow anxious about becoming overweight. Although those with the disorder initially do not want to eat, eventually they completely lose their desire for food. They diet continually and cannot stop even when they are so underweight that their lives are threatened. Frequently, the sight of food makes them nauseated.

Researchers believe that women are more likely than men to diet to control their weight. As a result, 90 percent of the sufferers of anorexia are women (Lucas, 1991).

bulimia Binge eating followed by laxatives or self-induced vomiting

Bulimia is an eating disorder related to anorexia. But while anorexic patients are usually painfully thin, bulimics are generally of normal weight. The bulimic person goes on an eating binge and then uses laxatives or tries to vomit.

Researchers have found that bulimics eat to control their anxiety. On one binge a bulimic person might consume several candy bars, an entire pie, three sandwiches, a large pizza, a jar of peanut butter, two donuts, and three bowls of cereal. Laxatives and self-induced vomiting are used to avoid getting fat. Bulimia is believed to be most common in college-age women. Estimates of the prevalence in this group range from 5 to 67 percent (Hart and Ollendich, 1985; Polivy and Herman, 1985).

Not all cases of dieting and binge eating are considered to be forms of anorexia or bulimia. For a person to be considered anorexic, he or she must lose at least 15 percent of original body weight. Many people who binge eat are not considered bulimic because they do not use laxatives or self-induced vomiting. As indicated in the excerpt in Feature 10-1, many women suffer from both anorexia and bulimia, and these eating disorders are closely related to other problems, including alcoholism.

FEATURE 10-1 PSYCHOLOGY IN THE NEWS

Eating Disorders—Part I

. . . Many women suffer from anorexia and bulimia at the same time or alternate between them. About half of anorectic patients also have bulimia, and about 40% of severely bulimic patients have a history of anorexia (usually, but not always, anorexia or at least restrictive dieting comes first). The combination is particularly debilitating both physically and emotionally. Bulimic anorectics are usually older and have been ill longer, and they are more likely to be anxious, depressed, emotionally unstable, or alcoholic. They are slower to recover and more likely to commit suicide. . . .

Bulimia is often accompanied by other psychiatric disorders, of which the most common and most important is alcoholism. In one study, one-third of bulimic women also had drug or alcohol problems. As many as one-third of alcoholic women may have had an eating disorder at some time; in two-thirds of the cases, the eating disorder comes first. A high rate of alcoholism is found in the families of bulimic patients—in one study, 28% as compared with 14% in families of controls. In another study alcoholism was found to be four times as common in the families of bulimic anorectics as in the families of restricting (nonbulimic) anorectics.

Source: (1992, December). Eating disorders—Part I. *The Harvard Mental Health Letter*, 2.

Obsessive-Compulsive Disorders

Have you ever been so concerned with a thought that you found concentrating on anything else impossible? Whether you were preoccupied by a broken romance, an illness of a close relative, or your own safety, many people would say you were obsessed with the thought. However, psychologists would argue that these thoughts were not true obsessions. You were dealing with real problems that most likely could be resolved.

Obsessions are persistent *ideas* or impulses that invade your mind against your will. They cannot be resolved. The ideas seem senseless but you cannot avoid them. One common obsession centers on being contaminated by germs. As a result of this obsession, a person would refuse to shake hands or come into contact with other people.

obsessions Unwanted but persistent thoughts or ideas

Obsessions often lead to *compulsions*. A compulsion is a persistent *behavior*. People who are obsessed with fears of contamination may become compulsive about hand-washing. They would feel they were never clean and would constantly wash and wipe their hands.

compulsion Repeated and persistent behavior ritual that a person feels compelled to carry out to avoid disaster

Compulsions often take the form of rituals. A hand-washing ritual might consist of two washings with soap and hot water, an antiseptic rinse, and waving the hands in circles to air-dry them. The ritual would be repeated whenever another person or object was touched. Failure to complete the ritual would cause intense anxiety. The compulsion would be more important than any other aspect of life.

Post-Traumatic Stress

Severe shocks or traumas cause anxiety. Sometimes the anxiety persists and becomes long-lasting. In these cases the person is considered to be suffering from a *post-traumatic stress disorder (PTSD)*. Symptoms include dreaming about the traumatic event, experiencing jumpiness, guilt, concentration problems, extreme suspicion, and overreacting to situations that stir memories of the trauma. Bower (1991) reported that about 12 million women in the United States have had PTSD resulting from rape, attempted sexual or physical assault,

post-traumatic stress Anxiety disorder that causes a person to constantly reexperience a traumatic or shocking event

FIGURE 10-1. His compulsion is stronger than any other need, including the need for silverware.

or a highly stressful experience, such as seeing someone killed. Post-traumatic stress disorder can also result from fire, an earthquake, or a bombing, as well as from rape; the condition is most common among wounded Vietnam veterans. Recent evidence has shown that PTSD contributes to family dysfunction (see Feature 10-2).

Exercise 10-4

Read each of the following symptoms, and indicate whether the person is likely to be suffering from anorexia nervosa, bulimia, obsessive-compulsive disorder, or post-traumatic stress disorder.

a. A woman who was raped in Bosnia still awakens with nightmares of the horror scenes.

_____

b. A woman is so concerned about being on time that she carries an alarm clock and checks the time every five minutes.

_____

c. A wounded Vietnam veteran is extremely jumpy. He has strong feelings of guilt about surviving while most of his friends were killed.

_____

d. A college student eats twenty-five pancakes, two large coffee cakes, three pounds of bacon, and two dozen blueberry muffins, and then takes a strong laxative.

_____

e. A teenager is extremely thin but believes she is overweight. She is starving herself.

_____

FEATURE 10-2 PSYCHOLOGY IN THE NEWS

Vietnam Combat Trauma: A Family Affair

Post-traumatic stress disorder (PTSD) continues to exact a psychological toll not just on a substantial number of Vietnam combat veterans, but on their families as well. . . . From late 1986 through May 1988, interviews were conducted with a random national sample of 1,200 Vietnam vets, 319 of whom suffered from PTSD, and with 376 spouses or live-in partners of the vets, including 122 married to or living with PTSD victims.

In the year prior to interviews, families of veterans diagnosed with PTSD experienced far more violent acts by both partners, more marital problems, more emotional distress, and a greater number of serious behavior problems among children. . . .

Source: (1993, January 9). Vietnam combat trauma: A family affair. *Science News.*

Occasionally a person will develop physical symptoms, and no organic or physical problem can be found. An estimated one in five health-care dollars is spent on the physical symptoms of psychological problems (Corr, 1992). One of the most dramatic (and fortunately, rare) examples is *conversion disorder*. The patient may suddenly lose sensation in an arm or leg, become paralyzed, or lose the sense of smell, hearing, or seeing. No physical findings can be found to explain the problem.

conversion disorder Anxiety disorder characterized by a loss of sensation without any physical cause

Sometimes people believe they are ill when in fact they are healthy. Have you ever known someone who constantly complained of a variety of ailments, yet physicians could find no problems? The person could be suffering from *hypochondriasis*. Hypochondriacs are totally preoccupied with health problems. They know the symptoms of an amazing assortment of diseases. It is not uncommon for hypochondriacs to believe they have symptoms of leprosy, heart disease, cancer, or other major disorders. A simple headache could be a signal of a heart attack or a brain tumor to a person with hypochondriasis.

hypochondriasis Anxiety disorder characterized by a total preoccupation with exaggerated health problems

Checkpoint

Use the following questions to check your understanding of this portion of the chapter. Choose and mark the one correct response to each question.

1. Which of the following factors is required for behavior to be considered abnormal?
   a. Rare
   b. Undesirable
   c. Distress
   d. All of the above

2. Mr. W. is a workaholic who lives alone. He stays at his office until 11 P.M. and then brings home additional work. He rarely gets more than four hours of sleep. Is his behavior abnormal?
   a. Yes, because it is rare
   b. Yes, because it is undesirable
   c. No, because it is not undesirable
   d. Yes, because most people need more sleep

3. What is the purpose of DSM IV?
   a. To determine disorders
   b. To determine causes of disorders
   c. To cure disorders
   d. To treat disorders

4. Which of the following classifications of disorders includes phobias, eating disorders, obsessive-compulsive disorders, and post-traumatic stress?
   a. Anxiety
   b. Anorexia nervosa
   c. Hypochondriasis
   d. Conversion disorder

5. What is the most common form of anxiety disorder?
   a. Eating disorders
   b. Phobias
   c. Obsessive-compulsions
   d. Post-traumatic stress

6. What is a phobia?
   a. A realistic fear
   b. A specific fear
   c. An unrealistic fear
   d. An eating disorder

7. Mr. A. suffers from agoraphobia. Which of the following statements is likely to be true?
   a. He is afraid of being stuck in a chimney.
   b. He is afraid of water.
   c. He does not have an anxiety disorder.
   d. He is afraid of leaving his house.

8. Which phobia is considered most severe?
   a. Acrophobia
   b. Agoraphobia
   c. Claustrophobia
   d. Zoophobia

9. What do patients suffering from anorexia nervosa and bulimia have in common?
   a. Both have obsessive-compulsive disorders.
   b. Both have eating disorders.
   c. Both suffer from post-traumatic stress.
   d. Both are normal.

10. Mrs. H. believes her hair is messy and is going to tangle and choke her. As a result she stops what she is doing every ten minutes and begins a hair-brushing ritual. Which of the following problems is she demonstrating?
    a. Post-traumatic stress
    b. Anorexia nervosa
    c. Obsessive-compulsive disorder
    d. Arachibutyrophobia

11. Which of the following persons might suffer from post-traumatic stress?
    a. A rape victim
    b. A woman surviving an earthquake
    c. A Vietnam veteran
    d. All of the above

Check your responses against the Checkpoint Answer Key at the end of the chapter. If you had difficulty with any question, reread the text. If you had little or no difficulty or have resolved the problems that you might have had, you are ready to continue with the second portion of the chapter.

You are most likely familiar with the famous story of Dr. Jekyll and Mr. Hyde. Dr. Jekyll suffered from a disorder called *multiple personality*. He had two distinct and quite different personalities. Each personality had its own memories, preferences, voice, facial expressions, and handwriting. Multiple personality is not fiction. Although extremely rare, it is a real disorder.

The most famous true story of multiple personality was documented in *The Three Faces of Eve* (Thigpen and Cleckly, 1954). Although cases of multiple personality provide material for dramatic books, films, and news stories, many psychiatrists and psychologists are skeptical about the popularity of the disorder. It is now used as an argument in legal defense. Prior to 1979, only 200 cases of multiple personality had been identified. Since 1979 more than 2500 cases have occurred. The disorder does not seem to exist outside of North America (Aldridge-Morris, 1989). Many professionals suspect that knowledge of the disorder has provided criminals with the ability to fake the symptoms. There are many theories about the causes of multiple personality. However, since the disorder has been so rare, research has been limited. The cause of multiple personality remains unknown.

multiple personality Rare disorder in which a person has two or more distinct personalities, each becoming prominent at a different time

FIGURE 10-2. It appears that Dr. Jekyll's "other" personality will give the second opinion.

amnesia Partial or complete loss of memory

Amnesia, a partial or complete memory loss, is another type of change in identity or consciousness. As explained in Chapter 4, amnesia can result from physical causes. Alcoholism, drug abuse, head injuries, and nutritional deficiencies are among the possible physical causes. Amnesia can also be caused by psychological factors. This form of amnesia is usually brought on by a highly stressful event and generally is only temporary. The duration varies; it can last for hours, days, or even years. The amount of memory loss also varies, from a very specific repression of the traumatic event to a complete loss of identity. People suffering from severe amnesia may forget who they are and totally lose contact with the real world. Schacter (1986) found that it is often difficult to determine whether people who claim a loss of identity are suffering from a severe form of amnesia or merely faking the symptoms.

Exercise 10-5

Describe two ways in which multiple personality and amnesia are alike.

a. _____

b. _____

Turn to the Feedback section to check your answers.

MOOD DISORDERS

Everyone has good moods and bad ones. You proably can recall feeling sad, gloomy, and listless. Perhaps you were terribly disappointed with your grades, had a serious argument with a good friend, or were fired from a job. You may have remained depressed and grumpy for days or even weeks. You were suffering from a mild form of *depression.*

depression Mood disorder in which a person feels overwhelming sadness

You might also recall some of your happier moods. The bliss of falling in love or winning an award may have kept you in an outstanding mood. Most days your moods are likely to be between the high of bliss and the low of gloom.

However, people with mood disorders are almost constantly coping with these severe moods. The moods are so severe that people do not have control of themselves. Some people suffer only from depression and experience only low moods. Others have both high moods (mania) and low moods (depression). They suffer from bipolar disorder.

Depression

Recall the last time you felt depressed. What brought on your depression? Maybe you were criticized by someone and went through a period of stress. Or perhaps you suffered a sense of personal loss resulting from the death of someone you loved. Depression is expected after the loss of a loved one, whether through death or divorce. Briscoe and Smith (1975) reported that divorced persons suffer even deeper and more extensive depression than widows and widowers do. Persons bereaved after the death of a loved one are

300

given an opportunity to mourn their loss with the support of family and friends. Divorced persons are usually expected to adjust without any condolences or help from others. As a result, divorced persons experience greater difficulty in recovering from their depression.

Sometimes depression has no apparent cause. You probably have had a down day and could not identify the reason. Possibly you were repressing the cause. Psychiatrists have also found that depression can occur regardless of outside events. Researchers have noted that certain hormonal and neurochemical changes can cause depression.

Some people suffer from severe depression during the winter season. During the 1980s psychiatrists labeled this winter mood change *seasonal affective disorder (SAD)*. SAD is a serious depression that usually begins in fall or winter and ends in spring. The disorder is more common in northern areas where seasonal changes are greater. Researchers have found the prevalence to vary from 1 to 2 percent in Florida to 4 percent in Washington, D.C., and 9 percent in Fairbanks, Alaska (*The Harvard Mental Health Letter*, 1993). Since victims of SAD seem to react favorably to treatment with light, researchers believe that this form of depression is triggered by shorter days rather than colder weather (see Feature 10-3).

seasonal affective disorder (SAD) Serious depression that usually begins in fall or winter and ends in spring

---

FEATURE 10-3 PSYCHOLOGY IN THE NEWS

Suffering from the Winter Blahs? A Bright Remedy Emerges

It doesn't get any worse than this. The holidays are over. The bright colored lights seem sadly dated. We get up in the dark and get home in the dark. December bills are arriving. Days are a boring gray. The leaves are gone. The grass is brown. Tax forms are coming. Some bones complain, and the flu is everywhere. . . .

Until recently even the name of the annual malady was boring: The winter blahs. Millions of Americans wallow in the blahs every winter. . . .

The blahs are now called SAD, for Seasonal Affective Disorder. Feel better already? According to Dr. Michael Terman, a Manhattan specialist who has treated hundreds of area residents, SAD's symptoms are increased desire for sleep, increased desire to stay asleep, increased desire for afternoon naps, increased desire to eat, especially carbohydrates, increased anxiety and gloom and increased lethargy, sometimes to the point where victims actually watch the Weather Channel. . . .

Mrs. Heyman, a New York native and an educational consultant here, began getting depressed at the end of Daylight Savings Time every year.

She was a dynamo all summer. But when the snow fences went up, "then I got like a bear," she recalls, "all fat and grumpy and lazy." Anything was too much for her. She always attributed her malaise to the weather, which was partly correct.

A few years ago Dr. Al Lewy of the Oregon Health Services University began experimenting by exposing winter-depressed patients to different timings and intensities of light. Within days their symptoms lifted. He estimated that 20 percent of North Americans, concentrated in the northern tier of states, could benefit from light treatments. . . .

As prescribed, Mrs. Heyman rises at 5 A.M. For 30 minutes from October through April she reads or exercises in front of lights 20 times brighter than a normal room. She also frequently walks outdoors without sunglasses. "I'm a different person," she says. "I just finished painting our new room. I play tennis. I'm P.T.A. president. Who cares about snow fences now?" . . .

Source: Malcolm, A. H. (1992, January 7). Suffering from the winter blahs? A bright remedy emerges. *The New York Times*, B-6.

FIGURE 10-3. One symptom of depression is a sense of hopelessness.

What are the symptoms of depression? A depressed person feels drained of incentives, tires easily, and lacks energy. Self-esteem is low, and the focus is on negative aspects of life. Somehow all positive features in life are lost. Personal achievements are minimized. Suppose you admired an oil painting by a depressed man. He would probably say it was easy to sketch or he had good brushes or super paints. He would never take personal credit for his achievement.

catastrophize Tendency to exaggerate things that may go wrong

Because confidence is low, depressed people tend to *catastrophize*, that is, exaggerate things that may go wrong. Assume you want to cheer up a depressed woman. You can recall that she once baked a delicious lemon meringue pie. You invite her to a covered-dish party at your home and ask her to bring her wonderful pie. She would probably begin by giving credit to the recipe rather than to her cooking talent. Then she would suggest that you bake the

---

FEATURE 10-4

Common Symptoms of Depression

Feelings of sadness, hopelessness

Insomnia, early wakening, difficulty getting up

Thoughts of suicide and death

Restlessness, irritability

Low self-esteem or guilt feelings

Eating disturbance—usually loss of appetite and weight

Fatigue, weakness, decreased energy

Diminished ability to think or concentrate

Loss of interest and pleasure in activities once enjoyed, such as sex

Chronic pains that fail to respond to typical treatment

pie. After you insisted that you did not have her baking talent, she might begin dwelling on all the possible mistakes she could make. Her thoughts might proceed, "I will probably ruin the crust or blow the mixing order. Once I burned the meringue. Nothing I do comes out right. How can I expect people to eat my food? I should not go to the party."

Depressed people prefer not to be cheered up and avoid doing anything pleasurable. Tears come easily, and sleeping and daydreaming can become excessive. One of the danger signals in depression is an unwillingness or inability to communicate with others. Sometimes depression brings on a sudden major change in behavior. A quiet person becomes boisterous or an easygoing person becomes antagonistic. Feature 10-4 lists the common symptoms of depression.

Brody (1991) reported that depression is twice as common in women as in men. In the United States alone, about 7 million women suffer from some form of depression. This sex difference holds for all races, and at all levels of income and education. Even unreported and unacknowledged depressions are twice as common in women. However, as the article in Feature 10-5 reveals, clinicians are more likely to diagnose women as depressed.

Since a depressed person does not want to be cheered up, you may be wondering what you can do to help. Although you can give personal support, victims of depression really need professional assistance. Treatment for depression is described in Chapter 11.

Exercise 10-6

Listed below are several symptoms. Put a check beside each symptom that suggests a possibility of depression.

_____ Lowered self-esteem

_____ Catastrophizing

FEATURE 10-5 PSYCHOLOGY IN THE NEWS

Personal Health: Recognizing Demons of Depression in Either Sex

Depression has long been considered primarily a woman's disease. The rate for women being treated and in community surveys, in fact, is two to six times as high as for men.

Now it looks as if men could be starting to catch up. Economic and social pressures and a greater willingness by men and doctors to recognize and discuss emotional problems may eventually whittle away the statistical difference. Still, according to a recent analysis involving more than 23,000 patients and 500 medical practitioners, many more mistakes are made in recognizing depression in men than in women.

The study . . . found that clinicians outside the mental health field failed to recognize symptoms of depression in two-thirds of the men as against half the women who were found to be suffering from it, using standardized tests. Furthermore, the clinicians in the study were more likely to diagnose depression in women when in fact they were not suffering from it, according to test results. . . .

Source: Brody, J. E. (1991, December 18). Personal health: Recognizing demons of depression, in either sex. *The New York Times,* C-21.

_____ Excessive energy

_____ Irritability

_____ Thoughts of death

_____ Good communication

_____ Strong motivation

_____ Proneness to tears

_____ Insomnia

_____ Hopelessness

You may compare your list to the one in the Feedback section.

Bipolar Disorder

At the opposite pole from depression is mania. Mania is an abnormally strong feeling of well-being. A manic person is full of energy, ambitions, plans, and power. Rapid speech and jokes are common. Perhaps this sounds like a wonderful state to be in. Actually the manic state is so extreme that behavior becomes irrational. Large sums of money may be spent or given away. Ideas often become outrageous. Hyperactivity is so strong that nothing is accomplished; the individual may not sleep for several days.

Mania almost always has a dark side. While someone can experience depression without ever feeling manic, it is rare for a person to experience only mania. People who have manic episodes almost always go through periods of depression. Their problem is labeled *bipolar disorder,* because their moods swing from a manic "pole" to a depressed "pole." On the positive side, people with bipolar disorder are likely to be highly creative.

bipolar disorder
Mood disorder involving mood swings between depression and mania

Exercise 10-7

Reread the first page of this chapter and diagnose Mindy's possible problem.

_____

_____

_____

You may check your response in the Feedback section.

SUBSTANCE ABUSE AND ADDICTION

About 15 percent of Americans have problems with drugs and alcohol, costing more than $110 billion each year. Each year more than 100,000 deaths result from alcohol-related violent crimes and accidents. (Lord, 1987; Gallant, 1987; Kamerow et al., 1986). Alcohol is the cause of 65 percent of murders and 40 percent of car accidents (Kent, 1990; Salisbury, 1990) and is the third major

Most new cases of alcoholism are with adolescents.

cause of death. About 200,000 new cases of alcoholism are diagnosed each year; most are in adolescents. Addiction had become such a major concern in the United States by 1993 that the American Board of Psychiatry and Neurology, with support from the American Psychiatric Association, began requiring a certification examination for psychiatrists specializing in addiction medicine.

The damage caused by alcohol and other drugs leads to a steady deterioration of the brain and other organs of the body, which will eventually cause death. Coleman (1972) reported that both alcoholics and drug users have low self-esteem and lack of confidence. Worried about failure, they have severe reactions to criticism and need constant praise and reinforcement. Alcohol is often consumed to reduce anxiety.

Williams (1966) found that nonalcoholics can reduce depression with up to 4 ounces of liquor, that is, about two drinks. However, after the third drink, depression is increased. Research by Nathan and O'Brien (1971) concluded that alcoholics become more depressed after their continued drinking. A more recent study by McKinney proposed that alcoholics are reinforced by the initial decrease in depression. They continue to consume alcohol in hopes that depression may be reduced, but depression only becomes deeper.

Alcoholics drink until they are completely intoxicated. Speech becomes slurred, coordination is impaired, and behavior and personality change noticeably. Alcoholics often go to work intoxicated and may even continue their drinking at their jobs. Alcoholics deny that they have a drinking problem. DSM IV lists *denial* as a key symptom of alcoholism. Since alcoholics deny their problem, they commonly drive while intoxicated, and accidents, injuries, and deaths result. Families of alcoholics also suffer. Spouses of alcoholics become resentful and controlling, parents experience grief and guilt, and children may suffer from verbal or physical abuse and are likely to have many difficulties throughout their lives (see Feature 10-6).

Several studies (Begleiter and Porjesz, 1990; Comings et al., 1991; Johnson et al., 1992) have indicated that a tendency toward alcoholism and substance abuse is inherited. Researchers feel that they are close to identifying specific gene abnormalities. Although heredity is a factor in creating a predisposition toward addiction, cultural and social factors can aggravate the condition (see Feature 10-7).

Recent improvements in technology have allowed researchers to learn more about the effects of alcohol and other drugs on the brain. Methods for controlling alcoholism are discussed in Chapter 11.

While alcohol deepens depression, many illegal drugs permit an immediate escape from anxiety and depression. But drugs clearly do not resolve any problems. Drug users suffer side effects and become addicted, while the original problem persists. Illegal drugs are generally more expensive than alcohol. As a result addicted drug users must find ways to come up with money to purchase drugs. Frequently, stealing and prostitution are the techniques chosen. Because of their addiction, drug users will use any method possible, whether legal or not, to keep themselves high. Methods used in drug therapy are described in Chapter 11.

Exercise 10-8

Use the text material to answer the following questions.

FEATURE 10-6 PSYCHOLOGY IN THE NEWS

Marital Woes May Await Children of Alcoholics

The children of "problem drinkers" are more likely to have marital and psychiatric problems when they grow up, a study of nearly 3,000 North Carolina residents has found. They are no more likely, however, to have difficulties with social relationships or on the job than the children of non-alcoholics.

The study . . . is among the few to separate the effects of problem drinking from other risk factors, such as poverty or physical abuse, that are sometimes associated with alcoholic families.

Previous smaller studies have found that heavy parental drinking is associated with a multiplicity of later problems for children, ranging from a higher rate of anxiety disorders to a greater likelihood of marrying an alcoholic. . . .

After controlling for various risk factors, as well as for age, race, and sex, researchers found that children of problem drinkers were more likely to have psychiatric problems as adults and were more likely to walk out on their spouses.

"Even after controlling for the effects of other childhood risk factors, we found that exposure to parental problem drinking in childhood was associated with a significantly higher lifetime prevalence of psychiatric symptoms," the authors wrote. "It is likely that the drinking parent's inconsistent and unpredictable behavior and availability place the child at risk for greater psychological distress later in life."

Source: Boodman, S. (1993, April 27). Marital woes may await children of alcoholics. *Washington Post Health.*

a. How are alcoholics and users of illegal drugs alike?

_____

_____

_____

b. How are they different?

_____

_____

Please turn to the Feedback section to check your answers.

SUICIDE

Substance abuse can lead to suicide. A long-term study by Aaron Beck and Robert Steer (1989) revealed that alcoholics had a five times higher than average chance of completing suicide. Characteristics such as age, sex, race, previous suicide attempts, level of depression, and most psychiatric disorders did not correlate well with completed suicides. Alcoholism was the only psychiatric diagnosis that made a clear difference in suicide completion. Unemployment alone did not increase the risk, but was associated with alcoholism.

FEATURE 10-7 PSYCHOLOGY IN THE NEWS

Addiction—Part II

Social conditions also help to determine who uses a drug and how it is used. Historical changes have greatly influenced the patterns and consequences of drug dependence. The extraction of pure chemicals from plant materials, which began two centuries ago, has created more powerful and dangerous addictive agents. The invention of the hypodermic needle in the middle of the last century allowed drug users to circumvent the body's natural biological defenses of bitter taste and slow absorption through the digestive tract. The many synthetic drugs invented in the twentieth century have created further opportunities for abuse and addiciton.

Culture affects patterns of drug dependence in other ways as well. One influence is the companionship and approval of other drug users. People who spend most of their time with heavy drinkers are more likely to become heavy drinkers themselves. . . . Some ethnic groups are more susceptible to alcoholism than others, possibly because of drinking practices that have been passed on from generation to generation. Any breakdown of social controls may promote a drug dependence. Addiction can become an epidemic when a drug is suddenly introduced, as alcohol was in Native American societies, to cultures that are unprepared for its effects and have no customs to guide its use. One reason for the high rate of addiction in modern industrial societies may be our lack of accepted rules about who should use drugs and when. . . .

Source: (1992, November). Addiction—Part II. *The Harvard Mental Health Letter,* 1.

Suicide is more likely among the lonely. Whether the loneliness results from being aged, divorced, or single and living alone, the person attempting suicide is often without friends. The suicide rate is highest among the elderly. However, incidence of suicide among adolescents has increased. Acute suicide is the second most frequent cause of death among young people between the ages of fifteen and twenty-four. (Accidents are number one.) The suicide rate for these young people has increased by more than 150 percent in the past twenty years (Harvard Medical School *Mental Health Letter*, 1986).

Suppose a friend or coworker indicated he was thinking about suicide. Psychologists suggest that any suicide threat should be taken seriously. Usually the person is calling for help. The first step should be to take him to a physician, psychologist, or psychiatrist. If he refused, it would be advisable to help him express his feelings and to show sincere concern and empathy. You might suggest that there are alternative solutions to his problem. It would be wise to determine whether he has a specific plan; if there is a plan, the situation is even more dangerous. Offer to hold the weapon (gun, razor, pills, or other) for a given time. Encourage your friend to seek help, and offer to acccompany him. If he is persistent about avoiding professionals, set another meeting time. Meanwhile you can get professional advice before the next meeting. The person attempting suicide needs assurances about his personal worth and importance to others. A friend who is supportive is crucial to survival.

Checkpoint

Use the following questions to check your understanding of this portion of the chapter. Choose and mark the one correct response to each question.

12. From which of the following disorders was Dr. Jekyll suffering?
    a. Split personality
    b. Multiple personality
    c. Bipolar disorder
    d. Amnesia

13. Which of the following is a possible psychological cause of amnesia?
    a. A traumatic event
    b. Alcoholism
    c. A head injury
    d. A vitamin deficiency

14. Which of the following amnesia victims is most likely to have memory restored?
    a. A drug addict
    b. A person who suffered brain damage
    c. A person with a severe nutritional deficiency
    d. A victim of an airplane crash

15. During which season are victims of SAD likely to feel depressed?
    a. Winter
    b. Spring
    c. Summer
    d. Fall

16. Which of the following persons is likely to experience the most severe depression?
    a. A person whose spouse just died
    b. A person who is suddenly divorced
    c. A person with type A personality
    d. A person with type B personality

17. Assume you have just admired an afghan crocheted by a depressed man. What is he most likely to do?
    a. Become invigorated because of your compliment
    b. Explain the intricacies and difficulties of crocheting
    c. Claim the pattern was so easy anyone could have done it
    d. Feel encouraged and tell you about his other accomplishments

18. What do most manics also experience?
    a. Multiple personality
    b. Amnesia
    c. Alcoholism
    d. Depression

19. Ivana has come home from work feeling depressed. She decides to have a few cocktails. How many can she have before becoming even more depressed?
    a. One or two
    b. Three or four
    c. Five or six
    d. None

20. Which of the following persons is most likely to steal?
    a. A guilty person
    b. An alcoholic
    c. A depressed person
    d. A drug addict

21. Which of the following persons is most likely to complete a suicide attempt?
    a. A person with multiple personality
    b. A person with bipolar disorder
    c. A person with amnesia
    d. An alcoholic

22. When should a suicide threat be taken seriously?
    a. When the person is elderly
    b. When the person is between 15 and 24
    c. When the person has a plan
    d. Always

Check your responses against the Checkpoint Answer Key at the end of the chapter. If you had difficulty with any question, reread the text. If you had little or no difficulty answering the questions or have resolved problems that you might have had, you are ready to continue with the final portion of this chapter.

personality disorder Pattern of negative traits that cause distress and an inability to get along with others, but the traits are not viewed as abnormal by the person exhibiting them

Personality disorders involve long-lasting traits or habits that interfere with relationships with other people. Most of these negative traits show up at an early age and strengthen with time. People with personality disorders do not recognize their problems. They think their behavior is normal and natural. Among the many forms of personality disorder are antisocial personality and borderline personality.

Antisocial Personality

antisocial personality Condition involving hurting others and breaking laws without any guilt

Persons with *antisocial personalities* seem to lack consciences and morals. They seem to feel no guilt when they hurt others or break laws. Most are attractive males with above-average intelligence. They manipulate other people and will seem sincerely sorry when they are caught in a lie or a crime. Some are even sociable and charming. As you might suspect, many young prisoners suffer from antisocial personality.

Borderline Personality

borderline personality Personality disorder involving instability, confused self-image, and problems in relationships

People with *borderline personalities* have trouble understanding who they really are. They are unstable and act impulsively. Their behavior is unpredictable, and they often feel empty and bored. It has been suggested that Adolf Hitler and Marilyn Monroe were borderline personalities (Sass, 1982).

Borderline personality is often difficult to diagnose. It seems to be close to depression and leads to such self-destructive behavior as drinking, gambling,

"Crime certainly doesn't pay. With me, it's always been a labor of love."
FIGURE 10-4. A victim of antisocial personality disorder.

sexual promiscuity, and even suicide. About two-thirds of the borderline patients are women. Incest appears to be an important factor. Females with borderline personality disorder are three to ten times as likely to have been victims of sexual abuse than are women in the general population. Although the symptoms usually last for many years, most borderline patients conquer their alcohol and drug habits and become stable in their mid-thirties. However, during the years before stability, borderline patients who are alcoholic and depressed are at great risk for suicide, with a staggering rate of 37 percent (Stone, 1990).

Exercise 10-9

Identify the personality disorders suggested by each of the following descriptions.

a. This person is almost entirely indifferent to the concerns of others and breaks laws freely.

    _____

b. This person has a constant feeling of emptiness and boredom.

    _____

c. This person is unstable and unpredictable.

    _____

d. This person will pretend to be sorry for a crime just to manipulate others.

    _____

Turn to the Feedback section to check your responses.

SCHIZOPHRENIA

The word *schizophrenia* literally means "split mind." But schizophrenia should not be confused with the "split" of multiple personality. The schizophrenic does not have two or more distinct personalities. Rather, in schizophrenia, the mind has split with reality and has become fragmented. The schizophrenic patient has thought disturbances and may suffer from delusions and hallucinations.

schizophrenia Severe disturbance involving hallucinations, delusions, or thought disturbances

Thought disturbances include odd associations, with jumbled ideas. This may result in speech that cannot be understood and is labeled "word salad." Words are left out and often there are no clear sentences. Word salads are often accompanied by bizarre behavior. A schizophrenic might giggle at a sad event or become furious when given joyous news. Some schizophrenics show no emotion at all.

A schizophrenic person who is having a *delusion* imagines something that is not true. Even when given proof to the contrary, the person continues imagining. For example, a woman may imagine she is Betsy Ross and insist that she made the first American flag. Evidence such as the dates that Betsy Ross lived, changes in the style and design of flags, the existence of Betsy Ross's tombstone, or any other contrary evidence will be ignored. The woman will persist in her delusion.

delusion Imagined idea that is not true and persists in spite of information to the contrary

A schizophrenic person suffering from *hallucinations* hears voices or sees images that do not exist in reality. A man who is hallucinating believes that he

hallucinations Voices or images that do not really exist

"You think you've got problems—this poor guy next to me thinks he's invisible."

FIGURE 10-5. Believing that he is Napoleon is an example of a delusion. The "poor guy" in the empty chair is a hallucination.

is seeing and hearing real images and voices. He may carry on a conversation and permit space for an imaginary person. Often the imagined voices and visions play a major role in a schizophrenic's experiences.

Symptoms of schizophrenia usually first appear in adolescence or early adulthood. Generally the symptoms become worse with each schizophrenic episode. But sometimes the symptoms come on abruptly and disappear with time. Schizophrenia varies greatly in types of symptoms, seriousness, and the length of the episodes.

There is evidence that people can inherit a genetic predisposition toward schizophrenia (Faraone and Tsuang, 1985). Researchers have also found that stress can trigger schizophrenic episodes (Warner, 1986). The article in Feature 10-8 reinforces that schizophrenia may result from a combination of a genetic predisposition and stress and may be a combination of diseases rather than a single disease.

Exercise 10-10

Two men have just seen a film about a woman who has two distinct personalities. She has a kind and wholesome personality and a dark, shady personality. She gives herself a different name when she experiences each of her two sides. One of the male viewers insists she is schizophrenic. Is he right?

Please compare your response to the one in the Feedback section at the end of the chapter.

Exercise 10-11

List three possible symptoms of schizophrenia.

_____

_____

You may check your list against the one in the Feedback section.

ORGANIC BRAIN DISORDERS

Organic brain disorders have a clear physical cause within brain tissue. Sometimes the problem is temporary, as in the case of vitamin deficiencies. A lack of the vitamin niacin can cause the brain disorder pellagra. Pellagra victims suffer from delirium and hallucinations. However, with a proper diet their behavior will become normal. Syphilis, a cause of brain damage, is treatable with penicillin.

However, organic brain disorders are often permanent and worsen steadily, perhaps leading to death. An example is *Alzheimer's disease,* which causes a gradual loss of memory, thinking, and motor ability. Most cases of senility in old age are caused by Alzheimer's disease (see Figure 10-6). Unfortunately, the diagnosis of Alzheimer's is difficult and is usually done by eliminating the possibility of other disorders. Some of the more advanced equipment for mag-

Alzheimer's disease Organic brain disorder causing a gradual loss of memory, confusion, and general mental deterioration

---

FEATURE 10-8 PSYCHOLOGY IN THE NEWS

Schizophrenia: Perplexing and Misunderstood

Even after decades of research, schizophrenia remains one of the most perplexing mental illnesses. The disease affects an estimated 2.8 million Americans—about 1 in 100 people—most of whom are stricken between the ages of 18 and 24.

It would be hard to overstate the emotional and financial toll that schizophrenia wreaks on its sufferers and on their families, many of whom exhaust their savings paying for treatment that may be little more than palliative. A minority of patients do recover after one or more episodes of schizophrenia. Most, however, are disabled, often severely, for life. While schizophrenia is a progressive disease that destroys portions of the brain, the worst symptoms, the tormenting voices, vivid hallucinations and unshakeable delusions—tend to become less intense in middle age. . . .

Many researchers now believe that schizophrenia is not a single disease but several illnesses. It appears to have a biological basis and seems to be triggered—but not caused—by emotional stress. Although some people believe it is genetic because the disease tends to run in families, no gene for schizophrenia has been discovered nor do researchers believe such a discovery is imminent. Certain features of the brains of schizophrenics look and function differently from those of people who don't have this disease, but no one knows precisely what that means. . . .

Source: Boodman, S. G. (1993, February 16). Schizophrenia: Perplexing and misunderstood. *Washington Post Health,* 13.

netic resonance imaging (MRI) gives three-dimensional images that are so vivid that researchers feel as if they are looking at brain tissue under a microscope. While experimental studies have been able to identify 95 percent of Alzheimer's victims when using this advanced equipment (Elias, 1992), the cost is prohibitive for most people and the advanced technology is not generally available. Even if a definite diagnosis of Alzheimer's is made, there is no known cure or treatment. Research suggests that at least some cases of Alzheimer's disease may be caused by a virus infection (Schmeck, 1988; and Stein, 1988). Although research has been extensive, the exact origin of Alzheimer's disease remains unknown.

Checkpoint

Use the following questions to check your understanding of the final portion of the chapter. Choose and mark the one correct response to each question.

23. Martin has a personality disorder. Which of the following statements is *most likely* to be true?
    a. He is concerned about his problem and has been seeking help.
    b. He does not recognize his problem.
    c. His problem came on suddenly and will probably disappear in a few days.
    d. He suffers from multiple personality.
24. Which of the following persons is likely to feel no guilt or remorse about breaking laws?
    a. Phil, who has an antisocial personality
    b. Nam, who has a borderline personality

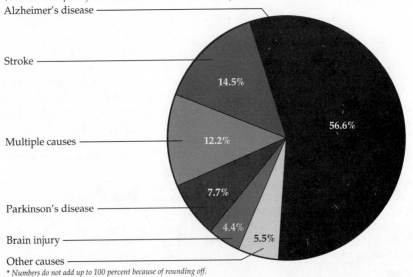

FIGURE 10-6. Causes of dementia among people in the United States between the ages of 65 and 93.
(*Source: Adapted from* Scientific American, *Sept. 1992.*)

Alzheimer's disease

Stroke

14.5%

56.6%

Multiple causes — 12.2%

7.7%

Parkinson's disease

4.4% 5.5%

Brain injury

Other causes
* Numbers do not add up to 100 percent because of rounding off.

   c. Janet, who is schizophrenic
   d. Barry, who has Alzheimer's disease

25. Hannah has borderline personality disorder. At what age is she most likely to improve?
   a. Sixteen
   b. Twenty-five
   c. Thirty-five
   d. Sixty-five

26. In schizophrenia, what is split?
   a. The personality
   b. The brain
   c. The mind and reality
   d. The memory and motor skills

27. A woman talks and listens to a Martian. What is she experiencing?
   a. Delusions
   b. Hallucinations
   c. Personality disorder
   d. Word salad

28. Which of the following persons with organic brain disorders is least likely to be cured by treatment?
   a. A woman with a vitamin deficiency
   b. A man with pellagra
   c. A man in an early stage of syphilis
   d. A woman with Alzheimer's disease

Check your responses against the Checkpoint Answer Key at the end of this chapter. If you had difficulty with any question, reread the text. If you had little or no difficulty answering the questions or have resolved problems that you might have had, you are ready to check yourself against the chapter inventory that follows.

CHAPTER INVENTORY

Use this list of objectives as a review checklist. You should be able to do the tasks outlined in the objectives and apply them to everyday examples. If you can, you may feel confident that you have mastered the material in the chapter.

1. List three criteria for abnormal behavior.
2. Describe the problems in diagnosis of abnormal behavior and the purpose of DSM IV.
3. Specify four forms of anxiety disorders.
4. Define phobia and identify the symptoms of common phobias.
5. Describe the symptoms of anorexia nervosa and bulimia.
6. Identify the symptoms of obsessive-compulsive disorders, and differentiate between obsessions and compulsions.
7. Specify the likely causes of post-traumatic stress.
8. Describe the symptoms of conversion disorder and hypochondriasis.

9. Describe the similarities and differences in multiple personality and amnesia.
10. Identify the symptoms of depression and bipolar disorder.
11. Describe the behavior of alcoholics and drug users.
12. State the methods that can be used to assist a person threatening suicide.
13. Identify two forms of personality disorder, and describe their symptoms.
14. Explain the symptoms and possible causes of schizophrenia.
15. Distinguish between schizophrenia and multiple personality.
16. Describe three types of organic brain disorders.

Feedback

The correct answers to the exercises follow. If you did not answer an exercise correctly, review the preceding pages and return to the exercise to correctly complete it.

10-1. a. Unusual or markedly different from normal
b. Undesirable
c. Causes personal emotional stress

10-2. DSM IV will provide descriptions of disorders that will help them diagnose the patient. It will not help them find the cause of the disorder.

10-3. Ms. P. has unrealistic and exaggerated fears that interfere with a normal life. Ms. F. has realistic fears that do not interfere with her everyday life.

10-4. a. Post-traumatic stress disorder
b. Obsessive-compulsive disorder
c. Post-traumatic stress disorder
d. Bulimia
e. Anorexia nervosa

10-5. Both involve a change in identity or consciousness. Both can be "faked" if convenient for a person.

10-6. Lowered self-esteem
Catastrophizing
Irritability
Thoughts of death
Proneness to tears
Insomnia
Hopelessness

10-7. Mindy is suffering from bipolar disorder. She is having mood swings from mania to depression.

10-8. a. Both are attempting to escape from their problems and/or relieve depression.
b. Drug users are more likely to behave illegally to support their addiction. Drug use does allow an immediate escape from depression, while the alcohol deepens depression.

10-9. a. Antisocial personality
b. Borderline personality
c. Borderline personality
d. Antisocial personality

10-10. No, the woman has multiple personality rather than schizophrenia. In schizophrenia the split is with reality and the personality is shattered.
10-11. Thought disturbances, delusions, and hallucinations

Checkpoint Answer Key

1. d; 2. c; 3. a; 4. a; 5. b; 6. c; 7. d; 8. b; 9. b; 10. c; 11. d; 12. b; 13. a; 14. d; 15. a; 16. b; 17. c; 18. d; 19. a; 20. d; 21. d; 22. d; 23. b; 24. a; 25. c; 26. c; 27. b; 28. d.

Getting Help

Neurotics build dream houses; psychotics live in
them; and psychiatrists collect the rent.
—Fritz Perls

Suppose you are the owner of a small business and want to hire someone to help keep your accounts in order. A middle-aged man with ten years of computer spreadsheet experience applies for the job. You find him to be qualified and a likable, friendly person. However, during the interview he confesses that he has suffered from depression and is presently receiving help from a psychiatrist. How would you react? Would you want more information about his depression or would you simply want to end the interview and forget about him? You would clearly be in the minority if you looked upon his getting help for mental problems as an asset.

Although it is fashionable in certain communities to discuss visits to a psychotherapist, for the most part people view mental problems negatively. Many associate mental problems with criminal behavior. Thoughts of raving maniacs and murderers are conjured up, and as a result irrational fears develop. Most people feel uncomfortable about visiting mental institutions or psychiatric wards in hospitals. People who are receiving help for mental problems definitely face a social stigma. They are subjects of jokes about crackpots, the nut house or funny farm, and men in white coats. Yet the majority of persons helped by professionals are not mentally ill; they are simply confronting problems that they cannot handle alone. They are wise to realize they need help.

Help comes in many forms but it usually begins with you yourself. You must admit you have a problem. Sometimes you can resolve the problem simply or use a self-help technique. In this chapter you will learn ways to help others, as well as yourself. But there are also times when professional assistance is essential, and you will examine the types of techniques professionals use. Finally, you will consider how community mental health programs can assist people.

SELF-HELP

Down on me, down on me
Looks like everybody in this whole round world
Is down on me.
            —JANIS JOPLIN

Yesterday all my troubles seemed so far away
Now it looks as though they're here to stay
        —JOHN LENNON AND PAUL MCCARTNEY

Have you ever listened to these lyrics and felt they were aimed at you? The popularity of these songs suggests that many people have shared your feelings. What do you do when you feel upset by your feelings, your surroundings, or your own behavior? The first step is to admit that you have a problem. For many people the solution is simple: self-help. Rather than seek help from a friend or relative or rush to a professional, often you can take some steps to help yourself.

Biofeedback

Assume that a middle-aged woman, Missy Hauser, has been told her apartment building is being converted into condominiums. Missy has been living there alone and comfortably for more than twenty years. There is less than $1000 in her savings account, and she can afford neither the down payment nor the monthly maintenance fee for a condominium. Although Missy knows she should be searching for a new place to live, tension headaches and hypertension are preventing her from thinking clearly and taking any action. According to her doctor, both her headaches and blood pressure are affected by stress.

What can Missy do to help herself out of this predicament? One beneficial self-help technique that her doctor might recommend is *biofeedback*. There are a number of devices and instruments available to help people monitor their blood pressure and heart rate. As you may recall from the discussion in Chapter 8, physiological changes always accompany emotional changes.

It is important that Missy follow her doctor's advice; biofeedback may not be recommended if she has certain other medical conditions. However, if her doctor suggests biofeedback, Missy could check her own blood pressure and then find some techniques to help her lower it. For example, she may want to check her blood pressure before and after such activities as a short walk,

biofeedback Technique that provides information on heart rate and blood pressure so that a person can control these internal processes

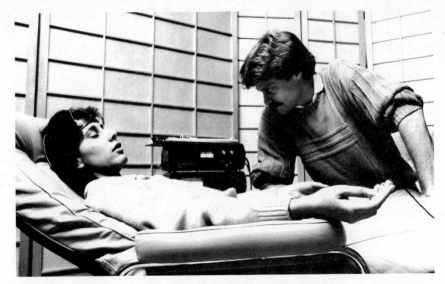

Some biofeedback measures require professional assistance. However, simple measures such as taking blood pressure and pulse rate can be evaluated by nonprofessionals.

watching an exciting hockey game, resting quietly, praying or meditating, or thinking about relaxing on a beach. After getting feedback information on how each activity affects her blood pressure, Missy can choose to spend more time in activities that lower her blood pressure and less time in stressful ventures. Chances are Missy may want to use more of her time for meditation and relaxing thoughts.

Many studies have shown that meditation can help relieve hypertension. Simply resting and concentrating on prayer or a relaxing experience can lower blood pressure significantly. Interestingly, blood pressure usually remains lowered long after the meditation experience, even if the person is bothered by stresses and strains. Somehow stress becomes less of a burden after a quiet experience. People can help themselves simply by learning how to relax.

Exercise 11-1

Listed below are some steps required to practice biofeedback for self-help. The steps are in a confused order. Specify the correct numerical order.

a. _____ Measure your pulse rate after each activity.

b. _____ Purchase or borrow a device for measuring physiological functions.

c. _____ Choose the activity that lowers your rate the most, and repeat the activity as often as possible.

d. _____ Obtain approval from your physician to begin a biofeedback program.

e. _____ Measure your rate before each activity.

f. _____ List a number of activities that you think may help lower your emotional responses.

Please turn to the Feedback section to check your responses.

Self-Control

Undoubtedly you have heard friends complain about lacking self-control. There probably have even been times when you yourself wished you had greater self-restraint. Whether you want to lose weight, stop smoking, hold on to your temper, or overcome your shyness, self-control is a possible solution. As you know, it is not easy to say no to a delicious snack. Likewise, watching everyone light cigarettes can entice a person trying to kick the habit to request one last cigarette. Taking charge of yourself is difficult, but according to psychologists, it is possible!

The first step in a self-control program is to find the type of event that triggers your problem. Suppose that a construction worker, Erica, is having trouble controlling her anger whenever her pushy, irksome foreman gives ridiculous orders. Erica can follow the advice of Novaco (1975) and use four steps:

1. *Prepare for the situation.* First Erica acknowledges the fact that her foreman's attitude makes her angry. She thinks about the type of dumb statements her foreman makes that are most aggravating. For example, she may recall her foreman shouting, "Hey, you, keep the plaster off the floor. It belongs on the wall."
2. *Think of ways to confront the provocation.* Before the annoying situation occurs again, Erica thinks of some ways she can handle herself. Then she imagines the actual confrontation or episode. When her foreman shouts a foolish order, Erica might imagine herself just shrugging and replying, "Whatever you say, sir," or "I guess that's why you're a foreman and I'm a laborer." By thinking about the situation beforehand, Erica will be prepared for the confrontation when it occurs.
3. *Cope with arousal and agitation.* When Erica spots her foreman heading in her direction, she will probably notice her heartbeat speeding up, her face flushing with anger, or her palms sweating—all signs of arousal. If she takes a few deep breaths and tries to relax the muscles, she will have a better chance of keeping calm and carrying out her plan.
4. *Reward yourself.* If Erica succeeds in controlling her anger, she rewards herself. Her reward can be anything that she really enjoys, perhaps fifteen minutes of listening to some favorite tapes, a shopping spree, an extra night of bowling, or tickets to an opera.

The same four steps could be used to handle many situations. A man who has difficulty getting rid of door-to-door salespersons and a teenage boy who has trouble asking girls to roller-skate could follow the same sequence to help themselves.

However, the sequence is not everyone's answer to self-help. Perhaps you are a smoker or drinker. Although you would prefer to eliminate these habits and be a healthier person, you find smoking or drinking extremely enjoyable and rewarding. Relaxing with a cup of coffee and a cigarette gives you comfort and gratification. Similarly, a cocktail, beer, or wine and some lively conversation with friends can bring pleasure and satisfaction. Eliminating habits that are enjoyable is particularly problematic.

Years ago, Nolan (1968) suggested that smoking could be controlled by removing the pleasurable aspect from the habit. For example, you would say that smoking is only permitted in a smoking chair. The smoking chair should be uncomfortable and located in a boring and inconvenient spot. A garage or basement corner usually qualifies as an uninteresting and undesirable atmosphere, ideal for a smoking chair. If you wish to smoke, you must go to your chair, sit down, and remain there the entire time you are smoking. You may leave your chair only after you are finished with your cigarettes.

Nolan's method is a variation of behavior modification (described in Chapter 3). The loneliness and bleak surroundings of the smoking chair remove the usual positive atmosphere of socializing while smoking.

Exercise 11-2

Fred is a police officer in a large city. He has been assigned to a high-crime area where many people are hostile toward police. Whenever people resist arrest and call him names, Fred loses his temper. He shouts back and often gets into physical fights. Because he has difficulty controlling himself, Fred is in danger of losing his job. List four steps Fred could take to control his anger.

a. _____

_____

b. _____

_____

c. _____

_____

d. _____

_____

You may check your responses against those in the Feedback section.

Exercise 11-3

Allison lives in a dormitory and wants to give up smoking. Her roommate suggested that Allison put an old chair in the corner of the dorm laundry room, facing a blank wall, and use it as a smoking chair. Why should Allison accept her roommate's recommendation?

_____

_____

Turn to the Feedback section to check your answer.

Jean Nidetch (1962) claimed she was overweight and had trouble sticking to her diet. She invited six overweight friends to chat about their difficulties and successes in dieting. The group then examined ways to help each other. The group expanded and soon became the international business, Weight Watchers. Whether you simply get together with friends who have similar problems or join an international organization, you are relying on a self-help group.

The purpose of self-help groups is to give social support to each member. During meetings, participants share their experiences and discuss problems and possible solutions. They socialize and encourage each other. Because of problems related to alcohol, drugs, eating, and the like, people often feel isolated. Group meetings provide an opportunity for affiliation and acceptance. Alcoholics Anonymous (AA) is the oldest, largest, and most famous self-help group. Founded in 1934, AA is found in 112 countries and serves several hundred thousand people each year (*Harvard Mental Health Letter*, 1993). More alcoholics are served by AA than by alcoholic clinics and physicians combined. AA is based on a twelve-step strategy that encourages members to meditate, be honest about their problems, take responsibility for them, change themselves, and help others.

Many self-help groups have adopted the twelve-step program of AA. Al-Anon is a support group for families and close friends of alcoholics. Among the other groups patterned after AA are: Batterers Anonymous, Emotions

FIGURE 11-1. Could this be another self-help group to add to the list?

Anonymous, Families Anonymous, Gamblers Anonymous, Homosexuals Anonymous, Impotents Anonymous, Narcotics Anonymous, Overeaters Anonymous, Rape Anonymous, Smokers Anonymous, and Workaholics Anonymous. There are also groups for child abusers, ex-convicts, widows and widowers, parents of twins, and parents without partners. Regardless of the specific purpose of the group, members help each other adjust and benefit from the encouragement and socialization at meetings. Computers have provided the newest contribution to self-help groups (see Feature 11-1).

Exercise 11-4

Imagine that an overweight friend asked you to join him in attending a meeting of his self-help group, "Weight Loss Anonymous." List three types of activities that you might expect to experience at the meeting.

a. _____

b. _____

c. _____

Please compare your list with the one given in the Feedback section.

FEATURE 11-1 PSYCHOLOGY IN THE NEWS

Finding Support Electronically

The room is hushed, expectant, and filled with unfamiliar faces. My confession cuts through the silence. "Hi, my name is Eden and I am a _____. (Fill in the blank with "compulsive overeater," "acrophobic," "shopaholic," "drug addict," etc.)" *Ugh.* You wouldn't find me at one of those meetings. I'm just not the type. I have a shy psyche. It doesn't like being naked in front of strangers. And, anyway, what if I managed to confess my darkest secrets and innermost pain to a whole gathering of people, then discovered I didn't *like* them? I mean, I don't talk about this stuff to my friends, let alone a roomful of strangers that for all I know includes religious fanatics and cat haters. No thank you.

At least that's how I felt before I discovered a new twist on the support group concept, an alternative to the programs that started with Alcoholics Anonymous and have expanded to encompass just about every sort of lifestyle and affliction. My support group, made up of diabetics such as myself, meets at all hours of the day and night. Members range in age from six to sixty-something. We hail from large cities and tiny rural burgs. Some of us participate only now and then. Others like me show up faithfully every day.

There are hundreds, maybe thousands, of such support groups, most accessible to anyone with a computer and a modem. As close as a keystroke and as distant as the relative anonymity of on-line communication, these groups have emerged as one of the latest uses for the electronic bulletin boards....

. . . Some of what we discussed in the group was practical information about doctors, self-care, and dealing with emotional ups and downs. At other times we engaged in mere fellowship, posting notes about our favorite novels, vacations we'd taken or hoped to take, family members, and pets.

. . . On the bulletin board, I could whine, vent, obsess, and ask questions to my heart's content. The responses were nearly always kind, insightful and extraordinarily helpful. If I needed to "talk" at three in the morning, I had only to turn on my computer....

Source: Stone, E. (1993, February). Finding support electronically. *New Age Journal.*

Although people sometimes need time to themselves to mull over problems, often they really need someone to listen to them. Troubles seem to get worse when they are held inside. Finding a good listener can be a solution to simple adjustments and confusions. However, volunteering to help your friends by listening requires some caution. Sometimes your help is not wanted. It is usually best not to pressure a person. Simply make your friends aware that you care, are concerned, and want to help and understand their difficulties.

Once a friend begins discussing problems with you, keep relaxed and friendly. Try not to pass judgment. A young man whose date walked out on him does not need to be reminded that he made stupid remarks. You could be more helpful by showing your understanding with statements such as, "I can imagine how you must feel; I would have felt let down and upset, too." A little tact can remove some of the sting and pain. If you stress the young man's strong points, he will be better able to plan to avoid similar mishaps in the future.

Sometimes a friend sits you down to listen to an apparently simple problem. As the conversation continues, the problem turns out to be severe. Although you should offer assurances that you respect privacy and will keep the conversation confidential, you would want to recognize situations that you cannot handle competently. In such cases, recommend professional help! Information on professional help follows in the next section of this chapter.

Checkpoint

Use the following questions to check your understanding of this portion of the chapter. Choose and mark the one correct response to each question.

1. Before using one self-help technique, a physician should be consulted. Which technique?
   a. Biofeedback
   b. Smoking chair
   c. Anger control
   d. Meditation

2. What is the purpose of biofeedback?
   a. To control anger
   b. To increase self-control
   c. To eliminate bad habits
   d. To reduce hypertension

3. What is the first step in a self-control program to overcome a problem?
   a. Rewarding yourself
   b. Thinking of many possible ways to confront the problem
   c. Determining the type of event that produces the problem
   d. Controlling your arousal by taking deep breaths

4. What is the purpose of a smoking chair?
   a. To increase the pleasant associations with smoking
   b. To decrease the pleasant associations with smoking
   c. To help a person give up drinking
   d. To permit a person to meditate

5. Which of the following methods involves a form of behavior modification?
   a. Preparation
   b. Listening
   c. Smoking chair
   d. Coping

6. Which of the following is the best example of a self-help group?
   a. Four pregnant unmarried teenage friends meet once a week to discuss their problems.
   b. Five middle-aged men sign up for a course in woodworking and carpentry.
   c. Six senior citizens purchase condominiums for the elderly in a nearby community.
   d. Seventy college students register for a psychology course required in their programs.

7. Assume your friend has just lost her job and has been crying for hours. You offer to help, but she does not want to talk about her problems. What should you do?
   a. Walk away and leave her alone.
   b. Tell her that her unwillingness to talk is probably the reason she lost her job.
   c. Insist that she talk to you, ask questions, and give her advice about finding another job.
   d. Tell her you are concerned about her, and suggest that she call you whenever she feels like discussing her problem.

Use the Checkpoint Answer Key to verify your responses. If you had any difficulty with a question, carefully reread the text. If you had little or no difficulty answering the questions or have resolved any problems that you might have had, you are ready to continue with the next portion of this chapter.

PROFESSIONAL HELP

Many problems cannot be cured, or even helped, by either self-help methods or a sympathetic, understanding listener. When people are upset, they often lose their self-control and have difficulty communicating with others. In such cases, professional help is needed. Lasting success in treatment usually requires a trained psychotherapist, although sympathetic nonprofessionals may help initially. An important factor in the success of psychotherapy is the client's belief that the emotional problems will be resolved (Prioleau, Murdock, and Brody, 1983).

Problems Requiring Professional Help

Simple Emotional Problems. Emotional problems are the simplest type of disorder that can profit from professional assistance. A person who is shy, has a poor self-image, or has difficulty adjusting to a marriage, children, a job, or

"*Yes, dear, of course, dear, yes, dear . . . .*"

FIGURE 11-2. It appears she believes her problems will be resolved, but he looks rather negative.

a new situation will feel confused and disturbed. Most people who seek professional help have no deeper disturbances. Psychologists recommend that help be received during the early stages of a problem; it is important not to wait. Time often brings further complications. The likelihood of improvement for persons with emotional problems is good. Everyone, including presidents, experiences instability in times of crisis. Seeking help is a sign of good judgment rather than of weakness.

Mental Disorders. People with the most severe problems are more likely to receive treatment than are those with lesser disorders. Among schizophrenics, 53 percent receive treatment, yet only 18 percent of alcohol and drug abusers are getting help (Shapiro et al., 1984). People with anxiety disorders and mood disorders are likely to recognize their problems and seek advice. However, unruly people, such as addicts and antisocial personalities, often deny their problems. Usually they are brought to treatment by others. Whether a person suffers from an anxiety disorder, a mood disorder, an addiction, a personality disorder, or schizophrenia, he or she can benefit from professional help.

Exercise 11-5

Read each of the following descriptions of people in need of professional help, and indicate the type of problem(s) the person is likely to have.

a. This person denies any problems and was brought to therapy by his wife. _____

b. This person lost her job and is having difficulty coping. _____

c. This person has felt overwhelmingly sad and is seeking help. _____

d. Fifty-three percent of people in this group receive help. _____

Please turn to the Feedback section to check your answers.

Techniques in Individual Psychotherapy

Psychotherapists use a broad variety of methods to help individuals. Some therapists have been trained heavily in one particular technique and use that method exclusively. Others have had more diverse training and choose techniques that they consider appropriate and most beneficial for each case. They have been labeled *eclectic therapists,* because they do not adhere to any one method. The most common forms of individual psychotherapy are psychoanalysis, humanistic counseling, rational-emotive therapy, and behavior therapy.

eclectic therapists Professionals who choose techniques appropriate for each case and do not adhere solely to one method

Psychoanalysis. A psychoanalyst is most often a psychiatrist, but occasionally, a psychologist, who bases treatment on the theories of Sigmund Freud. *Psychoanalysts* believe that the most important aspects of your personality are buried deep in your unconscious, and consequently you are not aware of them. In a typical visit to a psychoanalyst, you would be expected to rest comfortably on a couch and stare at a blank wall. You would become totally relaxed, although not fall asleep. You would then begin talking and say anything that comes into your mind, without blocking or censoring anything. Random ideas would flow into each other, and the therapist would look for hidden unconscious meanings. Psychoanalysts also interpret dreams. Since you are fully relaxed when asleep, you are less likely to inhibit your thoughts and feelings. For psychoanalysts, dreams help to reveal the unconscious. For successful treatment, past experiences, particularly painful memories, must be uncovered. Some therapists resort to hypnosis. Psychoanalysis has been losing popularity. It requires more time than other techniques do and is one of the most expensive forms of therapy.

psychoanalysis Psychotherapy technique that involves uncovering the unconscious

Humanistic Counseling. Did you notice the switch from the word "therapy" to the word "counseling"? One of the leading humanists, Carl Rogers, chose the word "counseling," and other humanistic psychologists agreed on the change. Humanists also prefer to call the person being helped a "client" rather than a "patient." The word "patient" implies helplessness, and *humanistic counseling* requires active, conscious participation by each client. The style of counseling used by Carl Rogers is labeled *client-centered,* because the client actually sets the direction for the therapy and can talk about feelings without fear of criticism. Rogers borrowed from Chinese philosophers the idea that each person must decide personally which direction to take in life. The counselor acts almost as a mirror, reflecting the feelings and emotions of the client.

humanistic counseling Psychotherapy approach that attempts to improve self-esteem and encourage personal growth

client-centered counseling Form of humanistic therapy where the client sets the direction without fear of criticism

Client-centered counseling takes a positive approach. Counselors focus on what is right with a client rather than on what is wrong. A major goal is to increase self-esteem. A person with a good self-image can find new solutions to problems. Independence is strongly encouraged. The past is disregarded, and the client gains insights into present feelings. The counselor often paraphrases the client and shows understanding and caring.

For example, imagine that Chip Moods visits a client-centered therapist. He begins by expressing his irritation with his stern mother-in-law who is visiting too often. The counselor might reply, "You are upset because you feel your mother-in-law is around too much." Chip then continues, expressing his annoyance that his wife encourages her crabby mother's frequent calls. The counselor adds, "You feel angry with your spouse because she does not consider your feelings." Ideally, by the end of his sessions, Chip will be better able to accept his feelings and resolve his problem.

Gestalt therapy and existential therapy also use humanistic approaches. Both are based on the eastern philosophy of Zen Buddhism and stress the present rather than the past or future. As humanistic therapists, gestaltists and existentialists emphasize understanding your own feelings. However, each of these two therapies has a slightly different focus.

According to Perls (1973), the founder of gestalt therapy, gestalt therapists should be on the alert for phoniness. Your physical gestures and inner feelings should match. For example, if you state that you are perfectly calm, while your voice quivers and your hands tremble, you are probably trying to cover your real feelings. A gestalt therapist would point out your physical shakes and allow you to reevaluate your true feelings.

The focus in *existential therapy*, according to Frankl (1955), is on the free will of each client. The therapist must help each person find meaning in life, develop values, and make responsible choices. There are no standardized procedures in existential therapy. Each therapy is a totally new experience and relationship.

Humanistic counseling requires far less time than does psychoanalysis. Clients meet with counselors only once each week. In most cases, problems are resolved in less than six months.

Cognitive Therapy. *Cognitive therapy* is based on the notion that psychological problems result from faulty thinking. In cognitive therapies, unlike in humanistic therapies, the therapist is active and does most of the talking, particularly in the beginning. The goal of the therapy is to correct unreasonable thinking. The treatment program usually consists of fifteen to twenty-five fiftyminute sessions. Aaron Beck, a leader in the cognitive approach to therapy, believes that almost all depression results from people's unrealistically negative views of themselves, the future, and the world (Sacco and Beck, 1985). In cognitive treatment, the therapist attempts to identify these negative thoughts and replace them with more realistic approaches. Clients are required to make lists of their thoughts and chart them. Feature 11-2 contains some negative thoughts and their replacements, from lists composed by a variety of individuals in cognitive therapy. Cognitive therapists believe that if thinking is changed, attitudes and behavior will also change.

Rational-emotive therapy (RET) is a variation on cognitive therapy, usually requiring only a few sessions. The goal of the therapist is to teach the client to think scientifically and rationally.

RET therapists assume people learn irrational and self-defeating proposi-

---

gestalt therapy
Form of humanistic therapy that focuses on consistency between behaviors and inner feelings

existential therapy
Form of treatment that focuses on free will and the meaning of life

cognitive therapy
Therapy that focuses on correcting unreasonable thinking

rational-emotive therapy Form of therapy that helps people think rationally and eliminate their self-defeating emotional thoughts

tions in their youth. For example, some people may assume that it will be disastrous if they fail in school, or a horrible catastrophe if they are unpopular. As a result, they limit and restrict themselves and are unwilling to take chances. A young engineering student may refuse to sign up for a required course in drafting because she fears she will fail. Or a young man may dread asking women for dates because he is horror-stricken by the possibility of being refused. In RET, the therapist would teach these people to reexamine their belief that one failure is a complete catastrophe. Clients are assigned homework; a shy young man may be told to strike up a conversation with a strange female before the next session. Even if he is unsuccessful, he can learn from his experience and hopefully realize that it is self-defeating not to continue trying.

RET is not for everyone. Ellis believes the approach is most profitable with clients who are above average in intelligence. The technique is clearly inappropriate for severe psychotics or anyone who has problems with thought patterns.

behavior therapy
Psychotherapy that uses techniques based on learning principles

Behavior therapy. *Behavior therapy* is based on the principle of behavior modification described in Chapter 3. Appropriate behavior is rewarded, and inappropriate or undesirable behavior is ignored and not reinforced. Behavior modification has been used successfully in mental institutions. Each time a

---

FEATURE 11-2 PSYCHOLOGY IN THE NEWS

Replacing Negative Thinking

Negative Thoughts	Realistic Thoughts
1. I'm completely self-centered and thoughtless. I'm just no good.	1. I'm thoughtless at times and at times I can be quite thoughtful. I probably do act self-centered at times. I can work on this. I may not be perfect but I'm not "no good."
2. What a lousy day!	2. A couple of bad things have happened, but everything hasn't been a disaster.
3. Nobody loves me.	3. Nonsense. I have many friends and family. I may not get *as much* love as I want when I want it, but I can work on this.
4. I'm a failure.	4. I've succeeded at some things and failed at others, just like everybody.
5. My boyfriend doesn't like me.	5. He doesn't like me enough for what? He may not want to marry me, but he takes me out on dates, so he *must* like me partially.

Source: Adapted from Burns, D. D. (1980). *Feeling good: The new mood therapy.* New York: William Morrow.

patient performs a chore, talks to a therapist, or behaves in any desirable way, he or she receives a token. Tokens may be used to purchase candy, desserts, additional recreation time, or any other items or activities that would be suitable rewards.

In severe cases, rewards are given directly. For example, a patient who makes eye contact with the therapist might be given a stick of chewing gum or a piece of candy. Next the patient is rewarded for answering questions. This technique is often used as a first step to get a patient into some form of treatment.

Another form of behavior therapy, systematic desensitization, was described in Chapter 3. Systematic desensitization is a gradual method that has been successful in removing some fears and phobias. For example, a man afraid of heights might at first imagine he is on a balcony one story above the ground and listen to some relaxing, enchanting music. At each session he moves up another story until his phobia is overcome. The strategy is a step-by-step approach.

Exercise 11-6

Read each of the following descriptions, and specify whether each is an example of psychoanalysis, client-centered counseling, gestalt therapy, existential therapy, cognitive therapy, rational-emotive therapy, or behavior therapy.

a. Abe's therapist points out every move he makes. He comments whenever Abe crosses his feet, folds his arms, bites his lip, or scratches his head. _____

b. Sasha is timid about selling things. Her therapist gave her homework. She must volunteer to work at an arts-and-crafts booth at her community-center bazaar. _____

c. Judy's therapist interprets her dreams. She must try to relax and recall as much as she can. _____

d. Todd's therapist dwells on values. Todd is trying to unravel the real meaning of his life. _____

e. Pablo hopes to gradually overcome his fear of flying. Last week his therapist took him on board an airplane. Next week he will taxi down the runway in the same plane. Eventually he hopes to fly without fear. _____

f. Jeanine does most of the talking in therapy, and her therapist is a good listener. He seems to really care about her feelings and shows immense understanding. _____

g. Marco is certain that his poor grades in college mean that he will never be successful in business. His therapist points out that many successful businesspeople were poor students.

Check your answers against the ones in the Feedback section.

Results of Individual Psychotherapies. As yet, there is no solid evidence that any one technique in therapy is superior to all others. The individual skills of each therapist and the relationship between the therapist and patient or client seem to be more important factors. Most of the time psychotherapy has good results.

Checkpoint

Use the following questions to check your understanding of this portion of the chapter. For each of the two sets that follow, match each term on the left with the expression on the right that provides the best description.

8. _____ Schizophrenics

9. _____ Alcoholics and drug abusers

10. _____ Persons with anxiety disorders

11. _____ Addicts and antisocials

a. Are likely to seek help themselves
b. Are treated in more than half the cases
c. Are usually brought to therapy by someone else
d. Are treated in less than 20 percent of cases

12. _____ Psychoanalysis

13. _____ Humanistic counseling

a. Involves therapist pointing and gesturing to help client evaluate true feelings

"Well, if you must know, I have trouble making friends, fatso!"

FIGURE 11-3. Obviously, it is not always easy for therapists to develop good relationships with their clients.

14. _____ Client-centered counseling

15. _____ Gestalt therapy

16. _____ Existential therapy

17. _____ Cognitive therapy

18. _____ Rational-emotive therapy

19. _____ Behavior modification

20. _____ Systematic desensitization

b. Focuses on past experiences and dreams

c. Prepares mental patients for other forms of therapy

d. Includes all therapies that focus on the present and require active participation of clients

e. Utilizes a gradual approach for overcoming phobias

f. Stresses free will and responsibility

g. Uses homework assignments to help clients eliminate self-defeating thoughts

h. Involves counselor restating feelings of client and being accepting

i. Has client make lists of negative thoughts

Check your responses against the Checkpoint Answer Key at the end of the chapter. If you had difficulty with any question, reread the text. If you had little or no difficulty or have resolved any problems that you might have had, you are ready to continue with the final portion of this chapter.

Group Approaches to Psychotherapy

Group therapy became popular after World War II when a large number of American veterans needed help for emotional problems. Since then, it has steadily gained popularity. For certain people, group therapy is less expensive and has some unique advantages. Methods used may include any, or a mixture, of the many individual techniques. Some use humanistic approaches, while others use rational-emotive therapy or behavioral methods. Usually six to twelve persons gather in an informal, comfortable seating arrangement. Members are carefully selected by the therapist. The group then talks openly about their ideas, their fears, and their troubles. The therapist directs the discussion and adds some insights and suggestions.

group therapy Situation where a therapist directs a discussion in a group of usually six to twelve persons, so that they may learn and profit from communication within the group

The group atmosphere helps individuals improve interpersonal relationships. Persons can share their thoughts, impressions, and experiences in a protected setting. Group techniques are particularly beneficial to people who are uncomfortable in social situations. As people learn appropriate roles for interacting with each other, they also become aware that others have similar problems. However, those who have trouble telling their feelings to even only one person probably will not find the sessions useful.

Group therapy is particularly suitable for persons sharing similar troubles. Groups have been developed for persons who are recently divorced, bereaved, or suffering from the same illnesses. As mentioned in Chapter 8, women suffering from terminal cancer who participated in group therapy doubled their life expectancies and felt more satisfied. People in uncomfortable situations can learn from the experiences of their peers. People who are in institutions are

Group therapy is an important part of most drug treatment programs. Recovering addicts learn from hearing about each others' problems and reactions.

usually involved in group therapy, since it helps them understand the problems of others in their institutional community.

Often, members of a family are treated together. Family problems frequently stem from relationships between members rather than from the troubles of one person within the family. Even when only one member of the family suffers from emotional problems or a mental illness, the others must make adjustments. By working together in a group session, family members can usually expose and resolve marital and family conflicts.

Exercise 11-7

List four advantages of group therapy over individual therapy.

a. _____

b. _____

c. _____

d. _____

Please turn to the Feedback section to check your answers.

Medical Approaches to Therapy

The importance of medical and biological factors in mental problems has been debated. Nonetheless there is clear evidence that medical assistance can benefit psychotic patients, depressed persons, and even those with certain types of phobias. There are basically three medical approaches used in psychotherapy:

drugs, electroshock, and psychosurgery. Although use of these techniques can bring relief to patients, it can sometimes also create added complications.

Drugs. For quite some time psychiatrists have prescribed mind-altering or *psychoactive drugs* to millions of patients. These chemicals can cause physical, emotional, or behavioral changes. Antipsychotic drugs are psychoactive drugs that are used to calm patients and make them less fearful, hostile, and excitable. Newer varieties of antipsychotic drugs are being developed that are more efficient and have few side effects. Although the drugs do not cure problems, they usually reduce symptoms and are helpful to the patients. Hospitals can allow more freedom among patients and can be less concerned about guarding and controlling patient behavior. However, these drugs are not totally without side effects. An added problem has arisen with the recent increase in psychotic persons being treated as outpatients. The costs of antipsychotic drugs have increased, and many mentally ill persons cannot afford them. Also, the dosage must be carefully monitored, since overdoses are dangerous.

psychoactive drug Chemical substance that causes physical, emotional, or behavioral changes

Another type of psychoactive drug, an antidepressant, is used for cases of depression. The purpose of these drugs is to stimulate and arouse patients who are feeling dejected and lethargic. Generally these drugs are slow to act, and they can sometimes cause fatigue and weight gain. There is some evidence that such drugs can be extremely helpful in the treatment of some phobias, although they do initially cause light-headedness.

Antianxiety drugs are psychoactive drugs that are used to reduce tension. They are often referred to as tranquilizers. The most common side effects are drowsiness, a loss of motor control, and unsteadiness. People who are taking them should not drive or drink alcohol. Antianxiety drugs exaggerate the effect of alcohol and can even cause death. The excerpt in Feature 11-3 describes some dangers and precautions for antianxiety drugs.

As researchers are learning more about the chemical nature of psychological disorders, they are developing new drugs. Through drugs, scientists are hoping to settle the brains of hyperactive children, increase the memory of senile patients, enhance the learning of dull students, and allow prisoners to be more readily rehabilitated. The article in Feature 11-4 reports on a drug that may reduce alcohol addiction.

With the widespread use of psychoactive drugs, new concerns are developing. Not everyone has the same reaction to the same drug. Since little is known about ethnic differences in drug reactions, a new center has been developed for research on physiological differences (see Feature 11-5).

Electroshock Treatment. In *electroshock treatment*, the patient is given an anesthetic. A brief electric pulse is then sent to certain areas in the frontal portion of the brain. The electric shock induces a convulsion, and memories are temporarily erased. During the recovery from the treatment, persons are less preoccupied with their previous problems. Although no one is certain of exactly what happens, electroshock treatment does seem to be beneficial to persons suffering from severe depression. However, this treatment has been controversial. Many patients suffer memory losses after ECT. But, some current research is finding that no structural brain damage occurs with this treatment.

electroshock treatment (ECT) Physiological therapy that delivers an electric shock to the brain to induce a convulsion or coma and reduce depression by erasing memories

In recent years, shock treatment has been used less, primarily because other types of therapy have been found to be equally effective in most cases.

Psychosurgery. About forty years ago a type of brain surgery called a "prefrontal lobotomy" gained fame. When neurons in the frontal lobes of the brain were severed, a severely disturbed patient was freed from guilt, anxiety, and violent behavior. However, the patient also became totally disoriented and unmotivated and could not function normally. Consequently, the technique has been little used in the past two decades.

psychosurgery Operations on the brain, performed to treat mental disorders

Newer forms of *psychosurgery* are still in the experimental stage. Some research has been done on implanting electrodes in certain parts of the brain believed to be "pleasure centers." The patient can use a control button to activate the electrode and bring on tranquil feelings. This form of surgery may benefit patients who cannot normally control their violence.

FEATURE 11-3 PSYCHOLOGY IN THE NEWS

High Anxiety

The woman we'll can Rachel G—now age 31—had experienced attacks of anxiety since she was a child. But those occasional incidents did not prevent her from marrying and taking a responsible job at an East Coast biotechnology company. Then, in late 1990 and early 1991, her life took a stressful turn. There was turmoil in the lab where she worked, her mother fell seriously ill, her grandmother committed suicide, and her marriage deteriorated.

"I broke into a cold sweat," she recalls. "My heart was palpitating. I swore I was having a heart attack. I was scared that I was dying. . . . I couldn't walk. I couldn't even move. The attacks went on for two days."

Rachel G. went to a psychologist for help, and simultaneously asked her regular internist for a pill to ease her suffering. Her physician prescribed *Xanax* (alprazolam). . . .

The drug gave her some relief, but she felt it really wasn't solving her problem. After about three months on *Xanax*, she tried to cut her dose in half. Within 48 hours she recalls, "I couldn't sleep. My heart was racing, and I was getting dizzy spells." Only going back up to an intermediate dose would suppress the withdrawal symptoms.

In February 1992, Rachel G. began having frightening thoughts of killing herself. She visited a psychiatrist, who prescribed . . . imipramine, an antidepressant that also works well against panic. Today she is doing well, still taking imipramine—and also *Xanax*. Though she feels the *Xanax* is no longer helping her, she can't bring herself to quit. . . .

RECOMMENDATIONS

. . . If you're suffering from panic disorder, agoraphobia, or chronic anxiety, you have a serious problem that requires professional evaluation and treatment by a psychiatrist or psychologist. It's not clear, however, that drug treatment should be your first option.

. . . Whatever your problem is, you should avoid *Xanax* and its chemical cousins if you have any history of alcohol abuse. . . .

. . . Inform your doctor immediately of any unexpected side effects, such as feelings of rage or agitation. And seriously consider trying some sort of psychotherapy to gain insight into your problem.

Source: (1993, January). High anxiety. *Consumer Reports.*

Opiate Blocker Boosts Alcoholism Treatment

A drug that diminishes the pleasure-inducing effects of the brain's naturally occluding opiates gives added punch to psychological treatments for alcoholism, at least over short periods of time, according to two separate studies.

The drug, naltrexone, may dampen the desire to continue drinking among alcoholics who slip up and consume an alcoholic beverage shortly after entering a treatment program. . . .

"Naltrexone appears to be a safe and effective adjunct treatment of alcohol dependence," hold psychiatrist Joseph R. Volpicelli . . . and his colleagues.

The team studied 70 men, mostly black and unemployed, who entered an outpatient treatment program following supervised alcohol withdrawal. The men reported an average of 20 years of heavy alcohol use. . . .

Half the men received naltrexone pills; the rest received placebo pills for the program's first three months.

At that point, one-quarter of the naltrexone group had returned to heavy drinking or alcohol binges, compared with one-half of the placebo group, the researchers report. Moreover, 19 of 20 placebo-treated men who reported taking a drink of alcohol after entering treatment experienced a relapse, compared with eight of the 16 naltrexone-treated men.

. . . A second study, directed by psychologist Stephanie S. O'Malley . . . suggests that naltrexone enhances alcohol abstinence rates when used in combination with psychotherapy.

. . . Volpicelli theorizes that naltrexone blocks the rush of naturally occurring opiates in the brain provoked by the first drink of alcohol, thus helping break the cycle in which one drink fuels the desire for another. . . .

Source: Bower, B. (1992, November 21). Opiate blocker boosts alcoholism treatment. *Science News.*

Ethnic Groups Respond Differently to Medication

Investigators at a new center funded by the National Institute of Mental Health (NIMH) are taking a close look at a little-studied topic: how different ethnic groups respond to psychotropic medications. . . .

. . . this center is unique in its primary focus on the way different ethnic groups psychologically process and respond to psychiatric medications, according to the center's director, Taiwanese-born psychiatrist Keh-Ming Lin.

. . . Lin became interested in ethnic differences in psychiatric drug processing and response during his residency at the University of Washington in the early 1970s. To his surprise, he found that his Caucasian patients were given 10 times the dose of antischizophrenic drug haloperidol that he normally gave his schizophrenic patients in Taiwan.

. . . the center's main focus will be on ethnic differences and similarities in metabolizing psychotropic drugs, mainly because none of the other NIMH-funded ethnically oriented centers address that subject, said Lin. . . .

Source: DeAngelis, T. (1991, August). Ethnic groups respond differently to medication. *APA Monitor.*

Exercise 11-8

Read each of the following cases and indicate one advantage and one possible disadvantage in the type of medical therapy used.

a. Lulu, a patient suffering from schizophrenia, has responded well to treatment with antipsychotic drugs. She has been released from an institution and given a prescription for continued use of antipsychotic drugs.

Advantage: _____

Disadvantage: _____

b. Guy had suffered from severe depression for the past two years. Since taking antidepressant drugs, he has found relief and has been able to return to work. He plans to take the drugs for the rest of his life.

Advantage: _____

Disadvantage: _____

c. Bobby has just had an electroshock treatment for his depression.

Advantage: _____

Disadvantage: _____

d. Vicky just read an article on a type of psychosurgery called a prefrontal lobotomy. She feels this will be an ideal treatment for her violent psychotic sister.

Advantage: _____

Disadvantage: _____

You may check your answers against those in the Feedback section.

COMMUNITY-HELP PROGRAMS

In 1963 the United States Congress passed the Community Health Centers Act, authorizing local communities to provide diverse services to prevent and treat mental problems. The services available in each community depend on the needs and interests of the people, as well as on the amount of funds available. Options include preventive approaches, outpatient services, and crisis management. In most communities, diminishing funds have caused a decrease in services. The American Pychiatric Association has placed the blame on federal, state, and local governments (Lamb, 1984). Why not contact your own community mental health center to find out exactly which types of services are available?

Preventive Approaches

The purpose of a preventive approach is to keep emotional problems from occurring in the first place. Kessler and Albee (1975) outlined four possible ways to accomplish this goal: (1) improve child-rearing practices, (2) reduce stress, (3) improve communications, and (4) build control and self-esteem. Some communities have organized training programs for paraprofessionals—persons who have had limited previous instruction in psychology, such as teachers, police officers, members of the clergy, or even bartenders and hairdressers. Although most participants have an associate's degree or a bachelor's degree, anyone with an interest in helping others can be trained to offer guidance in any or all of the four areas specified by Kessler and Albee. A study by Brown (1974) reported that paraprofessionals are often as effective as professionals are in the area of prevention.

Among the preventive services offered by community mental health centers are workshops, infant and child care, instruction on biofeedback methods for stress control, and courses in assertiveness training (discussed in Chapter 13). The article in Feature 11-6 describes one highly successful community program. Some communities have successfully used radio, television, and newspapers to reach additional people. There are undeniable advantages to preventive programs. Dodge and Rogers (1976) advised that communities with preventive facilities in their mental health centers had fewer admissions to psychiatric hospitals.

FEATURE 11-6 PSYCHOLOGY IN THE NEWS

Holistic in the 'Hood

It is not unusual to see a group of young people hanging out by a storefront on a street corner. It's a way of life in Chelsea, Massachusetts, a tough, poor city on the edge of Boston that has had severe and perennial youth problems. But at a corner storefront many blocks from the city center, there's a new way of life: More than 350 people are regularly greeted by a handshake, a placard depicting Che Guevara pointing a finger and saying, "You are not a minority," and—boldly painted in English, Spanish, and Khmer on the white walls—the seven ROCA principles: Safety, Respect, Integrity, Empowerment, Community, Multiculturalism, and Peace & Justice. That *is* unusual.

Founded in 1988 as a teen pregnancy prevention program in a three-room apartment, ROCA (Reaching Out to Chelsea Adolescents, and "rock" in Spanish) quickly earned national attention for its innovative multicultural approach, a necessity in a city of 34,000 people that is home to thirty-two nationalities. By March 1991, ROCA had expanded into a full-blown multi-service youth center. Open fourteen hours a day, the storefront seems a veritable candy store of opportunities: a high school equivalency program; job training; college coun-

seling; AIDS-prevention information; courses in Cambodian theater, African dance, martial arts, rock climbing, mask making, cooking, video production, and women's enpowerment. . . .

In viewing young people as resources rather than as problems to be fixed, ROCA differs radically from conventional youth programs. Its goal is social justice, not social service. "Social service is something you provide *to* people, social justice involves working *with* them to provide for themselves and the community," says the thirty-three-year-old [director] Baldwin. ". . . We believe that people feel good when they feel they belong, and when they feel they belong is when they participate in the world around them."

One measure of ROCA's success is its exponential growth. After twenty-one months, almost 10 percent of Chelsea's youth population were members. The organization believes in rigorous outreach: Staff and peers consistently go to extremes to bring hard-case kids into the process, and stay with them until they come around. . . .

Source: Howard, J. (1993, February). Holistic in the 'hood. *New Age Journal,* 61–62.

Most community mental health centers provide counseling and individual therapy. They strive to solve problems in early stages by working with children who are emotionally troubled or have alcohol or drug problems. Among the other outpatient services usually provided are family and marital counseling. Here, the focus is on resolving misunderstandings before they develop into disastrous problems. Some mental health centers focus on serving specific needs within the community, such as abstaining from alcohol, drugs, or gambling.

As a rule, community centers also provide outpatient care for former mental patients. To be sure, it is cheaper to look after patients who are living at home than it is to support staffs and institutional buildings. Some areas have halfway houses—temporary residences where people can readjust to living outside a mental institution. Patients receive psychotherapy and encourage one another to perform normal routines and work. But, unfortunately, too often community services are not available or patients are mentally unable to seek help. People suffering from chronic mental illness are thought to account for some 25 to 50 percent of the 250,000 to 3 million homeless in the United States (Lamb, 1984). Psychiatrist E. Fuller Torrey (1991) reported that the Pine Street Inn, a public shelter in Boston, is the largest "mental institution" in Massachusetts, with half of its 1000 nightly residents mentally ill.

Unfortunately, many mentally ill persons end up on soup lines at homeless shelters.

Torrey also noted that the largest "mental institution" in the United States is the Los Angeles jail, with 3600 mentally ill inmates in its total population of 24,000. An estimated 60 percent of people admitted to county jails suffer from clinically diagnosable addiction disorders (Freiberg, 1991). Unfortunately, fewer than one-third of the people suffering from mental illness ever seek help from physicians, mental health clinics, self-help groups, or other caregivers (Bower, 1993).

Outpatient community services can make a difference. Patients who have had the support of halfway houses usually learn to manage their lives. Even after patients return to their homes, most continue to benefit from day care, work, and recreation at halfway houses. About 80 percent of former mental patients who have resided at halfway houses have made successful adjustments.

Crisis Management

Some problems are urgent and cannot wait. If you are in a state of panic and terror over an exam you must take tomorrow, an appointment with a therapist next week is of no help. Similarly, persons who are severely depressed and suicidal should not be kept waiting for assistance and support. Many communities have hot lines, telephones answered by trained volunteers or paraprofessionals who are available twenty-four hours a day, seven days a week. Persons with drug, alcohol, marital, grief, or other immediate adjustment problems can be given instant aid and comfort. The article in Feature 11-7 describes one community's response to the crisis of domestic violence. Some college

---

FEATURE 11-7 PSYCHOLOGY IN THE NEWS

Domestic Violence: Battered Wives, Shattered Lives

. . . East Hampton, at the eastern end of Long Island, is best known as a resort community of shingled houses and beautiful white sand beaches. But in the past six years, it has distinguished itself—and won the praise of local activists and state experts—for its innovative efforts to fight domestic violence. This summer The Retreat, which had its beginnings in 1986 as a telephone hot line, becomes only the second residential shelter for battered women in Suffolk County (population 1.4 million). At a cost of $650,000, with 18 beds, The Retreat is proof that politicians, police, community service groups and activists can put their heads (and budgets) together in an all-out, no-nonsense effort to save lives. . . .

The hot line answering service almost immediately proved inadequate. Sherry Wolfe and the board of directors managed to squeeze $90,000 in grants from New York State and Suffolk County, and in 1988 she rented office space and hired a director, who trained volunteers. They helped battered women find safe houses and sign up for social services. Determined to create a permanent shelter, the board asked the town of East Hampton to donate land, which it did. The town also helped arrange for financing construction. With the village police chief now on the board, the group was able to work closely with the cops who were answering the distress calls. . . .

Source: Tivnan, E. (1992, July 21). Domestic violence: Battered wives, shattered lives. *Family Circle,* 100–101.

campuses maintain hot lines; not surprisingly the lines are usually busiest during final exam week!

Exercise 11-9

Imagine you have been elected to the board of directors of the community mental health center in Perfectown, U.S.A., a large prosperous community. Happily, Ben Evolant, a wealthy citizen, has just willed his entire fortune to be used for the improvement of community mental health programs. You must find ways to spend his money. Read the following description of existing programs in Perfectown, and suggest possible expansions and improvements in the three major areas listed below.

The Perfectown Mental Health Center offers courses in stress management, self-improvement, and communication skills. All three courses are popular, and many citizens enroll. The center also operates a therapy program for children with emotional and/or school problems. The program is considered successful. Recently one of the three mental institutions in the state closed, and patients with minimal disorders were released. Former mental patients living in Perfectown must travel more than 50 miles for treatment.

a. Improvements in preventive approaches (2):

_____

_____

b. Improvements in outpatient services (3):

_____

_____

_____

c. Improvements in crisis management (2):

_____

_____

Please compare your suggestions with those listed in the Feedback section.

SELECTING PROFESSIONAL THERAPISTS

When you are upset by problems, the task of deciding on the type of professional help needed can seem overwhelming. Indeed there are an enormous number of techniques, styles, and qualifications to consider. An important first step is to check with your physician. Although many problems have psychological causes, some may also be related to physical factors. For example, a headache could result from tension, but it could also be caused by a tumor, high blood pressure, or a visual disorder. Psychotherapy alone would not alleviate the problem.

If psychotherapy is needed, your family doctor is likely to be aware of the reputations and specializations of psychologists and psychiatrists in the community. If you do not have a family doctor or prefer not to use one in this way, seek a mental health clinic or a general hospital, which can usually provide a list of qualified professionals. As mentioned earlier in the chapter, specific techniques are less important than are overall qualifications and skills. If your background is other than Anglo-American, selecting a therapist who is sensitive to your culture is of prime importance. Most public libraries have directories of the American Psychiatric Association and the American Psychological Association that record the training and experience of each qualified therapist. In addition, the American Psychological Association publishes a directory of ethnic minority psychologists. The directory lists psychologists of four major ethnic groups: American Indian/Alaska native, Asian/Asian American/Pacific Islander, Black/African American, and Hispanic/Latino.

Checkpoint

Use the following questions to check your understanding of the final portion of this chapter. Indicate whether each statement is true or false.

21. _____ Group therapy is less expensive than individual therapy is.

22. _____ Group therapy is particularly beneficial for severely psychotic patients who cannot communicate or even maintain eye contact with another person.

23. _____ Antipsychotic drugs are used to keep patients calm.

24. _____ Antidepressant drugs have been beneficial in the treatment of phobias.

25. _____ Electroshock treatment is the most popular and effective method of controlling depression.

26. _____ A television program on child care is an example of a preventive approach.

27. _____ A paraprofessional must have an M.D. or a Ph.D.

28. _____ Halfway houses can help former drug addicts, alcoholics, or patients from mental institutions.

29. _____ A suicide-prevention center is an example of a crisis-management program.

30. _____ It is generally advisable to check with a family doctor before beginning psychotherapy.

Check your responses against the Checkpoint Answer Key at the end of this chapter. If you had difficulty with any question, reread the text. If you had little or no difficulty answering the questions or have resolved problems that you might have had, you are ready to check yourself against the chapter inventory that follows.

Use this list of objectives as a review checklist. You should be able to do the tasks outlined in the objectives and apply them to everyday examples. If you can, you may feel confident that you have mastered the material in this chapter.

1. Describe how biofeedback can be used to reduce stress.
2. Outline four steps to control anger, and suggest two possible methods for controlling bad habits.
3. Explain the purpose and give examples of self-help groups.
4. Recognize the cautions of counseling others.
5. Explain the importance of a trained therapist in a treatment program.
6. Distinguish between and describe the characteristics of simple emotional problems and mental disorders.
7. Explain the purpose and methods used in psychoanalysis, humanistic counseling, client-centered therapy, gestalt therapy, existential therapy, cognitive therapy, rational-emotive therapy, behavior therapy, and systematic desensitization.
8. Specify four advantages of group therapy.
9. Outline the advantages and limitations of drugs, electroshock, and psychosurgery.
10. List and give examples of three types of services that can be provided by community mental health centers.
11. Describe three possible methods for identifying qualified psychologists and psychiatrists.

Feedback

The correct answers to the exercises follow. If you did not answer an exercise correctly, review the preceding pages and return to the exercise to correctly complete it.

11-1. a. 5
      b. 2 or 3
      c. 6
      d. 1
      e. 4
      f. 2 or 3

11-2. a. Prepare himself by thinking about the types of situations and remarks that provoke his anger
      b. Think of ways to reply and handle himself
      c. Find ways to relax physically when he feels himself become agitated and upset
      d. Reward himself with something he enjoys whenever he handles a person calmly and successfully

11-3. The location of the chair sounds inconvenient and boring. It should remove some of the enjoyment of smoking.

11-4. a. Sharing successes and failures in dieting
      b. Encouraging and helping each other to continue dieting
      c. Socializing

11-5. a. Addiction or antisocial personality
      b. Simple emotional problem
      c. Mood disorder (depression)
      d. Schizophrenia

11-6. a. Gestalt therapy
      b. Rational-emotive therapy
      c. Psychoanalysis
      d. Existential therapy
      e. Behavior therapy
      f. Client-centered therapy
      g. Cognitive therapy

11-7. a. Cheaper
      b. Improves interpersonal relationships
      c. Allows participants to try out behaviors in a protected setting
      d. Allows learning from the experiences of others

11-8. a. Advantage: Lulu will probably be calmer and more controllable.
      Disadvantage: She could take an overdose or become overly dependent on the drug.
      b. Advantage: His depression is relieved by the drugs.
      Disadvantage: Prolonged use could worsen his depression and lethargy.
      c. Advantage: His unpleasant memories may be erased and his depression lessened.
      Disadvantage: There is no certainty about exactly what occurs during electroshock. There may be a danger.
      d. Advantage: Her sister would become less violent.
      Disadvantage: Her sister could never function as a normal person.

11-9. a. Preventive approaches: child-rearing course; training program for paraprofessionals (perhaps they could also expand into radio, television, and newspaper courses)
      b. Outpatient services: family and marital counseling; therapy program for mental patients; halfway houses
      c. Crisis management: suicide-prevention center; hot-line telephone system

Checkpoint Answer Key

1. a; 2. d; 3. c; 4. b; 5. c; 6. a; 7. d; 8. b; 9. d; 10. a; 11. c; 12. b; 13. d; 14. h; 15. a; 16. f; 17. i; 18. g; 19. c; 20. e; 21. true; 22. false; 23. true; 24. true; 25. false; 26. true; 27. false; 28. true; 29. true; 30. true.

Choosing Lifestyles

There is only one kind of love, but it has a thousand
guises.

—La Rochefoucauld

Almost every newspaper has a section devoted to wedding announcements. There is also coverage on famous people who are living together or considering marriage or divorce. If a celebrity has a homosexual relationship, the news is cause for headlines. People have a great curiosity about the lifestyles of others. Even if a recently divorced woman is only a casual acquaintance, people will wonder what caused the relationship to end, whether she has another lover, and if she will remarry.

Changes in lifestyles require adjustments that have a profound impact on the people involved. In this chapter you will learn more about gender attitudes and choices. You will also consider the many adjustments that are encountered in sexual lifestyles. After considering the many environmental factors that contribute to learning gender roles, you will read about various forms of love. Next you will probe into the stages of development in heterosexual relationships. Adjustments to cohabitation, marriage, death of a spouse, divorce, and singleness will be examined. Finally you will become acquainted with the nature of gay relationships.

The one thing you always remember about people is their gender. You might forget or not even notice their eye color, hair color, facial features, clothing, and jewelry. But you always notice and recall their gender. Obviously sex is more important than any other single characteristic.

Parental Influences on Gender Roles

Have you ever wondered when you first became aware of what sex you are? Psychologists have found that gender typing begins at birth. When parents are told that they have a son or a daughter, they have immediate feelings of what to expect from their child. Although it is impossible to detect sex differences in a covered or dressed baby, parents become annoyed if you think their infant son is a girl or vice versa. To avoid this type of irritation, parents frequently dress baby girls in pink and boys, in blue. Similarly, the baby's room is usually painted a sex-appropriate color, and female or male toys are selected.

As children develop, gender-appropriate behaviors tend to be encouraged and directly reinforced. Girls who play with dolls receive smiles of approval. Behaviors deemed inappropriate for the child's gender are discouraged and given direct negative reinforcements. A boy who is unwilling to fight is called a sissy. Likewise, a girl who climbs trees is called a tomboy. Interestingly, it is more acceptable to be a tomboy than to be a sissy. Often children learn from watching other children. This type of observation is called *vicarious learning*. Seeing a playmate ridiculed for being a sissy will discourage another boy from similar behavior.

vicarious learning Observing the positive and negative reinforcement of others

Children also learn gender roles by imitating the behavior of the same-sex parent. This type of learning is called *modeling*. Mothers who enjoy wearing frilly dresses and makeup are likely to see their little daughters dress similarly. Margaret Mead (1935) described a tribe in New Guinea with practices quite the opposite of traditional American gender roles. Among the Tchambuli tribe, men wore flowers and jewelry and tended to be dependent and flirtatious. Women worked at fishing and manufacturing and were expected to take the initiative in sex. Culture is a major factor in the development of gender roles. Think about the gender roles of your parents. Undoubtedly your parents' notions had a strong influence on your early attitudes.

modeling Learning that occurs by observing and imitating others

Exercise 12-1

Three methods of learning gender roles have been described: direct reinforcement (positive or negative), vicarious learning, and modeling. Read the following scenario and place the correct label on the line after each example.

a. Amanda's mother brought her into a day-care center for the first time. As the little three-year-old girl walked over to a group of boys playing with trucks, her mother reminded her "only bad girls play with boys."

_____

b. When Amanda joined two other little girls, her mother sighed, "That's a good girl."

_____

c. The two girls were struggling and fighting over a toy telephone. The teacher intervened and scolded, "You are acting more like naughty boys than like nice little girls." Amanda put her hands behind her back and would not touch any toys.

_____

d. Concerned that she may have frightened Amanda, the teacher patted her on the head and stated, "You are a perfect little lady."

_____

e. Amanda then noticed her mother was seated in the back of the room with her legs crossed. She pulled up a chair and imitated the way her mother was sitting.

_____

Please check your labels in the Feedback section.

Parents have a strong influence on their children's sex roles. Boys tend to imitate their fathers' behaviors.

"Gosh, Grandma, what a big office you have!"

FIGURE 12-1. If modeling occurs, the little girl may see herself as a future business executive.

Sex Differences

Aside from anatomy and hormones, how do males and females really differ? The existence of clearly inborn sex differences in abilities and personality has been a controversial topic. As reported by Begley and Carey (1979), there is considerable evidence that male hormones are related to aggressiveness in monkeys. However, none of these findings clearly indicates that differences in aggression can be linked only to hormones. In addition to aggressiveness, a number of other differences between males and females have been described. Most of these differences relate to specific abilities. Boys have been found to have superior mechanical aptitudes, while girls have better fine motor coordination and verbal ability. Although there might be a genetic explanation for these differences, most can be explained by environmental factors. The consensus among scientists is that most differences between males and females do not have a direct biological cause. Boys are encouraged to play with trucks and mechanical toys. Girls, on the other hand, are presented with dolls to be dressed. Some studies have found that mothers tend to sing and talk more often to baby girls than to baby boys. This behavior could influence verbal ability.

There is evidence that training can change the differences in abilities observed in boys and girls. Changes in education have narrowed the gap between males and females in verbal, mathematical, and spatial skills (Deaux, 1985). Most psychologists have found that sex differences are not large enough to predict skills and behavior (Hyde, 1981, 1984; Hyde and Linn, 1988; Matlin, 1987).

Exercise 12-2

A psychologist reported that eighth-grade girls earn lower scores than eighth-grade boys do on mathematics aptitude tests. A newspaper article concludes that there are innate differences in mathematical ability between males and females. From what you have learned about factors that influence sex differences, specify why the author of the article may not have drawn a valid conclusion.

_____

_____

_____

Turn to the Feedback section to check your answer.

Modifying Traditional Attitudes toward Gender Roles

In the past fifty years, gender roles have become less rigid. Traditional ideas required men to be tough, aggressive, and independent. It was part of the male role to make decisions, strive for achievement, and work outside the home. On the other hand, women were expected to be compassionate, understanding, gentle, tender, sensitive, and submissive. Female interests were to center on marriage, family, and the home.

One major reason for changes in gender roles has been the increase in the percentage of women who work outside the home. Attitudes on the role of women in making decisions have also changed. Most women now feel they should have a voice in family decisions. However, researchers have found that when mothers work outside the home, their daughters' attitudes remain similar to theirs. Women who take jobs because they need money would often really prefer not to work. They tend to convey traditional attitudes about gender roles to their children. However, women who have stimulating, interesting jobs and enjoy their work are more likely to encourage less traditional and more liberated attitudes in their children.

Ickes and Barnes (1978) compared communications among male and female students with traditional views of gender roles to those of students with more flexible values. They found that students with traditional values did not look at each other, smile, gesture, or talk to each other as often as those who did not adhere to the traditional view. The less traditional students were more relaxed and comfortable and enjoyed meeting members of the opposite sex. Further, women who adhere to traditional feminine roles are more likely to be anxious and low in self-esteem. Likewise, highly "masculine" men have been found to be anxious, neurotic, and low in self-acceptance (Unger and Crawford, 1992).

Although initial meetings are smoother and general adjustment is better when men and women have liberated attitudes toward their roles, a number of problems have been encountered by women who do not adhere to traditional values. An increasing number of women are complaining of sexual harassment at their jobs. Sexual harassment can range from being subjected to dirty jokes or lewd comments to sexual assault and rape. Some psychologists believe that

"O.K., you be the doctor, and I'll be the Secretary of Health and Human Services."

FIGURE 12-2. . . . and her children probably will have liberated attitudes, too.

sexual harassment has always been present and has not really increased. Rather, liberated women are now more willing to admit the problems and complain.

Married women and single mothers who work outside the home often experience stress. Although they have careers, they usually maintain primary responsibility for the house and children. Trying to do everything well can create a stress labeled "superwoman's disease." McBride (1990) suggested that important factors in this stress are the woman's attitude about her work, whether she is in an abusive or caring relationship, and whether she has friends that offer social support.

The liberation of women has also created a need for role changes in men. Many men have increased their involvement in both child care and household chores. An understanding of roles and gender attitudes is critical in maintaining a lasting relationship.

Exercise 12-3

Indicate whether each of the following persons is more likely to have a traditional or a flexible attitude toward gender roles.

a. Claude informed his wife that he accepted
a transfer in his job and that their family
must move to Liberia in two weeks.   _____

b. Madonna knows her mother hates her job, but their family needs the added income. _____

c. Jerome, a college sophomore, feels as relaxed with females as he does with males. _____

d. Thelma filed a complaint when her boss offered her a promotion if she would spend the night with him. _____

e. Mario intentionally stays at work longer so he will not have to concern himself with the children when he arrives home. _____

Turn to the Feedback section to check your answers.

LOVING

Compared with poets, psychologists do a poor job of defining love. After surveying couples in love, Lindzey, Hall, and Thompson (1975) described the feeling as "an intense affection or liking." From your own experience you probably realize that love is not limited to adults of the opposite sex. As a child you undoubtedly felt love toward your mother and father and perhaps some grandparents. You might even have loved a cat or dog or other pet.

As an infant you experienced selfish love: You needed to be loved by your parents rather than to give love. Infants need to be held firmly and have the security of knowing they will receive care. As you grew older you began to experience more mature forms of love. Mature love includes understanding and caring for the welfare of another. Perhaps you had a sick or injured pet. Recall the pain you experienced in your concern for the animal.

Mature human love requires even more than understanding, caring, and empathy. It also calls for trust and respect. Your complete interest is in the happiness of another person. Mature love should not expect reciprocity. You can give love without receiving it in return. Indeed there is a risk in loving!

In western culture, love brings feelings of possessiveness. If you love someone, you have a feeling that the person belongs to you. This possessiveness tends to lead to jealousy. This attitude is not the same in all cultures. In some societies men offer their wives to strangers as a sign of hospitality. Interestingly, American men have been found to be more jealous than women are. Completely possessive love is rare. But the next time you feel a twinge of jealousy, think of Maslow's (1970) statement: "We can enjoy a painting without wanting to own it, a rosebush without wanting to pluck from it, a pretty baby without wanting to kidnap it, a bird without wanting to cage it, and also can one person admire and enjoy another in a nondoing or nongetting way."

Checkpoint

Use the following questions to check your understanding of this portion of the chapter. Indicate whether each statement is true or false.

1. _____ Parents are the first influence on attitudes toward gender roles.

2. _____ Vicarious learning of gender roles requires observation of others.

3. _____ Attitudes toward gender roles are inherited.

4. _____ Gender roles are the same in all cultures.

5. _____ There has been little change in attitude toward gender roles in the past fifty years.

6. _____ Women who are unhappy at work but need the money usually are flexible in their attitudes toward gender roles.

7. _____ Male students with liberated attitudes toward sex roles are more relaxed when meeting women.

8. _____ A woman who feels pressured and stressed by the responsibilities of both a family and a full-time job may be suffering from super-woman's disease.

9. _____ Selfish love requires giving rather than receiving.

10. _____ Mature love is always reciprocal.

Use the Checkpoint Answer Key to verify your responses. If you had any difficulty with a question, carefully reread the text. If you had little or no difficulty answering the questions or have resolved any problems that you might have had, you are ready to continue with the next portion of this chapter.

HETEROSEXUAL RELATIONSHIPS

Have you ever thought of the stages you go through when you begin a relationship with someone of the opposite sex? Gagnon and Greenblat (1978) described three stages. Although the order may vary, you can probably identify some of them in your own relationships. One stage involves meeting a person and feeling the person is desirable. This is called the "attraction stage." Another stage occurs when an emotional closeness develops. This stage has been called "emotional commitment." The third stage described by Gagnon and Greenblat involves "sexual intimacy." These three stages may overlap and occur in any order. However, a complete heterosexual relationship will include all three stages.

Attraction

The process of socializing and pairing with the opposite sex usually begins in adolescence. Depending on the vogue of the times and the area, teenagers may choose gatherings, sports activities, clubs, concerts, dances, or dating as opportunities for meeting and selecting partners. You have probably participated in several of these activities. What attracted you to someone else at an event? Often people find themselves attracted to persons who remind them of old acquaintances whom they liked or admired.

Probably the most important factor in attraction is *proximity*. You tend to develop relationships with people who live near you, attend school with you, or work with you (Zajonc, 1968, 1970). You also tend to be attracted to people with similar attitudes and personal characteristics. After surveying husbands and wives, Berelson and Steiner (1967) reported that people were attracted to partners of the same race, religion, education, social class, and even previous marital status. A divorced man is likely to be attracted to a divorcee, a widow will be attracted to a widower, and a forever single is most likely to find appealing a person who has never married. If attitudes toward religion, drinking, and family size are similar, the attraction is apt to grow stronger. Not only does the attraction grow, but personalities and abilities also seem to grow more similar. Researchers say married couples grow more and more alike. They eventually adopt the same thoughts, perceptions, and even math skills (Schwartz, 1988).

Computer dating services are based on the notion that people with similar attitudes and backgrounds will find each other appealing. Usually a person is

Proximity is an important factor in attraction. Next-door neighbors are more likely to be friends than people who live at a distance.

FIGURE 12-3. Are his hopes realistic?

first asked to complete a questionnaire asking about a number of his or her personal characteristics, attributes, and attitudes. Next a questionnaire about an ideal mate must be completed. The computer is used to match the questionnaires of males and females. Occasionally the system goes awry. Imagine the surprise of a college student who won a computer date with his sister! Apparently the computer was not programmed to rule out dates for persons with the same parents.

Perhaps by now you are concerned about the truth of that old adage, "Opposites attract." If indeed people with similar backgrounds and attitudes tend to find each other appealing, how can the adage still hold? There may be a kernel of truth in grandmother's maxim. Often people with a weakness will find themselves attracted to persons with a strength in the same area. For example, a shy man might find a friendly, talkative woman appealing. Her chatter can cover his shyness. Similarly, a woman who has trouble making decisions may find herself attracted to a decisive male who prefers to show his authority. However, although the people in each couple may be opposite in their strengths and weaknesses, chances are they have similar backgrounds and attitudes on major issues.

Another old maxim on attraction has advised women to play hard to get. Here again, research gives only limited support for the principle. Although playing hard to get may increase a woman's desirability, it often causes males to retreat. Men are likely to assume that the woman is simply not interested in them. However, a woman who gives the appearance of being hard to get but focuses her attention on the person she cares for is likely to improve her desirability with him.

Exercise 12-4

Assume you have just accepted a job as a matchmaker at a dating bureau. The person you replaced left a list of recommended matches on your desk. Indicate whether you agree or disagree with each recommended match and specify your reason.

a. **Maurice L.** Male, 55 years old, divorced, three previous marriages, law degree from Harvard University, partner in law firm, atheist, wants to meet a younger woman, enjoys parties and drinking

and

Tanya M. Female, 20 years old, never married, high school graduate, clerk in department store, Mormon religion, likes older men, enjoys small gatherings with friends

b. **Julio Z.** Male, 48 years old, widower with three young children, operates a large laundry business, Jewish, seeking woman for permanent relationship (marriage)

and

Beta G. Female, 43 years old, widow with teenage daughter, employed as a beautician since death of her husband, Jewish, would like to find partner who will permit her to stay at home

c. **Dwayne R.** Male, 22 years old, never married, senior at Academia University, English major, Catholic, rigorous studying does not give him time to meet females, wants to meet someone intelligent and stimulating

and

Maria M. Female, 21 years old, never married, junior at Academia University, astronomy major, history minor, Catholic, desires an acceptable male companion to escort her to college lectures and functions

Please check your matchmaking abilities in the Feedback section.

Emotional Commitment

Emotional commitment occurs when people share their deepest feelings with others. Even if their feelings are not love, that commitment and sharing will create the illusion of being in love. Most people expect to fall in love and commit themselves emotionally to another person. Think of the many love stories you have read and heard in poems, novels, films, videos, and soap operas. Close relationships usually begin in high school. Larson et al. (1976) reported that 65 percent of White high school seniors and 77 percent of Black high school seniors had gone steady while in high school. According to Gilligan (1982), young men tend to be threatened by these attachments while young women tend to feel safer and more secure.

There are many fantasies associated with emotional commitments. Storybook romances are often described as complete bliss and perfection. As a result, falling in love seems extremely desirable and wonderful. Have you ever heard the song "Falling in Love with Love"? Perhaps you have known someone who constantly claimed to be in love, but the object of the love could change from month to month, week to week, or even day to day. Somehow this love seems more an illusion than a stage in a deep relationship.

infatuation Transient, temporary, selfish love

Transient love has been labeled *infatuation*. Infatuation is usually a temporary state. Assume that Jennifer is learning sculpting from Edgar. Jennifer believes that Edgar is perfect in every way. He is clearly the best-looking, most sensitive, intelligent, clever, artistic, and humorous person who ever existed.

"You have a truly magnificent scowl!"

FIGURE 12-4. A classic case of infatuation . . .

Jennifer cannot see any of Edgar's faults. Infatuation is a selfish love. Since Edgar is completely perfect, he could not possibly need Jennifer. She simply idolizes him. People who are infatuated usually cannot recognize the imperfections of those they adore.

Tennov (1979) introduced the term *limerance*. Limerance is a total emotional commitment that gives the experience of falling or being "in love." A limerant man will go out of his way to drive by the apartment or house of a woman he loves, even if he knows she is not at home. He will also become jealous if she spends time talking with other men. Most of his waking hours are spent thinking about her, and he wants to be with her as much as possible. He wants to do everything he possibly can to help her and make her happy. In most relationships, limerance only lasts from eighteen months to three years. Only rarely does limerance last a lifetime. However, you can love a person without being limerant.

Often one person is more emotionally committed, or limerant, than the partner. As a result the committed person will make sacrifices to preserve the relationship. However, Rubenstein (1981) reported that the happiness of persons making sacrifices dwindles after eighteen months, and their partners are even less satisfied as their relationship continues. For emotional commitment to endure happily, both partners need to work on communicating their feelings and continuing the relationship.

limerance Total emotional commitment that gives the experience of being or falling "in love"

FIGURE 12-5. Would you give this relationship more than eighteen months?

Exercise 12-5

In your own words, describe the key difference between infatuation and limerance.

_____

_____

_____

Please check your answer in the Feedback section.

Sexual Intimacy

Because of the increase in the number of pregnancies among unmarried teenagers, there has been a growing concern about adolescent sexual intimacy. A report from the House of Representatives Select Committee on Population stated that one-fifth of thirteen- and fourteen-year-old Americans have had sexual intercourse. The percentage of fifteen- to nineteen-year-old young women reporting premarital intercourse increased from 29 percent in 1970 to 52 percent in 1988 (Center for Disease Control, 1991). Less than one-third of sexually active teenagers ever use contraceptives. Every year one in every ten American teenage girls becomes pregnant (Dryfoos, 1985). The United States has one of the highest teenage birth rates in the western world and is the only industrial nation with an increasing rate of teenage pregnancy (Jones et al., 1985).

Premarital sex does not always result from a desire for intimacy. Peer pressure seems to be an important factor. For young males sexual intercourse is often considered a way to prove their manliness. Young females believe that sexual intimacy will prove they are sexy and desirable. Several studies have found that attractive girls are less likely to have sexual experiences in high school. Young women with poor self-images sometimes use sex as a method to feel better about themselves. Premarital sex is more prevalent among teens with poor grades, whose parents did not complete college, who drink alcohol and smoke marijuana, and who are not active in any religion (Harris and Associates, 1986; Orr et al., 1991). Simon et al. (1972) reported that females who plan to attend college are less likely to have sexual intercourse during high school than are females who do not plan to go to college. The most successful community programs for preventing teenage pregnancy have focused on improving self-esteem (Carrera, 1986).

Another important factor that increases the likelihood of premarital sex is hostility. For some young males and females, having sex relations without caring about the person is a way to belittle the opposite sex. Girls who feel hostile toward their parents will sometimes have sexual relations primarily to punish their parents. They feel their parents will disapprove of their behavior and perhaps feel hurt. The double standard of attitudes toward sex is fading. Teenagers hold similar standards for appropriate behavior for both sexes (Coles and Stokes, 1985).

Another changing trend has been an increased concern about the choice of sexual partners (Ehrenreich, Hess, and Jacobs, 1986). Fear of herpes and acquired immune deficiency syndrome (AIDS) have decreased the frequency of casual sex. While herpes is a bothersome condition, the AIDS virus is life-threatening. To date, there is no known cure for AIDS. Initially AIDS was considered a disease of homosexual men and drug abusers using needles. Although it is now widely known that the AIDS virus is spread through heterosexual intercourse, only a small percentage of people at risk use condoms for protection against the deadly disease (see Feature 12-1).

Emotional commitment and sexual intimacy do not always coexist. Sometimes one can lead to the other, but there are no guarantees. Marriages based on sex alone are rarely successful. Maslow (1970) strongly believed that sexual intimacy is more enjoyable and satisfying when accompanied by an emotional commitment.

Exercise 12-6

Janice, a sixteen-year-old, has just had sexual relations with Daryl, a boy who does not interest her. Specify three possible reasons for Janice's behavior.

a. _____

b. _____

c. _____

Turn to the Feedback section to check your responses.

Cohabitation

Some couples choose to cohabit, live together without marrying, during their developing relationship. Macklin (1972) surveyed students at a large university and described a variety of reasons for their cohabitation. Some couples wanted to try out their relationship before making a long-term commitment in marriage. Their cohabitation served as a trial marriage. Other couples simply did not believe in marriage. Among the other reasons listed were the need for a meaningful and convenient temporary relationship, avoiding loneliness, and sleeping with someone who cares about you.

Cohabitation is not limited to college students. It is becoming more common with all ages. Many elderly persons find it financially convenient to cohabit. According to the U.S. Census Bureau, the number of unmarried couples living together has more than tripled since 1970. Clayton and Voss (1977) interviewed males born between the years 1944 and 1954. Although only 5 percent of the men were cohabiting at the time of the survey, 18 percent had previously lived with a female for six months or longer. Results of the survey showed a high correlation between living with a woman and experimentation with lifestyles. In the 1970s, those who had cohabited were more likely to have "bummed around," studied ESP, astrology, or an eastern religion, demonstrated for a cause, lived in a commune, or meditated. But today, cohabitation is common and on the rise. In 1988, there were almost 3 million unmarried couples living together, as opposed to only about 523,000 in 1970 (U.S. Census Bureau, 1988). For many couples, living together is a modern version of "going steady" and is only temporary. Within a few years most cohabiting couples have either separated or married.

Will living together improve the chances for a successful marriage? The results of studies are mixed. One Canadian study found that the odds of divorce were less among those who married after cohabiting than among those who

---

FEATURE 12-1 PSYCHOLOGY IN THE NEWS

Risky Sex and AIDS

The first national survey of behaviors that increase the risk of contracting AIDS indicates that a large majority of people with multiple sex partners do not use condoms, particularly in black and Hispanic communities.

The 1990 survey, coordinated by researchers at the University of California, San Francisco, involved telephone interviews with two sample populations: a randomly selected group of about 2,800 adults across the nation, and a group of nearly 12,000 adults living in 20 major U.S. cities. The latter group, theoretically at greatest risk for developing AIDS, consisted of roughly equal numbers of whites, blacks, and Hispanics. . . .

Reports of multiple partners came from nearly 40 percent of unmarried white and black men between the ages of 18 and 45, and from 75 percent of unmarried Hispanic men between the ages of 18 and 29. These men represent prime targets for AIDS education programs, says Margaret Dolcini of UCSF.

Only 17 percent of all participants reporting multiple sex partners said they used condoms without fail in the past year. One in three used condoms in at least half of their sexual encounters. Among blacks and Hispanics, one-third of those with risky partners—who took drugs intravenously, had other sex partners or recently received a blood transfusion—never used condoms. . . .

Source: Bower, B. (1991, August 31). Risky sex and AIDS. *Science News*, 141.

had not lived together prior to marriage (Grant, 1988). However, results of more extensive surveys in Sweden and the United States suggest that married couples who have cohabited are at a higher risk for divorce (Hall, 1988; Bumpass and Sweet, 1988).

Marriage and Adjustments

According to recent reports, 95 percent of all Americans are married or will get married at some point. But the divorce rate has increased. For the first time in history, marriages are as likely to end from divorce as from death of a spouse (Weitzman, 1986). But even most divorced persons eventually remarry. Many people marry while they are in love or in a state of limerance. Tennov (1979) found that marriages that begin with limerance tend to last longer. Some marry for security and convenience rather than for love.

Successful Marriages

Have you ever wondered what makes some marriages more successful than others? Psychologists have identified a number of general characteristics that correlate with lasting happy marriages. Commitment to the institution of marriage appears to be one of the most important conditions. Previous general adjustment and ability to maintain a good relationship with parents also seem to be important factors. Children of happily married couples are more likely to have successful marriages. Although most people do not choose the year they plan to marry, age does make a difference. Marriages by persons under twenty-one are most likely to fail. The optimum age for successful marriages is twenty-one to twenty-nine for women, and twenty-four to twenty-nine for men. But, keep in mind that marriages by people of other ages can be successful. If you are over twenty-nine, do not despair; a happy marriage is still possible.

Choosing the right person to marry is crucial. Persons with the same attitudes and values will have fewer arguments. A computerized system called "Matesim" analyzes how a potential marriage might work out. The program includes questions in 180 areas, including goals, ambitions, attitudes toward life, job mobility, child discipline, and even television viewing habits. If the couple is in conflict in more than half the areas, the success of the marriage could not be predicted (Rice, 1980).

Besides having happily married parents, finding the right person, and marrying at the optimum age, what else could be required for a successful marriage? Psychologists have specified a number of personality characteristics that correlate with successful marriages. If you are an emotionally stable person with high self-esteem, you are off to a good start. Psychologists have found that people with low self-esteem tend to be more committed to partners who confirm their self-concepts (Swann et al., 1992). If you have a low opinion of yourself, you are likely to be more comfortable with a mate who agrees with your unfavorable view.

A successful marriage requires tolerance and understanding between partners. The first years of marriage require many mutual adjustments. Partners sometimes test each other by trying out their old freedoms. A man might intentionally plan a ski weekend with his old buddies and leave his wife at home alone. Similarly, a woman might circulate and flirt at a party to test her husband's reaction. Newly married couples need to consider the feelings of their spouses. Buss and his colleagues (1992) found that men experience more distress than women do when they believe their partner has been sexually unfaithful. Women feel more distress than men do when they believe their partner has been emotionally unfaithful.

Communication is critical to successful marriages. Too often men and women believe they can change their spouses after the wedding. If they are unhappy about habits and attitudes, they may say nothing until after the honeymoon. Only rarely are such marriages successful. Compromises can only be reached when both partners are flexible and willing to be open about their feelings. Good listeners who want to improve themselves are the best marriage partners. Most sex problems in marriages stem from poor communication.

Changing Role Structure in Marriage

Because there is more uncertainty in male and female roles today, it has become difficult for husbands and wives to distinguish their personal responsibilities during their marriages. Although the freedom from traditional structures can

"You say, 'off with her head,' but what I'm hearing is, 'I feel neglected.'"

FIGURE 12-6. Can they resolve their communication problem?

lead to richer relationships, the uncertainty can also be a source of frustration and anxiety. Many questions must be resolved. If both spouses work, which chores will the husband and wife assume responsibility for? Will there be children and who will care for them? How will the money be allocated? Interestingly, financial concerns have been the greatest single factor in divorce.

Psychologists and marriage counselors recommend that couples discuss and agree upon roles and responsibilities prior to the wedding. Even if roles are modified and changed during the course of a marriage, initial harmony helps the relationship last. Some couples draw up formal contracts agreeing on such mundane items as responsibility for ironing, housecleaning, and yard work, along with basic agreements on the distribution of money, amount of time for vacations, and future child care. Most couples do not sign contracts for their individual responsibilities, but hopefully they have an understanding about their general roles. Of course, contracts can be written and agreed upon anytime during a marriage.

Exercise 12-7

Read the following scenario. List eight factors that suggest a successful marriage and six factors that suggest an unsuccessful marriage.

Willy was thirty-five and Kelly was twenty-six when they decided to marry. Willy was limerant and in love with Kelly, but Kelly was marrying him only because her friends were married and she was feeling lonely. Both had graduated from college and had successful careers.

Willy's father had been married three times and his mother, twice. Most of his childhood was spent moving to new homes, and he had little opportunity to maintain friendships. Other than Kelly, Willy had no close friends, just a few casual acquaintances.

Kelly's parents are happily married. She and her sister recently arranged a family reunion to help their parents celebrate their thirtieth anniversary. She strongly believes in the institution of marriage. Her family has always been close and spent holidays together.

Kelly and Willy met at a church picnic. Both had been attending the same church but went to services at different times. They became fast friends when they realized they both enjoyed jogging and science fiction. They both joked and laughed easily.

Kelly has been upset and concerned about Willy's tendency to drink too much. However, she has not mentioned this to him. She figures she can change him after they are married. Although Kelly would like to have children as soon as possible, Willy feels they could purchase a magnificent sailboat if Kelly continued working and they did not need to support children. Kelly is certain he will change his mind after they are married.

a. Factors for a successful marriage: _____

_____

_____

b. Factors for an unsuccessful marriage: _____

_____

_____

Turn to the Feedback section to compare your lists.

Education for Marriage

Some psychologists have complained that more time is spent preparing people for a driver's license than for a marriage license. Although marriage gives opportunities for growth and happiness, it also requires many responsibilities. Preparation for making a decision to marry, accepting responsibilities, and communicating feelings has been minimal. As a result, expectations are often unrealistic. In the first flush of infatuation, some feel compelled to buy an engagement ring or apply for a marriage license. Franklin (1987) suggests that if the lovelorn male must do something, he should visit a florist! Newlyweds will be in a better position to cope if they recognize that limerance is temporary. The changing roles of males and females have made marriages more complicated. Few are prepared for the stresses and strains of even the first years of marriage. If someone you know is planning to marry, suggest some reading and open communication.

Checkpoint

Use the following questions to check your understanding of this portion of the chapter. Choose and mark the one correct response to each question.

11. What is the first stage of a heterosexual relationship?
    a. Emotional commitment
    b. Attraction
    c. Sexual intimacy
    d. Any one of the above

12. With whom would you be most likely to develop a close relationship?
    a. A person who looks like you
    b. A person who lives near you
    c. A person from an interesting, exotic country
    d. A person more intelligent than you

13. Gerry was recently divorced. To whom is he most likely to be attracted?
    a. Nelly, a divorcee
    b. Sheila, a widow
    c. Deirdre, who never married
    d. Frances, a happily married woman

14. In what way is the saying "opposites attract" true?
    a. People with opposite attitudes are attracted to each other.
    b. People from different cultures are attracted to each other.
    c. People with opposite personal experiences in life are attracted to each other.
    d. People with personality strengths and weaknesses that complement each other are attracted.

15. Lian, a high school junior, is attracted to a boy in her class. According to psychological research, how can she attract his interest?
    a. Ignore him and play hard to get.
    b. Smother him with attention, phone calls, and gifts.
    c. Give the illusion of being hard to get with others but show interest in him.
    d. Act interested in everyone else but play hard to get with him.

16. Every time Ira comes home from a party, he claims he just met the girl of his dreams. He has announced that he is in love eleven different times during the past month. What is Ira experiencing?
    a. Limerance
    b. Infatuation
    c. Emotional commitment
    d. Matesim

17. How long does limerance usually last?
    a. Less than one month
    b. Less than one year
    c. Less than three years
    d. A lifetime

18. Why has there been increased concern about adolescent sexual intimacy?
    a. There has been an increase in the number of pregnancies among unmarried teenagers.
    b. There have been increasing concerns about the double standard.
    c. The double standard has made adolescent girls feel immoral.
    d. Teenage girls who have sexual relations have strong emotional commitments to their partners.

19. According to surveys, which type of male is most likely to cohabit?
    a. One who is limerant
    b. One who is emotionally committed
    c. One who experiments with lifestyles
    d. One who never plans to marry

20. How are computers used in evaluating the success of potential marriages?
    a. Computers compare attitudes and values.
    b. Computers do family histories and check the happiness of the couple's parents.
    c. Computers analyze financial potential.
    d. Computers compare communication skills.

21. Which of the following is crucial for a successful marriage?
    a. Cohabitation prior to the wedding
    b. Communication of attitudes, goals, and responsibilities
    c. Limerance
    d. A written marriage contract specifying responsibilities and duties of each partner

Use the Checkpoint Answer Key to verify your responses. If you had any difficulty with a question, carefully reread the text. If you had little or no difficulty answering the questions or have resolved any problems that you might have had, you are ready to continue with the final portion of this chapter.

All relationships must come to an end. Even though many couples use such expressions as "until death do us part" at wedding ceremonies, few consider how their marriage will actually end. There are only two choices: separation or death. The ending of a relationship is more than just a change in marital status. Adjustments are required in financial responsibility, social activities, sex life, and possibly even such daily routines as sleeping and eating habits. The situation is usually further complicated by legal problems such as separation and divorce agreements, wills, and insurance settlements.

Death of a Spouse

Few people think about, or prepare for, the death of their spouses. Even if the subject is brought up in conversation, most people will avoid further discussion. Since women are usually two to three years younger than their husbands and have a longer lifespan, there are about four times as many widows as widowers. Emotional and financial stability do not spare grief; indeed they may intensify the negative feelings (see Feature 12-2). Whether the death is sudden or follows a prolonged illness, the spouse will experience a period of grief lasting at least two to three months.

FEATURE 12-2 PSYCHOLOGY IN THE NEWS

Bereavement: How Strength Saps Coping

A harmonious marriage, a solid bank account and a sense of control over life offer many rewards. But such sought after assets also set the stage for a particularly difficult adjustment to the death of a spouse, according to preliminary data from the first large-scale study of adults both before and after bereavement.

"People with considerable [psychological and financial] resources may be at most risk for negative reactions to the loss of a loved one," says psychology graduate student Vicki Gluhoski of the State University of New York at Stony Brook. "If someone views the world as predictable and safe, bereavement may hit them especially hard."

Gluhoski, who conducted the study with Stony Brook psychologist Camille B. Wortman and sociologist Ronald Kessler of the University of Michigan in Ann Arbor, presented the findings at the annual meeting of the American Psychological Society. . . .

Their findings suggest that people involved in conflict-ridden marriages suffer less emotional distress following a spouse's death than those in stable marriages. This contradicts the traditional assumption, based on clinical observations, that the survivor of a tumultuous relationship faces major difficulties in resolving the loss of his or her partner, Wortman points out.

The data also undermine the widespread notion that people armed with a sense of self-worth, confidence in their ability to overcome obstacles through hard work, and other emotional resources fend best in the face of severe stress, such as bereavement.

"So far, the findings fly in the face of most theories about grief," Wortman asserts. "A protestant work ethic type of world view can be very adaptive in many settings, but apparently not after the sudden loss of a loved one." . . .

Source: Bower, B. (1991, June 22). Bereavement: How strength saps coping. Science News, 390.

Cultural factors play an important role in how grief is handled. Japanese widows of Shinto and Buddhist religions tend to adjust comparatively well. The widow keeps in contact with her deceased spouse and most homes have altars dedicated to family ancestors. In contrast, Hopi Indians forget the deceased as soon as possible (Stroebe et al., 1992). In twentieth-century American culture, time is allowed for grieving. Widows who have few friends and do not have close relationships with children have the most difficult adjustment (Goldberg et al., 1988). Grieving spouses who have young children need to help the young ones cope. The article in Feature 12-3 offers some suggestions. Grief cannot be rushed, although friends and relatives can lend support and make the period less painful.

Psychologists have described four stages of grief that follow the death of a spouse. Throughout the four stages there are mixed feelings of agitation, anger, guilt, and depression (Parkes, 1972). The stages may overlap but they usually occur in order.

Stage 1: Shock. The first stage is a period of confusion. The spouse cannot understand the emotions being experienced. If the death followed a long period of illness, the widow or widower will worry that the death may have been caused by negligence or mistakes. They will think of things they could have done to prevent the death or blame doctors for poor treatment. They dwell on alternative actions even if the death was sudden or accidental. The shock in this stage often delays open expressions of grief. However,

---

FEATURE 12-3 PSYCHOLOGY IN THE NEWS

Helping Children Grieve

Bereavement is not for adults only. One out of 20 American children below the age of 15 suffers the loss of a parent. . . . According to researchers who conducted the Child Bereavement Study at Massachusetts General Hospital in Boston, adults must allow children to express their grief in their own way and time.

Over four years, the Massachusetts General team surveyed 125 children who had lost a parent; each child was interviewed with the surviving parent four months after the death and then one and two years later. "We found that the majority of these children manage very well," says Dr. Phyllis Silverman, a professor of human behavior at Massachusetts General's Institute of Health Professions, but about 20% may be at risk for behavioral and emotional problems during the first year following the parent's death.

The bereavement study revealed important ways in which loved ones can help grief-stricken children cope. For example, saving an object that had belonged to the deceased is a healthy response that encourages children to maintain an emotional connection. And because kids need to talk about their loss too, adults should let them know that discussing the deceased is okay. Adults should take their cues from the children, however, and not force them to open up.

While all youngsters need time to adjust following a loss, the interval varies. If after six months a child won't go to school, experiences a drop in grades, has trouble sleeping and eating or becomes withdrawn, it's time for the family to seek help. A guidance counselor or a support group for widowed parents is a good place to start.

Source: Springer, I. (1992, July/August). Helping children grieve. *American Health.*

the confusion of emotions leads to tears, sleepless nights, and a loss of appetite. Persons who normally drink or take sleeping pills are likely to take larger doses. Many widows and widowers wish for their own death.

Stage 2: Protest. During the second stage, bereaved spouses become easily irritated. A sense of unfairness is felt. They ask questions such as, "Why have I been left with all these responsibilities?" There is anger about changes in lifestyle, as well as paperwork and legal forms. Often there is no will or some confusion about the will. If there are financial burdens, the feelings of protest can become intense.

Stage 3: Depression and Withdrawal. Daydreaming about the past dominates the third stage. There is a strong tendency to tears, and widows and widowers prefer not to talk to others or socialize. They prefer to be left alone with their memories. During this stage there is often a resurgence of guilt. Spouses think of things they might have done to have been better partners. The bereaved experience many symptoms of depression described in Chapter 10. Support, warmth, and friendship from family and friends are crucial during this stage.

Stage 4: Recovery. Finally, the surviving spouse begins to function in a normal manner, completing routines and returning to work. Initially performance is somewhat less than usual, but going back to work usually helps a person feel more productive. Further, most working environments force some socializing, making it more difficult to remain depressed.

Exercise 12-8

Read the following descriptions and indicate the stage of bereavement for each widow and widower: shock, protest, depression and withdrawal, or recovery.

a. Jessica's husband died two weeks ago. She is furious that he never told her where he kept his insurance policies and securities. She feels he did not prepare her to handle family affairs and now has abandoned her. _____

b. Kevin returned to work today after a two-month leave of absence to bury his wife and settle legal and family problems. He still feels numb and listless but was able to accomplish some work and go out to lunch with his buddies. _____

c. Leroy was exhausted from his wife's long illness. She suffered so much during her last days. Leroy was hoping she would die to be spared further discomfort. When the doctor called him to tell him his wife had expired, Leroy was certain her death was caused by his wishes. _____

d. Ursula's spouse died more than three months ago. Although friends have invited her to dinner, she refuses to go anywhere. She prefers to stay home and go through picture albums and letters that her husband had sent her.

e. When Alberto heard his wife was killed in an automobile accident, he immediately poured himself a shot of whiskey. By the time his family arrived, he had consumed most of the bottle. He said he wanted to die, too.

Please check your answers in the Feedback section.

Divorce

The divorce rate has been high and is steadily increasing. Inglehart (1990) reported a divorce rate of 40 percent in Canada and 50 percent in the United States, with rates almost as high in Europe. The divorce rate increased 400 percent from 1965 to 1985. Many psychologists think the increased independence of women has been a leading factor in causing divorces. Hiller and Philliber (1978) found that working women with a positive self-concept and a sense of achievement are less dependent on their husbands for their own prestige. Since they do not need the emotional and economic support of their husbands, these women have become less willing to tolerate stresses in a marriage. Also, men often have problems in adjusting their roles to permit greater freedom for their wives and in taking on more daily responsibilities in the home. According to Kelly (1982), the wife is more likely to decide to end the marriage.

Adjustments to Divorce

Divorce is sometimes the only solution for a miserable relationship, but unfortunately it is always accompanied by additional pain. Divorce creates a sense of failure that leads to feelings of guilt and depression in both partners. Many states now have no-fault divorce laws. In a no-fault divorce, both partners agree that their marriage has severe problems that they cannot overcome. Although this helps to eliminate the problem of blaming one partner, it does not fully remove the burden of guilt and depression felt by both husband and wife.

As pointed out in Chapter 10, the depression after divorce is even more severe and longer lasting than is the depression that follows the death of a spouse. The divorced rarely receive sympathy and support from friends and relatives. While a bereaved spouse usually is allowed at least a one-week leave from work, a divorced person rarely takes more than a few hours. Some psychologists have suggested that ceremonies accompany divorces. The parted couple could vow to continue kindness and friendship toward each other and promise to support any children emotionally and financially. Friends and relatives would attend the ceremony and possibly a quiet reception would follow.

But a ceremony would be impossible for a group that suffers the greatest grief, the deserted. This is sometimes called "the poor man's divorce," since it is usually the woman who is abandoned. Since she is left with household bills and the economic responsibility of the children, the deserted woman faces economic as well as emotional problems. Today, women as well as men are deserting their spouses. Desertion creates special problems. The forsaken mate has the burden of not knowing whether the spouse is alive, physically or mentally ill, or troubled. Only costly, and often lengthy, investigations can help.

Regardless of the divorce method used, both partners must change their lifestyles. Divorced men often have problems performing household tasks. They feel a marked loss if they do not have custody of children. Hetherington et al. (1977) reported that divorced fathers work long hours, particularly if they have alimony payments. They also tend to sleep and eat poorly.

Women who have gained custody of their children often resent the father's freedom from responsibility. Many divorced wives see themselves as bogged down by household responsibilities while their husbands are allowed a carefree life. However, as Hetherington et al. (1977) reported, the fathers are far from happy. They become envious of their wives. They view their former spouses as fortunate, since they won the home and children. The result is often jealousy, bitterness, and hostility.

Divorced persons profit from support and encouragement from friends and relatives. Those who do not have close relationships to rely on can often be aided by counseling groups. Usually eight to ten recently divorced persons discuss their problems with a counselor. By listening to the troubles of others, people within the group feel less alone in their distress. They can also share their feelings and burdens with others. The benefits of group therapy were discussed in greater detail in Chapter 11.

Children of Divorced Parents

Divorce can be extremely painful for children. Often they feel responsible for the breakup of their parents' marriage and experience guilt. Since parents tend to argue about child rearing, children who have overheard arguments often assume that their misbehavior was the cause of the divorce. Children who have sided with one parent during an argument usually believe they have done the wrong thing. Often children fear they will be abandoned in the family breakup. Parents need to reassure their children and explain the custody arrangements in detail. Some children are embarrassed by their parents' divorce. They believe that divorce is proof that their family has failed, and they fear others will pity them. As a result, they will try to keep the divorce a secret and refuse to discuss it with anyone. In communities where divorce is common, children usually suffer less embarrassment. A number of books and novels have been written about children whose parents' marriages have failed. Reading about the experiences and feelings of others helps children understand their own emotions and feelings.

After divorce, children must adjust to separation from one parent. This adjustment is particularly difficult when parents continue to tear each other down. Although there have been many studies on the long-range effects of divorces on children, there are few clear conclusions. Bane (1976) acknowledged the initial guilt experienced by children but found no differences from children in intact families in social adjustment, school achievement, and susceptibility to delinquency. Wallerstein (1987) found that among sixteen- to eighteen-year-olds whose parents had divorced ten years earlier, three-quarters of the girls and half the boys had adjusted well. However, most were anxious about their love relationships and were afraid of being betrayed.

Hetherington (1972) reported that daughters of divorced parents who live with their mothers tend to have negative attitudes toward their fathers. These girls are also likely to have some difficulty relating appropriately to male peers and adults. According to Hetherington, they are prone to tenseness and promiscuity. As mentioned earlier in the chapter, having had divorced parents increases the likelihood that you will divorce someday.

Traditionally, mothers were usually awarded custody of their children. Currently, approximately 1 million children are in homes with a father only. As women have become more willing to relinquish their roles in child rearing, an increasing number of fathers have been assuming responsibilities for children. Joint custody is also gaining popularity. Children live with each parent for part of the year. When parents live near each other, children can visit in each home. Generally, children in joint custody have fewer adjustment problems. For divorced persons beginning their separate lives, the children from their previous marriage can create some awkward moments. Despite the many negative aspects of divorce, many psychologists feel that a broken home is better for children than a home of stress and conflict.

Exercise 12-9

Read the following scenario and describe how each underlined item is likely to improve adjustments to the divorce.

Nancy and John have decided that their marriage will never work. They argue constantly, and their relationship is miserable. They have decided on a (a) no-fault divorce. Nancy arranged for the (b) children of divorced friends to visit and chat with her youngsters; John purchased an interesting and appropriate novel for them. The divorcing couple explained to both children that (c) the failure of the marriage was the couple's responsibility as adults. The children were not to feel any blame. Nancy and John then agreed to plan (d) a short ceremony and pledge their continued devotion to their children. Members of their immediate families and a few close friends would be invited. (e) Guests would be asked to lend their support and friendship to both the couple and their children during the difficult months following the divorce.

a. _____

_____

b. _____

_____

c. _____

_____

d. _____

_____

e. _____

_____

Please turn to the Feedback section to check your answers.

Singleness

Singleness may be temporary, transitional, or permanent. For some, singleness is only a waiting period for marriage or remarriage. Singles comprise four groups: people who never married but will eventually; people who never married and never will; the divorced; and the widowed. The majority of divorced persons eventually remarry; however, only about half of the widowed give up their singleness.

Only a small group remains single permanently. Included in this small group are persons who stay with their parents, brothers and sisters living together, people who live alone, and members of religious orders. Single persons are not necessarily isolated. Even those who live alone usually enjoy close relationships with friends, relatives, nieces, nephews, and children of friends. People who live by themselves tend to have more friends and be less likely to become irked than people who live with others.

There are some clear advantages to singleness. To be sure, a single person who lives alone has more personal independence. Traveling or changing jobs and locations does not require another opinion. It is easier for singles to maintain privacy and please themselves.

However, there are also some problems. Single persons have to be emotionally independent and not need a long-term relationship. You have undoubtedly heard single persons pressured with questions such as, "When are you getting married?" "Haven't you found anyone yet?" Facing these questions, as well as such negative labels as "old maid," can be a chore!

Exercise 12-10

List two advantages and two disadvantages of remaining single.

a. Advantages: _____

_____

b. Disadvantages: _____

_____

Please compare your list with the one in the Feedback section.

GAY RELATIONSHIPS

Gay men and lesbians are attracted to people of the same gender; thus their intimate relationships are considered homosexual. Homosexuality is no longer considered a disorder and therapists do not encourage gay people to develop heterosexual relationships. Ellis and Ames (1987) reported that about 4 percent of the male population is gay and 1 percent of the female population is lesbian. The percentage of gays and lesbians has remained constant over many years and appears to be similar in most cultures studied (Hyde, 1986).

The causes of homosexuality are controversial and are not fully understood. It is known that male and female hormones are present in members of both sexes, and there is increasing evidence that homosexuality has biological roots (see Feature 12-4). Although there is some evidence that early family experiences could play a role in creating homosexual tendencies, research has had mixed results and therefore is not conclusive. At present most researchers believe that a predisposition to homosexuality is inborn and a natural trait, comparable to eye color or handedness.

Surveys of gay people found that between 40 percent and 75 percent have a long-term steady relationship with someone (Peplau, 1988). When compared with heterosexual couples, gay and lesbian couples show the same patterns of satisfaction in their relationships (Kurdek and Schmitt, 1986). Indeed, all couples face the same problems in developing and maintaining meaningful relationships.

Many gay and lesbian couples choose to raise children. In general, children raised in gay homes are no different than children raised by heterosexual couples, and according to the article in Feature 12-5, they may even have some advantages. However, they are often confronted with *homophobic* attitudes in the community. Too often people create negative stereotypes of homosexuals and develop irrational fears and contempt for them. Having parents who are

homophobia Irrational fear of, and contempt for, gay people

FEATURE 12-4 PSYCHOLOGY IN THE NEWS

Study of Twins Suggests Lesbianism Has a Genetic Component

Is homosexuality, at least in part, the product of biological causes? Researchers got closer to answering that furiously controversial question last week with a new study suggesting that genes may play a dominant role in determining whether a woman becomes a lesbian.

The findings, which parallel results of an earlier study of gay males, bolster the tentative but increasingly plausible theory that human sexual orientation—heterosexual as well as homosexual—is influenced to a significant degree by biology and is not exclusively a matter of upbringing or "lifestyle choice."

The study of lesbian twins "is the largest ever of female sexual orientation, and it suggests that genetic factors are as important in determining les-

bianism as they are in influencing male homosexuality," said psychologist J. Michael Bailey of Northwestern University.

Bailey conducted the study . . . with Richard Pillard of the Boston University School of Medicine. The men also collaborated on a similar 1991 study of gay male twins. . . .

"Based on our study, it looks as if genes are at least half the story. I think it's substantial. Before this study we didn't know any of the causes," Bailey said. But, he added, "We can't say what those genes are or what they are doing." . . .

Source: Daly, C. B. (1993, March 15). Study of twins suggests lesbianism has a genetic component. *The Washington Post*, A-3.

subject to prejudice and discrimination can make adjustments difficult for some children.

Checkpoint

Use the following questions to check your understanding of the final portion of this chapter. Choose and mark the one correct response to each question.

22. Bill's wife was hospitalized four days ago following a heart attack. He has just been told that his wife has died. Which of the following is likely to be his first reaction?
    a. Anger and resentment
    b. Confusion and shock
    c. Depression and guilt
    d. Protest and withdrawal

FEATURE 12-5 PSYCHOLOGY IN THE NEWS

Ozzie and Ozzie: What America Can Learn from Gay Families

What is still to be acknowledged is that more gays and lesbians than ever are rushing home after work to build a moral—yes, moral—family life.

To some the words "gay" and "family" are incompatible. But the reality is otherwise: Attorneys in the family law section of the American Bar Association estimate that 4 million gay and lesbian fathers and mothers are involved in the raising of 6 million to 10 million children in the United States. . . .

It's often assumed that homosexuals recruit their children to their lifestyle—which, besides being insulting to gays, appears to be empirically false. Psychologists who have studied population samples of children raised by gays and lesbians claim that the percentage of homosexual children is in keeping with the percentage of gays and lesbians in the general population. . . .

Other stereotypes don't withstand scrutiny. For example, children raised in gay-run households appear to cope reasonably well with parents who aren't mirror images of other moms and dads on the block. . . .

Much could be learned about family values and what enables families to stick together from gays and lesbians. Here are some examples:

- Because gays and lesbians are obliged to live in two worlds at once, surviving has meant embracing diversity—an enlarged perspective that, in the long run, is probably good for the country. And children raised by homosexuals are taught that self-worth needn't be tied to conformity. . . .

- Kids maturing in gay-run households clearly get expanded views of what behaviors are male and what are female, and their own skills are free to develop along lines of personal preference. A study by Pepper Schwartz and Philip Blumstein . . . found that lesbian couples split household chores more democratically than heterosexuals, who still cling to sex-determined notions of who does what. . . .

- Facing considerable intolerance, homosexuals have in many ways provided a model for what a real community is. The community has informed itself and others about the risk of AIDS; it has founded clinics and support groups to aid those who are HIV-positive; it has raised the money to give its ailing compassionate places to die; it has drawn attention to the alarmingly high gay-teen suicide rate and the discrimination gays often face as well as the violence they encounter. . . .

Source: Cunningham, A. (1992, September 27). Ozzie and Ozzie: What America can learn from gay families. *The Washington Post,* C-1, C-3.

23. Inez spends much of her time daydreaming about her deceased husband. Which stage of grief is she probably experiencing?
    a. Protest
    b. Shock
    c. Depression and withdrawal
    d. Recovery

24. According to psychologists, which of the following factors have contributed to the increase in the divorce rate?
    a. No-fault divorce
    b. Fewer children in marriages
    c. Changing male and female roles
    d. Books about divorce

25. Which of the following persons is likely to experience the most severe depression?
    a. A widow
    b. A divorcee
    c. A single woman
    d. A gay male

26. Under which circumstance does divorce cause greatest grief?
    a. When a partner is deserted
    b. When a no-fault divorce is filed
    c. When there is a ceremony
    d. When friends and relatives try to help

27. Last night twelve-year-old Mark overheard his parents arguing violently about the amount of time he spent watching television. This morning Mark's mother told him she was moving out of the home and divorcing his father. How will Mark probably feel?
    a. Furious with his mother
    b. Furious with his father
    c. Guilty about causing the divorce
    d. Relieved that there will be fewer arguments

28. Allison is upset and embarrassed about her parents' divorce. She does not want anyone to learn about it. Which of the following might help her?
    a. Receiving sympathy and pity from others
    b. Thinking about her own responsibility in causing the divorce
    c. Learning about the experiences of other children of divorced parents
    d. Ignoring the problem

29. Which group of single persons is most likely to marry?
    a. The divorced
    b. The widowed
    c. Members of religious orders
    d. People who wish to live alone permanently

30. From available information, what conclusion can be reached concerning the cause of homosexuality?
    a. Homosexuality is caused by an imbalance of hormones.
    b. Homosexuality is caused by childhood experiences.
    c. Homosexuality is not genetic.
    d. Homosexuality is probably at least partially genetic.

Check your responses against the Checkpoint Answer Key at the end of the chapter. If you had difficulty with any question, reread the text. If you had little or no difficulty answering the questions or have resolved problems that you might have had, you are ready to check yourself against the chapter inventory that follows.

CHAPTER INVENTORY

Use this list of objectives as a review checklist. You should be able to do the tasks outlined in the objectives and apply them to everyday examples. If you can, you may feel confident that you have mastered the material in this chapter.

1. Specify and give examples of three ways parents can influence the gender roles of their children.
2. Discuss the difficulty in distinguishing between environmental and genetic influences on gender differences.
3. Differentiate traditional gender roles from the newer, more liberated attitudes.
4. Describe the effects changed attitudes toward gender roles have had on lifestyles.
5. Identify the key differences between mature love and selfish love and between possessive love and nonpossessive love.
6. List and describe three stages in the development of heterosexual relationships.
7. Identify four factors that affect attraction.
8. Define and give examples of emotional commitment, infatuation, and limerance.
9. Specify three factors that influence the likelihood of premarital sex.
10. State reasons for cohabitation.
11. List three factors that correlate with successful marriages.
12. Describe personal characteristics required for a successful marriage, and identify pressures created by changing sex roles.
13. Explain the need for marriage education.
14. List and describe four stages of grief that follow the death of a loved one.
15. State one reason for the increasing divorce rate.
16. Describe the adjustments required after a divorce, and recognize the special problems associated with desertion.
17. Identify ways to improve adjustments to divorces.
18. Explain the problems confronting children of divorced parents.
19. Name the four groups of people described as singles.
20. List two advantages and two disadvantages of singleness.
21. Describe the evidence on the causes of homosexuality and explain why homophobia interferes with the adjustment of the families of gay people.

Feedback

The correct answers to the exercises follow. If you did not answer an exercise correctly, review the preceding pages and return to the exercise to correctly complete it.

12-1. a. Direct reinforcement
   b. Direct reinforcement
   c. Vicarious learning
   d. Direct reinforcement
   e. Modeling

12-2. Since there are many environmental differences that could have influenced the scores, the author cannot be certain that the differences were innate. The types of games boys play could aid their mathematical skills. Similarly, teachers may have favored boys.

12-3. a. Traditional
   b. Traditional
   c. Flexible
   d. Flexible
   e. Traditional
   f. Traditional

12-4. a. Disagree: a 35-year difference in age; differences in marital status, education, religious attitudes, and social interests
   b. Agree: similar ages, marital status, and religion; needs seem to complement each other
   c. Agree: similar ages, marital status, education, religion, and academic interests

12-5. Infatuation is unrealistic and selfish. The loved person is perfect and does not need you. Limerance is realistic and involves an emotional commitment. You want to help the loved person as much as possible.

12-6. a. She has low self-esteem and wants to prove she is sexy and desirable.
   b. She wants to belittle males.
   c. She feels hostility toward her parents.

12-7. a. Factors for a successful marriage: Kelly is 26; Willy is limerant; Kelly believes in the institution of marriage; Kelly's parents are happily married; Kelly has close family relationships; Kelly and Willy attend same church; they have the same interests: sailing, jogging, and science fiction; both have a good sense of humor.
   b. Factors for an unsuccessful marriage: Willy is 35; Kelly is marrying for convenience; Willy's family is unstable; Kelly is not communicating her feelings about his drinking; they have different attitudes about children; Kelly is not communicating her feelings about children.

12-8. a. Protest
   b. Recovery
   c. Shock
   d. Depression and withdrawal
   e. Shock

12-9. a. Neither partner will be forced to bear the blame.
   b. The children will learn that they are not alone in their problems and feelings and will have a better understanding of what to expect.
   c. The children will feel less guilt.

     d. The children will feel less abandoned and will be better able to acknowledge the finality of the divorce.

     e. The divorced couple and their children will be able to share their problems with friends and relatives.

12-10. a. Advantages: personal independence; privacy

     b. Disadvantages: need to be emotionally independent; negative attitudes of other people

Checkpoint Answer Key

1. true; 2. true; 3. false; 4. false; 5. false; 6. false; 7. true; 8. true; 9. false; 10. false; 11. d; 12. b; 13. a; 14. d; 15. c; 16. b; 17. c; 18. a; 19. c; 20. a; 21. b; 22. b; 23. c; 24. c; 25. b; 26. a; 27. c; 28. c; 29. a; 30. d.

Communicating

To have great poets, there must be great audiences,
too.

—WALT WHITMAN

Imagine the president of a packaging firm is overjoyed with the prospect of receiving a $10 million contract to enclose bubble gum in plastic wrappers. She feels she will be able to reward herself and her vice president with hefty salary increases. She calls in the vice president and announces, "The prospects for this contract look good. We may be able to raise our salaries enormously in a few months." The vice president, believing the word "our" meant all managers, rushes to the shop foreman and reports, "Next month, when the new contract is signed, we will all get huge raises!" The shop foreman in turn believes "we" are all employees. He announces to his workers, "Everyone is getting a big raise next month!" Workers rush out and purchase new cars, computers, dishwashers, and jewelry, all based on a series of misinterpretations.

Although this imaginary tale seemed to end in catastrophe, far worse disasters have resulted from faulty communications. Good communication is a key to positive relationships, whether between spouses, family members, students and teachers, management and labor unions, races, or nations. When communication breaks down, the result can be divorces, failures, strikes, riots, or even the devastation of wars.

The sequence of the first topics in this chapter follows the order in which you learned to communicate. First you learned to listen, then to speak, and finally to write. After studying ways to improve each of these skills, you will

"Plant manager speaking."

FIGURE 13-1. Cartoonists have long capitalized on misinterpretations and communication problems.

examine methods that psychologists have used to analyze communication. Next you will consider the various forms of communication without words. In the final portion of the chapter, patterns of communication are compared, and you will look at how good communication can reduce conflicts.

LISTENING

Although you probably have no recollection of how you originally learned to communicate, your first step was to listen. As an infant you spent many months hearing the voices of others. You spoke not a single word and only made babbling sounds or cried. Eventually you learned the language by listening to others and associating their words with objects and actions. Even today an immense amount of information can only be acquired by listening. On the other hand, by not listening, significant data can be lost.

Listening Problems

Why do you not listen? Undoubtedly someone has complained to you, "You never listen to me!" or, "See, you should have listened!" One reason for not listening is *preoccupation*. You may be so anxious to speak yourself that you totally miss the content of other people's remarks. Or something may be bothering you—perhaps a family argument, a sick pet, an overdue bill, or a sore toe.

Being *turned off* is another reason for not listening. Emotional factors, such as a dislike for a person's appearance or tone of voice, could cause you to ignore statements. Whining children, nagging spouses, and scolding parents are often turnoffs. Similarly, those with monotonous voices and lecturers or preachers with thick foreign accents will usually have problems holding your attention. Undoubtedly some topics bore you. A lecture on the history of angiosperms will be an intellectual turnoff if you have no interest in botany. Likewise if the lecturer uses unfamiliar terms, your listening will diminish further. There may also be a few topics that you might prefer to avoid for emotional reasons. Perhaps your mind would wander during discussions on cremation and cemetery plots.

Often people have set ideas and prefer not to hear anything contrary to their own thoughts. Rather than opening their minds to new suggestions, they become threatened and debate and argue. Have you ever tried to convince smokers that cigarettes are harmful? In spite of the evidence you presented, they probably turned you off and were not good listeners.

Improving Listening

Reik (1972) claims that "listening with a third ear" is the key to effective listening. Rather than just hearing words, the "third ear" listens and interprets feelings and meanings. The third ear focuses not only on what is being said but also on why and how the statements are made. To be sure, effective listening is not passive; rather, it is an active process that requires a concentrated effort. Psychologists have suggested several techniques to improve active listening.

Set a Purpose for Listening. Resolve to listen attentively. For example, if you know you must gain information from a boring lecture on soil tests in Greenland, decide beforehand that you will find out the composition of the dirt there.

Resist Distractions. Look directly at the speaker and avoid listening to other conversations or gazing out windows. In a classroom or lecture hall, seats in the front usually provide the least distraction, since you cannot see your classmates fidget or make comments. If you are listening at a noisy party, try to find a quiet corner!

Listen Openly and Reserve Judgment. Though you feel certain the speaker is a blockhead, give the person a chance. Even a clod can sometimes provide remarkable insights and information. Likewise a person may make some foolish statements initially but eventually may add important facts and opinions. If you follow the logic of speakers without interrupting, you will acquire a better understanding of their positions.

Paraphrase and Ask Questions. After a speaker is finished talking, wait before responding. Then summarize or rephrase the statement to be sure you understand. Also, ask any specific questions that might bother you. For example, suppose a man just mentioned a recipe for making beer bread, stating, "Just mix some beer, self-rising flour, and sugar. Throw it in a greased loaf pan and bake it at 350° for an hour." When his statement is completed, you should take a few seconds to envision the procedure. Then you might paraphrase: "Am I correct that there are only three ingredients, beer, self-rising flour, and sugar, and I bake the bread for an hour in a 350° oven?" You probably would also want to ask, "Just how much beer, flour, and sugar are needed?" Often speakers omit important details; by paraphrasing and asking questions, you can be more certain that you understand the information being communicated.

There are many fringe benefits to being a good listener. In addition to learning and being able to make more accurate statements, you are also showing that you care about others. As a result, other people are more likely to listen to you. People who talk but refuse to listen are likely to discover that they have lost their audience.

Exercise 13-1

Read the following scenario, and in the space provided list four ways Ms. Slicker could improve her listening.

Ms. C. T. Slicker took her new sports car for an afternoon drive in the country. Soon lost, she pulled into a service station and asked a mechanic for directions. As the mechanic began giving directions to the main road, Ms. Slicker began to wonder whether she had sufficient gas and began calculating the distance. She also checked the price of gasoline and pondered the possibility of getting to another filling station. The mechanic had a thick country twang, and Ms. Slicker feared that she did not have accurate information. When the mechanic finished giving her directions, Ms. Slicker thanked her and drove off, hoping to find another service station.

a. _____

b. _____

c. _____

d. _____

You may compare your list with the one in the Feedback section.

VERBAL COMMUNICATION

In spite of the enormous technological advances in communication across greater distances, problems in interpreting and understanding messages still exist. Clearly, effective listening can improve understanding. However, better speaking and writing skills are also needed.

Improving Speaking Skills

Speaking is without a doubt the most frequently used method of communication. Brenner and Sigband (1973) reported that even in organizations where written messages were stressed, spoken communications were more common. More than two-thirds of the persons surveyed claimed that at least 75 percent of their assignments were given by spoken orders from their bosses.

Speaking clearly requires more than pronouncing words distinctly. You must have a precise picture in your mind of exactly what you want to say. Then you must choose your words carefully, so your listener will hear an accurate statement. If you are giving a speech, you usually have some time for preparation. However, most oral communication requires spontaneous responses. These spontaneous responses often create uncertainty that leads to fear. The article in Feature 13-1 suggests that you practice facing these fears.

FEATURE 13-1 PSYCHOLOGY IN THE NEWS

Speak Up!

What is it about speaking to a room full of people that makes our knees turn to jelly and our palms sweat? Dr. Dennis Becker, director of the Speech Improvement Company (which has offices in Brookline, Massachusetts and Providence, Rhode Island), says that most bad public speakers suffer from a stubborn, preconceived notion that there is a "right" and "wrong" way of speaking before an audience.

The numbing fear of looking foolish reduces executives who are dynamic and commanding off-stage to awkward text readers on-stage, adds Carolyn Dickson, president of VOICE-PRO Associates in Cleveland, Ohio. In the workplace, Dickson says, the executive "thinks quickly and is a firm decision maker." But standing before a group of people, that same executive turns to stone and reads the script in a monotone flat enough to put his own mother to sleep." And the audience wonders, 'How did this guy become a CEO?' "

Sweaty-palmed speakers should first realize that without a doubt, they are going to make mistakes. But whether you trip your way to the podium or drop your notes all over the stage, Dickson says, your audience will forgive you if you handle the situation with aplomb. "The audience will forgive anything—even a fall off the stage—if the speaker treats his or her mistake with ease," she explains.

Learning to waltz through on-stage blunders when all you really want to do is dive under the nearest banquet table is certainly an acquired skill.

In public speaking instruction classes, for example, teachers sometimes "frame" their students into botching up. Students must "go through the pain," Dickson says, noting that "Conquering a fear means the systematic step-by-step approach of facing that fear."

Each person is his own worse critic, though. And in lieu of formal coaching, public speaking experts advise that executives take inventory of their speaking skills by using a tape recorder or video camera. During the playback, recommends Becker, who also teaches presentation and sales skills at Harvard and MIT, ask yourself if you would be impressed or swayed by you as a speaker, or if you would instead flip through the program to see who's up next. Try to determine what you do or don't like about your delivery, and watch for annoying habits—for example, a consistently dropped g at the end of "ing" words. A critical study of yourself can reveal speaking strengths and weaknesses that might not be evident to you at the podium, especially over the din of your knocking knees. You might discover, for instance, that you need to smile more, or that the last joke bombed because you really are not funny.

The goal of effective public speaking, Dickson and Becker agree, is that "the person up here on stage should be the same person your colleagues know in the office."

Source: Handley, A. (1988, January). 8 resolutions for '88: Speak up! USAIR.

One way to improve the accuracy of everyday speech is to increase your vocabulary. Evans (1963) stressed the importance of having more control over the words you use. If you have both a clear mental picture of what you want to say and a rich vocabulary, chances are you will be able to express yourself accurately, and misunderstandings will be avoided. Persons who have difficulty organizing their thoughts and expressing themselves clearly can suffer bitter results.

Perhaps you are concerned that flaunting a big vocabulary might make you appear stuffy and condescending. Certainly a person who chooses words that are not likely to be understood is probably trying to appear superior. However, having a plentiful supply of precise and punchy words at your command can help you communicate with a variety of types of audiences.

Another important aspect of speaking is holding the attention of your listeners. If you look someone directly in the eye, that person will find it difficult to ignore you. On the other hand, if you bury your head in your notes as you read your speech, you may find the audience has ignored your talk. An additional bonus of maintaining eye contact is learning the reactions of listeners. Frowns or puzzled expressions can inform you that you need to clarify your statements. Similarly smiles and nods of approval may permit you to give more details.

Face-to-face communication between two persons is usually the most effective. Political candidates have found that votes are most likely to be won by door-to-door campaigns. By meeting people individually, candidates can be sure they have the attention of each voter, while they also learn voter reactions and interests. In small communities residents are sometimes insulted if a candidate does not visit. But candidates for state and national offices can physically visit only a tiny percentage of their constituents.

Assuming that one-to-one communication is possible, how might a candidate best approach a voter? For that matter, how can anyone develop an effective conversation with someone else, whether a spouse, a teacher, a boss, or an intriguing person at a party? Psychologists have found that open questions are more conducive to improved conversation than closed questions. A closed question can be answered with a simple yes or no, where an open question requires a longer response. For example, "Do you like your job?" is a closed question. Once the person answers yes or no, the conversation is over. On the other hand if you asked "What do you like about your job?" or "How could working conditions be improved?" an extended reply would be required. As a result you would learn more and could continue the conversation intelligently.

Exercise 13-2

In your own words describe how each of the following techniques can help you improve your speaking and conversing abilities.

a. Developing a clear mental picture of what you want to say:

_____

_____

b. Increasing your vocabulary:

_____

_____

c. Using eye-to-eye contact:

_____

_____

d. Asking open questions:

_____

_____

Please turn to the Feedback section to check your answers.

Improving Writing Skills

Although written communication is not as popular as the spoken word is, a huge volume of messages is certainly written and read. Consider the number of books, newspapers, and magazines sold—as well as the reports, letters, and even junk mail received each day—and you will realize the influence of written communication. Skill in writing has had an increased emphasis in the past few years. With the increasing use of computer conferences rather than telephone calls, ability to write well is critical. More employers are looking for people with writing ability. If you have had to complete a job application form with essay questions, chances are the employer wished to check your writing competence.

There is one clear advantage of writing over speaking: You have time to think, organize, and even rewrite if necessary. However, there are two distinct disadvantages: You cannot use voice inflections or physical gestures, and you usually do not receive immediate feedback from your audience. To overcome the first disadvantage, you must incorporate an emotional tone in your language. As in spoken communication, a rich vocabulary is an undeniable advantage.

The second problem is not difficult to overcome if you know the interest, the reading level, and the vocabulary of your audience. Usually writing that is short and simple is easiest to understand. Nonetheless, authors sometimes use words to impress others rather than to communicate effectively. Gilmer (1975) related an amusing episode:

> No doubt, most of us are sympathetic with the plumber who wrote the Bureau of Standards in Washington to say he had found that hydrochloric acid opened clogged drains in a hurry and asked if it was a good thing to use. The reply came back: "The efficacy of hydrochloric acid is indisputable, but the corrosive residue is incompatible with metallic permanence." The plumber replied that he was glad to know it was all right to use acid. The scientist showed the letter to his boss, who replied to the plumber: "We cannot assume responsibility for the production of toxic and noxious residue with hydrochloric acid and suggest

you use an alternative procedure." The plumber thanked the Bureau and was glad they approved his use of acid. Finally, correspondence from Washington got through to the plumber: "Don't use hydrochloric acid. It eats the hell out of the pipes."

Checkpoint

Use the following questions to check your understanding of this portion of the chapter. Choose and mark the one correct response to each question.

1. How do infants learn to communicate?
   a. By using gestures
   b. By recognizing faces
   c. By listening
   d. By playing with objects
2. Ted is driving on a turnpike with his radio blaring loudly and turned to a news station. He is concerned about getting home before dark since the right front light of his car is not working. He checks his watch and the setting sun every few minutes. As he finally pulls into his driveway, Ted realizes he has not heard any news. What was his listening problem?
   a. Overload
   b. Preoccupation
   c. Turnoff
   d. Boredom
3. What does Reik mean by listening with a "third ear"?
   a. Active listening and interpreting
   b. Listening while also attending to distractions
   c. Listening to two conversations at the same time
   d. Using a hearing aid
4. If you want to listen attentively to a lecture, where is the best place to sit?
   a. In a back corner
   b. Directly in front of the speaker
   c. Near a window
   d. In the middle of the group
5. Assume your boss has just finished describing a complicated assignment. As an active listener, what should you do?
   a. Wait a few seconds, then paraphrase and ask questions.
   b. Wait a few seconds, then criticize and give your judgment.
   c. Immediately ask questions, then criticize.
   d. Immediately criticize, then ask questions.
6. What is the single most frequently used method of communication?
   a. Speaking
   b. Writing
   c. Gestures
   d. Facial expressions
7. Gladys has written a ten-page speech to deliver to her basket-weaving club. Which of the following methods will help her hold the attention of the group?

a. Keeping her eyes on her notes
b. Looking straight ahead into space
c. Keeping her eyes downcast
d. Maintaining eye contact with the group

8. Which of the following is an example of an open question?
   a. "Are you happy?"
   b. "Am I late?"
   c. "Why do you like me?"
   d. "Are you drinking coffee?"

9. For effective communication, which of the following is the best rule for writers?
   a. Impress others with big words.
   b. Assume your audience is intellectual.
   c. Keep your writing short and simple.
   d. Avoid taking time for rewriting

Check your responses against the Checkpoint Answer Key at the end of the chapter. If you had difficulty with any questions, reread the text. If you had little or no difficulty answering the questions or have resolved problems that you might have had, you are ready to continue with the next portion of this chapter.

Analyzing Verbal Expression

Having delved into listening, speaking, and writing, you may be wondering what else of importance is involved in communication. The actual words you choose can have a powerful impact. Likewise your attitude and intentions can convey messages to listeners. In this section of the chapter you will learn how psychologists have dissected language and conversations.

Denotations and Connotations

The *denotation* of a word is the dictionary definition. For example, Webster's New Collegiate Dictionary defines the word "father" as "a male parent." This definition is what the word denotes. The denotation of the word "communism" is "system [of social organization] in which goods are owned in common and are available to all as needed."

denotation Specific dictionary definition of a word

However, both the word "father" and the word "communism" have emotional overtones—meanings that are not in the dictionary. You may hear a man say "Don't give me an argument; I am your father!" He does not simply mean that he is a male parent. Or perhaps you have heard a politician claim that a vote for the opposition was a vote for communism. To be sure, the politician was not implying that his opponent shared property with the community. Rather, he probably was trying to associate his opponent with your negative feelings toward the word "communism." The feelings and emotions associated with words are called *connotations*.

connotation Emotional feelings and associations that a word arouses

You can experience some problems with denotations and connotations of words. Many words have more than one dictionary definition. Other words have been used in slang expressions and have taken on new meanings. Often you need to use the context to find the correct meaning. Suppose you were asked, "Would you like some grass?" Undoubtedly you would want to check on the speaker's definition of grass. If the speaker owned a golf course that was being replaced by a superhighway, you probably would be safe in assuming that you could improve your lawn. However, if the speaker seemed "spaced out," the other definition of grass was probably being used. Denotations are usually easier to discern if you are familiar with definitions.

Among those interested in the connotations of words are employers. Even though a job may require the same tasks, changing the job title can make a difference to a worker. For example, a job description may include activities such as dusting furniture, sweeping and vacuuming floors, scrubbing two bathrooms and a kitchen, and polishing silver. The title for the job could be "cleaning person," "maid," or "household technician." Clearly, the title "household technician" has more status and prestige than does either "cleaning person" or "maid"; the connotations of household technician are more favorable. Consider the difference in your attitude toward being labeled "clerk-typist," "secretary," "executive secretary," and "administrative assistant." Yet all four titles can be used to describe the same job. Psychologists have even advised businesses that although the word "corporation" has more prestige, the word "company" is considered friendlier.

In recent years feminist psychologists have uncovered the fact that language tends to devalue women (Unger and Crawford, 1992). A "govern*or*" is

FIGURE 13-2. "Mr. Stevens" probably has fewer negative connotations.

important and highly regarded, while a "governess" is little more than an educated nursemaid. Consider the difference in the meanings of "sir" and "madam" and "master" and "mistress." In each case the female version of the word has sexual connotations, while the male form adds prestige.

Another group intensely concerned about the connotations of words are advertisers. They seek words with both strong negative and strong positive emotional overtones. Whether the ad uses the word "grime," "bacteria," "congestion," "itch," "soreness," or "exhaustion," it is trying to draw out your negative feelings. Next the advertiser will offer a product that "cleanses," "relieves," "soothes," or "stimulates"—words with strong positive connotations.

Advertisers further capitalize on the connotations of words by means of voice inflections. A disgusted tone can make dirt and bacteria truly repulsive. Similarly, a low, comforting tone can make words such as "soothes" and "relieves" bring delight. Tone of voice can change both the denotation and connotation of words. A friend who sincerely states, "You really deserved that promotion" is delivering a different message from the person who makes the remark sarcastically. Yes, there may be truth to the old adage that it is not so much what you say, as the way you say it.

Exercise 13-3

What is the difference between the denotation and connotation of a word?

a. Denotation: _____

b. Connotation: _____

Exercise 13-4

Assume you want to find the real meaning of the word "mechanic."

a. How could you find the denotations? _____

b. How could you find the connotations? _____

Please turn to the Feedback section to check your answers.

Assertiveness

Assertiveness requires standing up for your own rights. Assertive behavior is not the same as aggressive behavior. When you act assertively, you respect the rights of others as well as your own individual rights. However, protecting your rights without offending others can be tricky. Deutsch (1993) suggests using three F's: When faced with conflict be "firm, fair, and friendly." Your firmness will allow you to resist being used or frightened by anyone. You can be fair by holding to your own moral principles and not being pulled into someone's immoral behavior even if you are provoked. Your friendliness will show that you are willing to cooperate.

assertiveness
Standing up for personal rights while respecting the rights of others

Psychologists suggest that you act on your feelings. If you are upset, hurt, and depressed, or if you feel unfairly criticized, tell the appropriate person. It is usually best to state rather than act out your feelings. Stating "I feel furious" will help release anger. It is not necessary to pound a table or punch someone.

By stating your own feelings rather than attacking or accusing another person, you avoid making others become defensive. Gordon (1970) recommended using "I" statements instead of "you" statements. "I feel upset and hurt when you are unwilling to share toys with your brother" is preferable to "You selfish child, you never share things with your brother." To be assertive, it is not necessary to attack the character of other people. After stating your feelings, it is helpful to offer a positive suggestion. You might add, "If you let your brother play with the toy telephone, maybe he will share his truck with you."

Exercise 13-5

Assume you have a spouse or a roommate who clutters your living space. This can be a ticklish situation, but with some effective assertiveness you can win. Describe how you might handle the situation.

_____

_____

_____

_____

_____

Please check your suggestions in the Feedback section.

MANKOFF

"No, Thursday's out. How about never—is never good for you?"

FIGURE 13-3. A humorous example of being firm, fair, and friendly.

Often people cannot find the words to describe their feelings, or they choose not to disclose information verbally. Anything that is communicated without the use of words is considered nonverbal communication. Whether you compose a symphony, yawn, wear a funny hat, stare into someone's eyes, or remain silent, you are sending a nonverbal message. Feelings and attitudes, as well as information, can be communicated by one or more of the nonverbal modes described in this section.

Artistic Forms and Symbols

Have you ever been moved by a symphony, religious music, or a popular tune? Perhaps it was the melody, the tone, or the rhythm that communicated a mood. To be sure, blues melodies have brought listeners to tears. Paintings, etchings, sculptures, and photographs have all been used to convey the feelings and attitudes of their originators. However, there is one problem with communicating through art forms: The original message is often misinterpreted.

CLOSE TO HOME   JOHN MCPHERSON

© 1993 John McPherson/Distributed by Universal Press Syndicate

3-19

***The Menlop brothers drop their dad some subtle hints
that they want a bigger TV.***

FIGURE 13-4. The Menlop brothers have mastered nonverbal communication.

Because there is no international language, efforts are being made to communicate essential information through picture symbols. Symbols that are easy to interpret have been chosen. Recently, the use of such symbols has become widespread. Poisons, restrooms, no-smoking areas, and highways now display international symbols.

Appearance and Body Language

Some aspects of your appearance and body language cannot be consciously controlled. For example, you cannot prevent yourself from blushing, flushing, quivering, or breaking out in goose bumps. If you are a bald male or have a receding hair line, without realizing it, you may be communicating maturity and status. On the other hand, if you have a beard, you may unconsciously be communicating unfriendliness (see Feature 13-2).

Other aspects of body language can be used purposefully and deliberately. You can raise an eyebrow, slump, lower your eyes, spit, or wave your arms. There are no precise interpretations of such facial expressions and gestures. The meaning varies among cultures and individuals (see Chapter 8). If you have ever played a game of charades, you know the difficulties in deciphering body language.

Psychologists have found that body language sends a far stronger message than verbal language does. If you burst into tears saying, "Everything is fine," your friends will heed your tears rather than your words.

The clothing you wear can advise others of your mood, feelings, and attitudes. A woman who outfits herself in a tight, slinky, low-cut dress on a date is conveying a message to her companion, whether or not she realizes it. Similarly, a man who shows up at a formal party in tennis clothes is communicating

---

FEATURE 13-2 PSYCHOLOGY IN THE NEWS

On the Pulse

If bald isn't beautiful, at least it makes a man appear intelligent. But bearded men beware, your whiskers may tell strangers you're not so nice. Those are some recent findings of psychologists who study the judgments people make when they see a strange face.

A study by psychologist Michael Wogalter, formerly of Rensselaer Polytechnic Institute in Troy, N.Y. found beards make men seem older, less attractive and less sociable than their clean-shorn counterparts. Wogalter ... said he didn't know why facial hair was viewed unfavorably.

The same study, in which Wogalter asked people to render their impressions of computer-generated mug shots, found that balding men were perceived as smarter and a little older and more mature.

A bit of extra good news for bald men is that the presence of cranial hair had no apparent effect on how viewers rated relative attractiveness.

Carol Keating of Colgate University has a theory that certain male features, like receding hairlines, may have evolved to attract mates. To this day, she said, such mature features are viewed as commanding because they imply age and status.

Source: Associated Press (1992, October 27). On the pulse. *Washington Post Health*, 5.

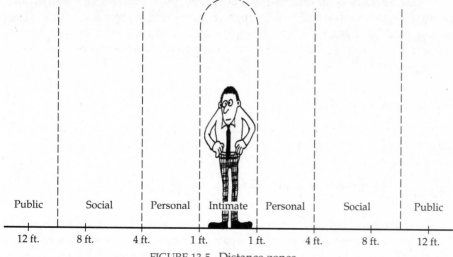

| Public | Social | Personal | Intimate | Personal | Social | Public |

| 12 ft. | 8 ft. | 4 ft. | 1 ft. | 1 ft. | 4 ft. | 8 ft. | 12 ft. |

FIGURE 13-5. Distance zones.

an attitude. Advertisers of perfumes and after-shave colognes insist that their products imply a message.

In addition to what you wear and how you stand, where you stand can communicate your attitude. Hall (1969) identified four types of personal zones or spaces.

Intimate Distance (1 Foot to Body Contact). This space is reserved for lovers, parents, children, and intimate friends. If a casual acquaintance came this close you would feel uncomfortable. Other than your dearest friends the only individuals usually permitted within this range are doctors, nurses, dentists, or other professionals responsible for your personal care. If you stand this close to another person, you are suggesting that you consider yourself an intimate friend or relative. One study found that happily married couples feel comfortable with each other within this distance. Troubled couples were too uneasy to come this close (see Feature 13-3).

Personal Distance (1 to 4 Feet). The actual size of this space can differ according to cultures. This space is primarily for personal conversations with your close friends. According to Fast (1970) most people believe this area belongs to them, and any unwelcome person who enters violates their privacy. People are within reach and can touch each other, shake hands, or pat each other on the back.

Suppose you were sitting in an empty cafeteria and a stranger sat in a chair next to you, within your personal space. You would probably feel awkward. Have you ever noticed that people in crowded areas, such as elevators, trains, or buses, tend to avoid eye contact with each other and stare into space? They undoubtedly are ill at ease with the invasion of their personal space.

Social Distance (4 to 10 Feet). Social distance is used for impersonal business and casual conversations. Most likely, you have heard the expression

"Keep your distance" or "Stay at arm's length." Personal or intimate conversations at this distance would indeed be strange. People at interviews and business meetings usually sit or stand at a social distance.

Public Distance (10 Feet and Beyond). If you are in a large lecture hall attending a town meeting or watching a play or a soccer game, you experience communication at public distance. At this distance, private behaviors or comments are inappropriate. It is even difficult to conduct business or an interview when the other person is so far away.

Exercise 13-6

Read each of the following descriptions of behaviors. From what you have learned about nonverbal communication, state the message that you think the individual is sending.

a. Jane was dressing for an interview. She pulled her long, blond hair into a tight bun, borrowed her mother's pin-striped suit and her grandmother's oxfords. She filled her father's briefcase with file folders and took it along.

_____

_____

b. After an argument with his wife, Andy painted an ugly portrait of her in blacks and grays. He hung it over her mirror.

_____

_____

FEATURE 13-3 PSYCHOLOGY IN THE NEWS

So Near and Yet So Far

When a wife complains that her husband seems "distant" it may literally be true. The emotional closeness of married couples can be measured, in inches, according to family therapist D. Russell Crane of Brigham Young University and colleagues.

The researchers tested 108 couples, asking partners to walk toward one another and stop when they got to a "comfortable conversation distance." After measuring the distance between them, the researchers gave each spouse several tests that tap marital intimacy, divorce potential and desire for change.

The greater the husbands' dissatisfaction with their marriage, the farther they stood from their wives, the researchers report (*Journal of Marital and Family Therapy*, Vol. 307, pp. 307-310). Or, to put it another way, the more emotional steps the husband had taken toward divorce, the fewer physical ones he would take to be near his wife.

The researchers also found that the average space between "distressed" couples (in which both were unhappy and had lots of unresolved conflict) was about 25 percent greater than that of "nondistressed" couples (both happy and low in conflict). The happy couples stood, on average, 11.4 inches apart; the unhappy ones stood 14.8 inches apart—but in their case, the inches felt like miles.

Source: Rosenfield, A. (1988, March). So near and yet so far. *Psychology Today.*

c. Gaya's boss patted her on the back and told her she was doing a great job. She immediately moved across the room from him.

_____

_____

d. Tessie looked over the uncrowded beach. She put down her beach towel and sat about 3 feet away from an attractive young man.

_____

_____

To check your interpretations, turn to the Feedback section.

CULTURAL DIFFERENCES

While the space allotments described above are comfortable for most American, German, and English people, Latin Americans, Arabs, Greeks, and French interact at closer distances. When two people of differing cultures try to adjust their comfort zones as they communicate, the result can be amusing. One researcher (Rumpel, 1988) referred to the "Latin Waltz," a constant space adjustment made as a Mexican moved closer and an American moved away during a conversation.

Miscommunication between cultures has created many awkward business situations. In public addresses, most Americans begin speaking by describing their expertise and study on the topic. For people of Asian backgrounds, these openings are considered boastful. Asians prefer to introduce themselves humbly and with modesty.

The article in Feature 13-3 provides pointers for African Americans who are adjusting to rules of White businessmen. But the suggestions can be generalized to anyone who needs to communicate in an unfamiliar culture.

Checkpoint

Use the following questions to check your understanding of this portion of the chapter. Choose and mark the one correct response to each question.

10. Which of the following is the denotation of the word "mother"?
    a. Sensitive and fair
    b. An authority
    c. A female parent
    d. A soft, friendly person

11. What is the connotation of a word?
    a. The dictionary definition
    b. The emotional associations
    c. The slang usage
    d. The cultural expression

12. Which of the following factors can influence the connotation and denotation of words?

Business Etiquette: A Refresher Course

There was once a young brother, fresh out of graduate school and newly arrived in corporate America, at dinner with his work compatriots. When asked whether he would like to try some chateaubriand, he replied no thank you, he did not drink. This well-educated young lad wanted to crawl under the table when he was told later that chateaubriand was not a well-aged, very expensive red wine but a nicely prepared, pricey red meat. That young fellow violated one of my five cardinal rules of business etiquette.

The way you present yourself in the corporate world signals whether or not you understand the unwritten rules of how business really gets done in America. . . . When the white people who made up these rules (and they are made up) go to Japan or the Middle East and do business, they find their business etiquette rules altogether different. This is how they separate the winners from the losers. . . .

I've pulled these guidelines together over the years and have passed them down to younger entrants into the business world. Take a look at them; you may want to send them to a few of your colleagues.

1. **Don't be a perpetrator.** . . . nothing makes one look more foolish than trying to put on airs. This perpetration comes about because some people think they will be looked at askance if they don't know everything. Therefore, it is more important to learn quickly what you do not know than to worry about whether someone thinks differently about you because for the moment you are unaware. . . .

2. **Don't talk too much and listen too little.** Folks do this for two reasons: 1) nervousness and 2) an unwarranted belief that what you have to say is more important than what anyone else has to say. . . .

3. **No talkin' like you're rappin' with the boyz n the hood.** Why, oh why do I even need to say this one? When one is in a corporate setting, formal English is required for good etiquette. . . . Use slang sparingly in very informal settings. And, if you must use it, wait until you've been on the job at least six months and only with people who know you know how to talk.

4. **When it's Monday morning don't dress like it's Friday night.** . . . Sometimes I think what is operating here is the desire not to be dressed "boringly." Trust me. At work, boring is OK, especially for junior employees. Calling attention to yourself in any other way than by your stellar job performance does you a disservice.

   For the fellows, follow this advice and you'll be all right: dress the way your boss's boss dresses.

5. **No matter what your home is like, keep your office neat.** While we may think that an empty desk makes for an empty mind, many think that a messy desk makes for a cluttered mind, and a lot of those people who keep their desks neat become bosses. Go figure.

   Regardless, a neat-looking desk probably makes a better impression.

The way you talk, the way you look, the way your office appears, all tell the story about you. Follow these guidelines and you'll have a much better chance of your story having a happy ending.

If that's the case, when you go out to celebrate, order some chateaubriand (medium rare) and some Chateau-Figesc, a very lovely red table wine, and enjoy.

Source: Jamison, C. N., Jr. (1992, October/November). Business etiquette: A refresher course. *Upscale*, 62-63.

   a. Context and tone of voice
   b. Recognition and familiarity
   c. Recognition and context
   d. Context and familiarity

13. Which of the following techniques have been used to measure the connotations of words?
   a. Looking up words in a dictionary
   b. Checking associations on a questionnaire
   c. Analyzing transactions
   d. Using "I" statements rather than "you" statements

14. Assume a neighbor borrowed Jim's chain saw three months ago. Jim wants to cut wood and notices that his neighbor has still not returned the saw. Which of the following would be the most desirable assertive behavior for Jim?
   a. Ignore the problem and cut the wood some other day.
   b. Borrow a chain saw from another neighbor.
   c. Tell his neighbor he is disappointed and ask that the saw be returned.
   d. Accuse the neighbor of being careless and inconsiderate and refuse to ever lend anything again.

15. Which of the following is an example of nonverbal communication?
   a. A symphony
   b. A textbook
   c. A phone call
   d. A fax message

16. A woman laughs as she reports on having lost her temper. What will she communicate?
   a. Anger
   b. Hostility
   c. Confusion
   d. Humor

17. Assume you are having a personal conversation with your best friend. About how many feet apart are you likely to be standing?
   a. 18
   b. 12
   c. 8
   d. 4

18. Which aspect of communication differs according to cultures?
   a. Both verbal and nonverbal
   b. Neither verbal nor nonverbal
   c. Only verbal
   d. Only nonverbal

Check your responses against the Checkpoint Answer Key at the end of the chapter. If you had difficulty with any question, reread the text. If you had little or no difficulty answering the questions or have resolved problems that you might have had, you are ready to continue with the final portion of this chapter.

**one-way communi-
cation** Speaker
speaks and receives
no feedback from
the listener

**two-way communi-
cation** Speaker
speaks and receives
feedback from a lis-
tener, who then be-
comes a speaker

Whether the communication is verbal or nonverbal, there are basically only two patterns of communication, one-way and two-way. In *one-way communi-cation*, the speaker speaks, the listener listens, and the communication is complete. The speaker does not receive any feedback from the listener. Mary talks to Bob and Bob listens but does not respond.

In *two-way communication*, the listener and speaker alternate roles; the result is a conversation. The speaker receives feedback from the listener. Mary speaks and Bob listens; then Bob gives his feedback while Mary listens. His feedback might include a question, a comment, an opinion, or his interpretation.

Both Leavitt (1951) and Tesch et al. (1972) have studied the efficiency of one-way and two-way communications. They found that one-way communication is faster, but it is also less accurate. The speaker cannot be certain that the listener understands the message. One-way communication also protects power, since the speaker can be neither questioned nor criticized. Classrooms where the lecturer speaks and students take notes are orderly, quiet, and free of interruptions. However, the lecturer will not know whether the students understood his message until he receives some feedback. Unfortunately for the students, the feedback may be in the form of a midterm or final exam.

In two-way communication the speaker receives immediate feedback. From the feedback, the speaker can decide if it is necessary to modify statements. Mistakes, inaccuracies, and oversights can be detected. If a lecturer is using jargon that students cannot understand, students will ask questions and the words can be defined. Because they can ask questions, listeners feel more sure of themselves in two-way communication. Problems can be alleviated immediately.

Two-way communication is clearly more accurate than one-way communication. Businesses are more successful when workers have a complete understanding of their jobs. Similarly, problems can be resolved as they arise rather than later in a union confrontation or a grievance procedure. However,

FIGURE 13-6. A one-way communication problem.

there are two shortcomings: two-way communication takes more time, and the speaker is vulnerable to criticism.

Exercise 13-7

For each of the following situations, indicate whether one-way or two-way communication would be preferable.

a. A newly appointed sergeant wants to assert his power over new soldiers. _____

b. An accountant wants to be sure his clients understand how to keep financial records. _____

c. An employer wants to avoid a strike. _____

d. A businesswoman is in a hurry and wants to leave a message with her secretary. _____

e. A newly hired man wants to be certain that he understands his job requirements. _____

Please turn to the Feedback section to check your answers.

Networks

Whenever two-way communication involves more than two people, there must be a system, or *network*, for sending and receiving messages. Sometimes the network is formal, but more often it is informal and haphazard. Among the more popular informal networks is the grapevine, where the news or rumor is spread to anyone who might be interested. It often becomes difficult to identify the original source of the information. Hence, the expression, "I heard it from the grapevine." Surprisingly, Davis's research (1973) found that the grapevine is both fast and efficient. He noted that 75 to 95 percent of grapevine information is correct.

network Communication involving more than two people

Leavitt (1951) identified and studied four types of formal communication networks. He then experimented to determine the amount of accuracy and personal satisfaction that each type of network created.

Circle. In a circle network, each person can communicate only with two other persons (see Figures 13-7 and 13-8). Information must then be relayed through the circle. No one person leads or coordinates. Each person in the circle is equal in power to the others.

Y Arrangement. According to their position on the Y arrangement, members can communicate with either one, two, or three other persons (see Figure 13-9). The person at the bottom and the two persons on the diagonals converse with only one other person. The person at the head of the line where the diagonals form a junction communicates with three others. This individual clearly has the most power. All others communicate with two people.

Wheel. The person in the center of a wheel communicates with all others (see Figures 13-10 and 13-11). Persons along the rim of the wheel cannot converse with each other. All information must flow to and from the center.

FIGURE 13-7. Circle.

You may be more familiar with the wheel as an organization chart. The owner of a business communicates with the manager of each division.

Concom. The concom arrangement is similar to a circle in that all members are equal (see Figure 13-12). However, in a concom arrangement, individuals can communicate with three rather than two others.

By now you may be wondering about the consequences of using each of these different networks. Leavitt found that the most accurate network was the

FIGURE 13-8. An example of a circle network.

FIGURE 13-9. Y arrangement.

Y arrangement. Circle arrangements made the most mistakes, probably because no single person could coordinate a solution. However, members of circle networks were among the most satisfied. Members of circle and concom groups were more satisfied with their interactions. The most highly satisfied person within all groups was the person in the center of the wheel. The next most satisfied was the person at the top junction of the Y arrangement. Persons on the rim of the wheel proved to be least satisfied. Leavitt concluded that participation was a key to satisfaction. People were more content if they felt they shared in decisions.

Exercise 13-8

Illustrate each of the following communication networks. Specify whether the illustration demonstrates a circle, a Y arrangement, a wheel, or a concom.

a. Carol is selling cosmetics. Money that she earns from orders is reported to Meg, and orders must be filled by Charlotte. Carol receives her first order and money from

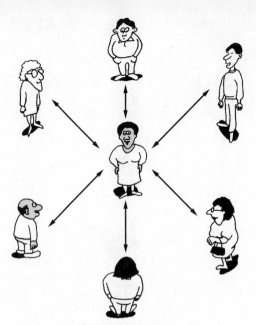

FIGURE 13-10. Wheel.

Ann. When Ann told Beth about her super new makeup, Beth gave money to Ann and asked her to place an order through Carol. Beth in turn told Jan about the new makeup, and Jan asked Beth to pass her money and order through Ann to Carol.

b. When Goldie inherited her fortune, she hired a chauffeur to care for her three cars, a trainer to manage her stables and horses, a tax attorney to give her financial advice, a social secretary to handle her invitations,

FIGURE 13-11. Wheel organization chart.

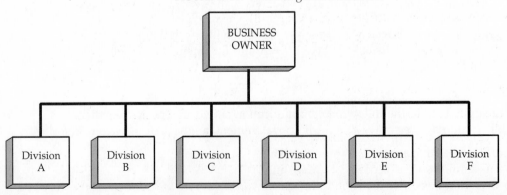

FIGURE 13-12. Concom.

and a household technician to keep her home in good order.

c. When the high school debating team prepares for a challenge with another school, Ted and Juan prepare some arguments. Then Juan goes over their presentation with Chris. Chris checks it with Scott. Scott contacts Paul for new ideas. Paul works with Len who gets back to Ted. Next, Ted works with Scott. Paul calls Juan, and Len and Chris work together.

Exercise 13-9

Of the networks described in Exercise 13-8,

a. Which two persons would be most satisfied with their interactions?

b. Who would be least happy?

c. Which network type would be the most efficient?

Turn to the Feedback section to compare your illustrations and answers.

Participation

Leavitt's research clearly emphasized the importance of participation. People who were actively involved in a network were more satisfied with their interactions. Consequently, employers have developed a keen interest in increasing participation by improving both downward and upward communication.

downward communication Passing messages from upper management down to workers

upward communication Passing information from workers up to management

Downward communication is the passing of messages from upper management down to workers. Messages may include goals, praise, comments on achievements, or criticisms and suggestions for improvement. Downward communication is usually direct. *Upward communication* can move in a number of patterns. Sometimes employees work upward through a line of managers. Other times there are opportunities for direct encounters with the top person, as in coffee-with-the-boss meetings. Individual workers are invited to comment and make suggestions openly.

Suggestion boxes, questionnaires, and open-door policies are all attempts at improving upward communications. However, often these techniques are not effective. Employees sometimes feel their suggestions are ignored. Thus it is considered best to reply to suggestions with reasons why the proposal was

"Let's make this new substitute teacher regret the day she was born."

FIGURE 13-13. The substitute teacher has both physical and psychological size.

accepted or rejected. Unfortunately, according to Davis (1977), an open-door policy too often means the door is open for the manager to walk out.

Upward communication is sometimes difficult because of a problem labeled *psychological size*. Bosses often seem overwhelmingly important. Talking with someone of great importance makes you feel anxious and small by comparison. The problem worsens if the boss must be addressed by an impressive title, such as "Your Honor" or "Professor." A professor who sits on a platform behind a lectern increases not only physical size but also psychological size. Upward communication becomes difficult and unlikely.

psychological size Perceived importance of a person

Perhaps you have been able to detect differences in attitudes toward upward communication by checking seating arrangements. Often the professor behind a lectern on a platform has little concern about the opinions of students. On the other hand, an instructor who arranges seats in a circle and sits among students is probably trying to encourage communication. Psychologists have found that circular formations encourage the most communication.

But back to the boss. What seating arrangement will reduce psychological size sufficiently to permit an employee to speak freely and easily? Sommer (1969) has checked out some possibilities: To encourage communication, the best arrangement is to be seated across the corner of a desk from each other. Next best is seating directly across a desk. The worst is side by side.

Some employers prefer to delegate upward-communication problems. Harriman (1974) reported that some organizations assign specific persons to work on upward communication. Employees can contact the persons anonymously by telephone or letter and discuss difficulties. The assigned person then works on the problems.

Exercise 13-10

Imagine you are the mayor of a small town. Newspapers give excellent coverage to your town meetings, and members of the community are fully aware of town ordinances and changes. However, you are concerned because people do not attend your town meetings, and you are therefore not aware of their concerns and problems. List six techniques you could use to improve upward communication.

a. _____

b. _____

c. _____

d. _____

e. _____

f. _____

Compare your strategies with the ones listed in the Feedback section.

Self-Disclosure

Self-disclosure requires an ability to speak honestly and fully about yourself. When you disclose yourself, you show yourself and your feelings so that others

self-disclosure Speaking honestly and revealing true feelings to others

can understand you. Jourard (1971) claims that self-disclosure is essential for effective communication. To be sure, there is a risk in self-disclosure. You must supply even embarrassing information and give others a chance to view your vulnerable self. If you are afraid of being rejected or ridiculed, you are not likely to provide such insights.

However, there are also clear benefits. By self-disclosure you show that you trust the other person. This usually deepens a relationship. The other person is then more likely to develop trust in you and disclose private thoughts. The process is slow and gradual. As the relationship grows, each person reveals more. Disclosure steadily increases, and the result is a mutually intimate relationship.

The Johari Window

Johari window
System of quadrants used in the study of self-disclosure

One way of studying self-disclosure is with a *Johari window* (see Figure 13-14). Although it may have a strange name, the Johari window is simply a square with four quadrants. According to Luft (1970) the name was derived from a combination of the first names of its inventors, Joe Luft and Harry Ingham. Each quadrant of the Johari window describes an aspect in relationships between people.

Quadrant I: Open. Quadrant I describes behavior that is known to both yourself and others. The color of your eyes, your sex, and other obvious physical information would be in this quadrant. Also included would be any information you wished to disclose to others. For example, suppose you scheduled a conference with your English instructor. The instructor knows nothing about you other than your appearance. If you open the conference by stating honestly, "I feel nervous when I have to come for a conference," you immediately increase the size of quadrant I. Quadrant I then reflects your self-disclosure.

Quadrant II: Blind. In quadrant II lies information that is obvious to others but is concealed from yourself. It might include some annoying mannerisms. Perhaps you pace the floor or tap your foot or your pencils without realizing it. Many people are unaware that they constantly use words and expressions such as "um," "you know," or "okay?" However, everyone else is fully aware! Undoubtedly, you have seen people make complete fools of themselves. They may have thought they were extremely clever,

FIGURE 13-14. The Johari window.

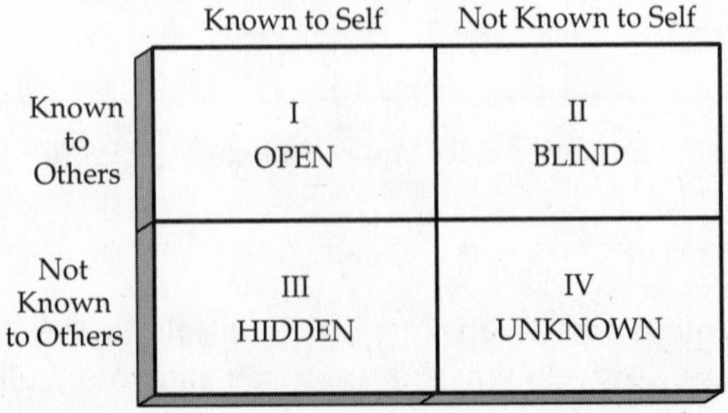

	Known to Self	Not Known to Self
Known to Others	I OPEN	II BLIND
Not Known to Others	III HIDDEN	IV UNKNOWN

but observers shook their heads in disbelief. Or maybe you know people who cannot see that friends or relatives are manipulating them. In each of these cases, the individuals are blind to their own behavior.

Quadrant III: Hidden. This quadrant describes information that is known to you but unknown to others. It may include such unimportant facts as the amount of coffee you drank yesterday or the brand of underwear you prefer. It will also include thoughts, feelings, and information that you are afraid to share because you fear embarrassment and ridicule. Most likely there are a few things that you are not proud of. You might hold back this information because you fear rejection.

Hidden information can complicate communication. Suppose three recreation workers, Peppy, Snaps, and Buddy, are setting up a schedule for their community center this month. Peppy wants to be sure she is free on her birthday but will not admit it to Snaps and Buddy. Although supposedly their agenda is to develop a practical schedule for the month, Peppy has a *hidden agenda,* or a special personal interest. She wants to schedule a day off on her birthday. As you might imagine, their meeting will probably last much longer than is necessary. Peppy will reject any proposal that schedules her to work on her birthday.

hidden agenda Important personal information that is not revealed to other members of a group

If someone has a hidden agenda, the conversation becomes overly lengthy. Other people become frustrated and conflicts can result. Bradford (1972) suggested watching for such clues to hidden agendas as increased tension or long discussions. If a hidden agenda is suspected, try to surface it with remarks such as, "Why is this problem taking so long? Perhaps we should discuss our feelings about it," or "Do you think we should discuss some other related problem?" It is usually best not to make others feel guilty about their hidden agendas. There will always be differences in opinions and perceptions.

Quadrant IV: Unknown. In quadrant IV are your underlying motivations that are not known to anyone, even yourself. This quadrant comprises primarily unconscious feelings. For example, you might find yourself constantly arguing with your kid brother. You may not realize that you are really jealous of the attention he draws from your parents. He does not recognize your jealousy either and just sees you as a grouch.

The sizes of the quadrants in the Johari window change according to the type of relationship you are sharing with another person. Clearly you are more open with your lover or spouse and more hidden with casual acquaintances. Indeed, a casual acquaintance would probably be put off by your personal disclosures.

Exercise 13-11

Read each of the following descriptions of behavior and state in which quadrant of the Johari window each belongs.

a. A computer science instructor constantly raps his fingers on his students' monitors. He seems totally unaware of this behavior but it irritates his class.

b. Dick had too much to drink last night. He has a severe headache but is smiling and acting cheerful. He fears people will think he has a drinking problem. _____

c. Mrs. Goode screamed, "I'm scared to death of these little creatures" when one of her second-grade students put his collection of frogs and worms on her desk. _____

d. Jane, an excellent actress, always fears she will forget her lines. She has no reason for this fear and never has missed a line or a cue. _____

Please turn to the Feedback section to check your answers.

RESOLVING CONFLICTS

What happens when communication breaks down? The outcome can be hurt feelings, frustration, anger, fighting, and even wars. Each month about 40,000 healthy humans are killed in wars around the world. When leaders of countries resort to name-calling and become rigid and refuse to listen to each other's ideas, the result can be a devastating loss of lives. Can this be avoided? Psychologists recommend a technique called *GRIT,* or *Graduated and Reciprocated Initiatives in Tension Reduction.* The GRIT process begins when the leader of one side states that both sides will benefit if tensions are reduced; for example, if people's lives will be spared and money will be saved. This leader then offers to begin the process of peacemaking by making some small adjustment toward reducing tensions. This opens the door for the leader of the opposing side to reciprocate with a similar offer. If the opposing leader responds with hostility, the process ends. However, if the enemy reciprocates with another step toward reducing hostility, the first leader begins a second round of compromises. The reduction in nuclear arms resulted from many rounds of conciliatory acts. In laboratory experiments, GRIT strategy was found to increase trust and cooperation (Lindskold, 1978, 1985).

GRIT (Graduated and Reciprocated Initiatives in Tension Reduction) Technique for resolving conflicts; it can be useful in peacemaking

Although GRIT was desiged to aid communication and negotiation between nations, the strategy is also effective in day-to-day communications between people. When you feel uncomfortable from tensions with another person, express your feelings and suggest that you both would benefit from a more peaceful relationship. Then start the compromise process by offering to make some adjustment and wait for a response. It just may work!

Checkpoint

Use the following questions to check your understanding of the final portion of this chapter. Indicate whether each statement is true or false.

19. _____ One-way communication is faster than two-way communication.

20. _____ One-way communication is more accurate than two-way communication.

21. _____ In two-way communication the speaker is open to criticism.

22. _____ The grapevine is an informal communication network.

23. _____ A circle network has no leader.

24. _____ In a Y arrangement network, everyone has equal power.

25. _____ Members of wheel networks are most satisfied with their communications.

26. _____ An upper-level increase in psychological size makes upward communication easier.

27. _____ A suggestion box is an example of upward communication.

28. _____ There is no risk to self-disclosure.

29. _____ Self-disclosure builds trust.

30. _____ Sizes of the quadrants in a Johari window can change.

31. _____ Unconscious motives are included in quadrant II (blind) of a Johari window.

32. _____ Hidden agendas usually shorten meetings.

33. _____ It is best to try to surface hidden agendas.

34. _____ GRIT begins with mutual agreement that reducing tension is beneficial.

35. _____ GRIT increases trust and cooperation.

Check your responses against the Checkpoint Answer Key at the end of the chapter. If you had difficulty with any question, reread the text. If you had little or no difficulty answering the questions or have resolved problems that you might have had, you are ready to check yourself against the chapter inventory that follows.

CHAPTER INVENTORY

Use the list of objectives as a review checklist. You should be able to do the tasks outlined in the objectives and apply them to everyday examples. If you can, you may feel confident that you have mastered the material in this chapter.

1. Describe the role of listening in communication.
2. Identify and provide examples of two types of listening problems.
3. List and discuss four ways to improve listening skills.
4. Identify and describe four ways to improve speaking skills.
5. Specify one advantage and two disadvantages to writing rather than speaking.
6. Differentiate between the denotation and connotation of words.
7. Distinguish between assertive and aggressive behavior.
8. Identify one limitation of art as a nonverbal form of communication.

9. Explain the role of appearance and body language in nonverbal communication.
10. List and describe four types of distance zones.
11. Describe cultural factors that affect communication.
12. Compare the advantages and disadvantages of one-way and two-way communication.
13. Describe one type of informal communication network and four types of formal networks.
14. Distinguish between, and provide examples of, upward and downward communication.
15. List six possible ways to improve upward communication.
16. Define and explain the importance of self-disclosure.
17. Describe and provide examples for each quadrant of a Johari window, and identify one method for bringing hidden agendas to the surface.
18. Explain how GRIT can be used to resolve conflicts.

Feedback

The correct answers to the exercises follow. If you did not answer an exercise correctly, review the preceding pages and return to the exercise to correctly complete it.

13-1. a. Ms. Slicker should set a purpose for listening.
    b. She should avoid distractions while someone is talking. She should worry about the status of her gas gauge later.
    c. She should be more open-minded. Even though the mechanic has a twang, she might know her way around the countryside.
    d. She should ask questions if she feels she missed something. If she thinks she understood, she could paraphrase to be certain.

13-2. a. By thinking ahead, you can plan what you want to say.
    b. You will have greater control over the words you use and are more likely to be understood.
    c. You are more likely to hold the attention of listeners.
    d. You will get a more informative response.

13-3. a. The denotation is the dictionary definition.
    b. The connotation is the emotional association.

13-4. a. Look up "mechanic" in the dictionary.
    b. Hand out questionnaires asking people to measure the word on a number of dimensions.

13-5. Rather than accuse the person of being sloppy, you might begin by reporting, "I feel depressed when I sit in a messy room." Next add a positive suggestion, such as, "If we put two bags in the corner, one for trash and one for dirty clothes, we will have more room to walk around." You could use the three F's of assertiveness by expressing your opinions firmly, being fair in dividing the chores, and having a friendly attitude toward cooperation.

13-6. a. Jane is using her clothing and appearance to communicate that she is businesslike.

    b. Andy is using art to communicate his negative attitude toward his wife.

    c. Gaya is telling her boss she does not want a personal relationship.

    d. Tessie is telling the young man she would like to have a personal conversation.

13-7. a. One-way

    b. Two-way

    c. Two-way

    d. One-way

    e. Two-way

13-8. a. Y arrangement (Figure 13-15)

    b. Wheel (Figure 13-16)

    c. Concom (Figure 13-17)

13-9. a. Carol and Goldie

    b. The chauffeur, the horse trainer, the tax attorney, the social secretary, and the household technician

    c. The Y arrangement

13-10. a. Advertise "coffee with the mayor."

    b. Put up suggestion box.

    c. Send out questionnaires.

FIGURE 13-15. Y arrangement.

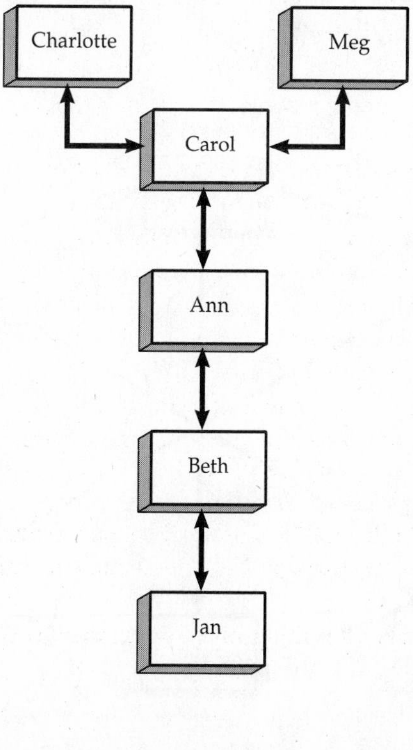

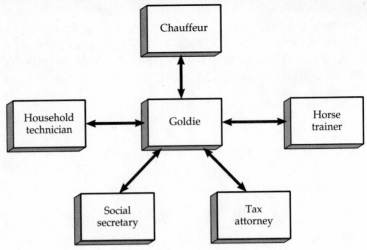

FIGURE 13-16. Wheel.

    d. Announce an open-door policy and be available.
    e. Have people call you by your first name rather than "Your Honor" or "Mayor."
    f. Rearrange furniture to make it more conducive to communication.

13-11. a. Quadrant II: blind
    b. Quadrant III: hidden
    c. Quadrant I: open
    d. Quadrant IV: unknown

FIGURE 13-17. Concom.

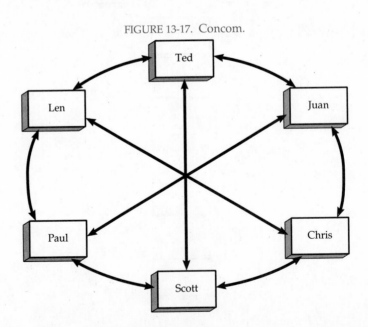

Checkpoint Answer Key

1. c; 2. b; 3. a; 4. b; 5. a; 6. a; 7. d; 8. c; 9. c; 10. c; 11. b; 12. a; 13. b; 14. d; 15. a; 16. d; 17. d; 18. a; 19. true; 20. false; 21. true; 22. true; 23. true; 24. false; 25. false; 26. false; 27. true; 28. false; 29. true; 30. true; 31. false; 32. false; 33. true; 34. true; 35. true.

Using Attitude Theories

A great many people think they are thinking when
they are merely rearranging their prejudices.
—WILLIAM JAMES

Have you ever been influenced by a television commercial? Try to analyze why your attitude was swayed by the ad. Why did you want to buy the product advertised? Perhaps it was endorsed by an expert. Or maybe some ordinary people like yourself claimed it was crackajack. Or you were impressed by some scientific research. Whether the product was a tennis racquet, mouthwash, plastic trash bags, spaghetti sauce, or tofu, the advertiser was probably using one of the many persuasion techniques found through research to influence people's attitudes. After reading this chapter you will be better able to examine the causes of people's attitudes and the inducements toward attitude change.

The chapter begins by differentiating between attitude, prejudice, and discrimination. Next, the causes of prejudice and positive, or helping, attitudes are explored. You will consider the many factors that influence people's attitudes toward each other. Finally, you will look at some methods that are used to persuade people and change their attitudes. Attention will focus on advertisements, along with a brief description of brainwashing techniques.

ATTITUDES, PREJUDICE, AND DISCRIMINATION

To be sure, the three words in the heading are closely related. Prejudice is a type of attitude. Discrimination is the result of attitudes and can be caused by prejudice. But there are some clear distinctions in the meanings of the words.

Next you will look at their meanings, along with some limitations in their relationships.

Attitudes

Harrison (1976) identified three components in *attitudes*: beliefs, emotions, and behavior. Your *beliefs* are your basic values, or what you consider desirable and undesirable. Undoubtedly you have some stable underlying values. Perhaps you have strong convictions about freedom, independence, good health, close family relationships, money, or success. Any one of these values can influence many beliefs. For example, if good health is one of your important values, you probably believe people should eat nutritious foods, exercise, rest, and avoid alcohol and drugs. Similarly, if you value family relationships and success, you will no doubt hold an assortment of beliefs that will promote better relationships within families and permit job advancement. Beliefs are the preferences that result from your values.

Emotions separate attitudes from opinions. Suppose a pollster asks a woman if she thinks colleges should have book collections on the greenhouse effect. She stops for a moment to think and replies, "Sure, why not." She then continues with her daily activities. She values education but does not have any emotional commitment about knowledge of global warming. If, on the other hand, she had become upset about the lack of library books on the greenhouse effect, her opinion would have developed into an attitude. Even if she felt annoyed that too many books on global warming were already available, she would be showing emotion. Feelings that accompany attitudes may be positive or negative, but they are never neutral.

Because attitudes are accompanied by emotions, there is almost always some form of *behavioral* result. You might simply speak out for or against an issue. If you feel more strongly, you might write a letter or contribute to a campaign. If you really have intense emotions, you might even run for public office. Even attitudes that do not bring on such noticeable actions have behavioral results. For example, suppose a man believes that a wealthy suburb is an ideal place to live. He loves the area but cannot afford any of the houses. Nonetheless, he spends some time daydreaming about his ideal home. His daydreaming is a behavior. Of course, you can probably guess how he will behave if he ever inherits a fortune from a rich relative!

attitude Conviction based on beliefs, emotions, and behavior toward an object, person, or idea

Exercise 14-1

Three components of attitudes have been described: *beliefs, emotions,* and *behavior.* Read the following scenario about a woman's attitude about abortion. In the space provided, identify signs of each of the three aspects of her attitude.

Adele feels that everyone should be entitled to personal freedom and total independence. Recently she has been arguing with friends who are members of the right-to-life movement. Adele contends that women should be permitted to decide for themselves whether or not they wish to bear a child. Disputes have become heated, and Adele once burst into tears when a friend called her a murderer. She feels angry that more women do not support her views.

a. Beliefs: _____

_____

_____

b. Emotions: _____

_____

_____

c. Behavior: _____

_____

_____

The answers may be found in the Feedback section.

Prejudice

prejudice Negative attitude based on a hasty judgment without facts

stereotype Overgeneralized belief about a group of people

The word *prejudice* is derived from the Latin *praejudicium*, "a judgment based on previous experience." Translated into English, the word has come to mean a premature or snap judgment that is made before examining the facts. This snap judgment is usually based on an overgeneralized belief, or *stereotype*, about a group of people. Today the meaning also usually includes a negative connotation.

The negative attitude of prejudice is usually directed toward an out-group, people who are perceived to be different in some way. You may be prejudiced against people who are extremely overweight or are flashy dressers or those who receive welfare checks. Most prejudices are against races, ethnic groups, religious minorities, and women. But many people even have negative stereotypes of the disabled individuals and blame them for being victims (Bronstein and Quina, 1988).

racism Belief that one race is superior and entitled to special privileges

History records several examples of *racist* prejudice. Racists believe that their group is superior to all others and therefore is entitled to special privileges. An extreme example of racism is the attitude of German Nazis toward the Jewish people prior to World War II. Even in the United States, racism had been legalized through segregation laws. As the article in Feature 14-1 describes, even today, long after segregation laws have been abolished, voluntary segregation occurs on many campuses.

sexism Belief that women are inferior to men

Sexism refers to prejudice against women. Sexists maintain that women are inferior to men. A man who is sexist would feel extremely uncomfortable about working for a female boss and would not vote for a woman regardless of her abilities. Sexism is considered responsible for keeping women in traditionally female professions, such as teaching and nursing, and preventing women from rising to executive and management positions.

homophobia Irrational fear of, and contempt for, gay people

Recently there has been a rise in *homophobia*, hostile feelings against gay men and lesbians. Homophobia is an irrational fear and contempt for gay people. Among gay students at Rutgers University, 55 percent reported that

Race on Campus

... To be sure, the new segregation is perpetuated by choice not by law. "It makes a great deal of difference whether segregation is voluntary or if it is imposed on you," says Robert Hill, a vice president of Syracuse University. "For kids who have not had much contact before college with European-Americans, living with other African-Americans raises the comfort level." But voluntary or not, the result is often the same: two universities—one black and one white—existing side by side on the campus. "We have a campus of 25,000 students and there is no mixing across cultural and racial lines," reports Christine Romans, 22, the thoughtful editor of the student newspaper at Iowa State University, scene of one of last spring's worst racial skirmishes. "Afterward," she adds, "they had a rally for unity, but all the blacks clustered together and all the whites clustered together."

Romans was one of 550 student editors who participated in a recent *U.S. News* survey of race relations on campus. The results clearly indicate that many of those glowing photos in college promotional material showing blacks and whites strolling on peaceful fall afternoons present a distorted picture—particularly at the larger institutions. For example 64 percent of the editors at schools enrolling more than 10,000 students and 49 percent of all respondents characterized the state of race relations on their campuses as "fair" or "poor."

Nine out of 10 editors at the larger schools—75 percent overall—reported that self-segregation among blacks was common on their campuses; 53 percent at the larger schools—and 37 percent overall—agreed that blacks on their campuses feel "white students are hostile and aloof"; 33 percent at the larger schools—24 percent overall—said the white students were physically afraid of blacks. And 85 percent of the respondents at larger schools—71 percent overall—reported that there had been at least one incident on campus that could be characterized as racial during the past year. While the new segregation is not the sole cause of conflict, among the editors at larger institutions, the survey showed a statistically significant relationship between the degree of self-segregation by race and the number of racial incidents. ...

Source: Elfin, M. & Burke, S. (1993, April 19). Race on campus. *U.S. News & World Report.*

---

they had been verbally abused and 42 percent stated that they had been harassed by their roommates (Dodge, 1989). The excerpt in Feature 14-2 points out that prejudice against gay people is intense.

Because prejudices, like all attitudes, are emotionally charged, they are difficult to change. In spite of information and evidence to the contrary, people stick to their old unjustified attitudes. Prejudices are acquired gradually and become a habitual way of thinking.

Perhaps by now you are looking around for those "awful" prejudiced people. You need not search far; everyone has some prejudices. Most people tend to favor their own race, religion, sex, and ethnic background and exclude others. Even those who accept and enjoy the diversity of others will at some time demonstrate a prejudice. For example, a woman may have a favorable attitude toward donating money to people who beg on street corners. She always has a coin for an outstretched hand. One day a man smelling of liquor asks for a handout. She has heard tales of alcoholics who ask for money to buy cheap wine and feels repulsed. She knows nothing about this particular man but is clearly biased against beggars with an aroma of alcohol. Her prejudice is based on an unjustified overgeneralization. But it is reasonable, in spite of her lack of sufficient evidence.

Exercise 14-2

In your own words describe the relationship between attitudes and prejudice.

_____

_____

_____

You may check your reply in the Feedback section.

Discrimination

discrimination Determining differences and sorting objects or people into categories

Discrimination simply means deciphering differences or sorting items into categories. Undoubtedly you can discriminate between apples and peaches, adults and children, and males and females. Discrimination reflects an opinion but not necessarily a prejudice. For example, you probably differentiate between people whom you address by their first names and those whom you address by their titles and last names. A best friend would be shocked if you called him "Mr. Whoever" instead of "Moe" or "Harry." Similarly, unless your physician is a personal friend you probably call her "Doctor Whatsyourname" instead of "Jezabel" or "Tammy." Such discrimination is not related to negative attitudes.

FEATURE 14-2 PSYCHOLOGY IN THE NEWS

Homophobia: Scientists Find Clues to Its Roots

. . . One of the most troubling findings for those trying to combat anti-gay bias is data showing that hostility is far more accepted among large numbers of Americans than is bias against other groups. In surveys, about three-quarters of homosexuals say they have been harassed by people calling them names, and as many as one in four say they have been physically assaulted.

"Anti-gay violence is still acceptable because while leaders decry racial and religious bigotry, they ignore violence against gays and lesbians," said Matt Foreman, executive director of the New York City Gay and Lesbian Anti-Violence Project.

A 1988 study by the State of New York for the Governor's Task Force on Bias-Related Violence concluded that of all groups, "the most severe hostilities are directed at lesbians and gay men."

In "one of the most alarming findings" the report found that while teenagers surveyed were reluctant to advocate open bias against racial and ethnic groups, they were emphatic about disliking homosexual men and women. They are perceived "as legitimate targets which can be openly attacked," the report said.

In a survey of 2,823 students from 8th to 12th grade, three-quarters of the boys and half the girls said it would be bad to have a homosexual for a neighbor. The feelings were as strong among 12-year-olds as among 17-year-olds. Many students added gratuitous vicious comments about homosexuals; that was not the case with the other groups. . . .

Source: Goldman, D. (1990, July 10). Homophobia: Scientists find clues to its roots. *The New York Times*, C-1.

Discrimination in hiring is inevitable. Jobs have qualifications, and an employer must distinguish among candidates who can do the job. A person who has completed courses and worked in data processing is probably a better candidate for a computer-programmer job than is a person who studied wastewater treatment. Discrimination is clearly biased behavior, but it can be fair.

However, too often, discrimination is unfair and stems strictly from prejudiced attitudes. A woman who chooses graduates of her alma mater over other job applicants is discriminating unfairly. Regardless of their education, experience, and abilities, graduates of other schools are not being considered. This form of discrimination has resulted not only in unequal hiring but also in unequal justice in the courts. Juries, as well as judges, have reflected prejudice and discrimination in their decisions. Prejudice is an attitude, and discrimination is a behavior.

Have you ever served on a jury? If so, you are likely to be aware of the lengthy process involved in jury selection. Lawyers for both the prosecution and the defense ask extensive questions of all potential jurors. Both want to be certain that any discrimination will be in their favor. For example, assume a man is suing the owner of a poodle who bit his son. His lawyer would prefer a jury of parents who dislike dogs. The defense attorney would no doubt like

"Actually, Lou, I think it was more than just my being in the right place at the right time. I think it was my being the right race, the right religion, the right sex, the right socioeconomic group, having the right accent, the right clothes, going to the right schools . . ."

FIGURE 14-1. Looks as if he was a winner in unfair discrimination.

to pick a jury of dog owners and humane society members who do not care for children. Each lawyer questions every potential juror and refuses to permit assignment of anyone who is likely to discriminate in an unfavorable way.

However, often people are either unaware of their prejudices or unwilling to admit to them. Bahr and Chadwick (1974) questioned White people about their attitudes toward American Indians. Although almost all stated that they wanted Indians to become part of the American culture, they did not want their children to have a close association with them. And although most health-care professionals consider themselves fair, Black people are less likely than White people to receive coronary bypass surgery, kidney transplants, and other major treatments (Council on Ethical and Judicial Affairs, 1990).

What can be done to reduce unfair discrimination? Clearly this unfair behavior stems from prejudice. Although laws forbid discrimination based on sex, race, ethnic origin, or religion, prejudice and unfair behavior exist. An employer may unwillingly hire a person purely to conform with the law. The employer may then make unfair demands on the new employee. Legislation alone is not effective in removing discrimination caused by prejudice. Although the Civil Rights Act of 1964 guarantees equal employment opportunity, large differences in the salaries and job levels between men and women continue.

It is clear that laws alone cannot end unfair discrimination. One study (Langer, Bashner, and Chanowitz, 1985) attempted to teach sixth graders to use discrimination fairly. The researchers described this as *mindful discrimination*. They encouraged the sixth graders to be mindful by encouraging inventive thinking. The children discussed physical disabilities. They then decided whether specific disabilities would be an advantage or disadvantage in different situations. In one instance, the researchers showed the children pictures of two boys, one in a wheelchair and the other without a physical handicap. The students were then asked which boy they would prefer as a partner in checkers, soccer, and a wheelchair race. The researchers compared the responses of the trained children with another group of untrained sixth graders. The trained children made far more appropriate choices, or discriminations. Perhaps future school programs will use these methods to increase "mindful" discrimination.

Another creative plan to reduce unfair bias was developed for elementary school classes with diverse ethnic populations. Aronson (1987) used a strategy called the *jigsaw classroom*, where children of different ethnic backgrounds had to cooperate to earn good grades. Each class was divided into groups. Each group had representatives from as many ethnic groups as possible. The teacher presented each member of the group wih different important information on a subject that the class was learning. The group then had to put all the pieces of information together to complete their report (like pieces of a jigsaw puzzle). Conversations between children of different ethnic groups increased and the children began to appreciate the skills of people of diverse backgrounds.

Occasionally people overreact to prejudices. They will bend over backwards to prove they are not prejudiced. As a result, they will discriminate in favor of a group they feel negatively about, or use *reverse discrimination*. For example, suppose a White man is prejudiced against Black people. He often flies on business trips and prefers to work rather than converse with fellow passengers. On one trip an African-American man sits next to him. Although

mindful discrimination Discrimination based on training and sound reasoning

jigsaw classroom Technique to encourage children of diverse backgrounds to work for their grades together, on an equal status

reverse discrimination Favoring a group that elicits negative feelings

In a jigsaw classroom, children of diverse ethnic backgrounds must work together for their grades.

ordinarily he would not speak to the person next to him, he does not want the African-American to think his silence is caused by prejudice. As a result, he starts a conversation. When people overreact to prejudice, they engage in behavior that they would not ordinarily. Interestingly, often this behavior leads to a reduction of prejudice and discrimination. The two men will probably talk about things they have in common and learn to appreciate each other as individuals rather than as part of a stereotyped group.

Exercise 14-3

Discrimination can be caused by fair distinctions, prejudiced attitudes, or reverse discrimination. For each of the following examples, indicate which of these three factors is probably the cause of discrimination.

a. Nathan, a new student at college, does not want his fellow students to think he is prejudiced. Whenever he sees minority students in the cafeteria or at a library table he joins them, even though he prefers to eat and work alone.

b. Lakefront Summer Camp will only hire swimming counselors who have passed a swimming test and have a lifesaving certificate. _____

c. Arnold Livingston Cooper III does not want to have Jim Common accepted in his fraternity, since Jim's parents are not college graduates. _____

d. Elvira refuses to hire any men. She claims men will not work well for a woman. _____

Exercise 14-4

Sometimes people who claim they are not prejudiced against a group will discriminate unfairly against them. Why might this occur?

_____

_____

Exercise 14-5

Identify three strategies that can reduce unfair bias.

a. _____

b. _____

c. _____

To check your answers, please turn to the Feedback section.

FORMING ATTITUDES

Initially we all copy the attitudes of our parents. If your parents enjoyed jokes or fairy tales or books or intricate toys, you probably mimicked them. The location of your home and the school you attended were selected by your parents. Parents choose the influences on their children. Many a mother and father have admonished their offspring to avoid playing with a rowdy child.

After parents select a school, their influence begins to decrease, while teachers and friends begin to contribute to the formation of attitudes. By adolescence, peers clearly become the most important influences on attitudes. Teenagers tend to assert their independence by rebelling against their parents' attitudes and clinging to the opinions of their friends. Newcomb (1963) studied the attitudes of Bennington College students over twenty-five years. Most students had come from families with conservative attitudes. The school faculty, however, had liberal attitudes and influenced the students. During their years at Bennington, students became more liberal and conformed to their faculty and peers. Newcomb found that over the twenty-five-year period, students stuck to their liberal attitudes. They did not revert to their parents' views.

Adolescents even conform in their attitudes toward clothing. Have you ever noticed their similarity in appearance? Adolescents feel more secure when they look alike. Zajonc (1968) concluded that people tend to have positive attitudes toward things and people who are familiar; the unfamiliar will be disliked. Perhaps this explains one reason for dressing in similar styles.

Exercise 14-6

In Figure 14-2, why might the sons have different attitudes from the fathers?

_____

_____

Turn to the Feedback section to check your response.

First Impressions

Often, first impressions are based on past experiences. If you are accustomed to talking with women in jeans, you will feel more comfortable with, and probably like, women in jeans. Similarly, if you meet someone who reminds you of an old buddy, he will probably make a good first impression. Have you ever met someone you instantly disliked? Think about some of the characteristics that have created positive and negative first impressions.

People often form strong first impressions for unusual reasons. A study reported by Horn (1980) found that waitresses could win heavier tips by wearing a flower in their hair. Another study reported by Bozzi (1988) noted that teachers rated tall boys and slim girls more favorably than short boys and heavy girls.

"Yeah, my son's the same kind of phony liberal—billions for the Third World, zip for Chrysler."

FIGURE 14-2

Checkpoint

Use the following questions to check your understanding of this portion of the chapter. Choose and mark the one correct response to each question.

1. According to Harrison, what are three essential ingredients in attitudes?
   a. Beliefs, prejudices, and values
   b. Values, emotions, and prejudices
   c. Beliefs, emotions, and behavior
   d. Beliefs, values, and convictions

2. The owner of a grocery store believes that shoplifters should be arrested or fined. What is this belief based on?
   a. A prejudice
   b. A basic value
   c. Racism
   d. An overgeneralization

3. How do attitudes differ from opinions?
   a. Attitudes involve emotions.
   b. Opinions involve emotions.
   c. Opinions are usually negative.
   d. Attitudes are usually negative.

4. Which of the following definitions best describes the current meaning of "prejudice"?
   a. A negative snap judgment that is not based on facts
   b. A positive or negative premature judgment
   c. A judgment based on previous experience
   d. A negative attitude toward other races

5. The owner of an apartment building claims that she has no prejudices against any groups. Yet she will not rent apartments to Jewish people. How can her behavior be explained?
   a. She may be unaware of her prejudices or unwilling to admit them.
   b. She is discriminating fairly and not showing prejudice.
   c. She is overreacting to her prejudices and showing reverse discrimination.
   d. Her discriminating behavior is consistent with not being prejudiced.

6. Which type of discrimination is most widespread and intense?
   a. Racism
   b. Sexism
   c. Homophobia
   d. Ethnic discrimination

7. Who was first to influence your attitudes?
   a. Your parents
   b. Your friends
   c. Your teachers
   d. Your brothers and sisters

8. Who is most likely to make the best first impression?
   a. A person who dresses differently
   b. A person who wears elaborate or dressy clothing

c. A person who looks unfamiliar
d. A person who looks familiar

Check your responses against the Checkpoint Answer Key at the end of the chapter. If you had difficulty with any question, reread the text. If you had little or no difficulty answering the questions or have resolved problems that you might have had, you are ready to continue with the next portion of this chapter.

Negative and Positive Attitudes

Since attitudes cannot be neutral (remember the emotion factor), your parents, schools, and friends have instilled in you either positive or negative attitudes. Your negative attitudes lead to disagreements, arguments, conflicts, or other confrontations. Prejudice is a key factor in negative attitudes. On the other hand, positive attitudes can induce you to assist other people, to be caring and unselfish. Next you will consider the reasons behind prejudices (negative attitudes) and helping behavior (positive attitudes).

Forming Prejudices

Allport (1958) described two general sources of prejudice: personal concerns and group conformity. *Personal concerns* include fears and worries about another group being a threat to you as an individual. *Group conformity* implies that you go along with your peers in disliking an out-group, even though the out-group is not a personal threat to you. Psychologists have studied the causes of prejudice in each of these categories.

Personal Concerns. A prime cause of personal prejudice is the concern for economic survival. Assume you are working as a window washer at $7 an hour. An immigrant from Ugliopia is willing to complete your hourly tasks for only $4. You begin to develop a dislike for Ugliopians. They are a threat to you and can steal your job.

Bettelheim and Janowitz (1950) studied the attitudes of White, gentile World War II veterans. Veterans who did not obtain jobs as good as the ones they had before the war were more anti-Semitic and anti-Black than were veterans who found as good or better jobs. The minorities were blamed for taking jobs and opportunities away from others.

In large cities, *overcrowding* has been a cause of personal prejudice. If there had been an influx of Ugliopians and you could not find a seat on the subway, were pushed off sidewalks, and never had a place to park your car, you would likely blame the newcomers. The most recent immigrants are blamed for the overcrowding. In the United States during the early 1900s the Irish, Italians, and Jews were the victims of prejudice and discrimination. Later, Blacks and Puerto Ricans were considered the culprits. Now often Mexican-Americans and Central Americans are the targets.

Another cause of personal prejudice is *conflict and competition*. If you fear a group is threatening your life or the lives of your group, you will undoubtedly

"Of course, for a little more money I could probably have gotten some big-name portraitist."

FIGURE 14-3. Feeling underpaid, the artist has a negative image of his client.

develop some very strong negative attitudes. Consider the attitudes of Americans toward the Japanese and German people during World War II. Iranians were unpopular during the hostage crisis of 1979–1980 and Iraqis were out of favor after the invasion of Kuwait in 1991. Conflicts and battles clearly promote prejudice.

Groups that compete with each other generally develop prejudices against each other. Even when money or lives are not involved in the competition, strong negative attitudes can be generated. People who navigate sailboats are often irritated by owners of motorboats who do not give them the right-of-way or who create unnecessary waves. Skippers of sailboats refer to motorboats as "stinkpots" and often consider their owners inferior. Similarly it is common for fraternity brothers and sorority sisters to have prejudiced attitudes against members of other fraternities and sororities. Consider the attitudes of Republican and Democratic activists toward each other!

Another cause of prejudice is *fear of the unknown*. Most people are comfortable in familiar situations with persons who are similar to themselves. A person who wears unusual native dress or has different cultural customs can seem a threat. Reasons for not associating are conjured up, and prejudices result. Studies have found varying attitudes of preschool children toward the elderly. Children who are unfamiliar with older people show clear prejudices.

Individuals can derive personal satisfaction from their prejudices. Anger

THE FAR SIDE GARY LARSON

*To Ernie's horror, and the ultimate disaster of all,
one more elephant tried to squeeze on.*

FIGURE 14-4. Ernie is likely to develop a prejudice
against elephants.

and hostility can be released. The target of prejudice becomes a *scapegoat* and is blamed for economic, social, and achievement problems. The prejudiced person can feel superior to the scapegoat. Because satisfaction accompanies personal prejudice, the prejudice is difficult to change. Further, as disclosed by Merton (1948), a *self-fulfilling prophecy* is also associated with prejudice. If you are prejudiced against a person, you will undoubtedly be unkind and unfair. The person in turn will respond in a negative way. This will convince you that your original attitude was accurate. A teacher who dislikes the young boys in her class might punish them unnecessarily. As a result they might become disrespectful toward her, perhaps using obscenities or making rude remarks. Their behavior woud assure her that she was correct in assuming that little boys are rude and not to be trusted.

self-fulfilling prophecy Making a prediction and acting in a way to ensure that it will come true

Exercise 14-7

Four possible causes of personal prejudice have been described: economic survival, overcrowding, conflict and competition, fear of the unknown. Read each of the following descriptions of prejudice and indicate the probable cause.

a. Mark is fed up with the increasing bumper-to-bumper traffic when he commutes to work. He is convinced it is caused by too many women working. He claims women are poor drivers and are inefficient and un-coordinated. _____

b. The Hatfords were upset when a family from Saudi Arabia moved next door. They are afraid to talk with their new neighbors, who appear to be quite different. _____

c. Nigel's soccer team, the Kicks, lost to the Stops, 8–0. Nigel claims all the team members of the Stops are rude and snobbish. _____

d. The women's club of Biastown voted not to allow women to join until they have lived in Biastown for at least five years. They claimed they want to be sure of their members. _____

e. Eliza quit her job to stay home and raise her children. When she decided to go back to work, she had trouble finding a position at the same salary. She claims that incompetent Mexican men and women are stealing jobs. _____

Exercise 14-8

List two reasons why it is difficult to change personal prejudices.

a. _____

b. _____

You may find the correct answers in the Feedback section.

Group Conformity. Often people change their beliefs to make them agree with the beliefs of a group. As mentioned earlier, adolescents will switch their attitudes to conform with their peers. Even youngsters with open-minded parents can be convinced to comply with the thinking of a few prejudiced friends. The out-group can even be former friends. But group conformity is not limited to adolescents. Adults also adopt the prejudices of their groups. A man who is promoted and now eats in the executive lounge may feel uncomfortable about bringing one of his former coworkers to dine with his new group. He may even shun his former buddies, since they are not accepted in his new social class.

Similarly, if your neighbors are upset about too many minorities moving into the community, you may begin to feel the pressure even if you are not prejudiced yourself. When selling your house, you might discourage minorities by pointing out the negative features. Chapter 15 covers the influence of groups on attitudes in more detail.

Macho College, a traditional all-male school, began admitting women ten years ago. The alumni association maintains several college clubs throughout the country. None of these clubs admits women. A survey found that since women have been enrolled in the school, individual male students view the women as equals. Why might the prejudice persist in the alumni association?

_____

_____

_____

To check your response, turn to the Feedback section.

Helping Attitudes

Have you ever had car trouble and felt helpless? You may have raised the hood, flashed the blinkers, and wondered if someone—anyone—would come along and offer some assistance. Assuming you were not waving $10 at passers-by, the help you needed would stem from a person's altruism. *Altruism* is helping without expecting any reward or benefit. According to psychologists, whether or not you received altruistic help would depend on the following factors:

altruism Concern for others; helping others without expecting a reward or benefit

The Number of Observers. If you were on a crowded highway, your chances of getting help would decrease. Surprisingly, if cars went by you infrequently, you would have a better chance of someone stopping. A shocking murder case in Queens, New York, in 1964 sparked the interest of social psychologists concerned with altruism. A young woman, Kitty Genovese, was stabbed during an attack that lasted more than thirty minutes. More than thirty-eight neighbors in an apartment building admitted witnessing the struggle. Twice, people turned on lights and almost scared the attacker away. But he returned to murder her. Not one person called the police or tried to help the victim. Psychologists claim there is a "bystander effect": The more people who witness a problem, the less likely that someone will interfere and help.

In an experiment on the bystander effect, Latane and Darley (1968) sent subjects into a room to complete a questionnaire. Supposedly, they were to fill in the forms while waiting for an interviewer. In one situation, subjects were alone in the room. Irregular bursts of smoke came out from under a door that led to another room. Fully 75 percent of the subjects reported the problem promptly. In a second experimental condition, a subject was sent to a room with two confederates (fake subjects assisting the experimenter). The confederates ignored the bursts of smoke initially. As it continued, they remained calm and apathetic and just brushed it away. Ten different subjects were used individually with the confederates; only one reported the problem. In the third situation two subjects were sent to the questionnaire room. Thirty percent reported the smoke, but they took much longer than subjects did who were alone.

In another experiment involving the bystander effect, Latane and Darley

(1970) observed helping behavior among subjects who overheard another subject suffer a (fake) epileptic seizure. To begin, each subject was assigned to a cubicle and seated in front of a microphone. The experimenter described the experimental conditions over an intercom. Subjects were told they simply were discussing adjustment problems with other students. One group of subjects believed they were communicating with only one other subject. Another group believed there were two others. A third group believed there were five subjects. In each situation, subjects believed a person in their communication network had epilepsy. A recording described epileptic problems; the voice began to choke, called for help, and expressed fears of dying. The subjects' reactions varied according to how many listeners they thought were present. All subjects who believed they were the only person to hear the seizure responded quickly. Subjects who believed another person overheard the seizure took longer and only 85 percent responded. When subjects thought four others were listening, they took more than three times longer, and only 62 percent responded.

People seem to be reluctant to help if they believe others are available. Responsibility can be shared with the others. Each person looks to another and no one helps. Since no one is helping, one person does not want to appear different or foolish. The result is a bystander effect.

Location. Back to your car problem. Would you rather break down in the city or in the country? As you might have suspected, help is more likely in the country. Milgram (1970) and Korte and Kerr (1975) found that city dwellers are more indifferent and apathetic than rural residents. The general level of friendliness and socializing seems to be much higher when a country atmosphere is introduced, even in a city. Rubenstein (1981) reported that shoppers at a city farmers market are far more outgoing than those in a city supermarket.

Levine et al. (1976) concluded that city residents are less friendly and helpful because they are more vulnerable and threatened. Clearly there is more crime in cities. City people were less willing to let a stranger in their home than were people from small towns. Nonetheless, city residents were willing to assist strangers by making a phone call while the stranger waited outside.

Appearance. How you are dressed when your car breaks down could also make a difference. As mentioned earlier, people tend to be more trusting and accepting of someone who looks similar to them. A man with a button-down oxford shirt is more likely to be helped by another conservative than by the leader of a motorcycle gang. On the other hand, a young man in a leather jacket, boots, and a hard helmet will more probably be assisted by a motorcycle gang member rather than by an executive in a pin-striped suit.

Previous Observations. If someone else has car problems on the highway and is receiving assistance, you are more likely to get help. In a number of different studies, psychologists have noted that people who see another person giving help are more likely to be altruistic themselves. In an interesting study by Macauley (1970), donors to a sidewalk Santa Claus and a Salvation Army kettle were observed. People who had seen another person making a donation were more likely to contribute.

Weather. Unfortunately, if you are standing out in the rain with your broken-down car, you are less likely to receive any help. Although it is difficult to reason why, people are less altruistic on cloudy and rainy days. Apparently sunshine brings out the goodness and kindness in people.

Self-Esteem. Suppose all the conditions for help were negative. Imagine you were in heavy city traffic on a cloudy day, dressed as Dracula on your way to a costume party. Several people had car problems, but no one was receiving help. Sound hopeless? Psychological studies offer some encouragement. Researchers have found that people with high self-esteem are more likely to help others, regardless of the situation. Take heart. In your moment of despair a person with a good self-image could come along and repair your car.

Exercise 14-10

In each of the following sets of cases, one person is more likely to receive help. Indicate which person has a better chance, and explain the reason for your choice.

a. Jim dropped his comb on a crowded sidewalk in the zoo.

or

Mitch's pen dropped out of his pocket while he was taking a closer look at a tulip at the flower show. There were only three other people at the tulip exhibition.

_____

_____

_____

b. Gertrude falls and cuts her knee. She notices that Michelle, the president of the senior class and star of the soccer team, is coming along the walkway.

or

Naomi slips on a banana peel and her books are spread all over the grass. Eunice is out for a stroll on the green, trying to shake her depression.

_____

_____

_____

c. Richard's umbrella blows inside out in a severe rainstorm.

or

Edward is having difficulty setting up his beach umbrella on a hot sunny day.

_____

_____

_____

d. Cecilia cannot find a restaurant in Chicago.

or

Paula is having difficulty finding a hotel in Staple, New Mexico.

_____

e. The entire ski patrol was out helping people who were skidding on the icy trails. Janice also skidded and was having trouble getting up.

or

Lots of fallen skiers were along the trails. People were skiing around them. Edith slipped and joined the ranks of the fallen.

_____

f. Ben was letting his hair and beard grow for a part in a local play. He was wearing shabby old clothes, since he expected to paint sets and move equipment. When he realized he had forgotten his wallet, he decided to ask people coming out of office buildings if he could borrow change for a phone call.

or

Luke was wearing his school varsity football jacket when he realized he had left his car keys back in his locker. When he returned to the athletic building he realized that it was locked for the night. He decided to try to borrow taxi fare from some young men outside the building.

_____

You may check your choices in the Feedback section.

Developing Altruistic Attitudes

To be sure, altruistic attitudes are extremely desirable. But with fears and personal concerns, people do not always behave in the best interest of others. Psychologists have found that altruistic behavior is present in young children. One study examined the altruistic behavior of children from six countries: India, Kenya, Mexico, Japan, the Philippines, and the United States (Whiting and Edwards, 1988). American children were the least altruistic. Societies where children had family responsibilities and strong respect for their parents had the most altruistic children.

A more recent study (Oliner and Oliner, 1988) compared non-Jewish Europeans who had risked their lives to rescue Jews in the Nazi occupied countries of the 1930s and 1940s with people who did not help the Jewish people. The rescuers reported closer family relationships. Their parents behaved altruistically and stressed compassion, caring, and fairness even to strangers. Rescuers were more likely to be disciplined using reasoning and explanations rather than spankings. Their families put less emphasis on obedience, money, and self-importance.

Often people fail to behave altruistically because they simply do not know what to do. Suppose you are in a supermarket and hear a whining child. The obviously overstressed mother begins to violently beat the three-year-old. It looks like a clear case of child-abuse to you. Do you remain an "innocent bystander" or do you interfere? Criticizing the parent is risky. If the mother is already under severe strain, your opinions may further aggravate her. On the other hand the three-year-old child is helpless and needs someone to intervene. Read Feature 14-3 for some useful suggestions on what to do.

Checkpoint

Use the following questions to check your understanding of this portion of the chapter. Choose and mark the one correct response to each question.

9. What types of attitudes can you have?
   a. Positive and neutral
   b. Neutral and negative
   c. Positive and negative
   d. Positive, negative, and neutral

FEATURE 14-3 PSYCHOLOGY IN THE NEWS

What to Do

... What's the best approach for the bystander to take in public incidents of child abuse?

Part of the trouble for advice columnists and experts alike is there's no easy answer. A misstep by the witness might further endanger the child. Some out-of-control parents might need only a gentle reminder that they've gone too far; others may be hardened child abusers who've tipped their hand in public. What experts do agree on is that if the abuse is severe, if a child is being harmed or in danger, bystanders should alert the store manager or a security guard—or simply call the police.

In the more common incidents that aren't so clear-cut, neither is the solution. "We found that the most effective types of intervention tended to be comments that were helpful," says San Francisco psychologist Harrison Voigt. "Like 'Gee I see you're having a really difficult time with your child. Is there anything I can do to help?' That type of response is less likely to provoke anger because it is not a criticism. It's better than saying don't dare do that!'"

Parents Anonymous (PA), a Los Angeles-based nonprofit group that offers free support to parents who feel overwhelmed, frustrated, or inadequate, recommends bystanders avoid making negative remarks and giving bad looks. Instead it advises striking up a conversation with the adult to steer attention away from the child with comments like "My child gets upset like that too" or "Children can wear you out, can't they? Can I help?"

"When parents feel stress they do a lot of things they shouldn't be doing," says Lisa Pion-Berlin, PA's national director. "Bystanders need to try to be more supportive and not judgmental. . . . It really is detrimental to go up and say, 'Get a life. You're a horrible parent.' Everybody has been there. Parenting is a very stressful job.'"

Some parents mistreating their children can benefit from a model of good parenting. Arkansas psychologist Patricia Petretic Jackson watched a restaurant owner and waitress handle an abusive mother nicely by volunteering to hold the crying baby for her. "They said it's hard to eat when you have a baby that wants to be held," she says. "They talked about what a good boy he was. They did a nice educational intervention. Their example provided her with a better way to deal with the child. . . .'"

Source: Oldenburg, D. (1992, October 6). What to do. *The Washington Post,* B-5.

10. Bettleheim and Janowitz found that veterans who could not find satisfactory jobs after World War II were more prejudiced than veterans who were content with their jobs. What was the likely cause of prejudice?
    a. Overcrowding
    b. Economic survival
    c. Fear of the unknown
    d. Group conformity

11. Personal prejudice can result from hostility. What is the target of this hostility called?
    a. A self-fulfilling prophet
    b. A conformist
    c. An altruist
    d. A scapegoat

12. You tend to treat people unfavorably if you are prejudiced against them. As a result they often behave badly toward you. What is this interaction called?
    a. Fear of the unknown
    b. Group conformity
    c. Self-fulfilling prophecy
    d. Altruism

13. A person who has no cause for personal prejudice often has biased attitudes against a group. Which of the following could contribute to this prejudice?
    a. Group conformity
    b. Altruism
    c. The bystander effect
    d. Weather

14. Raj saw a man drop a grocery bag on the sidewalk. Raj helped him pick up the products and offered to get a new bag for the man. Which term best describes Raj's attitude?
    a. Conformity
    b. Altruism
    c. Overcrowding
    d. Competition

15. What is a bystander effect?
    a. When many people view a problem, help is likely.
    b. When many people view a problem, help is unlikely.
    c. A city atmosphere encourages helping behavior.
    d. Bystanders with high self-esteem are unlikely to help.

16. Which type of weather seems to encourage helping behavior?
    a. Clouds
    b. Rain
    c. Sunshine
    d. Snow

17. Which of the following parental behaviors is likely to lead to altruism in children?
    a. Spankings
    b. Competition for money

c. Boasting about themselves

d. Reasoning about discipline

Check your responses against the Checkpoint Answer Key at the end of the chapter. If you had difficulty with any questions, reread the text. If you had little or no difficulty answering the questions or have resolved problems that you might have had, you are ready to continue with the next portion of this chapter.

INFLUENCING AND CHANGING ATTITUDES

Whether your attitudes are good or bad (and you know they cannot be indifferent), they can be changed. Within a single day you probably shift and alter attitudes several times. Perhaps you want to go to a party but your friend prefers a movie. After your buddy provokes your interest in the film by listing the outstanding cast and discussing the intriguing plot, you become convinced the movie is a better idea. Or maybe you rarely read magazines. Your television blares an ad claiming people who read *Popularity* magazine are more successful and happier. You find yourself agreeing and calling their toll-free number to order a subscription.

Both the advertiser and your buddy were making deliberate attempts to change your attitudes. Such deliberate attempts constitute persuasion. As you probably suspect, some methods of persuasion are more effective than others. The type of person persuading you and the method being used can both influence whether or not you change your attitude.

Persuaders

The most crucial characteristic of a person who is trying to persuade others is credibility (Aronson et al., 1963). You must be able to trust the person and believe statements if you are to change your attitude. To be sure, an expert in a field has credibility. When Stefie Graf claims a brand of tennis shoes is durable and comfortable, she will be believable. Likewise, if a famous doctor recommends a particular brand of medication, he will be convincing.

Attractive people usually have more credibility than unattractive people. You may have noticed that magazine ads often show attractive men and women with products. Frequently the alluring people have nothing to do with the product. Their presence is expected to give the ad credibility. A study reported by Pecoraro (1981) concluded that jurors are more likely to believe attractive people who are either defendants or victims.

Even people who are neither experts nor overwhelmingly attractive will be believed if they are famous or well-known. You are more likely to be convinced by a statement from someone with a familiar face than one from someone you have never seen before. You are also more likely to vote for a name you have heard. As a result, before an election, bumper stickers and posters with candidates' names are everywhere.

Have you ever noticed how famous people and experts seem down-to-earth in television advertisements? Several studies have shown you are more likely to be persuaded by a person who you believe is much like yourself. A person who is similar to you is more convincing. Because advertisers are attempting to appeal to average television viewers, a single ad may have several different types of people endorsing a product. A bar of soap will be proclaimed "terrific" by a toddler, a teenager, a working man, a homemaker, a career woman, and a senior citizen.

Persuasion is most effective when a listener thinks the speaker has nothing to gain from the attitude change. If a car dealer raves about the car she sells, you might be skeptical. Clearly, she will profit if you buy one of her cars. However, if a woman who is not in the automobile business recommends a type of car, you are more likely to believe her. Walster and Festinger (1962) found that messages that are overheard are more convincing than ones spoken directly to you. When you overhear a conversation, you assume the message is not being directed at you. Thus, the person is not really trying to convince you. Commercials that show people who are supposedly unaware of the cameras are aimed at convincing viewers that they are witnessing and overhearing an actual conversation.

Exercise 14-11

List five characteristics that would make a person a successful persuader.

a. _____

b. _____

c. _____

d. _____

e. _____

You may compare your list to the answers in the Feedback section.

Persuasion Techniques

Suppose you wanted to convince people to sign up for a course in applied psychology. As a first step you could attempt to combine the characteristics of a successful persuader. You might have a famous, attractive, down-to-earth psychologist whisper loudly that applied psychology courses are super. But you may also want to consider some other strategies. As you are aware, people have reasons for not taking courses: insufficient time and money, work pressures, and other responsibilities. Should the psychologists present the opposite side of the argument as well? Research has shown that if the audience is well-informed and intelligent, its members are more likely to be persuaded if they hear a two-sided argument. If the audience is clearly opposed to a view, discussing their view first helps. For example, your famous psychologist may begin, "I know most of you have many personal pressures and responsibilities and that money is tight. But if at all possible, you really would benefit from an applied psychology course. The course can actually help you reduce pressures and be more successful. Why I know one student who. . . ." The many arguments in favor of the course could then be presented. The psychologist shot down the opposing argument before presenting the case. Research shows that an audience that is leaning toward you may not need to hear the opposing view. Also, people of limited intelligence can become confused by a lengthy two-sided argument.

Psychologists and advertisers have discovered a number of specific techniques that effectively persuade people.

Emotional Appeals. Television commercials often use emotional appeals. Some ads scare you into buying products, others make you feel homey, still others promise you popularity. Janis and Feshback (1953) experimented on the effects of scare tactics in changing attitudes. They divided subjects into two groups. The first group was given some mildly upsetting information. They were presented statistics on the relationship between poor oral hygiene and dental and gum problems. The second group was given more threatening and fear-arousing information. They were shown actual photographs of decayed teeth and diseased gums. Subjects in the first group improved their dental hygiene habits more than the people in the second group did. The experimenters concluded that weak or moderate fear is more effective in changing attitudes than are intense threats. No doubt you can recognize some mildly fearful ads. Commercials for deodorants, soaps, mouthwash, denture adhesive, tires, and batteries usually begin with someone suffering rejection or facing a problem.

Other emotional appeals have been pleasant. Products are sometimes associated with a warm, loving, old-fashioned, homey atmosphere. Recall commercials that refer to products that grandmother wanted to use. Whether cookies, bread, fruit punch, or spaghetti sauce, the product that can be linked to a family in the olden days has added appeal. Indeed, sales will no doubt increase if grandmother endorses a product as tasting "homemade."

Another common emotional appeal is to a need for popularity. If you use a softener in your washing machine, everyone will thank you and appreciate you. This type of ad also insinuates that fabric softeners are important. Or an ad might give the impression you would gain popularity by looking sexier in a certain brand of jeans. Then again, according to the ads, wearing the right perfume and purchasing the correct brand of sherry will also win intimate friendships.

Dissonance. Changing attitudes through *dissonance* was suggested by Festinger (1962). Festinger held that if you do the opposite of what you believe, you will become uncomfortable and tense. As a result of your tension, you will change your attitude. For example, suppose that you always believed that people who collect insects are rather strange. You find that an insect collection is required in your biology class. You spend several months collecting crawling creatures and pinning them in an old box. Festinger claims that if you continue to behave in a way that is the opposite of your attitude, you will create a dissonance. Chances are you will change your attitude about insect collectors and recognize that there may be some reason and merits to their work.

Acknowledging that your own behavior does not comply with your atti-

dissonance Discomfort that occurs from two inconsistent thoughts or beliefs tude is an important part of creating dissonance. As described in Feature 14-4, students who spoke on AIDS prevention and admitted that they had neglected to use condoms in the past were more likely to use condoms in the future.

McGuire (1961), using analogies, found that people who agreed with logic in one situation would transfer the same reasoning to another situation. Dissonance and attitude change would result. Advertisers have capitalized on the method. The commercial may begin with the statement that engines need oil or they will dry out and age prematurely. You are nodding your head in agreement. Next a picture of human skin is flashed. The ad continues warning you that skin that is not fed oil will also dry out and age. Even if you had not been keen on skin preparations, the motor analogy created a dissonance and there is a chance you will purchase the product.

In one instance, the analogy-dissonance method was used to improve relationships between normal children and handicapped children. In trying to bring handicapped children into the mainstream of public schools, leaders found that normal children were fearful of the handicapped and had negative attitudes about them. A Washington, D.C. group began giving puppet shows about the handicapped. Each puppet represented a person with a different disability. One puppet was in a wheelchair, another was retarded, and another was missing limbs. The children were encouraged to converse with the puppets and ask questions. Organizers of the shows found that normal children showed

FEATURE 14-4 PSYCHOLOGY IN THE NEWS

Practice What You Preach

Preliminary data suggest that an enlightened focus on hypocrisy fosters condom use and AIDS awareness among sexually active young adults. AIDS education campaigns in schools might profit by holding discussions in which each student first tries to persuade others of the need for sexual safety precautions and then acknowledges his or her own past failures in that regard, asserts a team led by psychologist Elliot Aronson of the University of California, Santa Cruz.

Well-intended information about AIDS typically elicits fear from young adults, who then deny the threat rather than change their sexual behavior. . . . This denial also stems from the widespread belief that condoms wreck the romance and spontaneity of sex, they say.

The scientists recruited 40 female and 40 male sexually active college students. Half composed speeches advocating condom use, based on a fact sheet about AIDS, and delivered their talk in front of a television camera. An experimenter told them

an AIDS prevention program would use the tape. Researchers began the exercise by asking half of these 40 volunteers to describe recent situations in which they failed to use condoms, thereby creating a sense of hypocrisy.

The remaining students composed pro-condom speeches from the fact sheet but only rehearsed them silently. Again, half of this group first told of their recent failures to use condoms.

After the exercise, the 40 students who revealed their hypocrisy—particularly those who gave a taped speech—reported more past failures to use condoms than the other 40 and a greater willingness to use them in the future. Among 39 participants contacted three months later, the 12 who taped the message in the hypocrisy condition reported significantly more condom use since the experiment.

Source: (1992, January 18). Practice what you preach. *Science News*, 44.

marked changes in attitudes after chatting with puppets. The analogy was made between the puppets and live children.

Foot-in-the-Door Tactics. Everyone is familiar with the image of a traveling salesman sticking his foot in a doorway so the person cannot close the door. The salesman's method is obvious. Psychologists have discovered several subtle ways to achieve the same purpose. A salesperson can get you to agree on a number of unrelated things. Maybe the weather is getting colder, the cost of gasoline is increasing, skiing is a wonderful sport, or Hawaii is a beautiful vacation spot. Since you are in agreement on so many issues, you begin to feel that you both think alike. Next the salesperson pulls out a contract and gets you to agree to make a purchase.

Freedman and Fraser (1966) suggested that requests can be used similarly. A salesperson begins by making small requests such as, "Could I have just two or three minutes of your time?" "Would you take a second and look at this folder?" "May I ask you a few questions?" After you have been continually agreeing and complying, you are asked to sign a contract for a purchase.

Recently, psychologists have worked as court consultants for lawyers. They help lawyers construct strong opening statements that will set a framework. This helps lawyers get a foot in the door as they slide in their evidence.

Negative Psychology. Have you ever been irritated by a high-pressure salesperson? Brehm (1966) claimed that if you get high-pressure treatment you will resist and try to assert your freedom and independence. He labeled this resistance and assertiveness *reactance*. When salespeople suspect reactance, they often use negative psychology. A woman selling small economy cars might ask people browsing in the showroom, "Have you ever felt they are putting too much emphasis on economy in cars?" or "You probably are not concerned about mileage." Knowing that most people are plagued with high-pressure sales pitches in junk mail, a home-improvement advertiser might realize they will read the first sentence of a flier and assert their independence by tossing it in the trash. Therefore, use of a negative approach would be a more effective weapon against their reactance. The letter might begin, "If you are wealthy and don't mind wasting thousands of dollars each year on home repairs, don't read any further."

reactance Strong resistance that results from receiving high-pressure persuasion and often causes a person to do the opposite of what is asked

Group Pressure. Just as groups can pressure you into prejudiced attitudes, they can change and influence your other attitudes each day. Groups and peers reinforce you when you conform. Bob Sober may prefer to go home directly after work. His coworkers chide him about being henpecked and suggest he join them for a few beers or shooters after work. When he shows up, they cheer and buy him drinks. As mentioned in the previous section of this chapter, adolescents are more susceptible to group pressure than any other age category.

Implications. Whether intentional or not, many advertisements are misleading. Advertisers frequently use implications rather than facts. Implications avoid giving specific information. For example, the advertiser may claim a product "may help eliminate colds" or "fights blemishes." If you still have a

FRANK & ERNEST® by Bob Thaves

FIGURE 14-5. Confusing implications and assertions can be costly.

cold and blemishes after careful use of the products, you cannot complain to the advertisers. The products may have been helping your cold and fighting your blemishes, but without success.

Implications are often incomplete sentences. A claim may state "Cure-yourills gives more relief." More relief than what? Or you may hear a claim, "Cleanup gives 30 percent more suds." More than what? Again the comparison is unclear. Perhaps it makes more suds than motor oil does. Harris (1977) compared college students' reactions to asserted and implied claims in ads. The students heard phony tape-recorded commercials that either made an assertion (a definite statement) or an implied claim. Students were then given test sentences and asked to mark them true or false. Feature 14-5 gives examples of an assertion, an implication, and a test sentence. There was no significant difference in the responses of students who heard implications and those who heard assertions: Students who heard implied statements were just as likely to mark the test sentence true. Harris also found that people who heard implied statements tended to remember the implications as facts.

Exercise 14-12

Read each of the following examples of persuasion attempts. Indicate the persuasive technique or techniques being used: emotional appeal, dissonance, foot-in-the-door, negative psychology, group pressure, or implication.

FEATURE 14-5 PSYCHOLOGY IN THE NEWS

Assertions and Implications

Assertion: "In a survey of 500 doctors, over half reported that they recommended Knockout Capsules."

Implication: "In a survey of 500 doctors, over half reported that they recommended the ingredients in Knockout Capsules."

Test Sentence: (Answer true or false) "A majority of doctors in a survey recommended Knockout Capsules."

Source: Harris, R. J. (1977). Comprehension of pragmatic implications in advertising. *Journal of Applied Psychology, 62,* 603–608.

a. Oscar is serving jury duty. It is 3 A.M. and the rest of the jury is convinced the defendant is guilty. Oscar still thinks she may be innocent. Everyone wants to go home. Jury members are yawning and ignoring Oscar's statements.

---

b. Mrs. Cash answers the telephone. The caller announces, "If you can answer this question, you can win a valuable prize. The question is, 'What color is a lemon?' " Mrs. Cash answers correctly. The caller then requests her name, occupation, salary, and the types of encyclopedias in her home. He then offers her, as a prize, a set of encyclopedias for only $850.

---

c. A radio ad begins, "Do you remember the lovely sweet smell of your grandmother's hands and the softness of her touch? For centuries family women have used Roses-in-Springtime hand cream. You too can prove you are a family woman! Roses-in-Springtime cream is twice as effective and lasts longer."

---

d. Mr. Charity is trying to collect money for the Society for the Preservation of Old Timepieces. He meets his friend Sam and announces, "Sam, you probably don't care much about history and changes that have taken place. Remember that lovely old Victorian mansion that was torn down to make way for a high-rise apartment building? And how some people were all worked up about destroying the past. People just get themselves in a panic. They're afraid to live in a crowded world of concrete. I'll bet you don't mind seeing the past crumble. So I won't even bother to ask you for a small donation to preserve old watches and clocks."

You may check your answers in the Feedback section.

Propaganda and Brainwashing

If you are aware of the persuasion techniques that can be used, you will not be as susceptible to advertisements. Often advertisers intentionally mislead the public with emotional appeals, incorrect analogies, and implications. Information that is deliberately deceptive or erroneous is called *propaganda*. Propaganda is usually associated with institutions and governments, but is also used by advertisers who deliberately distort facts for selfish purposes; they are spreading propaganda.

A particularly vicious and dangerous use of propaganda is involved in *brainwashing*, a technique sometimes used by governments and religious cults. Schein et al. (1961) pointed out the method used. First a person is isolated so that old attitudes and beliefs will not be supported. The person is dependent on the attitude changers for food, drink, sleep, facilities, and other basic needs.

propaganda Information that is deliberately deceptive or erroneous

brainwashing Dangerous technique used in spreading propaganda

Lacking sleep and food, the victim feels helpless. The propaganda program begins when the person is exhausted. Rewards of food, privileges, and praise are given when the victim cooperates and changes toward the desired attitude. Perhaps the most disastrous results of brainwashing occurred in Jonestown in 1978 and Waco in 1993.

Checkpoint

Use the following questions to check your understanding of this portion of the chapter. Indicate whether each statement is true or false.

18. _____ Persuasion is a deliberate attempt to change an attitude.

19. _____ Unattractive people are more successful at persuasion than attractive people are.

20. _____ Overheard conversations are more effective in changing attitudes than direct messages are.

21. _____ Two-sided arguments are most effective on intelligent and informed people.

22. _____ It is best to use only a one-sided argument if an audience seems to share your views.

23. _____ An advertiser who warns that perspiration odor can cause unpopularity is using a foot-in-the-door technique.

24. _____ Presenting intensely frightening information is the most effective method for changing attitudes.

25. _____ Dissonance occurs when your behavior is different from your attitude.

26. _____ Salespersons who have you agree with them on a number of unrelated matters are using dissonance.

27. _____ Reactance often occurs after a high-pressure sales pitch.

28. _____ Negative psychology is a method of dealing with reactance.

29. _____ Studies have shown that people clearly differentiate between assertions and implied statements in advertisements.

30. _____ "Seventy percent of children prefer Chewy chewing gum" is an example of an assertion.

31. _____ Propaganda is a deliberate attempt to change attitudes with false or deceptive information.

32. _____ Brainwashing is often used by advertisers.

Check your responses against the Checkpoint Answer Key at the end of the chapter. If you had difficulty with any question, reread the text. If you had little or no difficulty answering the questions or have resolved problems that you might have had, you are ready to check yourself against the chapter inventory that follows.

Use this list of objectives as a review checklist. You should be able to do the tasks outlined in the objectives and apply them to everyday examples. If you can, you may feel confident that you have mastered the material in this chapter.

1. Define and differentiate among the terms "attitude," "prejudice," and "discrimination."
2. Specify three components of attitudes.
3. Define sexism, racism, and homophobia and provide examples of each.
4. Provide examples of three causes of discrimination.
5. Identify three ways to reduce unfair bias.
6. Explain how attitudes develop.
7. Describe the role of first impressions.
8. List two general causes of prejudice.
9. Describe four personal concerns that can cause prejudice.
10. Define altruism and explain six factors that influence helping behavior.
11. Identify parental factors that help children develop altruistic attitudes, and describe effective altruism for child abuse.
12. Define persuasion and outline five characteristics of effective persuaders.
13. Compare usefulness of one-sided and two-sided arguments in persuasion.
14. List and provide examples of six persuasion techniques.
15. Define and describe the applications of propaganda.
16. Outline the technique used in brainwashing.

Feedback

The correct answers to the exercises follow. If you did not answer an exercise correctly, review the preceding pages and return to the exercise to correctly complete it.

14-1. a. Beliefs: Adele values freedom and independence and has developed the belief that women should be permitted to decide whether or not they want abortions.
   b. Emotions: Adele must have had some feelings about the issue or she would not have begun arguing. Bursting into tears gives further evidence of her emotional involvement. Finally, her anger about the lack of support from other women is a clear indication that emotions accompany her opinions.
   c. Behavior: Adele's arguing and crying were both outward behaviors that resulted from her attitude toward abortion.

14-2. A prejudice is a type of attitude. Prejudice is based on a belief that is either not supported by facts or is contrary to facts. Prejudice is accompanied by negative emotions, whereas other attitudes can bring on either positive or negative feelings.

14-3. a. Reverse discrimination
   b. Fair distinctions
   c. Prejudiced attitudes
   d. Prejudiced attitudes

14-4. They may not be aware of their feelings, or they may be ashamed to admit their prejudices.

14-5. a. Mindful discrimination
   b. Jigsaw classroom
   c. Reverse discrimination

14-6. Parental influence on attitudes tends to lessen after adolescence. Possibly their sons attended liberal schools or had friends who had liberal attitudes. Peers have the strongest influence on attitude formation from adolescence on.

14-7. a. Overcrowding
   b. Fear of the unknown
   c. Conflict and competition
   d. Fear of the unknown
   e. Economic survival

14-8. a. Prejudice provides a scapegoat for anger and hostility and helps a person feel superior.
   b. Through self-fulfilling prophecy aspect of prejudice, prejudiced person becomes convinced of correctness.

14-9. Although individual students may be open-minded about admitting women, their attitudes may change when they vote with a group. After graduating, male students become part of a new group—the alumni. The alumni club members have traditionally been males, and group members tend to conform.

14-10. a. Mitch: The bystander effect suggests that the more people who witness a problem, the less likely anyone will help.
   b. Gertrude: People with high self-esteem are more likely to be altruistic. (A class officer and star athlete probably has higher self-esteem than a depressed person.)
   c. Edward: People are more willing to help on sunny days.
   d. Paula: People in the country tend to be friendlier and more helpful than people in a city.
   e. Janice: People who have witnessed someone else being helpful are more likely to offer assistance themselves.
   f. Luke: People are more likely to help someone who is dressed similarly to them.

14-11. a. Being an expert
   b. Being attractive
   c. Being famous or familiar
   d. Acting down-to-earth
   e. Speaking to someone else and being overheard

14-12. a. Group pressure
   b. Foot-in-the-door
   c. Emotional appeal and implication
   d. Negative psychology and dissonance

Checkpoint Answer Key

1. c; 2. b; 3. a; 4. a; 5. a; 6. c; 7. a; 8. d; 9. c; 10. b; 11. d; 12. c; 13. a; 14. b; 15. b; 16. c; 17. d; 18. true; 19. false; 20. true; 21. true; 22. true; 23. false; 24. false; 25. true; 26. false; 27. true; 28. true; 29. false; 30. false; 31. true; 32. false.

Working with Groups

There are two ways of spreading light: to be
The candle or the mirror that reflects it.
—EDITH WHARTON

Suppose you were chosen to work on a committee to select street names and street signs for a small-town community. The community is tightly knit, but committee members clash over the types of signs and street names that would be most suitable. Some want to retain the pastoral atmosphere, with wooden signposts and names like Meadow Lane. Others prefer to modernize, with numbered streets and iridescent signs that will be visible at night. Within the committee, some people are leaning toward iridescent signs with pastoral names, while others prefer wooden posts with numbered streets. All seem rigid and unbending in their opinions.

What would you do to help the group agree? Think about how you usually behave in groups. Perhaps you like to generate new ideas, or maybe you just prefer to make jokes and help release tension. Within most groups there are both leaders and followers. If you tend to organize people's ideas and make suggestions about assignments, you are taking a leadership role. If you would rather do routine jobs and carry out orders carefully, you are clearly a follower. As you will learn in this chapter, whether one is a leader or follower usually depends on the situation and the task set before a group. You may be a great leader in a group planning a fund-raiser for AIDS research, but your leadership qualities are not turned on by signposts for a small town.

In this chapter you will study the nature of leadership along with interactions and behaviors within groups. You will begin by considering the nature of groups and their goals. Some goals help groups stick together, while others seem to break up friendships and cause hostility. Next you will study factors that either aid or inhibit the productivity of groups. Finally you will examine leadership. Two possible types of leadership emphasis are discussed. The techniques used by leaders are related to the types of assumptions they can make. A brief summary on the pros and cons of groups closes the chapter.

THE NATURE OF GROUPS

group Two or more people who interact or are aware of each other and share a common goal

Two or more people who interact or are aware of each other are a *group.* Usually, group members have a common goal. The students in your class probably share a goal of passing the course. Theatergoers standing in line all want to be admitted to the theater. A congregation gathered in a church probably is hoping for inspiration or a religious experience. Even people riding a bus form a group. Whether or not they interact, they are aware of each other and share a goal of being transported.

Clearly, every person must interact with groups. People need and rely on each other constantly. Some groups are formal and establish rules. Political parties and organizations such as the League of Women Voters, the United Fund, taxpayers' associations, and labor unions are established for specific purposes. However, there are far more informal groups: your family, friends, coworkers, and any people you see, hear, or interact with during the course of a day.

Some groups have leaders, while others do not. To be sure, audiences, crowds shopping, or people waiting for a train do not need a leader. But, orchestras, classes of students, and governments generally like to have someone in charge. Whether or not they have leaders, groups are dynamic; that is, they are constantly changing. As people interact with others, they change their attitudes and behaviors.

Exercise 15-1

Indicate which of the following are examples of groups.

a. _____ Two men are reupholstering a sofa.

b. _____ A mother is helping her two daughters with their homework.

c. _____ Three hundred people are watching a high school basketball game.

d. _____ A man is making phone calls to solicit money for a cancer fund.

e. _____ Five women are collecting trash to clean up a neighborhood.

f. _____ Two students are completing their project in a biology laboratory.

g. _____ Ten youngsters are practicing teamwork in soccer.

Please check your answers in the Feedback section.

Group Norms

Group norms are rules of behavior. The norm for a group of passengers in an elevator is to face the door without making eye contact or conversing with other passengers. Although there is no written rule, this is the proper way to behave in an elevator. If you faced the rear wall of the elevator and introduced yourself to each passenger, you would be breaking an informal, unwritten rule. There are many informal group norms. Hairstyles, clothing selection, and how and where to eat are usually not written but are rules that group members keep. Can you imagine combing your hair over your face, wearing pajamas, and facing your chair away from the table at a restaurant!

Some group norms are written and formalized. Laws, traffic regulations, and community housing restrictions are examples of written norms. Newly formed groups often want to be certain that members understand their purpose and rules. Many hours are spent drafting a constitution or bylaws to provide a formal set of group norms. The bylaws may require members to wear funny hats, give unusual handshakes, or attend social functions.

If people want to continue as members of the group, they must accept and adhere to the norms, whether written or unwritten. Most likely, you are unaware of the many norms you comply with. You may have one group of friends that likes to study, another that is critical, and still another that jokes. In all probability, you study with the first group, criticize with the second, and clown with the third.

When you first join a group, you are usually uncertain of their norms. You want to be included but feel ill at ease because you have not determined the accepted behavior. New members usually initially appear quiet and aloof. In reality they are sizing up the group and trying to decipher the norms. Groups are accepting of people who adhere to their norms and tend to reject people who disregard those norms.

group norms Rules of behavior for two or more people

"Could you walk a little faster, buddy? This is New York."

FIGURE 15-1. New York must have a group norm for walking pace.

447

With the recent increase in international businesses, air travel, tourism, immigration, and international students, there has been a growing concern about how people can best adjust to the norms of new cultures. As described in Chapter 13, people of differing cultures require unequal amounts of personal space for comfortable communication. In addition, the cultural norms may also have different requirements for punctuality and schedules. For example northern European and Japanese cultures require a faster pace and more precise timing than do the relaxed norms of Latin American and Mediterranean countries. Read the article in Feature 15-1 for a description of how differences in cultural norms can present personal problems.

Exercise 15-2

Observe the informal norms of the group in the courtroom (Figure 15-2). What might Mr. Scrooge do to be accepted by the group and have a fair trial?

_____

_____

_____

Please check your answer in the Feedback section.

Group Goals

cooperative goal
Objective that a group works together to achieve

Groups can have *cooperative goals* or competitive goals. Imagine that your psychology instructor has directed your class to work on a project together. The instructor plans to judge the completed project and decide whether the entire class should receive A, B, C, D, or F for their efforts. The class will be working together toward the same goal: developing an excellent project. Each person will have some responsibility in reaching the group goal. To be successful, class members must cooperate with each other. The instructor has established a cooperative goal for the class.

competitive goal
Objective that people in a group work against each other to achieve

Now suppose your psychology instructor wanted to set a *competitive goal* for the group. The instructor might announce an individual test and state that only one person in the class would receive an A grade. There would be two B's, three C's, and four D's; everyone else would fail. Everyone has the same goal: to receive an A on the test. However, each person hopes that others will be unsuccessful. In a competitive setting, each person's success results in someone else's failure. Only one person will receive the A.

When a group has a cooperative goal, people work together. When the goal is competitive, people work against one another. Crombag (1966) found that cooperative groups have better communication and their members are friendlier to each other. Deutsch (1968) found that cooperative groups were also more productive and generated better results. Cooperative-group members contributed more diverse ideas, felt more pressure to achieve, and were more concerned about other members. Rivalry and opposition prevented members of competitive groups from exchanging ideas. However, competition is not without some benefits. It can create challenges, diminish boredom, and add interest.

The Productive American

Peter Reed is a computer software specialist who had developed a good reputation as a programmer in the United States. His specialties were data management for hospitals and computer-assisted diagnosis. Seeking new challenges, he accepted an appointment as a software specialist in his company's branch office in Tokyo. In his own country Peter had a reputation as a very productive programmer, and part of his preferred work style involved working on a number of different projects at the same time. If there was a stumbling block in one project, Peter often found that he could clear his mind by working on one or even two other projects. His mind refreshed, he could then return to the original project with a fresh outlook and a range of potential solutions to problems. Managers in the American branch encouraged his work style since they saw that Peter was very productive when allowed to work in his own preferred manner. The American managers were also very tolerant when Peter (and other productive workers) deviated from written policy in such activities as lateness to work, lunch hours that extended beyond 60 minutes, number of work breaks during the day, and so forth. As long as the employees were productive, rules were loosely enforced.

Peter arrived in Tokyo and met his immediate supervisor, Mr. Hirumi Watanabe. The relationship between the two started out well since Mr. Watanabe recognized Peter's abilities and the quality of his work. After about three months, however, tensions began to arise. Peter enjoyed going off by himself when faced with a difficult problem, sometimes sequestering himself in the company library and forgoing lunch with his coworkers. When he did have lunch with coworkers, he was surprised that males usually ate with males, and the females in the company with other females. Accustomed to more integration of males and females in his own country, he would sometimes ask females to join his lunch group, but his invitations were received with obvious discomfort. When he was late coming back from lunch or late coming to work, Mr. Watanabe reacted negatively. At first, negative reactions consisted of frowns. Finally, Mr. Watanabe had to ask Peter to be more careful about observing company policy. Mr. Watanabe was also frustrated at Peter's habit of working on different projects at the same time and not giving enough attention to the one that he (Watanabe) considered the most important. Mr. Watanabe did not seem to appreciate Peter's preferred style in which working on a second and third project would eventually solve difficulties encountered in the first and highest-priority project. It was clear to everyone who knew of Peter's work that he was one of the most productive workers in the company. He was clearly not abrasive, or unpleasant, and he clearly enjoyed interacting with his Japanese coworkers. Yet he was unhappy in his assignment, and Mr. Watanabe was not pleased with Peter's contributions. Peter recognized that he was unhappy, and that he was not getting along very well with Mr. Watanabe, but he was unable to "put his finger on" the reasons for the difficulties. Eventually, Peter was forced to consider changing companies. What are the reasons, all involving cultural differences, for Peter's difficulties?

Source: Brislin, R. (1992). The productive American. *Understanding culture's influence on behavior.* Fort Worth, Tex.: Harcourt Brace Jovanovich.

No doubt you can think of many examples of cooperative and competitive goals. A campaign committee working to have their candidate elected has a cooperative goal. However, three candidates for the same office have a competitive goal. Teams present an example of both cooperative and competitive goals. Team members must cooperate among themselves but compete with other teams. For example, the Dallas Cowboys must cooperate to understand strategies and carry out plays. However, they clearly are competing when they play the Washington Redskins or the Philadelphia Eagles!

FIGURE 15-2.

How can competitive teams be prompted to cooperate with each other? To be sure, there would be no fun and no advantage to cooperation between the Cowboys and the Redskins or the Yankees and the Red Sox. But cooperation among competing nations could reduce the likelihood of wars and save lives. There are clear advantages to reducing competition and hostility in some situations.

Sherif et al. (1961) studied cooperative and competitive goals among groups of twelve-year-old boys. They divided the boys into two groups. Each group was sent to its own boy scout summer camp. The camps were actually operated by psychology experimenters. The psychologists selected counselors to observe and report on the boys. The experiment had three phases.

Soccer teams use both cooperative and competitive goals. Each team must work together to beat the opposing team.

Phase 1: Cooperative Goal Development within Groups. During the initial phase the experimenters suggested activities with a common cooperative goal for each group. The boys worked cooperatively at their own camps, fixing up swimming holes and building bridges. One group called themselves the Rattlers, the other the Eagles. within each group the boys became friendly with each other and felt a spirit of belonging together.

Phase 2: Competitive Goal Development between Groups. Next the experimenters arranged conflicts between the Eagles and the Rattlers. Sports competitions such as baseball games and tugs-of-war were scheduled. As expected, a strong sense of competition developed between the two groups. Hostilities led to name calling and arguments.

Phase 3: Cooperative Goal Development between Groups. In the final stage of the experiment the psychologists attempted to reduce the hostility between the Rattlers and the Eagles. They brought the two groups together for meals, but this did not work. The groups remained hostile. Next they found a common enemy for the two groups, namely, a neighboring camp. Although the common enemy brought the groups closer, hostility still remained. Finally the experimenters had the two groups work together for a

451

common goal on ventures similar to the tasks in phase 1. They arranged for a truck to break down at the bottom of a hill. The strength of both groups was needed to push the truck back up the hill. As a result of the cooperative activities, the boys from the two groups became closer to each other and hostility was reduced significantly.

Working toward a common goal is usually the best method to reduce hostility between groups. People realize they need each other to achieve their goal. The result is cooperation, better communication, and a friendlier attitude.

You may be wondering whether working on cooperative goals could be used to reduce tensions in multicultural schools. Johnson and Johnson (1987) reported that cooperative classroom situations clearly promoted interracial friendships. And as an added bonus, cooperative education also increased student achievement (Slavin, 1989).

Exercise 15-3

Imagine that a community has two local high schools. The two schools are openly competitive in both academics and sports. Recently their hostility toward each other has resulted in name calling, crank phone calls, and vandalism. You have been asked to help remedy the hostility. From what you learned about Sherif's experiment with the two boy scout camps, describe one technique that might help reduce the hostility.

_____

_____

_____

_____

Please turn to the Feedback section to check your answer.

Cohesiveness

cohesiveness Ability to stick together in a group

The _cohesiveness_ of a group is its closeness or ability to stick together. Highly cohesive groups have a sense of identity. Their members stick close together, are loyal, and help each other. Shaw (1971) reported that people in cohesive groups are more likely to attend meetings and take an active role. They feel emotionally involved in the group, delight in group successes, and are upset by failures. The morale of cohesive groups is higher.

As you might have suspected, groups with cooperative goals are more cohesive than groups with competitive goals. Cohesiveness is further improved if the goals are precisely defined. Groups with clearly established norms also are more likely to be cohesive. Since members have an understanding of their expected behavior, they are more likely to participate.

Cohesiveness is desirable; it keeps a group together. Groups with low cohesiveness have difficulty with attendance at meetings. Members do not show up. If they do attend, they are often bored and fail to interact with each other.

Checkpoint

Use the following questions to check your understanding of this portion of the chapter. Choose and mark the one correct response to each question.

1. How many people are required to form a group?
   a. At least one
   b. At least two
   c. At least three
   d. At least five

2. Which of the following is an example of a formal group?
   a. A family of four
   b. Five friends at a cafeteria table
   c. A political committee of twenty
   d. Thirty people riding a public bus

3. Why are groups described as dynamic?
   a. They rarely have leaders.
   b. They are usually informal.
   c. They are usually competitive.
   d. They are constantly changing.

4. Why are new members of groups often quiet?
   a. Formal group norms do not permit them to speak.
   b. New members are learning both formal and informal norms.
   c. New members are usually more competitive than older members.
   d. New members are usually more cooperative than older members.

5. Courier and Becker are playing for a singles tennis championship. How would you describe their goal?
   a. Cooperative
   b. Competitive
   c. Team
   d. Both cooperative and competitive

6. A group of competing wrestlers often quarrel and act hostile toward one another. Which of the following would best reduce their hostility?
   a. Spending more time together
   b. Competing with each other
   c. Finding a common enemy
   d. Working cooperatively on a job

7. Which of the following is characteristic of cohesive groups?
   a. Loyalty
   b. Competition
   c. Aloofness
   d. Poor attendance

Use the Checkpoint Answer Key at the end of the chapter to verify your responses. If you had any difficulty with a question, carefully reread the text. If you had little or no difficulty answering the questions or have resolved any problems that you might have had, you are ready to continue with the next portion of this chapter.

Groups have clear advantages over individuals working alone. Information from individuals can be pooled, and insights can be gained from other members. In solving problems, groups make fewer errors than do individuals. However, groups are not without limitations. A key disadvantage to groups is time. Although they are more accurate, groups take longer to solve problems and complete tasks.

The size of the group is an important factor in productivity. Research on small groups has concluded that five is an ideal size. Larger groups tend to become cumbersome and divide into factions. Also, quiet people are less likely to talk in a large group. Berelson and Steiner (1964) noted that groups with an odd number of members are more efficient than groups with an even number of members. Groups of four, six, or eight members are not as efficient as groups of five or seven. Psychologists have concluded that one reason five is ideal is that a minority of two people will feel free to discuss their opinions. Since only three form a majority, the majority does not overpower the rest of the group.

Time constraints can also help group productivity. Rice (1981) reported that groups that claim they need overtime are usually less efficient during regular hours. If groups are given realistic time limits, they can be more productive.

A number of other factors also influence the productivity of groups. Too much conformity and obedience can stifle new or original ideas. People in groups often give up their own beliefs to comply with others, even when they feel certain they are right. Similarly, people will obey rules and strong authorities against their own consciences.

Conformity

Suppose you walk up to join a line for a movie. There are about thirty people in the line, all facing the wrong way. Their backs are to the theater and cashier. What would you do? Would you go along with the group, or would you assert your independence by facing the usual direction?

To be sure, you would have some serious questions about why the group was facing the wrong way. But even if you thought the group was mistaken, you would probably go along with them rather than appear different. However, the next time you lined up for a movie, you would revert back to your normal behavior and face the cashier.

Conformity and Compliance

conformity Accepting the beliefs of a group and behaving accordingly

compliance Publicly behaving in accordance with a group while privately disagreeing with their beliefs

Psychologists distinguish between compliance and conformity. Kelman (1958) explained that *conformity* requires people to accept the information and beliefs of a group. Because they accept the beliefs of the group, their behavior changes. However, sometimes people will change their behavior publicly to go along with a group but privately maintain their own beliefs. They are demonstrating compliance. *Compliance* implies that the person is following the conventions of the group either for approval or to avoid embarrassment.

FIGURE 15-3.

The most famous research on social pressure and compliance was performed by Asch (1956). Asch told subjects they were participating in an experiment on perception. Groups of seven students sat in a semicircle around an easel. For each trial, two large cards were presented on the easel. One card contained a standard line. The other card contained three lines, only one of which was equal to the standard (see Figure 15-4). Students were instructed to name the line that was equal to the standard.

Although there were seven students in each group, only one was actually a subject. The other six were confederates, that is, persons helping the experimenter. They had been instructed to agree unanimously on correct and incorrect choices. The one genuine subject answered last and believed that the six confederates were also subjects. The confederates answered correctly for the first few trials. Naturally, the subject agreed. But then the confederates began to agree on incorrect responses. The subject was in an awkward position. The correct answer seemed obvious; the subject had to decide whether to go along with the group or to stick with the correct response. Fully 37 percent of the subjects yielded to group pressure and gave incorrect responses.

After the experiment, compliant subjects were interviewed. They stated that they knew their responses were incorrect. They complied with the group so they would not look different. They could not believe that everyone else was wrong and that they were the only ones who could see the correct answers.

Factors Affecting Conformity and Compliance

Why did some people refuse to go along with the incorrect responses of the group? Psychologists believe that group conformity and compliance are related to self-esteem. People with high self-esteem are less likely to follow a group when they believe the group is wrong. People with lower self-esteem are less sure of themselves. As a result, they are more likely to conform to pressure.

Overcrowded prisons provide an example of conformity to negative behavior (Footlick, 1981). Since many inmates were imprisoned for violent be-

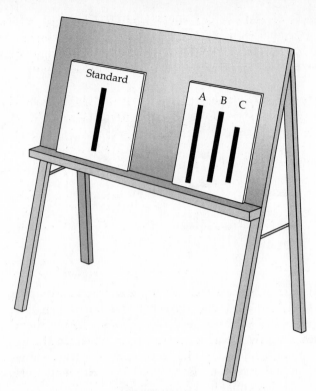

FIGURE 15-4.

havior, assaults, rape, and other violence become the norm. Persons jailed for nonviolent crimes sometimes become hardened criminals after a single jail sentence. As you might suspect, inmates at penitentiaries tend to have low self-esteem.

In addition to the self-esteem of the person being pressured by the group, certain conditions and characteristics of the group can affect the tendency to conform.

Size of the Group. Gerard et al. (1968) found that the likelihood of conformity increases rapidly as the size of the group approaches five members, then increases at a slower pace as the group size approaches eight people. In a slightly different experiment on conformity, Milgram et al. (1969) had people stand on a sidewalk and stare up at the sixth-floor window of a building. The experimenters observed the percentage of passersby who conformed with the staring-upward behavior. When a group of five people gazed upward, 16 percent of the people passing by joined them. When the group size was fifteen people, 40 percent of the passersby conformed. Beyond this point, the size of the group no longer seemed to be a powerful influence on conformity.

Presence of Another Dissenter. Allen and Levine (1971) did a variation on Asch's experiment on compliance. Rather than having six confederates give an incorrect response, one dissented and agreed with the subject. However, this dissenter was wearing thick glasses and struggling to peer at the lines. But even with this minimal support, subjects showed less group compliance and were more willing to stick with their independent judgments. Other research has also provided evidence that the presence of even one other dissenter makes nonconforming more comfortable and therefore more likely.

Public Choices versus Secret Choices. If Asch had allowed his subjects to use a secret ballot when choosing the correct line, he might have had different results. Deutsch and Gerard (1955) found that subjects who had to express their opinions openly were more likely to conform with the group. A secret ballot spares the embarrassment of appearing different or strange to the other members of the group.

Exercise 15-4

In your own words explain why Asch's experiment studied compliance rather than conformity.

_____

_____

_____

_____

CLOSE TO HOME   JOHN MCPHERSON

"Dee Dee Vershay's dog is having a hernia operation. Everybody's signing this get-well card and kicking in $10."

FIGURE 15-5. Would you predict that he will comply?

Exercise 15-5

Willy is participating in an experiment on group pressure. All other group members are confederates of the experimenter. The group will be asked to name the second President of the United States. A wrong answer, "Abraham Lincoln," will be given by the first member of the group. Others will conform. You are asked to decide whether Willy will comply with the wrong answer. List four factors you would like information on before making your decision.

a. _____

b. _____

c. _____

d. _____

Please turn to the Feedback section to check your responses.

Obedience

Obedience requires complying or conforming to rules or to the commands of an authority. No doubt, from the time you were a child you practiced obedience. You submitted to orders from parents, teachers, baby-sitters, crossing guards, and any other adult who appeared to have authority. You may even have succumbed to obeying a neighborhood bully. You probably still are an obedient person. If you are driving along a highway and a police officer raises her hand ordering you to stop, you certainly would obey. But suppose the police officer ordered you to move forward, possibly harming other people. Would you do it?

Milgram (1963, 1974) experimented to learn whether people would be obedient, even if another person might be harmed as a result. Milgram advertised in a New Haven, Connecticut, newspaper, offering to pay men $4.50 to participate in a learning experiment. Forty men aged twenty to fifty, from a variety of occupations and educational levels, were chosen as subjects for the experiment. Subjects were told the purpose of the experiment was to study the effects of punishment on memory.

In reality, the purpose was to see whether subjects would give increasingly higher levels of electric shocks to another person, following orders and urges from an experimenter. When each subject arrived for the experiment, he met with the experimenter and someone he believed was another subject. Actually the other person was a confederate of the experimenter. The experimenter explained that a learner and a teacher would be required. A fake drawing was set up so that the subject became the teacher and the confederate, the learner. The subject discovered that the learner was being strapped into a chair that appeared to be wired with electricity. The learner's electric chair was behind closed doors.

The subject was then instructed to sit in front of an electric-shock device. His goal was to have the learner memorize pairs of words. Whenever the learner made a mistake, the subject was to give an electric shock. Voltage level was to be increased with each error. Warnings appeared above fake switches on the electric-shock devices: At 390 volts and above was "Danger! Severe shock"; at 435 volts, "xxx."

In the beginning of the experiment the learner answered correctly; then he made a few mistakes. At a planned point in the experiment the learner acted as if he were suffering from the shocks and began screaming out in pain. The experimenter urged the subject to continue increasing the levels of shock. Eventually the learner shrieked and pleaded that he wanted to quit. Again the experimenter directed the subject to continue. What would you have done?

Although Milgram's experiment did not really offer shocks to the "learners,"the results did shock psychologists. All forty subjects went at least to the 300 voltage level of shocks. Only five refused to go above 300 volts. Twenty-six men, almost two-thirds of the subjects, went all the way to 450 volts, beyond the "danger" and "xxx" warnings.

The experiment was later repeated with undergraduate students and women and had similar results. In all situations, subjects were hesitant and unhappy but continued when encouraged. Milgram reported that they did show signs of stress. They bit their lips, sweated, trembled, stuttered, and laughed inappropriately. Nonetheless, they were obedient.

Milgram's study showed the power of authority and the limitations of individual freedom and choice. Subjects were willing to harm another person against their own conscience. The results of the experiment have been used to explain the willingness to follow harmful orders in Nazi Germany, Vietnam, the Watergate scandal, and among members of the Mafia. Compliance is really widespread!

Exercise 15-6

Suppose you are driving along the highway and come upon an accident. The police officer in charge orders you to drive through the accident scene, inconveniencing many injured people. After reading the results of Milgram's experiment do you expect that you would be obedient?

_____

_____

Please turn to the Feedback section to check your response.

Groupthink

Not only do conformity and obedience often lead to harm, they can also limit group productivity. A group that is constantly conforming will find itself in a rut. The members begin to think alike and neglect to look outside the group for ideas. Janis (1973) labeled this type of rut _groupthink_. According to Janis, groupthink is more likely to occur in cohesive groups when no one wants to break up the cohesiveness. Members feel loyal to the group and do not want to raise controversial issues, even if they think the group is wrong. Everyone conforms and rubber-stamps group ideas.

groupthink Conformity that keeps a group in a rut

Janis blames poor political decisions on groupthink. The lack of preparation for Pearl Harbor, the invasion of North Korea, the Vietnam War, the Bay of Pigs invasion, and the Watergate scandal are his examples. The people working

LEESCAPES   **BILL LEE**

FIGURE 15-6. At least his extreme obedience is harmless to others.

on these decisions were more concerned about being unanimous than about consulting outside experts and considering other alternatives. No member of the group was willing to express any doubts or criticisms.

What can be done to avoid a groupthink? How can a group get out of a rut? One technique that has been recommended is called *brainstorming*. The goal in a brainstorming session is to generate different ideas and develop creative solutions to problems. Members are instructed to withhold criticism until the end of the session. First they are to let their imaginations stretch and be as creative as possible. Even seemingly outlandish ideas should be discussed. Suggestions can be mixed and combined. The session is freewheeling and spontaneous. Ideas are neither squelched nor criticized. Finally, at the end of the session, all ideas are evaluated.

brainstorming Technique for generating new and creative ideas without fear of criticism

Exercise 15-7

Polly Tish Chen is running for Congress. Her campaign committee has been mailing brochures and literature to her constituents. The committee is always unanimous in suggestions for her campaign. Committee members are close friends, respect each other, and rarely argue. Polly is falling behind her opponent in the polls. The committee met last night and unanimously agreed to increase the number of brochures and other types of literature they are mailing. Polly is concerned that her committee is in a rut and it may cost her the election. Describe what Polly might suggest to get some creative new ideas for her campaign.

Compare your suggestions with those in the Feedback section.

Risk Taking

Stoner (1961) found that groups are willing to take greater risks than individuals are. He gave a number of risk-taking problems to individuals and to groups (see Feature 15-2). In each case the group chose a riskier solution. Stoner suggested that people feel less responsible in a group than they do as individuals. In a group, if the solution fails, no one person is responsible and each member feels less blame.

Suppose you were considering quitting your job and investing your savings in a small business. You have $5000. Two of your friends have the same savings and are willing to form a corporation with you. There are some definite risks in starting the business. If you fail, you cannot have your job back. Sitting by yourself, you may dwell on the risks and decide to stick with your job. However, if you meet with your friends, you are more likely to go ahead with the new plan. Psychologists hold that most people are unwilling to admit to not being as risky as others. Group pressure can cause risk taking.

Exercise 15-8

List two reasons why groups may be willing to take greater risks than individuals would.

a. _____

_____

b. _____

_____

Check your reasons in the Feedback section.

FEATURE 15-2

A Stoner Risk-Taking Problem

A college senior planning graduate work in chemistry may enter University X, where, because of rigorous standards, only a fraction of the graduate students manage to receive a Ph.D.; or he may enter University Y, which has a poorer reputation, but where almost every graduate student receives a Ph.D. What chance of success would you require before recommending that the student enter University X?

Source: Kogan, N., & Wallach, M. (1964). *Risk Taking.* New York: Holt Rinehart & Winston.

Panic behavior occurs in a group when members are frightened and are competing for something scarce. Mintz (1951) concluded that panic results from a breakdown in cooperation. Imagine there is a fire in an old movie theater. There is only one exit, in the back of the theater. Who do you suppose would be more likely to panic, the people near the exit or the people up front? The people near the exit have little to fear; they know they can leave safely. However, the people up front will probably begin pushing if they fear that by waiting for their turn, they will burn before reaching the exit.

Riot behavior is an extension of panic behavior. Riots are usually based on fear and panic. But with riot behavior the panic is coupled with long-standing frustrations, in addition to a triggering event.

What can possibly be done to prevent groups from panicking? A technique commonly used by airlines is to prepare ahead. If you have ever traveled by air, you are aware of the location of oxygen masks, flotation cushions, and emergency exits. As the plane taxis on the runway, flight attendants spend a few minutes explaining plans for an emergency. The technique is effective.

Riot behavior results from a combination of long-standing frustrations and a triggering event. The Rodney King trial was the triggering event in Los Angeles.

People tend to be reasonable and orderly in airplane emergencies. Fortunately, panic behavior in disasters is becoming rare.

Checkpoint

Use the following questions to check your understanding of this portion of the chapter. Choose and mark the one correct response to each question.

8. Which of the following is a disadvantage of groups solving problems?
   a. Groups make more mistakes than an individual does.
   b. Groups take more time than an individual does.
   c. Groups have fewer insights than an individual does.
   d. Groups cannot pool information.

9. Which size group is likely to be most productive?
   a. Three people
   b. Five people
   c. Ten people
   d. Fourteen people

10. Which of the following terms best describes the behavior advocated by the expression "When in Rome, do as the Romans do"?
    a. Compliance
    b. Conformity
    c. Obedience
    d. Panic

11. How does conformity differ from compliance?
    a. Conformity does not require obedience to an authority.
    b. Conformity requires obedience to an authority.
    c. Conformity requires accepting the beliefs of a group.
    d. Conformity does not require accepting the beliefs of a group.

12. What did the results of Asch's experiment demonstrate?
    a. Perceptual ability changes when an individual joins a group.
    b. The perception of groups is a composite of the perceptions of individuals in the group.
    c. A person will go along with a group even when he or she feels certain the group is wrong.
    d. A person will go along with a group if he or she is rewarded.

13. Which of the following persons is most likely to conform or comply when pressured by a group?
    a. Jon, who has a poor self-concept
    b. Lon, who has a good self-concept
    c. Ron, who knows his best friend will always agree with him
    d. Don, who knows the vote will be by secret ballot

14. Milgram showed that subjects would give electric shocks to a person even if they believed it could be harmful. Why were the subjects harming others?
    a. They wanted a reward.
    b. They feared punishment.
    c. They were pressured by a group.
    d. They were obedient to an authority.

15. Which of the following groups is suffering from groupthink?
    a. A group of women who are pooling all their savings on chances in a state lottery
    b. A group of men who always agree unanimously to the same solution
    c. A group of women who argue among themselves continuously
    d. A group of men who start a riot

16. What is the purpose of brainstorming?
    a. To help a group reach a unanimous decision
    b. To avoid panic behavior
    c. To develop creative new ideas
    d. To maintain obedience to an authority

17. In which situation would you probably be willing to take the greatest risks?
    a. Alone
    b. In a group
    c. With an authority
    d. With a confederate

18. Imagine you own an old wooden dance hall with only two exits. You want to be sure that people will not panic in the event of a fire. Which of the following techniques would be most effective?
    a. Station a police officer with a gun near the exit.
    b. Mark the exits with large signs.
    c. Schedule brainstorming sessions.
    d. Explain the emergency procedure at the beginning of each dance.

Use the Checkpoint Answer Key to verify your responses. If you had any difficulty with a question, carefully reread the text. If you had little or no difficulty answering the questions or have resolved any problems that you might have had, you are ready to continue with the next portion of the chapter.

LEADERSHIP

leader Person who gives guidance or direction to others and influences or changes their behavior

A *leader* is a person who gives guidance and direction to a group, influencing or changing people in the group. Some groups have a formal leader, a person elected or appointed to manage the group. A leader is perceived as an authority by the group. Leaders, as you recall from the discussion of obedience in the previous section of this chapter, can have a powerful influence on behavior. In corporations the names of formal leaders are listed on organizational charts. But there are also informal leaders, people who emerge from groups and have a powerful influence on other members. Perhaps you have worked with a group where the formal leader was useless. Frequently, a member of the group will make up for the leader's inadequacy and provide some direction.

Although research has provided limited evidence of specific qualities found in leaders, there are some rather general characteristics. Surveys have found that most formal leaders are above average in height (Crenshaw, 1980). Shaw (1971) claimed leaders have enthusiasm, initiative, verbal ability, persistence, and sociability. Most leaders are intelligent, sincere, and have high self-esteem.

Leadership Emphasis

Have you ever noticed that some groups have more than one informal leader? Often groups have two informal leaders or one formal and one informal leader. Each of the leaders has a different area of emphasis. Bales (1958) identified two types of leaders: task and socioemotional. A *task leader* presents new ideas and keeps the group working toward goals. A leader with a task orientation wants to get the job done efficiently. The emphasis is on defining problems, collecting information, opinions, and suggestions, and evaluating and summarizing the group's work. Most formal leaders are assigned task roles. A leader with a *socioemotional* orientation is concerned about the personal and social needs of members of the group. The goal for this leader is group harmony and cohesiveness. Attempts are made to build an atmosphere of trust and friendliness. The leader is concerned about hurt feelings and soothes and comforts members. Praise is common, and jokes are used to release tension. Japanese managers have been known to demonstrate a stronger leaning toward socioemotional emphasis than have their American counterparts.

task leader Person who keeps a group working toward a goal

socioemotional leader Person who directs a group primarily according to the personal and social needs of the members

Exercise 15-9

Read each of the following descriptions and indicate whether each leader is formal or informal and task-oriented or socioemotionally oriented.

a. Ima Principal was appointed headmistress of a private school. She was aware of the problem with teacher turnover: Because of a limited budget, teachers left for higher-paying jobs at public schools. She is trying to keep teachers happy by having friendly gatherings and developing school spirit. She encourages them and gives them many privileges.

_____

b. Bertha is one of four young women sharing an apartment in a large city. She was concerned about her roommates' disorganization in paying bills. She decided to take over by keeping records of the accounts and billing each woman every month.

_____

c. When Harry Hatchet was appointed director of the Dreamy Day-Care Center, he vowed to get the center out of debt. He is holding weekly meetings to discuss improvements. Thus far he has fired five teachers because their enrollments declined and he felt they were unpopular. The remaining teachers are handling more children.

_____

To check your answers turn to the Feedback section.

Assumptions of Leaders

McGregor (1960) claimed that leaders base their methods on assumptions they make about people. He divided assumptions into theory X and theory Y. *Theory X* is a pessimistic view of human nature. Managers who adhere to theory X

theory X Belief that people are basically lazy and must be controlled and directed by management

believe that people are basically lazy and will avoid work and responsibility. These managers hold that individuals have selfish interests in their own security and do not care about the organization. People will avoid making decisions and prefer to be directed by others. As a result the manager who holds the assumptions of theory X will check on people's work and direct and control them, feeling that because people dislike work, they must be directed, coerced, and threatened with punishment if they do not show effort.

theory Y Belief that people are naturally interested in work and can direct their own behavior

On the other hand, *theory Y* holds a more positive set of assumptions about people. Theory Y assumes that people have a natural interest in work and are capable of directing their own behavior, that under proper conditions, people will seek responsibility, make decisions, and show imagination and creativity. A leader who believes the assumptions in theory Y will not threaten or pressure a group, but rather will allow them freedom.

theory Z Belief that people work most efficiently when given appropriate direction

More recently Ouchi (1981) introduced another set of assumptions that he labeled *theory Z*. Leaders who rely on theory Z believe that workers do not dislike work but they will not work efficiently without appropriate direction. Theory Z managers try to develop trust and cooperation among workers and leaders. They make an effort to develop loyalty and commitment to the workplace and include a consensus of management and employees in making critical decisions.

Leaders may choose the assumptions of either theory X, theory Y, or theory Z; the three are not compatible. Assume you are a manager of a secretarial staff and believe the assumptions of theory X. You probably would have employees sign in and out or punch a time clock. If they came in late or left early, you would dock money from their paychecks. Coffee breaks and lunch hours would

FIGURE 15-7. A theory X boss.

also be monitored carefully. You probably would provide the secretaries with folders of sample letters to be sure they typed correctly. You also would edit their work for errors. As you might suspect, you would probably find that the members of the secretarial staff indeed would conform to theory X: As you got tougher in handling them, they would become even further entrenched in their theory X characteristics.

But the opposite is also true. If the same group of secretaries were managed assuming theory Y characteristics, they would probably work accordingly. If permitted to create original letters, they would. They would also edit and check their own work. Being motivated and finding the job interesting, they would be more likely to arrive on time and complete their day's work. So as a theory Y manager, you would also be convinced that your assumptions were correct.

As a theory Z manager, you would argue that your method was most effective. You would ask the secretaries about their preferred hours and based upon their responses, you might change the working day, split jobs, or use flex-time. Workers would share their ideas on how they develop effective letters, comment on the software packages they are using, and develop friendships among their colleagues. Feeling satisfied that the company was trying to accommodate them, they would have a sense of loyalty and a commitment to work harder.

Exercise 15-10

Read each of the following statements and indicate whether it is based on assumptions from theory X, theory Y, or theory Z.

a. "Be sure to tell the carpenters to clean up when they are finished; otherwise they will probably leave a mess." _____

b. "Always carry a map in a strange city. Taxi drivers will take you all over town just to make some fast money." _____

c. "I always give my basketball team a pep talk and ask them which shots they need to practice. They usually spend more time on the court this way." _____

d. "Let the boy scout troop develop its own plan for cleaning up the neighborhood. Adults just get in the way." _____

Please turn to the Feedback section to check your answers.

Leadership Styles

Psychologists have identified three styles of leadership: authoritarian, democratic, and laissez-faire. Generally, authoritarian leaders are task-oriented and believe theory X assumptions about people. Laissez-faire leaders are more socially oriented and accept the assumptions of theory Y. Democratic leaders fall somewhere between these two extremes in their orientation and hold to theory Z assumptions. In each of these styles, the leader accepts a different role.

authoritarian leader Person who gives direct orders and is solely in charge of a group

democratic leader Leader who expects group members to participate in decisions

laissez-faire leader Coordinator who gives a group free rein

Authoritarian. This style of leadership is also referred to as "autocratic." The leader is the sole person in charge of the group and has complete responsibility. Direct orders are given and are expected to be carried out by the group. The leader remains aloof from the rest of the group and is considered an expert.

Democratic. Democratic leaders expect group participation; hence this style is sometimes labeled "participative." The leader offers an overview or philosophy and sets objectives for the group. The group must then decide how best to implement the objectives. Group members draw on the expertise and experience of each other.

Laissez-Faire. In a laissez-faire style of leadership, the leader is more of a coordinator. The group has complete freedom and free rein. The laissez-faire leader acts as liaison with external groups but exerts no power or influence on the group.

Lewin et al. (1943) compared these three styles of leadership as used with boys' clubs. Lewin formed three equal groups of boys, with adult leaders using one of the three leadership styles. In the authoritarian group the leader made policies and instructed the boys but never socialized with them. The democratic leader held group discussions on policy and allowed the boys to choose their own work groups for projects. In the laissez-faire group, the leader provided information when it was requested but generally let group members do as they pleased.

The results of Lewin's experiment showed that the authoritarian leaders had smooth and well-organized groups. However, the members were unhappy and were hostile to each other. Members of the democratic groups liked their leaders and tried hard. The groups with laissez-faire leaders had very little constructive activity.

Although the results of Lewin's experiment seem to recommend a democratic style of leadership, there are situations where authoritarian and laissez-faire styles would be more appropriate. For example, if you were leading people out of a plane crash or a fire, you would hardly want to stop to take a vote. Giving direct authoritarian orders would be more realistic. Similarly, in professional areas, a laissez-faire system of leadership is suitable. Physicians, dentists, and college professors rarely need direction from a leader.

While men tend to emerge as leaders more often than women, extensive research by Eagly and her colleagues (1991) revealed that women in leadership roles are at least as effective as their male counterparts. In general, women use a more democratic style of leadership than men do and both men and women tend to be slightly more satisfied with female leaders. While women seem more concerned with social relationships than men do, when jobs are traditionally female (as nursing supervisor), women are more task-oriented.

Most leaders maintain flexibility. Even the most authoritarian boss will permit employees to plan their own company picnic and decide on the date, the food, and entertainment. Similarly, a laissez-faire leader could recognize the potential chaos if a town permitted everyone to build houses, roads, office buildings, and high-rises wherever they wished.

Imagine you have been assigned to lead a group in planting a vegetable garden on a five-acre plot of land. Six people are assigned to your group. Describe what you would do as a leader if you used each of the three possible leadership styles.

a. Authoritarian: _____

_____

_____

_____

b. Democratic: _____

_____

_____

_____

c. Laissez-faire: _____

_____

_____

_____

Compare your leadership plans with those listed in the Feedback section.

Leadership Strategies

One of the goals of good leadership is to improve the quality of the work performed. Many businesses have adopted a technique called *Total Quality Management (TQM)*. TQM applies quality principles to every aspect of a company, from customer satisfaction to the quality of innovative ideas and employee satisfaction. Clearly, this is not a simple task. Increasing quality often requires a major upheaval of old business methods. The original concept of TQM was invented by an American, W. Edwards Deming, during World War II. Deming outlined fourteen points for quality improvement (shown in Feature 15-3). The approach was widely adopted in Japan during the 1950s and 1960s but did not become popular in the United States until the 1980s.

Although organizations use the same fourteen steps, there is no single formula for how to best carry out the steps; each business must develop its own program. Adopting TQM is costly both in time and money (Port et al., 1992); however, as reported in Feature 15-4, TQM has saved companies. Typical TQM programs may include report cards from supervisors with grades for production and attitude, employees' evaluations of their managers, certificates or awards for outstanding work, and requests for employees' suggestions for improvement (Bloch, 1993).

Total Quality Management (TQM) Technique that applies quality principles to every aspect of an organization

Deming's Fourteen Points for Total Quality Management (TQM)

1. Create constancy of purpose towards improving product and service.
2. Adopt a new philosophy.
3. Cease dependence on mass inspection.
4. End the practice of awarding business on the basis of price tag.
5. Improve constantly and further the system of production of service.
6. Institute training on the job.
7. Institute leadership.
8. Drive out fear.
9. Break down barriers between departments.
10. Eliminate slogans, exhortations, and targets asking for zero defects and new levels of productivity.
11. Eliminate work standards which prescribe numerical quotas—substitute leadership.
12. Remove barriers which rob hourly workers of their right to pride of workmanship.
13. Institute a vigorous program of education and self-improvement.
14. Everybody in the company must work to accomplish this transformation.

Source: Adapted from Akande, A. (1992). Applying Deming to service. *Management Decision, 30,* 3, 3–8.

Continuous Quality Improvement (CQI) Management technique that views quality as an ongoing process

Not every organization that has attempted TQM has met with success. A new variation on TQM, *Continuous Quality Improvement (CQI),* stresses a complete commitment to the customer, from the design of a product to after-sales services. CQI views quality as an ongoing process. While TQM focuses on "zero defects" and seeks perfection, CQI is based on a never-ending journey toward improvement.

Exercise 15-12

Assume you are the manager of a pizza delivery service that has been losing money because of a decrease in business. You have decided to implement a TQM program. Indicate which of the following steps would be part of your strategy.

a. _____ Survey customers to learn what they like and dislike about your pizzas.

b. _____ Tell your chefs to save money by using less cheese.

c. _____ Give all workers a salary increase.

d. _____ Ask employees how service can be more efficient.

e. _____ Reward employees who have innovative ideas for making and delivering pizzas.

f. _____ Sponsor training programs where your chefs can have fun learning from each other.

g. _____ Offer a bonus to the employee who delivers the most pizzas each week.

h. _____ Ask customers to complete a questionnaire on the quality of your service.

'A Little Bit of Smarts, A Lot of Hard Work'

Get lost. That's essentially what Buick Motor Div. told Michael A. Plumley in 1983. Citing poor-quality parts, the General Motors Corp. unit dropped Plumley Cos. which since 1967 has been a supplier of hoses and other rubber gear. But instead of quitting, Plumley fought back. It stepped up worker training and started a quality drive that has taken it to the front ranks of America's auto-parts industry. Today the $80 million company holds quality awards from GM, Chrysler, and Nissan, and is one of 16 suppliers in the world to have earned Ford's Total Quality Excellence (TQE) Award.

Pushed by their customers, a handful of small U.S. parts makers have remade themselves into industry pacesetters. They have retrained their employees, upgraded equipment, and worked to make their own suppliers comply with ever more demanding standards. . . . "It's a little bit of smarts, a lot of hard work, and constancy of purpose," says Plumley, chairman and CEO of Plumley Cos. . . .

Source: Treece, J. B. (1992, November 30). 'A little bit of smarts, a lot of hard work.' *Business Week,* 71–72.

i. _____ Lower the prices of your pizzas.

j. _____ Ask employees to rate you as a manager.

Please compare the items you checked with the list in the Feedback section.

THE PROS AND CONS OF GROUPS

Although groups are effective in reaching goals and providing helpful information, you probably have also been identifying some shortcomings. Buys (1978) outlined several negative influences of groups. Groups lose their sense of responsibility and tend to make risky and impulsive decisions. There is often a sense of conformity in groups, and members will go along with others even if others are wrong. Also, groups often encourage panic behavior. Since responsibility is shared, group members sometimes loaf, letting others do their work. This slowdown has been labeled *social loafing* (Latane, Williams, and Harkins, 1973).

social loafing Tendency of individuals to exert less effort when they work together than when they work alone

Harkins and Petty (1983) examined ways to make social loafing less likely. They suggested giving each group member a different important job so that each will have a strong sense of personal responsibility. Latane and associates called attention to the methods used by the Ohio State University football team. The coaches observe and score each play. They then compute the average performance score for each player. The scores are made public and high-scoring players are awarded honors at weekly luncheons. Outstanding players are rewarded with "buckeye" decals to wear on their helmets. Group members are recognized as individuals as well as cooperative group members. The Ohio State football team has become highly successful using this approach to avoid social loafing.

In spite of their limitations, groups are here to stay!

Checkpoint

Use the following questions to check your understanding of the final portion of the chapter. Indicate whether each statement is true or false.

19. _____ A formal leader is either elected or appointed.

20. _____ The name of an informal leader is likely to appear on a company's organizational chart.

21. _____ Most leaders have a good self-concept.

22. _____ Formal leaders usually have a socioemotional emphasis.

23. _____ A leader with task emphasis is likely to joke to release tension.

24. _____ Theory X leaders are usually authoritarian.

25. _____ Leaders who believe theory X usually find out they are wrong.

26. _____ Laissez-faire leaders are task-oriented.

27. _____ Authoritarian leaders draw on the experience of group members.

28. _____ Democratic leadership is the most effective in all situations.

29. _____ Total Quality Management is based on fourteen points for improvement.

30. _____ Groups can have negative influences.

Check your responses against the Checkpoint Answer Key at the end of the chapter. If you had difficulty with any question, reread the text. If you had little or no difficulty answering the questions or have resolved problems that you might have had, you are ready to check yourself against the chapter inventory that follows.

CHAPTER INVENTORY

Use this list of objectives as a review checklist. You should be able to do the tasks outlined in the objectives and apply them to everyday examples. If you can, you may feel confident that you have mastered the material in this chapter.

1. Define a group, and distinguish between formal and informal groups and group norms.
2. Explain why people new to a group often do not participate.
3. Differentiate between cooperative and competitive goals, and list their advantages and disadvantages.
4. Describe one method to reduce hostility among groups.
5. Define cohesiveness, and specify conditions that are conducive to its existence.
6. Discuss group size and time constraints as factors that affect group productivity.
7. Distinguish between conformity and compliance and describe one experiment on compliance.

8. Identify four factors that influence compliance.
9. Explain why Milgram's experiment showed the power of authority and the limitations of free choice.
10. List five factors that contribute to a groupthink, and describe a technique for avoiding group ruts.
11. State two reasons why groups take greater risks than individuals do.
12. Identify the causes of panic behavior and riots, and describe a method to avoid panic behavior in groups.
13. Differentiate between formal and informal leaders and task-oriented and socioemotional leaders.
14. Explain the differences among theory X, theory Y, and theory Z.
15. Describe three styles of leadership, and relate them to the assumptions in theory X, theory Y, and theory Z.
16. Discuss the usefulness and application of the three leadership styles.
17. Describe the purposes of Total Quality Management (TQM) and Continuous Quality Improvement (CQI).
18. List two advantages and three disadvantages of groups.
19. Define social loafing and describe how it can be avoided.

Feedback

The correct answers to the exercises follow. If you did not answer an exercise correctly, review the preceding pages and return to the exercise to correctly complete it.

15-1. All seven are examples of groups. Two or more people are interacting or are aware of each other.
15-2. Mr. Scrooge should suggest a court recess. He might go home and put on a Santa Claus suit before returning. Groups reject people who disagree with them!
15-3. Activities that require the cooperation of students from both schools would help reduce hostilities. You might suggest a community project, such as collecting money for the entire town, improving a local park, building a picnic area, or painting the town offices.
15-4. It is doubtful that subjects in Asch's experiment changed their behavior permanently. Those who did go along with the group admitted that their reason was to avoid embarrassment. They were aware of the correct response but were complying because of pressure from the group.
15-5. a. The level of Willy's self-esteem
    b. The size of the group
    c. Whether anyone else in the group will give a correct response
    d. Whether Willy can write his answer secretly
15-6. If you are like most of the subjects in Milgram's study, chances are you would obey the police officer. Undoubtedly it would bother you and you would show some signs of stress.
15-7. Polly needs to get her campaign committee out of their groupthink. She should suggest a brainstorming session. Members can mention any campaign suggestions they can conjure up, even those that seem ridiculous. At the end of the session, the committee could evaluate all the original ideas and perhaps find a more creative solution than more literature.

15-8. a. Group members can share the responsibility. If their risky decision fails, no one person will be blamed.

b. Group members succumb to group pressure. No one wants to admit they are not as risky as the other members of the group.

15-9. a. Formal; socioemotional

b. Informal; task-oriented

c. Formal; task-oriented

15-10. a. Theory X

b. Theory X

c. Theory Z

d. Theory Y

15-11. a. Authoritarian: Decide how and what you want planted in the garden. Draw a plan and purchase seeds. Assign group members specific tasks.

b. Democratic: Discuss garden plans with the group. Allow members to choose vegetables and jobs they prefer. Members who wish can work together.

c. Laissez-faire: Turn the group loose on the plot of land and let them do as they wish.

15-12. a; d; e; f; g; h; j.

Checkpoint Answer Key

1. b; 2. c; 3. d; 4. b; 5. b; 6. d; 7. a; 8. b; 9. b; 10. a; 11. c; 12. c; 13. a; 14. d; 15. b; 16. c; 17. b; 18. d; 19. true; 20. false; 21. true; 22. false; 23. false; 24. true; 25. false; 26. false; 27. false; 28. false; 29. true; 30. true.

Planning Careers

The human being is by nature active,
and when inactive begins to die
—ERICH FROMM

Assume you are at a party. The host begins the introductions and tells you something about each person. You meet Maureen, a nurse's aide who assists retarded children; Clark, who picks grapes at a vineyard; Isaac, a chef and author of two cookbooks; and Joanne, a rocket scientist. Based on their occupations, you probably form some first impressions. People are often identified with their jobs. Introductions are more likely to include information about occupations than other facts about people.

People are usually stereotyped according to their occupation: Rocket scientists are expected to be intelligent; nurse's aides to retarded children are imagined to be patient and considerate. Indeed, a dumb rocket scientist and an impatient nurse's aide would not be suited for their jobs. But there are also some unfair stereotypes. Clearly, it is wrong to assume that male hairdressers and ballet dancers are gay. Likewise, female executives are no less sensitive than female homemakers are. But such stereotypes persist. Even within the harmony of a symphony orchestra, some rather negative job stereotypes endure. Davis (1976) found that string players view brass players as coarse, unrefined, loud-mouthed, clowning, heavy-drinking, and less intelligent. On the other hand, brass players stereotype string players as oversensitive, touchy, physically delicate, and too serious.

Psychologists have evaluated people successful in occupations to determine their abilities and interests. In the first part of this chapter you will learn ways to use their findings to help you recognize the types of occupations that are likely to be suitable for you.

This chapter begins with a description of how to analyze both yourself and some possible career choices to be sure that you select a job that suits your abilities, interests, and needs. Next is a focus on how to get the job: letters of application, resumes, references, interviews, and follow-up letters. Factors involved in job satisfaction and decisions to change careers are also discussed. Finally, you will consider the effects of unemployment and ways to use your leisure to prepare for retirement.

CHOOSING A CAREER

career Set of experiences that permit the use of abilities for profit

Psychologists describe a *career* as a set of experiences that permit you to use your abilities for profit. Profit is a crucial word in the definition of a career. A career for one person may be a leisure hobby for another. If you do needlework solely for pleasure, you have a hobby, not a career. However, as soon as you sell an embroidered pillowcase or apron, you could be on the brink of starting your career.

Your choice of career is clearly among your most important decisions. The job you select will not only affect how you are introduced at parties, it will also affect your standard of living and financial security. Your friends and your status in the community will also be decided by your career choice. Likewise your own self-concept and sense of worth will be strongly affected by your work. Your career decision might also influence where you live. It would be difficult to be a farmer in downtown Chicago or a marine biologist in Bolivia.

Career decisions are not just a problem for high school and college students. Although early choices of a major may point to future career options, most people retrain, expand, and go into new areas during their lives. Many people change careers in their twenties, thirties, forties, or fifties. Some even begin new careers after they have retired.

Regardless of when career decisions are made, they clearly have a crucial impact on your entire lifestyle. To be sure, you would not want to make such a decision in haste or under pressure. The best way to avoid being trapped into an unsuitable career is to take two steps: Analyze yourself, and analyze jobs. Hopefully, the result will be a career choice that satisfies your needs and interests.

Analyzing Yourself

Although it may seem in bad taste to begin with the subject of money, to a large extent your career choice will be limited by the finances available to you. If you have wealthy parents or other relatives who are willing to invest in your future, or if you have accumulated your own fortune, your possible career choices will be limited only by your own abilities and interests. However, if you must borrow money or have only a small supply, you need to think about the costs of training programs and education. Institutions that offer scholarships and organizations that offer on-the-job training or tuition benefits deserve consideration. A college degree does not in itself offer better job opportunities. Successful careers also require ability and interest.

Assessing Abilities

The easiest way to determine your strengths and weaknesses is to recall your successes and failures. No doubt some school subjects seemed easy to you, while others were a dismal chore. If you always did well in biology classes but struggled through Spanish, you probably have more scientific ability than language ability. The only defect in this method is that your success in school subjects could also have been influenced by teachers and classmates. For example, you may have had an excellent biology teacher and been in a class with friendly, outstanding students. The Spanish teacher, on the other hand, may have been a misfit, and your Spanish classmates may have been poor students who joked and wasted class time. However, if you had studied science and Spanish with a variety of different teachers and students, you could be more certain of a correct assessment.

You might also recall abilities that friends and teachers noticed and commented on. Perhaps you have a clever writing style, or you are a skillful salesperson or an efficient organizer. Friends and instructors also notice weak points. Can you think of areas of criticism? If people consistently agree on your positive and negative qualities, they probably are reliable assessments.

Psychologists have developed tests to measure abilities. The three types of ability tests most commonly used for career counseling are intelligence tests, achievement tests, and aptitude tests. Intelligence tests, described in detail in Chapter 5, measure your general potential. *Achievement tests* assess the level of your past accomplishments, usually in academic subjects. *Aptitude tests* are designed to predict future achievements in specific areas. Aptitude tests have been devised to measure mechanical, artistic, musical, and literary ability, as well as potential in certain professions, such as medicine, law, education, and engineering. There are aptitude tests available to forecast your abilities in almost every career. Research has found that if people use their skills at work, they will develop a sense of competence that increases self-esteem.

achievement test Test designed to assess past accomplishments, usually in academic subjects

aptitude test Test designed to measure individual potential and to predict future achievements in a given area.

Determining Values and Interests

Suppose a man has a beautiful bass voice. He also inherits a tremendous fortune. Several fine music colleges offer him scholarships, but he hates to sing and thinks music is a waste of time. He prefers working with animals. His values and interests would probably prevent his success in music. Even if he did accept one of the scholarships and pursued a career as a singer, he would undoubtedly be unhappy.

It is wise to examine your values and interests before choosing a career course. If you value the opinions of your family and friends, you most likely will want a job that pleases them. But you also want to please yourself. Do you prefer to work alone or in a group? Would you like a structured job, or would you rather manage and organize your work yourself? Oldham et al. (1976)

reported that people with security needs usually prefer structured, routine jobs. Others with achievement needs enjoy controlling their own methods and techniques. You also want to consider the salary and status level you are seeking. Some people are interested in working for large corporations, while others find small companies preferable. Willingness to travel is yet another concern; many jobs require heavy travel commitments.

Just as tests are available to measure your abilities and aptitudes, inventories developed by psychologists are used to check your values and interests. The purpose of these inventories is to help you sort out your interests and focus on your preferences and dislikes. The most commonly used *interest inventories* are the Strong-Campbell Interest Inventory for high school seniors and adults; the Kuder Preference Records for high school juniors, seniors, and adults; and the Vocational Interest Survey for students in grades 8 through 12. A self-test, The Self Directed Search, allows you to assess your own interests without the aid of a counselor. This test, available from the Consulting Psychologists Press, divides occupations into five categories: realistic, investigative, artistic, social, and enterprising. You rate your interests in each of these areas and search through a list of occupations in an "Occupation Finder" to find a field that fits the pattern of your interests. Although all of these tests have some usefulness in reflecting your interests, they have been widely criticized. Many psychologists believe interest inventories are not reliable: They only reflect how you felt at the time of testing. With additional education or new experiences, your interests will change. Matteson (1975) pointed out an additional limitation. People taking the tests are required to stretch their imaginations. Often they have had no experiences comparable to the test items. They must fantasize about what they would like to do, since they have never really tried it.

Sorting your interests will help you determine whether or not you would enjoy a job. But keep in mind that interest alone does not indicate that you have the ability or are suited for a job. A man may be interested in interior design, but if he is color blind and lacks artistic ability, he will not get very far in his career.

interest inventory Test designed to determine personal values, likes, and dislikes

Evaluating Gender and Cultural Factors

Although in the past many women have worked outside the home, currently there are more women in the work force than ever before. Matthews and Rodin (1989) reported that the percentage of women in the labor force rose from 33 percent in 1950 to 56 percent in 1987. Women are getting jobs in business and the professions. In 1975, 13 percent of physicians were female, compared with 20 percent in 1988 (Rix, 1990). Nonetheless, a large portion of women are still doing low-paid work. Women are six times as likely than men are to be clerks and twice as likely to have service jobs (Unger and Crawford, 1992). Women do not advance in their jobs as quickly as men do. In the United States only 3 percent of top executives at Fortune 1000 corporations are women; yet women comprise 97 percent of nurses and 99 percent of secretaries (Castro, 1990; Williams, 1989).

For some women, remaining in low-paying jobs is attributed to their need to juggle their jobs with their family responsibilities. Travel requirements often present a particular problem for women. A study by Crowley et al. (1973)

found that women have the same concerns as men about their jobs, but several other studies have reported that, for women, outside pressures can interfere with their achievements. Crowley noted that women are equally concerned with their personal growth on the job, opportunity for advancement, and intellectual challenge. In a paper presented to the American Psychological Association, Pines and Kafry (1977) highlighted the special concerns of women, pointing out their problems in balancing marital, parental, and work roles. Although men also share roles of spouses and parents, both Stafford et al. (1977) and Heckman et al. (1977) noted that most couples give the wife primary responsibility for household chores and child rearing. The findings of Mueller and Campbell (1977) will be no surprise: Women who have achieved high positions in their careers are more likely to remain single. Women need to consider their level of interest in family life before choosing a career. Many women decide to rear children first and then go to work. Others prefer to start their careers before choosing marriage. Still others are interested in careers that will be compatible with family life.

Whether Black or White, women face the same problems; but Black women are more likely to be employed in domestic or service work. Only in recent years have Black women moved into white-collar jobs and away from domestic work. In 1965 only 24 percent of Black women were in white-collar jobs, while in 1977, 46 percent were in white-collar jobs (Betz and Fitzgerald, 1987). By the year 2003, women and African-American, Hispanic, and Asian men will all increase their share of the work force, although White males will still hold the largest portion, with about 32 percent (Lindsey, 1992). Clearly the changing percentages will require a better distribution of diversity among workers at all levels. As the article in Feature 16-1 stresses, improving education is a key to greater job equity.

FEATURE 16-1 PSYCHOLOGY IN THE NEWS

Education: The Key to Our Future

Once dependent on the cost free labor afforded by slavery, America again finds that its economic destiny is intertwined with the availability and performance of African-Americans. . . .

The source of consternation can be found in Work Force 2000, a report commissioned by the U.S. Department of Labor, which predicted that corporate America and its labor market will undergo the most sweeping changes in U.S. industrial history. The results are particularly disturbing because the nation remains ill-prepared to cope with forecasts regarding the demographics of the 21st century work force. For example, by the year 2000, most of the entry-level workers in the labor-force will be minorities and, to a large extent women. Yet, capital investment for the education of these key groups lags noticeably behind the requirements needed to produce a skilled, proficient and sizable workforce. . . .

To their credit, an increasing number of companies are forging partnerships with local schools in an attempt to bolster academic performance and career choices. In establishing these mentor programs, corporate executives along with school officials, hope to turn the tide of drug addiction, teen-age pregnancy, low self-esteem and gang violence—all of which have a reverse impact on the learning process. . . .

Source: Conigland, K. (1992, October/November). Education: the key to our future. *Upscale*, 38–40.

While in North America most physicians and dentists are male, in the Soviet Union most physicians are female, as are most dentists in Denmark. Cultural influences are important in determining whether women will be allowed time to pursue careers. Often women in low-paying jobs are not personally rewarded by their jobs and feel more fulfilled in the time they spend with their families. As a result they are less motivated at work and put their energies into their families.

Exercise 16-1

Read each of the following descriptions and indicate what steps each individual should take to improve his/her self-analysis in choosing a career.

a. Boyd, an eighteen-year-old high school senior, wants to be a dentist. He has an A average in school and a high score on his college aptitude tests. Results of an interest inventory suggested that he is fascinated by teeth and enjoys working with individual people. He is well-organized and prefers to work at his own pace.

_____

_____

b. Hilda's mother is a policewoman and wants Hilda to join her on the force. Her mother has emphasized that Hilda would receive excellent on-the-job training. Hilda feels it is best to do what her mother wants.

_____

_____

c. Grant likes to work in his own home. He has decided that carpentry would be an excellent field for him, since he could set up a shop in his own basement.

_____

_____

d. Dwanda is a high school freshman and wants to drop out of school. She is uncertain of her interests but claims that women in her African-American community never get decent jobs.

_____

_____

Please turn to the Feedback section to check your responses.

Analyzing Jobs

A prime concern in rating a job is opportunity. Not many people will become secretary general of the United Nations. Similarly, aspiring to become the queen of Britain is limiting; it appears that job will be filled for quite some time. Even jobs that are currently plentiful may be eliminated in the future because of expansions in technology. Other positions are more stable. It is not likely that careers in cosmetics, funeral services, religion, or police science will ever become obsolete. However, the future for longshore workers, railroad ticket agents, toll collectors, and bookkeepers looks shaky.

Effects of Technology

In addition to eliminating some jobs, advances in technology will also cause changes in the nature of jobs. Factory work has become more fragmented as machines replace humans. Many jobs require workers to constantly update themselves. For example, twenty-five years ago computer programmers were expected to wire heavy plug boards to be inserted in the early computers. This aspect of their job has clearly been simplified, but anyone who did not update his or her training is out of work. The excerpt in Feature 16-2 spells out some changes that you can expect.

Current estimates suggest that within the next few years more than 75 percent of all jobs will require some form of interaction with a computer. These estimates suggest that most people will need to retrain and become more knowledgeable about computers. However, with improved technology new problems have been added.

Job Requirements

Once you have assured yourself that a job will still exist a few years hence, you will want to learn more about the job requirements and working conditions. First, you need to determine the skills and training required. Some jobs require good vision, good hearing, or physical strength. If you are considering certain professions, you will need to have extensive schooling. Air-traffic controllers and management trainees usually have long periods of on-the-job training.

If you are satisfied with the training and skills required for a job, you are ready to check the working conditions. Whether you will be required to work indoors or outdoors, in a private office or an open area, or alone or with others

---

FEATURE 16-2 PSYCHOLOGY IN THE NEWS

Managing Your Life

1. Most people will change careers several times.
2. Higher levels of skill will be required.
3. Greater emphasis will be placed on transferable skills.
4. Jobs will require more adaptive skills.
5. Workers will be more involved with quality and productivity.
6. New jobs will require more education.
7. Workers will be called on to make more decisions.
8. Human needs will be given greater priority.
9. Employment opportunities will continue to grow, but at a slower rate.
10. The service sector will grow most rapidly.
11. The makeup of the workforce will change.
12. Flexible work patterns will continue to expand.

Source: Hecklinger, F. J., & Black, B. M. (1990). *Training for life: A practical guide to career and life planning.* Dubuque, Iowa: Kendall/Hunt.

"All I did was hit the delete button!"

FIGURE 16-1. A future technology problem?

are important considerations. Jobs requiring uniforms—for example, the military, nursing, and work with an airline—are sought by some and shunned by others. Working hours are another important factor. Some careers require shift-work, others require evening hours, and still others require your availability twenty-four hours each day.

Where can you learn about job requirements and working conditions? The most widely used source is the *Occupational Outlook Handbook*,* published by the U.S. Bureau of Labor Statistics and revised and updated every two years. More than 850 occupations are briefly and concisely described. Descriptions include the employment outlook, the type of work involved, qualifications, training, salary, working conditions, locations, advancement possibilities, and sources of additional information.

Another source is the *Dictionary of Occupational Titles*,* which is published by the U.S. Department of Labor and describes more than 22,000 jobs. Information includes aptitude requirements, physical demands, and the interests and traits of people currently working on the jobs.

Although these two volumes may provide some insights, it is preferable to get first-hand information. Most colleges have career centers with brochures and videotapes on different job groups. Interviewing people in jobs of interest to you would give you more specific information. If possible, try to spend a few days observing the work. Often what seems to be a glamorous or exciting career can be a dull routine on a day-to-day basis.

* Available at most libraries or may be ordered from the Superintendent of Documents, U.S. Government Printing Office, Washington, DC 20402.

Prepare a list of ten questions you would want answered in analyzing a job.

a. _____

b. _____

c. _____

d. _____

e. _____

f. _____

g. _____

h. _____

i. _____

j. _____

Compare your list with the one in the Feedback section.

Matching Jobs to People

Finding a suitable career is critical to both your success and your happiness. Only through an honest appraisal of yourself and each job is this possible. Often the stereotypes associated with jobs are incorrect. Careful job appraisal and self-analysis may seem tedious, but it is time well spent!

Checkpoint

Use the following questions to check your understanding of this portion of the chapter. Indicate whether each of the following questions is true or false.

1. _____ Leisure hobbies are examples of careers.

2. _____ Your self-concept is affected by your career choice.

3. _____ Career choices must be made before completing high school.

4. _____ Consistent success in school subjects can be an indicator of ability.

5. _____ Intelligence tests measure potential abilities.

6. _____ Aptitude tests cannot measure artistic abilities.

7. _____ Ability is more important than interest in choosing a career.

8. _____ People with achievement needs prefer routine jobs with close supervision.

9. _____ Female executives are more likely to be married and have families than to be single and childless.

10. _____ Interest inventories have been criticized because they only measure interests at the time of the testing.

11. _____ Interest is more important than ability in choosing a career.

12. _____ Gender and cultural background do not affect job opportunities.

13. _____ Improvements in technology will eliminate or change many jobs.

14. _____ Salary is the most important consideration in selecting a job.

15. _____ The best way to learn about a career is to interview a person performing a job and observe the working conditions.

16. _____ Self-analysis and job analysis are crucial in choosing a career.

Use the Checkpoint Answer Key to verify your responses. If you had any difficulty with a question, carefully reread the text. If you had little or no difficulty answering the questions or have resolved any problems that you might have had, you are ready to continue with the next portion of this chapter.

APPLYING FOR JOBS

Assuming you have selected and prepared yourself for a career, your next step is to find a job. Inform your friends of your search; they might have a good lead. But if you already have a job and would rather your current employer not learn that you are job hunting, exercise some restraint in spreading the word. There are many sources that provide information on job options. You can check classified ads in newspapers, professional journals, and trade magazines. Or you can visit your school or college placement office, a state employment agency, or a private employment agency. Keep in mind that private agencies charge fees: Sometimes the employer pays, but often you are expected to forfeit some of your initial salary.

Once you have located a few opportunities, you are ready to send letters of application and resumes to prospective employers. Next, you must prepare yourself for interviews. Finally, you should follow up interviews with letters of appreciation. Each of these three steps must be performed properly to be sure you optimize your chances of winning the job you want.

Letters of Application

Letters of application should be short and factual. A letter addressed to a specific person is more likely to attract attention and be read. If you do not know anyone at a company, a quick phone call could determine the name of the person in charge of your area or of the director of hiring. Feature 16-3 shows a sample outline of a letter of application.

A few cautions about application letters. Try to avoid sounding either hopeless and desperate or pompous and egotistical. Your letter will convey a

Sample Outline for a Letter of Application

Name of Person (Employer)
Title
Name of Organization
City, State, Zip Code

Dear _____:

Paragraph 1   State the name of the position for which you are applying and how you heard of the opening.

Paragraph 2   Indicate the reasons for your interest in the type of work, the employer, and the location.

Paragraph 3   Relate the information on your resume to the job description. Point out how your experience and qualifications match the job.

Paragraph 4   Ask for an interview and indicate when you will be available or state when you will call for an appointment.

first impression of you to a prospective employer. Also, avoid copying a form letter verbatim from a textbook. A letter that is written by you will be more informative. If possible, type the letter on plain white, $8^1/_2 \times 11$ inch paper, and never send a machine-copied version.

Since a letter of application should be brief, rarely more than one page, most of the information on your background should be recorded on your resume. A resume should accompany your letter of application and give full details about your education and experiences. The sample outline in Feature 16-4 provides guidelines for writing your resume.

Brohard (1981) recommends *brainstorming* before writing a resume. She claims the process requires several days of reflecting on your past accomplishments. During the brainstorming period, jot down every attainment you can recall—volunteer work, clubs, political work, courses, and extracurricular work. Then review your list and be sure to include everything relevant to the job you seek.

brainstorming
Technique for generating new and creative ideas without fear of criticism

Many organizations require you to complete their own application forms. It is wise to check dates beforehand to be certain that you are accurate. Some applications require lengthy responses. Often the employer is evaluating not only your responses but also your ability to write, so be sure to check your spelling and sentence structure! (See Feature 16-5.)

Application forms almost always request the names of references. As a courtesy and for your own protection, ask permission from any person you plan to use as a reference. Send a letter reminding the person being used as a reference about yourself. Former employers and teachers sometimes have difficulty recalling every worker and student. One or two facts might help jog their memories. Also mention a time when you will call to be certain you have their permission to use their names. The chances of receiving a positive reference will improve if you have permission.

Sample Outline for Resume

Name
  Home address   Business address
  Phone number   Business phone number

Job specification	State concisely the type of job you desire.
Employment	List previous relevant jobs in reverse chronological order, explaining precisely what you did on each job.
Education	List schooling in reverse chronological order, and include any schooling that may have a bearing on the job you seek.
Special Skills	Include equipment you have used and special skills you have acquired.
References	Indicate that references will be furnished upon request.

Exercise 16-3

    Assume Greg Loser asked you to read and criticize his letter of application. Comment on each of the areas listed below.

To who it may concern:

    I think you should know that I am an outstanding student and would be an exceptional asset to your company. I had the highest grade in my high school history classes and was the best bowler in my league. I am also very popular with everyone I meet. I would like to be an executive.

    I know if you meet me you will probably want to hire me. I desperately

Bad Grammar Can Ground You

Remember when your grade school teacher told you it was important to learn to read and spell correctly so that you could grow up to be *somebody*? Bet you didn't expect to hear her words echoed by CEOs and corporate executives. But a recent poll of 100 Fortune 1000 executives revealed that a job candidate's chances of landing a job or a promotion could depend on the quality of her grammar and writing skills.

    According to the results of the survey . . . 80 percent of the executives said they have declined to interview candidates *solely* because of poor grammar, spelling or punctuation found on their resumes or cover letters. And 99 percent said they

believe that poor writing and grammar will hinder a person's ability to be promoted.

    While you may know how smart you are, mixing up *who* and *whom*, *they* and *their*, *me* and *I* can overshadow your talents. Nearly two-thirds of the executives thought that bad grammar and writing skills reflect poorly on a person's intellectual ability. So if you suspect that your grammar and writing need work, buy a grammar book. . . . Polish up on your grammar and let your talents shine through.

Source: Agyemang-Badu, N. A., Hawkins-Bond, P., & Manuel-Logan, R. (1992, August). Bad grammar can ground you. *Essence*, 128.

*Ted felt it was important to have a resume that
would catch the personnel manager's eye.*

FIGURE 16-2. Not a good way to catch attention.

need a job, since I have been out of work for three weeks. I cannot even afford
food for my parakeet.

Hear are some references: Professor Mercy, Mr. Hope, and Charity Love.
Their addresses are in the phone directory. If they don't remember me, try Mr.
Grinch, Ebenezer Grump, and B. Nasti.

I will be in town next week, and you could interview me on Tuesday or
Wednesday. My phone number is (555)123-4567. Please let me know if I can
send or bring any additional information.

a. Addressee: _____

_____

b. Opening paragraph: _____

_____

c. Reference to resume: _____

_____

d. Tone and attitude: _____

_____

e. Spelling and grammar: _____

_____

f. References: _____

_____

g. Closing paragraph: _____

_____

Please check your critique in the Feedback section.

Types of Interviews

Most interviews take less than thirty minutes, but within the brief time period, opinions are formed and important decisions are made. There are as many types of interviews as there are interviewers. Each person puts some individual style into the exchange. However, most interviews can be categorized as either informal, standardized, or situational. There are distinct differences among these three types.

informal interview Verbal exchange without a specific structure or standard form

Informal Interviews. An *informal interview* has no set agenda. The interview either is not planned at all or is mapped out rather loosely. The employer and applicant converse and exchange questions and answers. Each applicant is asked to provide different information, according to the direction of the conversation. This technique is often used to size up applicants rather than to gather information. Comparing applicants is difficult, since each applicant may have been asked an entirely different set of questions.

standardized interview Personal exchange based on a prepared set of questions

Standardized Interviews. In a *standardized interview*, the employer asks every applicant the same prepared set of questions. The interviewer begins by attempting to put the applicant at ease with some informal conversation. Next the questioning begins with requests for specific details on work and educational experiences. A sample set of questions might be:

- Why did you major in _____?
- Why did you leave your previous job?
- What did you enjoy most about your job?
- How do you feel about being pressured to meet deadlines?

situational interview Observation of an applicant in a specific situation set up by an interviewer

stress interview Situational interview in which the applicant is confronted with anxiety-provoking events

Situational Interviews. *Situational interviews* are usually limited to large organizations wishing to select people for upper-management jobs. Many of these organizations have assessment centers to handle their screening. The applicant is put in a specific situation, and the interviewer observes reactions. A rather amusing type of situational interview is the *stress interview*, where the applicant is confronted with events that are likely to cause anxiety. The interview is amusing if you are not the applicant. The applicant might be seated in a chair with a broken leg. As the chair rocks and almost tumbles, the applicant is observed. Those applicants who survive the initial stress may then be handed a leaky coffee mug. The events that occur in a stress interview are limited only by the imagination of the interviewer.

"This isn't going to be one of those 'stress' interviews, is it?"

FIGURE 16-3. It helps to prepare for the type of interview you are confronting.

Another type of situational interview is the *in-basket* interview. Here applicants must go through a series of memos, requests, and orders that they find in their in baskets. Time is limited and they must take action on them. Applicants are observed carefully, and notes are made on whether they are systematic or haphazard in approach. The observer also notes whether they perform tasks themselves or delegate some of the work. After the session each applicant must justify and explain the rationale for all actions taken.

The *leaderless-group interview* is another type of situational interview. Six to twelve applicants are instructed to work together to solve a business problem. They are provided some initial information, and throughout the session the information is updated. Just when they are on the brink of an important decision, new information is sent in to wipe out their conclusions. Leadership and reactions to pressure are observed.

in-basket interview Situational interview in which an applicant must, within a limited time, make decisions based on memos and notes

leaderless-group interview Situational interview in which several applicants are observed as they work together to solve a problem

Exercise 16-4

Read each of the following descriptions of interviews, and indicate whether each is an example of an informal, standardized, stress, in-basket, or leaderless-group interview.

a. The interviewer handed Martino a pen and asked him to complete an application. The pen immediately broke. He was handed another pen and it also fell apart. A third pen spilled ink all over the application. _____

b. When Jinx was applying for a job as a receptionist, her employer was cordial and friendly. They had a delightful chat about summer vacations, families, and football. At the end of the interview the employer shouted, "You're hired!" _____

c. Cloris was sent to a testing center for her interview. She was seated at a desk and told to handle the work in front of her. An interviewer sat across the room and observed her.

_____

d. Manuel felt at ease when his interviewer chatted with him about the weather last winter. Then the interviewer began reading a long list of questions.

_____

Please turn to the Feedback section to check your responses.

Preparing for Interviews

It is wise indeed to learn as much as possible about the company before your interview. You will appear more interested and ask better questions. As in other emotional situations, preparing ahead can spare you stress and anxiety. Make a checklist to be certain you remember to bring your resume, a list of references, and a list of questions for your potential employer. Put questions about salary and fringe benefits on the bottom of the list. Jot down some notes on why you want the job and why you feel you qualify. Be prepared to justify and expand on any items in your resume.

To create the best impression, dress conservatively, preferably similar to the workers in the company. Of course, if you are being interviewed for a job in landscaping, you do not need to show up in mud-stained overalls. Practice a firm handshake; it will set a good tone. Show interest, stand properly, and avoid fidgeting. The article in Feature 16-6 provides additional tips.

FEATURE 16-6 PSYCHOLOGY IN THE NEWS

Handling the Job Interview: Interview Traps to Avoid

- Never criticize your (former) company or management.
- Do not debate or argue various points, notions, ideas, or opinions.
- Do not show dissatisfaction in the interview; make it productive and evaluate it immediately afterward.
- Avoid verbosity and heavy gesturing. Try to be brief and focus on relevant aspects that are commensurate with your background highlights. Do not talk with your hands.
- Never underestimate "third-party interviews"—search firms, human resources—they can represent important shareholders in the total process and in the ultimate decision.

- Do not bring up compensation. It will come up in the second or subsequent interviews when it is appropriate.
- Be a good listener. Do not try to take control of the interview—it is a give and take process.
- Avoid negative behavior—don't have a chip on your shoulder, and don't be overconfident.
- Be relaxed and willing to share vocational interests, personal pursuits, etc. But do not get too relaxed and show pictures of your children.

Source: Sweeney, S. (1992, October/November). Handling the job interview: Interview traps to avoid. _Upscale,_ 46.

At the end of the interview, pull out the firm handshake again and thank your interviewer. Thank the secretary, receptionist, and anyone else who had a role in processing your application or scheduling the interview. If you hear nothing within ten days, you are entitled to call to determine whether the position has been filled.

Following Up on Applications

Immediately after the interview, send a thank-you note to your interviewer. You might restate your interest in the company and show appreciation for the time and information. Your note may make a difference if you are in a close race with other applicants. Also be sure to thank your references. Not only does your appreciative note show courtesy, but it might be helpful if you need your references again.

Exercise 16-5

Assume you are being interviewed for a magnificent job next Monday. Prepare a checklist of at least five items that you want to remember.

a. _____

b. _____

c. _____

d. _____

e. _____

Please compare your list with the list in the Feedback section.

Holding a Job

After the application and interview process, most people are relieved if they learn they have been hired. However, most organizations have a probation period. New employees are observed and reconsidered for a set period of time, usually between one week and six months. It is during this period that you must prove you can do the work. To perform any job well, you must organize time efficiently and set priorities.

Checkpoint

Use the following questions to check your understanding of this portion of the chapter. Choose and mark the one correct response to each question.

17. Which of the following agencies is most likely to charge you a fee for locating a job?
    a. College placement office
    b. State employment agency
    c. Private employment agency
    d. High school employment agency

18. Which of the following should accompany a letter of application?
    a. A thank-you note
    b. A resume
    c. A fee
    d. A transcript

19. A young man is applying for a job at the Builtwell Hardware Company. The personnel director is Mr. Chain. How should the young man address his letter?
    a. "Dear Builtwell Hardware Company:"
    b. "Gentlemen:"
    c. "Dear Personnel Director:"
    d. "Dear Mr. Chain:"

20. How should a letter of application conclude?
    a. With a final plea about how you need the job
    b. With a request for an interview
    c. With a detailed description of your education
    d. With a summary copied from a text

21. Which of the following is an example of a situational interview?
    a. A leaderless group
    b. An informal interview
    c. A structured interview
    d. A formal interview

22. What advice would you give a friend who wanted to know how to dress for an interview?
    a. Wear clothing that will attract attention.
    b. Wear expensive clothes.
    c. Wear conservative clothes.
    d. Wear casual clothes.

Use the Checkpoint Answer Key to verify your responses. If you had any difficulty with a question, carefully reread the text. If you had little or no difficulty answering the questions or have resolved any problems that you might have had, you are ready to continue with the next portion of this chapter.

JOB SATISFACTION

Have you ever been unhappy about a job or a course in school? Perhaps you had a bad year in sixth grade or a boring part-time job for a cranky boss. To be sure, your unhappiness affected the work you were doing, but your dissatisfaction probably also affected your relationships off the job or out of school.

Iris and Barrett (1972) studied two groups of foremen. One group was happy and satisfied and the other, unhappy and dissatisfied. Both groups were given a questionnaire to rate the importance of their jobs and a questionnaire on job and life satisfaction. They found that job satisfaction had a stronger influence on life satisfaction than life satisfaction had on job satisfaction. The impact of job satisfaction on life satisfaction was strongest for foremen who considered their jobs extremely important.

Both psychologists and corporations have been focusing more interest on the relationships between job satisfaction and life satisfaction. Indeed, job dissatisfaction can be hazardous to your health. Thompson (1991) reported that people with the lowest scores in job satisfaction were 330 percent more at risk for back injury than those who scored highest. Many companies are now offering counseling services to their employees. Employees may discuss areas of dissatisfaction at work, as well as personal matters that may be bothering them.

Lawler (1970) reported that more than 5000 articles have been published on job satisfaction. Most studies conclude that job satisfaction is relative to expectations and needs. People can be satisfied with some aspects of their work and dissatisfied with others.

Common Needs and Expectations

Resources and Comfort. Working conditions are basic to job satisfaction or dissatisfaction. If you have a problem locating a parking space or must walk a half mile from the parking lot to your office, you can get off to a poor start each day. Poor lighting, uncomfortable chairs, and noisy surroundings can all create dissatisfaction. Herzberg (1968) referred to such working conditions as *hygiene factors.* Hygiene factors also include the availability of equipment, supplies, and help. If you must waste time waiting in line to use a copy machine or must work with a faulty printer, you could easily become irritated and unhappy. If you work in attractive surroundings, in a convenient location, at acceptable hours, with ample resources, these hygiene factors cannot create dissatisfaction. A ten-year study by Kohn and Schooler (1983) revealed that positive hygiene factors can increase self-esteem, job commitment, and motivation.

hygiene factors External conditions that contribute to job satisfaction

Challenge and Stimulation. Although some individuals prefer the security of a routine job, most people seek some stimulation and challenge from their work. Dignity and pride are attached to achievements, and people search for ways to show some initiative. If a job becomes overly dull, people will look for some stimulation by perhaps getting a cup of coffee, strolling over to the water fountain, or starting up a social conversation with a coworker.

In the past two decades the level of education in the United States has increased markedly. Many people are overeducated for the jobs they perform (Rice, 1980). There are individual differences in needs for challenge. Some people are satisfied if they feel they are using their talents and their work is meaningful. Others have higher expectations and struggle for advancement.

Relations with Coworkers. Work offers opportunities for socializing. Lasting, close relationships with coworkers can make a dismal job acceptable. However, productivity generally decreases. If you are dissatisfied with the challenge of your work and the general working conditions, you are likely to spend more time socializing than working. Nonetheless, there are some people who prefer to work among friends. These people will become dissatisfied with their jobs if their coworkers are hostile or unfriendly.

The working conditions in this office most likely will create job dissatisfaction.

sexual harassment
Unwelcome sexual advances, requests for sexual favors, and other verbal or physical behavior of a sexual nature

Sexual harassment is a prevalent problem for women. In a large survey that sampled more than 1200 workers, 53 percent of the women claimed they had been sexually harassed by men on the job. Men were far less likely than women to be sexually harassed (Gutek, 1985). Matlin (1993) noted that for every complaint that is filed, hundreds of harassment incidents probably go unreported. Sexual harassment includes sexual advances, requests for sexual favors, and other verbal and physical behavior of a sexual nature. It may include obscene remarks, dirty jokes, or suggestive comments. It may also involve grabbing, fondling, or even rape. In the work setting, the harasser is usually a person of power, an immediate boss or a higher-level supervisor. Sometimes sexual harassment includes threats about job loss for failure to grant sexual favors. More than 20 percent of women either have quit their jobs, requested a transfer, or were fired as a result of harassment (Gutek, 1985).

Escape. For some people, work is an escape from their homes. Some want to break loose from a tense family; others who live alone want to escape from their loneliness. By keeping busy, people can avoid facing unpleasant realities. If providing nothing else, a job can provide this escape, which is usually temporary.

Financial Reward and Security. Supposedly everyone has a price. What salary would you require to work in dreadful conditions? For some, money is more important than the nature of the work. Others will accept a lower salary if the job is stable and they can have a sense of security. Clearly, companies attempt to lure workers away from other companies, with offers of better salaries and fringe benefits. There probably has never been a perfect job that fulfilled every need and expectation described. But job satisfaction does not rely entirely on factors beyond your control. You can increase your satisfaction by focusing on positive aspects of an organization. If you are unhappy about an aspect of your work, try to criticize constructively. Describe problems to a person with authority and offer one or two possible solutions. Hopefully, you can help your job meet your needs.

Exercise 16-6

A psychologist and an architectural designer just completed individual surveys at a large corporation. The psychologist concluded that job satisfaction was low, and the architect claimed satisfaction was high. Explain how the two professionals could have come to such opposite conclusions.

_____

_____

_____

_____

_____

You may check your explanation in the Feedback section.

CAREER CHANGES

Renwick and Lawler (1978) surveyed magazine readers and concluded that people do not give sufficient time in their youth to studying careers. Many just take jobs that are convenient. As a result, most people rethink and consider changing their careers sometime during their lives.

Some careers come to a natural end. Athletes must look for new jobs by middle age. Similarly, women who remained home to rear children find their careers in motherhood end when the children are off on their own careers.

Sometimes people are forced to make changes. A business may shut down from bankruptcy or may need to lay off workers. The article in Feature 16-7 reports how one man resolved his forced career-change problem and provides some tips. Many women are forced into career changes when they become displaced homemakers as a result of divorce, widowhood, or their spouse's unemployment. The National Commission on Working Women (1990) reported that in 1989 alone about 10 million women over the age of forty-five were displaced homemakers.

After working on a job for a decade or more, people sometimes reach a dead end. They realize they cannot progress any further. Because of the limited opportunity for advancement or promotion, they consider changing careers. Janis and Wheeler (1978) suggested that people draw up a balance sheet on their alternatives and list the pros and cons of a career change. They suggested four categories for comparison:

- Gains and losses for yourself
- Gains and losses for important others (spouse, children, parents, and the like)
- Self- approval or disapproval
- Approval or disapproval of others

FEATURE 16-7 PSYCHOLOGY IN THE NEWS

The Self-Employment Solution

Ask Rick Rouault about the secrets of starting a successful business and he'll tell you what worked for him: "First thing is to work for a company that goes belly up," says Rouault. "Second is to be over 55 and not find another job."

Rouault wasn't as desperate as that sounds. A corporate controller for a New Jersey car dealer, he'd already helped friends with tax returns and bookkeeping problems so had the outline of his business—Reliable Bookkeeping Services—already in place.

Now he pushes himself during tax season, takes time off during the slow periods, and manages to make ends meet.

It's best to start the way Rouault did: small, at home, consulting, writing or providing services in a field you already know. Consider these pointers:

- Talk to your spouse. If you're not both behind the idea, forget it.
- Start low budget, not big picture. If the business

takes off you can rent fancy offices and hire help.
- Use all the networking skills you would use looking for a job to find clients for your business.
- Ask other small-business owners about pros and cons and the start-up mistakes they made.
- Study the small-business section of the library; call the Small Business Administration for information on SBA publications, videotapes, and other services.
- Do market research to find out if there's a demand for your services.
- Remember, you'll get tax breaks for the business but you'll pay for your own benefits.
- Nothing ventured, nothing gained. Even if your business doesn't make it, you'll probably have some great contacts to turn to for your next job-search.

Source: Stern, L. (1993, June–July). The self-employment solution. *Modern Maturity*, 30.

This type of exercise helps people recognize the features and drawbacks of both their present jobs and other potential jobs. A more interesting job for you may not be worth the sacrifice of making your family move and your children change schools. Likewise, you want to consider whether you need the respect of others for your work.

UNEMPLOYMENT

Because western cultures value work, unemployment usually leads to guilt. Worse, people who are unemployed are not respected. Many stereotype the unemployed as lazy or parasitical. As a result, losing a job is traumatic. Several studies have found increased incidences of suicide, mental illness, alcoholism, and death from heart and kidney diseases among the unemployed.

For many persons, retirement is really unemployment. A surprising number of persons are being pushed into retirement (Selby, 1987). If not prepared, persons who are forced into retirement suffer from depression and illnesses similar to those of the unemployed. Many retired persons feel energetic and productive. Since they are unemployed, they must use their own imaginations and initiative. Returning to college, leisure activities, hobbies, and even finding a new career are all possibilities!

Exercise 16-7

Mr. Oldham is seventy years old. Although he is intelligent and energetic, he was retired from his company because of their mandatory retirement policy. Mr. Oldham felt the company was unfair, since he is more productive than most younger workers. He is rapidly becoming more depressed.

a. Why is Mr. Oldham likely to be depressed?

_____

_____

b. What do you recommend he do?

_____

_____

_____

Please turn to the Feedback section.

LEISURE

Not only are leisure activities essential in retirement, they are important throughout your life. Yankelovich (1978) reported that 80 percent of Americans find more enjoyment in their leisure activities than in their work. Everyone needs relaxation and a change of pace to release tension. The amount of time spent in leisure activities usually increases as you age. Young couples with children have little free time to themselves. By middle age it is healthy to

FIGURE 16-4. Those who have read this text will never spend their leisure time here.

develop a hobby. Sports and exercise will make you feel better both physically and psychologically. Whether ceramics, bird watching, stamp collecting, painting, or playing computer games, the hobby can be carried into retirement. Free time that can be enjoyed is never depressing!

Checkpoint

Use the following questions to check your understanding of the final portion of this chapter. Indicate whether each of the following questions is true or false.

23. _____ There has been very little research on job satisfaction.

24. _____ According to Herzberg, hygiene factors include physical working conditions.

25. _____ People in dull jobs search for stimulation.

26. _____ Middle-aged managers have a strong need to socialize at work.

27. _____ People can be satisfied with some aspects of their work but dissatisfied with others.

28. _____ Women are more likely than men to be sexually harassed.

29. _____ Few people change the careers that they originally chose.

30. _____ A balance sheet can be used to help make a decision about a career change.

31. _____ Unemployed people have fewer health problems.

32. _____ Developing a hobby can improve your adjustment to retirement.

Check your responses against the Checkpoint Answer Key at the end of the chapter. If you had difficulty with any question, reread the text. If you had little or no difficulty answering the questions or have resolved any problems that you might have had, you are ready to check yourself against the chapter inventory that follows.

CHAPTER INVENTORY

Use this list of objectives as a review checklist. You should be able to do the tasks outlined in the objectives and apply them to everyday examples. If you can, you may feel confident that you have mastered the material in this chapter.

1. Discuss the importance of career decisions, and describe two basic steps required in making them.
2. List three considerations in analyzing yourself, and specify three ways to analyze your abilities.
3. Identify a technique used by psychologists to assess interests and needs.
4. Describe the influences of gender and culture on job choice.
5. List two general considerations in analyzing jobs.
6. Describe the probable impact of technology on jobs.
7. Identify three sources of information on the nature of jobs.
8. Identify ways to learn of possible job opportunities.
9. Write a letter of application, a resume, and a request for a reference.
10. Recognize the importance of brainstorming before writing a resume.
11. Distinguish among informal, standardized, and situational interviews.
12. Describe the procedure used in in-basket and leaderless-group interviews.
13. Prepare for an interview.
14. Recognize the relationship between job satisfaction and satisfaction in life.
15. Describe five aspects of job satisfaction.
16. State three reasons why people might change careers.
17. Recognize the effects of unemployment and forced retirement on health.
18. Specify the importance of leisure activities both while working and in retirement.

Feedback

The correct answers to the exercises follow. If you did not answer an exercise correctly, review the preceding pages and return to the exercise to correctly complete it.

16-1. a. Boyd should check his bank account or find out if any friends, relatives, or institutions are willing to finance his education. (Equipping a dental office is an added expense.)
  b. Hilda needs to determine her own interests and abilities before making a career choice.
  c. Grant should find out if he has a talent for carpentry.

d. Dwanda should stay in school and learn more about her interests and abilities. With the changing labor requirements in the coming years, Dwanda's talents will be needed.

16-2. Your list should include any ten of the following:

Are there many openings for the job?

Will the job be in demand in the future?

Will continuous retraining be required?

How will technology affect the nature of the work?

What skills and abilities are required?

What previous training is required?

Will there be lengthy training periods on the job?

Is most of the work performed indoors or outdoors?

Is travel required?

What are the office facilities like?

Is a uniform required?

What are the working hours?

Are there unpleasant or hazardous working conditions?

16-3. a. Greg should find out the name of the person who will be most interested in his letter.

b. The opening paragraph should tell more about the type of position he wants. "Executive" is too vague. Experience should appear on his resume. The assets he mentions do not seem relevant.

c. What resume? Greg should have a brainstorming session and enclose a resume.

d. The tone and attitude sound both puffed up and desperate. He should stick to relevant facts.

e. Greg used "who" instead of "whom" and "hear" instead of "here."

f. Greg needs to contact his references and obtain permission to use their names. He should also include addresses.

g. The closing paragraph is the best feature of the letter. He might suggest his interest in visiting the organization even if he cannot be interviewed.

16-4. a. Stress interview

b. Informal interview

c. In-basket interview

d. Standardized interview

16-5. Your list should include any five of the following:

Take a resume.

Take a list of references.

Prepare a list of questions to ask at the interview.

Prepare notes on why you want the job and how you qualify.

Review the resume.

Have conservative clothes ready.

Work on a positive attitude.

Listen attentively.

Practice shaking hands.

Thank everyone involved.

16-6. The architectural designer probably focused on resources and comfort, while the psychologist probably questioned employees on job stimulation, relations with coworkers, and, possibly, escape value of the job. It appears the physical setting is pleasant, but the work itself leaves much to be desired!

16-7. a. Mr. Oldham's retirement is really unemployment for him. He is showing a normal reaction to unemployment.

b. He could use his intelligence and energy in a productive way. Volunteer work, a hobby, or another job are possibilities. He may even consider starting his own business.

Checkpoint Answer Key

1. false; 2. true; 3. false; 4. true; 5. true; 6. false; 7. false; 8. false; 9. false; 10. true; 11. false; 12. false; 13. true; 14. false; 15. true; 16. true; 17. c; 18. b; 19. d; 20. b; 21. a; 22. c; 23. false; 24. true; 25. true; 26. false; 27. true; 28. true; 29. false; 30. true; 31. false; 32. true.

Glossary

achievement need Motivation to accomplish tasks and be a success.

achievement test Test designed to measure past accomplishments, usually in academic subjects.

affiliation need Motivation to associate and belong with other people and feel loved.

ageism Negative stereotyping of older adults.

aggression Behavior that hurts or destroys another person, either verbally or physically, or both.

agoraphobia Most severe phobia, usually accompanied by panic attacks; inability to go out of the house.

altruism Concern for others; helping others without expecting a reward or benefit.

Alzheimer's disease Organic brain disorder causing a gradual loss of memory, confusion, and general mental deterioration.

amnesia Loss of memory or memory gap that includes forgetting personal information that would normally be recalled.

amniocentesis Procedure involving the removal of fluid samples from the uterus of an expectant mother to detect possible disease or genetic defects.

anorexia nervosa Prolonged refusal to eat, resulting in a severe weight loss.

antisocial personality Condition involving hurting others and breaking laws without guilt.

anxiety disorder Continuous state of tension, stress, and fearfulness.

applied psychology Approach involving practical uses of the study of behavior and thought.

approach-approach conflict Conflict that results from choosing between two desirable goals.

approach-avoidance conflict Conflict that results from weighing the positive and negative aspects of a single goal.

aptitude test Test designed to measure individual potential and to predict future achievements in a given area.

artificial intelligence Computer programs that solve problems.

assertiveness Standing up for personal rights while respecting the rights of others.

attitude Conviction based on beliefs, emotions, and behavior toward an object, person, or idea.

authoritarian discipline Regulating the behavior of others by rigid rules.

authoritarian leader Person who gives direct orders and is solely in charge of a group.

avoidance-avoidance conflict Conflict that results from being forced to choose between two undesirable goals.

behavior modification Technique that uses principles of conditioning to reach a desirable goal.

behavior therapy Psychotherapy that uses techniques based on learning principles.

behaviorism Belief that psychology should be scientific and based on observable events.

biofeedback Technique that provides information on heart rate and blood pressure so that a person can control these internal processes.

bipolar disorder Mood disorder involving mood swings between depression and mania.

borderline personality Personality disorder involving instability, confused self-image, and problems in relationships.

brain stem Lower part of the brain that controls heartbeat and breathing.

brainstorming Technique for generating new and creative ideas without fear of criticism.

brainwashing Dangerous technique used in spreading propaganda.

bulimia Binge eating followed by laxatives or self-induced vomiting.

career Set of experiences that permit the use of abilities for profit.

case study In-depth study of one individual, usually including tests, biographical and family histories, and interviews.

catastrophize Tendency to exaggerate things that may go wrong.

cerebellum [sehr-uh-BELL-um] Small section attached to the brain stem that controls balance.

cerebrum [seh-REE-bruhm] Upper part of the brain that is the center of thinking.

chunking Grouping individual items together into units, to increase short-term retention.

clairvoyance Ability to perceive objects or events that are not within the reach of the senses.

classical conditioning Form of learning based on pairing a stimulus that elicits a reflex or emotional response with a neutral stimulus, so that the neutral stimulus will eventually elicit the reflexive or emotional response.

client-centered counseling Form of humanistic therapy where the client sets the direction without fear of criticism.

cognition Mental or thought process.

cognitive psychology View that focuses on how the mind processes information.

cognitive therapy Therapy that focuses on correcting unreasonable thinking.

cohesiveness Ability to stick together in a group.

compensation Healthy defense mechanism that allows persons who are inadequate in one area to turn to areas where they can excel.

competitive goal   Objective that people in a group work against each other to achieve.

compliance   Publicly behaving in accordance with a group while privately disagreeing with their beliefs.

compulsion   Repeated and persistent behavior ritual that a person feels compelled to carry out to avoid disaster.

conformity   Accepting the beliefs of a group and behaving accordingly.

connotation   Emotional feelings and associations that a word arouses.

Continuous Quality Improvement (CQI)   Management technique that views quality as an ongoing process.

control group   Group of research participants that are the same as the experimental group, with the exception of the variable being studied.

conversion disorder   Anxiety disorder characterized by a loss of sensation without any physical cause.

cooperative goal   Objective that a group works together to achieve.

corporal punishment   Inflicting bodily harm to decrease undesirable behavior.

corpus callosum [KOR-pus kah-LOW-sum]   Bundle of nerves that connects the right and left hemispheres of the brain.

correlation   Relationship between scores on two variables.

cortex   Outer surface of the brain that processes all perception and complex thoughts.

cortisol   Hormone released in times of stress that converts protein to energy, maintains blood pressure, and weakens the immune system.

creativity   Ability to see things in a new way and come up with unusual solutions.

culture   Norms, beliefs, values, and ways of life that are shared by a group of people.

culture-bound   Limited to one culture.

culture-fair test   Test that uses experiences common to many cultures.

culture-free test   Test with no culture-linked content.

defense mechanisms   Variety of unconscious techniques used to avoid anxiety and protect self-esteem.

delusion   Imagined idea that is not true and persists in spite of information to the contrary.

democratic approach   Method using explanations and reasoning for rules.

democratic leader   Leader who expects group members to participate in decisions.

denotation   Specific dictionary definition of a word.

depression   Mood disorder in which a person feels overwhelming sadness.

desensitization   Therapeutic approach that uses a gradual method of classical conditioning to remove fears.

discrimination   Determining differences and sorting objects or people into categories.

displacement   Redirection of feelings to a substitute person or object when the true cause of the feelings is either an unacceptable or unavailable target.

dissonance   Discomfort that occurs from two inconsistent thoughts or beliefs.

downward communication   Passing messages from upper management down to workers.

drug   Chemical substance that causes physical, emotional, or behavioral changes.

dysfunctional family   Family that changes behavior in reaction to the stress of abnormal behavior of one or more members.

dyslexia   Perceptual impairment that results in reading, writing, and/or listening problems; reversed, scrambled, or confused message is sent to the brain.

eclectic therapists   Professionals who choose techniques appropriate for each case and do not adhere solely to one method.

eclectic view   Belief that psychology should select among appropriate findings of behavioral, gestalt, psychoanalytic, humanist, cognitive, and other views.

electroshock treatment (ECT)   Physiological therapy that delivers an electric shock to the brain to induce a convulsion or coma and reduce depression by erasing memories.

emetic   Substance that causes vomiting.

emotion   Feeling that arouses an individual to act or change.

emotional respondent   Emotion that is always elicited by a given stimulus and does not require learning; an emotional reflex.

ethnic group   Group that shares common nationality, culture, or language.

existential therapy   Form of treatment that focuses on free will and the meaning of life.

experiment   Research technique using controls to find the causes of specific behaviors.

experimental group   Group that receives treatment being investigated in an experiment.

extinction   Weakening or diminishing of a response; removal of a positive reinforcer to decrease the likelihood of a behavior.

extrasensory perception (ESP)   Ability to perceive and/or influence objects without using external senses.

extrinsic motivation   Performing activities only for an outside, or external, reward.

fantasy   Defense mechanism that involves withdrawing to an imaginary world through daydreams.

fetal alcohol syndrome (FAS)   Disorder characterized by physical, mental, and behavioral abnormalities in babies whose mothers drank large amounts of alcohol during pregnancy.

flex-time   Program that permits employees to schedule their own hours of work.

flow   State of concentration that permits complete absorption in an activity.

free association   Following a sequence of associated, spontaneous personal thoughts.

frustration   Feeling that results whenever you cannot reach a desired goal.

functional fixedness   Using objects only for their known purposes and being unable to think of other possible uses to solve problems.

gestalt   School of psychology that emphasizes patterns of organization in behavior.

gestalt therapy   Form of humanistic therapy that focuses on consistency between behaviors and inner feelings.

global demential amnesia   Type of amnesia characterized by an absentmindedness about present events.

GRIT (Graduated and Reciprocated Initiatives in Tension Reduction)   Technique for resolving conflicts; it can be useful in peacemaking.

group   Two or more people who interact or are aware of each other and share a common goal.

group norms   Rules of behavior for two or more people.

group therapy   Situation in which a therapist directs a discussion in a group of usually six to twelve persons, so that they may learn and profit from communication within the group.

groupthink   Conformity that keeps a group in a rut.

hallucinations   Voices or images that do not really exist.

halo effect   Bias that causes a person to overlook another person's specific deficiencies because of one favorable characteristic.

hidden agenda   Important personal information that is not revealed to other members of a group.

homeostasis   Ability of vital functions to maintain a stable condition.

homophobia   Irrational fear of, and contempt for, gay people.

hospice   Place for terminally ill patients where understanding, feelings, and dignity are primary concerns, along with health care.

humanistic counseling   Psychotherapy approach that attempts to improve self-esteem and encourage personal growth.

humanistic psychology   View that emphasizes the importance of self-direction and personal growth.

hygiene factors   External conditions that contribute to job satisfaction.

hypochondriasis   Anxiety disorder characterized by a total preoccupation with exaggerated health problems.

hypothesis   Educated guess that gives a tentative explanation and a basis for research.

hysterical amnesia   Amnesia that has no organic or physical cause; usually occurs after a trauma and is temporary.

ideal self   Person's goal or dream self.

illusion   Misinterpretation or error in perception.

in-basket interview   Situational interview in which an applicant must, within a limited time, make decisions based on memos and notes.

incentive   Reward that motivates behavior.

infatuation   Transient, temporary, selfish love.

informal interview   Verbal exchange without a specific structure or standard form.

informed consent   Document signed by subjects in an experiment after the nature of the research and any risks have been explained.

insomnia   Difficulty getting to sleep, staying asleep, or both.

intelligence   Ability to learn or adapt.

intelligence quotient (IQ)   Score on an intelligence test that is used to classify individuals.

interest inventory   Test designed to determine personal values, likes, and dislikes.

interpretation   Inferring meaning from what is sensed by comparing it with previously stored information.

intrinsic motivation   Performing activities because they are, in themselves, rewarding and enjoyable.

jigsaw classroom   Technique to encourage children of diverse backgrounds to work for their grades together, on an equal status.

Johari window   System of quadrants used in the study of self-disclosure.

laissez-faire leader   Coordinator who gives a group free rein.

Lamaze method   Preparation for active and conscious participation in the birth process.

leader   Person who gives guidance or direction to others and influences or changes their behavior.

leaderless-group interview   Situational interview in which several applicants are observed as they work together to solve a problem.

learning   Relatively lasting changes in behavior that are caused by experience or practice.

Leboyer method   Childbirth method that attempts to minimize shock to the newborn infant.

life structure   Basic pattern of a person's life.

limerance   Total emotional commitment that gives the experience of being or falling "in love."

loci   Mnemonic device that associates locations along a familiar path with items to be remembered.

long-term memory   Third stage of memory; items remembered more than five minutes are likely to be stored there indefinitely.

magical thinking   Irrational thought processes.

management   Conditioning method that allows a person to choose alternatives of reward or punishment.

management by objectives (MBO)   System that requires managers to set goals and employees to develop their own strategies to accomplish the goals.

mental set   Limited view of possible solutions and a tendency to respond in the same way regardless of the problem.

mindful discrimination   Discrimination based on training and sound reasoning.

mnemonics   Method that gives meaning and organization to help memory.

modeling   Learning that occurs by observing and imitating others.

motivation   Needs and incentives that cause people to behave as they do.

multiple personality   Rare disorder in which a person has two or more distinct personalities, each becoming prominent at a different time.

negative correlation   When one variable increases, the other decreases.

negative reinforcement   Removal of an unpleasant stimulus to increase the likelihood of a behavior.

neonate   Newborn infant, usually less than two weeks old.

network   Communication involving more than two people.

normal curve   Bell-shaped frequency distribution.

observation   Research method that requires watching and recording behavior without interference or interpretation.

obsessions   Unwanted but persistent thoughts or ideas.

one-way communication   Speaker speaks and receives no feedback from the listener.

operant (instrumental) conditioning   Type of learning that occurs because of positive or negative reinforcements.

organic amnesia   Amnesia that has physiological causes.

parapsychology Field of psychology that focuses on extrasensory perception.

peak experience Brief sense of overwhelming total fulfillment, approximating self-actualization.

pegword Method for improving memory, using a poem to attach mental image associations with items on a list that is to be retained.

perception Process that combines both sensing and interpreting.

permissive approach Method using little or no discipline.

personality disorder Pattern of negative traits that cause distress and an inability to get along with others, but the traits are not viewed as abnormal by the person exhibiting them.

phobia Intense, exaggerated, and unrealistic fear.

placebo Inert substance or fake treatment often used on a control group in an experiment.

polygraph Instrument commonly known as a lie detector that measures changes in heartbeat, blood pressure, breathing, digestive activity, and electric resistance on the skin surface.

positive correlation When one variable increases, the other also increases.

positive reinforcement Rewards that increase the likelihood of a behavior.

post-traumatic stress Anxiety disorder that causes a person to constantly reexperience a traumatic or shocking event.

power need Motivation to dominate and rule others.

precognition Ability to foresee future events.

predicate thinking Nonlogical thought that unconsciously associates subjects of sentences that have the same predicates or endings.

prejudice Negative attitude based on a hasty judgment without facts.

premise Belief.

primacy effect Explanation of why the first things learned are easier to remember.

proactive interference Forgetting that occurs because of confusion with previously learned material.

projection Defense mechanism, based on guilt, that involves accusing another of one's own weakness.

projective test Personality test that uses ambiguous stimuli and is designed to measure unconscious feelings.

propaganda Information that is deliberately deceptive or erroneous.

psychoactive drug Chemical substance that causes physical, emotional, or behavioral changes.

psychoanalysis View that psychology should focus on unconscious feelings; psychotherapy technique that involves uncovering the unconscious.

psychokinesis (PK) Ability of the mind to manipulate physical objects without the use of any physical contact.

psychological size Perceived importance of a person.

psychology Scientific study of human behavior and thought processes.

psychosurgery Operations on the brain, performed to treat mental disorders.

punishment Unpleasant stimulus that decreases the likelihood of behavior.

race Genetic background of Caucasoid, Negroid, or Mongoloid.

racism Belief that one race is superior and entitled to special privileges.

random assignment Assignment based on chance alone.

rational-emotive therapy Form of therapy that helps people think rationally and eliminate their self-defeating emotional thoughts.

rationalization Defense mechanism that distorts truth to provide excuses for a situation that is unacceptable.

reactance Strong resistance that results from receiving high-pressure persuasion and often causes a person to do the opposite of what is asked.

reaction formation Defense mechanism that causes people to behave in a manner opposite to their unacceptable impulses.

recency effect Explanation of why the last things learned are easier to remember.

reflex Response that is always elicited after a given stimulus and does not require learning.

regression Defense mechanism that involves the use of immature and childlike behaviors to cope with problems.

repression Forgetting that is caused by unconscious blocking of thoughts or events that are threatening or frightening.

retroactive interference Forgetting that occurs because of confusion with newly learned material.

reverse discrimination Favoring a group that elicits negative feelings.

seasonal affective disorder (SAD) Serious depression that usually begins in fall or winter and ends in spring.

schizophrenia Severe disturbance involving hallucinations, delusions, or thought disturbances.

script Brief story that requires you to fill in information.

self-actualization Highest need on Maslow's hierarchy; need to grow and fulfill potential.

self-concept Collection of beliefs that a person has about his or her own self-image.

self-disclosure Speaking honestly and revealing true feelings to others.

self-esteem Personal regard that people have for their own worth.

self-fulfilling prophecy Making a prediction and acting in a way to ensure that it will come true.

sensation Bringing stimuli from the outside world into the nervous system.

sensitivity training Form of group therapy that requires total honesty and trust among members.

sensory register First stage of memory when information that is sensed is briefly recorded and rapidly decays if not passed along to short-term memory.

set point Mechanism that maintains a person's usual weight.

sexism Belief that women are inferior to men.

sexual harassment Unwelcome sexual advances, requests for sexual favors, and other verbal or physical behavior of a sexual nature.

shaping Rewarding each behavior in a sequence that will eventually lead to a target behavior.

short-term memory   Second stage of memory when information is stored for less than thirty seconds.

sibling rivalry   Competition among brothers and sisters in a family.

situational interview   Observation of an applicant in a specific situation set up by an interviewer.

social loafing   Tendency of individuals to exert less effort when they work together than when they work alone.

socioeconomic class   Level of financial and social power.

socioemotional leader   Person who directs a group primarily according to the personal and social needs of the members.

SQ3R   Mnemonic for survey, question, read, recite, and review; a successful approach to studying.

standardized interview   Personal exchange based on a prepared set of questions.

standardized test   Test that has a uniform set of instructions for administration and scoring; the results can be compared with the scores of a larger population.

stereotype   Overgeneralized belief about a group of people.

stress   Tension caused by intense emotion.

stress interview   Situational interview in which the applicant is confronted with anxiety-provoking events.

sublimation   Healthy defense mechanism that channels unacceptable impulses into positive, constructive areas.

subliminal   Stimulus beneath a person's sensory threshold.

suppression   Consciously and intentionally avoiding unpleasant thoughts and memories.

survey   Poll to determine attitudes and behaviors of a group of people.

task leader   Person who keeps a group working toward a goal.

telepathy   Ability to understand what another person is thinking, without the use of the senses; mind reading.

theory X   Belief that people are basically lazy and must be controlled and directed by management.

theory Y   Belief that people are naturally interested in work and can direct their own behavior.

theory Z   Belief that people work most efficiently when given appropriate direction.

threshold   Smallest amount of stimuli that a person is aware of; stimulus a person can barely sense.

Total Quality Management (TQM)   Technique that applies quality principles to every aspect of an organization.

trace   Memory impression stored in the brain.

two-way communication   Speaker speaks and receives feedback from a listener, who then becomes a speaker.

type A personality   Behavior characterized by competitiveness and aggression.

type B personality   Behavior characterized by a relaxed manner.

type T personality   High-thrill-seeking personality.

type t personality   Low-thrill-seeking personality.

unconscious Motives, feelings, and impulses that are not in a person's awareness but nonetheless may influence the individual's behavior.

upward communication Passing information from workers up to management.

vicarious learning Observing the positive and negative reinforcement of others.

withdrawal Defense mechanism that involves escaping and removing oneself from unpleasant situations.

workaholic Person who prefers work to socializing and relaxing.

Bibliography

Adams, A. J., & Stone, T. H. (1977). Satisfaction of need for achievement in work and leisure time activities. *Journal of Vocational Behavior, 11,* 174–181.

Adelson, J. (Ed.) (1980). *Handbook of adolescent psychology.* New York: Wiley.

Adler, T. (1991, July). Women's expectations and menopause villains. *APA Monitor, 14.*

Albee, G. W. (1985, February). The answer is prevention. *Psychology Today,* 60–64.

Aldridge-Morris, R. (1989). *Multiple personality: An exercise in deception.* Hillsdale, N.J.: Erlbaum.

Allen, V. L., & Levine, J. M. (1971). Social support and conformity: The role of independent assessment of reality. *Journal of Experimental Social Psychology, 7,* 48–58.

Allport, G. (1958). *The nature of prejudice.*Garden City, N.Y.: Anchor/Doubleday.

Allport, G. (1961). *Pattern and growth in personality.* New York: Holt, Rinehart & Winston.

American Psychological Association (1990). Guidelines for providers of psychological services to ethnic, linguistic, and culturally diverse populations. Office of Minority Affairs.

American Psychological Association (1992). Ethical principles of psychologists. *American Psychologist, 45,* 3, 390–395.

Anastasi, A. (1988). *Psychological testing* (6th ed.). New York: Macmillan.

Andreason, N. (1987). Creativity and mental illness: Prevalence rates in writers and their first degree relatives. *American Journal of Psychiatry, 144,* 1288–1294.

Angell, M. (1985). Disease as a reflection of the psyche. *New England Journal of Medicine, 312* (24), 1570–1572.

Aronson, E. (1987). Teaching students what they think they already know about prejudice and desegregation. In V. P. Makosky (Ed.), *The G. Stanley Hall lecture series,* Vol. 7, 69–84. Washington, D.C.: American Psychological Association.

Aronson, E., Turner, J., & Carlsmith, M. (1963). Communicator credibility and communicator discrepancy as determinants of opinion change. *Journal of Abnormal and Social Psychology, 67,* 31–36.

Asch, A. (1988). Disability: Its place in the psychology curriculum. In P. Bronstein & K. Quina (Eds.), *Teaching a psychology of people.* Washington, D.C.: American Psychological Association.

Asch, S. E. (1956). Studies of independence and conformity: A minority of one against a unanimous majority. *Psychological Monographs, 70* (9, Whole No. 416).

Ashley, W. R., Harper, R. S., & Runyon, D. L. (1951). The perceived size of coins in normal and hypnotically induced economic states. *American Journal of Psychology*, 64 (4), 564–572.

Associated Press. (1987, December 4). Seat belt statistics. *Arlington Journal*.

Averill, J. R. (1976). Emotion and anxiety: Social, cultural, biological and psychological determinants. In M. Zuckerman & C. Spielberger (Eds.), *Emotion and anxiety*. Hillsdale, N.J.: Lawrence Erlbaum Associates.

Bahr, H. M., & Chadwick, B. A. (1974). Conservatism, racial intolerance, and attitudes toward racial assimilation among whites and American Indians. *Journal of Social Psychology, 94,* 45–56.

Bales, R. F. (1958). Task roles and social roles in problem-solving groups. In E. E. Maccoby, T. M. Newcomb, & E. L. Hartley (Eds.), *Readings in social psychology*. New York: Holt, Rinehart & Winston.

Bandura, A. (1969). *Principles of behavior modification*. New York: Holt, Rinehart & Winston.

Bandura, A., Ross, D., & Ross, S. A. (1963). Imitation of film-mediated aggressive models. *Journal of Abnormal and Social Psychology, 66,* 3–11.

Bandura, A., & Walters, R. H. (1959). *Adolescent aggression*. New York: Ronald.

Bandura. A., & Walters, R. H. (1963). *Social learnings and personality development*. New York: Holt, Rinehart.

Bane, M. J. (1976). Marital disruption and the lives of children. *Journal of Social Issues, 32,* 103–117.

Barron, F., & Harrington, D. M. (1981). Creativity, intelligence, and personality. *Annual Review of Psychology, 32,* 439–476.

Baum, A., Greenberg, N. E., & Singer, J. E. (1992). Biochemical measurement in the study of emotion. *Psychological Science, 3,* 1, 56–60.

Baumrind, D. (1967). Child care practices anteceding three patterns of preschool behavior. *Genetic Psychology Monograph, 75,* 43–88.

Baumrind, D. (1970). Socialization and instrumental competence in young children. *Young Children, 26* (2).

Beck, A. T., & Steer, R. A. (1989). Clinical predictors of eventual suicide: A 5- to 10-year prospective study of suicide attempters. *Journal of Affective Disorders, 17,* 203–209.

Beecher, H. K. (1959). *Measurement of subjective responses: Quantitative effects of drugs*. New York: Oxford University Press.

Beers, T. M., & Karoly, P. (1979). Cognitive strategies, expectancy, and coping style in the control of pain. *Journal of Consulting and Clinical Psychology, 47,* 179–180.

Begley, S., & Carey, J. (1979, November 26). The sexual brain. *Newsweek*.

Begleiter, H., & Porjesz, B. (1990). Neuroelectric processes in individuals at risk for alcoholism. *Alcohol and Alcoholism, 25,* (2/3), 251–256.

Bennet, W., & Gurin, J. (1982). *The dieter's dilemma: Eating less and weighing more*. New York: Basic Books.

Berelson, B., & Steiner, G. (1964). *Human behavior*. New York: Harcourt Brace Jovanovich.

Berkowitz, L. (1968). *Roots of aggression: A re-examination of the frustration-aggression hypothesis*. New York: Atherton.

Berry, J. W., & Bennett, J. A. (1992). Cree conceptions of cognitive competence. *International Journal of Psychology, 27* (1), 73–88.

Betancourt, H., & Lopez, S. R. (1993). The study of culture, ethnicity, and race in American psychology. *American Psychologist, 48* (6), 629–637.

Bettelheim, B., & Janowitz, M. (1950). *Dynamics of prejudice: A psychological and sociological study of veterans*. New York: Harper & Row.

Betz, N. E., & Fitzgerald, L. E. (1987). *The career psychology of women*. New York: Academic Press.

Birnbaum, I. M., Parker, E. S., Hartley, J. T., & Noble, E. P. (1978). Alcohol and memory: Retrieval processes. *Journal of Verbal Learning and Verbal Behavior, 17,* 325–335.

Birns, B., Blank, M., & Bridger, W. H. (1966). The effectiveness of various soothing techniques on human neonates. *Psychosomatic Medicine, 28*, 316–322.

Bloch, J. (1993, Spring). The truth about quality programs. *Smart Business, 1*, II, 1, 7.

Bower, B. (1993, February 27). Mental disorder numbers outpace treatment. *Science News, 143*, 143.

Bower, B. (1991). Women's trail of trauma. *Science News, 140*, 9, 141.

Bower, B. (1991, May 4). Emotional aid delivers labor-saving results. *Science News, 139*, 277.

Bower, G. (1973, October). How to . . . uh . . . remember! *Psychology Today*, 62–70.

Bozzi, V. (1988, February). A sizable advantage. *Psychology Today*.

Bradford, L. (1972). The case of the hidden agenda. *Group Development Selected Reading Series*. Washington, D.C.: National Training Laboratories.

Brazelton, T. B. (1970). Effects of prenatal drugs on the behavior of the neonate. *American Journal of Psychiatry, 126* (9), 95–100.

Brehm, J. W. (1966). *A theory of psychological reactance*. New York: Academic Press.

Brenner, M. H., & Sigband, N. B. (1973). Organizational communication: An analysis based on empirical data. *Academy of Management Journal, 325*.

Brewer, M. B., & Lui, L. (1984). Categorization of the elderly by the elderly: Effects of perceiver's category membership. *Personality and Social Psychology Bulletin, 10*, 585–595.

Briscoe, C. W., & Smith, J. B. (1975). Depression in bereavement and divorce: Relationship to primary depressive illness, a study of 128 subjects. *Archives of General Psychiatry, 32*, 439–443.

Broberg, D. L., & Bernstein, I. L. (1987). Candy as a scapegoat in the prevention of food aversions in children receiving chemotherapy. *Cancer, 60* (9), 2344–2347.

Brody, J. E. (1991, December 18). Recognizing demons of depression in either sex. *The New York Times*, pp. C21.

Brohard, E. B. (1981). The job application process. Unpublished manuscript, Northern Virginia Community College, Sterling, Va.

Bronstein, P., & Quina, K. (1991). *Teaching a psychology of people: Resources for gender and sociocultural awareness*. Washington, D.C.: American Psychological Association.

Brown, W. F. (1974). Effectiveness of paraprofessionals: The evidence. *Personnel and Guidance Journal, 53* (4), 257–263.

Bugelski, B. R., & Alampay, D. A. (1961). Professor Ahman Oramouz. *Canadian Journal of Psychology, 15*, 206.

Bumpass, L. L., & Sweet, J. A. (1988). Preliminary evidence on cohabitation. *NSFH Working Paper No. 2*. Center for Demography and Ecology, University of Wisconsin-Madison.

Buss, D. M., Larsen, R. J., Westen, D., & Semelroth, J. (1992). Sex differences in jealousy: Evolution, physiology, and psychology. *Psychological Science, 3* (4), 251–255.

Buys, C. J. (1978). Humans would do better without groups. *Personality and Social Psychology Bulletin, 4*, 123–125.

Cangemi, J. (1974). Futuristics: A brief view of some aspects of the field of psychology circa the year 2000. *Psychology, 11* (1), 52–55.

Carrera, M. A. (1986, April 11). Future directions in teen pregnancy prevention. Talk presented to the annual meeting for the Scientific Study of Sex, Eastern Region.

Castro, J. (1990, Fall issue on women). Get set: Here they come. *Time*, 50–52.

Center for Disease Control (1991, January 5). Data from the National Survey of Family Growth, report by Associated Press release.

Chambless, D. (1986). Fears and anxiety. In C. Tavris (Ed.), *Every woman's emotional well-being*. New York: Doubleday.

Chase, W. G., & Simon, H. A. (1973). The mind's eye in chess. In W. G. Chase (Ed.), *Visual information processing*. New York: Academic Press.

Clarke-Stewart, A. (1989). Infant day care: Maligned or malignant. *American Psychologist, 44*, 266–273.

Clayton, R. R., & Voss, H. L. (1977). Shacking up: Cohabitation in the 1970's. *Journal of Marriage and the Family, 39* (2), 273–283.

Cohen, S., & Hoberman, H. M. (1983). Positive events and social support as buffers of life change stress. *Journal of Applied Social Psychology, 13*, 99–125.

Coleman, J. C. (1972). *Abnormal psychology and modern life.* Glenview, Ill.: Scott, Foresman.

Coles, R., & Stokes, G. (1985). *Sex and the American teenager.* New York: Harper & Row.

Comings, D. E., Comings, B. G., Muhleman, D., Dietz, G., Shahbahrami, B., Tast, D., Knell, E., Kocsis, P., Baumgarten, R., Kovacs, B. W., Levy, D. L., Smith, M., Borison, R. L., Evans, D., Klein, D. N., MacMurray, J., Tosk, J., Sverd, J., Gysin, R., & Flanagan, S. D. (1991). The dopamine D2 receptor locus as a modifying gene in neuropsychiatric disorders. *Journal of the American Medical Association, 266*, 1793–1800.

Coombs, B., Hales, D., & Williams, B. (1980). *An invitation to health.* Menlo Park, Calif.: Benjamin/Cummings.

Coopersmith, S. (1967). *The antecedents of self-esteem.* San Francisco: W. H. Freeman.

Corr, J. M. (1992). Somatization: Mind over matter. *Harvard Health Letter, 17* (6), 4.

Council on Ethical and Judicial Affairs. (1990). Black-white disparities in health care. *Journal of the American Medical Association, 263*, 2344–2346.

Crawford, M., & English, L. (1984). Genetic versus specific inclusion of women in language: Effects on recall. *Journal of Psycholinguistic Research, 13*, 373–381.

Crenshaw, A. (1980, February 24). "Big men" really are. *The Washington Post.*

Cressen, R. (1978). Artistic quality of drawings and judges' evaluation of the DAP. *Journal of Personality Assessment, 42*, 597–603.

Crombag, H. F. (1966). Cooperation and competition in means-independent triads. *Journal of Personality and Social Psychology, 4*, 692–695.

Crowley, J. E., Levitin, T. E., & Quinn, R. P. (1973, March). Seven deadly half-truths about women. *Psychology Today*, 94–96.

Crowne, D. P., & Marlowe, D. (1964). *The approval motive: Studies in evaluative dependence.* New York: Wiley.

Darley, C. F., Tinkleberg, J. R., Roth, W. T., Hollister, L. E., & Atkindon, R. C. (1973). Influence of marihuana on storage and retrieval processes in memory. *Memory and Cognition, 1*, 196–200.

Davidson, R. J. (1992). Emotion and affective style: Hemispheric substrates. *Psychological Science, 3* (1), 39–43.

Davies, J. (1976, February 8). Stereo-phonic. *The Washington Post.*

Davis, K. (1973, July). The care and cultivation of the corporate grapevine. *Dun's.*

David, K. (1977). *Human behavior at work.* New York: McGraw-Hill.

Deaux, K. (1985). Sex and gender. *Annual Review of Psychology, 36*, 49–81.

Deci, E. L. (1971). Effects of externally mediated rewards on intrinsic motivation. *Journal of Personality and Social Psychology, 18*, 105–115.

Deci, E. L. (1975). *Intrinsic motivation.* New York: Plenum Press.

Deci, E. L. (1972, August). Work: Who does not like it and why. *Psychology Today*, 56–68.

DeLongis, A., Coyne, J. C., Dakof, G., Folkman, S., & Lazarus, R. S. (1982). Relationship of daily hassles, uplifts, and major life events to health status. *Health Psychology, 1*, 119–136.

Deutsch, M. (1968). The effects of cooperation and competition upon group process. In D. Cartwright & A. Zander (Eds.), *Group dynamics: Research and theory.* New York: Harper & Row.

Deutsch, M. (1993). Educating for a peaceful world. *American Psychologist, 48* (5), 510–517.

Deutsch, M., & Gerard, H. B. (1955). A study of normative and informational social influences upon individual judgment. *Journal of Abnormal and Social Psychology, 51,* 629–636.

Diagnostic and statistical manual of mental disorders. (DSM III-R). (1987). Washington, D.C.: American Psychiatric Association.

Disabling panic attacks (agoraphobia). How is agoraphobia treated? (1979, August). *Harvard Medical School Health Letter.*

Dodge, J. R., & Rogers, C. W. (1976). Is NIMH's dream coming true? Wyoming centers reduce state hospital admissions. *Community Mental Health Journal, 12* (4), 399–404.

Dodge, S. (1989, December 13). Rutgers panel outlines ways to fight homophobia. *The Chronicle of Higher Education,* A51.

Drillien, C. M., & Ellis, R. W. B. (1964). *The growth and development of the prematurely born infant.* Baltimore: Williams & Wilkins.

Dryfoos, J. (1985). What the United States can learn about prevention of teenage pregnancy from other developed countries. *SIECUS Report, XIV,* 1–7.

Duran, R. P. (1983). *Hispanics' education and background: Predictors of college achievement.* New York: College Board Publications.

Eagly, A., Johnson, B., Makhijani, M., Karau, S., & Klonsky, B. (1991). Gender and leadership. Paper presented at American Psychological Association Convention Science Weekend, San Francisco.

Ehrenreich, B., Hess, E., & Jacobs, G. (1986). *Re-making love.* Garden City, N.Y.: Anchor/ Doubleday.

Ekman, P. (1980). *The face of man.* New York: Garland STPM Press.

Ekman, P. (1982). Methods for measuring facial action. In P. Ekman & K. Scherer (Eds.), *Handbook of methods in non-verbal behavior research.* New York: Cambridge University Press.

Ekman, P. (1992). Facial expressions of emotion: New findings, new questions. *Psychological Science, 3* (1), 34–38.

Ekman, P. (1993). Facial expression and emotion. *American Psychologist, 48* (4), 384–392.

Ekman, P., & Friesen, W. (1978). *FACS investigators guide.* Palo Alto, Calif.: Consulting Psychologists Press.

Ekman, P., Friesen, W., & Ancoli, S. (1980). Facial signs of emotional experience. *Journal of Personality and Social Psychology, 39,* 1125–1134.

Ekman, P., Friesen, W. V., & O'Sullivan, M. (1988). Smiles when lying. *Journal of Personality and Social Psychology, 54,* 414–420.

Elias, M. (1992, July). Aging and memory: When to worry about forgetting. *Harvard Health Letter, 17* (9), 1–3.

Ellis, A. (1979). Rational emotive therapy. In R. Corsini (Ed.), *Current psychotherapies.* Itasca, Ill.: Peacock.

Ellis, M., & Ames, M. A. (1987). Neurohormonal functioning and sexual orientation: A theory of homosexuality–heterosexuality. *Psychological Bulletin, 101,* 233–258.

Engstrom, L., Geijerstam, G., Holmberg, N. G., & Uhrus, K. A. (1964). A prospective study of the relationship between psycho-social factors and the course of pregnancy and delivery. *Journal of Psychosomatic Research, 8,* 151–155.

Ennis, R. H. (1985). Critical thinking and the curriculum. *National Forum, 65* (1), 28–30.

Evans, B. (1963). *Word-a-day vocabulary builder.* New York: Random House.

Fantz, R. L. (1958). Pattern vision in young infants. *Psychological Record, 8,* 43–47.

Faraone, S. V., & Tsuang, M. T. (1985). Quantitative models of genetic transmission of schizophrenia. *Psychological Bulletin, 98* (1), 41–66.

Farley, F. (1986, May). The big T personality. *Psychology Today.*

Fast, J. (1970). *Body language.* New York: Pocket Books.

Festinger, L. (1962). Cognitive dissonance. *Scientific American, 207,* 93–98.

Footlick, J. K. (1981, March 23). Lock 'em up—but where? *Newsweek.*

Foster, H. C., Hillbrand, M., & Silberstein, M. (1992, August). Neuropsychological deficit and aggressive behavior: A prospective study. Paper presented at American Psychological Association Centennial Meeting, Washington, D.C.

Frankl, V. (1955). *The doctor and the soul.* New York: Knopf.

Freedman, J. (1978). *Happy people: What happiness is, who has it and why.* New York: Harcourt Brace Jovanovich.

Freedman, J., & Fraser, S. C. (1966). Compliance without pressure: The foot in the door technique. *Journal of Personality and Social Psychology, 4,* 195–202.

Freedman, M., & Rosenman, R. (1974). *Type A behavior and your heart.* New York: Knopf.

Freiberg, P. (1991, March). Better service urged for mentally ill criminals. *APA Monitor,* 29.

Frerichs, R. R., Aneshensel, C. S., & Clark, V. A. (1981). Prevalence of depression in Los Angeles County. *American Journal of Epidemiology, 113,* 3, 691–699.

Gagnon, J. H., & Greenblat, C. S. (1978). *Life designs: Individuals, marriages and families.* Glenview, Ill.: Scott, Foresman.

Gallant, D. M. (1987). *Alcoholism.* New York: Norton.

Gardner, H. (1983). *Frames of mind: The theory of multiple intelligences.* New York: Basic Books.

Gardner, H. (1985). *Frames of mind.* New York: Basic Books.

Geisinger, K. F. (1992). *Psychological testing of Hispanics.* Washington, D.C.: American Psychological Association.

Gelman, D., Carey, J., Gelman, E., Melamud, P., Foote, D., Lubenow, G., & Contreras, J. (1981, May 18). Just how the sexes differ. *Newsweek.*

Gerard, H. B., Wilhemy, R. A., & Conelley, E. S. (1968). Conformity and group size. *Journal of Personality and Social Psychology, 8,* 79–82.

Gilligan, C. (1982). *In a different voice.* Cambridge, Mass.: Harvard University Press.

Gilmer, B. (1975). *Applied psychology: Adjustments in living and work.* New York: McGraw-Hill.

Ginott, H. G. (1969). *Between parent and child.* New York: Avon Books.

Glass, D. C. (1977). *Stress and coronary prone behavior.* Hillsdale, N.J.: Lawrence Erlbaum Associates.

Gold, P. W., Gwirtsman, H., Avgerinos, P. C., Nieman, L. K., Gallucci, W. T., Kaye, W., Jimerson, D., Ebert, M., Rittmaster, R., Loriaux, L., & Chrousos, G. P. (1986). Abnormal hypothalamic-pituitary-adrenal function in anorexia nervosa. *New England Journal of Medicine, 314,* 1335–1342.

Goldberg, E. L., Comstock, G. W., & Harlow, S. D. (1988). Emotional problems in widowhood. *Journal of Gerontology, 43* (6), S206–208.

Goldberger, L. (1982). Sensory deprivation and overload. In L. Goldberger & S. Breznitz (Eds.), *Handbook of stress: Theoretical and clinical aspects.* New York: Free Press.

Goleman, D. (1986, November 9). A different sort of IQ test. *The New York Times.*

Gordon, T. (1970). *Parent effectiveness training.* New York: Peter Wyden.

Gould, R. (1975, August). Adult life stages: Growth toward self-tolerance. *Psychology Today.*

Grant, E. (1988, March). Marriage: Practice makes perfect? *Psychology Today.*

Greenberg, M., & Morris, N. (1974). Engrossment: The newborn's impact upon the father. *American Journal of Orthopsychiatry, 44* (4), 520–531.

Greenfield, P. (1992, June 18). Making basic texts in psychology more culture-inclusive and culture sensitive: Notes and references for developmental psychology. E-mail. Calif.: UCLA.

Greenwald, A. G., Spangenberg, E. R., Pratkanis, A. R., & Eskensi, J. (1991). Double-blind tests of subliminal self-help audiotapes. *Psychological Science, 2,* 119–122.

Gurman, A. S., & Kniskern, D. P. (1976). Research on marital and family therapy. In S. L. Garfield & D. E. Bergin (Eds.), *Handbook of psychotherapy and behavior change*. New York: Wiley.

Gutek, B. A. (1985). *Sex and the workplace*. San Francisco: Jossey-Bass.

Gyllenhammer, P. G. (1977). How Volvo adapts work to people. *Harvard Business Review, 55*, 102–105.

Haire, D. (1972). The cultural warping of childbirth. *International Childbirth Association News, 35*.

Hall, E. T. (1969). *The hidden dimension*. Garden City, N.Y.: Anchor/Doubleday.

Hall, H. (1987, December). Wedded faces. *Psychology Today*.

Hall, H. (1988, July/August). Marriage: Practice makes imperfect? *Psychology Today*.

Hamilton, M. C., & Henley, N. M. (1982). Detrimental consequences of generic masculine usage. Effects on the reader/hearer's cognitions. Paper presented at a meeting of the Western Psychological Association, Sacramento, Calif.

Harkins, S. G., & Petty, R. E. (1983). Social context effects in persuasion. In P. Paulus (Ed.), *Basic group processes*. New York: Springer-Verlag.

Harriman, B. (1974). Up and down the communication ladder. *Harvard Business Review, 52*, 147–148.

Harris, L., & Associates. (1986). American teens speak: Sex myths, TV, and birth control: New York: The Planned Parenthood Poll.

Harris, R. J. (1977). Comprehension of pragmatic implications in advertising. *Journal of Applied Psychology, 62*, 603–608.

Harrison, A. A. (1976). *Individuals and groups*. Monterey, Calif.: Brooks/Cole.

Hart, K. J., & Ollendich, T. H. (1985). Prevalence of bulimia in working and university women. *American Journal of Psychiatry, 142* (7), 851–854.

Hartley, D., Roback, H., & Abramowitz, S. (1976). Deterioration effects in encounter groups. *American Psychologist, 31*, 247–255.

Harvard Medical School Mental Health Letter (1986, February). Suicide, Part I and II, 2 (8), 1–4.

Harvard Mental Health Letter (1993, February). Seasonal affective disorder. 1–3.

Harvard Mental Health Letter (1993, March). Self-help groups, Part I, 1–3.

Haskins, R. (1985). Public aggression among children with varying day care experience. *Child Development, 56*, 689–703.

Heckman, N. A., Bryson, R., & Bryson, J. B. (1977). Problems of professional couples: A content analysis. *Journal of Marriage and the Family, 39* (2), 323–330.

Helms, J. E. (1992). Why is there no study of cultural equivalence in standardized cognitive ability testing? *American Psychologist, 47* (9), 1083–1100.

Herzberg, F. (1968, March). Motivation morale. *Psychology Today*, 42–45.

Hetherington, E. M. (1972). The effect of father absence on personality development in adolescent daughters. *Developmental Psychology, 7*, 313–326.

Hetherington, E. M., Cox, M., & Cox, R. (1977, April). Divorced fathers. *Psychology Today*, 42.

Hettlinger, R. F. (1975). *Human sexuality: A psychosocial perspective*. Belmont, Calif.: Wadsworth.

Hill, W. F. (1985). *Learning: A survey of psychological interpretations* (4th ed.). New York: Harper & Row.

Hiller, D. V., & Philliber, W. W. (1978). The derivation of status benefits from occupational attainments of working wives. *Journal of Marriage and the Family, 40* (1), 63–68.

Holmes, T. H., & Rahe, R. H. (1967). The social readjustment rating scale. *Journal of Psychosomatic Research, 2*, 213–218.

Holtzman, W. H. (1975). New developments in the Holtzman Inkblot Technique. In P. McReynolds (Ed.), *Advances in psychological assessment*, Vol. 3. San Francisco: Jossey-Bass.

Horn, J. C. (1980, June). Dining: What tips tippers to tip. *Psychology Today*, 32.

Horn, P., et al. (1973, October). The phony Doctor Fox. *Psychology Today*, 19–20.

Horner, M. (1969, March). Women's will to fail. *Psychology Today*, 36–38.

Hunt, M. (1974). *Sexual behavior in the 1970's*. Chicago: Playboy Press.

Huston, T., Ruggiero, M., Conner, R., & Geis, G. (1981). Bystander intervention into crime: A study based on naturally occurring episodes. *Social Psychology Quarterly, 44*, 14–23.

Hyde, J. S. (1981). How large are cognitive gender differences? *American Psychologist, 36* (8), 892–901.

Hyde, J. S. (1984). How large are gender differences in aggression? A developmental meta-analysis. *Developmental Psychology, 20*, 722–736.

Hyde, J. S. (1986). *Understanding human sexuality* (3rd ed.). New York: McGraw-Hill.

Hyde, J. S., & Linn, M. C. (1988). Gender differences in verbal ability: A meta-analysis. *Psychological Bulletin. 104*, 53–69.

Ickes, W., & Barnes, R. (1978). Boys and girls together and alienated: On enacting stereotyped sex roles in mixed sex dyads. *Journal of Personality and Social Psychology, 36* (7), 669–683.

Inglehart, R. (1990). *Culture shift in advanced industrial society*. Princeton, N.J.: Princeton University Press.

Iris, B., & Barrett, G. (1972). Some relationships between job and life satisfaction. *Journal of Applied Psychology, 56* (4), 301–304.

Ismail, A. H., & Gruber, J. J. (1967). *Integrated development: Motor aptitude and intellectual performance*. Columbus, Ohio: Charles E. Merrill.

Janis, I. L. (1973). *Victims of groupthink: A psychological study of foreign policy discussion and fiascos*. Boston: Houghton Mifflin.

Janis, I. L., & Feshbach, S. (1953). Effects of fear-arousing communications. *Journal of Abnormal and Social Psychology, 48*, 78–92.

Janis, I. L., & Wheeler, D. (1978, May). Thinking clearly about career choices. *Psychology Today*, 67–68.

Johnson, D. W., & Johnson, R. T. (1987). *Learning together and alone: Cooperative, competitive and individualistic learning* (2nd ed.). Englewood Cliffs, N.J.: Prentice-Hall.

Johnson, J. P., Comings, D. E., Flanagan, S. D., Nessman, D. G., Tosk, J. M., & Kelly, J. T. (1992, August). Genetic influence on P300 latency in substance abusers. Paper presented at American Psychological Association Convention, Washington, D.C.

Johnson, W. G. (1971). Some applications of Homme's covariant control therapy: Two case reports. *Behavior Therapy, 2*, 240–248.

Jones, E. F., Forrest, J. D., Goldman, N., Henshaw, S. K., Lincoln, R., Rosoff, J. I., Westoff, C. F., Wulf, W., & Wulf, D. (1985). Teenage pregnancy in developed countries: Determinants and policy implications. *Family Planning Perspectives, 17*, 53–63.

Jourard, S. (1971). *Self-disclosure*. New York: Wiley-Interscience.

Jourard, S. (1971). *The transparent self*. New York: Van Nostrand Reinhold.

Judd, C. M., & Park, B. (1988). Out-group homogeneity: Judgments of variability at the individual and group levels. *Journal of Personality and Social Psychology, 54*, 778–788.

Kalish, R. A., & Reynolds, D. K. (1976). *Death and ethnicity: A psychocultural study*. Los Angeles: University of Southern California Press.

Kamerow, D. B., Pincus, H. A., & Macdonald, D. I. (1986). Alcohol abuse, other drug abuse, and mental disorders in medical practice. *Journal of American Medical Association, 225*, 2054–2057.

Kaminoff, R. D., & Proshanky, H. M. (1982). Stress as a consequence of the urban physical environment. In L. Goldberger & S. Breznitz (Eds.), *Handbook of stress: Theoretical and clinical aspects.* New York: Free Press.

Kanner, A. D., Coyne, J. C., Schaefer, C., & Lazarus, R. (1981). Comparison of two modes of stress measurement: Daily hassles and uplifts versus major life events. *Journal of Behavioral Medicine, 4,* 1–39.

Kastenbaum, R., & Costa, P. T. (1977). Psychological perspective on death. *Annual Review of Psychology, 28,* 225–249.

Katzell, R. A., & Thompson, D. E. (1990). Work motivation. *American Psychologist, 45* (2), 144–153.

Kelly, J. B. (1982). Divorce: The adult perspective. In B. Wolman (Ed.), *Handbook of developmental psychology.* Englewood Cliffs, N.J.: Prentice-Hall.

Kelman, H. C. (1958). Compliance, identification and internalization: Three processes of attitude change. *Journal of Conflict Resolution, 2,* 51–60.

Kent, D. (1990, May). A conversation with Claude Steele. *APS Observer,* 11–17.

Kessler, M., & Albee, G. W. (1975). Primary prevention. *Annual Review of Psychology, 26,* 557–592.

Keys, A. B., Brozek, J., Henschel, A., Michelson, O., & Taylor, H. L. (1950). *The biology of human starvation,* Vol. 2. Minneapolis: University of Minnesota Press.

King, K., Balswick, J. O., & Robinson, I. E. (1977). The continuing premarital sexual revolution among college females. *Journal of Marriage and the Family, 39,* 455–459.

Kitayama, S., & Markus, H. R. (1992, May 6–8). Construal of the self as a cultural frame: Implications for internationalizing psychology. Prepared for: Symposium on Internationalization and Higher Education, University of Michigan.

Klatzky, R. L. (1975). *Human memory: Structures and processes.* San Francisco: Freeman.

Klatzky, R. L. (1980). *Human memory: Structures and processes* (2nd ed.). San Francisco: Freeman.

Koch, K. (1977). *I never told anybody.* New York: Random House.

Kohlberg, L. (1969). Stage and sequence: The cognitive developmental approach to socialization. In D. A. Goslin (Ed.), *Handbook of socialization theory and research.* Chicago: Rand McNally.

Kohlberg, L. (1976). Moral stages and moralization. In T. Lickona (Ed.), *Moral development and behavior.* New York: Holt, Rinehart & Winston.

Kohn, M., & Schooler, C. (1983). *Work and personality.* Norwood, N.J.: Ablex.

Korte, C., & Kerr, N. (1975). Response to altruistic opportunities in urban and nonurban settings. *Journal of Social Psychology, 95,* 183–184.

Kubler-Ross, E. (1969). *On death and dying.* New York: Macmillan.

Kurdek, L. A., & Schmitt, J. P. (1986). Relationship quality of partners in heterosexual married, heterosexual cohabiting, and gay and lesbian relationships. *Journal of Personality and Social Psychology, 51,* 711–721.

Lamb, H. R. (1984). *Homeless mentally ill.* Washington, D.C.: American Psychiatric Association.

Lamb, M. (1979). Paternal influences and the father's role: A personal perspective. *American Psychologist, 34* (10), 938–943.

Langer, E. J., Bashner, R. S., & Chanowitz, B. (1985). Decreasing prejudice by increasing discrimination. *Journal of Personality and Social Psychology, 49* (1), 113–120.

Langer, E. J., & Dweck, C. S. (1973). *Personal politics: The psychology of making it.* Englewood Cliffs, N.J.: Prentice-Hall.

Lapp, D. (1987). *Don't forget! Easy exercises for a better memory at any age.* New York: McGraw-Hill.

Larson, D. L., Spreitzer, E. A., & Snyder, E. E. (1976). Social factors in the frequency of romantic involvement among adolescents. *Adolescence, 11,* 7–12.

Latané, B., & Darley, J. M. (1968). Group inhibition of bystander intervention. *Journal of Personality and Social Psychology, 10,* 215–221.

Latané, B., & Darley, J. M. (1970). *The unresponsive bystander: Why doesn't he help?* New York: Appleton-Century-Crofts.

Latané, B., Williams, K., & Harkins, S. (1979). Many hands make light work: The causes and consequences of social loafing. *Journal of Personality and Social Psychology, 37,* 822–832.

Lawler, E. E. (1970). Job attitudes and employee motivation: Theory, research and practice. *Personnel Psychology, 23,* 223–237.

Leavitt, H. J. (1951). Some effects of certain communication patterns on group performance. *Journal of Abnormal and Social Psychology, 46,* 38–50.

Leboyer, F. (1975). *Birth without violence.* New York: Random House.

Levanway, R. W. (1955). The effect of stress on expressing attitudes toward self and others. *Journal of Abnormal and Social Psychology, 50,* 225–226.

Levine, M. E., Villena, J., Altman, D., & Nadien, M. (1976). Trust of a stranger: An urban/small town comparison. *Journal of Psychology, 92,* 113–116.

Levinson, D. (1986). A conception of adult development. *American Psychologist, 41* (1), 3–13.

Levinson, D. J., Darrow, C. N., Klein, E. B., Levinson, M. H., & McKee, B. (1978). *The seasons of a man's life.* New York: Knopf.

Levinson, R. W. (1992). Autonomic nervous system differences among emotions. *Psychological Science, 3* (1), 23–27.

Lewin, K. (1935). *A dynamic theory of personality.* K. E. Zener & D. K. Adams (Trans.). New York: McGraw-Hill.

Lewin, K., Lippitt, R., & White, R. (1943). Patterns of aggressive behavior in experimentally created social climates. *Journal of Social Psychology, 10,* 271–299.

Lewis, M. (1992). *Shame: The exposed self.* New York: Free Press.

Liebert, R. M., & Sprafkin, J. (1988). The early window (3rd ed.). Elmsford, N.Y.: Pergamon.

Lindskold, S. (1978). Trust development, the GRIT proposal, and the effects of conciliatory acts on conflicts and cooperation. *Psychological Bulletin, 85,* 772–793.

Lindskold, S. (1985). GRIT: Reducing distrust through carefully introduced conciliation. In S. Worchel & W. G. Austin (Eds.), *Psychology of intergroup relations,* 305–322.

Lindsey, F. (1992, November). An outlook on employment. *Upscale,* 42.

Lindzey, G., Hall, C., & Thompson, R. (1975). *Psychology.* New York: Worth.

Linville, P. W., & Jones, E. E. (1980). Polarized appraisals of outgroup members. *Journal of Personality and Social Psychology, 38,* 689–703.

Loftus, E. F. (1975). Leading questions and the eyewitness report. *Cognitive Psychology, 1,* 560–572.

Loftus, E. F., Miller, D. G., & Burns, H. J. (1978). Semantic integration of verbal information into visual memory. *Journal of Experimental Psychology: Human Learning and Memory, 4,* 19–31.

Lonner, W. J. (1988, October). The introductory text and cross-cultural psychology: A survey of cross-cultural psychologists. Kalamazoo: Center for Cross Cultural Research, Western Michigan University.

Lord, L. J. (1987, November). Coming to grip with alcoholism. *U. S. News and World Report,* 55–63.

Lucas, A. R. (1991). Eating disorders. In Melvid Lewis (Ed.), *Child and adolescent psychiatry: A comprehensive textbook.* Baltimore: Williams & Wilkins.

Luft, J. (1970). *Group process: An introduction to group dynamics.* Palo Alto, Calif.: National Press Books.

Lynn, D. (1974). The father: His role in child development. Monterey, Calif.: Brooks/ Cole.

Macauley, J. R. (1970). A shill for Santa Claus. In J. Macauley & L. Berkowitz (Eds.), *Altruism and helping behaviors: Social psychological studies of some antecedents and consequences*. New York: Academic Press.

Maccoby, E. E., & Jacklin, C. N. (1974). *The psychology of sex differences*. Stanford, Calif.: Stanford University Press.

Mackenzie, B. (1984). Explaining race differences in IQ: The logic, the methodology, and the evidence. *American Psychologist, 39*, 1214–1233.

Macklin, E. D. (1972). Heterosexual cohabitation among unmarried college students. *Family Coordinator, 21*, 463–472.

Madigan, C. O., & Elwood, A. (1984). *Brainstorms and thunderbolts*. New York: Macmillan.

Mahoney, M. J. (1971). The self-management of covert behavior: A case study. *Behavior Therapy, 2*, 575–578.

Maier, S. F., & Laudenslager, M. (1985, August). Stress and health: Exploring the links. *Psychology Today*, 44–45.

Marcus, M. G. (1976, May). The power of a name. *Psychology Today*, 75–76.

Marion, R. W., Wiznia, A. A., Hutcheon, G., & Rubinstein, A. (1986). Human T-cell lymphotropic virus Type III (HTLV-III) embryopathy. *American Journal of Diseases of Children, 140* (7), 638–640.

Markides, K. S., & Kraus, N. (1986). Older Mexican Americans. *Generations, 10* (4), 31–34.

Martin, R. A., & Lefcourt, H. M. (1983). Sense of humor as a moderator of the relation between stressors and moods. *Journal of Personality and Social Psychology, 45*, 1313–1324.

Maslow, A. H. (1970). *Motivation and personality*. New York: Harper & Row.

Mason, R. A. (1985). Artificial intellience: Promise, myth, and reality. *Library Journal, 110* (7), 56–57.

Mathews, K., Helmreich, R., Beane, J., & Lucker, W. (1981). Making it in academic psychology: Demographic and personality correlates of attainment. *Journal of Personality and Social Psychology, 39*, 896.

Matlin, M. M. (1987). *The psychology of women*. New York: Holt, Rinehart & Winston.

Matlin, M. M. (1993). *The psychology of women*. Fort Worth: Harcourt Brace Jovanovich.

Matteson, D. R. (1975). *Adolescence today: Sex roles and the search for identity*. Homewood, Ill.: Dorsey Press.

Matthews, K. A., & Rodin, J. (1989). Women's changing work roles: Impact on health, family, and public policy. *American Psychologist, 44* (11), 1389–1393.

Mayer, R. E. (1983). *Thinking, problem solving, cognition*. New York: W. H. Freeman.

McBride, A. B. (1990). Mental health effects of women's multiple roles. *American Psychologist, 45* (3), 381–384.

McClelland, D. C. (1961). *The achieving society*. Princeton, N.J.: Van Nostrand.

McClelland, D. C. (1985). How motives, skills, and values determine what people do. *American Psychologist, 40*, 812–825.

McClusky, H. Y., Milby, J. B., Switzer, P. K., et al. (1991, January). Efficacy of behavioral versus triazolam treatment in persistent sleep-onset insomnia. *American Journal of Psychiatry, 148*, 121–126.

McGaugh, J. L. (1970). Time-dependent processes in memory storage. In J. L. McGaugh & M. J. Herz (Eds.), *Controversial issues of memory trace*. New York: Atherton.

McGaugh, J. L. (1983). Preserving the presence of the past: Hormonal influences on memory storage. *American Psychologist, 38*, 161–174.

McGregor, D. (1960). *The human side of enterprise*. New York: McGraw-Hill.

McGuire, W. J. (1961). Resistance to counter-persuasion conferred by active and passive prior refutation of the same alternative counter-arguments. *Journal of Abnormal and Social Psychology, 63*, 326–332.

Mead, M. (1935). *Sex and temperament in three primitive societies.* New York: Morrow.

Menninger, K. (1938). *Man against himself.* New York: Harcourt Brace Jovanovich.

Merikle, P. M., & Reingold, E. M. (1990). Recognition and lexical decision without detection: Unconscious perception? *Journal of Experimental Psychology: Human Perception and Performance, 16*, 574–583.

Merton, R. (1948). The self-fulfilling prophecy. *Antioch Review, 8*, 193–210.

Milgram, S. (1963). Behavior study of obedience. *Journal of Abnormal and Social Psychology, 67*, 371–378.

Milgram, S. (1970). The experience of living in cities. *Science, 167*, 1461–1468.

Milgram, S. (1974). *Obedience to authority.* New York: Harper & Row.

Milgram, S., Beckman, L., & Berkowitz, L. (1969). Note on the drawing power of crowds of different size. *Journal of Personality and Social Psychology, 13*, 79–82.

Miller, G. (1969). On turning psychology over to the unwashed. American Psychological Association Paper.

Miller, M. E., Adesso, V. J., Fleming, J. P., Gino, A., & Lauerman, R. (1978). Effects of alcohol on the storage and retrieval processes of heavy social drinkers. *Journal of Experimental Psychology: Human Learning and Memory, 4*, 246–255.

Mintz, A. (1951). Non-adaptive group behavior. *Journal of Abnormal and Social Psychology, 46*, 150–159.

Monahan, K. D., & Shaver, P. (1974). Interpsychic versus cultural explanations of the "fear of success" motive. *Journal of Personality and Social Psychology, 29*, 60–64.

Moreno, J. L. (1953). *Who shall survive?* New York: Beacon House.

Morris, D., Collett, P., & O'Shaughnessy, M. (1979). *Gestures.* New York: Stein & Day.

Mueller, C. W., & Campbell, B. G. (1977). Female occupational achievement and marital status: A research note. *Journal of Marriage and the Family, 39* (3), 587–593.

Mussen, P. H., Conger, J. J., & Kagan, J. (1978). *Child development and personality.* New York: Harper & Row.

Myers, D. G. (1980). *The inflated self.* New York: Seabury Press.

Myers, D. G. (1992). *Well-being: Who is happy—and why.* New York: William Morrow.

Nahas, G. G. (1979). *Keep off the grass.* Elmsford, N.Y.: Pergamon Press.

Nathan, P. E., & O'Brien, J. S. (1971). An experimental analysis of the behavior of alcoholics and nonalcoholics during prolonged experimental drinking: A necessary precursor of behavior therapy? *Behavior Therapy, 2*, 455–476.

Nathan, P. E., O'Brien, J. S., & Lowenstein, I. M. (1971). Operant studies of chronic alcoholism: Interaction of alcohol and alcoholics. In P. J. Creaven & M. K. Roach (Eds.), *Biological aspects of alcohol.* Austin: University of Texas Press.

National Center for Health Statistics. (1986). Maternal weight gain and the outcome of pregnancy, United States, 1986. *Vital statistics (Series 21,* No. 44, DHHS Pub. No. 86-1922), Washington, D.C.: U.S. Government Printing Office.

National Commission on Working Women. (1990). *Women, work, and age.* Washington, D.C.

National Institutes on Alcohol Abuse and Alcoholism (NIAAA). (1981). *Fourth special report to the U.S. Congress on alcohol and health.* Washington, D.C.: U.S. Government Printing Office.

National Institute on Alcohol Abuse and Alcoholism (NIAAA). (1982). *Alcohol and Health Monograph Nos, 1,2,3,4.* Washington, D.C.: Department of Health and Human Services.

National Institutes of Health. (1984). *Drugs and insomnia. NIH consensus development statement, 4* (10). Washington, D.C.: U.S. Government Printing Office.

Nemy, E. (1973, April 16). Suicide now no. 2 cause of deaths among young. *The New York Times*, p. 1.

Neugarten, B. (1980, April). In E. Hall (Interviewer), Acting one's age: New rules for the old. *Psychology Today*, 66–80.

Newcomb, T. (1963). Persistence and regression of changed attitudes: Long-range studies. *Journal of Social Studies, 19*, 3–14.

Newman, L. F., & Buka, S. L. (1991, Spring). Clipped wings. *American Educator, 27–33*, 42.

Nidetch, J. (1962). *The story of weight watchers.* New York: New American Library.

Nisbett, R. E. (1993). Violence and U.S. regional culture. *American Psychologist, 48*, 4, 441–449.

Nolan, J. D. (1968). Self-control procedures in the modification of smoking behaviors. *Journal of Consulting and Clinical Psychology, 32*, 92–93.

Nord, W. (1970). Improving attendance through rewards. *Personnel Administration, 33*, 37–41.

Norton, A. J., & Glick, P. C. (1976). Marital instability: Past, present and future. *The Journal of Social Issues, 32*, 5–20.

Novaco, R. W. (1975). *Anger control: The development and evaluation of an experimental treatment.* Lexington, Mass.: Heath, Lexington Books.

O'Hara, K., Johnson, C. M., & Beehr, T. A. (1985). Organization behavioral management: A review of empirical research and recommendations for further investigation. *Academy of Management Review, 10*, 848–864.

Oldham, G., Hackman, J. R., & Pearce, J. F. (1976). Conditions under which employees respond positively to enriched work. *Journal of Applied Psychology, 61* (4), 395–403.

Oliner, S. P., & Oliner, P. M. (1988). *The altruistic personality: Rescuers of Jews in Nazi Europe.* New York: Free Press.

Olshan, N. H. (1980). *Power over your pain without drugs.* New York: Rawson, Wade.

Orr, D. P., Beiter, M., & Ingersoll, G. (1991). Premature sexual activity as an indicator of social risk. *Pediatrics, 87*, 141–147.

Osgood, C. E. (1957). A behavioristic analysis of perception and language as cognitive phenomena. In *Contemporary approaches to cognition.* Cambridge, Mass.: Harvard University Press.

Ouchi, W. (1981). *Theory Z: How American business can meet the Japanese challenge.* Reading, Mass.: Addison-Wesley.

Papalia, D., & Olds, S. (1988). *Psychology.* New York: McGraw-Hill.

Parker, E. S., Birnbaum, I. M., & Noble, E. P. (1976). Alcohol and memory: Storage and state dependency. *Journal of Verbal Learning and Verbal Behavior, 15*, 691–702.

Parkes, C. M. (1972). *Bereavement: Studies of grief in adult life.* New York: International Universities Press.

Paul, R. W. (1984, September). Critical thinking: Fundamental to education for a free society. *Educational Leadership.*

Pearlin, L., & Schooler, C. (1978). The structure of coping. *Journal of Health and Social Behavior, 19*, 2–21.

Pecoraro, T. (1981, October). Beauty I: Jurors go easy on handsome rapists and homely victims. *Psychology Today.*

Pedalino, E., & Gamboa, V. U. (1974). Behavior modification and absenteeism. *Journal of Applied Psychology, 59*, 694–698.

Perls, F. S. (1973). *The gestalt therapy and ex-witness to therapy.* Palo Alto, Calif.: Science & Behavior Books.

Peplau, L. A. (1988, July). Research on lesbian and gay relationships: A decade review. Paper presented at the International Conference on Personal Relationships, University of British Columbia, Vancouver, Canada.

Peterson, R. C. (1984). Marijuana overview. In M. D. Glantz (Ed.), *Correlates and conse-quences of marijuana use* (DHHS Pub. No. ADM84-1276). Washington, D.C.: U.S. Government Printing Office.

Phares, E. J. (1976). *Locus of control in personality.* Morristown, N.J.: General Learning Press.

Phillips, D., McCartney, K., & Scarr, S. (1987). Child-care quality and children's social development. *Developmental Psychology, 23,* 537–543.

Piaget, J. (1952). *The origins of intelligence in children.* New York: International Universities Press.

Pick, H. I., & Pick, A. D. (1970). Sensory and perceptual development. In P. H. Mussen (Ed.), *Carmichael's manual of child psychology,* Vol. 1. New York: Wiley.

Pines, A., & Kafry, D. (1977). Burn-out and life tedium in three generations of profes-sional women. American Psychological Association Paper.

Plateris, A. (1978). Divorce and divorce rates, United States vital health statistics (Series 21, No. 29, National Center for Health Statistics). Washington, D.C.: U.S. Govern-ment Printing Office.

Pogrebin, L. C. (1980, June 30). Celebrating ourselves. *Bottom Line Personal.*

Polivy, J., & Herman, C. (1985). Dieting and bingeing: A causal analysis. *American Psychologist, 40,* 193–201.

Prioleau, L., Murdock, M., & Brody, N. (1983). An analysis of psychotherapy versus placebo studies. *Behavioral and Brain Sciences, 6,* 275–285.

Port, O., with Carey, J., Kelly, K., & Forest, A. (1992, November 30). Quality: Small and midsize companies seize the challenge—not a moment too soon, 67–74.

Pyke, S. W., & Kahill, S. P. (1983, Winter). Sex differences in characteristics presumed relevant to professional productivity. *Psychology of Women Quarterly, 8,* 189–192.

Raudsepp, E. (1980, July). More creative gamesmanship. *Psychology Today,* 71–76.

Reik, T. (1972). *Listening with the third ear.* New York: Pyramid Publications.

Relman, A. S. (1982). Marijuana and health. *New England Journal of Medicine, 306* (10), 603–604.

Renne, K. S. (1970). Correlates of dissatisfaction in marriage. *Journal of Marriage and the Family, 32,* 54–67.

Renwick, P., & Lawler, E. (1978, May). What you really want from your job. *Psychology Today,* 58–66.

Rice, B. (1980, January). Dear Miss C-3PO. *Psychology Today.*

Rice, B. (1980, July). Work: Education for restlessness. *Psychology Today.*

Rice, B. (1981, August). Management: Overtime is underproductive. *Psychology Today.*

Rix, S. E. (Ed.). (1990). *The American woman 1990–1991: A status report.* New York: Norton.

Robins, L. N., Helzer, J. E., Weissman, M. M., Orvalschel, H., Greenberg, E., Burke, J. D., & Regier, D. A. (1984). Lifetime prevalence of specific psychiatric disorders in three sites. *Archives of General Psychiatry, 41,* 949–958.

Rogers, C. (1970). *Carl Rogers on encounter groups.* New York: Harper & Row.

Rogers, D. (1972). *Adolescence: A psychological perspective.* Monterey, Calif.: Brooks/Cole.

Rorschach, H. (1942). *Psychodiagnostics: A diagnostic test based on perception.* New York: Grune & Stratton.

Rosenbaum, B. (1980, September 22). Self-esteem gets the job done. *Chemical Engineering.*

Rosser, P., with the staff of the National Center for Fair and Open Testing. (1987). *Sex bias in college admissions tests: Why women lose out* (2nd ed.). Cambridge, Mass.: National Center for Fair and Open Testing.

Rotter, J. B. (1966). Generalized expectancies for internal vs. external control of reinforce-ment. *Psychological Monographs, 80* (Whole No. 609).

Rovner, S. (1991, March 26). Acting out your anger. *The Washington Post, Health,* p. 17.

Rubenstein, C. (1981, January). Relationships: Martyrdom's brief glow. *Psychology Today*, 82.

Rubenstein, C. (1981, July). Alienation in supermarkets. *Psychology Today*.

Rumpel, I. (1988, August). A systematic analysis of the cultural content of introductory psychology textbooks. Thesis presented to the Faculty of Western Washington University, Bellingham, Wash.

Sacco, W. P., & Beck, A. T. (1985). Cognitive theory of depression. In E. E. Beckham & W. R. Leber (Eds.), *Handbook of depression*. Homewood, Ill.: Dorsey.

Salisbury, S. (1990, March–April). Alcoholism: In the genes? *State University of New York Research*, 8–10.

Sampson, H. A., & Jolie, P. L. (1984). Increased plasma histamine concentrations after food challenges in children with atopic dermatitis. *New England Journal of Medicine*, 311, 372–376.

Sass, L. (1982, August 22). The borderline personality. *The New York Times Magazine*, pp. 12–15, 66–67.

Scarr, S., Pakstis, A. J., Katz, S. H., & Barker, W. B. (1977). The absence of relationship between degree of white ancestry and intellectual skills within a black population. *Human Genetics*, 39, 69–86.

Scarr, S., & Weinberg, R. A. (1976). IQ test performance of black children adopted by white families. *American Psychologist*, 31, 726–739.

Schacter, D. L. (1986). Amnesia and crime: How much do we really know? *American Psychologist*, 41, 286–295.

Schank, R., & Abelson, R. (1983). Scripts, plans and knowledge. In R. Mayer (Ed.), *Thinking, problem solving, cognition*. New York: W. H. Freeman.

Schank, R. C., & Hunter, L. (1985). The quest to understand thinking. *BYTE*, 10 (4), 143–155.

Schein, E. H., Schneier, I., & Barker, C. H. (1961). *Coercive persuasion*. New York: Norton.

Schmeck, H. (1988, July 23). Research hints at link to Alzheimer's disease. *The New York Times*.

Schmidt, S. M., & Kipnis, D. (1985, April). The language of persuasion. *Psychology Today*.

Schwartz, J. (1988). Birds of a feather. *Omni*.

Segal, M. H., Dasen, P. R., Berry, J. W., & Poortinga, Y. H. (1990). Human behavior in global perspective: An introduction to cross-cultural psychology. New York: Pergamon.

Selby, H. (1987, March). Work: Retiring from unemployment. *Psychology Today*.

Seligman, M. E. P. (1974, January). Submissive death: Giving up on life. *Psychology Today*, 80–85.

Shapiro, S., Skinner, E. A., Kessler, L. G., Von Korff, M., German, P. S., Tischler, G. L., Leaf, P. J., Benham, L., Cottler, L., & Regier, D. A. (1984). Utilization of health and mental services. *Archives of General Psychiatry*, 41 (10), 971–978.

Shaver, P., & O'Connor, C. (1986). Problems in perspective. In C. Tavris (Ed.), *Every woman's emotional well-being*. New York: Doubleday.

Shaw, M. E. (1971). *Group dynamics*. New York: McGraw-Hill.

Sheehy, G. (1976). *Passages: Predictable crises of adult life*. New York: Dutton.

Shekelle, R. B., Raynor, W. J., Ostfield, A. M., Garron, D. C., Beliauskas, L. A., Lin, S. C., Malizia, C., & Paul, O. (1981). Psychological depression and 17-year risk of death from cancer. *Psychosomatic Medicine*, 43 (2), 117–125.

Sherif, M., Harvey, O. J., White, B. J., Hood, W. R., & Sherif, C. W. (1961). *Intergroup conflict and cooperation: The robbers' cave experiment*. Norman, Okla.: Institute of Group Relations, University of Oklahoma.

Sherman, L. M., & Berk, R. A. (1984). The specific deterrent effects of arrest for domestic assault. *American Sociological Review*, 49, 261–271.

Simon, W., Berger, A. S., & Gagnon, J. H. (1972). Beyond anxiety and fantasy: The coital experiences of college youth. *Journal of Youth and Adolescence, 1* (3), 203–221.

Sirpola, E. M. (1935). A study of some effects of preparatory set. *Psychological Monographs, 46* (Whole No. 210).

Skinner, B. F. (1938). *The behavior of organisms: An experimental analysis.* Englewood Cliffs, N.J.: Prentice-Hall.

Sklar, L., & Anirman, H. (1951). Stress and cancer. *Psychological Bulletin, 89,* 369–406.

Slavin, R. E. (1989). Cooperative learning and student achievement. In R. E. Slavin (Ed.), *School and Classroom Organization.* Hillsdale, N.J.: Erlbaum.

Sommer, R. (1969). *Personal space.* Englewood Cliffs, N.J.: Prentice-Hall.

Spiegel, D., Bloom, J. R., Kraemer, H. C., & Gottheil, E. (1989, October 14). Effectiveness of psychosocial treatment on survival of patients with metastatic breast cancer. *The Lancet, 2,* 888–891.

Spielberger, C. D. (1992, August 14). Anger/hostility, heart disease and cancer. Presidential address, American Psychological Association Centennial Convention, Washington, D.C.

Spitz, R. (1965). *The first year of life.* New York: International University Press.

Stafford, R., Backman, E., & Dibona, P. (1977). The division of labor among cohabiting and married couples. *Journal of Marriage and the Family, 39* (11), 40–47.

Stein, R. (1988, July 22). Study suggests virus is involved in at least some Alzheimer's cases. *The Philadelphia Inquirer.*

Steinberg, L., Dornbusch, S. M., & Brown, B. B. (1992). Ethnic differences in adolescent achievement: An ecological perspective. *American Psychologist, 47* (6), 723–729.

Sternberg, R. J. (1984). *Beyond IQ: A triarchic theory of human intelligence.* New York: Cambridge University Press.

Stone, L. (1992, August). Relation of racial identity states to self-esteem in black working class women. Paper presented at American Psychological Association Convention, Washington, D.C.

Stone, M. H. (1990). *The fate of borderline patients.* New York: Guilford Press.

Stoner, J. A. F. (1961). A comparison of individual and group decisions involving risk. Unpublished master's thesis, Massachusetts Institute of Technology, Cambridge, Mass.

Stroebe, M., Gergen, M. M., Gergen, K. J., & Stroebe, W. (1992). Broken hearts or broken bonds: Love and death in historical perspective. *American Psychologist, 47* (10), 1205–1212.

Stuart, R. B., & Davis, B. (1972). *Slim chance in a fat world.* Champaign, Ill.: Research Press Company.

Swann, W. B., Hixon, J. G., & DeLaRonde, C. (1992). Embracing the bitter "truth": Negative self-concepts and marital commitment. *Psychological Science, 3* (2), 118–121.

Szapocznik, J., & Kurtines, W. M. (1993). Family psychology and cultural diversity: Opportunities for theory, research, and association. *American Psychologist, 48* (4), 400–407.

Taylor, S., Lichman, R., & Wood, J. (1984). Attribution, beliefs about control and adjustment to breast cancer. *Journal of Personality and Social Psychology, 46,* 489–502.

Tennov, D. (1979). *Love and limerance.* Briarcliff Manor, N.Y.: Stein & Day.

Tesch, F., Lansky, L. M., & Lundgren, D. C. (1972). The exchange of information: One-way versus two-way communication. *Journal of Applied Behavioral Science, 8,* 4.

Thigpen, C. H., & Cleckley, H. (1954). *The three faces of Eve.* New York: McGraw-Hill.

Thompson, L. (1991, March 5). Job dissatisfaction increases likelihood of back injury. *The Washington Post, Health,* p. 5.

Thorndike, P. W. (1977). Cognitive structures in comprehension and memory of narrative discourse. *Cognitive Psychology, 9,* 77–110.

Torrey, E. F. (1991). Care of the mentally ill. *Harvard Mental Health Letter, 7* (9), 8.

Triandis, H., Brislin, R., & Hui, H. C. (1988). Cross-cultural training across the individ-ualism-collectivism divide. *International Journal of Intercultural Relations, 12,* 269–289.

Turok, M. (1972). Handicrafts: A case study on weaving in the highlands. Manuscript on file, Harvard Chiapas Project, Department of Anthropology, Harvard University, Cambridge, Mass.

Tyhurst, J. S. (1951). Individual reactions to community disaster. *American Journal of Psychiatry, 10,* 746–769.

Unger, R., & Crawford, M. (1992). *Women and gender: A feminist psychology.* New York: McGraw-Hill.

U.S. Census Bureau. (1979). *Perspectives on American husbands and wives.* Washington, D.C.: U.S. Government Printing Office.

U.S. Census Bureau. (1988). *Households, families, marital status and living arrangements: March 1988.* Washington, D.C.: U.S. Government Printing Office.

Vokey, J. R., & Reed, J. D. (1985). Subliminal messages: Between the devil and the media. *American Psychologist, 40,* 1231–1239.

Wagner, R. K., & Sternberg, R. J. (1985). Practical intelligence in real-world pursuits: The role of tacit knowledge. *Journal of Personality and Social Psychology, 49* (20), 436–458.

Wallerstein, J. S. (1987). Children of divorce: Report of a ten-year follow-up of early latency-age children. *American Journal of Orthopsychiatry, 53* (2), 230–243.

Walster, E., & Festinger, L. (1962). The effectiveness of "overheard" persuasive com-munications. *Journal of Abnormal and Social Psychology, 65,* 395–402.

Walster, E., Walster, G. W., Piliavin, J., & Schmidt, L. (1973). "Playing hard to get": Understanding an elusive phenomenon. *Journal of Personality and Social Psychology, 26,* 113–121.

Warner, R. (1986, June). Hard times and schizophrenia. *Psychology Today.*

Weisman, A. D. (1972). *On dying and denying: A psychiatric study of terminality.* New York: Behavioral Publications.

Weitzman, L. (1986). *The divorce revolution.* New York: Free Press.

Wetzel, C. D., Janowsky, D. S., & Clopton, P. L. (1982). Remote memory during mari-juana intoxication. *Psychopharmacology, 76,* 278–281.

Whiting, B. B., & Edwards, C. P. (1988). *Children of different worlds: The formation of social behavior.* Cambridge, Mass.: Harvard University Press.

Williams, A. F. (1966). Social drinking, anxiety and depression. *Journal of Personality and Social Psychology, 3,* 689–693.

Williams, C. L. (1989). *Gender differences at work: Women and men in nontraditional occu-pations.* Berkeley: University of California Press.

Wingfield, A., Labar, C. J., & Stine, E. A. L. (1989). Age and decision strategies in running memory for speech: Effects of prosody and linguistic structure. *Journal of Gerontol-ogy: Psychological Science, 44,* 106–113.

Wolfe, J. M. (1983). Hidden visual processes. *Scientific American, 218* (2), 94–103.

Wylie, R. C. (1957). Some relationships between defensiveness and self-concept discrep-ancies. *Journal of Personality, 25,* 600–617.

Yankelovich, D. (1978, May). The new psychological contract at work. *Psychology Today,* 4.

Zajonc, R. (1968). Attitudinal effects of mere exposure. *Journal of Personality and Social Psychology, 9,* 1–27.

Zajonc, R. B. (1970, February). Brainwash: Familiarity breeds comfort. *Psychology Today,* 32–35, 60–62.

Zuckerman, M. (1990). Some dubious premises in research and theory on racial differ-ences: Scientific, social, and ethical issues. *American Psychologist, 45,* 1297–1303.

Acknowledgments

For permission to use copyrighted materials, the author is indebted to the following:

Chapter 1

Page 2   Quotation from George Miller. Reprinted by permission of George Miller.

Page 3   Feature 1-1. Copyright 1987 by the American Psychological Association. Reprinted by permission.

Page 7   Feature 1-2. Adapted from the Eastern Washington University catalog with permission from Eastern Washington University.

Page 12   Figure 1-2. © 1994, The Washington Post Writers Group. Reprinted with permission.

Page 13   Figure 1-3. Reprinted courtesy *OMNI* Magazine © 1990.

Page 15   Figure 1-4. Reprinted from *The Saturday Evening Post* © 1987 BFL&MS, Inc.

Page 18   Feature 1-4. Reprinted with permission from *Psychology Today* Magazine. Copyright © 1988 (P.T. Partners, L.P.).

Page 19   Figure 1-7. Drawing by Drucker, © 1987 *The New Yorker* Magazine, Inc.

Page 20   Feature 1-5. Reprinted with permission from *Psychology Today* Magazine. Copyright © 1981 (P.T. Partners, L.P.).

Page 22   Feature 1-7. Reprinted with permission from *Science News*, the weekly newsmagazine of science, copyright 1990 by Science Service, Inc.

Page 23   Figure 1-8. FRANK AND ERNEST reprinted by permission of NEA, Inc.

Page 27   Figure 1-9. FRANK AND ERNEST reprinted by permission of NEA, Inc.

Page 29   Feature 1-8. Copyright © 1992. Reprinted by permission.

Page 29   Feature 1-9. Reprinted with permission from THE HARVARD MENTAL HEALTH LETTER, 164 Longwood Avenue, Boston, MA 02115. Excerpted from the *HARVARD MENTAL HEALTH LETTER*, © 1991, President and Fellows of Harvard College.

ACKNOWLEDGMENTS

Chapter 2

Page 38   Feature 2-1. Reprinted by permission of *OMNI,* © 1990, OMNI Publications International, Ltd.

Page 40   Feature 2-2. Reprinted with permission from *Science News,* the weekly news-magazine of science, copyright 1992 by Science Service, Inc.

Page 41   Figure 2-3. Drawing by Vietor; © 1988 *The New Yorker* Magazine, Inc.

Page 45   Figure 2-4. Reprinted from *The Saturday Evening Post* © 1992 BFL&MS, Inc.

Page 46   Figure 2-5. Copyright 1961 Canadian Psychological Association. Reprinted by permission.

Page 48   Feature 2-4. Reprinted with permission from *Psychology Today* Magazine. Copyright © 1987 (P.T. Partners, L.P.).

Page 49   Figure 2-7. *The Far Side* © 1992 Universal Press Syndicate. Reprinted by permission.

Page 51   Feature 2-5. © 1992 *The Washington Post.* Reprinted by permission.

Page 61   Feature 2-6. Copyright © 1990 by the New York Times Company. Reprinted by permission.

Page 62   Feature 2-7. Reprinted with permission from *Science News,* the weekly news-magazine of science, copyright 1992 by Science Service, Inc.

Page 63   Feature 2-8. Reprinted with permission from *Science News,* the weekly news-magazine of science, copyright 1991 by Science Service, Inc.

Chapter 3

Page 71   Figure 3-2. Reprinted from *The Saturday Evening Post* © 1987 BFL&MS, Inc.

Page 72   Figure 3-3. Reprinted from *The Saturday Evening Post* © 1992 BFL&MS, Inc.

Page 78   Feature 3-1. Reprinted with permission from *Science News,* the weekly news-magazine of science, copyright 1978 by Science Service, Inc.

Page 79   Exhibit 3-2. Copyright 1987 by *Omni* Magazine and reprinted with the permission of Omni Publications International, Ltd.

Page 82   Figure 3-7. Reprinted with special permission of King Features Syndicate, Ltd.

Page 83   Figure 3-8. Reprinted with special permission of King Features Syndicate, Ltd.

Page 85   Feature 3-3. © 1993 *The Washington Post.* Reprinted by permission.

Page 88   Feature 3-4. Copyright 1987 by the American Psychological Association. Reprinted by permission.

Page 93   Figure 3-9. Reprinted from *The Saturday Evening Post* © 1993 BFL&MS, Inc.

Chapter 4

Page 102   Feature 4-1. Reprinted with permission from *Psychology Today* Magazine. Copyright © 1988 (P.T. Partners, L.P.).

Page 108   Figure 4-3. Drawing by W. Miller. © 1987 *The New Yorker* Magazine, Inc.

Page 112   Feature 4-2. Reprinted with permission from *Psychology Today* Magazine. Copyright © 1987 (P.T. Partners, L.P.).

Page 122   Feature 4-3. Copyright 1988 by *Omni* Magazine and reprinted with the permission of Omni Publications International, Ltd.

Page 125   Feature 4-4. Copyright © 1991 by the New York Times Company. Reprinted by permission.

Page 128   Feature 4-5. Reprinted with permission of the Associated Press.

Chapter 5

Page 136   Figure 5-3. Drawing by Bernard Schoenbaum; © 1991 *The New Yorker* Magazine, Inc.

Page 139   Feature 5-1. Reprinted with permission from *Science News,* the weekly newsmagazine of science, copyright 1991 by Science Service, Inc.

Page 140   Figure 5-4. *Doonesbury* © 1990 Universal Press Syndicate. Reprinted with permission. All rights reserved.

Page 141   Figure 5-5. Reprinted from *The Saturday Evening Post* © 1980 BFL&MS, Inc.

Page 145   Feature 5-2. Copyright © 1991 by the *New York Times* Company. Reprinted by permission.

Page 145   Feature 5-3. Reprinted from *The Saturday Evening Post* © 1992 BFL&MS, Inc.

Page 146   Figure 5-7. Reprinted from *The Saturday Evening Post* © 1987 BFL&MS, Inc.

Page 149   Figure 5-8. *Calvin and Hobbes* © 1992 Universal Press Syndicate. Reprinted with permission. All rights reserved.

Page 154   Feature 5-4. Reprinted with permission from *Science News,* the weekly newsmagazine of science, copyright 1991 by Science Service, Inc.

Pages 155–156   Feature 5-5. Copyright © 1986 by the *New York Times* Company. Reprinted by permission.

Page 157   Figure 5-9. *The Far Side* © 1992 Universal Press Syndicate. Reprinted with permission. All rights reserved.

Page 158   Figure 5-10. Drawing by M. Twohy; © 1991 *The New Yorker* Magazine, Inc.

Chapter 6

Page 165   Figure 6-1. Reprinted from *The Saturday Evening Post* © 1992 BFL&MS, Inc.

Page 167   Feature 6-1. Reprinted with permission from *The Harvard Mental Health Letter* © 1992, the President and Fellows of Harvard College.

Page 170   Feature 6-2. Reprinted with permission from *Science News,* the weekly newsmagazine of science, copyright 1991 by Science Service, Inc.

Page 171   Feature 6-3. Copyright 1992 by the American Psychological Association. Reprinted by permission.

Page 176   Figure 6-2. Reprinted from *The Saturday Evening Post* © 1980 BFL&MS, Inc.

Page 181   Feature 6-4. From *How to Eat Like a Child* by Delia Ephron. Reprinted by permission of Viking Penguin, Inc.

Page 183   Figure 6-4. Drawing by John O'Brien; © 1991 The *New Yorker* Magazine, Inc.

Page 186   Figure 6-5. Drawing by M. Twohy; © 1987 The *New Yorker* Magazine, Inc.

Page 190   Feature 6-5. From *Newsweek,* December 12, 1992 and © 1992, Newsweek, Magazine, Inc. All rights reserved. Reprinted by permission.

Page 192   Poem by Mary Zaharjko. Reprinted from *I Never Told Anybody* by K. Koch © 1977 with permission from Random House, Inc.

Page 193   Feature 6-6. Reprinted from *The Saturday Evening Post* © 1992 BFL&MS, Inc.

Chapter 7

Page 201   Figure 7-1. Reprinted by permission of NEA, Inc.

Page 204   Feature 7-1. Copyright 1991 by the American Psychological Association. Reprinted by permission.

Page 205   Figure 7-2. Reprinted from *The Saturday Evening Post* © 1988 BFL&MS, Inc.

Page 209   Feature 7-2. © 1992. Reprinted by permission of *Upscale* Magazine. One time usage. All rights reserved.

Pages 212–213   Feature 7-3. Reprinted with permission from Marilyn Machlowitz © 1980.

Page 219   Copyright © 1989 by the *New York Times* Company. Reprinted by permission.

Page 221   Figure 7-5. Reprinted from *The Saturday Evening Post* © 1988 BFL&MS, Inc.

Chapter 8

Page 230   Figure 8-1. Picture credit: Paul Ekman.

Page 231   Feature 8-1. Reprinted with permission from *Science News*, the weekly newsmagazine of science, copyright 1991 by Science Service, Inc.

Page 234   Feature 8-2. Copyright 1991, *U.S. News & World Report*. Reprinted by permission.

Page 235   Figure 8-3. Reprinted from *The Saturday Evening Post* © 1988 BFL&MS, Inc.

Page 245   Figure 8-7. Reprinted from *The Saturday Evening Post* © 1954 BFL&MS, Inc.

Page 246   Feature 8-3. From *Anger Kills: Seventeen Strategies for Controlling Hostility that Can Harm Your Health.* Reprinted by permission of Redford Williams and Virginia Williams.

Page 250   Feature 8-4. Reprinted with permission from *Journal of Psychosomatic Research*, 3. Thomas H. Holmes and Richard H. Rahe "The Social Readjustment Rating Scale" copyright 1967, Pergamon Press, Ltd. and with permission of Thomas H. Holmes.

Page 251   Feature 8-5. Adapted with permission from Plenum Press copyright, 1981.

Page 253   Figure 8-8. Drawing by Mankoff; © 1987 *The New Yorker* Magazine, Inc.

Page 254   Figure 8-9. Reprinted by permission of *The New England Journal of Medicine*, 1991.

Page 254   Feature 8-6. Copyright © 1991 *The New York Times* Company. Reprinted by permission.

Page 254   Feature 8-7. Copyright © 1991 *The New York Times* Company. Reprinted by permission.

Page 255   Figure 8-10. Reprinted from *The Saturday Evening Post* © 1987 BFL&MS, Inc.

Chapter 9

Page 262   Figure 9-1. Drawing by C. Barsotti; © 1980 *The New Yorker* Magazine, Inc.

Page 264   Figure 9-2. Reprinted with permission from *Psychology Today* Magazine. Copyright © 1988 (P.T. Partners, L.P.).

Page 265   Feature 9-1. Copyright © 1991 *The New York Times* Company. Reprinted by permission.

Page 265   Figure 9-3. Reprinted from *The Saturday Evening Post* © 1992 BFL&MS, Inc.

Page 269   Figure 9-4. Reprinted from *The Saturday Evening Post* © 1979 BFL&MS, Inc.

Page 271   Figure 9-5. Reprinted from *The Saturday Evening Post* © 1987 BFL&MS, Inc.

Page 271   Figure 9-6. Reprinted by permission of NEA, Inc.

Page 279   Feature 9-2. Excerpted from the January 1992 issue of the *Harvard Heart Letter* © 1992, President and Fellows of Harvard College.

Page 282   Feature 9-3. Reprinted from the *Harvard Mental Health Letter.* Excerpted from the March 1991 issue; © President and Fellows of Harvard College.

Page 285   Figure 9-7. Drawing by D. Reilly; © 1991 *The New Yorker* Magazine, Inc.

Page 286   Feature 9-4. Reprinted by permission of author.

Chapter 10

Page 294 Feature 10-1. Reprinted from the *Harvard Mental Health Letter*. Excerpted from the November 1992 issue; © 1992 President and Fellows of Harvard College.

Page 295 Figure 10-1. Tank McNamara © 1988 Universal Press Syndicate. Reprinted with permission. All rights reserved.

Page 296 Feature 10-2. Reprinted with permission from *Science News*, the weekly news-magazine of science, copyright 1993 by Science Service, Inc.

Page 299 Figure 10-2. Reprinted courtesy *OMNI* Magazine © 1987.

Page 301 Feature 10-3. Copyright © 1992 by *The New York Times* Company. Reprinted by permission.

Page 302 Figure 10-3. Reprinted courtesy *OMNI* Magazine © 1987.

Page 303 Feature 10-5. Copyright © 1991 by *The New York Times* Company. Reprinted by permission.

Page 306 Feature 10-6. © 1993. *The Washington Post*. Reprinted with permission.

Page 307 Feature 10-7. Reprinted from the *Harvard Mental Health Letter* © 1992, President and Fellows of Harvard College.

Page 310 Figure 10-4. Drawing by Ross; © 1987 *The New Yorker* Magazine, Inc.

Page 312 Figure 10-5. Reprinted from *The Saturday Evening Post* © 1979 BFL&MS, Inc.

Page 313 Feature 10-8. © 1993 *The Washington Post*. Reprinted with permission.

Chapter 11

Page 319 *Down on Mew* (Janis Joplin), quotation used by permission of Slow Dancing Music, Inc., c/o BSA. All rights reserved.

Page 319 *Yesterday* (John Lennon and Paul McCartney) © 1965 Northern Songs Limited. All rights for the U.S.A., Mexico, and the Philippines controlled by Maclen Music, Inc., c/o ATV Music. Used by permission. All rights reserved.

Page 323 Figure 11-1. Reprinted courtesy *OMNI* Magazine © 1988.

Page 324 Feature 11-1. Copyright © 1993. Reprinted with permission from Eden Stone.

Page 327 Figure 11-2. Reprinted from *The Saturday Evening Post* © 1988 BFL&MS, Inc.

Page 330 Feature 11-2. From *Feeling Good: The New Mood Therapy* by David Burns, M.D. © 1980 by David Burns by permission William Morrow Publishers.

Page 332 Figure 11-3. Reprinted courtesy of Hoest and *Parade Magazine* © 1989.

Page 336 Feature 11-3. "High Anxiety" Copyright 1992 by Consumers Union of U. S., Inc., Yonkers, N. Y. 10703-1057. Reprinted by permission from *Consumer Reports*, January 1992.

Page 337 Feature 11-4. Reprinted with permission from *Science News*, the weekly news-magazine of science, copyright 1992 by Science Service, Inc.

Page 337 Feature 11-5. Copyright 1991 by the American Psychological Association. Reprinted by permission.

Page 339 Feature 11-6. Copyright © 1993 by *New Age Journal*. Reprinted by permission.

Page 341 Feature 11-7. Copyright 1992. Reprinted by permission of Ed Tivnan.

Chapter 12

Page 349 Figure 12-1. Drawing by Ross, © 1987 *The New Yorker* Magazine, Inc.

Page 351 Figure 12-2. Drawing by Bernard Schoenbaum; © 1993 *The New Yorker* Magazine, Inc.

Page 355 Figure 12-3. FRANK AND ERNEST. Reprinted by permission of NEA.

Page 357   Figure 12-4. Drawing by Koren; © 1993 *The New Yorker* Magazine, Inc.

Page 358   Figure 12-5. Drawing by Ziegler, © 1987 *The New Yorker* Magazine, Inc.

Page 360   Feature 12-1. Reprinted with permission from *Science News*, the weekly news-magazine of science, copyright 1991 by Science Service, Inc.

Page 362   Figure 12-6. Reprinted with permission of *Modern Maturity* copyright 1993, American Association of Retired Persons.

Page 366   Feature 12-2. Reprinted with permission from *Science News*, the weekly news-magazine of science, copyright 1991 by Science Service, Inc.

Page 367   Feature 12-3. *American Health* © 1992 by Ilene Springer.

Page 373   Feature 12-4. © 1993 *The Washington Post*. Reprinted with permission.

Page 374   Feature 12-5. © 1992 *The Washington Post*. Reprinted with permission.

Chapter 13

Page 380   Figure 13-1. Reprinted from *The Saturday Evening Post* © 1993 BFL&MS, Inc.

Page 383   Feature 13-1. Reprinted from *USAir Magazine,* Pace Communications, Inc., Greensboro, North Carolina, with permission from Ann Handley.

Page 388   Figure 13-2. Reprinted with permission of Peter Steiner.

Page 390   Figure 13-3. Drawing by Mankoff; © 1993 *The New Yorker* Magazine, Inc.

Page 391   Figure 13-4. *Close to Home* © 1993 Universal Press Syndicate. Reprinted by permission. All rights reserved.

Page 392   Feature 13-2. Reprinted with permission of Associated Press.

Page 394   Feature 13-3. Reprinted with permission from *Psychology Today* Magazine. Copyright © 1988 (P.T. Partners, L.P.).

Page 396   Feature 13-4. Reprinted by permission of *Upscale* Magazine. One time usage. All rights reserved.

Page 398   Figure 13-6. Reprinted courtesy *OMNI* magazine © 1987.

Page 400   Figure 13-8. Drawing by Leo Cullum; © 1980 *The New Yorker* Magazine, Inc.

Page 404   Figure 13-13. Reprinted from *The Saturday Evening Post* © 1992 BFL&MS, Inc.

Page 406   Figure 13-14. From *Group Process: An Introduction to Group Dynamics* by Joseph Luft by permission of Mayfield Publishing Company. Copyright © 1963, 1970 by Joseph Luft.

Chapter 14

Page 417   Feature 14-1. Copyright 1993. *U.S. News & World Report*. Reprinted by permission.

Page 418   Feature 14-2. Copyright 1990 by *The New York Times* Company. Reprinted by permission.

Page 419   Figure 14-1. Drawing by W. Miller; © 1992 *The New Yorker* Magazine, Inc.

Page 423   Figure 14-2. Drawing by D. Reilly; © 1980 *The New Yorker* Magazine, Inc.

Page 426   Figure 14-3. Reprinted from *The Saturday Evening Post* © 1993 BFL&MS, Inc.

Page 427   Figure 14-4. *The Far Side.* © 1987 Universal Press Syndicate. Reprinted by permission. All rights reserved.

Page 433   Feature 14-3. © 1992 *The Washington Post*. Reprinted by permission.

Page 438   Feature 14-4. Reprinted with permission from Science News, the weekly newsmagazine of science, copyright 1992 by Science Service, Inc.

Page 440   Figure 14-5. Reprinted by permission of NEA, Inc.

Page 447   Figure 15-1. Drawing by M. Stevens; © 1987 *The New Yorker* Magazine, Inc.

Page 449   Feature 15-1. Excerpts from *Understanding Culture's Influence on Behavior* by Richard Brislin, copyright © 1993 by Harcourt Brace Jovanovich. Reprinted by permission of the publisher.

Page 450   Figure 15-2. Drawing by Chas. Addams; © 1980 *The New Yorker* Magazine, Inc.

Page 457   Figure 15-5. *Close to Home* © 1993 Universal Press Syndicate. Reprinted by permission. All rights reserved.

Page 460   Figure 15-6. Reprinted by permission: Tribune Media Services.

Page 461   Feature 15-2. From N. Kogan and M. Wallach *Risk Taking,* Holt Rinehart and Winston, 1964. Reprinted by permission of Holt Rinehart and Winston.

Page 466   Figure 15-7. Reprinted from *The Saturday Evening Post* © 1993 BFL&MS, Inc.

Page 470   Feature 15-3. Reprinted with permission of MCB University Press.

Chapter 16

Page 479   Feature 16-1. Reprinted by permission of *Upscale* Magazine. One time usage. All rights reserved.

Page 481   Feature 16-2. From Hecklinger & Black, *Training for Life: a Practical Guide to Career and Life Planning.* Copyright 1990 by Kendall Hunt Publishing. Used with permission.

Page 482   Figure 16-1. Reprinted from *The Saturday Evening Post* © 1993 BFL&MS, Inc.

Page 487   Figure 16-2. *Close to Home* © 1993 Universal Press Syndicate. Reprinted by permission. All rights reserved.

Page 486   Feature 16-5. Reprinted with permission from *Essence* © 1992.

Page 489   Figure 16-3. Reprinted from *The Saturday Evening Post* © 1993 BFL&MS, Inc.

Page 490   Feature 16-6. Reprinted by permission of *Upscale* Magazine. One time usage. All rights reserved.

Page 496   Feature 16-7. Reprinted by permission of Linda Stern, copyright 1993.

Page 498   Figure 16-4. Drawing by Handelsman; © 1980 *The New Yorker* Magazine, Inc.

PHOTO CREDITS

Page 9: Ken Robert Buck/The Picture Cube. Page 50: Jean-Claude Lejeune. Page 114: Frank Fournier/Woodfin Camp. Page 126: Frank Siteman/The Picture Cube. Page 191: Jaye R. Philips/The Picture Cube. Page 203: Peter Southwick/Stock, Boston. Page 230: Paul Ekman. Page 232: *(top)* David H. Wells/The Image Works; *(bottom)* Doug Mason/Woodfin Camp & Associates. Page 275: © 1943 by the President and Fellows of Harvard College; © 1971 by Henry A. Murray. Page 283: Eastcott/The Image Works. Page 305: Alan Carey/The Image Works. Page 320: Joel Gordon. Page 334: Joel Gordon. Page 340: J. Berndt/The Picture Cube. Page 348: Beringer-Dratch/The Picture Cube. Page 354: M. Antman/The Image Works. Page 421: Elizabeth Crews/Stock, Boston. Page 451: Bruce M. Wellman/Stock, Boston. Page 462: Paul Sakuma/AP/Wide World Photo. Page 494: Wojnarowicz/The Image Works.

Index